Why Do You Need This New Edition?

Whatever your major or interests, the new edition of *Beyond Words* offers strategies for figuring out how contemporary media and cultural texts are shaping your life and attitudes. *Beyond Words* explains how to respond to these pressures with powerful language of your own—verbal and visual.

1. With updated images and readings, most of them new to this edition, you'll find high-interest texts and topics you'll want to discuss, from the Wiimote and *Daily Show* to Second Life and *On the Road*.

2. Chapter 1, heavily revised to provide more accessible advice, offers a direct method for responding to cultural texts so you know where to begin when you're intrigued or puzzled by a book, movie, video—you name it.

3. Readings in Chapter 1 present serious authors defending their cultural values the way you might yourself, standing up for blockbuster summer movies or TV shows like *The Sopranos* and *24*.

4. Chapter 2 gives you a sensible process to apply to writing academic papers or composing in other media. It provides you with efficient checklists for a wide variety of projects, all in one place.

5. The six extensively updated anthology chapters (Chapters 3 to 8) cover topics you'll recognize because you talk about them every day: from identity to the environment to media, technology, design, and politics. Just the good stuff.

6. The anthology chapters open with provocative new "Gallery" sections designed to raise your interest and suggest topics for projects. Images in this edition are larger, too, for more impact and they are more closely tied to background information and study questions.

7. Chapters 3 to 8 offer thoroughly revised "Writing About" sections, which provide instruction tailored to specific topics and projects, not generic advice. The material is carefully cross-referenced to the writing instruction in Chapter 2.

8. Chapters 3 to 8 include twelve student writing projects (nine of them new to this edition) that show how students like you successfully completed their assignments. Each chapter includes two such projects in full, one of them annotated by an instructor showing you the key moves the student made.

PEARSON

BEYOND WORDS

Cultural Texts for Reading and Writing

SECOND EDITION

John Ruszkiewicz
University of Texas at Austin

Daniel Anderson
University of North Carolina at Chapel Hill

Christy Friend
University of South Carolina

Longman
New York San Francisco Boston
London Toronto Sydney Tokyo Singapore Madrid
Mexico City Munich Paris Cape Town Hong Kong Montreal

Executive Editor: Lynn M. Huddon
Senior Development Editor: Katharine Glynn
Senior Marketing Manager: Sandra McGuire
Senior Supplements Editor: Donna Campion
Production Manager: Ellen MacElree
Project Coordination, Text Design, and Electronic Page Makeup: Nesbitt Graphics, Inc.
Cover Designer/Manager: Wendy Ann Fredericks
Cover Photo: © Richard Cummins/Corbis, All rights reserved. To learn more about this photo, please turn to page 235.
Senior Manufacturing Buyer: Alfred C. Dorsey
Printer and Binder: Courier/Kendallville
Cover Printer: Phoenix Color Corp./Hagerstown

Library of Congress Cataloging-in-Publication Data

Ruszkiewicz, John J., 1950-
 Beyond words : cultural texts for reading and writing / John Ruszkiewicz, Daniel Anderson, Christy Friend. -- 2nd ed.
   p. cm.
   ISBN-13: 978-0-205-57662-3
   ISBN-10: 0-205-57662-1
   1. College readers. 2. English language--Rhetoric--Problems, exercises, etc. 3. Report writing--Problems, exercises, etc. 4. Critical thinking--Problems, exercises, etc. 5. Readers--Multiculturalism. 6. Readers--Current events. I. Anderson, Daniel. II. Friend, Christy. III. Title.
   PE1417.R87 2008
   808'.0472--dc22
                                                                                2008045927

For permission to use copyrighted material, grateful acknowledgment is made to the copyright holders on pp. 551–553, which is hereby made part of this copyright page.

Copyright © 2009 by Pearson Education, Inc.

All rights reserved. No part of this publication may be reproduced, stored in a retrieval system, or transmitted, in any form or by any means, electronic, mechanical, photocopying, recording, or otherwise, without the prior written permission of the publisher. Printed in the United States.

Longman
is an imprint of

PEARSON

http://www.ablongman.com

1 2 3 4 5 6 7 8 9 10—CRK—11 10 09 08
ISBN 13: 978-0-205-57662-3
ISBN 10:   0-205-57662-1

Contents

Preface   xi

Introduction   1

Understanding How We Read and Write Today   3
Looking at the History of Words and Images   4
Using *Beyond Words*   7

CHAPTER 1
Reading Texts   8

Identifying subject or focus   10
Identify the subject   10
Find focal points   11
Examine and interpret the details   11
Notice what is missing   12
  PAINTING Pere Borrell del Caso, *Escaping Criticism*   13
  PHOTO James Evans, *Hallie's Hands*   14
  PHOTO Donald Judd, *Fifteen Untitled Works in Concrete*   15

Considering audience   16
Note how a text signals its audience   16
Assess the level of the message   17
Note the demographics   17
Understand the original or intended audience   17
Notice how the audience has changed   18
  WEB PAGE *Daily Kos*   19
  AD Nike, *My Butt Is Big*   20
  AD 1956 Dodge *La Femme*   21
  PHOTO Leni Riefenstahl, *Triumph of the Will*   22

Understanding purpose   24
Understand texts that inform and analyze   24
Understand texts that persuade   25
Understand texts that teach and delight   26
  WEB SITE Michael Jordan's The Steakhouse N.Y.C.   27
  PHOTO Frank Gehry, Stata Center, Massachusetts Institute of Technology   28

Identifying genres   30
Identify the conventions of the genre   30
Recognize changing conventions   30
  POEM William Shakespeare, "Sonnet 130"   31
  POEM Seamus Heaney, "Clearances"   31

Examining media   32
Understand media   32
Appreciate language as a medium   32
  WEB PAGE *Lara Croft Tomb Raider* Online Game   33
  WEB PAGE Barak Obama Presidential Announcement, 2007   34
  PHOTO John McCain Presidential Announcement, 2007   35

Understanding contexts   36
Understand the context   36
Explore personal associations   36
  EDITORIAL CARTOON Thomas Nast, *The American River Ganges*   37

Examining structure and composition   38
Examine the parts   38
  PHOTO Shakespeare at Winedale, *Henry V, 2001*   40
  PHOTO Grid Lines Showing the Rule of Thirds   41
  PAINTINGS Mark Ulriksen, *Puppy Love* and *Little Dog*   42
  PAINTING Michelangelo da Caravaggio, *David and Goliath*   43

Understanding and Reading Media   44
  ESSAY Thomas Washington, "A Librarian's Lament: Books Are a Hard Sell"   45
  ESSAY Manohia Dargis, "Defending Goliath: Hollywood and the Art of Blockbuster"   47
  ESSAY Steven Johnson, "Watching TV Makes You Smarter"   50

CHAPTER 2
Composing Texts 47

Choosing a Subject or Focus 56
Stretch your comfort zone 56
Define your subject 56
- **AD** Oreck Special Edition XL Ultra Vacuum Cleaner 57
- **POSTERS** S. Mirzoyan, A. Ivanov, *Help Build the Gigantic Factories*; Raul Martínez, *Fidel* 58

Reaching an Audience 60
Know your audience 60
Figure out what your audience needs 61
Earn the interest of your audience 61
- **PHOTO** Cover of *Rolling Stone*, November 16, 2006 62

Deciding on Your Purpose and Context 64
Understand your assignment 64
Respond to opportunities 65
Explain the context of your project 65
- **PHOTO** Dorothea Lange, *Migrant Mother* 66

Choosing a genre and structure 67
Writing a description 67
Writing a narrative 68
Writing a comparison and/or contrast project 68
Writing a report 69
Writing a response or position paper 70
Preparing a problem/solution project 71
Writing a rhetorical analysis 71
Writing an ad analysis 72

Writing an argument 73
Preparing an oral presentation 74
- **PHOTO** Fake Nissan Altima Keys 76

Choosing a medium 77
Choose the spoken word 77
Choose written words 77
Choose the fine arts 77
Choose the graphic arts 78
Choose photography 78
Choose film 78
Choose video 78
Choose the World Wide Web 79
Choose multimedia 79
- **REPORT** Opening pages of Chapter 9 from *The 9/11 Commission Report* 80
- **GRAPHIC ADAPTATION** Sid Jacobson and Ernie Colón, *The 9/11 Report: A Graphic Adaptation* 81
- **WEB PAGE** NASA Multimedia Page 83

Doing research and documenting sources 84
Scope out your topic 84
Be methodical in your research 84
Use the library 85
Use the Internet 85
Learn from experts 86
Prepare a field observation 86
Document your sources 87

Revising and editing 88
Evaluate and revise your work 88
Sweat the details 89

Project 2.1: Analyzing a Visual Text 90
- **STUDENT PROJECT** Jacqueline Cruz, "She's Very Charlie" 90

CHAPTER 3
Identities 94

READING TEXTS ABOUT IDENTITY 96

Gallery | Representations of Identity 97
- Dorothea Lange, *Drought Refugees Camping* 97
- Pepsi Advertisement Featuring David Beckham 98
- Jim Borgman, *I Want to Be. . . .* 99
- *Love Me Tender* Movie Poster 100
- Judy Syfers-Brady, "Why I Want a Wife" 101
- Razanne Doll and Muslim Girl 103
- Edward Hopper, *Nighthawks* 104
- Gordon Parks, *American Gothic* 105

CLUSTER 3.1 | LIFE STORIES 106
- **ESSAY** Patricia Hampl, "I Could Tell You Stories" 107
- **GRAPHIC NOVEL** Marjane Satrapi, From *Persepolis*, "The Veil" 110
- **PAINTING** Albrecht Dürer, Self-Portraits 117
- **ESSAY** Alison Stateman, "Postcards from the Edge" 118
- **PHOTO ESSAY** Jim Goldberg, Images from *Raised by Wolves* 122
- **PHOTO** Harry Benson, *Jubilant Clay* 124
- **ESSAY** Annie Dillard, From *An American Childhood* 125

CLUSTER 3.2 | BODIES 128
- **ESSAY** Susan Bordo, "The Empire of Images in Our World of Bodies" 129
- **PHOTO MONTAGE** On the Cover of *Rolling Stone* 137
- **ESSAY** Josie Appelton, "The Body Piercing Project" 138
- **PHOTO** A. Ramey, *Holding Cell, Maricopa County Jail* 142
- **PHOTO** Uwe Krejci, *Teenagers with Facial Piercings* 143
- **ESSAY** Henry Louis Gates, Jr., "In the Kitchen" 144
- **PHOTO** Bob Marley Performing in Stockholm 148
- **PHOTO** Nat King Cole 149

CLUSTER 3.3 | GROUPS AND ETHNICITIES 150
- **ESSAY** Lan Tran, "Lone Stars" 151
- **PHOTO** Matthias Clamer, *Young Men Entering Cowboy Saloon* 155
- **SHORT STORY** Alice Walker, "Everyday Use" 156
- **PHOTO** *AIDS Quilt*, Washington, DC 161
- **PHOTOS** Edward Curtis, *A Navaho* and *White Duck*; Gertrude Käsebier, *Zitkala-Sa* 162
- **SHORT STORY** Sherman Alexie, "I Hated Tonto (Still Do)" 163
- **PHOTO** Hulleah J. Tsinhnajinnie, *Damn!* 165

WRITING ABOUT IDENTITY 166

Project 3.1: Composing a Personal Memoir 167
- **STUDENT PROJECT** Allen Shannon, "Uncle Duane" 168

Project 3.2: Researching and Profiling an Artist 172
- **STUDENT PROJECT** Billy Smith, "Gordon Parks: Using Photographs to Spark Social Change" 173

Additional Projects 179

vii

CHAPTER 4

Places and Environments 180

READING TEXTS ABOUT PLACES AND ENVIRONMENTS 182

Gallery | Places and Environments 183

- Paris Casino, The Strip, Las Vegas 183
- Smiley N. Pool, *The Dallas Morning News*, "The Water Is Rising" 184
- David Muench, *Grand Prismatic Spring, Yellowstone National Park* 185
- Melissa Ann Pinney, *Disney World, Orlando, Florida* 186
- *Tapei 101* 187
- Bobby Troup, "Route 66" 188
- Richard Harrod, *Café, Montmartre* 189
- Alice Attie, From *Harlem in Transition* 190

CLUSTER 4.1 | PLACES WE INHABIT 192

- **PHOTO** Sears Catalog, *The Dover* 193
- **ESSAY** David Brooks, "Our Sprawling, Supersize Utopia" 194
- **PHOTOS** Images from Suburban Life 200
- **ESSAY** Jenny Attiyeh, "My Ghost Town: A Vanishing Personal History" 202
- **PHOTO** Jonathan Levine, *Jelly! Austin* 204
- **ESSAY** Glenn Reynolds, "The Comfy Chair Revolution" 205
- **ESSAY** Michael Gerson, "Where the Avatars Roam" 212
- **WEB PAGE** Ryan Bretag, *Welcome to the Texas State University Second Life Campus* 213

CLUSTER 4.2 | BORDERLANDS 214

- **EDITORIAL CARTOONS** On Immigration 215
- **ESSAY** Charles Bowden, "Our Wall" 216
- **PHOTO** Diane Cook and Len Jenshel, *Tijuana, Mexico* 221

- **POEM** Benjamin Alire Sáenz, "War (in the City in Which I Live)" 222
- **PHOTO** Joe Grossinger, From *El Paso Street Art* 224
- **ESSAY** Randal C. Archibold, "Far from Home, Mexicans Sing Age-Old Ballads of New Life" 226
- **PHOTO** Chad Chase, *Jose F. Garcia and His Son Benjamin* 227

CLUSTER 4.3 | ROADS WE TRAVEL 230

- **POSTER** *Road Trip* Movie Poster 231
- **FICTION** John Steinbeck, From *The Grapes of Wrath* 232
- **PHOTO** *Cadillac Ranch* 235
- **FICTION** Jack Kerouac, From *On the Road* 236
- **PHOTO** Jack Kerouac 241
- **ESSAY** Holland Cotter, "On My Road" 242
- **PHOTOS** Ben Shahn, *Sign on a Restaurant, Lancaster, Ohio 1938*; Russell Lee, *Man Drinking at a Water Cooler in the Street Car Terminal, Oklahoma City, Oklahoma, July 1939* 246

WRITING ABOUT PLACES AND ENVIRONMENTS 248

Project 4.1: Analyzing a Representation of a Place 259

- **STUDENT PROJECT** Jenna Williamson, "Gainesville: Selling Small-Town America" 251

Project 4.2: Observing and Analyzing a Public Space 255

- **STUDENT PROJECT** Kruti Parekh, "India: A Culinary Experience" 257

Additional Projects 261

viii CONTENTS

CHAPTER 5
Media 262

READING TEXTS ABOUT THE MEDIA 264

Gallery | Messages in the Media 265
- *Got Milk?* 265
- Crowd Gathered Outside an Outdoor TV Set in India 266
- CNN/YouTube Democratic Presidential Debate 267
- Personality Identification Playing Cards 268
- Lewis Hine, *Girl Worker in Cotton Mill* 269
- Philip Greenberg, Viagra Model Car 270
- Human Rights Watch Web Site 271
- *Princess Mononoke* Still 272
- Filming an Episode of *Survivor* 273

CLUSTER 5.1 | STORIES OF WAR 274
- **INTERVIEW** Gene Santoro, "A Conversation with Ken Burns" 275
- **PHOTO** Watching a Medic, *Sicily, August 9, 1943* 278
- **WEB PAGE** Public Broadcasting Service, *The War* Web Site 279
- **ESSAY** David Carr, "Telling War's Deadly Story at Just Enough Distance" 280
- **PHOTO** George Bush Meeting with Burned Soldier 282
- **ESSAY** Susan Sontag, From *Regarding the Pain of Others* 284
- **PHOTO** Nick Ut, *Vietnam Napalm* 290
- **PHOTO** Iraqi Prisoner Consoles His Son 291

CLUSTER 5.2 | FILM STORIES OVER THE YEARS 292
- **PHOTOS** Still Images from *Casablanca* and *North by Northwest* 293
- **ESSAY** Amy Taubin, "Fear of a Black Cinema" 296
- **PHOTOS** Still Images from *Do the Right Thing* 300
- **ESSAY** Brian D. Johnson, "The Collateral Damage of *Crash*" 302
- **PHOTOS** Still Images from *Crash* 304
- **PHOTOS** Still Images from *Brokeback Mountain* 305

CLUSTER 5.3 | CITIZENS MAKING MEDIA 306
- **ESSAY** Henry Jenkins, "From YouTube to YouNiversity" 307
- **WEB PAGE** Newbie's Guide to Literacy Theory 312
- **PHOTO** Oh Yeon-ho, founder of OhmyNews 313
- **ESSAY** Brad Stone, "MySpace Data Mining" 314
- **ESSAY** Scott Adams, "Giving Stuff Away on the Internet" 316
- **CARTOON** Scott Adams, *Dilbert* cartoon 317

WRITING ABOUT MEDIA 318

Project 5.1: Exploring a Filmmaker 319
- **STUDENT PROJECT** Virginia Wooten, "*North by Northwest* and *Spellbound: Identifiably Hitchcock*" 320

Project 5.2: Composing a Photo Essay 327
- **STUDENT PROJECT** Michael Lee, "Images of History: The Hmong" 328

Additional Projects 330

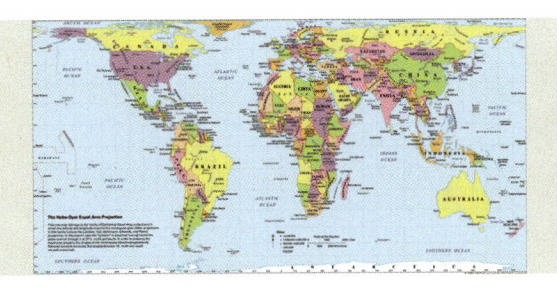

CHAPTER 6
Technology and Science 332

READING TEXTS ABOUT TECHNOLOGY AND SCIENCE 334

Gallery | Technology and Science 335
- PocketX Software, Cell Phone Instructions 335
- LCD Screen on a Lexus GS 450h 336
- Bar Graphs and Table, File Sharing 2002–2003 337
- AMA Poster *Girlie Drinks, Women's Diseases* 338
- MRI Brain Images 339
- Kiosk with Informational Flyers 340
- Newspaper Rock, Utah 341
- Ready.gov images 342
- National Geographic *EarthPulse* Web Site 343

CLUSTER 6.1 | MAPPING KNOWLEDGE 344
- **PHOTO** NASA, *Blue Marble* 345
- **PHOTO** Images from *Blue Marble, Next Generation* 346
- **ESSAY** Evan Ratliff, "Google Maps Is Changing the Way We See the World" 348
- **PHOTO** Aerial Streetview Photo 352
- **EDITORIAL** *The Denver Post*, "Now on Google Maps: You" 353
- **POEM** Elizabeth Bishop, "The Map" 354
- **ESSAY** Susan Neville, "On Maps and Globes" 355

CLUSTER 6.2 | LIFE SCIENCE 360
- **POSTERS** Movie Posters from *Frankenstein*, *Blade Runner: The Final Cut* and *Gattaca* 361
- **ESSAY** Nicholas Wade, "Genetic Engineers Who Don't Just Tinker" 362
- **PHOTOS** Photos of Genetically Engineered Animals 364
- **PHOTOS** Art Works from *Gene(sis): Contemporary Art Explores Human Genomics* 365
- **ESSAY** Natalie Angier, "Pursuing Synthetic Life, Dazzled by Reality" 366
- **ESSAY** Max M. Houck, "*CSI* Reality" 368
- **PHOTO** Television Still from *CSI: Miami* 373

CLUSTER 6.3 | LIVING IN VIRTUAL WORLDS 374
- **WEB PAGE** Screenshot from Guild Wars 374
- **ESSAY** Andrea L. Foster, "The Avatars of Research" 375
- **WEB PAGES** Screenshots from Second Life 378
- **ESSAY** Alan Sipress, "Does Virtual Reality Need a Sheriff?" 379
- **ESSAY** Steven Johnson, "This is Your Brain on Video Games" 381
- **ESSAY** Kevin Spivey, "Baby, You Mean the World of Warcraft to Me" 385

WRITING ABOUT TECHNOLOGY AND SCIENCE 386

Project 6.1: Explaining a New Development in Technology or Science 388
- **STUDENT PROJECT** Beau Faulkner, "*Year Zero*: A Viral Marketing Promotion" 389

Project 6.2: Composing a Set of Instructions 394
- **STUDENT PROJECT** Hannah Bailey, "Fitting and Preparing Pointe Shoes" 395

Additional Projects 399

CHAPTER 7
Style, Design, and Culture 400

READING TEXTS ABOUT STYLE, DESIGN, AND CULTURE 402

Gallery | Style, Design, and Culture 403
- Screensaver, *The Devil Wears Prada* 403
- Greg Marting, Giro Atmos Bicycle Helmet 404
- Nintendo Wii Controller 405
- Mary J. Blige, Gap (PRODUCT) RED Collection Ad 406
- Still from *King Kong*, 1933; Poster for *King Kong*, 1976 407
- Jeep Design Language: 1940–Present Day 408
- Jay B. Sauceda, "Let Me Learn Ya Somethin'" 409

CLUSTER 7.1 | THE DESIGN OF EVERYDAY THINGS 410
- **PHOTO** F-16 Fighting Falcon 411
- **ESSAY** Michael Bierut, "To Hell with the Simple Paper Clip" 412
- **DRAWING** The Freedom Chair 414
- **INTERVIEW** Pilar Viladas, "Questions for Niels Diffrient" 415
- **PHOTO** Le Corbusier, Villa Savoye at Poissy, France 416
- **ESSAY** Cathleen McGuigan, "The McMansion Next Door: Why the American House Needs a Makeover" 418
- **PHOTO** "HeadOn, Apply Directly to the Forehead" 420
- **ESSAY** Seth Stevenson, "Head Case: The Mesmerizing Ad for Headache Gel" 421

CLUSTER 7.2 | THE EYES OF THE BEHOLDER 424
- **PHOTOS** Still from Dove's Campaign for Real Beauty 425
- **ESSAY** "The Campaign for Real Beauty Background" 426
- **PHOTO** Nikki Blonsky, star of the film *Hairspray* 428
- **ESSAY** Virginia Postrel, "The Truth about Beauty" 429
- **CARTOON** Christo Komarnitski, *Obesity Planet* 432
- **ESSAY** Daniel Akst, "Looks *Do* Matter" 433

CLUSTER 7.3 | THE CULTURE AND POLITICS OF DESIGN 442
- **PHOTO** GMC Yukon Hybrid Logo 442
- **MANIFESTO** "First Things First Manifesto 2000" 444
- **WEB PAGE** Adbusters Web site, Blackspot Sneakers 446
- **ESSAY** Linda Baker, "Salon.com asks 'Are you ready for some 'unswooshing'?" 447
- **PHOTO** Torin Boyd for *The New York Times*, Japanese Vending Dress Used as Urban Camouflage 452
- **ESSAY** Martin Fackler, "Fearing Crime, Japanese Wear the Hiding Place" 453

WRITING ABOUT STYLE, DESIGN, AND CULTURE 456

Project 7.1: Analyzing the Design of an Everyday Text 458
- **STUDENT PROJECT** Dylan Ellis, "June 23, 1989" 459

Project 7.2 Studying Design and Its Contexts 463
- **STUDENT PROJECT** Sean Nixon, "The Transformation of American Architecture during the 1920s and 1930s" 464

Additional Projects 469

CHAPTER 8
Politics and Advocacy 470

READING TEXTS AND IMAGES ABOUT POLITICS AND ADVOCACY 472

Gallery | Politics and Advocacy 475
- Political bumper stickers 475
- Andrew Parsons, *An Iraqi Woman Shows Her Inked Finger after Casting Her Ballot in a Polling Station in Baghdad* 476
- Todd Heisler, *Reno, Nevada* 477
- PETA, *Fur is Dead* poster 478
- Margaret Bourke-White, *At the Time of the Louisville Flood* 479
- USA Today, "Debate: College Affordability" Opposing Editorials 480
- Dick Locher, Cartoon 482
- Screenshot From Pottercast, the Harry Potter Podcast 483

CLUSTER 8.1 | GETTING OUT THE VOTE 484
- **AD** Urban Outfitters T-Shirt 485
- **ESSAY** The Onion, "Huge Democracy Geek Even Votes in Primaries" 486
- **ESSAY** Thomas Friedman, "Generation Q" 487
- **ESSAY** Courtney Martin, "Generation Overwhelmed" 489
- **AD** "Rock the Vote" Official T-shirt 491
- **WEB PAGE** Redeem the Vote 492
- **WEB PAGE** Voto Latino 493
- **WEB PAGE** PunkVoter 493
- **ESSAY** Mike Connery, "Journalist Cheat Sheet: Eleven Tips for Reporting the Youth Vote" 494

CLUSTER 8.2 | THE POLITICS OF FOOD 496
- **ESSAY** Michael S. Rosenwald, "Why America Has to Be Fat" 497
- **PHOTOS** Lauren Greenfield, Images from *Thin* and *Camp Shane* 500

- **ESSAY** Gary Shteyngart, "Sixty-nine Cents" 502
- **ESSAY** Kim Severson, "Be It Ever So Homespun, There's Nothing Like Spin" 504
- **ESSAY** Michael Pollan, "Why Bother?" 507
- **ESSAY** Jonathan Rauch, "Will Frankenfood Save the Planet?" 512
- **PHOTOS** Peter Menzel and Faith D'Aluisio. Images from *Hungry Planet: What the World Eats* 519

CLUSTER 8.3 | TAKING ACTION 522
- **PHOTO** Bono Speaking on Third-World Debt Relief at the U.S. Capitol 523
- **ESSAY** Mark Yaconelli, "Christian Megastar: Bono on Record" 524
- **ESSAY** David Heim, "Breakfast with Bono" 526
- **PHOTO** Bono Greets George W. Bush after Speaking at the National Prayer Breakfast, 2006 527
- **ESSAY** Paul Theroux, "The Rock Star's Burden" 528
- **PRESS KIT** The New York City Street Memorial Project/Ghost Bike Project 531
- **ESSAY** Alex Williams, "Realistic Idealists" 534

WRITING ABOUT POLITICS AND ADVOCACY 538

Project 8.1: Analyzing a Political Argument 540
- **STUDENT PROJECT** Jonathan Butler, "Visual Images of National Identity: Propaganda Posters of the Great War" 541

Project 8.2: Creating a Public Service Announcement 545
- **STUDENT PROJECT** Meixia Huang, "Pay Attention to Them" 545

Additional Projects 549

Image Credits 550
Text Credits 551
Index 553

Preface

Beyond Words is an anthology built on the assumption that the most dynamic writing classes grow from encounters with contemporary culture and media. Writers naturally want to write about issues and materials they come up against daily and can do so powerfully, given appropriate tools for analysis and composition. That's what the first edition of *Beyond Words* proved to instructors and students alike. This second edition extends that realization by offering materials more concise and practical in their pedagogy, richer in their presentation, and in many cases eagerly suggested or endorsed by students. It is a collection even better adapted to contemporary writing courses.

What's New to This Edition

- A fresh opening chapter on "Reading Texts" introduces **key rhetorical concepts** and terms used systematically throughout the book including *subject, audience, purpose, genre, media, context,* and *structure/composition.*
- A chapter on "Composing Texts" more thoroughly explains **composing processes** and includes detailed checklists (all in one place) for key assignments offered in *Beyond Words.* The chapter concludes with an annotated student project.
- A cluster of readings in Chapter 1 on culture and media introduces **key issues** explored in *Beyond Words.*
- The six extensively updated anthology chapters are **simpler in structure** and more precisely organized around specific contemporary themes.
- **"Galleries"** in the opening sections of the anthology chapters offer images and texts to jump-start class discussions. Each gallery item is supported by exercises and is cross-referenced to introductory material in the chapters.
- **Reorganized and better focused clusters** in each anthology chapter provide effective teachable units. These revised clusters serve as "casebooks," offering readings, images, exercises, and writing projects that encourage students to explore important issues in depth.
- New "Writing About . . ." sections in each anthology chapter provide **instruction tailored to support major student projects**. The material is also cross-referenced to general writing instruction in Chapter 2, "Composing Texts."
- **New sample student papers** or projects are given in every anthology chapter. Each chapter concludes with two full models, one of them annotated to highlight key points or rhetorical features.
- Gallery items, visual texts, clusters, and projects are **systematically numbered** for quick identification and reference.
- Larger images throughout the anthology feature an enhanced, **magazine-style format and design**.
- The second edition offers dozens of new visual and verbal texts with more than **50 percent new**.

In concept and coverage, these changes describe a book as fully innovative as the first edition and yet more welcoming to instructors who are looking for a fresh approach to their established composition courses, whether beginning or advanced. The familiar terminology in *Beyond Words*, its cleaner pedagogical structure, and its detailed writing projects make focusing on culture and media intuitive and appealing. Yet the revised materials also guarantee a consequential engagement with ideas and attitudes writers today find central to their studies, whatever their majors or interests: an inquiry into cultural values and priorities, a critique of media influence, an interest in political engagement, and a concern for social and intellectual diversity.

Indeed, we wrote *Beyond Words* in large part to respond to challenges raised by transformations in technology, communication, and composition sweeping the academic and professional worlds—challenges that call for both students and instructors to develop fresh protocols for understanding culture and media. So this anthology presents a rich array of visual and verbal texts that invite writers to respond in innovative ways. But *Beyond Words* does much more.

Readings and Organization

What distinguishes *Beyond Words* is the powerful way it connects new cultural phenomena and media to traditional rhetorical concepts and themes. Instructors who offer thematic courses will find timely subjects in every chapter—with six full chapters focused on topics central to many composition pedagogies these days: Identities; Places and Environments; Media; Technology and Science; Style, Design, and Culture; and Politics and Advocacy. If they structure their courses rhetorically, instructors will find ample materials in the two introductory chapters "Reading Texts" and "Composing Texts" as well as in detailed explanations that support major writing projects at the end of each anthology chapter.

The readings and assignments in Chapter 4, "Places and Environments," for example, examine various definitions of "place" and different ways of embodying these spaces, in words, pictures, digital environments, even songs. Students might respond to these materials with narratives about home, political arguments over borderlands, photo essays of urban environments, or other types of compositions. The texts in the chapter and the responses to them might serve as examples of expressive, informative, or argumentative writing—but they do not have to.

We've taken a similar approach with subsequent chapters, encouraging instructors to follow different paths, depending on their pedagogical inclinations. An instructor interested in culture and identity might emphasize Chapters 3 through 5, which focus on people, their environments, and their stories. An instructor more invested in political and social themes might prefer the technology, design, and social advocacy topics explored in Chapters 6 through 8. We believe that the flexible design of the book, built around thematic concerns and detailed writing activities, will help students explore a variety of texts, allowing them to say, "Wow, let me think. . . ." rather than "Whoa, what do I do with this?"

We want students to be surprised and challenged by the materials in *Beyond Words*. We include essays in numerous traditional nonfiction genres: personal reflections, manifestos, newspaper columns, op-ed pieces, news stories, technical analyses, reviews, and arguments. We also offer fiction of several kinds, including poems and selections from novels. But we have added many examples of texts less common in collections for writing courses:

photographs, photo essays, Web sites, YouTube videos, magazine covers, song lyrics, film stills, print ads and TV commercials, cartoons, graphic novels, street art, maps, MRIs, bumper stickers, and much more. In this edition, many such texts—for example, the Chris Jordan images that introduce Chapter 1 and the Hipster PDA in Chapter 7—came from students using the first edition of *Beyond Words*.

Pedagogical Strategy

Beyond Words offers all the support most students will require to move from reading to writing. That's no small claim. The eye-catching selections throughout the anthology certainly invite students to think about a wide range of topics and issues. But the tougher challenge is moving students to respond to the selections intelligently or to create texts of their own. Checklists and exercises alone won't do it—though *Beyond Words* offers such features. What's required is a strategy for instruction built deep into the structure of the book that gives students the concepts, tools, and examples they need to compose successfully. That instruction begins with "Reading Texts" and "Composing Texts," the opening pair of chapters that frame the book's key rhetorical terms and concepts. The sequence of concepts introduced in "Reading Texts" (*subject, audience, purpose, genre, media, context,* and *structure/composition*) is echoed (with sensible variations) in "Composing Texts," where additional topics are also introduced: *doing research and documenting sources* and *revising and editing.* These important concepts then reappear in "Writing About . . ." sections, which conclude each of the anthology chapters and provide detailed support for major writing projects.

The anthology chapters (3–8), of course, draw upon the two opening chapters to guide students through texts many will find unfamiliar and challenging. Indeed, the small cluster of readings in Chapter 1—featuring essays by a librarian, film critic, and media critic—models a range of responses readers may have to contemporary culture.

The anthology chapters themselves have their own pedagogical sequence.

- **Signature images selected to provoke response.** Each chapter begins with a provocative pair of images, followed by a brief analysis.
- **Introductory section and gallery.** The theme of the chapter is explained and explored, keyed to supporting items in a gallery of texts and images that follow. The gallery items resonate with chapter themes but also provoke response in many directions through their evocative subjects and accompanying exercises.
- **Clustered selections.** Following the gallery, each anthology chapter presents three focused clusters, which use texts and images to give students multiple perspectives on a topic, making for more nuanced responses. In Chapter 3, "Identities," for example, the clusters are "Life Stories, "Bodies," and "Groups and Ethnicities."
- **Innovative Assignments and Projects.** Each anthology chapter ends with the "Writing About . . ." section discussed above followed by two major assignments—each of them illustrated by authentic and complete student models. We believe that these projects are among the most useful features in the book, providing students with believable examples of the kind of projects they might pursue. The samples vary from traditional essays to multimedia projects. They also demonstrate a range of sophistication and media savvy.

Supplements

The new **MyCompLab** Website integrates the market-leading instruction, multimedia tutorials, and exercises for writing, grammar and research that users have come to identify with the program with a new online composing space and new assessment tools. The result is a revolutionary application that offers a seamless and flexible teaching and learning environment built specifically for writers. Created after years of extensive research and in partnership with composition faculty and students across the country, the new MyCompLab provides help for writers in the context of their writing, with instructor and peer commenting functionality, proven tutorials and exercises for writing, grammar and research, an e-portfolio, an assignment-builder, a bibliography tool, tutoring services, and a gradebook and course management organization created specifically for writing classes. Visit www.mycomplab.com for more information.

The **Instructor's Resource Manual** provides teachers with clear and concise strategies for using *Beyond Words* in a variety of courses. The IRM outlines practical classroom approaches to help teachers prepare their students to read, analyze, and write about verbal and visual texts in several genres. To this end, the manual includes sample course syllabi as well as specific teaching ideas, reading and writing exercises and prompts, and lists of additional resources for each chapter of *Beyond Words*, including resources found in MyCompLab.

Acknowledgments

Obviously, a book as wide-ranging as *Beyond Words* required the talents and assistance of many people. The book simply would not exist without the determination of our editor, Lynn Huddon, who had a spirited vision for the original project and has carried it through into this second edition. The book also owes much to the encouragement, creativity, and expertise of our development editor, Katharine Glynn, and our production editor, Kathy Smith.

Among the students who in one way or another contributed ideas, suggestions for images, or short passages from papers to this second edition are the following from the University of Texas at Austin: Jordyn Brown, Tzer-Shiuan Chiang, Maxine Defforey, Vincent Didaniele, Solomon Fong, Michael Gould, Ryan Hailey, Mexia Huang, Benjamin Orlansky, Andres Sada, and Gregory Webb. Contributing full essays are Jacqueline Cruz, Dylan Ellis, Beau Faulkner, Kruti Parekh, and Jenna Williamson from the University of Texas and Jonathan Butler and Hannah Bailey from the University of South Carolina. Thanks as well go to students at the University of North Carolina for their contributions, especially Michael Lee, Sean Nixon, and Billy Smith. And special thanks to research assistants Cindy Anderson, Lisa Bailey, Christopher Broadbent, John Erik Metcalf, and Bradley Stratton, who suggested many ideas and images for this project.

The design and production of *Beyond Words* demonstrate the creative energy of a talented team, including Ellen MacElree, Julie Tesser, Rona Tucillo, Alisha Webber, and Jerilyn Bockorick. We appreciate the skill and pedagogical expertise of those who revised and updated the Instructor's Manual for *Beyond Words*.

We are indebted to our colleagues who reviewed the book for their generous and useful insights: Barclay Barrios, Rutgers University; David Beach, George Mason University; Amy

Braziller, Red Rocks Community College; Mike Chaser, University of Iowa; Ron Christiansen, Salt Lake Community College; Keith Comer, Idaho State University; Karen Culver, University of Miami; Trevor Dodge, Clackamas Community College; Jay Dolmage, West Virginia University; Patrice Fleck, Northern Virginia Community College; Patricia M. Garcia, Our Lady of the Lake University; Judith Gardner, University of Texas, San Antonio; Brenda Helmbrecht, California Polytechnic State University, San Luis Obispo; Bruce Henderson, Fullerton College; Ellen Hendrix, Georgia Southern University; Brook Hessler, Oklahoma City University; Charlie Hill, University of Wisconsin, Oshkosh; Van Hillard, Duke University; Bryan Hull, Portland Community College; Edward Joyce, Suffolk County Community College; Kate Maurer, University of Minnesota, Duluth; John Faber McAlister, University of Iowa; Gloria McMillan, Pima Community College; Tamara Miles, Orangeburg-Calhoun Technical College; Hildy Miller, Portland State University; Nancy Morrow, University of California, Davis; Michael Neal, Florida State University; Stephanie Paterson, California State University, Stanislaus; Dara Perales, Mira Costa College; Beverly Reed, Stephen F. Austin State University; Thomas Rickert, Purdue University; Patricia Roby, University of Wisconsin, Washington County; Catherine E. Ross, The University of Texas at Tyler; Kathleen J. Ryan, University of Montana; Sara Safdie, Bellevue Community College; Sherry Suisman, San Francisco State University; Deborah Coxwell Teague, Florida State University; Lou Thompson, Texas Women's University; Monica Parrish Trent, Montgomery College; Mark Tursi, University of Denver; Greta Vollmer, Sonoma State University; Eve Wiederhold, University of North Carolina, Greensboro; and Xiaoye You, Purdue University.

John Ruszkiewicz    **Daniel Anderson**    **Christy Friend**

INTRODUCTION

Digital media and technology have altered the way we interact with the world. Many of us now take devices such as smart phones and iPods for granted; routinely converse with friends via instant messages; share our lives on Facebook; amuse ourselves with video games; pull weather information we need off the Internet; and track political and cultural events via blogs and YouTube. We download music to our computers, take photographs with cell phones, and do much academic work online. But being immersed in new media is not the same as comprehending all its messages or knowing how to respond to them critically. For centuries, people were considered literate if they could just read and write. And that's still the case. But reading and composing sure look different today.

Beyond Words is designed to help you to negotiate such differences—to make you a more self-conscious participant in a culture that is growing ever more complex. Our title itself tells you that we intend to explore literacy in its many forms—verbal, visual, tactile, aural. But words remain at the heart of the enterprise, the medium that enables us to talk about all the rest. We ask you to examine a wide range of provocative items—as different as a HeadOn ad, an Iraqi wall mural on Abu Ghraib, and a chapter from *On the Road*—because such diverse and challenging works invite critical response and provoke the kinds of inquiry common in academic courses and environments. Our aim is to give you systematic strategies for dealing with all of them. But just as the texts presented throughout *Beyond Words* routinely cross media boundaries, the activities and assignments in this anthology also encourage you to bend the meaning of "text" and challenge you to explore an expanded notion of literacy, one that may push you to consider reading and composing in more than words alone. Why? Because you already live in an environment that assumes you *are* literate in this way.

Understanding How We Read and Write Today

One marker of the new literacy is the ease with which people are expected to shift between and among media. Once again, for good or ill, the boundaries have largely disappeared between knowledge, art, news, and commerce.

Consider how complicated the phenomenon of launching a major movie such as *Iron Man* or the latest *Indiana Jones* sequel has become. It usually starts with a Web site for the forthcoming film, requiring Flash plug-ins to experience the cast interviews, interactive games, chat rooms, screen savers, and contests tied to the launch of the product. The site will also give you access to the film's trailers—noisy, fast-paced teasers often more entertaining than the film itself—which will play in movie houses (and on YouTube) months before the epic itself opens. As the movie premiere nears, the lead actors drop in on news/talk programs to show clips, and their action figures appear in stores and fast-food outlets. When the film opens its run in theaters, critics review it in print, online, and on TV ("Two thumbs up!"). Whether a success or a bomb in its initial release, the film will reappear a few months later on Blu-ray discs, usually including enhancements—possibly a director's cut—and lots of extras. The film might spawn a sequel or two, a book, a music CD, a TV series, a video game, a board game, maybe even a Broadway musical. How many media is that?

Even something as "simple" as a Web page can be a multimedia event. A single screen of CNN.com, for example, features not only headlines, news, and photographs but also links to audio and video files. It may also include ads that move and change depending on who has logged in, as well as innumerable paths to more pages and still more visual and aural kicks. The screen might look like a mess to someone accustomed to the sober front pages of the print-version of the *Wall Street Journal* or *New York Times*. But most Web users probably find it lively, inviting, and highly readable.

Not surprisingly, when you compose in digital environments yourself, you're as much a conductor or juggler as a writer. You've adapted to the unprecedented speed and fluidity of media and know, almost intuitively, how to move from reading an article to taking notes to responding to e-mails to checking a calendar to watching a film clip, and on and on. The process isn't so much linear as simultaneous; its very ease conceals the brain's remarkable power to assimilate and manipulate information.

But there may be a downside to all this velocity. What do you do when you encounter a demanding text, one that can't be read hurriedly or clarified by a quick Google search—the sort of work essayist Francis Bacon (1551–1626) advised should "be read wholly, and with diligence and attention"? You slow down, you pay attention, you read with diligence and care, taking the time necessary to appreciate what you are learning, to see the details, and to think critically. This kind of reading remains essential to your academic work and to your thoughtful encounters with ideas and culture.

Looking at the History of Words and Images

If visual and technical complexity strike you as uniquely modern, however, think again. We didn't invent multimedia in the past decade, nor are we the first generation to live with texts and images. Perhaps the ancient Egyptians led the way. Thousands of years before the Greeks built the Parthenon (432 BCE) or the Romans their Coliseum (75 CE), the Egyptians were ornamenting their sculptures, buildings, and books with images and hieroglyphics. This glossing of physical objects was routine: almost no wall went undecorated.

Ideas and images met on papyrus too. A page from the *Book of the Dead*, for instance, is as visually rich as any modern text. Such mergers of text and images are also a feature of Japanese painting and art.

Page from the *Book of the Dead*, 1040–945 BCE

Detail from Trajan's column, 106–113 CE

The ancient Greeks and Romans, too, shuttled easily between media. The Greeks, of course, invented principles of rhetoric still influential today and created public spaces for both oratory and theater. The Romans, who imitated and extended Hellenic accomplishments in language, were also warriors and builders. So when the emperor Trajan decided to memorialize his conquests in the early second century CE, he did so on a 100-foot column on which the story of his conquests winds around the shaft in an ascending spiral, even if no one could see the ending once the monument was erected. (According to art historian Paul Johnson, citizens in Rome could learn more about Trajan's victories at a nearby library, a very modern multimedia touch.)

Centuries later, during an era inappropriately dubbed the Dark Ages, monks in Northumbria (northern England) produced what may be Western culture's most beautiful book, the *Lindisfarne Gospels* (715–720 CE). The monks who illuminated the gospels were doing more than adding pictures to biblical stories. Their rich designs embodied complex theological concepts and mysteries, and deepened the experience of reading the scriptures.

The European Middle Ages also produced a multimedia experience perhaps never quite equaled: the Gothic cathedral. The largely illiterate population knew how to "read" the Bible

Page from the *Lindisfarne Gospels*

stories on the elaborately sculpted facades and stained-glass windows of the cathedrals. Inside, the faithful could hear a Mass, which, on the greatest feast days, might incorporate appeals to every sense:

- music and bells for the ears
- candles, decorated altars, and processions of clerics in colorful robes for the eyes
- incense for the olfactory sense
- readings and sermons for the mind and heart

Such spectacles earned the ire of Reformation theologians, many of whom objected strongly to the presence of statues, images, music, and art in churches. These reformers joined a long list of "iconoclasts" over the ages who were suspicious enough of the power of the visual to forbid or even destroy "graven images." The most recent of these iconoclasts may be the Taliban in Afghanistan, who in 2001 demolished centuries-old statues of Buddha carved into a mountainside.

Statue of Buddha before and after destruction by the Taliban in Afghanistan, 2001

Over the centuries, too, media themselves have mutated and developed—and thinkers such as Marshall McLuhan (1911–1980) have argued that such shifts have far-reaching consequences, even changing how we think and relate to one another. The story of writing and printing alone could fill an encyclopedia, as texts migrated from papyrus and scrolls to early handwritten books on vellum to Gutenberg's printing press to personal computers. And each medium of expression and communication—sculpture, painting, architecture, landscaping, photography, film, graphic design—has its own equally complex history, usually tied inextricably to other arts. Today, all these stories and streams of influence come together when you—the heir of great traditions refreshed by new technologies—read and compose.

Using *Beyond Words*

Given the vast scope of our subject—and we genuinely hope you'll be surprised by the diversity of material you'll find in *Beyond Words*—we needed a structure that would be both familiar and roomy, one that would accommodate an exciting variety of images and readings but still lead you through a thoughtful succession of cultural texts and assignments, whether you read the book in sequence or just browse.

We've based our structure on the familiar rhetorical pyramid to remind you that any act of communication involves relationships (always changing) among an **author** or creator (*you*), a **subject** matter, an **audience**, and a **medium** of communication. We've positioned this structure inside a globe because all communication occurs within a tangle of social, political, and cultural **contexts**—which together make up our world. And if this weren't a book, we'd set our pyramid and globe spinning together to suggest the dynamic relationships among all these elements.

The first two chapters of *Beyond Words* use the key concepts embodied in this rhetorical pyramid—as well as a few familiar terms such as **purpose**, **genre**, and **structure**—to present the general issues you'll face in reading and reacting to materials of all sorts. The subsequent chapters then direct you to texts (alone and in clusters) that focus on six areas of cultural significance: Identities; Places and Environments; Media; Technology and Ideas; Style, Design, and Culture; and Politics and Advocacy. Each of the anthology chapters concludes with detailed instruction for writing about its themes, several major writing assignments, and two sample student projects, one of them annotated. So we hope you will react to the texts we have assembled with words and images of your own. After all, potentially, everyone is a printer, publisher, cartoonist, editor, and designer today. Everyone is a would-be sports reporter, artist, journalist, filmmaker, or musician. And, of course, everyone's a writer.

Our intention in *Beyond Words*, then, is to offer you a fresh way of addressing texts that reflect the cultural currents of our time. We want you to learn to appreciate the introspection of the portrait photographer, the sense of space of the architect, the steady gaze of the mapmaker, the cunning of the advertiser, the grace of the designer, the passion of the activist. No book can cover every motive for composing or explore every intriguing theme. But we hope you'll find much in this book that expands the way you think about literacy and writing, about images and art, indeed, about all media. But, most of all, we hope *Beyond Words* encourages you to write.

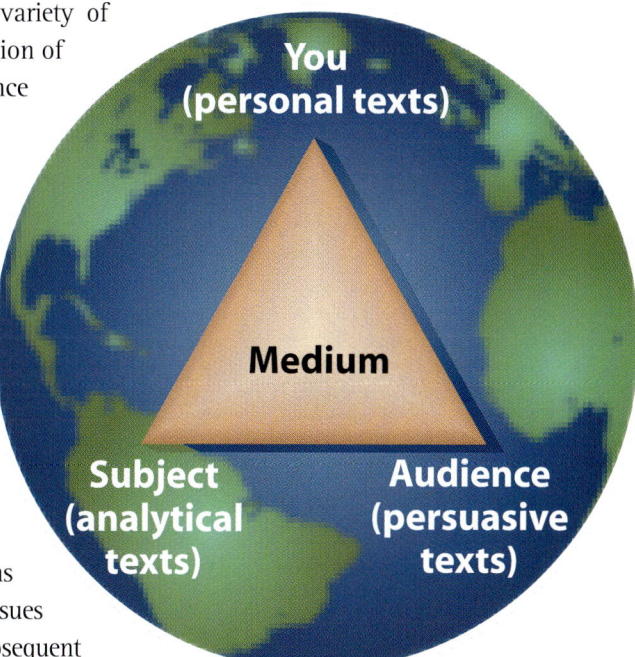

CHAPTER 1

READING TEXTS

ITEM 1.1 ■ Chris Jordan, *Cans Seurat*, 2007

Has artist/photographer Chris Jordan gotten your attention with his work entitled *Cans Seurat* (see Item 1.1)? You might recognize it is an adaptation of a famous painting by Georges Seurat entitled *A Sunday Afternoon on the Island of La Grande Jatte* (1884-86), one of the most celebrated works in the Art Institute of Chicago. Like Seurat's masterpiece, Jordan's photograph is huge, five feet tall and almost eight feet wide. But whereas Seurat painted with oil, using a remarkable technique called pointillism to create an image entirely from dots of color, Chris Jordan worked in a wholly different medium. As the close-ups show, *Cans Seurat* is built from aluminum cans.

What is Jordan's point? A caption explains all: "Depicts 106,000 aluminum cans, the number used in the US every thirty seconds." And this item is part of an ongoing series of photographs by Jordan graphically depicting the awesome maw of American culture—from the two million plastic bottles we use every *five* minutes to the eight million trees harvested every month to make mail order catalogs. Jordan uses his startling photographs to break through the media clutter, to get us to pause for a moment and *reflect* in a world that numbs our responses by the sheer volume of messages it sends.

Just in moving from a classroom to your dorm or apartment, you encounter so many texts that you may not notice any of them—not the posters on the classroom walls, EXIT signs above doors, headlines in the campus paper, logos on T-shirts, shouts from activists on the mall, banners strung across the street, and on and on. To gain attention, a text practically has to bully its way into our minds. Think of that endlessly repeated ad for a headache treatment: *HeadOn—Apply directly to the forehead*.

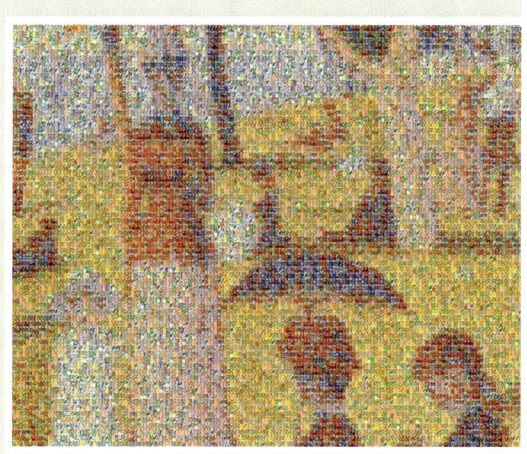

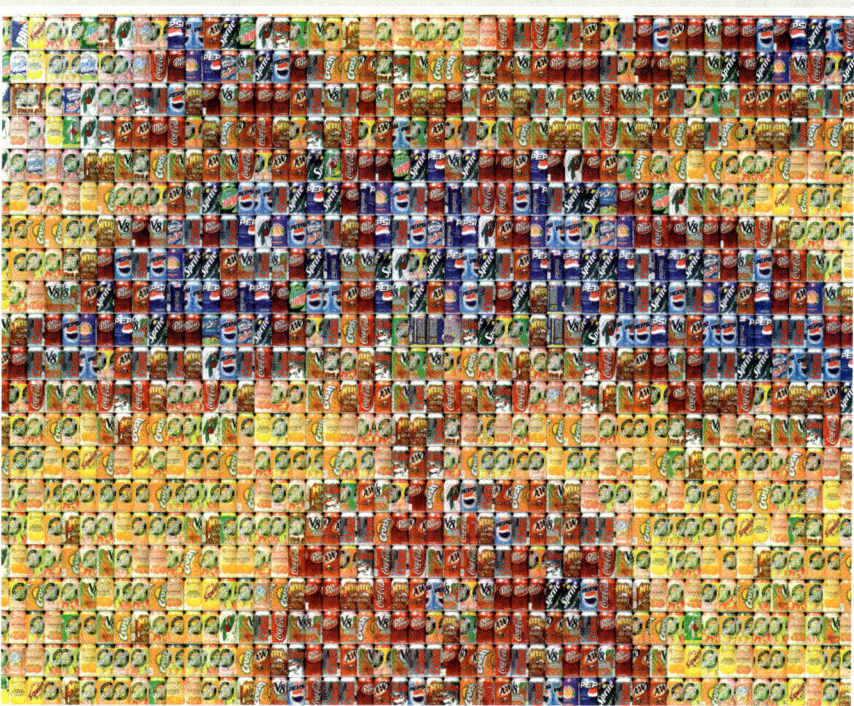

But even less aggressive (and perhaps more worthy) texts regularly invite us to take the initiative as readers, to look more closely at them, and to figure out what they have to offer. Throughout this book, we define *text* very broadly to include *anything deliberately fashioned by human beings to convey an idea, a message, or even a feeling*. By our definition, then, a forest isn't a text, but a photograph of one could be. A city in itself might be too vast and random to be a coherent text, but it contains many messages worth reading and writing about. Movies, paintings, posters, murals, songs, symphonies, sculptures, advertisements, bumper stickers, T-shirts, video games, and e-mails are all texts. Most important for our purposes, words and images are texts that carry messages and make meaning. We read and explore these works by looking at them closely, and by seeing how they connect with and illuminate other texts.

You may already have training in what is called *critical reading* and might want to review some of the general techniques careful readers use—such as pre-reading, annotating, summarizing, and paraphrasing. But we'd also like you to begin reading texts rhetorically (see the Introduction) to appreciate how exactly they inform, influence, and persuade you. In this chapter, we present seven rhetorical dimensions for you to consider whenever you encounter works you find especially intriguing, challenging, or puzzling—including, we hope, the readings and images you'll find in Chapters 3–8. Those rhetorical elements are *subject, audience, purpose, genre, medium, context*, and *structure and composition*.

Identifying subject or focus

If someone handed you a slide rule today to figure out your taxes or do the calculations for a math test, you might feel confused and disoriented. What is this contraption, with its tiny numbers and parallel scales? How does it operate? What's it for? The moving ruler and clear plastic slides might tempt you to experiment with it, but you'd need plenty of assistance before you'd know how to use this unfamiliar object, which was common in American high schools prior to the invention of the pocket calculator.

Such a feeling of disorientation (or wonder) is actually a good place to begin your encounter with any new text—verbal, visual, aural, tactile. An intriguing text *should* attract your attention and provoke specific questions.

- What is it about? The question seems so basic because it is the one most of us ask when we encounter a new and unfamiliar text. Sometimes the answer is obvious; on other occasions you'll have to work to discover a clear-cut answer.
- What do you focus on in the work? Your reading of a text usually begins with a spark of interest. Can you identify what caused it—what the **focal point** of the work might be?

IDENTIFY THE SUBJECT

Books, articles, movies, images, and even ads must offer a subject worthy of your attention, one that gets you thinking. The subject matter of a text can be signaled in an almost infinite number of ways. A topic may be simply and clearly announced—as is the case in reference works, textbooks, and research reports. Titles, too, can help to define subject matter, even though they can also be mysterious, deliberately elusive, or provocative (see Item 1.2).

Often, the subject matter of a work such as a painting, novel, or film has to be inferred or interpreted. A book or movie may just seem to tell a story. What is the subject matter of the *Lord of the Rings* trilogy? In some ways, it's the tale of a Hobbit with a mission to destroy a sinister ring. But on other levels, it may be a reiteration of the heroic myths of Western culture or a retelling of the Second World War or yet another unfurling of a good-versus-evil saga. The effort to understand the subject matter of a complex text is one of the pleasures of reading. Great works tempt us to return to them often to discover new, different, and sometimes contradictory meanings.

Of course, you also need to be able to explain *how* you found those meanings in a text. A text should provide evidence for the interpretations you offer.

FIND FOCAL POINTS

One way to identify the subject of a text is to locate and examine its focal points. Writers, artists, designers, architects, and musicians know how important it is that their works converge on some thesis or theme. To be a good reader, you need to pay attention to their signals. If you've ever written a paper with a thesis statement or a paragraph with a topic sentence, you are familiar with one simple device for focusing with words: a sentence or two that clearly announces what the writer intends to discuss.

But there are dozens of other techniques for focusing attention. On a printed page, a big headline, an underscored heading, boldfaced or italicized type, or a four-color photo might entice your eye. In a photograph, an artist might use light and shadow to seduce your gaze or manipulate depth of focus (see Item 1.3), whereas a painter might align objects to direct your eyes (and thoughts) in a specific direction. On a Web page, you might first encounter a striking graphic or a tempting menu of options to focus your attention.

You can begin your encounters with texts by noting where you look first and then asking *why*. But be prepared, too, to be puzzled or deliberately thrown off balance. Many texts will resist your efforts to understand them at a glance, to pluck out the heart of their mysteries.

EXAMINE AND INTERPRET THE DETAILS

Sometimes details will reveal the subject and scope of a work. Successful texts get you thinking beyond your first impressions by offering up rich details. You may not notice these items initially because they are deliberately secondary—like the separate stones that make up an arch. But remove one stone and watch what happens. In written texts, it's often the details that provide support for a claim or make a story plausible. In music, the backbeat may be what defines a song and makes it memorable or tuneful. In visual texts, the details enrich or complicate our initial experience and encourage us to look again and again—like those aluminum cans in the Chris Jordan photograph.

But because of the sheer variety of texts, it's hard to provide general directions for paying attention to details beyond the obvious: read, look, and listen carefully. Still, some guidelines might be useful in helping you to assemble the numerous fine points of a text into a coherent statement about its subject matter or theme.

- Don't trust first impressions. They may very well be wrong or misleading, especially when something you are reading is truly new or moves contrary to your expectations.

- Assume that more may be going on than you initially surmise. Read any text imaginatively and creatively to appreciate how a writer or artist is developing a subject. Take for granted that someone has paid careful attention while creating it and that all its elements develop an idea or theme. In particular, look for connections between the primary subject or thesis of the work and all the supporting details.

- Approach every text, especially a familiar or conventional one, as if you were encountering it for the first time. Sometimes we stop paying attention when the terrain we are covering seems familiar—like driving the same road every day.

- Examine how the finer details help to define the subject of a work. Study the lighting technique used by the photographer, the brushstrokes of a painter, the similes and metaphors of a writer, and so on. Learn as much as you can about any texts you encounter often.

NOTICE WHAT'S MISSING

Sometimes what's *not* in a text is a key to its meaning—to appreciating its success, failure, or appeal. Perhaps the artistic movement *Minimalism* is the best expression of exclusion as a subject matter. Minimalists sought to reduce their art, architecture, literature, or music to core and necessary elements—and nothing more. An absence or empty space in such a work could be an important element (see Item 1.4)

But there are other kinds of omissions worth noticing when examining the subject matters of texts. Studying portraits of Renaissance men and women in a museum, you might see lots of aristocrats and churchmen, but very few commoners or laborers. American cinema for many decades rarely included native or minority groups, except as stereotypical figures: the subject matter of these films clearly represented the world of a majority culture. We notice such omissions today because of our greater focus on diversity. But we are probably overlooking other kinds of absences in texts currently being produced.

So think about what a text has excluded or left out. Pay attention to the framing or cropping of an image, the topics not covered in an article or newspaper, the people whose names or faces aren't represented in a work. These omissions may prove to be more than a matter of missing details. They may be clues to what's really going on in a text.

ITEM 1.2 ■ Pere Borrell del Caso, *Escaping Criticism*, 1874

Pere Borrell del Caso entitled this 1874 painting in the popular trompe d'oeil (fool the eye) style *Escaping Criticism*. How does the title shape your perception of its subject matter? Would your reading of the work change if its title were *Playing Hooky*?

1 | READING TEXTS

ITEM 1.3 ■ **James Evans,** *Hallie's Hands*, **1996**

The title of this photograph by James Evans seems almost superfluous given the way he has manipulated its depth of field to identify his subject so clearly. What stories might those hands tell? Where do you look next after gazing at them? Use the Web to learn more about Evans's subject: Hallie Stillwell.

14   IDENTIFYING SUBJECT OR FOCUS

ITEM 1.4 ■ Donald Judd, *Fifteen Untitled Works in Concrete*, 1980–84

Artist Donald Judd (1929–94) was a key figure in an art movement called *Minimalism*, which sought to create works stripped down to their fundamental elements. One of Judd's works is this installation of concrete shapes along a remote highway. How might you define its subject matter? Is it significant that the individual works are untitled?

CONSIDER

1. Working in a group, imagine some thoughtful alternative titles for Pere Borrell del Caso's *Escaping Criticism* (Item 1.2). How do your new titles change the subject matter of the piece or the way viewers might encounter it?

2. We're accustomed to seeing titles on papers, books, paintings, and poems. But where else do you find titles or "subject lines" that help you understand what a text might be about? Describe several of these items and how they function. Be open-minded, considering a wide variety of media.

3. Describe a time when you found yourself completely unable to figure out the subject of some text you encountered. It might have been a puzzling object like a slide rule, spork, or quirt, or perhaps a puzzling sculpture or film. How did you figure out what it was you were dealing with?

4. Using the Web, find a copy of Vermeer's painting entitled *Woman Holding a Balance*. Its title probably tells you what to examine first in the painting: the woman's delicate fingers holding a balance in the very center of the work. But what else in the painting moves you to look there? What devices does the artist employ to direct your attention to that spot? Consider elements such as light, shadow, gestures, and other objects in the painting. Then examine a painting or photograph by an artist of your choosing, preferably a more contemporary work. How does it focus your attention and help you to identify its subject?

5. What devices do radio and television programs use to signal their content or subject matters? How long do you have to attend to a program to know what you are hearing or watching?

1 | READING TEXTS

Considering audience

Any text you might encounter—whether a book, editorial, Web site, song, online video, painting, or even an e-mail message—is going to have a complex relationship with the people who encounter it. These readers, usually carefully selected, but sometimes random or even unintended, constitute the *audiences* for texts. You can't really say that you understand a text until you have come to grips with its relationship to its readers and viewers—an essential rhetorical perspective. Moreover, this relationship is dynamic, working in both directions and shifting all the time. Texts are constructed to reach and influence audiences who, in their turn, reshape the report, sculpture, or social network by the reception they give it and the assumptions they bring to it.

All this might sound abstract and drearily academic. When you write a personal e-mail to a friend, the relationship of your message to its audience seems completely transparent, doesn't it? But consider what happens if she forwards it to other acquaintances or you accidentally send this private note to everyone on a much longer recipient list? Or your friend prints out the document (which she cherishes), files it away among her personal papers, and it turns up in the hands of great-grandchildren a hundred years from now? Is the e-mail the same message in all these circumstances? Not really.

NOTE HOW A TEXT SIGNALS ITS AUDIENCE

You may remember moving up from the children's reading room in your library to the young adult section and then finally on to the adult materials. Someone was making judgments about audience appropriateness for you, categorizing texts according to what people your age could appreciate and handle. But texts send the same sorts of signals themselves, enabling you to react to them appropriately. For instance, you don't have to read too deeply into most political blogs before you figure out their orientations—and whether you're going to feel comfortable with the slice of the world they present (see Item 1.5).

You can also tell a lot about texts by *where* they appear. Even before you read a word, you know what kind of audiences academic journals or scholarly books attract—and how they will differ from the readership for supermarket check-out tabloids, with their lurid headlines and gaudy covers. The scholarly works appeal to readers who want fact-based, carefully reasoned, and thoroughly documented arguments offered in sober language; the tabloid magazines don't. Yet the same person *might* read both types of texts, because people play many different roles in their lives and often cross readily from one audience to another.

Of course, as a critical reader, you'll often have to interpret the signals unfamiliar texts may be sending about their implied audiences. You couldn't just guess that articles in *The New Yorker* are written for an intellectually upscale clientele or that films released by independent distributor Lionsgate tend to be edgy. Fortunately, you can discover a lot about texts of all kinds just by doing a little research—finding out what they do, to whom they appeal, what their cultural orientation might be, and who publishes or supports them.

Understand, though, that some texts aren't eager to win wide acclaim or appreciation. They cultivate the outsider's cachet, the sense of offering a counterculture point of view. They may even set out deliberately to shock the sensibilities of the masses—or of older generations—to win a select audience. One generation's *Mad* magazine is another's *Vice*. You won't get it unless you get it.

ASSESS THE LEVEL OF THE MESSAGE

It goes without saying that when a text signals a welcome to one group of readers, it may be excluding others. But this discrimination is often quite practical and helpful. A writer or artist reaching to a broad general audience will work differently from someone aiming to serve a more specialized clientele: the subject matter may be more accessible, the themes more conventional, the language colloquial and unchallenging. But addressing popular audiences isn't easy. Casual readers don't bring the same enthusiasm or commitment to a subject that experts or professionals may. So a writer or artist has to give them reasons to pay attention and then work hard keep them invested in the project.

In contrast, you may notice that works aimed at more expert or elite audiences make far fewer explanations and concessions: their authors assume readers or viewers who bring an interest to the subject and substantial background information and expertise—whether it's a microbiologist writing for fellow microbiologists or a Nine Inch Nails Web site talking to Trent Reznor fans. As a reader, you'll need to assess the level of expertise and engagement between texts and audiences.

NOTE THE DEMOGRAPHICS

The great appeal of the Web to marketers is that it gives them an unprecedented ability to target precisely the people they hope to reach. They assume if you browse specific sites, you may be signaling all sorts of characteristics that could be exploited commercially—among them, your gender, age, religion, political or sexual orientation, technical interests, hobbies, musical tastes, education, maybe even your level of income. Such measurements may seem crude, but the fact is that many of the texts we encounter appeal to similar demographic markers. Your response to such a text may be thrown off if you don't notice such an appeal (possibly because you aren't included in the intended demographic). But you're just as likely to find the outsider's perspective helpful in reading a text in an intriguing way (see Item 1.6).

When considering the make up of any audience, do remember that demographics shouldn't be confused with identity. Indeed, texts or products that make that mistake often don't last long. In 1955, Dodge introduced an orchid-colored sedan called *La Femme*, complete with rain cape and hat and made especially for women. It survived only until model year 1956 (see Item 1.7).

UNDERSTAND THE ORIGINAL OR INTENDED AUDIENCE

There's an entire scholarly industry dedicated to explaining how the audiences in Shakespeare's day would have responded to his plays. Obviously, you can learn a lot about a text by seeing it through the eyes of the people for whom it was originally created—their tastes, expectations, values, and behaviors. Even much more recent works can seem odd, quaint, and remarkably dated simply because we don't recognize what was perfectly evident to audiences in their time. All those bizarre films of the 1950s featuring oversized monsters (like Godzilla) destroying cities make better sense when understood in the context of the Cold War, with the threat of nuclear devastation seeming quite real to audiences at the time. So expect to do some library or online research to figure out what an older book, manifesto, poster, building, or song might have meant to people for whom it was the latest thing. You could learn a lot.

NOTICE HOW THE AUDIENCE HAS CHANGED

Just as important as appreciating the original audiences for texts from the past—whether they be books, movies, buildings, fine arts, or crafts—is understanding that the audiences for these texts can change significantly over time. New audiences bring different assumptions, traditions, and values to such texts, and so they read them differently, applying the standards of their own time. In effect, the works themselves are altered by such shifts in audience appreciation. One famous and troubling example of shifting audience response is raised by Leni Riefenstahl's 1935 film *Triumph of the Will*, a gripping and technically brilliant documentary that captured the rise of a charismatic German politician, Adolf Hitler. Celebrated in its own time, *Triumph of the Will* today is a different film: audiences cannot watch it without seeing in it portents of World War II and the Holocaust. To them, it has become art in the service of evil (see Item 1.8).

FYI

ITEM 1.5 ■ *Daily Kos*, August 17, 2007

Daily Kos may be the most influential political blog in the United States. Its topics, theme, and language on any given day clearly signal its intention to serve a left wing audience. Many blogs, including *Daily Kos*, include a link called "About" or "About Us"—which will give you additional information about audiences and purpose. (The link is not shown here.) How else might you infer the intended audiences of Web sites?

DAILY KOS

The President's Radio Address
by BarbinMD
Sat Aug 18, 2007 at 12:34:27 PM PDT

As the date for the ~~much anticipated Petraeus~~ White House report on the success of the "surge" in Iraq draws near, the message from George Bush during today's radio address was, don't give up, stay the course, progress is happening throughout the country. And after his heart-warming stories of new construction, growing commerce and local governments, Bush finished by saying:

> Unfortunately, political progress at the national level has not matched the pace of progress at the local level. The Iraqi government in Baghdad has many important measures left to address, such as reforming the de-Baathification laws, organizing provincial elections, and passing a law to formalize the sharing of oil revenues.
>
> America will continue to urge Iraq's leaders to meet the benchmarks they have set. Yet Americans can be encouraged by the progress and reconciliation that are taking place at the local level. An American politician once observed that "all politics is local." In a democracy, over time national politics reflects local realities. And as reconciliation occurs in local communities across Iraq, it will help create the conditions for reconciliation in Baghdad as well.

Now let's compare that to what Bush said eight months ago when he first announced the "surge":

> The most urgent priority for success in Iraq is security, especially in Baghdad...So I've committed more than 20,000 additional American troops to Iraq. The vast majority of them -- five brigades -- will be deployed to Baghdad.
>
> I've made it clear to the Prime Minister and Iraq's other leaders that America's commitment is not open-ended...Now is the time to act...To establish its authority, the Iraqi government plans to take responsibility for security in all of Iraq's provinces by November. To give every Iraqi citizen a stake in the country's economy, Iraq will pass legislation to share oil revenues among all Iraqis...To empower local leaders, Iraqis plan to hold provincial elections later this year. And to allow more Iraqis to re-enter their nation's political life, the government will reform de-Baathification laws, and establish a fair process for considering amendments to Iraq's constitution.

How things have changed. That once, "most urgent priority," will happen when it happens. The clear message that America's commitment isn't open-ended has become urging the Iraqi government to try harder. But we should all be encouraged and most importantly, stay the course, or as Bush warned America about the cut-and-runners eight months ago.

MY BUTT IS BIG
AND ROUND LIKE THE LETTER C
AND TEN THOUSAND LUNGES
HAVE MADE IT ROUNDER
BUT NOT SMALLER
AND THAT'S JUST FINE.
IT'S A SPACE HEATER
FOR MY SIDE OF THE BED
IT'S MY AMBASSADOR
TO THOSE WHO WALK BEHIND ME
IT'S A BORDER COLLIE
THAT HERDS SKINNY WOMEN
AWAY FROM THE BEST DEALS
AT CLOTHING SALES.
MY BUTT IS BIG
AND THAT'S JUST FINE
AND THOSE WHO MIGHT SCORN IT
ARE INVITED TO KISS IT.
JUST DO IT.

NIKEWOMEN.COM

ITEM 1.6 ■ Nike, *My Butt Is Big*, 2005

This famous ad couldn't be clearer about its appeal to a specific demographic and audience. Readers are even directed to the URL of Nikewomen.com. Whom might such a single-minded ad offend or exclude? Might it appeal to people beyond the audiences invoked in its text and images?

ITEM 1.7 ■ Dodge, *La Femme* Ad, 1956

Print advertisements like this announced the 1956 Dodge *La Femme*, a product designed specifically for one demographic: women. What does the item say about its creators' perceptions of women as consumers and drivers? Are there differences in the way cars are marketed to women today?

La Femme

now for the first time anywhere, a car glamorously, *Personally Yours*

Never a car more distinctively feminine than *La Femme* . . . first fine car created *exclusively* for women! In this superbly designed car, Dodge brings together luxurious, delicately-toned interiors and ultra-fashionable appointments . . . every sophisticated touch your heart could desire! Here is, truly, the ultimate in fine motoring.

22 CONSIDERING AUDIENCE

FYI

ITEM 1.8 ■ Leni Riefenstahl, *Triumph of the Will,* **1935**

Leni Riefenstahl's 1935 documentary *Triumph of the Will* used the spectacle of the 1934 National Socialist Party Congress in Nuremberg to present party leader Adolf Hitler as the savior of Germany. Audiences and critics alike responded to the director's groundbreaking techniques, camera angles, and editing—and her message. Should audiences today be willing to separate Riefenstahl's technical achievement from the ethical and moral dilemma posed by a documentary that may have been too successful?

CONSIDER

1. You probably belong to many different audiences, depending upon your interests and habits as a reader or consumer of texts. Identify some of those audiences. Do any of them cross over? Where and how?

2. When you encounter a book, magazine, Web site, or any other text that is new to you, how do you determine whether you are a part of its intended audience? What signals do you look for? What characteristics of an unfamiliar text might make you risk a new experience?

3. What counterculture magazines, Web sites, graphic novels, music, or experiences do you identify with? What precisely makes these items cool—perhaps their subject matter, language, attitude, irony?

4. With what demographic groups do you especially identify when you encounter texts? Does being a woman draw you to feminist Web sites, women's magazines, or so-called "chick" cars? Are there portions of your demography that you routinely ignore? Perhaps you have Scottish ancestry, for example: Do you look for books or journals that cover Scotland? How do you determine which aspects of your life make you a potential audience for texts?

5. Describe a text that you believe is read differently today than it was in the past. If you can, identify a fairly complicated case—a text that has been treated in many different ways. One good example might be the Constitution of the United States, which seems to be read and interpreted somewhat differently by almost every generation.

Understanding purpose

When you encounter an unfamiliar text, you are usually curious about its purpose—what it is trying to achieve. As you might guess, a text can be up to just about anything. It may evoke personal reflection, like a family portrait or photograph. It may arouse memories, like an urban cityscape or a rural scene. It may be quietly decorative, like a piece of sculpture on a lawn, or robustly informative and pushy, like a traffic sign. A text may try to seduce you, change you, persuade you, amuse you, or move you to action. And it may do several things at once or different things at different times: a figure such as Uncle Sam may evoke good humor at a Fourth of July parade, protest at an anti-war rally, and patriotic fervor on a recruitment poster.

But unless you can figure out what a text is up to at a given moment, you may have a difficult time appreciating and responding to it. So we're going to cut broadly and suggest three general purposes drawn from tradition: texts inform and analyze; texts persuade; texts teach and delight. These categories at least give you a place to begin. But be ready for endless permutations. They make life interesting.

UNDERSTAND TEXTS THAT INFORM AND ANALYZE

Much that you'll read and encounter in academic and professional worlds will have the goal of conveying and sharing information. We expect such data to be accurate and clear. It also helps if information has the value of *surprise* because then we know we have learned something. A text that sets out to present information should do it in an appropriate format, and so the variations in format and medium can be enormous. Some information is conveyed most effectively in words: a news report, a court transcript, a treaty, a contract, an historical account, even a textbook all rely on the meticulousness of language to convey meaning. But a great deal of information is numerical and, hence, best collected, arrayed, and interpreted when presented in tabular or graphic form. Thus spreadsheets and databases have become indispensable records for people in every field. Consider, too, the innumerable texts that add images to words and data: road maps and weather maps can be remarkably complex texts, conveying reams of facts; so can photo essays and film documentaries. Even YouTube videos can serve as informative texts, distributing you-are-there accounts of news events and more mundane happenings.

Many important texts then take the next step up from gathering information to analyzing and interpreting it. This is the daily work of scholars, scientists, conscientious journalists, and artists making meaning out of the world. In some sense, any presentation of data is an interpretation: someone chooses what's to be included or excluded in any assembly of facts, and readers respond to that purposeful selection. But more formal analysis is inevitable and essential: someone has to put together all the numerical data and images a tropical storm is generating in order to project what its path may be. Someone has to sift through the archives and records of past wars or presidential administrations and turn them into history. As a reader, you simply want to be aware when interpretation is occurring and recognize how it affects your perception of an informative text. Eyes wide open—that's the ticket.

Knowing that a text is informative gives you important criteria for reading and assessing it. Informative texts need to be well organized and appropriately titled. They need clear headings, helpful links, or accurate captions to direct users to information. They often need some authentication too—perhaps verified by the organizations that publish them or the work of referees or editors who vet them. Texts that claim to convey information become immediately suspect if their facts prove unreliable or inaccurate or if they provide no means for verifying their data. Obviously your academic research papers would fall into this category.

UNDERSTAND TEXTS THAT PERSUADE

Some theorists have claimed that all texts make arguments, persuading us to respond to them in some way. Even if you don't accept this blanket claim, it is obvious that we're surrounded by texts (and people) who want something from us: our agreement, approval, affection, vote, or money. Texts that make disputable claims are arguments; when they offer evidence and substantive reasons for their claims, they become *good* arguments. In most cases, you'll at least suspect when you are being overtly persuaded. But when you encounter a persuasive text, it still helps to understand the ways it goes about achieving its purposes. Again we'll fall back on tradition and identify three familiar appeals you'll find in many texts: appeals to *logos*, *ethos*, and *pathos*.

- Appeals to *logos* are those that rely on evidence, testimony, and good reasons to make a case. Texts that present facts and evidence generally win wide approval. Our court system, for example, relies on the presentation (and refutation) of verifiable evidence. But this strong evidence also needs to be supported by sensible assumptions and logical reasons before people will take action. So you will see general principles offered, for example, that we should, in a given situation, choose the greater good or the lesser evil, or, perhaps, that we should invest in the future by prudent spending now. In general, texts that rely primarily on appeals to *logos* tend to be low-key in language, heavily qualified in their claims, data-heavy, and documented in some way.

- Appeals to *ethos* focus on persuading us through the good character of the person or entity (corporation, institution, organization) making the appeal (see Item 1.9). We tend to listen to or agree with people we like and believe we can trust. Or we tend to go along with people or groups we find that share our values or raise our own sense of self worth. Writers (or politicians) make ethical appeals when they in some way demonstrate their authority, integrity, or honesty—talking about their families or upbringing, parading their credentials, acknowledging their failings, using appropriate language, and so on. Institutions may hire celebrity spokespersons to give them a familiar face or craft careful logos to capture their *ethos*. Some companies may even create entire campaigns to bolster their images: see Nike's *My Butt Is Big* on page 20 and Dove's *Campaign for Real Beauty* on page 425. When you see strategies like these, you're almost surely reading a persuasive text.

- Appeals to *pathos*, that is, to emotions, may provoke the greatest skepticism when we find them in persuasive texts. We've been trained to think with our heads. But appeals to the human heart (and other parts of the anatomy) can be equally convincing: our desires for love, power, pleasure, excitement (even food), as well as our numerous fears and doubts can motivate us to believe and do just about anything. We jump when we hear the threat of "lawsuit"; spend a fortune on Valentine's Day gifts; volunteer eagerly to help puppies at the shelter. Should we be leery of emotional appeals? Sure. But would we be concerned about Darfur and the environment if our hearts weren't at least somewhat invested in the images we see or scenarios we are asked to imagine? Pay attention to the numerous ways that texts play upon our feelings. Chances are, acts of persuasion are in the offing.

Of course, persuasive texts work in other ways as well with appeals that are just plain hard to categorize—especially when media images are so pervasive and techniques of advertising constantly break new ground. We can be seduced purely by style and cleverness—the choice of typefaces on a poster, the pounding repetition of a radio message, the planting of a CD or flash drive at a concert to cue us in to a viral campaign, the sheer visual impact of an object. It's almost as if people were built to persuade and be persuaded.

UNDERSTAND TEXTS THAT TEACH AND DELIGHT

This is, fortunately, a huge (and ancient) category. Texts give us instruction and pleasure in many ways: they can illuminate us with their wisdom, befuddle us with their artistic vision, amuse us with their wit, and surprise us with their provocative depictions of the human condition. In recent years much attention has been given to the works of architects like Santiago Calatrava and Frank Gehry (see Item 1.10) because of the sheer enchantment of their structures. Of course, their work is practical too: they build usable houses, college buildings, museums, and bridges. But one misses the whole point of their "texts" if one doesn't experience the innovation in the designs and the statements they make about architecture. Texts that teach and delight obviously encompass all the literary and fine arts, performing arts and crafts, and so on, but may also include works that fall into the informative and persuasive categories as well.

FYI

ITEM 1.9 ■ **Web Site for Michael Jordan's The Steak House N.Y.C., 2003–04**

What is *ethos*? It's what makes it possible for a great athlete to put his name on a restaurant "designed to reflect [his] sense of taste and style." Would you dine here? What does the design of the Web site itself suggest about Jordan's *ethos*?

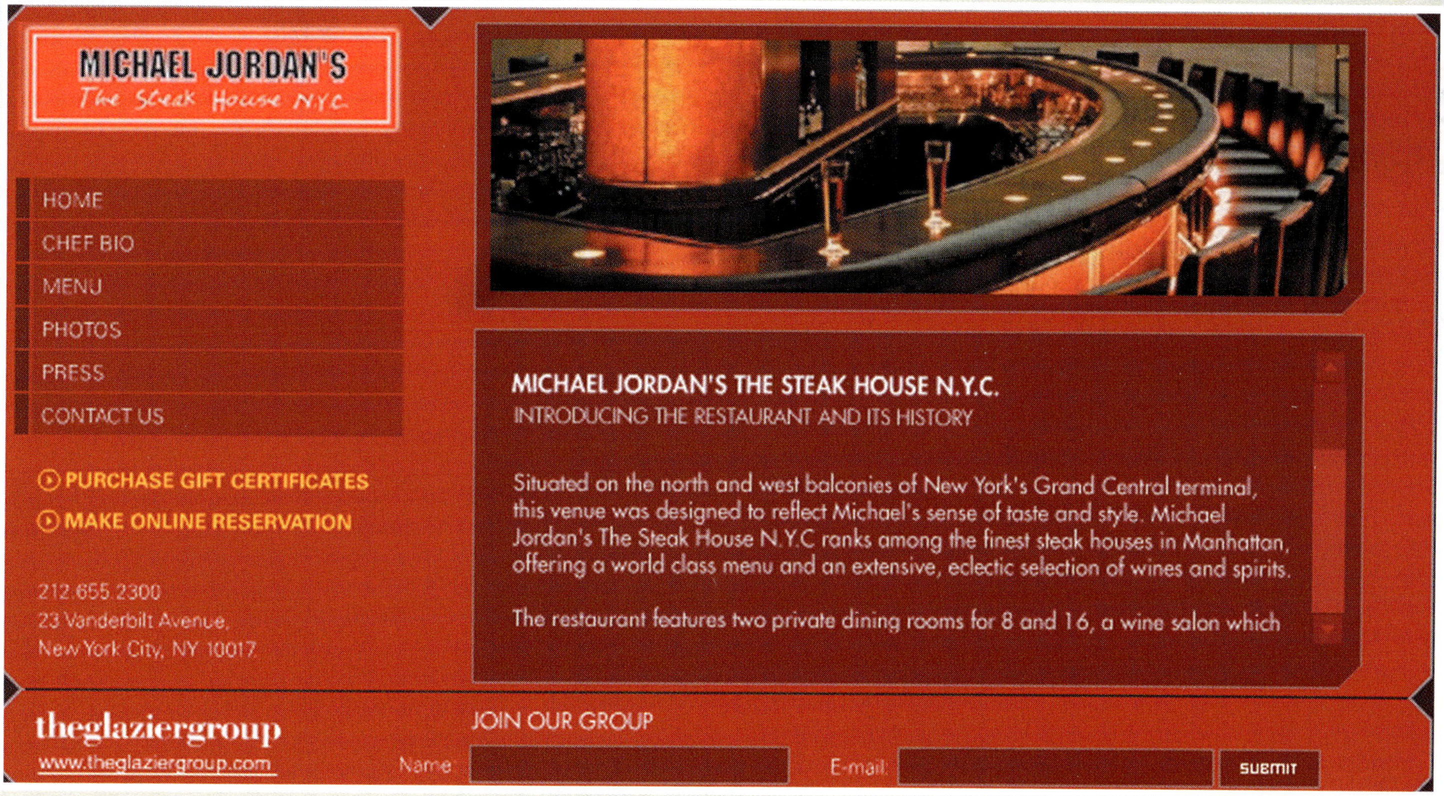

MICHAEL JORDAN'S The Steak House N.Y.C.

- HOME
- CHEF BIO
- MENU
- PHOTOS
- PRESS
- CONTACT US

◉ PURCHASE GIFT CERTIFICATES
◉ MAKE ONLINE RESERVATION

212.655.2300
23 Vanderbilt Avenue,
New York City, NY 10017

MICHAEL JORDAN'S THE STEAK HOUSE N.Y.C.
INTRODUCING THE RESTAURANT AND ITS HISTORY

Situated on the north and west balconies of New York's Grand Central terminal, this venue was designed to reflect Michael's sense of taste and style. Michael Jordan's The Steak House N.Y.C ranks among the finest steak houses in Manhattan, offering a world class menu and an extensive, eclectic selection of wines and spirits.

The restaurant features two private dining rooms for 8 and 16, a wine salon which

theglaziergroup
www.theglaziergroup.com

JOIN OUR GROUP Name _____ E-mail _____ SUBMIT

1 | READING TEXTS

ITEM 1.10 ■ **Frank Gehry, Stata Center, Massachusetts Institute of Technology, 2004**

MIT hired noted architect Frank Gehry to replace its famous but aging Building 20 with a new structure that might reflect the institute's research. Building 20 had little style; in contrast, Gehry's Stata Center was pure whimsy. Check out other images of the Stata Center on the Web. Is the building a text that persuades or instructs and delights? Why or why not?

CONSIDER

1. Browse through this textbook—or a convenient newspaper or magazine—and try to identify a dozen or so different kinds of texts. What specific purposes do they serve?

2. How well do the items you identified in the previous exercise fit into the general categories identified in this section: texts that inform and analyze, texts that persuade, texts that teach and delight?

3. Understanding the term broadly, *maps* convey information: they may display terrain, show converging weather fronts, outline battle plans, show economic trends, and so on. Can these graphics be persuasive as well? Give examples of maps that might do more than provide a visual representation of data.

4. Identify several persuasive texts you may have written yourself that rely primarily on logical appeals. In what persuasive situations, if any, might you avoid logical appeals?

5. Study the elements used to generate an *ethos* that represents Michael Jordan in Item 1.9. Choose a celebrity whose character and reputation strike you as significantly different and describe how you would modify a similar site to reflect that shift in *ethos*.

6. Texts that teach and delight are extremely common. But what role do they play in your academic major or professional life? Are such texts mainly recreational? Discuss and dispute.

Identifying genres

When we meet a dog, most of us immediately try to identify its breed or mix in order to appreciate its looks, temperament, and characteristics. We do the same with texts we encounter fresh, substituting genre for breed. Genres are expressed through conventions—the identifiable features and structures that make them what they are. For instance, when we see a text with an address, greeting, message, and signature, we think *letter*. Or we once did.

IDENTIFY THE CONVENTIONS OF A GENRE

In encountering a text, old or new, you want to ask questions about what it *is*. Sometimes a text will identify itself—as movies frequently do. You don't accidentally walk into a *superhero blockbuster* or *low-budget indie noir homage*. Similarly, without much effort, you could enumerate the features of the typical business letter and personal letter because you've seen so many. And you could likely identify other specific types of missives (in paper or electronic form), each with distinctive missions or features: job application letters, letters to the editor, "Dear John" letters, and so on.

But other genres may be more challenging. The first time you enter Second Life or pick up a tragedy or sonnet, you've got a lot to learn. It's likely you'll need to explore "Help" menus or do library research to understand the rules and conventions of these genres if they are new to you (see Item 1.11). You may even have to define genres on the fly for some very recent kinds of texts, thinking critically about their shape, asking yourself what they resemble and how they work. What, after all, is an iPhone? Or Facebook? Or Radar.net?

RECOGNIZE CHANGING CONVENTIONS

Once you recognize a genre or subgenre of a text, you know what to expect and how to read some of its features. With a romance novel, for instance, you'll anticipate a tale of passionate lovers set in exotic locales; a mystery better have a crime, a detective, and appropriate punishment. But the fun starts when writers and artists start stretching, defying, or parodying conventions or forming new genres. Not infrequently, new genres borrow their wardrobes from existing ones. Very old movies, for instance, sometimes look like stage plays because that's how early filmmakers imagined stories should be told visually. Pioneer screenwriters also drew upon novels and plays for their scripts, again using well-established conventions to help invent new ones. Today, creators of video games sometimes take their inspiration from movies—and, amazingly, vice versa. Indeed, the electronic revolution of the past few decades has spawned many fresh ways of sharing words and images: the $8\frac{1}{2}$" × 11" paper letter morphed into a stream of electrons we called *e-mail*, visible immediately on someone else's computer screen. It surely resembles a letter, but it's different too. And it's just this tendency of contemporary genres to evolve radically that makes texts today so worthy of your careful scrutiny.

ITEM 1.11 ■ Sonnets

A genre of poetry you probably recognize is the sonnet—by tradition, *a love poem in fourteen lines with a specific pattern of rhyme*. With a little research, you could discover that they often use conventional imagery (like *ruby lips* and *cherry cheeks*) and sometimes come in sequences that tell of a man's pursuit of an ideal woman. Recognizing these conventions helps when reading a text such as Shakespeare's "Sonnet 130" (1609), a poem addressed to a mysterious "dark lady," who may have played a role in the poet's life. Later poets have also employed the sonnet form, but they have moved it in new directions. Their poems are not always about romantic love, don't always run for just fourteen lines, or may not rhyme conventionally. But they do claim the brevity, concentration, and intricacy of the original genre. What genre connections can you find between "Sonnet 130" and "Clearances," a poem by Nobel laureate Seamus Heaney? What differences?

Sonnet 130

My mistress' eyes are nothing like the sun;
Coral is far more red than her lips' red;
If snow be white, why then her breasts are dun;
If hairs be wires, black wires grow on her head.
I have seen roses damask'd, red and white,
But no such roses see I in her cheeks;
And in some perfumes is there more delight
Than in the breath that from my mistress reeks.
I love to hear her speak, yet well I know
That music hath a far more pleasing sound.
I grant I never saw a goddess go;
My mistress, when she walks, treads on the ground.
And yet, by heaven, I think my love as rare
As any she belied with false compare.

—William Shakespeare

Clearances

When all the others were away at Mass
I was all hers as we peeled potatoes.
They broke the silence, let fall one by one
Like solder weeping off the soldering iron:
Cold comforts set between us, things to share
Gleaming in a bucket of clean water.
And again let fall. Little pleasant splashes
From each other's work would bring us to our senses.
So while the parish priest at her bedside
Went hammer and tongs at the prayers for the dying
And some were responding and some crying
I remembered her head bent towards my head,
Her breath in mine, our fluent dipping knives—
Never closer the whole rest of our lives.

—Seamus Heaney

CONSIDER

1. Make a list of genres that you work with routinely today that did not exist ten or twenty years ago. Which are totally new, and which share features with earlier texts and genres—the way e-mail resembles traditional business and personal letters?

2. Find a page of TV listings, and create a list of genres into which the programs on that page fit. Then briefly try to define several of the genres by identifying their purpose and enumerating their conventions. For example, *The O'Reilly Factor* might be placed in the news/talk or news/opinion genre, in which hosts with political axes to grind debate hot-button political issues with figures in the news.

Examining media

A medium is the material, vehicle, or technology that conveys an idea. It can be as substantive as stone or brick, as delicate as watercolors, as ethereal as radio waves, as abstract as numbers, letters, and words. Texts have always communicated through a vast array of media. Artists decorated the walls of caves, writers left marks on tablets of stone and wax, bishops used stained glass to teach moral lessons, queens wove their thoughts into tapestries, and players turned a humble wooden stage into all the world. But no prior era was as aware of media as ours is, perched as we are at a moment when digital technologies are daily revolutionizing how ideas are shaped and shared. New media can be scary, but, in fact, many of us seem to be adapting well to watching movies on cell phones, sharing our life stories (with pictures) on social networks, or living in fictional worlds we create with others. The only constant seems to be change.

UNDERSTAND MEDIA

The medium a text uses is not a small matter. You cannot really understand a text apart from its mode of transmission. Nor should we think of texts as having messages separable from their media: they are a single package. Of course, concepts and ideas have long migrated from medium to medium and that trend has only accelerated thanks to electronic technologies. For example, you've probably encountered Shakespeare's *Romeo and Juliet* on the page, on stage, and on film. What changes? Almost everything. Each medium makes its own demands on your imagination and your senses. Read the play, and you create most of the work in your head. Watch it from a front-row theater seat, and you might duck when the swords start clashing. See *Romeo + Juliet* on DVD, and Leonardo DiCaprio becomes the default Romeo in your mind.

Media deliver messages in particular ways and we process and experience those texts so differently that they can become different works entirely (see also "Choosing a Medium" on pages 77–79). That's why not every good book translates into a successful film, why receiving an e-mail isn't quite the same experience as receiving a handwritten letter, why going to a concert is a different event than listening to a CD. Or consider how differently you experience a news event if you learn of it via a magazine, a newspaper, a nightly news program, a twenty-four-hour news channel, or a Web site or blog. The medium shapes the message, or at least a good part of it (see Item 1.12).

So in encountering a new or puzzling text, take a moment to consider how well it works within its medium. Ask why a writer, artist, scholar, or politician has selected one medium rather than another to present his or her ideas to the world (see Item 1.13). Could another medium have been more effective or memorable? Note, too, that media play to different senses and sensibilities: photographs and paintings to our eyes, operas and oral poetry to our ears, sculpture and textiles perhaps to our fingertips. How do you encounter a text and what part does the medium play in your response to it?

APPRECIATE LANGUAGE AS A MEDIUM

All the attention paid to visual and electronic media makes it easy at times to forget that words remain our most common and subtle tool of communication and expression. But sometimes it takes stepping back and looking closely at the medium of language to appreciate how it works. Everything you read has a style that you can analyze, though it may take some practice to recognize the elements that give writing its character. Here are some features of the medium to look for in a document:

- **Voice.** How individual is the voice you *hear* as you read? Some writing is very cordial, other writing has a manufactured personality, and much academic work is deliberately impersonal, purged of character. You can look to features such as pronouns (*I, you, we, us, it*), contractions (*we're, you'll, won't*), or dialogue to discover and describe voice.

- **Tone.** Words can express both emotions and emotional distance. Look for specific words or phrases in writing that make a piece warm or cold, friendly or intimidating, and so on.

- **Word choice.** Words are a medium that can send many signals, and the level and choice of vocabulary items reveal much about a text. Vocabulary items may indicate much about writers: their age or experience, the social groups to which they belong, the audiences they wish to reach, and their sensitivity to difference. A word like *underprivileged* has a denotative meaning; it comes across as objective, and we can agree on its meaning. A word like *downtrodden* has a more connotative meaning; it strikes us as more opinionated and emotional.

- **Level of formality.** Formality in writing is related to tone and voice. You might characterize the language as casual and easy (as in a personal letter); direct and professional (as in business writing and journalism); or serious and formal (as in academic writing, legal writing, or writing for special occasions).

- **Level of technicality.** Some writing tries to explain every detail to readers new to a subject, some works hard to accommodate the needs of generally educated readers, and some is written specifically for experts.

- **Figures of speech.** Writing of all kinds relies on metaphors, analogies, and other figures of speech to convey thoughts, ideas, and emotions. You can learn much about a given piece by identifying its most characteristic devices of language.

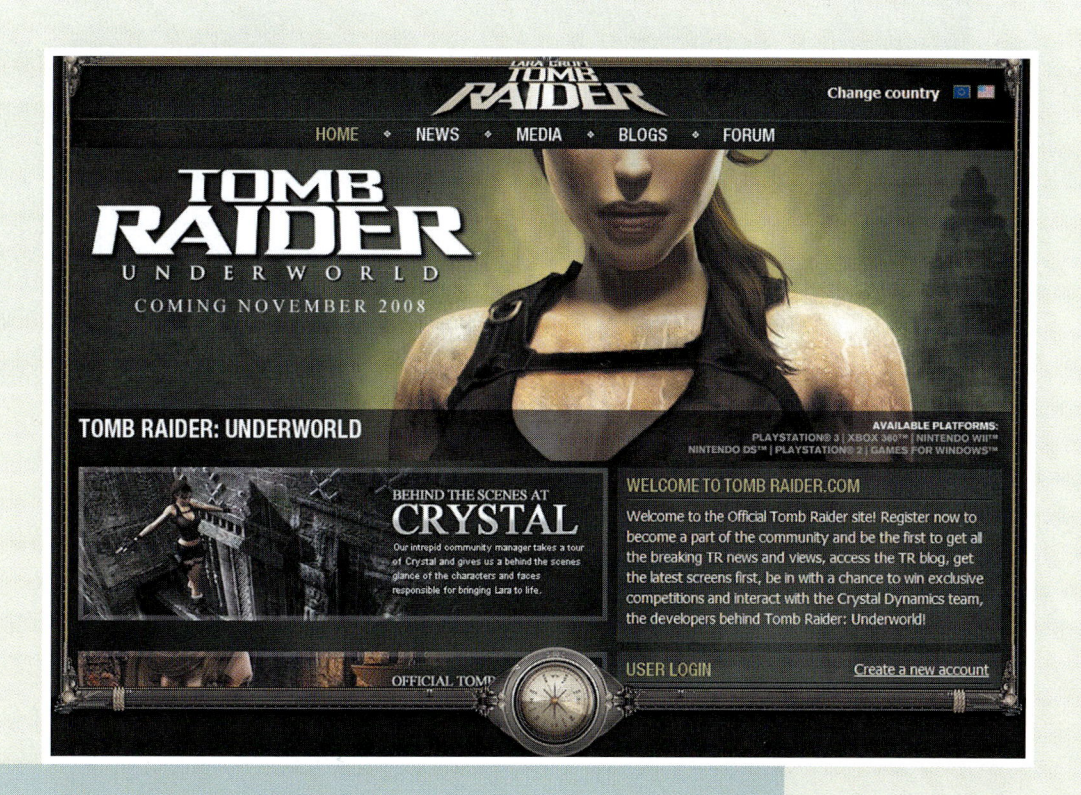

ITEM 1.12 ■ *Lara Croft Tomb Raider* Online Game

A number of popular video games have been translated into films, some more successfully than others. What are the differences between these two media? How might those differences translate into potential problems when turning a game into a movie? Why would movie producers go to the trouble?

FYI

ITEM 1.13 ■ Barack Obama and John McCain Presidential Announcements, 2007

Early in 2007, Democrat Barack Obama used a video posted on YouTube to announce his intention to run for President of the United States. The medium gave him complete control of his words and images. A few months later, Republican John McCain made his announcement more traditionally, speaking outdoors to an audience from behind a podium. The images from his event were created by photographers, with the power to fashion their own take on the candidate. Which medium do you suspect candidates will use in the future?

Barack Obama 2007 Presidential Announcement

CONSIDER

1. When does a physical substance—such as stone or metal—become a medium rather than merely a material? Can you give examples? Is the distinction between medium and material useful or important?

2. Can you think of several other texts like *Romeo and Juliet* that you may have experienced in various media? Which medium provided the best environment for the text? Why?

3. In recent years, many photographers have experienced a major change in their work process as they made the adjustment from film-based to digital photography. Given what you may know about photography, would you regard this shift as a change in technique or medium? Discuss and explore the differences with colleagues.

EXAMINING MEDIA

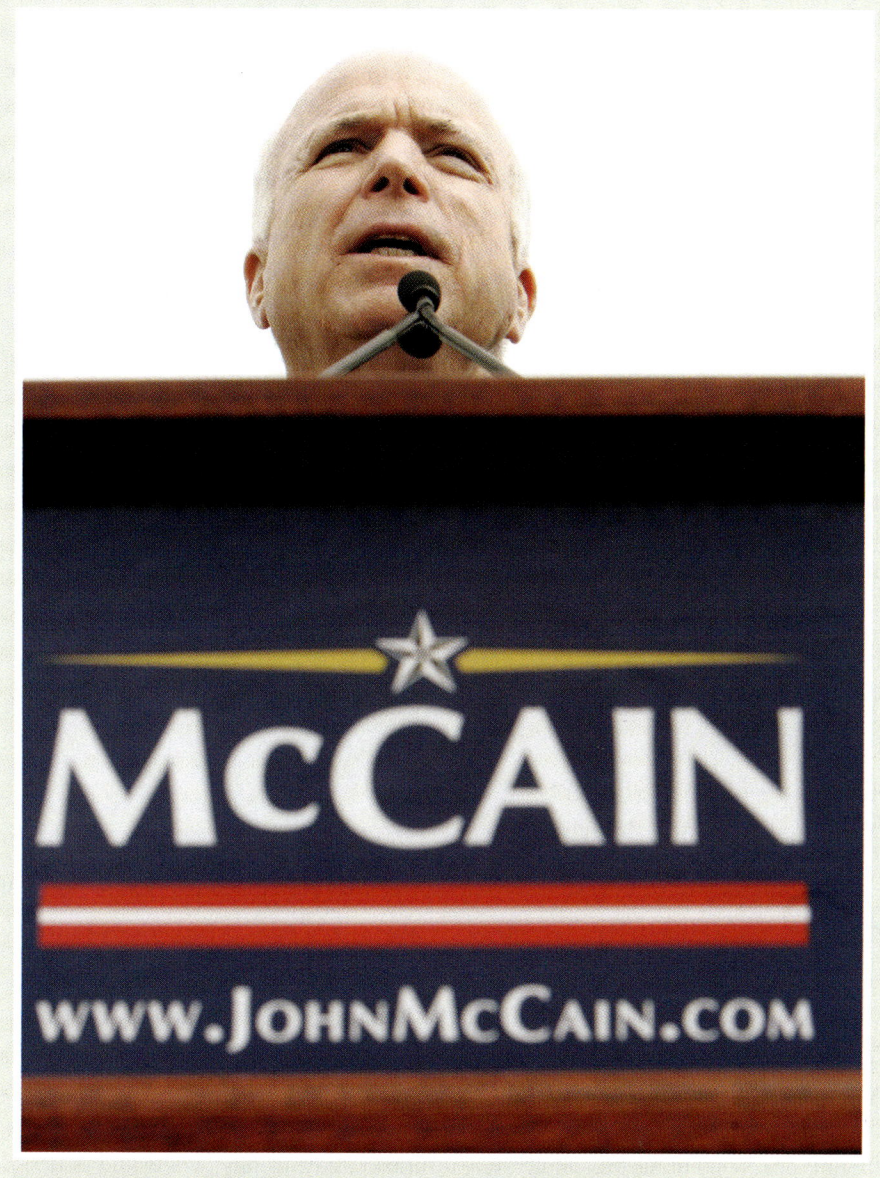

John McCain 2007 Presidential Announcement

4. Try to identify situations, personal or professional, in which choosing one medium for a message might be more socially appropriate or effective than another. For instance, is it defensible to complain about a grade via e-mail or is a face-to-face approach more principled? Would you consider breaking up a long-term relationship (or an engagement) via a text message? Why or why not?

5. Many people feared that the popularity of electronic and visual media might reduce the value of the printed word as a medium (see "A Librarian's Lament" in on pages 45–46). How might you respond to this concern? For instance, have environments such as Facebook and YouTube changed the quantity and character of the reading you typically do?

6. Do media such as video games and TV drama make you dumber—as some critics have argued? Or do they, in fact, place significant cognitive demands on users and viewers? Discuss the point *before* reading the essay by Steven Johnson on pages 50–53.

Understanding contexts

Every book, article, painting, sculpture, cartoon, photograph—you name it—exists within a context. Several, in fact. Context is nothing more nor less than the *who, what, where, when,* and *why* that surround every word, image, or artifact. We read every text wanting to know how it engages with the world, both now and in the past (if it has a past yet). In grasping this context, we may also come to appreciate the reason it was created and the goals it was meant to achieve.

UNDERSTAND THE CONTEXT

You probably notice context most when you're missing some part of it. Works that are anonymous or not reliably dated leave us guessing about their origins and wanting to know more. But centuries don't have to pass to erase a text's neighborhood. So much stuff gets lost or displaced in our daily lives that there is even a periodical—*Found* magazine, with a Web site at FoundMagazine.com—for people eager to share displaced objects they discover in odd places, from garbage cans to cluttered attics.

In presenting such fragments of people's pasts, *Found* raises just the sorts of questions you should consider when encountering a text unfamiliar to you:

- Who made it?
- When was it composed?
- To what does it respond?
- What trends, fashions, or attitudes does it represent?
- How did people react to it initially?

In some ways, uncovering the context of a text breathes new life into it. This renewal makes an important point about context: *it always changes.*

But context isn't only a matter of discovering in what year the original *Shrek* was released, how popular "Thriller" was when it debuted, or why Dorothea Lange photographed migrant workers during the Great Depression. Sometimes you also have to connect a work to current events or popular culture simply to understand it. Editorial cartoons in newspapers demonstrate this principle well. Any item published today or tomorrow would likely stump most readers a decade from now simply because such items are deliberately attuned to day-to-day events and issues. But a little background information might quickly make the point clear again (see Item 1.14).

EXPLORE PERSONAL ASSOCIATIONS

You may bring your own highly personal associations to reading and responding to texts, creating yet another context for a work. Writers and artists may stimulate your imagination, but they cannot control it. Nor can they anticipate the layers of history and memory that any individual or group brings to the world. Because of our distinct birth, educational, and life experiences, we all come to texts differently, find different things in them, and react to them in unique ways. These personal connections are so important that they shape many of the responses you bring to a work. A Chicana may identify more powerfully with a work by Sandra Cisneros than an Italian American, who might in turn have plenty to say about *The Sopranos*, much of it critical. And so on down the line through a full roster of religious, ethnic, gender, cultural, and even physical differences. The key here is *differences.* The contexts we bring to texts personally aren't a matter of right and wrong; they are crucially distinct ways of seeing.

ITEM 1.14 ■ Thomas Nast, *The American River Ganges*, 1871

You'd need plenty of information to understand the context of this editorial cartoon by noted caricaturist Thomas Nast. It expresses the fear that efforts to give public assistance to Catholic schools in states with large immigrant populations threatened to turn the country over to an exotic foreign religion. You can find more details at http://cartoons.osu.edu/nast/river_ganges.htm. What elements do you find most puzzling? How does this cartoon differ from most contemporary editorial cartoons? Might the cartoon make any connections with contemporary attitudes and issues?

CONSIDER

1. Examine an editorial cartoon in a newspaper today. What events have prompted the item? What kinds of knowledge does a reader need in order to understand the cartoonist's point? How well informed does the cartoonist assume the reader is? How self-explanatory will the drawing be a decade from today?

2. Go to *The Onion* (print or online) and pick a story at least a few paragraphs long. Then list all the cultural connections a reader would need to recognize in order to understand it fully. You might want to work on this assignment with a group since one person may not catch all the allusions. How funny will the story be a year from now, five years from now, a century from now? Will it even be comprehensible?

3. Find a personal object in your closet, attic, or elsewhere that has not aged well—it might be a piece of clothing, an ugly radio, a picture of an old car, a graduation present, or a souvenir. As well as you can, explain how the object is connected to you through memories and associations. What might you want other people to know about the object if it showed up in *Found* magazine?

4. Pick a film released prior to 1975, and do as much research as you can to describe the world into which it premiered and the way it is regarded now. Be sure to choose a film that has some standing today. For example, what attracted audiences to *The Wizard of Oz* in 1939? What struck them as new or different? What other films debuted that year? Did producers of the film anticipate that *The Wizard of Oz* would become a classic? How is the film regarded now?

Examining structure and composition

Many kids go through a phase during which they take things apart. Even if the results are sometimes catastrophic, the impulse is a good one. Seeing how the pieces of a clock, camera, or talking doll fit together can give a hands-on feel for the way the object works. The same principle holds for your encounters with texts. Sooner or later, you've got to examine them closely enough to appreciate what holds them together or makes them tick.

EXAMINE THE PARTS

When it comes to texts, the parts can sometimes be obvious—like the chapters in a book or the sections in a report introduced by titles, headings, and subheadings. With other texts, you may have to learn new terms and concepts to appreciate that operas may have their acts, arias, ballets, and leitmotifs; buildings their domes, facades, hallways, columns, and terraces; and films their opening sequences, narrative arcs, tracking shots, and montages. Moving from medium to medium, you'll discover how complex composition can be. You need knowledge of a genre and medium and, often, a new vocabulary to argue knowledgeably about what makes a particular video game amazing or a photograph intriguing. Certain strategies for reading structure and organization apply to a wide variety of texts.

- Look for elements that give **unity** to a text. A work that is unified seems to develop a dominant idea, theme, or feeling. That doesn't mean that a work expresses only one notion, but rather that its elements seem coherent or stay on message.

- Look for **sequences** that link events or different parts of a text. For example, a story may be organized by a plot that explains what happened first, what happened second, and so on. Even when flashbacks or reminiscences (techniques especially common in movies) interrupt such tales, you can still usually assemble a coherent sequence. Many other kinds of works use numbers or progressions to keep things in order, from timelines and sonnet sequences to slide shows and movies on DVD. Even chapters and other divisions in books are numbered to give order to a work.

- Look to the way a **whole is divided into parts**. Many texts are organized by some principle of division that helps us see relationships. Sometimes that division is quite simple—just a breakdown of an idea or object into separable items, like the tracks on a CD or rows in a garden. But texts can also be organized by more thoughtful principles based on a rigorous classification of ideas, images, or even colors and shapes.

- Look for **patterns** that organize a text. Repetitions of any kind stick in our minds and help us read texts. Consider the power of repetition and rhythm in music—and how easily you can distinguish between the verses of a song and its chorus. You'll also find patterns, large and small, in written texts that help organize them. Any work written to a formula, from a biology lab report to a screenplay for a movie, is following a template that readers are trained to recognize. And, naturally, patterns play an enormous role in organizing visual texts. The facades of buildings, for instance, typically present us with many patterns, subtly varied to keep us interested. Look for both: pattern and variation.

- Look for **arrangement** and **balance**. The physical layout of elements in a text can be an important structural feature. In an image such as a photograph, a single dominant figure front and center has a different impact than two figures who are balanced, positioned off center, or counterbalanced by other elements. Your eye moves in different ways in encountering and reacting to such arrangements. As a result some texts seem static; others feel more dynamic (see Item 1.15).

  Photographers may also arrange their shots using what they call the "rule of thirds." Employing this principle, they avoid centering the most important elements in a photograph. Instead, they position them roughly at the points where imaginary lines, both horizontal and vertical, divide an image into thirds. The rule is not hard and fast. Sometimes an image requires more balance or symmetry. But the eye seems to respond well to structures that promote complex or intriguing relationships, as the rule of thirds does (see Item 1.16).

- Look for the **point of view**. By highlighting one element or perspective at the expense of others (see Item 1.17), writers and artists can shape the structure of a text (and how people will interpret it). Such decisions aren't necessarily sinister: most writers must choose an angle on a subject to give their work coherence or focus. But as a reader, always consider what view of a subject an author is offering you. Is the perspective flat and patterned like a medieval painting, rich and full-bodied like a Renaissance fresco, or deliberately spontaneous and disruptive like a Surrealist film or Post-Modern installation?

- Look for **contrasts** that organize information by focusing attention. Contrast is what makes black text on a white page stand out. Many texts are organized on the same principle: that we see things more clearly when they stand next to their opposites. That is as true of ideas as it is of colors and shapes. Contrast is a device in many kinds of works, from traditional comparison-and-contrast essays and pro-and-con arguments to visual and aural pieces of all sorts (see Item 1.18).

- Look for a **hierarchy** in texts. Some things are more important than others, and texts use various devices to signal what is of greater and lesser rank within them: size, color, highlighting, positioning, placement, length, and so on. All of these cues help guide you through a text. For instance, consider how the size and style of headlines and photographs in a newspaper determine what you choose to read—and in what order.

FYI

ITEM 1.15 ■ Shakespeare at Winedale, *Henry V*, 2001

These photographs taken at a production of William Shakespeare's *Henry V* suggest how structure can express content: the king (left), alone and centered, looks contemplative; the middle characters stand in conflict, balanced around a center point; the moving figures (right) are off center, full of action and energy. What other factors give character to these shots?

40 EXAMINING STRUCTURE AND COMPOSITION

ITEM 1.16 ■ **Photo with Grid Lines Showing the Rule of Thirds**

In another photo from *Henry V*, note that the head of the French king is exactly at one of the intersections between lines drawn to illustrate the rule of thirds. How would the photograph have been different had the king been centered? What other visual relationships do you see in the shot?

FYI

ITEM 1.17 ■ Mark Ulriksen Paintings

Graphic designer and painter Mark Ulriksen manipulates both perspective and point of view in his images of man's best friend. We see the puppy from far above at a high angle; the little dog is right in our face, close up at a low angle. These elements in his paintings encourage us to imagine our relationships with dogs in new ways. How might the titles and colors also shape our reading of these texts?

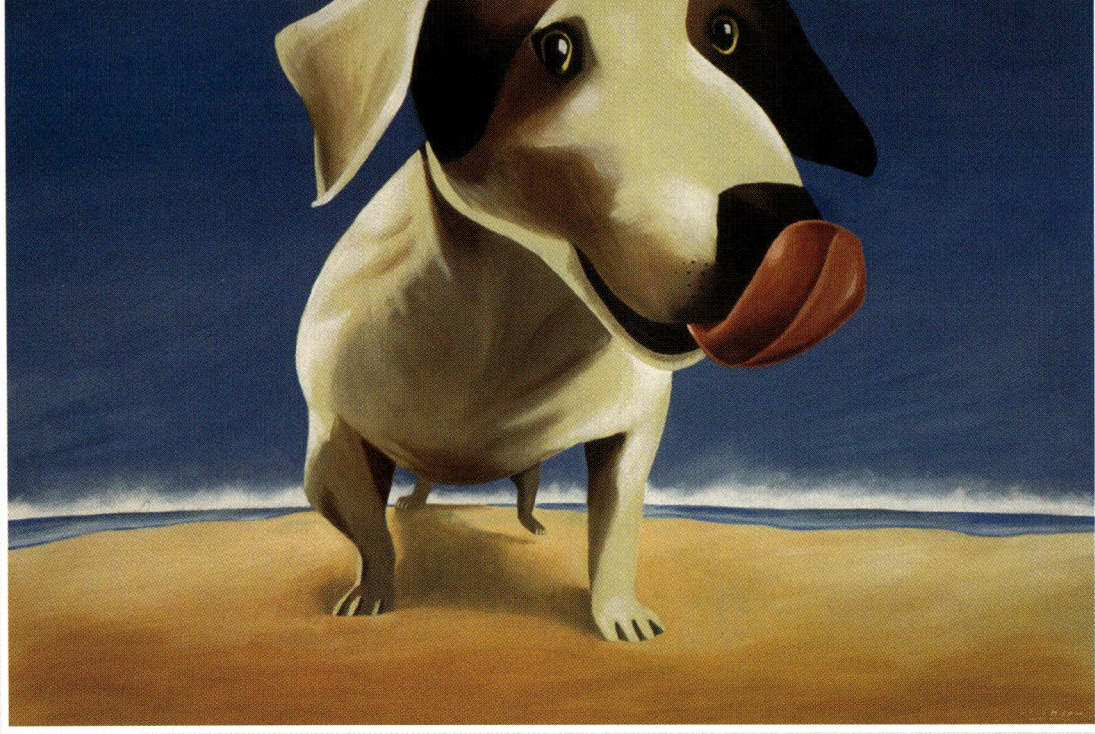

Puppy Love, 2001

Little Dog, 2000

42 EXAMINING STRUCTURE AND COMPOSITION

ITEM 1.18 ■ **Michelangelo da Caravaggio,** *David and Goliath,* **c. 1600**

The painter Caravaggio invented sensational lighting effects to create graphic scenes of unusual power in his works, emphasizing strong contrasts between light and dark. Photographers, particularly those working in black and white, use similar contrasts between light and dark to structure their images and make us more aware of patterns. What is the focal point of *David and Goliath*? How does light organize your response to the work?

CONSIDER

1. In writing courses, you've probably been introduced to patterns and structures such as description, narration, process analysis, classification, comparison and contrast, and analogy. Try to apply two of the patterns you recognize or recall to a medium other than writing. For instance, a process analysis explains how something is done. In what other media might you expect to see explanations of how to do or create something?

2. Look for photographs in magazines or online—or perhaps some you have taken yourself—that seem to violate the rule of thirds. Would the photographs have been more dynamic if they followed the guideline? Why or why not? Try to explain when it might feel right to center a subject.

3. Point of view and perspective can be easy to spot in a photograph. Try to detect these principles operating in other media: a novel, a professional article, a film, a painting, a TV commercial, a public monument, and so on. In what different ways can point of view be expressed?

4. Examine the front page of a newspaper or home page of a Web site to see how different font sizes and types (as well as different sizing and placement of images and other decorative elements) lead your eye toward specific stories or features. What do you notice first, second, third? Why?

Understanding and Reading Media

Reading "texts" well may sound like an academic concern, but it's not. People do care about the kinds of materials adults and children alike are encountering these days and what they may be learning from them—if anything. Major magazines and newspapers routinely run articles lamenting the hours young people are wasting, for example, playing video games, communicating on social networks, and watching reality TV. But, as always, the bigger picture may be more complex and, perhaps, even encouraging.

In this brief cluster, we offer three readings about our cultural engagement with media of various kinds. In the first piece, a former English teacher worries that books are no longer getting the kind of attention they deserve even in libraries where they've been displaced by a focus on information technologies and popular entertainment. But contemporary texts may have much to offer. That's the argument made in the other two articles, one by a distinguished film critic contemplating the charms of the blockbuster summer movie and the other by a media critic who argues that watching *The Sopranos* makes people smarter. All three authors and their texts deserve your close attention as well as your creative responses.

A Librarian's Lament: Books Are a Hard Sell

Thomas Washington
(2007)

> **FYI** Thomas Washington is a librarian at a private school in the Washington DC area. His opinion piece originally appeared on WashingtonPost.com on January 21, 2007.

I'm a librarian in an independent Washington area school. We're doing all the right things. Our class sizes are small. Most graduating seniors gain admission to their college of choice. The facilities are first-rate.

Yet from my vantage point at the reference desk, something is amiss. The books in the library stacks are gathering dust.

When I started in this profession five years ago—I used to teach English—I presumed that librarians were mostly united in their attraction to books. But as I moved along in my library science program, I found that books weren't really our focus. Information management, database networking and research tools claimed the largest share of the curriculum. In other words, literacy today is defined less by how English departments or a librarian might teach Wordsworth or Faulkner than by how we find our way through the digital forest of information overload.

Typically, many people in my line of work no longer have the title of librarian. They are called media and information specialists, or sometimes librarian technologists. The buzzword in the trade is "information literacy," a misnomer, because what it is really about is mastering computer skills, not promoting a love of reading and books. These days, librarians measure the quality of returns in data-mining stints. We teach students how to maximize a database search, about successful retrieval rates. What usually gets lost in the scramble is a careful reading of the material.

Students are still checking out the standard research fare—the Thomas Jefferson biography, the volume of literary criticism on Jane Austen—but few read it. The library checks the books back in a day later, after the students have extracted the information vitals—usually an excerpt or two to satisfy the requirement that a certain number of works be cited in their papers.

Conventional wisdom has it that teenagers don't read because they're too busy. Only after high school, sometime midway through college, do young adults reconnect with their childhood love of reading and make books their partners for life. I don't think so anymore. The 2004 *Reading at Risk* report by the National Endowment for the Arts concluded that literary reading was in serious decline on all fronts, especially among the youngest adults, ages 18 to 24, whose rate of decrease was 55 percent greater than that of the total adult population.

To counter this trend we set up a "new arrivals" display shelf this school year. It's stocked with bestsellers, young-adult fiction and DVDs. We also maintain a top-shelf lineup of books that we hope will entice young minds and bring them back to the reading table. We position the books on tiny stands and place notecard teasers underneath, much as Borders bookstores promote the managers' top choices.

> **"These days, librarianship is all about making the sale."**

No, I'm not foolish enough to think that the books are going to move off the shelves like jeans at Abercrombie, but any school librarian who hasn't figured out some way to market his goods probably needs to find another line of work.

These days, librarianship is all about making the sale. Public libraries have caught on: In Fairfax County, *The Washington Post* recently reported, they're tossing out volumes that have gone unchecked for two years in favor of books that can "generate the biggest buzz."

Recent front-runners in my school library include "The Boy Who Fell Out of the Sky," Ken Dornstein's memoir about his brother's death aboard Pan Am Flight 103; "The Overachievers," on how our culture of high-stakes education has spiraled out of control; and "Bob Dylan: The Essential Interviews." While I wait for nibbles on these and other books, my colleague and I paste eye-catching posters on the walls. These aren't literary quotes, either. Today the American Library Association's posters have employed Denzel Washington to encourage kids to read. But how many of these students really buy the message?

I recently spoke with a junior who was stressed about her decreasing ability to focus on anything for longer than two minutes or so. I tried to inspire her by talking about the importance of reading as a way to train the brain. I told her that a good reader develops the same powers of concentration that an athlete or a Buddhist would employ in sport or meditation. "A lot out there is conspiring to distract you," I said.

> "To her, the idea that reading might benefit the mind was, well, lame."

She rolled her eyes. "That's your opinion about books. It doesn't make it true." To her, the idea that reading might benefit the mind was, well, lame.

A library's neglected shelves reveal the demise of something important, especially for young readers starved for meaning—for anything profound. Still, I'm not ready to throw in the towel just yet. I'm turning the new-arrivals shelf into a main attraction in my school's library. Recently I stood Charles Dickens's "Bleak House" next to the DVD version produced by the BBC. Lady Dedlock (Gillian Anderson) graced both covers. A senior fingered the DVD for a minute, then turned it over to read the blurb. "The book is too long," she said. "Is the movie any better?"

"You're right. The book is long," I said. "But once you start this one, you won't be able to put it down, right from that first page about the London fog."

"I think I'll watch the DVD," the student said.

And in my library ledger, I'll register this as a sale.

CONSIDER

1. Does Washington describe your own recent experience with libraries and research? Do you in fact spend more time with databases and Web sites than actual books? Do you read books mainly to extract information and, if so, is that really a problem? How regularly do you read a book, cover to cover?

2. Is it a sign of cultural decline that librarians recommending books have to think about "making the sale"? Or does it make sense that books have to compete in the same marketplace of texts as other forms of media? What, if anything, marks books as special?

3. Many critics of visual or electronic media focus on the fact that such texts don't put sustained intellectual demands on readers: instead, they cater to (or perhaps foster) short attention spans and superficial opinions. Is this a legitimate criticism or a misreading of the way people use media? Provide specific evidence for any response you offer.

CHALLENGE

4. Online, look for a copy of "Reading at Risk: A Survey of Literary Reading in America." (Search the phrase "NEA report: reading at risk.") Review the document and write an essay responding to it in the same personal style that Thomas Washington employs in "A Librarian's Lament." Draw freely on your personal experiences.

Defending Goliath: Hollywood and the Art of the Blockbuster

Manohla Dargis
(2007)

> **FYI** — Manohla Dargis is a film critic for the *New York Times*. She has previously written for the *The Village Voice* and *The Los Angeles Times*. Her essay on the summer blockbuster film appeared in the *New York Times* on May 6, 2007. A writing course she took while pursuing a Masters in Cinema Studies at NYU led to her career as a film critic.

Summertime and the viewing is lousy and noisy and deedle-dee dumb, or so the received wisdom has it. It is our season of stupidity, summertime, that interminable stretch when adults surrender the nation's theaters to hordes of popcorn-chugging, sugar-jonesing, under-age nose-pickers for whom the cinematic experience means nothing more than recycled big, bigger, biggest bangs. It is the season of mass distraction, of the tent pole, the event movie, the blockbuster.

Blockbuster is really just descriptive, but it often carries with it a down-market whiff, as do many pop-cultural products that come with eye-catching price tags and seem precision-tooled for young audiences. Critics, including, yes, yours truly, often use blockbuster as easy (too easy) shorthand for overinflated productions that rely more on special effects than words and characters, and that distract rather than engage the audience. At its most reductive the negative spin on blockbusters is that they signal the death of cinema art and mark the triumph of the corporate bottom line, of marketing strategies, product placements and opening-weekend returns. And here you thought you were just watching Tobey Maguire run around in a unitard.

But just because a movie blows stuff up doesn't mean it automatically stinks. A good blockbuster, like the recent Bond flick "Casino Royale," takes you places you might never otherwise go and shows you things you could never do. It brings you into new worlds, offers you new attractions. It takes hold of your body, making you quiver with anxiety, joy, laughter, relief. When great blockbusters sweep you up and away—I'm thinking about watching "The Matrix" for the first time with a few hundred other enraptured souls—they usher you into a realm of communal pleasure. In a culture of entertainment niches, they remind you of what going to the movies can still be like.

They also remind you that without the human factor a blockbuster is nothing but a big empty box. Blockbusters that endure strike a balance between the spectacular and the ineffably human, whether it's Peter O'Toole framed against the never-ending desert in "Lawrence of Arabia" or Keanu Reeves coming down to earth in "The Matrix" as he realizes that he knows kung fu. It's the epic story of America refracted through one family in the "Godfather" films. It's a mechanical shark and Robert Shaw remembering the U.S.S. Indianapolis in "Jaws." It's Tom Cruise hanging by a thread in "Mission: Impossible" and Christian Bale standing amid a cloud of bats in "Batman Begins." It's Leonardo DiCaprio's wild eyes in "Titanic" and Kirsten Dunst's sad ones in "Spider-Man."

Blockbuster usually describes products sold in enormous quantities, like movies, but also theater productions, museum shows, hit songs, books and even pharmaceuticals. The word probably originated with the powerful bombs that the British Royal Air Force used to decimate German cities during World War II, the so-called blockbusters. It soon entered the vernacular, appearing in advertisements before the end of the war, and as a clue in a 1950 crossword

Source: Manohla Dargis, "Defending Goliath: Hollywood and the Art of the Blockbuster." From *The New York Times*, May 6, 2007. © 2007 The New York Times. All rights reserved. Used by permission and protected by the Copyright Laws of the United States. The printing, copying, redistribution, or retransmission of the material without express written permission is prohibited.

puzzle in this newspaper (46 across). In the early 1950s the heavyweight champion Rocky Marciano was known as the Brockton Blockbuster, after the city where he was born, and the word blockbuster routinely appeared in articles about the Hollywood vogue for super-size entertainments.

These days highbrows dismiss movie blockbusters because they are often based in fantasy rather than reality, which is generally a bad thing unless the fantasy comes with a literary pedigree like "The Lord of the Rings." Blockbusters tend to be made for adolescents instead of adults, which is also a bad thing because youngsters are untrustworthy cultural consumers. (One exception: blockbusters based on children's books that also appeal to adults, like the Harry Potter cycle.) Blockbusters based on comics are invariably questionable unless they are called graphic novels and then not always. Blockbusters that open on thousands of screens are also considered dubious because anything that appeals to a wide audience is inherently suspect. I'm joking, but not really.

> **Blockbusters based on comics are invariably questionable unless they are called graphic novels and then not always.**

In recent years it has become axiomatic that the 1970s special-effects-laden blockbusters "Jaws" and "Star Wars" helped bring an end to New Hollywood's flirtation with creative freedom (think of "Nashville"), ushering in the era of juvenile diversions like "Raiders of the Lost Ark." Never mind that "Jaws" is a good movie, far better at least for some than "Nashville." As Martin Scorsese says in "Easy Riders, Raging Bulls," Peter Biskind's history of 1970s American cinema: "'Star Wars' was in. Spielberg was in. We were finished." Well, not exactly, as suggested by the little gold statue presented to Mr. Scorsese in February by Steven Spielberg, George Lucas and Francis Ford Coppola, whose 1972 blockbuster, "The Godfather," also happens to be a masterpiece.

The movie industry has been in the business of big—big stars, big stories, big productions, big screens and big returns—about as long as it's been a business. And as long as the movies have told stories, they have used spectacle to sell those stories. In the silent era motion-picture producers employed spectacle to help distinguish the new medium from that of the theater, creating what were essentially protoblockbusters. In the 1950s the faltering movie industry went into the business of the supercolossus, delivering epic-size stories on ever-widening big screens in part to distinguish itself from that small-screen menace called television. Much has changed about the movies in the decades since, but not so the uses of pyrotechnics, sweeping landscapes and all manner of cinematic awesomeness.

Nowadays the armies of sword-brandishing soldiers may be largely computer generated, as in "300," but film spectacle works more or less the same now as it did in 1912 when the Italian epic "Quo Vadis?" hit screens with a cast of literally thousands and extreme action in the form of a chariot race. That film's pageantry, its gladiators and sacrificed Christians earned an enthusiastic thumb's up from the sculptor Auguste Rodin, who declared it "a masterpiece." (Everyone really is a critic.) The Italians were among the first in the film-spectacle business, but the Americans soon jumped in with costly productions like D. W. Griffith's benighted masterpiece, "The Birth of a Nation," which dramatically advanced the art.

Spectacle didn't just enthrall audiences; it was instrumental to the very development of feature filmmaking, as directors learned how to make longer-running entertainments. Not that spectacle and narrative always mesh, then or now. In 1923 an anonymous critic for *The New York Times* wrote that Cecil B. DeMille's "Ten Commandments" was divided into two sections, "the spectacle and the melodrama," that might as well have been directed by two different men. The critic's admiration for the spectacle ("done with meticulous precision") tempered the larger criticism. ("It would have needed an unusually perfect modern drama to stand up in comparison.") Somewhere the producer Jerry Bruckheimer is shaking his head, wondering why he can't catch a similar break with today's reviewers.

Yet if audiences dig spectacle, critics often view it with suspicion, as sneers about the modern blockbuster suggest. The negative rap on blockbusters is partly due to the literary bent of a lot of critics, who privilege words over images and tend to review screenplays, or what's left of them, rather than the amalgamation of sights and sounds in front of them. But the sneers also suggest an underlying and familiar contamination anxiety. In the 1980s "Top Gun" wasn't just a glib divertissement; it was evidence that MTV had infected the movies like a deadly virus. In the same grim light "300" isn't just a shell of a movie; it's proof that the movies have been infiltrated by an outside force, namely video games.

The threats have changed over the years—from television to music videos, comic books, digital technologies and so on—yet what has remained constant is the idea that the movies are under siege. But if the movies have taught us anything it is that they are brilliant adapters. They mutate and shift, stretch and adjust, and they neutralize those threats the way an organism absorbs nutrients, by assimilating them. We call some of these movie mutations comic-book flicks and compare still others to music videos, sometimes with a sigh, sometimes with a smile. We complain about car chases and forget that D. W. Griffith was among the first to put pedal to the metal on screen. And we condemn blockbusters for, if we're lucky, doing the very thing we say we want from the movies: giving us a reason to watch.

CONSIDER

1. How does the first paragraph of Dargis's essay get your attention? Do you find yourself in any way offended by it or excluded from her intended audience?

2. How well does Dargis define the blockbuster film? Could you list a dozen films from the past several summers that fit into this category?

3. Dargis presents herself as a serious critic. Are you surprised when her argument turns to defend the blockbuster experience? What kinds of evidence does she offer to defend big summer movies?

4. What cultural contexts does Dargis explain for first understanding the term *blockbuster* and then for appreciating the history of the genre? Is the information new or surprising to you? Is it relevant to her claim?

5. Dargis in part structures her argument by imagining a cultural divide, with serious or elite critics of films on one side and ordinary viewers who like big movies on the other. Examine the way she uses this device throughout the essay. Does she stack the deck in favor of one side or the other? With which group do you identify?

COMPOSE

6. Can you identify another type of text that, like the action or superhero film, is typically unappreciated or disliked by the cultural elites—perhaps a genre you enjoy yourself? Write in its defense, as Dargis does for blockbuster movies. Take the time to research your subject.

Watching TV Makes You Smarter

Steven Johnson
(2005)

SCIENTIST A: *Has he asked for anything special?*
SCIENTIST B: *Yes, this morning for breakfast . . . he requested something called "wheat germ, organic honey and tiger's milk."*
SCIENTIST A: *Oh, yes. Those were the charmed substances that some years ago were felt to contain life-preserving properties.*
SCIENTIST B: *You mean there was no deep fat? No steak or cream pies or . . . hot fudge?*
SCIENTIST A: *Those were thought to be unhealthy.*
— From Woody Allen's "Sleeper"

> **FYI** "Watching TV Makes You Smarter" is adapted from Steven Johnson's book *Everything Bad Is Good for You: How Today's Popular Culture Is Actually Making Us Smarter* (2005). The full article appeared in the *New York Times Magazine* on April 24, 2005. Included here are its complete opening section (on TV narrative structure) and the conclusion of the essay. Johnson, a writer on media and technology topics, is also the author of *Mind Wide Open: Your Brain and the Neuroscience of Everyday Life* (2004) and several other books.

On Jan. 24, the Fox network showed an episode of its hit drama "24," the real-time thriller known for its cliffhanger tension and often-gruesome violence. Over the preceding weeks, a number of public controversies had erupted around "24," mostly focused on its portrait of Muslim terrorists and its penchant for torture scenes. The episode that was shown on the 24th only fanned the flames higher: in one scene, a terrorist enlists a hit man to kill his child for not fully supporting the jihadist cause; in another scene, the secretary of defense authorizes the torture of his son to uncover evidence of a terrorist plot.

But the explicit violence and the post–9/11 terrorist anxiety are not the only elements of "24" that would have been unthinkable on prime-time network television 20 years ago. Alongside the notable change in content lies an equally notable change in form. During its 44 minutes—a real-time hour, minus 16 minutes for commercials—the episode connects the lives of 21 distinct characters, each with a clearly defined "story arc," as the Hollywood jargon has it: a defined personality with motivations and obstacles and specific relationships with other characters. Nine primary narrative threads wind their way through those 44 minutes, each drawing extensively upon events and information revealed in earlier episodes. Draw a map of all those intersecting plots and personalities, and you get structure that—where formal complexity is concerned—more closely resembles "Middlemarch" than a hit TV drama of years past like "Bonanza."

For decades, we've worked under the assumption that mass culture follows a path declining steadily toward lowest-common-denominator standards, presumably because the "masses" want dumb, simple pleasures and big media companies try to give the masses what they want. But as that "24" episode suggests, the exact opposite is happening: the culture is getting more cognitively demanding, not less. To make sense of an episode of "24," you have to integrate far more information than you would have a few decades ago watching a comparable show. Beneath the violence and the ethnic stereotypes, another trend appears: to keep up with entertainment like "24," you have to pay attention, make inferences, track shifting social relationships. This is what I call the Sleeper Curve: the most debased forms of mass diversion—video games and violent television dramas and juvenile sitcoms—turn out to be nutritional after all.

I believe that the Sleeper Curve is the single most important new force altering the mental development of young people today, and I believe it is largely a force for good: enhancing our cognitive faculties, not dumbing them down. And yet you almost never hear this story in popular accounts of today's media. Instead, you hear dire tales of addiction, violence, mindless escapism. It's assumed that shows that promote smoking or gratuitous violence are bad for us, while those that thunder against teen pregnancy or intolerance have a positive role in society. Judged by that morality-play standard, the story of popular culture over the past 50 years—if not 500—is a story of decline: the morals of the stories have grown darker and more ambiguous, and the antiheroes have multiplied.

The usual counterargument here is that what media have lost in moral clarity, they have gained in realism. The real world doesn't come in nicely packaged public-service announcements, and we're better off with entertainment like "The Sopranos" that reflects our fallen state with all its ethical ambiguity. I happen to be sympathetic to that argument, but it's not the one I want to make here. I think there is another way to assess the social virtue of pop culture, one that looks at media as a kind of cognitive workout, not as a series of life lessons. There may indeed be more "negative messages" in the mediasphere today. But that's not the only way to evaluate whether our television shows or video games are having a positive impact. Just as important—if not more important—is the kind of thinking you have to do to make sense of a cultural experience. That is where the Sleeper Curve becomes visible.

TELEVISED INTELLIGENCE

Consider the cognitive demands that televised narratives place on their viewers. With many shows that we associate with "quality" entertainment—"The Mary Tyler Moore Show," "Murphy Brown," "Frasier"—the intelligence arrives fully formed in the words and actions of the characters on-screen. They say witty things to one another and avoid lapsing into tired sitcom cliches, and we smile along in our living rooms, enjoying the company of these smart people. But assuming we're bright enough to understand the sentences they're saying, there's no intellectual labor involved in enjoying the show as a viewer. You no more challenge your mind by watching these intelligent shows than you challenge your body watching "Monday Night Football." The intellectual work is happening on-screen, not off.

But another kind of televised intelligence is on the rise. Think of the cognitive benefits conventionally ascribed to reading: attention, patience, retention, the parsing of narrative threads. Over the last half-century, programming on TV has increased the demands it places on precisely these mental faculties. This growing complexity involves three primary elements: multiple threading, flashing arrows and social networks.

According to television lore, the age of multiple threads began with the arrival in 1981 of "Hill Street Blues," the Steven Bochco police drama invariably praised for its "gritty realism." Watch an episode of "Hill Street Blues" side by side with any major drama from the preceding decades—"Starsky and Hutch," for instance, or "Dragnet"—and the structural transformation will jump out at you. The earlier shows follow one or two lead characters, adhere to a single dominant plot and reach a decisive conclusion at the end of the episode. Draw an outline of the narrative threads in almost every "Dragnet" episode, and it will be a single line: from the initial crime scene, through the investigation, to the eventual cracking of the case. A typical "Starsky and Hutch" episode offers only the slightest variation on this linear formula: the introduction of a comic subplot that usually appears only at the tail ends of the episode, creating a structure that looks like this graph. The vertical axis represents the number of individual threads, and the horizontal axis is time.

"STARSKY AND HUTCH" (ANY EPISODE)

A "Hill Street Blues" episode complicates the picture in a number of profound ways. The narrative weaves together a collection of distinct strands—sometimes as many as 10, though at least half of the threads involve only a few quick scenes scattered through the episode. The number of primary characters—and not just bit parts—swells significantly. And the episode has fuzzy borders: picking up one or two threads from previous episodes at the outset and leaving one or two threads open at the end. Charted graphically, an average episode looks like this.

"HILL STREET BLUES" (EPISODE 85)

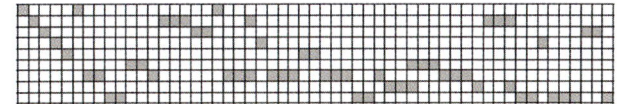

Critics generally cite "Hill Street Blues" as the beginning of "serious drama" native in the television medium—differentiating the series from the single-episode dramatic programs from the 50's, which were Broadway plays performed in front of a camera. But the "Hill Street" innovations weren't all that original; they'd long played a defining role in popular television, just not during the evening hours. The structure of a "Hill Street" episode—and indeed of all the critically acclaimed dramas that followed, from "thirtysomething" to "Six Feet Under"—is the structure of a soap opera.

"Hill Street Blues" might have sparked a new golden age of television drama during its seven-year run, but it did so by using a few crucial tricks that "Guiding Light" and "General Hospital" mastered long before.

Bochco's genius with "Hill Street" was to marry complex narrative structure with complex subject matter. "Dallas" had already shown that the extended, interwoven threads of the soap-opera genre could survive the weeklong interruptions of a prime-time show, but the actual content of "Dallas" was fluff. (The most probing issue it addressed was the question, now folkloric, of who shot J.R.) "All in the Family" and "Rhoda" showed that you could tackle complex social issues, but they did their tackling in the comfort of the sitcom living room. "Hill Street" had richly drawn characters confronting difficult social issues and a narrative structure to match.

Since "Hill Street" appeared, the multi-threaded drama has become the most widespread fictional genre on prime time: "St. Elsewhere," "L.A. Law," "thirtysomething," "Twin Peaks," "N.Y.P.D. Blue," "E.R.," "The West Wing," "Alias," "Lost." (The only prominent holdouts in drama are shows like "Law and Order" that have essentially updated the venerable "Dragnet" format and thus remained anchored to a single narrative line.) Since the early 80's, however, there has been a noticeable increase in narrative complexity in these dramas. The most ambitious show on TV to date, "The Sopranos," routinely follows up to a dozen distinct threads over the course of an episode, with more than 20 recurring characters. An episode from late in the first season looks like this.

"THE SOPRANOS" (EPISODE 8)

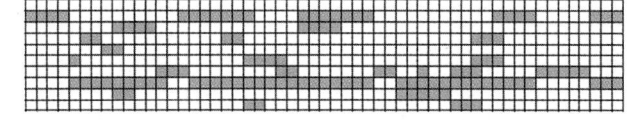

The total number of active threads equals the multiple plots of "Hill Street," but here each thread is more substantial. The show doesn't offer a clear distinction between dominant and minor plots; each story line carries its weight in the mix. The episode also displays a chordal mode of storytelling entirely absent from "Hill Street": a single scene in "The Sopranos" will often connect to three different threads at the same time, layering one plot atop another. And every single thread in this "Sopranos" episode builds on events from previous episodes and continues on through the rest of the season and beyond.

Put those charts together, and you have a portrait of the Sleeper Curve rising over the past 30 years of popular television. In a sense, this is as much a map of cognitive changes in the popular mind as it is a map of on-screen developments, as if the media titans decided to condition our brains to follow ever-larger numbers of simultaneous threads. Before "Hill Street," the conventional wisdom among television execs was that audiences wouldn't be comfortable following more than three plots in a single episode, and indeed, the "Hill Street" pilot, which was shown in January 1981, brought complaints from viewers that the show was too complicated. Fast-forward two decades, and shows like "The Sopranos" engage their audiences with narratives that make "Hill Street" look like "Three's Company." Audiences happily embrace that complexity because they've been trained by two decades of multi-threaded dramas.

Multi-threading is the most celebrated structural feature of the modern television drama, and it certainly deserves some of the honor that has been doled out to it. And yet multi-threading is only part of the story...

[Johnson goes on the discuss how contemporary TV shows make increasing demands on viewers' attention and intelligence by explaining fewer plot elements and forcing viewers to follow faster and more allusive dialogue. Even reality shows place greater cognitive demands on participants and viewers than in the past. Johnson's conclusion follows.]

THE REWARDS OF SMART CULTURE

The quickest way to appreciate the Sleeper Curve's cognitive training is to sit down and watch a few hours of hit programming from the late 70's on Nick at Nite or the SOAPnet channel or on DVD. The modern viewer who watches a show like "Dallas" today will be bored by the content—not just because the show is less salacious than today's soap operas (which it is by a small margin) but also because the show contains far less information in each scene, despite the fact that its soap-opera structure made it one of the most complicated narratives on television in its prime. With "Dallas," the modern viewer doesn't have to think to make sense of what's going on, and not having to think is boring. Many recent hit shows—"24," "Survivor," "The Sopranos," "Alias," "Lost," "The

Simpsons," "E.R."—take the opposite approach, layering each scene with a thick network of affiliations. You have to focus to follow the plot, and in focusing you're exercising the parts of your brain that map social networks, that fill in missing information, that connect multiple narrative threads.

Of course, the entertainment industry isn't increasing the cognitive complexity of its products for charitable reasons. The Sleeper Curve exists because there's money to be made by making culture smarter. The economics of television syndication and DVD sales mean that there's a tremendous financial pressure to make programs that can be watched multiple times, revealing new nuances and shadings on the third viewing. Meanwhile, the Web has created a forum for annotation and commentary that allows more complicated shows to prosper, thanks to the fan sites where each episode of shows like "Lost" or "Alias" is dissected with an intensity usually reserved for Talmud scholars. Finally, interactive games have trained a new generation of media consumers to probe complex environments and to think on their feet, and that gamer audience has now come to expect the same challenges from their television shows. In the end, the Sleeper Curve tells us something about the human mind. It may be drawn toward the sensational where content is concerned—sex does sell, after all. But the mind also likes to be challenged; there's real pleasure to be found in solving puzzles, detecting patterns or unpacking a complex narrative system.

In pointing out some of the ways that popular culture has improved our minds, I am not arguing that parents should stop paying attention to the way their children amuse themselves. What I am arguing for is a change in the criteria we use to determine what really is cognitive junk food and what is genuinely nourishing. Instead of a show's violent or tawdry content, instead of wardrobe malfunctions or the F-word, the true test should be whether a given show engages or sedates the mind. Is it a single thread strung together with predictable punch lines every 30 seconds? Or does it map a complex social network? Is your on-screen character running around shooting everything in sight, or is she trying to solve problems and manage resources? If your kids want to watch reality TV, encourage them to watch "Survivor" over "Fear Factor." If they want to watch a mystery show, encourage "24" over "Law and Order." If they want to play a violent game, encourage Grand Theft Auto over Quake. Indeed, it might be just as helpful to have a rating system that used mental labor and not obscenity and violence as its classification scheme for the world of mass culture.

Kids and grown-ups each can learn from their increasingly shared obsessions. Too often we imagine the blurring of kid and grown-up cultures as a series of violations: the 9-year-olds who have to have nipple broaches explained to them thanks to Janet Jackson; the middle-aged guy who can't wait to get home to his Xbox. But this demographic blur has a commendable side that we don't acknowledge enough. The kids are forced to think like grown-ups: analyzing complex social networks, managing resources, tracking subtle narrative intertwinings, recognizing long-term patterns. The grown-ups, in turn, get to learn from the kids: decoding each new technological wave, parsing the interfaces and discovering the intellectual rewards of play. Parents should see this as an opportunity, not a crisis. Smart culture is no longer something you force your kids to ingest, like green vegetables. It's something you share.

CONSIDER

1. The title of Johnson's article—"Watching TV Makes You Smarter"—is a claim. What was your initial response to it? Why did you respond as you did?

2. Do you find Johnson's mapping of the narrative structures of television dramas helpful and illustrative? (See pages 51-52.) Do you agree that multi-threaded dramas make greater (and appreciated) cognitive demands on viewers? Why or why not?

COMPOSE

3. Write a short essay in which you apply the observations and claims in the concluding section of "Watching TV Makes You Smarter" to a media activity you engage in routinely. It may involve engagement with traditional texts (books, poems, *I Love Lucy* reruns) or the multi-threaded, multi-tasking entertainments Johnson champions. In either case, apply his thoughts to your world. Do you welcome Johnson's conclusions or feel uneasy about them or their implications?

CHAPTER 2

COMPOSING TEXTS

ITEM 2.1 ■ **Holechek Bros.,** *The 305,* **2007**

This screenshot is from a fanfilm version (available on YouTube) of Zach Snyder's studio film, *300*.

Have you seen a movie recently that you liked a lot? How did you respond? Did you go back for a second viewing? Recommend it to your friends, hoping they'd share your enthusiasm? Buy it when it came out on DVD? Sensible reactions, all.

But did you ever consider creating your own version of the film? You could borrow a digital video camera; persuade friends to play Leonidas or Spiderman; rework the original story to suit the local scenery; and start shooting your prequel, sequel, or reimagined epic. Sound weird? Perhaps. Yet a surprising number of people have been doing exactly that for years, creating a phenomenon called "fan films" (see Item 2.1).

Or you could review the film on your own Web site, sharing your love and appreciation for movies the way Siskel and Ebert did for many years on TV or Harry Knowles does at AintItCool.com. Not long ago, it was tough to find an audience or medium for what you wanted to write or compose. That's not the case anymore (see Item 2.2). With honest ideas and a little cheek, you can easily respond to movies, books, editorials, or athletic events, or create texts of your own—and people will actually read (or view) your stuff. Writing has never been a passive activity, but now it's a *remarkably* interactive and social one. So you want to be good at it—really good.

In this chapter, we offer advice for meeting that challenge. Our assumption is that, in most cases, you will be using this material to write reactions to images, readings, and writing assignments throughout this book. But the guidelines here aren't narrow or specialized; rather, they walk you through elements that shape every message and aspect of communication: *subject*, *audience*, *purpose and context*, *genre and structure*, *medium*, *research and documentation*, and *editing*.

ITEM 2.2 ■ *Cole and Bobby . . . at the Movies!, 2007*

This Web project began as a school prank but has since evolved into an ongoing film review site with a growing audience.

Choosing a subject or focus

It's easy to be excited when an assignment, topic, or text appeals to you personally. Consider the messages you text to friends on Twitter to bring them up to speed on your life or the latest must-see video on YouTube. You don't worry about choosing a topic or considering your purpose. You just type sentence after sentence because you already know what you want to communicate. The subject seems obvious.

Such passion for composing can't be manufactured, but it can be cultivated. The advice we offer in Chapter 1 is, in part, designed to make you push back against the words and images pummeling you every day. When you read any text critically and attentively, chances are you will find something in it that sparks a critical response. *Critical* here is not a negative term. It means experiencing something with the metaphorical equivalence of *eyes wide open*. Such a gaze prepares you to write with intelligence and grip about a topic that matters. Here's a writer opening a paper by explaining why she found a pink vacuum cleaner, of all things, an intriguing subject (see Item 2.3).

> In high school, I went through a phase when everything that was pink caught my eye. One day while shopping with a friend, we passed by a store that had the most interesting pink accessory I had ever seen: a vacuum cleaner. I was further intrigued by the connection that the product had with breast cancer research. Almost in unison, my friend and I shouted out, "I want that." I couldn't help but ask myself what kind of marketing genius came up with a way to make a vacuum cleaner appealing to two bored teenage girls. As it turns out, the design, color, and style of the Oreck "Clean for the Cure" machine help to explain its success. . . .
> —Jordyn Brown, "Vacuum-N-Pink"

The personal angle here works well both as a means of finding a subject and as a way to make readers focus on it.

STRETCH YOUR COMFORT ZONE

You've probably been told to work with topics you know well, and that's fine advice in many cases: we all like to write to our strengths. But a major reason for engaging with other texts is to expand what you know and extend your reach as a thinker. As you mull over general topics for writing, let curiosity lead you to more specific subjects. Ask pointed questions about what you are examining and then turn them into provocative claims of your own.

DEFINE YOUR SUBJECT

Don't push too far into a project with your topic just dimly lit. True, your ideas may change as you learn more about a subject through library or online research (see pages 84–87). But at any given point, you should be able to describe your subject to an instructor or colleague in a sentence or two. If you can't, pull back, read more about your topic, and then decide what you might do with it.

Sometimes, projects go off track because they are too ambitious. For example, you might begin with a general interest in poster art—those vibrant sheets plastered on campus walls to announce concerts or rouse political activity. It's a worthy subject, but way too big to cover in just five or ten pages or through a simple Web site. But if you investigate the topic you'll discover that artists, groups, or movements have used poster art for different reasons. So pick a reason that intrigues you: your generic "poster art" project might evolve into a historical study comparing and contrasting the style of Soviet-era and Cuban political posters (see Item 2.4). With such a focal point, your subject will become both more manageable and more appealing.

As you narrow a topic, begin thinking, too, about the point you want to make. Writers will often use a thesis statement to identify their claim about a subject or explain to readers what a project will cover. A thesis usually works best as a complete and complex sentence with all its claims and reasons attached—not as a sentence fragment or simple question (although a question might be used to focus on a thesis idea). Here, at the end of the first paragraph of a paper examining a breakthrough perfume ad campaign from the 1980s, writer Jacqueline Cruz leads up to a topic sentence that defines the claim her paper will prove (see the full annotated paper on pages 90–93):

> . . . You also notice that she [the Charlie woman] is poised. She is fun and free. She is active. Most important, she looks empowered. You want to be her. The agency responsible for this ad campaign wanted women to aspire to be the independent Charlie woman with a self-possessed identity. **Therefore it is no surprise that the ad agency allied itself with the feminist movement of the latter part of the century to create the Charlie woman's personality and to push their perfume sales**.
>
> —"She's Very Charlie"

But a thesis statement is not the only way to bring a subject to a point. Sometimes you may need an entire paragraph (or more) to define the focus of a project. Or you may leave it to readers to infer the theme of a piece, depending upon your genre: very few movies, novels, or photographs, for instance, have thesis statements, but many such works make clear and memorable claims. In different media, you might use headlines or headings, dialogue or images, even colors and lighting to snap a topic into focus.

ITEM 2.3 ■ Oreck Special Edition XL Ultra Vacuum Cleaner

Complete with a "Clean for the Cure" ribbon, this pink Oreck vacuum cleaner was sold with the manufacturer's promise to donate $50 for each machine sold to the Susan G. Komen for the Cure® organization to fight breast cancer. What potential topics might such an item suggest to you? Can you identify other similar items sold to advance social or political causes that might provoke a strong and critical reaction?

FYI

ITEM 2.4 ■ Soviet and Cuban Political Posters

Even a casual glance at the Soviet-era political poster (left) and the Cuban poster (right) suggests differences in perspective and style that might lead to intriguing topics. What might account for such differences in art produced by two closely related communist regimes? (More posters can be viewed on the International Institute of Social History Web site.)

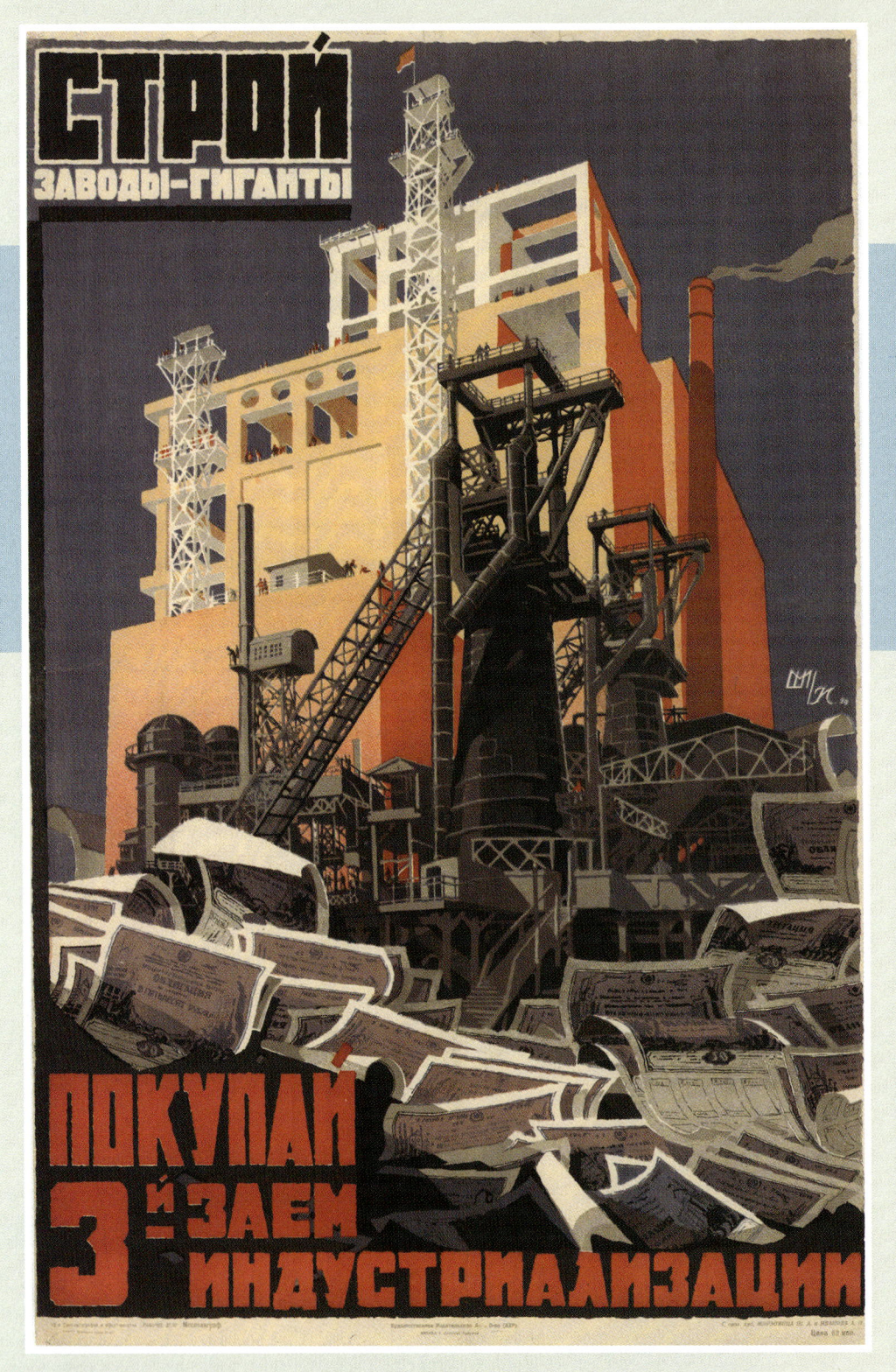

S. Mirzoyan, A. Ivanov, *Help Build the Gigantic Factories*, 1929

CHOOSING A SUBJECT OR FOCUS

Raul Martínez, *Fidel*, 1968

CONSIDER

1. List a number of people whose work or accomplishments you know well enough that you would feel comfortable making them the subject of a lengthy blog posting or full Web page. What angle might you take in presenting these artists, athletes, politicians, entrepreneurs, or just ordinary folk to readers? What aspect of their lives would you focus on?

2. First, identify a subject you know a lot about, perhaps one that others even associate with you. Then, from your position of expertise, explain what else you'd like to know about that subject. What aspects would you willingly explore on your own, given the time and the available resources?

3. Check out the first few pages of your local newspaper or the online version of a national newspaper to find an allusion to an event, institution, or object that you don't recognize. Do a quick search on the item and decide how you might turn it into a paper. What aspects of the issue or topic might merit additional exploration?

4. Look for an advertisement or public service announcement for one item that piggybacks on another—for example, a fast-food promotion on a cereal box or a missing-child label on a milk carton. Briefly discuss the relationship between the appeals. Who is trying to get you to respond, and why? How is the main subject enhanced or changed by its relationship with another product, sponsor, or institution? Then offer some topic ideas for a paper on the technique used.

COMPOSE

5. Choose a film that you've seen recently, preferably one that got you thinking, and then write a quick review—no more than 200 words. If you prefer, focus this assignment on a provocative editorial cartoon or an attention-getting advertisement or series of ads.

Reaching an audience

Big corporations and political parties alike conduct demographic studies to pinpoint the age, sex, income level, hobbies, and inclinations of potential consumers or voters. Such efforts don't always pay off because people are far more complicated and unpredictable than researchers would like. But the idea makes sense: the more attention you pay to audiences, the greater your chance of influencing them (see Item 2.5). It's a principle no writer can ignore.

KNOW YOUR AUDIENCE

Who is likely to respond to the writing you are doing or a project you are considering? An instructor? Colleagues in a class? Family? Members of campus organizations? An Internet community? You'll find yourself tailoring your ideas and words to readers as you *imagine* them to be. But that's not always easy.

Consider how tough it can be to figure out what a teacher wants. Assignment sheets and in-class comments may provide some clues about what an instructor expects. But chances are you won't get a good read on the teacher until you've received feedback from him or her on a test or paper. And then, what a difference a few comments can make. It works the same way with other audiences, if you can figure out how to get timely feedback on your work—for example, through topic proposals, peer editing, or professional workshops.

But sometimes you can do no better than anticipate their responses. Are you writing to colleagues or classmates? You'd hope they'd be something like you—a bit casual, freewheeling, and down to earth. Writing to family? You might need to clean up your act just a bit. Addressing the smart and ambitious people who read a campus newsletter or a local music magazine? For these more anonymous populations, you'd better get your ducks in a row: strangers will usually cut you less slack than family and friends. It's just a fact of life: whenever you're producing texts, you'll be analyzing readers this way and making constant adjustments. You might modify your subject, provide more (or less) background information, change the technicality of your vocabulary, or, maybe, alter the medium for the target audience: instant messages for your best friends; stamped letters on quality stationery for Aunts Rose and Mildred.

And you should probably anticipate multiple audiences too, especially when your project is built for an electronic environment. A conventional research paper might address just your classmates and instructor. Turn that paper into a Web project, however, and you have to imagine a larger and more diverse readership. The same would hold true for the viewers of photographs or videos you create, paintings you exhibit, or multimedia projects on which you collaborate.

Alternatively, you may shape a project for quite specific audiences, even deliberately excluding others. Maybe you are drafting e-mail appeals intended to stir up core supporters for a political candidate—so you deliberately make fewer concessions to independent voters or members of an opposing group. But even so, remember that other readers may eventually come across your work and hold you accountable for ill-advised language—as many hot-headed online bloggers have discovered.

FIGURE OUT WHAT YOUR AUDIENCE NEEDS

Audiences may have specific needs, depending on the genre or medium you have selected. Readers of paper documents, for example, usually expect a logical title and headings, appropriate formatting, and so on. Web readers might look for well-organized links, a site map, or a way to respond to your work. But you will have to make lots of judgments. Provide too little background information in a report, for instance, and readers may be confused; give too much, and you might lose their attention. Here, for example, writer Beau Faulkner opens a paper on "viral marketing" by taking a moment to explain the concept for readers to whom it might be unfamiliar.

> With the advent of the Internet a new term has been coined in advertising: **viral marketing. Viral marketing describes any strategy relying on individuals to pass on a marketing message to others, thereby creating an exponential growth in the message's exposure and influence**. Before the Internet, similar strategies had been referred to as "word-of-mouth," "creating a buzz," or "network marketing." Hotmail is one of the first services to employ viral marketing by including information on getting a free hotmail account at the bottom of all e-mails sent from hotmail addresses. Using the free e-mail service was the incentive for passing on the advertising message. One of the newer strategies in the realm of viral marketing is to use alternate reality games (ARGs).
>
> —"Year Zero: A Viral Marketing Promotion"

You won't be surprised that the next paragraph in Faulkner's paper goes on to explain ARGs.

Be sure, too, that your projects always give due consideration to audiences with disabilities, especially when you are working with new media. On the Web, for instance, your material can be readily accessible to the blind if you pay attention to the arrangement of information on your pages and to the tagging of visual items. To learn about accessibility issues, search the phrase "Web accessibility" on the Internet.

EARN THE INTEREST OF YOUR AUDIENCE

Even when you've created something important, you can't assume that audiences will care. Sometimes your readers will need the media equivalent of a good kick in the pants to take notice. Since texts are always competing for attention (see Chapter 1), give your work the equivalent of stage presence. In some circumstances, you can gain notice through powerful language alone; in others, an image can be worth the proverbial thousand words. Or maybe you need to combine media, amplifying your ideas through photographs, animating them with videos, or making them a part of a Web presentation, poster, or collage. Do whatever works.

DR. EVIL'S PLAN TO STOP GLOBAL WARMING

Rolling Stone

rollingstone.com
Issue 1013 >> November 16, 2006 >> $3.95

HIP-HOP REPORT
JAY-Z
NAS
DIDDY
YOUNG JEEZY
TUPAC

THE WHO RETURN!

Jon Stewart & Stephen Colbert
AMERICA'S ANCHORS
By Maureen Dowd

BORAT
COMEDY OF THE YEAR

FYI

ITEM 2.5 ■ Cover of *Rolling Stone*, November 16, 2006

How does a magazine that focuses chiefly on music and entertainment persuade its readers to pay attention to political and social issues? It designs a cover that sends the right signals to its hip and still relatively young audience. How well does this item from *Rolling Stone* appeal to its typical readers? Do you consider yourself in *Rolling Stone*'s demographic?

CONSIDER

1. Select several magazines from a library rack or elsewhere and examine them carefully to identify how they signal their appeal to specific readers. Try to look at a range of periodicals, from mass-market monthlies such as *Reader's Digest* and *Spin* to enthusiasts' magazines such as *Hooked on Crochet!* and *Popular Woodworking*. Why, for example, do many men push away from *Cosmo* while women roll their eyes at *Maxim*? What are the visual differences between *Vogue* and *Men's Vogue*? Can you recognize signals concerning the gender, income, class, age, or other characteristics of intended readers?

2. Find a text in your local or campus environment, and consider how you might make it accessible or comprehensible to someone who does not experience it the way you do. For example, how would you make a large bronze statue accessible to someone who is not sighted? Could you help a sighted person appreciate a Braille text? Can you imagine sharing an opera or rock concert with someone who is hearing impaired?

COMPOSE

3. Find an instruction manual for a product you own, and write a paragraph analyzing how well it serves its potential readers. Does it explain how to use the product effectively or safely? Does the manual assume that the user is reasonably intelligent, technically sophisticated—or an idiot? How well, if at all, does the manual deal with the problem of readers with different levels of experience with the product? How much of the manual is genuinely aimed at the buyer of the product, and how much is written in response to product liability lawyers who are eager to sue?

Deciding on your purpose and context

You have a topic. Now what do you do with it? No doubt you've seen and read enough to appreciate how expansive your opportunities could be, limited only by your ambitions, time, talent, and budget. But in most situations, your options will be more restricted. For school, you'll usually be preparing projects that inform, analyze, or persuade your readers—or please an instructor (see "Understanding Purpose" on pages 24–26).

But on some occasions, even in school or on the job, your work may take different paths. You might draw editorial cartoons to educate audiences about politics, create video games to amuse them, or design photo essays to enlighten or even anger them. In fact, some of your work might cross boundaries, accomplishing several goals simultaneously. (Consider how material written for children ordinarily has to be both educational *and* entertaining.) But in any case, you'll want to begin most projects with a clear sense of purpose, one that you can convey confidently to readers.

UNDERSTAND YOUR ASSIGNMENT

You often don't have a choice about how to respond to a text or writing situation. You've got a job to do. If an instructor asks for a report on a subject, you don't respond with a personal narrative or a one-sided argument. And when you don't understand an assignment, you should ask for more details or for a model to examine. Study the way any such examples work (see also "Choosing a Genre and Structure" on pages 67–75).

Obviously, some types of assignments will limit you more than others. When writing an academic report, for example, you'll have to deliver factual information to readers clearly, comprehensively, and objectively. You'll probably follow a specified format too, with a limit on length that will define the scope of your research (consider the difference between a five-page report on African folk masks and a fifty-page report on African folk art). The style of the report will be impersonal because your opinion may not matter: after all, you're relying mainly on research done by other people, usually more knowledgeable than yourself.

Instructed to analyze a subject—a book, ad campaign, or museum installation, for example—you'll have more breathing space. You still bear the responsibility to learn something about your subject and treat it fairly, but you've been invited to render a judgment too. So you have to think about ways to interpret texts or ideas and then find appropriate (though still moderate) language for your response. You'll need to signal, too, when you are offering an opinion or making a judgment of your own.

Asked to prepare an argument, you face even more choices and opportunities. First, you have to find a claim to defend as well as reasons and evidence to support it and then think about how to convey this material to readers who are as overwhelmed by media appeals as you are. You might have an opportunity to select the medium for your work—creating an ad, filming a video, designing a poster, or writing an editorial. Which will work best to sway audiences to your way of thinking? And how will you present yourself in the argument? Readers won't be persuaded unless they believe and trust you.

RESPOND TO OPPORTUNITIES

People do react to texts and ideas without being pushed by formal assignments. They may simply be intrigued by a concept, struck by an image, or perhaps disturbed by a change in their lives. They notice something and want to respond. That's just fine. Consider, for example, how you might be moved by a provocative photograph such as Dorothea Lange's famous *Migrant Mother* (1936)—see Item 2.6. You might slip into a conventional genre or create a new one.

- You could express your personal reactions to *Migrant Mother* as a human portrait, explaining what you see in it and how its depiction of hard times and human endurance touches your life.

- You could try to create a portrait that captures similar concerns today, using a digital camera or your skills with collage or oil paints.

- You could describe the scene that Dorothea Lange presents in the image and explore the harsh environments in which this and others of her Depression-era photographs were taken for the Farm Security Administration (FSA).

- You could locate the image within an older tradition of "Madonna and child" portraits and explore similarities and differences, doing research necessary to find comparable images.

- You could narrate the cultural history that explains *Migrant Mother*, placing it in the context of similar works, such as the film version of John Steinbeck's *The Grapes of Wrath* (1940).

- You could explain the technical aspects of Lange's craft as a photographer, reporting information about her career, techniques, and her body of work.

- You could analyze the enduring impact that photographs by Lange and others of the Depression era have had on viewers both in the United States and worldwide.

- You could argue that artists do or do not have a responsibility to address social concerns in their work.

EXPLAIN THE CONTEXT OF YOUR PROJECT

Don't expect readers to guess your reasons for responding to a text or creating a project. Give them the background information they need to understand it. In a personal or expressive essay, you might open by identifying what motivated you to take on a subject. Here, for example, Maxime Defforey supplies the context for his review of a French restaurant in Texas, his purpose being to correct some false impressions.

> French cuisine has a well-established reputation around the world. Undeniably recognized as the pinnacle of gastronomy, it is also associated with a refined setting and an irreplaceable ambiance embodied in the United States by Chef Rochat's Alizé and Andre's in Las Vegas, or by Le Bernardin (Chef Le Coze) in New York.
>
> Nevertheless, this is only one aspect of French cuisine. The sophistication of these places is not always a correct portrayal of how the French live in everyday life. Many people may develop stereotypes too from Hollywood pictures or their own trips to France when they carefully selected their restaurants. As a consequence, some do not consider Austin's Chez Nous *a* "real" French place, and often are disappointed because it wasn't what they expected.
>
> —"Chez Nous: Real French Cuisine in Austin"

In a report or analysis, you might need to situate your work within a current social or political controversy. Or, in an argument, you could simply explain that your letter to an editor or op-ed piece is a response to someone else's editorial or essay.

FYI

ITEM 2.6 ■ **Dorothea Lange, *Migrant Mother*, 1936**

During the Great Depression of the 1930s, Dorothea Lange worked as a photographer for the Farm Services Administration. *Migrant Mother* became her most famous photograph. What might be the purpose of such a work? What could a photographer hope to achieve with such a shot? Can you point to similar work presented to the public today?

CONSIDER

1. Review the types of projects you develop during a typical term in school or several months on the job. How much of your work serves a single and identifiable purpose: *to inform, analyze,* or *persuade*? How much of it crosses boundaries or has multiple aims? Is any of your work designed to entertain or amuse readers?

2. Make a list of the limitations placed on your work by a typical academic assignment—a lab report, a book review, a term paper? What would quickly get you into trouble? How did you learn these conventions or rules?

COMPOSE

3. Keeping in mind Dorothea Lange's *Migrant Mother*, identify a more recent photograph or work of art (painting, movie, TV episode) and list the various ways you might respond to it. Choose something with a high and perhaps controversial profile: the final episode of *The Wire*, the final novel in the Harry Potter series, *High School Musical 2*.

DECIDING ON YOUR PURPOSE AND CONTEXT

Choosing a genre and structure

A genre is a particular type of writing defined by specific goals, features, and conventions. Genres do change over time, adapting to new situations and needs, but their predictable structures and elements make them useful. When someone asks you to compare and contrast two items, write a movie review, or analyze an advertisement, you can look to examples of these genres, study their features, and then approximate their patterns, allowing yourself latitude to adapt them to your purposes. Here we offer guidelines for a number of genres you might want to use in responding to texts in this anthology.

WRITING A DESCRIPTION

You may have relatively few occasions to write purely descriptive papers. But descriptive passages can play important roles in other kinds of writing, especially when you deal with visual media. For example, you might need to describe a painting you intend to analyze, inventory the details of a design, or explain the specific environmental consequences of global warming. In all such situations, readers will be more responsive if you include specific details rather than page after page of generalities. This is especially true when writing about places. When you take readers to a specific locale, you become their guide. They can see, hear, taste, smell, and feel only what you set before them. And if you omit these sensory details, their experience of the place will be flat and forgettable.

If you haven't already, you'll probably soon hear a teacher talk about the difference, in writing, between showing and telling. The most common scenario goes something like this: telling—simply writing about something ("it was 95 degrees in the shade")—is not as effective as showing—letting readers share an experience with you ("I felt my skin liquefy as I stood unprotected in the Mojave sun"). Telling isn't always a bad technique, however. Often, for reasons of pacing, priority, and space, telling works well because readers can't experience everything. Consider this example from Margaret Cezair-Thompson's essay "Geography Lessons," describing her experiences in Jamaica.

> I went back for Christmas 1997. I had lived most of my adult life in the United States, and the violence in Jamaica in the '70s had alienated me. As I was driving from the airport, familiar sights reassured me: the noisy commerce of cart men, roadside hagglers and crowded buses. The island seemed more lush and beautiful than ever; the violence of men had not denuded the landscape.

Although her trip from the airport is important, it isn't the central point of her essay, so Cezair-Thompson tells readers what she wants them to know in a few sentences. Showing all of this might have taken a few pages. Notice, however, that even in her telling, Cezair-Thompson appeals to readers' senses by using such words as *noisy* and *lush*. And don't you pause over *hagglers*?

And that's the point: the best descriptive writing combines showing and telling, using strong verbs, evocative adjectives and adverbs (in small doses), and lots of sensory details.

As you write descriptions, keep the following in mind to bring people and places to life.

- Think about the particulars of a description. If you're writing about a place, list the critical details unique to that place, that set it off from other locales.
- Group your list by sense (sight, sound, taste, smell, touch). How many of the details are visual? Probably most of them, since we rely most heavily on what we can see when describing places. Try to think of details that appeal to the other senses as well.

- Decide which of these details you want to show and which you want to tell. These choices will depend upon your purpose, the amount of space you have, and, in some cases, your audience.
- Keep your descriptions lean and accurate. Don't pile on the adjectives or fall back on the obvious cliché. Spend the time necessary to find an arresting word, spot-on and specific: *Mojave sun*, not *blazing sun*.
- Make sure readers can follow the movements within your descriptions. Be directional if it helps—left-to-right, top-to-bottom, east-to-west. Or make it clear that you've focused on a few arresting details.
- Use media to replace words when appropriate. Substitute images for words whenever they work better. For instance, most readers prefer a map to verbal directions. Of course, images and words often work together well, enriching the experience of readers.

WRITING A NARRATIVE

Like descriptions (see above), narratives need to provide readers with a careful and memorable set of details. But narratives don't just present scenes or capture images. They also tell a story or record an incident, usually by moving readers through a sequence of events—with a beginning, middle, and end. So although narratives will usually include descriptive passages, you'll also need to pay attention to an entirely different set of issues. Here are some guidelines.

- Choose events that best support a point you'd like your narrative to make. You can't cover every detail in telling even a simple story. Decide what readers or viewers must know and focus on those incidents.
- Give your narrative a trajectory. Open with an incident that will interest an audience, build toward a climax, and end with an action, comment, or observation that leaves the audience thinking about your story.
- Link events with transitions (preferably subtle) that enable readers to keep track of changes in time and location.
- Provide necessary background information, especially early in the narrative. When relevant, describe the setting, the time, and the context for events. (For example, does the narrative occur during your college orientation?) But keep background information brief.
- Take a moment to introduce important characters. Briefly explain who they are and what they look like. Give them names.
- Use dialogue if necessary, but keep it lean and realistic. Check a handbook for conventions for handling dialogue in a written text.

WRITING A COMPARISON AND/OR CONTRAST PROJECT

Throughout your college and professional career, you'll be asked to compare items or ideas, sometimes as a specific project (*Which film school is better?*), but often as part of a larger report, evaluation, or analysis (*Which film school should I attend?*). Here's how to approach comparison-and-contrast projects.

- Understand the terms of any comparison/contrast assignment. Strictly speaking, *compare* might be taken as an order to look for similarities between objects; *contrast* as a directive to find differences. But *compare* commonly implies both meanings. Given an assignment to compare objects or ideas, you might want to determine whether the term is being used narrowly or broadly.

- Introduce readers to the items you will compare/contrast and explain what you expect to demonstrate by the comparisons. For example, if your purpose is to compare European and American political cartoons, you need to explain why. Will it be to determine which culture produces the more sophisticated, frank, or critical commentaries? Or are you more interested in variations in the style of the drawings? Be specific.

- Explain how you chose the particular items to compare or contrast. With political cartoons, you might select those most highly honored in their respective countries or make a sampling from newspapers regarded as the most influential or popular. Share this information with readers so they can assess the quality and validity of your selection.

- Decide which features you will compare or contrast in all the items. Readers will expect your choices to be fair and sensible. There'd be little point, for example, in comparing political candidates by height or hair color, sports cars by their off-road ability, or paintings by their prices. Comparisons should be meaningful—that is, relevant to the function or purpose of your subjects. So politicians might be examined according to their records of achievement, personal character, or policy recommendations.

- Decide how you will organize your comparisons. You can look at the items one at a time or feature by feature. Decide which structure will give readers the data they need most efficiently. It's always a tough call. Object-by-object comparisons look at subjects sequentially in their entirety: first you discuss President Nixon (his foreign and domestic policies), then Ford, then Carter. Feature-by-feature comparisons focus on differences: first you discuss President Nixon's foreign policies, then Ford's, then Carter's; then you discuss their domestic policies.

- Provide evidence for the comparisons and contrasts you make. Use tables and charts to convey numerical data. Use pictures or drawings for comparisons that are best explained visually.

- Use headings, subheadings, and other markers to guide readers through your work. Help them find the information they need.

- Summarize your key points and help readers to see their significance. Draw conclusions that reflect the complexity of your data and acknowledge any weaknesses or flaws in your methodology.

WRITING A REPORT

Your purpose in writing a report is usually to convey information. While there are many specific types of reports—from lab reports in science courses to history term papers and even insurance reports—all the various genres share some conventions. For instance, most reports announce their subjects clearly in an opening section or paragraph and then provide background information readers will need, answering such questions as *who, what, where, when, how,* and *why*. Since reports share data and ideas, they tend to be based on documented research, reliable testimony and eyewitness accounts, repeatable experiments, and so on. Reports generally strive to be objective (or at least to appear so). Consequently the style of reports tends to be plain and pokerfaced, relatively free of the connotative language that bends words in emotional directions. Overall, a report needs to exhibit accuracy, thoroughness, and competence. So, in preparing a report, consider these guidelines.

- Use a conventional pattern of organization in a report—such as sequence, comparison/contrast, classification, division, etc.—to cut readers a predictable path through the information you will share and to give shape to your work.

- Use headings, subheadings, and other markers to keep readers on track. Internally, use transitional words and phrases to make the report easy to read.

- Write in a plain style, editing your drafts to eliminate wordiness. Take care, too, to define terms your readers won't recognize. But don't hesitate to use any technical language that your intended audience should know.

- Check with an instructor or editor before using the first person "I" or "we" or second person "you" in the report. Some readers object strongly to such personal language.

- Find ways to present or array information efficiently. Use tables, charts, and graphs to summarize data. Use photographs, drawings, slides, or video to convey visual information *necessary* to the report. Label and caption these items following whatever style sheet you must use: MLA, APA, AP, etc.

- Document the project, giving due credit not only for direct quotations but also to any ideas not considered *common knowledge*. (If you find a concept mentioned repeatedly in professional sources and without explicit documentation, it's probably considered common knowledge in the field.) Follow the assigned documentation format down to the smallest detail—getting even the punctuation perfect.

- Since your report will be a source of information to your readers, be sure your facts are spot on. Pay special attention to the spelling of names, the titles for source materials, and the precise dates for events. In fact, cross check such details in at least two reliable sources.

- Format the project correctly. A written report needs unwavering margins, a title page or correct headings on the first page, consistent page numbers, and, quite likely, a list of sources at the end.

WRITING A RESPONSE OR POSITION PAPER

Sometimes an instructor will ask you to examine a reading, a visual text, or some other item, and then respond with a short and focused paper—often fewer than five hundred words. Less formal than a report and more tentative than an argument, such a response or position paper assignment typically encourages you to explore an idea and take some risks with it.

- Develop a coherent idea in your response or position paper. Response papers should be thoughtful, reflecting your careful reading of texts, but they may also be tentative and intellectually playful.

- Since response papers usually react to particular texts or ideas, make sure your paper demonstrates that you have, in fact, read that text carefully. For example, you might quote from the assigned material or summarize (briefly) what you have seen or discovered.

- Make connections between the item you are examining and other similar texts you have seen or read. Explore those relationships.

- Feel free to use the first person (*I* or *we*) unless specifically directed otherwise. Position papers usually encourage personal reflection.

- Although a position paper may be informal, be sure to present it professionally. Proofread the item carefully, making sure you get the spelling right. Unless directed otherwise, double space the paper and be sure it has margins wide enough (at least 1") to allow a reader to write comments.

- If you are asked to post your position paper online in a discussion forum, keep your response frank, but consider your audience. And take the time to respond to a few of your colleagues' postings.

PREPARING A PROBLEM/SOLUTION PROJECT

This genre is more common than you might think. Many works you'll encounter represent attempts to address a problem: it can be a design challenge faced by an architect or a communication issue a politician, film-maker, or writer may need to confront. The elements listed here won't fit every problem/solution paper you write, but they do offer a structure for such projects.

- Describe the problem you or someone else seeks to fix. Be precise about the difficulty that needs to be addressed. Play the journalist here, answering such factual questions as *who, what, where, when, how,* and *why.*

- Explain why the problem needs to be resolved. Readers will have to be convinced that the issue deserves their attention. Don't take it for granted that they will be concerned, for example, about handicapped access problems at your school or a graphic artist's attempts to make signage more readable. When possible, explain how readers might be personally affected by the problem.

- Explain how the problem has been addressed (unsuccessfully) before. If a problem has been around for a long time, review the history of attempts to fix it. For example, designers have puzzled for decades over the need to make complex audio equipment in cars easier to use. Solutions have ranged from lots of tiny square buttons to touch-screen interfaces. Readers need to know not only what's been tried in the past but also that you are aware of those efforts.

- Explain why previous solutions have failed. What's wrong with a radio with dozens of buttons or a touch-screen interface? Don't assume that readers will know.

- Describe the proposed solution (yours or someone else's) and how it was arrived at—briefly chronicling its trials and errors. Be sure to explain what the new approach accomplishes. Don't get argumentative yet. Once again, play the journalist, answering *who, what, where, when, how,* and *why.*

- Explain the advantages of the solution and suggest its implications (if any) for society and culture. Indicate what objections people may have to the solution or what roadblocks might stand in the way of its adoption.

- Defend the feasibility of the solution or innovation. Will it work? Is it cost effective? Legal? Can it be applied broadly enough to make a difference?

- Explain how the solution might be implemented. Once you've persuaded readers that an approach to a problem is sensible and feasible, show that it might become a reality. Who has to approve, fund, and administer this new approach? Over what period of time?

WRITING A RHETORICAL ANALYSIS

In a rhetorical analysis, you examine how a text actually works. Depending on the assignment, you can simply describe how a text (often a persuasive one) uses various devices of language, rhetoric, or design to achieve its aims. Or you can inquire into the strategies and motives behind a particular text. Or you can go a step farther and actually judge the rhetorical success of your subject, whether it be an essay, article, photograph, building, mural, public space, or any other object that might have an impact on readers or audiences.

Not long ago, rhetorical analysis seemed pretty much just an academic exercise. But Web sites and blogging have drawn the activity into the mainstream: on a huge number of sites you can now watch writers, from *DailyKos* on the political left to *Power Line* on the right, scrutinizing news stories, editorials, and other political discourse intensely, sometimes line by line and picture by picture. The immediacy of the Web can make these rhetorical inquisitions hasty and unbalanced at times, but it's also clear that such extremely close readings of texts have influenced the utterances of journalists and politicians. It's much harder now to get away with *anything.*

If you're assigned to prepare a rhetorical analysis, you'll likely have more time than a typical blogger to look closely at a text and to treat it fairly. Following is some general advice for approaching such a task.

- Examine the subject of your rhetorical analysis very closely, reading or viewing it several times, carefully noting its features and strategies (see Chapter 1 "Reading Texts"). You may want to photocopy a written text so that you can annotate its features.

- So far as you can, identify the purpose of the text you are examining and determine the context in which it was originally offered. If necessary, do research on this question.

- Consider the basic rhetorical features of the item and identify any that might account for its appeal or lack thereof. Begin by considering how the text deals with its potential audience. How does it signal to them? What devices does it use to make that appeal? Does it seem to exclude any readers or viewers—and is that exclusion significant?

- Determine the genre and medium of the text. How does the genre affect your expectations for the text (for example, you expect a report to be factual, an editorial to offer an opinion). Does the medium suit the subject matter or, perhaps, challenge the audience's expectations—for example, is a cartoon used to treat a serious topic? (See Item 2.8.)

- Examine the types of evidence or appeals employed in the text: *ethos*, *pathos*, *logos* (see pages 25–26). Does the text rely mainly on hard facts, testimony, verifiable sources, and reasoned argument? Do the people or institutions presenting the appeal represent themselves as honest, trustworthy, and knowledgeable? Does the text target readers or viewers through strong emotional appeals?

- After a close examination of your subject, focus your analysis around a specific claim you can support with evidence from the text itself. Make the claim specific enough to teach your readers something about the text that they probably wouldn't notice in a casual reading.

- Early in your analysis, be sure to identify the text you are analyzing by author/creator and name. If necessary, briefly describe or summarize the work and share with readers any background information about it that you have uncovered in your research. Readers need to know exactly what you are talking about. Provide an image when appropriate.

- Present the detailed evidence you need to support your claim. Quote freely from a written text or present any images that might help readers appreciate the points you are making.

WRITING AN AD ANALYSIS

An ad analysis is a subcategory of rhetorical analysis (see pages 71–72) and uses many of the same techniques. Of course, you've seen so many ads, whether on TV or in print, that you may already feel qualified to judge them. After all, in most cases, you are their target audience. But when you write about an advertising spot or campaign, you still need to make a point, present evidence for any claims you make, and show an appreciation for detail.

- In an ad analysis, describe the item as if the reader has not seen it. Taking the time to summarize the spot will also sharpen your appreciation of its structure and strategies. A short description near the opening of the analysis usually helps to orient readers. Use images, too, to supplement or clarify your words. Provide readers with the URL (or search terms) for a TV ad available on YouTube or elsewhere.

- Make a specific and complex point about the ad, a coherent and stimulating claim that is richer than *this campaign uses good* ethos, pathos, *and* logos. Compose a thesis to explain why exactly the ad might succeed, fail, insult, obfuscate, confuse, celebrate, or persuade. Then prove it.

- Understand the point of the ad. Examine its elements closely and look for any strategies that bring them together—whether verbal, visual, thematic, or stylistic. Assume that there is a deliberate strategy in the ad, even if you don't initially detect it.

- Understand the audience of the ad. How specifically does the spot signal its demographic boundaries, and how well does it appeal to the targeted group? Consider that you might not be the target audience of the commercial. Don't assume you should be.

- Appreciate the savvy of a professional ad. Not all pitches work, and even professional efforts fail spectacularly at times. But you will perform a sharper analysis if you assume, at least at the outset, that the creators of the spot weren't stupid.

- Understand the persuasive tools used. Does the spot rely on facts? On emotions? On an appeal to the reputation or authority of its sponsor? On the *ethos* of a celebrity spokesperson? What does the choice of tactics say about the advertising spot or campaign?

- Analyze the medium selected. Advertisers are picky about where they place their spots, hoping to target the maximum number of their desired viewers for the least amount of money. But media do work differently (see pages 77–79). An interactive Web ad or an alternative reality game (ARG) demands more from viewers than a 15-second spot repeated endlessly on talk radio. Does it accomplish any more (see Item 2.7)? You can explore such differences in your analysis.

- Understand the visual tools used. How is the spot arranged or narrated? How are images and words connected? How are key ideas highlighted? How is color employed? What fonts are selected and why?

- Understand the way sound is used. For a TV or radio spot, consider what the soundtrack or dialogue contributes to the ad. What type of music is offered and why? Might any silences be significant?

- Present evidence for the points you offer. Show precisely how any claim you make is supported by describable elements of the ad. Don't hurry through your presentation of evidence or assume that it is obvious to your readers. Give all the details required.

WRITING AN ARGUMENT

In an argument, you offer readers evidence and reasons to accept a claim you support. Arguments are diverse and demanding, pressing upon readers at every turn, from the pop-up ads on Web sites (*Buy me!*) to the book-length treatises of serious scholars, politicians, and thinkers eager to change the world (*Earth in the Balance*). When writing an argument, you ordinarily begin with an *arguable proposition*—that is, a claim that a reasonable person finds worth discussing. Sometimes the claim is offered in a thesis statement early in the argument. But arguments—especially those in media other than words—often lead readers toward a claim stated at the end of the work or embedded in it. The claim might be merely (but usually quite strongly) implied.

Once you have a claim or point you want to argue, you'll need to gather and arrange evidence to make your case. Here is some advice.

- In writing an argument, have a clear sense of what your position is and what evidence you'll need to make it appealing to your intended audience. Study your audience, but don't pander to it.

- For academic projects, base your arguments chiefly on facts and evidence. Do the research necessary to know your subject cold and to command the data likely to convince readers that your claim is reasonable or perhaps even right.

- Offer sensible reasons for accepting your claims and evidence. For instance, show that an action you are proposing is the best of several choices, or the lesser of two evils, or that it follows long-established precedents. Generate as many such arguments as you can initially, and then use the three or four most likely to convince a skeptical audience.

- Think about ways to make your readers identify with your argument. When appropriate, appeal to their emotions, needs, and desires. Or use these appeals to move them to action once you have convinced them that your claim may be right or valid. Getting people to act is tougher than getting them to believe.

- Give listeners a reason to trust you. Use sources responsibly (documenting them, for instance), explain your credentials for offering an argument (experience, education), and speak in a moderate yet confident voice. Sound like someone who knows his or her material.

- Offer specific evidence for the claims you make. Present numbers or testimony for the logical claims. Provide illustrations and examples that enhance your emotional appeals. When possible, choose evidence that is memorable—stuff audiences will take away with them.

- Arrange your arguments and evidence for maximum impact. Open strong, but save your very best material for the end. Use transitions to move readers through the piece. Don't be afraid of *first, second, on the other hand, to the contrary,* or *finally*. An argument should always feel as if it has a trajectory—that it is leading to a powerful conclusion.

- Respect opposing arguments enough to learn them and to describe them fairly in your own work. You'll win over many wavering readers by this admirable strategy.

- Pay attention to style, both verbal and visual. You can win arguments by making points clearly and efficiently and illustrating them vividly. But don't overdo it. If you grow long-winded, you'll lose an argument.

PREPARING AN ORAL PRESENTATION

Quite often in school and on the job, you will be asked to present your ideas directly to an audience. Any such oral presentation requires preparation and organization. Never try to wing such an assignment or assume that you can just read a paper to the group. If you give the occasion your full attention, you may even find that you enjoy the experience.

- For an oral report, choose a clear and limited subject that fits the time allotted for the presentation. Plan to cover a small topic thoroughly.

- Organize the presentation with a simple pattern of exposition—one an audience can follow easily and remember. You might make a single claim about a controversial building and then support it with three or four major points. Or you might compare and contrast the design of several structures.

- Have a clear beginning, middle, and end and let readers know where you are in the presentation. Use the opening to introduce yourself, announce your subject, and outline the presentation. In the body of the presentation, cover all the territory you promised in the introduction. Then use the conclusion to summarize your points (briefly) and to suggest any implications.

- Use media sensibly. Not every presentation must be based on PowerPoint slides. But do use media to present charts, relevant images, or pertinent (and short) video clips to illustrate your points. Be careful not to let visual items dominate the presentation.

- Be sure any charts, film clips, or slides can be seen, heard, or read by your audience. Words and drawings on slides should be bold and highly visible.

- If you use software such as PowerPoint, choose a simple style for the slides. Open with one that presents your title, your name, and any other pertinent information (date, institution). Then list your major points—with subsequent slides covering each one in sequence. A summary slide at the end is also helpful. *Don't read from your slides or present long prose passages on them.* And avoid the elaborate sound effects or slide transitions available on presentation software: they can seem amateurish.

- Watch the clock. Don't go over your allotted time; if necessary, edit your remarks as you go rather than deliver them so fast no one can understand you. Allow time at the end for questions too.

- Speak clearly and deliberately and maintain eye contact with members of the audience. Don't pace the stage, rock at the podium, or punctuate every sentence with *ya know* or *ummmm*.

- Practice your presentation, speaking it exactly as you expect to deliver it to the audience so that you get an accurate estimate of its length. Be sure you know how to operate any equipment you plan to use.

- Dress for the occasion. Show respect for your audience by selecting more formal clothes for the presentation.

FYI

ITEM 2.7 ■ **Fake Nissan Altima Keys, March 2007**

What do you call an ad that doesn't seem like an ad? "Nontraditional" and "viral" are terms the *New York Times* applied to a campaign by Nissan Motors that involved deliberately losing 20,000 key rings like the one below to promote a new Altima sedan that started with a pushbutton rather than a traditional key. Nissan could even target specific audiences by deciding where to spread the fake keys. The *Times* notes that they were distributed "in bars, concert halls, sports arenas, and other public places in seven large markets" ("A Promotion to Sell Cars by 'Losing' the Keys," March 19, 2007).

CONSIDER

1. The Nissan campaign described in Item 2.7 is an example of "viral marketing," a type of advertising that breaks rules and crosses traditional genres. Use the resources of the Web to explore the genre of viral marketing. To what groups might such campaigns appeal?

2. What writing genre might you use to respond to the fake Nissan Altima keys in Item 2.7 and to the concept of viral marketing itself? (See Beau Faulkner's essay on pages 389–394.)

3. What new genres of writing or communication have you explored in recent years? Would you consider the exchanges in a social network such as Facebook or Twitter to represent a new genre? Why or why not?

4. Pick a particular genre or media you know well and try to explain its distinctive features to someone outside its normal demographic. You might try to explain a genre of video game to someone who has never played one or outline what a women's fashion magazine story must include to a person who prefers *Field and Stream* (or vice versa).

76   CHOOSING A GENRE AND STRUCTURE

Choosing a medium

To convey ideas, you'll choose some physical means of transmission, a *medium*. As recently as a decade ago, your choice of medium for responding to texts or assignments would have been limited to what was really a choice among genres, most of which involved language: you could compose a lab report, research paper, essay, book review, journal entry, and so on. Yet even then, texts like these might have included charts, graphs, and illustrations, even if it took considerable skill and patience to handcraft the images and integrate them. Today it's far easier to compose in various media simply because of stunning improvements in technology.

So you have more choices and opportunities than ever when thinking about how you might deliver a project to readers. Of course, you have to appraise your skills when selecting a medium. Making a Web site or creating podcasts for an academic assignment might seem cooler than writing a conventional paper. But these projects could have a steeper learning curve for you: better a solid paper than a poor PowerPoint presentation. You simply have to make intelligent choices, fitting the medium to the aims and audiences of your project. Following is a review of the strengths and limitations of major media.

CHOOSE THE SPOKEN WORD

This remains a powerful medium because it involves direct human contact. Words can be delivered with whatever tone, volume, or pace a speaker chooses and at whatever length, and with accompanying body language and gestures (though these movements might be invisible if the words are delivered via radio, yet another medium). In a live performance, speakers may use visuals or other aids (PowerPoint slides, for example) to reinforce their words; speakers also receive immediate feedback from their audiences, which influences their performances. Dialogue is an even more active form of the spoken word, with participants learning from the give and take of discussion. Unless recorded, however, speech evaporates into memory. So, in cultures that do not value memory, spoken words and testimony are considered less reliable than written documents and "hard evidence."

CHOOSE WRITTEN WORDS

Written words allow for the precise expression of complex ideas. Thoughts can be set down in endless detail, complete with supporting evidence and meticulous qualifications. Words can also record and inspire subtle human feelings and emotions. On paper, words can preserve ideas for millennia under ideal conditions. However, written language is a relatively static medium, less conducive than speech to the interplay of ideas—except, perhaps, in some electronic forums. Printed words are also, as Plato noted, mute and unvarying and the enemies of memory. They can also be clumsy devices for describing physical objects or conveying proportion, perspective, or spatial relationships.

CHOOSE THE FINE ARTS

The fine arts, which typically include drawing, painting, sculpture, dance, and so on, provide conduits for expressing human thoughts and feelings. Appealing to the senses as well as the imagination, the fine arts encourage interpretation and provoke dialogue. These arts tend to be tactile—objects or activities with a physical dimension or quality. Some, like oil paintings or pieces of sculpture, are permanent; others, like a dance or a musical production, exist in the moment of performance. Most of these works can be transmitted in some form, especially the performing arts. But many lose their impact when they are reproduced: the original work in oil, stone, or wood or the live performance or concert represent the ultimate expression of the artist's achievement. Copies are not the same.

CHOOSE THE GRAPHIC ARTS

These arts often serve other media—for example, when a designer selects appropriate fonts, colors, and elements for a book. Yet, increasingly, the graphic elements of texts are recognized as part of the message. This is clearly the case for presentation software such as PowerPoint, which enables writers to use charts, graphs, and design elements to deliver lectures, sales reports, and education. But almost every item we now create in digital form requires an appreciation of and expertise in graphic design.

CHOOSE PHOTOGRAPHY

Photographs provide a relatively accurate means of recording aspects of the physical world using equipment available to most anyone, including rank amateurs. Photographers can produce work that is scientific, personal, or commercial, preserving on film everything from cellular structures and news events to crime scenes and vacation memories. Yet they also reach into the realms of high art. By its nature, photography is a static medium, and its images are open to interpretation, sometimes requiring words to explain them or give them context.

CHOOSE FILM

Movies are an ideal medium for capturing and embodying movement and action. Like still photography, film can record important events, activities, and processes; yet it is also (or simultaneously) an artistic medium, one that can tell stories, shape opinions, and provide entertainment. Film can be cut and spliced to manage the flow of ideas and time; each shot also provides opportunities for artistic (or other) manipulation. So film can convey ideas powerfully and serve as a medium for documenting events. But films can also distort, falsify, or create "reality."

CHOOSE VIDEO

This medium shares many of the qualities of film. Like film, video can capture and edit movement. But the images in a video medium are stored and reproduced on a screen electronically rather than through the projection of light. Images shot with video cameras have a different quality than works captured on film—video feels more immediate and "realistic" than film but also cruder, colder, and less sharp. These differences are obvious enough to affect the response of audiences, although the distinctions between digital video and film are rapidly breaking down. Video is immediate, too. Images can be captured even on a cell phone and distributed immediately worldwide via YouTube and other Web sites.

CHOOSE THE WORLD WIDE WEB

The Web is without a doubt the most important new medium spawned by the computer and digital revolutions of the past two or three decades. Although the Web uses many media—including the printed word, sound, and video—it does not simply combine them. It transforms them. The Web can convey up-to-date information and entertainment in stunningly original and interactive ways, but it can also be distressingly confusing, invasive, and even coercive. Long texts are hard to read on the screen, and the Web still has to prove its ability to archive materials over time. Yet it is remarkable that the same medium that offers to download pop music and provides moment-by-moment updates of stock prices can also reach deeply into library and museum collections. We still haven't fathomed all the dimensions of this medium.

CHOOSE MULTIMEDIA

Multimedia is a catch-all term for any combination of genres and media. As we point out in our introduction, such combinations are nothing new. Images and words have worked together since at least the time of the Egyptian pharaohs. Digital technologies now enable almost anyone to integrate words, images, and sounds into texts. These hybrid media can create environments nicely adapted to specific subject situations: the online version of the *New York Times* provides not only words and pictures but also audio and video files and slide shows of news events, depending on the story covered. The downside of multimedia is that the technology can easily swamp the content if it draws too much attention to itself.

ITEM 2.8 ■ **Opening Pages of Chapter 9 from *The 9/11 Commission Report*, 2004, and from Sid Jacobson and Ernie Colón, *The 9/11 Report: A Graphic Adaptation*, 2006**

The official report of the National Commission on Terrorist Attacks on the United States was released in summer 2004. A best seller praised for its readability, it nonetheless ran for 567 thickly printed pages. In 2006, with the blessing of Commission chairs Thomas H. Kean and Lee H. Hamilton, a much shorter "graphic version" appeared, its purpose to reach an even broader audience. But is a medium usually associated with comic books appropriate to a subject as serious as the 9/11 attacks?

9

HEROISM AND HORROR

9.1 PREPAREDNESS AS OF SEPTEMBER 11

Emergency response is a product of preparedness. On the morning of September 11, 2001, the last best hope for the community of people working in or visiting the World Trade Center rested not with national policymakers but with private firms and local public servants, especially the first responders: fire, police, emergency medical service, and building safety professionals.

Building Preparedness
The World Trade Center. The World Trade Center (WTC) complex was built for the Port Authority of New York and New Jersey. Construction began in 1966, and tenants began to occupy its space in 1970. The Twin Towers came to occupy a unique and symbolic place in the culture of New York City and America.

The WTC actually consisted of seven buildings, including one hotel, spread across 16 acres of land. The buildings were connected by an underground mall (the concourse). The Twin Towers (1 WTC, or the North Tower, and 2 WTC, or the South Tower) were the signature structures, containing 10.4 million square feet of office space. Both towers had 110 stories, were about 1,350 feet high, and were square; each wall measured 208 feet in length. On any given workday, up to 50,000 office workers occupied the towers, and 40,000 people passed through the complex.[1]

Each tower contained three central stairwells, which ran essentially from top to bottom, and 99 elevators. Generally, elevators originating in the lobby ran to "sky lobbies" on higher floors, where additional elevators carried passengers to the tops of the buildings.[2]

Stairwells A and C ran from the 110th floor to the raised mezzanine level of the lobby. Stairwell B ran from the 107th floor to level B6, six floors below ground, and was accessible from the West Street lobby level, which was one

278

The 9/11 Commission Report, 2004

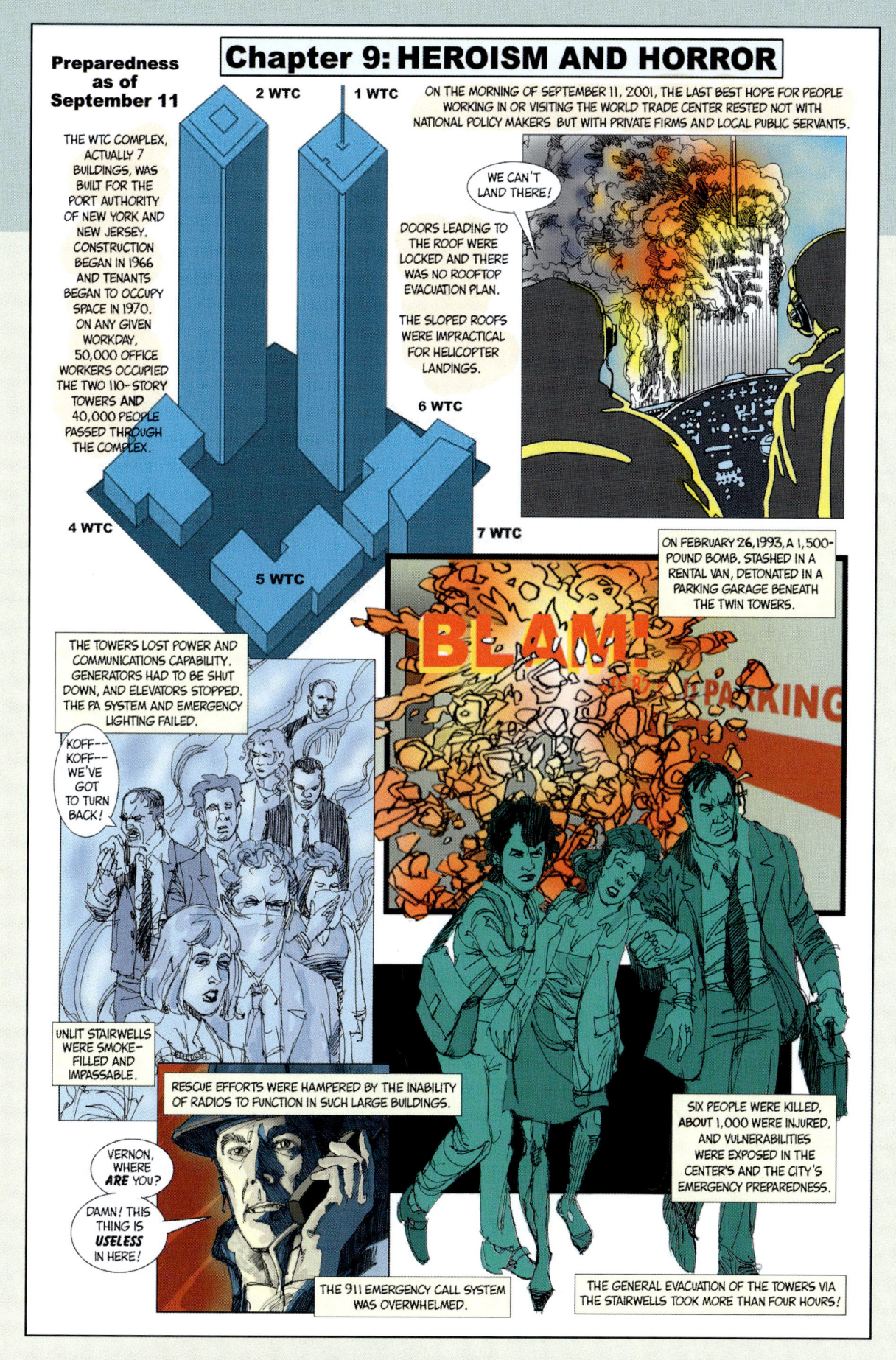

The 9/11 Report: A Graphic Adaptation, 2006

CHOOSING A MEDIUM

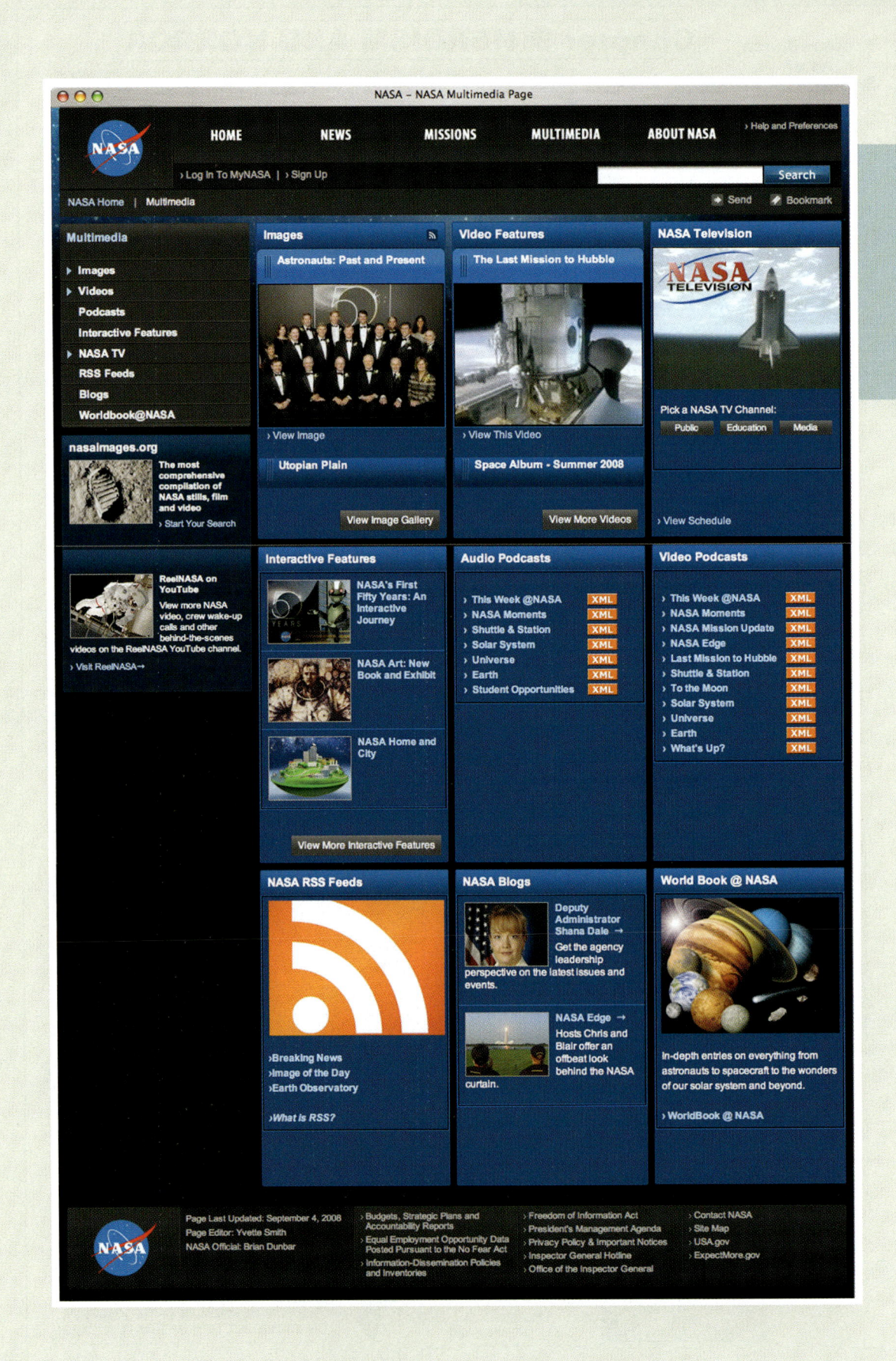

FYI

ITEM 2.9 ■ NASA Multimedia Page, June 13, 2008

As the federal agency charged with pioneering "the future in space exploration, scientific discovery and aeronautics research," NASA also has an important educational mission for the scientific community, the general public, and even school children. What does this "Multimedia Page" from NASA's Web site reveal about its educational strategies? What different purposes and audiences do the different media presented on the page serve? Which medium would you be inclined to try first? Why? This page is available at <http://www.nasa.gov/multimedia/index.html>.

CONSIDER

1. Can you identify another non-fiction book or publication that might benefit from a graphic version such as that shown in Item 2.8? What features could the graphic text offer that might be lacking in a typical verbal medium?

2. Asked to explain either your academic major or some special interest of yours through a media document such as the NASA Web page in Item 2.9, what media would you choose, and how might you employ them? What media wouldn't work well for your subject?

3. Plato observes that "oratory is the art of enchanting the soul." Use this formula to compose definitions of several other media, especially modern ones. For example, "PowerPoint is the art of making important ideas seem trivial" or "Writing e-mail is the verbal equivalent of dropping in uninvited." Compare your aphorisms with those composed by others in the class. Then choose one of your observations and defend it in a paragraph.

4. Choose one of the nine categories of media discussed in this section (*spoken word, printed word, film*, and so on), and annotate the description with additional examples that either illustrate or undercut the claims made. For example, you have grown up with video, thanks to TV productions, videotapes, and camcorders. Is it true that "images shot with video cameras have a different quality than works captured on film"? Or that "video feels more immediate and 'realistic' than film"? What evidence would you use to confirm these claims or make others think twice about them?

COMPOSE

5. Write a brief proposal explaining how you would take a text already famous in one medium and move it to another. Filmmakers have been doing this for decades, turning novels, plays, or even comic books into movies. Argue the value of doing the same with some other text, but be imaginative in your migration from medium to medium. For example, could you turn Grant Wood's well-known painting *American Gothic* into a TV sitcom? What would be the rationale for doing that? What would be the theme for your *American Gothic* series? Who would the supporting characters be—in addition to the couple in the painting—and who would play them? Or how about turning a political show such as *Hardball* or *The O'Reilly Factor* into a video game? Again, what would be the challenge? How would players score? What would be the interface? And for any such shift of medium, what would be the point of the transformation?

Doing research and documenting sources

Writers need to know what they are talking about. Gut reactions are fine when you are just offering an opinion. But you'll need to move well beyond that basic level of response in your academic or professional work. Readers will expect you to know enough about a subject to present verifiable evidence for any claims you make. In many cases, that will mean doing research both in a library and online. For some projects, you may even need to do a field observation.

SCOPE OUT YOUR TOPIC

Determine what you already know about it, what you need to figure out, and where you might locate that information. Be sensible too. It's tempting to make sweeping claims about subjects, and such bold statements certainly do appeal to audiences. For instance, you may think that *The Lord of the Rings* is the finest film trilogy ever made—and some readers might agree. But to make that argument in a paper or on a Web site, you'll need to earn real expertise. Digging into film history, you'd soon discover that some of the world's most distinguished filmmakers have made trilogies, including Ingmar Bergman, Hiroshi Inagaki, and Michelangelo Antonioni. Then there is *The Godfather* trilogy, two of which won Best Picture Oscars. Things just got complicated.

Your initial claim, bold and unlimited, would obligate you to track down and watch films you'd never have heard of and then read stacks of articles of film criticism. And then you'd need to weigh any worthy trilogies by some reasonable criteria against *The Lord of the Rings*. Can you do it? Sure. Will it be easy? No one said it would be. But you could also modify your thesis to make your research much more focused and manageable: after all, *The Lord of the Rings* might well be the best *English-language fantasy-adventure film trilogy of modern times*. That's a claim you could more likely handle in the few weeks available for most academic papers.

Research is, in many ways, easier to do today than ever before, thanks to the fluidity of digitized information—which can be archived, shared, and searched with ease. But you still have to read what you find, evaluate it, and then draw it together into a coherent project. So a key to successful research is to begin with a manageable project. Don't bite off more than you can chew.

BE METHODICAL IN YOUR RESEARCH

A few decisions made early in the process can save you time and energy later.

- Read the assignment sheet carefully and follow it exactly. Pay attention to any due dates (for a topic proposal, bibliography, draft, and final project). Note, too, whether you must follow a particular style sheet or system of documentation: APA, MLA, Chicago, or AP.

- Keep a record of sources you've consulted. In the past, researchers used note cards to manage the books and articles they read. Today, you might use a database instead to keep track of the authors, titles, journals, dates of publication, and page numbers of sources you'll cite in a paper. Photocopy or download key sources or pages.

- Carefully summarize and paraphrase *in your own words* the materials you've read so that you don't accidentally plagiarize your sources. Use quotation marks around borrowed language. And remember that in an academic paper you must document any words and ideas you borrow (except those considered common knowledge).

USE THE LIBRARY

Because you search your local library via an online catalog, you might assume that it doesn't offer much more than the Web. In fact, the resources are quite different. Most of the books, journals, older magazines, and print sources of a library still aren't available online. Nor is online information as deliberately collected and organized for research as are the materials in a library—where you will also find librarians to help you. So whatever the project, plan to spend some time working in a library.

- For a quick but professional overview of a project, consult specialized encyclopedias such as the *Encyclopedia of Art* or *The New Grove Dictionary of American Music.* Librarians can suggest the best resource. But don't rely on encyclopedias as sources: they are only a starting point.

- Get familiar with the *Library of Congress Subject Headings* (known as the *LCSH*). This is a multi-volume set of subject headings used to organize library material. By figuring out the subject terms used to describe your topic, you can search the library catalog more efficiently. Ask a librarian for assistance.

- Learn to use library databases. Some library databases aren't available online. They may also have fairly complicated interfaces. Read the instructions and ask for help if necessary.

- Explore the special collections. Libraries may have extensive selections of video, audio, and photographic materials—as well as maps, microfilm archives of newspapers and magazines, and more.

USE THE INTERNET

The Web is a splendid tool for generating ideas and finding information—especially about current topics and popular culture. But you have to be careful in figuring out how to find the links that lead to the data you need. Imagine, for example, that you find an amazing image by a photographer whose name you don't recognize. You'd probably search for the name on the Web, using Google or Yahoo. Then you need to decide what links to follow: look for other works she has produced or galleries where she has exhibited. One of those galleries might have an online catalog with more links to artists who do similar work. Before you know it, you may discover an entire school of photography you didn't even know existed, one you might want to write about or imitate.

But you can also waste lots of time browsing this way. You need to be both open to the richness of the Web and focused on the needs of your project when doing research there.

- Learn to search efficiently with keywords. By combining search terms that accurately describe your subject, you can narrow the hits you'll receive from either the Web at large or a more specialized database. Most tools of this kind offer user's guides: read them.

- Use Web tools prepared by your campus library or national sources. For example, many major university libraries provide extensive subject-by-subject bibliographies of online materials. To find these useful materials, just search "subject guides" or "library research guides" on Google or any similar Web site. Or go to the New York Public Library site at <www.nypl.org> and search for "subject guides."

- Rely on credible sources. For factual information, use resources tied to well-known institutions. The federal government, for example, offers extensive online materials. So do major libraries, museums, and galleries. Don't quote from sources you can't verify. If you do choose to use blogs or personal sites, clearly identify them as such so readers can exercise their own judgment.

LEARN FROM EXPERTS

People can be valuable resources for your projects, especially when you are dealing with artists, filmmakers, or other creative types who may give you a first-hand look at the work they do. Again, the Web can help jump-start the process, helping you to identify local people who may have a connection to your project. You might also want to explore discussions archived at the Google Groups pages, where you can tap into many of the conversations of experts or interested amateurs.

But don't go unprepared into an interview with an expert. And don't bother an expert with elementary queries. You'll need sufficient background information on your subject to ask worthwhile questions.

- Make a formal appointment by phone or e-mail.

- Do some background reading about the interviewee. Find out what you can about his or her work or accomplishments.

- Have a set of questions prepared. If you're smart, they won't be the kind that can be answered by "yes" or "no."

- Be prepared to take notes. If you want to record the interview, clear it with your subject ahead of time.

- Get to the point: don't waste the expert's time. And send a follow-up e-mail or card to thank your subject for talking with you.

PREPARE A FIELD OBSERVATION

Assignments to describe a place or situation accurately may require field research involving systematic observation. For social scientists, such field observation is a technique conducted according to well-established, formal research methods. As a nonspecialist, you probably won't adhere to such strict conventions in most academic projects. But by following steps similar to those used by social scientists, you can build a detailed survey of a place or situation.

- Preview your site and make a plan. Figure on at least two visits where you can observe without distractions for at least one hour. Decide in advance what times you'll go, where you'll sit, and how you'll record your observations. Try observing at different times of the day and on different days of the week to get a sense of whether activities at the site vary.

- Draw a map of the space, showing the location of key structures, surfaces, paths, objects, and other permanent features.

- Take careful field notes. Buy a notebook expressly for this purpose, and describe each visit on a separate page marked with the date and time. Look carefully at the space and what goes on there, and take as many notes as possible. Decide in advance how you'll organize your materials. Many researchers use a two-column format, writing factual observations in the left-hand column and personal interpretations and comments in the right-hand column.

- Review your notes as soon as possible after the observation session, filling in details, words, or other items that you've left out.
- Analyze your observations after a few hours or days have passed, looking for interesting patterns or unexpected findings.

Repeat your field observation process each time you visit the site. And as you analyze each set of notes, look for commonalities and differences from one session to the next.

DOCUMENT YOUR SOURCES

In gathering information for any project, you must respect intellectual property concerns and understand the conventions for documenting information. Working with written texts, you likely know your responsibilities to keep track of your sources, to document your use of ideas or words borrowed from others, to use quotation marks around word-for-word borrowings, and to provide a list of sources used in your project. You probably have a handbook that explains the conventions of various systems of documentation—Modern Language Association (MLA), American Psychological Association (APA), *The Chicago Manual of Style* (CMS), Council of Science Editors (CSE), and perhaps some others—one of which you should use in any paper or project requiring formal documentation. (Your instructor will tell you which style to follow.)

But you also need to give proper credit to any photographers, filmmakers, musicians, or other artists you borrow from, especially when those items might appear in a publicly displayed work. A photograph or a film must be documented as carefully as a journal or newspaper article—though that credit might be handled differently, with a credit line, for example, rather than a footnote. Handbooks now explain how to document many nontraditional sources. Remember, too, that readers may want some background information about the images you use, especially the name of the artist responsible for the image and the date when it was produced, simply to give them context for reading it. Help them out with a caption or note.

CONSIDER

1. From the following list, choose a person or subject about which you'd like to know more. Then spend an hour in the library and some time online learning more about the topic—enough for you to make a brief in-class oral presentation. Keep track of your sources of information, and identify those that proved to be most helpful, comparing what you found in the library to online resources.

   - Georgia O'Keeffe (painter)
   - iPhone
   - Marshall McLuhan (media theorist)
   - *Dogtown and Z Boys* (2001, film)
   - Jonathan Ives (designer)
   - Dorothea Lange (photographer)
   - Art Deco movement
   - Gordon Parks Sr. (photographer)
   - Edward Curtis (photographer)
   - Hybrid gas-electric cars
   - The Glass House (1939)
   - Philip Johnson (architect)
   - Al Jourgenson (musician)
   - Hiroshi Inagaki (filmmaker)
   - *The Sixth Sense* (1999, film)

2. In a current writer's handbook that covers MLA and APA documentation, review the standards for documenting online and nonprint works (films, plays, cartoons). How do the systems differ in their treatment of these items? How are they alike?

Revising and editing

No matter what your project, whether it is as different as creating a photo essay, analyzing a print advertisement, or designing a Web site to encourage voter registration, you'll be making choices that determine your process of composing. No "one size fits all" formula works when you are responding to texts or assignments. As we've suggested throughout this chapter, you will need to decide the following issues.

- What your subject or content will be
- What audiences you'll want to reach (or ignore)
- What strategies you might use to achieve your ends
- What genre and structure you'll adopt
- What medium will best convey your material
- What research you'll need to do

You also should understand that the whole business of composing is messy, and often involves false starts, dead ends, uncooperative technologies, unpredictable audiences, and so on. Composing is very much a process of rethinking and revising as you move ahead toward a product that comes close to meeting your expectations (even if it never quite gets there).

EVALUATE AND REVISE YOUR WORK

Test your project at various stages, drawing on the expertise of knowledgeable colleagues, friends, or even potential members of your audience. Begin with a topic proposal, for example, in which you explain to an instructor or classmates what you intend to do. Get responses on drafts or prototypes of your project. Show a brochure you are creating to a test group, and ask members if they understand its point or can find essential information easily. Review a Web page you have created to see if it travels well from Mac to PC platforms. Ask someone who hasn't seen Steven Spielberg's *Indiana Jones and the Kingdom of the Crystal Skull* to judge how well your review explains the film.

The same care is important with projects in nonprint media. Here a second or third opinion may encourage you to pull back a bit when you use images for their own sake or insist on embedding an audio file on a page just because you've recently learned that skill. You might excuse a little graininess in a photograph you took because you really like the subject. A more experienced photographer could bring you down to earth or suggest how you might adjust the image to take advantage of its roughness.

And, naturally, you'll have to review your work on your own. Before you revise, put a paper aside for a few days; then you will be far more likely to detect gaps and problems. Trust your instincts and be honest about them: when you suspect something isn't working, you're probably right. Here's a list of big-ticket items you should review carefully.

- Check that the project makes a point. You don't have to have a thesis at the beginning of a paper or a comparable explicit statement of theme in other projects. But your audience needs to know what you are up to. A clear title can do some of the work.
- Check that you haven't omitted essential information. Have you anticipated any serious *who*, *what*, *where*, *when*, *how*, and *why* questions readers might have about your work? Have you fully identified the people or texts you're discussing?

- Check that the transitions or navigation within the project work. You can provide easy and natural transitions between sentences and paragraphs (*first, next, on the other hand*), while you might use headings and captions to identify bigger sections and parts. When creating a Web site, you'll need logical links as well as a site design that neatly segregates different kinds of information.

- Edit for a clear and efficient style in academic papers. Your tone and vocabulary may change from piece to piece as you shift between levels of formality. But readers always appreciate a lean and clear style. Keep most verbs active, avoid strung-out noun phrases, and cut any words not pulling their weight.

SWEAT THE DETAILS

With a paper, that means checking facts and proofreading. On a Web project, test all the links. In a slide show, be certain the images are in the right order and have the correct captions. Make sure everything is spelled right in any project. Overlooked details that seem insignificant to you may well damage your work in the eyes of viewers accustomed to quality work. Your best guide could be a handbook of grammar and writing. But here's a checklist of items you can't afford to miss.

- Get the format right. Academic papers are usually double-spaced, with one-inch margins. They require titles, page numbers, and your name and course information on a title or opening page. But just about every type of medium has comparable conventions. Your film may need credits, your PowerPoint presentation an introductory slide.

- Treat titles correctly. Italicize or underscore the titles of books, newspapers, magazines, TV shows, movies, and major works of art—an opera, a painting, a CD. Put lesser titles in quotation marks: book chapters, TV episodes, and songs. But these conventions do vary, depending on the style sheet you use, for example, MLA, APA, or AP, so check a handbook to be sure.

- Check your spelling. The spell checker won't catch every error, and people react very strongly to misspelled words. So give every page or screen one last careful look.

- Check your punctuation. Commas, apostrophes, and quotation marks probably cause more problems in academic papers than misspelled words. Review these items in a handbook. The rules are fairly clear—and certainly not rocket science. There's no reason to mistake *it's* for *its*.

CONSIDER

1. Most of us have strengths and weaknesses as writers. At the editing stage, it obviously makes sense to give extra attention to the problems you typically have or the errors you make habitually. Make a list of your characteristic blunders. Compare it with your colleagues' lists.

COMPOSE

2. Fan films (see Item 2.1) are mostly amateur efforts, but some are nicely plotted or show imaginative use of special effects. Do a Web search of "fan films" to locate some works you might review, and examine several. Then respond to one as if you have been asked by the director to look at a rough cut and suggest improvements. Summarize your recommendations in a short, but specific document. Begin by affirming what works: explain what you would not change. Next, make comments about the film as a whole: Does the story work? Is the narrative coherent? Are the characters appropriately motivated and cast? Is the pacing right? How about the lighting, the setting, the costumes? Then offer specific suggestions about production details that might be improved or corrected. Are there any obvious slips?

Project 1.1

Analyzing a Visual Text

In the following paper, writer Jacqueline Cruz responds to an assignment to analyze a visual text. Her purpose is to explain how a famous 1980s ad for *Charlie* perfume works. But since the item is twenty years old, she puts it in context for her readers, drawing on research she has previously done on second-wave feminism. Cruz models her analysis on similar essays about advertising by writer Seth Stevenson, who employs the genre routinely at Salon.com (see pages 421–422). Like Stevenson, Cruz uses a personal voice throughout her work and even ends her piece with a grade.

STUDENT PROJECT
Jacqueline Cruz, "She's Very Charlie"

Cruz 1

Jacqueline Cruz
Prof. John Ruszkiewicz
RHE 315 Rhetoric and Writing
March 26, 2007

She's Very Charlie

It is 1988. You're a woman flipping through the pages of <u>Vogue</u> or <u>Cosmopolitan</u>. You see images of fashion-forward women looking back at you. They may be in a normal pose, or they may be in odd poses with their thin arms placed at awkward angles. Their job is to look pretty, to communicate to you what beauty is supposed to be. But then you flip to this unusual image of a young, confident woman walking alongside a man whose bum she is patting (see fig. 1). You think to yourself, "Women don't pat men's bums. They simply don't." But you can't help but admire the woman for doing something that at the time was--dare I say--ballsy. You also notice that she is poised. She is fun and free. She is active. Most important, she looks empowered. You want to be her. The agency responsible for this ad campaign for Revlon wanted women to aspire to be the independent Charlie woman with a self-possessed identity. Therefore it is no surprise that the ad agency allied itself with the feminist movement of the latter part of the century to create the Charlie woman's personality and to push their perfume sales.

- The paper is edited to conform to MLA style.
- The title hints at the subject of the ad analysis: Charlie perfume.
- The opening ¶ provides a context for the analysis, drawing readers in.
- The writer uses the correct MLA form (see fig. 1) to point readers to the visual text included in the paper.

90 REVISING AND EDITING

Cruz 2

When Revlon's Charlie ad campaign started in the 1970s, it wanted to associate itself with modern, progressive women. The genius of the campaign was its ability to portray a message memorably, and this ad released in 1987 during the campaign's peak is a classic example of the agency's ability to communicate its message successfully. The ad itself is very simple. It consists of a large picture, the campaign slogan at the top, and a smaller picture of the product at the bottom corner. That's it. It was designed to be eye-catching,

Fig. 1. This advertisement, introduced in 1988 in various publications such as Vogue and Cosmopolitan, featured a confident, young working woman. (Advertising Archive, 1988).

Cruz 3

clever, and instantly understood. We can infer from the picture that the Charlie woman is a successful corporate twenty-something because she is wearing a stylish business suit and she carries a briefcase. She is not a docile housewife. Her hair is flowing freely, and if you look closely, she is looking down at the man next to her. When you compare the pair's shoulders, you notice that she is taller than the man too. She does not have overstyled, helmet hair to impress a man she pines for. Instead, she oozes self-assurance and power. This model represents what second-wave feminism strove for.

> **Even though the writer includes the ad itself in the paper, she carefully interprets its details to explain its strategies.**

Second-wave feminism began in the 1960s and continued through the late 1980s. It concentrated not only on de jure inequality, but also on de facto inequality. This movement wanted equality in the law and equality in the general perception of a woman's place and potential. So how do the advertisers simultaneously reject the traditional representations of women while embracing this newfound female bravado and still sell perfume? That is where the butt pat--one of the manliest gestures--comes in. The fact that the model in the ad is a woman challenges the norm associated with that symbolic gesture. She communicates, "If a man can do it, then why can't I?" When we think of a butt pat, we usually imagine it occurring in a sports setting--a male-dominated arena. It is a friendly gesture given to show support or provide encouragement and reassurance. It is common to see it in a football game after a player scores a touchdown, or when a player in a baseball game returns to home plate.

> **Having introduced the term "second-wave feminism" at the end of the preceding ¶, the writer provides the necessary background information.**

In the ad, though, the Charlie woman defies these norms and yet the man next to her does not seem to mind. In fact, he is smiling. Hence, she is able to get away with the violation of this norm, and give it a whole new meaning. In essence, the Charlie woman is capable of doing anything she pleases. After all, "She's very Charlie." Ironically, of course, feminism--a movement not normally associated with cosmetics and beauty products--is being successfully employed to help sell perfume.

> **The writer is at the heart of her analysis here, bringing together second-wave feminism and the Charlie ad.**

The reason Charlie ads were so successful in selling perfume was that they explored territory that had not been fully charted before.

Cruz 4

The Charlie ad campaign recognized that women were growing tired or bored of stereotypical representations of what women do, or how they should be. Women were joining the work force in greater numbers than ever before, either for necessity or personal satisfaction. They did not have the time to stay home and bake pies while wearing puffy sundresses and three-inch heels. Women were working hard, turning in their sales reports and closing deals with clients while wearing business suits with shoulder pads. However, this did not mean they were unconcerned about being considered feminine and attractive. Revlon adjusted accordingly, associated Charlie with this active lifestyle, and promised women that they could have it all: confidence, power, beauty, and allure. Needless to say, this premise helped sell thousands of the golden bottles.

Looking back, had I been old enough to buy a bottle of Charlie in the 1980s, I probably would have. Besides, the fragrance is strong but pleasant, so it would work nicely in small doses. The idea of the modern and attractive working woman would have appealed to me too. I definitely would have liked to be "very Charlie." Moreover, who does not like to feel celebrated and empowered?

Grade: A. Simple design with powerful cultural message.

CHAPTER 3
IDENTITIES

ITEM 3.1 ■ Matthew Rolston, Johnny Depp, Cover of *Rolling Stone*, July 13–27, 2006

We seem to fixate on personalities. We categorize those we meet: introvert, extrovert, good dancer, loudmouth, bore. We might be attracted to charismatic leaders, tuning in to their every television appearance. We might be fascinated by a face in the crowd or on the magazine rack at the checkout aisle. In all of these instances we're interested in people's identities. Consider the allure of the portrait of Johnny Depp (Item 3.1) on the cover of *Rolling Stone* magazine. Perhaps it's Depp's celebrity status. Maybe it's the gaze directed outward toward the viewer. It could be the colorful pirate garb. Whatever the reason, the image calls to us, projecting a compelling sense of identity. But identities are more complex than anything that might be captured in a photograph. To understand something about identities, we need to look beyond outward appearances and untangle the many threads that weave together to create personalities.

Think about the elements that make up the *Rolling Stone* portrayal of Johnny Depp. We see Depp as pirate actor, complete with braided goatee, crimson head scarf, and prop sword. The image points to the inscrutable difference between a person's outward appearance and his inner self, what philosophers have long pondered as the problematic split between our minds and our bodies. That we can "act" as another person reveals that our identities are not fixed as much as they are constructed or projected, depending on circumstance—think of how you behave differently around friends, family, or coworkers.

Consider the screenshot representing the Wikipedia entry for Depp (Item 3.2). Facts like Depp's date of birth, home town, and family structure establish a sense of history that affirms something concrete about his identity. Additional details tell us more about Depp's history, but remain open to interpretation—his family moved a lot; his parents divorced when he was fifteen.

In many ways, our identities are not our own. They are shaped by our families, our friends, the events that have befallen us, and even by strangers who wish to interpret us in their own ways. We may never grasp all of the elements that make up our identities, but at least we'll never be bored trying.

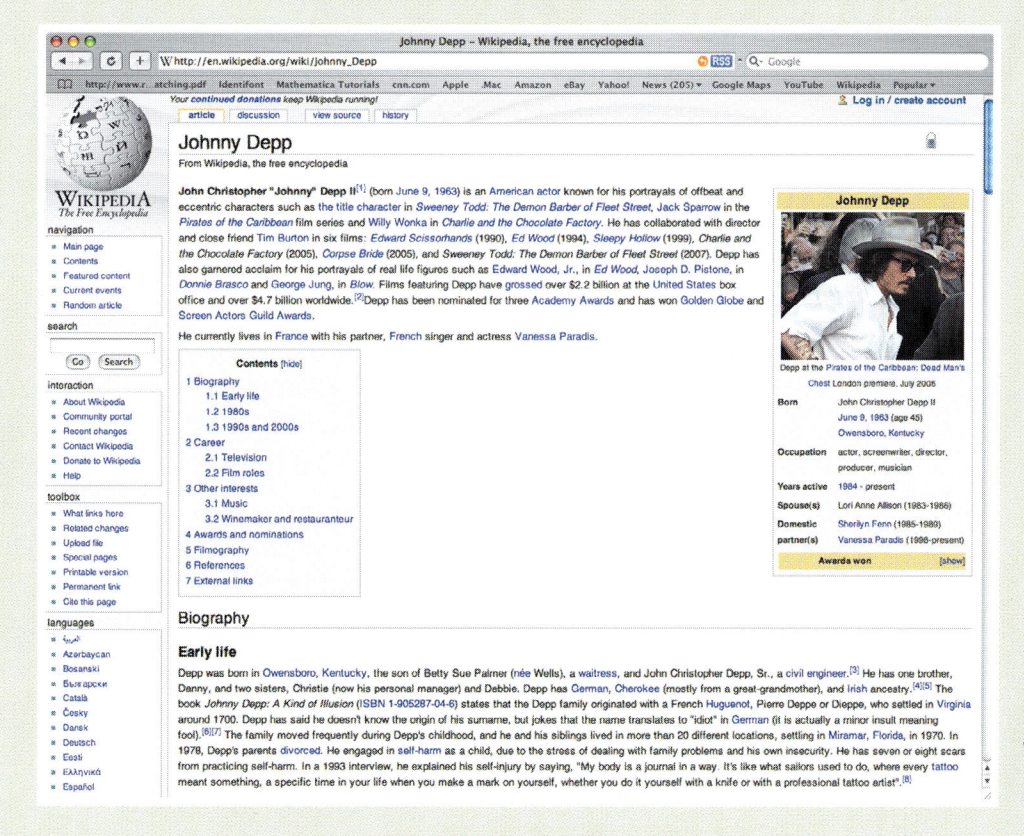

ITEM 3.2
Wikipedia, "Johnny Depp," 2007

Reading Texts About Identity

Because conceptions of self are so complex, it might seem an impossible task to develop a reading of an identity. Indeed, thinking about even a single person might require us to consider multiple identities—brother, son, choir singer, angler, waiter, whatever. And these identities are woven together from many strands of influence—families, bodies, friends, ethnic groups, cultural expectations, and so on.

In fact, as you read individuals, you might begin by asking questions about the **subject**. Is this a well-known person? Is this person more or less unknown in the public eye? If so, what kind of situation do you find the person in? Dorothea Lange's photographs (Item 3.3) became famous precisely because they represented the shared distress of displaced individuals during the Depression—the common person in an uncommon situation. Looking at **contexts** like this allows us to talk about identity in terms of the cultural connections that shape individuals and color our interpretations. Similarly, we can read individuals in terms of traditions they carry forward or challenge. A Pepsi advertisement (Item 3.4) identifies soccer player David Beckham with ancient gladiators.

You can also ask questions about the physical makeup of individuals as you construct readings of identity. Is this person a small child, a teen, a thirtysomething, a retiree? Is the person male or female? Of course, these questions just open more avenues for exploring the complexities of identity. Constructions of gender, for instance, often lead us to interpretations focusing more on cultural expectations than the physical characteristics of individuals. We're likely to focus on questions of **genre** or **medium** as we explore these texts. Consider, for instance, the "I Want to be...." cartoon in Item 3.5. The cartoon juxtaposes two competing claims made on our bodies, the unreal representation of beauty encapsulated in a Barbie doll and the counterintuitive pitch that consuming fast food will translate into a Happy Meal. Reading such representations requires us to weigh concerns of **purpose** and **audience**. The short piece, "Why I Want a Wife" (Item 3.7), for instance, explores the institution of marriage and the ways it shapes identities. Similarly, we can think about the ways that culture shapes conceptions of identity. It's well known that women and men go to extremes to shape their bodies to meet cultural expectations—expectations often constructed around insecurities and consumerism rather than conceptions of good health. No wonder we're confused about identity.

You'll also need to think about the ways identities are shaped by the groups in which we participate. Think about the complexities of categories like Hispanic, Anglo, Muslim, or agnostic (see Item 3.8). How can thinking about the memberships people have in multiple groups help us read their identities? Consider the cast of characters in Edward Hopper's painting *Nighthawks* (Item 3.9). To create a reading of the identity of one or more of these individuals would require you to stretch your interpretive skills—you might think about common traits among the characters, the shared setting they inhabit, the activities they undertake.

All of these concerns demonstrate how rich a topic identity can be. Again, you'll have no trouble if you understand that identities are twisted together from strands that include the personal, the public, appearances, physical traits, and the influences of cultures and groups, and then follow these strands carefully to develop your readings.

Gallery: Representations of Identity

ITEM 3.3 ■ **Dorothea Lange, *Drought Refugees Camping by the Roadside*, 1936**

Dorothea Lange is best known for her images depicting victims of the Great Depression. (Her iconic photograph, *Migrant Mother*, appears on page 66.) Lange began her career as a portrait photographer, and much of this background comes through in her work. Circumstances dominate images like the one above, but still the focus of the photographs is the human drama that plays out within these situations.

1. Look closely at Lange's photograph. What can you infer about the identities and circumstances of the family members it depicts? Who is the focal point of the portrait, in your opinion? How do you know?

2. Lange was interested in promoting government reforms to help refugees from the Depression. Do you think the political motives behind Lange's photograph enrich or detract from the artistic qualities of the image?

3. Can you think of artists and writers today whose work reflects their social or political commitments? What do you think of these artists' work?

ITEM 3.4 ■ **Pepsi Advertisement Featuring David Beckham, 2004**

Sports figures have long been associated with product pitches—think of the images of Jerry West or Michael Jordan that have been translated into marketing icons for the NBA or Nike. Produced for a magazine campaign, this image of David Beckham represents the athlete as a modern-day warrior.

1. How much does this image rely on viewers' recognizing the celebrity figure of David Beckham? Why might the creators of the ad have left any identifying text off of the image?

2. What roles do the leather body armor and soccer ball play in the image? How are these items related to notions of identity?

3. What is the significance of the presence of the Pepsi logo in the image? How does knowing who the sponsor is influence your thinking about the image in terms of identity?

ITEM 3.5 ■ Jim Borgman, *I Want to Be. . . .*, 1998

Cartoons have long offered insights into identity. From lampoons of political figures to roasts of celebrities, the undercurrent of humor has enabled cartoons to offer social commentary and pointed critiques of people. Jim Borgman's cartoon questions aspects of identity and culture.

1. Do you think it's fair to argue that objects like dolls strongly influence our notions of identity? Why or why not?

2. To which groups would you say this cartoon is designed to appeal? Would you say the cartoon is meant simply to evoke humor or does it have a more serious message? Do you think the cartoon is likely to influence anyone? Why or why not?

3. What questions arise when people argue about marketing products to children? How would you read the cartoon in terms of such questions?

ITEM 3.6 ■ *Love Me Tender* Movie Poster, 1956

Visit Graceland and you'll see that the phenomenon of Elvis is alive and well. Elvis still represents a major celebrity, a cultural icon who bridged the realms of popular music and film to become an international figure. *Love Me Tender* debuted in 1956 and the song by the same name went to number one on the charts.

1. What notion of identity is constructed for the figure of Elvis Presley in the poster? What strategies does the creator of the poster use to create this impression?

2. Would it be fair to say that Elvis still has a strong influence on contemporary society? Why or why not? What factors give an individual staying power as a cultural icon?

3. How has media marketing changed in the fifty-plus years since this poster sold tickets to *Love Me Tender*? What influences might these marketing changes have on our identities?

ITEM 3.7 ■ Judy Syfers-Brady, "Why I Want a Wife," 1971

"Why I Want a Wife" has an interesting history. Judy Syfers-Brady first read the essay at a celebration of the fiftieth anniversary of the passing of the 19th amendment. The piece then appeared in the inaugural issue of *Ms Magazine*. After its publication, the essay soon became widely circulated in feminist circles, taking on a life of its own.

Why I Want a Wife

I belong to that classification of people known as wives. I am A Wife.

And, not altogether incidentally, I am a mother. Not too long ago a male friend of mine appeared on the scene fresh from a recent divorce. He had one child, who is, of course, with his ex-wife. He is looking for another wife. As I thought about him while I was ironing one evening, it suddenly occurred to me that I, too, would like to have a wife. Why do I want a wife?

I would like to go back to school so that I can become economically independent, support myself, and if need be, support those dependent upon me. I want a wife who will work and send me to school. And while I am going to school I want a wife to take care of my children. I want a wife to keep track of the children's doctor and dentist appointments. And to keep track of mine, too. I want a wife to make sure my children eat properly and are kept clean. I want a wife who will wash the children's clothes and keep them mended. I want a wife who is a good nurturing attendant to my children, who arranges for their schooling, makes sure that they have an adequate social life with their peers, takes them to the park, the zoo, etc. I want a wife who takes care of the children when they are sick, a wife who arranges to be around when the children need special care, because, of course, I cannot miss classes at school. My wife must arrange to lose time at work and not lose the job. It may mean a small cut in my wife's income from time to time, but I guess I can tolerate that. Needless to say, my wife will arrange and pay for the care of the children while my wife is working.

I want a wife who will take care of my physical needs. I want a wife who will keep my house clean. A wife who will pick up after my children, a wife who will pick up after me. I want a wife who will keep my clothes clean, ironed, mended, replaced when need be, and who will see to it that my personal things are kept in their proper place so that I can find what I need the minute I need it. I want a wife who cooks the meals, a wife who is a good cook. I want a wife who will plan the menus, do the necessary grocery shopping, prepare the meals, serve them pleasantly, and then do the cleaning up while I do my studying. I want a wife who will care for me when I am sick and sympathize with my pain and loss of time from school. I want a wife to go along when our family takes a vacation so that someone can continue care for me and my children when I need a rest and change of scene. I want a wife who will not bother me with rambling complaints about a wife's duties. But I want a wife who will listen to me when I feel the need to explain a rather difficult point I have come across in my course of studies. And I want a wife who will type my papers for me when I have written them.

I want a wife who will take care of the details of my social life. When my wife and I are invited out by my friends, I want a wife who will take care of the baby-sitting arrangements. When I meet people at school that I like and want to entertain, I want a wife who will have the house clean, will prepare a special meal, serve it to me and my friends, and not interrupt when I talk about things that interest me and my friends. I want a wife who will have arranged that the children are fed and ready for bed before my guests arrive so that the children do not bother us. I want a wife who takes care of the needs of my guests so that they feel comfortable, who makes sure that they have an ashtray, that they are passed the hors d'oeuvres, that they are offered a second helping of the food, that their wine glasses are replenished when necessary, that their coffee is served to them as they like it. And I want a wife who knows that sometimes I need a night out by myself.

I want a wife who is sensitive to my sexual needs, a wife who makes love passionately and eagerly when I feel like it, a wife who makes sure that I am satisfied. And, of course, I want a wife who will not demand sexual attention when I am not in the mood for it. I want a wife who assumes the complete responsibility for birth control, because I do not want more children. I want a wife who will remain sexually faithful to me so that I do not have to clutter up my intellectual life with jealousies. And I want a wife who understands that my sexual needs may entail more than strict adherence to monogamy. I must, after all, be able to relate to people as fully as possible.

If, by chance, I find another person more suitable as a wife than the wife I already have, I want the liberty to replace my present wife with another one. Naturally, I will expect a fresh, new life; my wife will take the children and be solely responsible for them so that I am left free.

When I am through with school and have a job, I want my wife to quit working and remain at home so that my wife can more fully and completely take care of a wife's duties.

My God, who wouldn't want a wife?

---

1 What conclusions can you draw about the identity of the author of "Why I Want a Wife"? What details in the text lead you to these conclusions?

2 How would you compare the attitudes toward gender roles reflected in "Why I Want a Wife" with those of today? What would you say to someone who argued that little has changed in the intervening years? How would you back up your points?

3 "Why I Want a Wife" is written from a woman's perspective. If you were writing from the perspective of a man, what kind of response might you compose? What details would you include and why?

ITEM 3.8 ■ Razanne Doll and Muslim Girl, 2003

Think of girls' dolls and you might imagine a shapely figure with flowing blonde hair, perhaps seated in a Jeep or American sports car, a Barbie. The doll here represents no such identity. Razanne is designed to appeal to Muslim children. The doll lacks the buxom figure of a Barbie and comes in three versions: blonde with fair skin or dark haired with olive or black skin.

1. How would you describe the doll in the photograph in terms of identity? Would you say the doll represents a Muslim identity? Why?

2. How would you characterize the identity of the young girl in the image? What role does the doll play in your characterization? What other elements in the image shape your reading?

3. Mattel, the creator of Barbie, also produces a Moroccan Barbie, along with a number of Barbies designed to appeal to non-Western cultures. What are your thoughts on the differences between a doll like Razanne, and a Moroccan Barbie created by Mattel?

ITEM 3.9 ■ Edward Hopper, *Nighthawks*, 1942

Edward Hopper is frequently characterized as presenting a visual sense of alienation and American life. His works are often sparsely populated with figures set against urban or human backdrops. One of his best-known American paintings, *Nighthawks,* represents a diner Hopper claims to have seen in New York City.

1. *Nighthawks* dates from the same time as the photograph, *American Gothic* (page 105). Which do you find portrays a more compelling representation of identity? How would you compare the two images in terms of identity?

2. Is it possible to determine whether *Nighthawks* emphasizes any of the individuals in the diner? If you had to pick a figure to discuss in the image, which would you choose and why?

3. Hopper's painting has often been described as a depiction of alienation. Would you agree? What details in the image would support your reading?

ITEM 3.10 ■ Gordon Parks, *American Gothic*, 1942

Gordon Parks led an accomplished life as a photographer and filmmaker. His film credits include the original version of the movie *Shaft*, a film offering a strong statement about African American identity in its protagonist, the street-savvy private detective John Shaft. His photographs similarly focus on the identity of both celebrities and everyday people.

1. How would you describe the figure in the photograph? Would you say you are able to understand a good deal about her identity from this single image? Why or why not?

2. Compare Parks's photograph with the iconic painting of the husband and wife farmers by Grant Wood. How does the tradition established by Wood's painting contribute to the representation of identity in the photograph?

3. What objects in the photograph call out for more interpretation? Is it fair to say the objects contribute more to the message of the image than the figure of the woman does? Why or why not?

Cluster 3.1
Life Stories

When did you realize you were an individual? Can you remember your first experience with language or your first lengthy separation from a parent or sibling? Most of us can't dredge up such foundational moments. But we can cast back into memory, pulling out events that have marked our development and made us who we are. You may not remember learning to read, but you might remember learning to ride a bike, and you'll probably have a hard time forgetting your first kiss. Memory is a rich field we can mine to discover elements of our identities, as Patricia Hampl demonstrates in her essay, "I Could Tell You Stories" in which she explores the power of memory.

Annie Dillard offers similar insights based on recollection in an excerpt from her memoir, *An American Childhood*. What was once a childhood afternoon in the neighborhood becomes a lesson in perspective as we bring it forward and put it into words. When we look to these accounts of events and personal histories, we're called on to determine the relationships between facts and storytelling. What seemed to be fact can be turned into fiction as we translate memories into stories for others. But whether recollections map perfectly with the facts, or whether they represent creative constructions of an idealized past, there is no disputing that they combine to represent much of who we are.

And we're fascinated by the stories of others. Despite the number of works of fiction, science fiction, and fantasy lining the shelves of every bookstore, the best sellers regularly depict the lives of real people, and not just celebrities. What happens when someone gives up fast food for thirty days or meat for a year? What was it like growing up in Afghanistan during the reign of the Taliban or serving in Iraq in 2008? Marjane Satrapi delivers just such an account as she reflects on childhood memories of the Islamic Revolution in Iran using the medium of the graphic novel.

Of course, part of the fascination with personal accounts is the way they reveal lives unlike our own. The images from Jim Goldberg's *Raised by Wolves* as well as Alison Stateman's "Postcards from the Edge" both depict the not-so-comfortable realities of life on the streets. These and other works in this cluster evoke our responses not only for the stories they present, but also for the insights they provide into the complex constructions that make up our identities.

I Could Tell You Stories

Patricia Hampl
(1999)

> **FYI** Patricia Hampl has been a leading author of memoirs over the last decade. Her books include *A Romantic Education*, *Virgin Time*, and *Blue Arabesque*. Her works on memory stand out for the way they not only chart Hampl's own experiences but also offer insights into what it means to write about the self. "I Could Tell You Stories" is an excerpt from Hampl's 1999 book of the same name.

Years ago, in another life, I woke to look out the smeared window of a Greyhound bus I had been riding all night, and in the still-dark morning of a small Missouri river town where the driver had made a scheduled stop at a grimy diner, I saw below me a stout middle-aged woman in a flowered housedress turn and kiss full on the mouth a godlike young man with golden curls. But I've got that wrong: *he* was kissing *her*. Passionately, without regard for the world and its incomprehension. He had abandoned himself to his love, and she, stolid, matronly, received this adoration with simple grandeur, like a socialist-realist statue of a woman taking up sheaves of wheat.

Their ages dictated that he must be her son, but I had just come out of the cramped, ruinous half sleep of a night on a Greyhound and I was clairvoyant: This was that thing called love. The morning light cracked blood red along the river.

Of course, when she lumbered onto the bus a moment later, lurching forward with her two bulging bags, she chose the empty aisle seat next to me as her own. She pitched one bag onto the overhead rack, and then heaved herself into the seat as if she were used to hoisting sacks of potatoes onto the flatbed of a pickup. She held the other bag on her lap, and leaned toward the window. The beautiful boy was blowing kisses. He couldn't see where she was in the dark interior, so he blew kisses up and down the side of the bus, gazing ardently at the blank windows. "Pardon me," the woman said without looking at me, and leaned over, bag and all, to rap the glass. Her beautiful boy ran back to our window and kissed and kissed, and finally hugged himself, shutting his eyes in an ecstatic pantomime of love-sweet-love. She smiled and waved back.

Then the bus was moving. She slumped back in her seat, and I turned to her. I suppose I looked transfixed. As our eyes met she said, "Everybody thinks he's my son. But he's not. He's my husband." She let that sink in. She was a farm woman with hands that could have been a man's; I was a university student, hair down to my waist. It was long ago, as I said, in another life. It was even another life for the country. The Vietnam War was the time we were living through, and I was traveling, as I did every three weeks, to visit my boyfriend who was in a federal prison. "Draft dodger," my brother said. "Draft resister," I piously retorted. I had never been kissed the way this woman had been kissed. I was living in a tattered corner of a romantic idyll, the one where the hero is willing to suffer for his beliefs. I was the girlfriend. I lived on pride, not love.

My neighbor patted her short cap of hair, and settled in for the long haul as we pulled onto the highway along the river, heading south. "We been married five years and we're happy," she said with a penetrating satisfaction, the satisfaction that passeth understanding. "Oh," she let out a profound sigh as if she mined her truths from the bountiful, bulky earth, "Oh, I could tell you stories." She put her arms snugly around her bag, gazed off for a moment, apparently made pensive by her remark. Then she closed her eyes and fell asleep.

I looked out the window smudged by my nose which had been pressed against it at the bus stop to see the face of true love reveal itself. Beyond the bus the sky, instead of becoming paler with the dawn, drew itself out of a black line along the Mississippi into an alarming red flare. It was very beautiful. The old caution—*Red sky in the morning, sailor take warning*—darted through my mind and fell away. Remember this, I remember telling myself, hang on to this. I could feel it all skittering away, whatever conjunction of beauty and improbability I had stumbled upon.

It is hard to describe the indelible bittersweetness of that moment. Which is why, no doubt, it had to be remembered. The very word—*Remember!*—spiraled up like a snake out of a basket, a magic catch in its sound, the doubling of the m—*re memmemem*—setting up a low murmur full of inchoate associations as if a loved voice were speaking into my ear alone, occultly.

Whether it was the unguarded face of love, or the red gash down the middle of the warring country I was traveling through, or this exhausted farm woman's promise of untold tales that bewitched me, I couldn't say. Over it all rose and remains only the injunction to remember. This, the most impossible command we lay upon ourselves, claimed me and then perversely disappeared, trailing an illusive silken tissue of meaning, without giving a story, refusing to leave me in peace.

Because everyone "has" a memoir, we all have a stake in how such stories are told. For we do not, after all, simply *have* experience; we are entrusted with it. We must do something—make something—with it. A story, we sense, is the only possible habitation for the burden of our witnessing.

The tantalizing formula of my companion on the Greyhound—*oh, I could tell you stories*—is the memoirist's opening line, but it has none of the delicious promise of the storyteller's "Once upon a time. . . ." In fact, it is a perverse statement. The woman on the bus told me nothing—she fell asleep and escaped to her dreams. For the little sentence inaugurates nothing, and leads nowhere after its *dot dot dot* of expectation. Whatever experience lies tangled within its seductive promise remains forever balled up in the woolly impossibility of telling the-truth-the-whole-truth of a life, any life.

Memoirists, unlike fiction writers, do not really want to "tell a story." They want to tell it *all*—the all of personal experience, of consciousness itself. That includes a story, but also the whole expanding universe of sensation and thought that flows beyond the confines of narrative and proves every life to be not only an isolated story line but a bit of the cosmos, spinning and streaming into the great, ungraspable pattern of existence. Memoirists wish to tell their mind, not their story.

The wistfulness implicit in that conditional verb—*I could tell*—conveys an urge more primitive than a storyteller's search for an audience. It betrays not a loneliness for someone who will listen but a hopelessness about language itself and a sad recognition of its limitations. How much reality can subject-verb-object bear on the frail shoulders of the sentence? The sigh within the statement is more like this: I could tell you stories—if only stories could tell what I have in me to tell.

For this reason, autobiographical writing is bedeviled. It is caught in a self which must become a world—and not, please, a narcissistic world. The memoir, once considered a marginal literary form, has emerged in the past decade as the signature genre of the age. "The triumph of memoir is now established fact," James Atlas trumpeted in a cover story on "The Age of the Literary Memoir" in the *New York Times Magazine*. "Fiction," he claimed, "isn't delivering the news. Memoir is."

> **Maybe a reader's love of memoir is less an intrusive lust for confession than a hankering for the intimacy of this first-person voice, the deeply satisfying sense of being spoken to privately.**

With its "triumph," the memoir has, of course, not denied the truth and necessity of fiction. In fact, it leans heavily on novelistic assumptions. But the contemporary memoir has reaffirmed the primacy of the first person voice in American imaginative writing established by Whitman's "Song of Myself." Maybe a reader's love of memoir is less an intrusive lust for confession than a hankering for the intimacy of this first-person voice, the deeply satisfying sense of being spoken to privately. More than a story, we want a voice speaking softly, urgently, in our ear. Which is to say, to our heart. That voice carries its implacable command, the ancient murmur that called out to me in the middle of the country in the middle of a war—remember, remember (*I dare you, I tempt you*).

Looking out the Greyhound window that red morning all those years ago, I saw the improbable face of love. But even more puzzling was the cryptic remark of the beloved as she sat next to me. I think of her more often than makes sense. Though he was the beauty, she is the one who comes back. How faint his golden curls have become (he also had a smile, crooked and charming, but I can only remember the idea of it—the image is gone). It is she, stout and unbeautiful, wearing her flowery cotton housedress with a zipper down the middle, who has taken up residence with her canny eye and her acceptance of adoration. To be loved like that, loved improbably: of course, she had stories to tell. She took it for granted in some unapologetic way, like being born to wealth. Take the money and run.

But that moment before she fell asleep, when she looked pensive, the red morning rising over the Mississippi, was a wistful moment. *I could tell you stories*—but she could not. What she had to tell was too big, too much, too *something*, for her to place in the small shrine that a story is.

When we met—if what happened between us was a meeting—I felt nothing had ever happened to me and nothing ever would. I didn't understand that riding this filthy Greyhound down the middle of bloodied America in the middle of a mutinous war was itself a story and that something *was* happening to me. I thought if something was happening to anybody around me it was happening to people like my boyfriend: They were the heroes, according to the lights that shined for me then. I was just riding shotgun in my own life. I could not have imagined containing, as the farm woman slumped next to me did, the sheer narrative bulk to say, "I could tell you stories," and then drifting off with the secret heaviness of experience into the silence where stories live their real lives, crumbling into the loss we call remembrance.

The boastful little declaration, pathetically conditional (not "I'll tell you a story" but "I could") wavered wistfully for an instant between us. The stranger's remark, launched in the dark of the Greyhound, floated across the human landscape like the lingering tone of a struck bell from a village church, and joined all the silence that ever was, as I turned my face to the window where the world was rushing by along the slow river.

CONSIDER

1. Hampl's piece begins with a striking opening scene. Do you believe such a striking episode is necessary for a compelling piece of personal writing? Why or why not?

2. At several points, Hampl seems to suggest that it is impossible to accurately capture in words the experiences represented by our personal stories. Is it fair, then, to ask, "Why bother?" What might be Hampl's response to such a question?

COMPOSE

3. Recall a vivid episode from your own past. Think about what that episode represents for you as a person. Write a paragraph or two in which you recount and reflect on the experience.

ITEM 3.11 ■ **Marjane Satrapi, Excerpt from *Persepolis*, 2004**

Often our past experiences are colored with multiple sensations ranging from the touch of a loved one to the site of an accident to the smell of baking bread. Capturing these moments sometimes calls for more than words. Marjane Satrapi has long been an innovator in expressing identity and memory in the form of the graphic novel. The excerpt below is taken from *Persepolis*, Satrapi's 2004 novel that has recently been made into a feature film.

THE VEIL

This is me when I was 10 years old. This was in 1980.

And this is a class photo. I'm sitting on the far left so you don't see me. From left to right: Golnaz, Mahshid, Narine, Minna.

In 1979 a revolution took place. It was later called "the Islamic Revolution".

Then came 1980: the year it became obligatory to wear the veil at school.

"Wear this!"

We didn't really like to wear the veil, especially since we didn't understand why we had to.

"It's too hot out!"

"Execution in the name of freedom."

"Give me my veil back!"

"You'll have to lick my feet!"

"Ooh! I'm the monster of darkness."

"Giddyap!"

3

110   3.1 | LIFE STORIES

AND ALSO BECAUSE THE YEAR BEFORE, IN 1979, WE WERE IN A FRENCH NON-RELIGIOUS SCHOOL.
WHERE BOYS AND GIRLS WERE TOGETHER.
AND THEN SUDDENLY IN 1980...
ALL BILINGUAL SCHOOLS MUST BE CLOSED DOWN.
THEY ARE SYMBOLS OF CAPITALISM.
BRAVO!
WHAT WISDOM!
OF DECADENCE.
THIS IS CALLED A "CULTURAL REVOLUTION."
WE FOUND OURSELVES VEILED AND SEPARATED FROM OUR FRIENDS.
AND THAT WAS THAT...

4

EVERYWHERE IN THE STREETS THERE WERE DEMONSTRATIONS FOR AND AGAINST THE VEIL.
the veil!
the veil!
the veil!
the veil!
the veil!
freedom!
freedom!
freedom!
freedom!
freedom!
AT ONE OF THE DEMONSTRATIONS, A GERMAN JOURNALIST TOOK A PHOTO OF MY MOTHER.
I WAS REALLY PROUD OF HER. HER PHOTO WAS PUBLISHED IN ALL THE EUROPEAN NEWSPAPERS.
AND EVEN IN ONE MAGAZINE IN IRAN. MY MOTHER WAS REALLY SCARED.
HAVE YOU SEEN THIS?
DON'T WORRY, DARLING.
SHE DYED HER HAIR,
AND WORE DARK GLASSES FOR A LONG TIME.
5

I REALLY DIDN'T KNOW WHAT TO THINK ABOUT THE VEIL. DEEP DOWN I WAS VERY RELIGIOUS BUT AS A FAMILY WE WERE VERY MODERN AND AVANT-GARDE.
I WAS BORN WITH RELIGION.
AT THE AGE OF SIX I WAS ALREADY SURE I WAS THE LAST PROPHET. THIS WAS A FEW YEARS BEFORE THE REVOLUTION.
O' Celestial light!
BEFORE ME THERE HAD BEEN A FEW OTHERS.
I AM THE LAST PROPHET.
A WOMAN?
I WANTED TO BE A PROPHET...
BECAUSE OUR MAID DID NOT EAT WITH US.
BECAUSE MY FATHER HAD A CADILLAC.
AND, ABOVE ALL, BECAUSE MY GRANDMOTHER'S KNEES ALWAYS ACHED.
COME HERE MARJI! HELP ME TO STAND UP.
DON'T WORRY. SOON YOU WON'T HAVE ANY MORE PAIN. YOU'LL SEE.
6

LIKE ALL MY PREDECESSORS I HAD MY HOLY BOOK.
THE FIRST THREE RULES CAME FROM ZARATHUSTRA. HE WAS THE FIRST PROPHET IN MY COUNTRY BEFORE THE ARAB INVASION.
YOU MUST BASE EVERYTHING ON THESE THREE RULES: BEHAVE WELL, SPEAK WELL, ACT WELL.
I ALSO WANTED US TO CELEBRATE THE TRADITIONAL ZARATHUSTRIAN HOLIDAYS. LIKE THE FIRE CEREMONY,
BEFORE THE PERSIAN NEW YEAR, NOROUZ, ON MARCH 21ST, THE FIRST DAY OF SPRING.
ONLY MY GRANDMOTHER KNEW ABOUT MY BOOK.
RULE NUMBER SIX: EVERYBODY SHOULD HAVE A CAR.
RULE NUMBER SEVEN: ALL MAIDS SHOULD EAT AT THE TABLE WITH THE OTHERS.
RULE NUMBER EIGHT: NO OLD PERSON SHOULD HAVE TO SUFFER.
IN THAT CASE, I'LL BE YOUR FIRST DISCIPLE.
REALLY?
BUT TELL ME HOW YOU'LL ARRANGE FOR OLD PEOPLE NOT TO SUFFER?
IT WILL SIMPLY BE FORBIDDEN.
7

EVERY NIGHT I HAD A BIG DISCUSSION WITH GOD.
GOD, GIVE ME SOME MORE TIME. I AM NOT QUITE READY YET.
YES YOU ARE, CELESTIAL LIGHT, YOU ARE MY CHOICE, MY LAST AND MY BEST CHOICE.
EXCEPT FOR MY GRANDMOTHER I WAS OBVIOUSLY THE ONLY ONE WHO BELIEVED IN MYSELF.
WHAT DO YOU WANT TO BE WHEN YOU GROW UP?
vion
A - a
I'LL BE A PROPHET.
HAHA! HAHA! HAHA!
SHE'S CRAZY.
MY PARENTS WERE CALLED IN BY THE TEACHER.
YOUR CHILD IS DISTURBED. SHE WANTS TO BECOME A PROPHET.
WHAT ABOUT IT?
DOESN'T THIS WORRY YOU?
NO ! NOT AT ALL !
?
8

CONSIDER

1. How does the veil function as a symbol? Is it fair to say the veil limits conceptions of identity? Why or why not?

2. The events in "The Veil" are both religious and political. How are institutions like religion and politics portrayed in the memoir? How do they relate to identity?

CHALLENGE

3. Using your own writing and drawing skills or comic creation software, develop your own graphic representation of an episode in your life. Select an episode that represents aspects of your identity. Storyboard the comic to organize the events. Compose the comic and share it with classmates or post it on the Web.

3.1 | LIFE STORIES

ITEM 3.12 ■ Albrecht Dürer (1471–1528), Self-Portraits at Ages 22, 26, and 28

Think of the collections of school portraits you might find on the mantle at your grandparents' house. What might you discover by looking at yourself over the years? Would the identity of the person in your first grade picture be substantially different than what was framed in your portrait from third grade? How about fifth or seventh grade? Our identities shift over time; the images here represent one artist's attempts to stop and take stock of the changes.

CONSIDER

1. What specific differences can you see in Dürer's three paintings? What elements stay more or less the same? What do these similarities and changes suggest about his circumstances, his career, and his identity?

2. Compare Dürer's paintings to a sequence of formal portraits you have had taken, such as school photographs, yearbook or graduation pictures, or wedding portraits. How well do these portraits capture you? How much control did you have over the images?

COMPOSE

3. Write three paragraphs, with each one describing yourself at a different age or period in your life. Imagine that these paragraphs could become part of a family album or perhaps the narrative portion of a video.

Postcards from the Edge

Alison Stateman
(2003)

It's one of those bone-numbing rainy days, the kind that gets under your fleece and rain gear, rendering all attempts at warmth futile. Julie, 26, is in a mood as foul as the weekend weather.

"This is ridiculous," she said, her words punctuated with four-letter invectives. "You would think that people would be more willing to help out, but it's not like that."

"Actually," she added, gesturing toward her plastic cup, clearly disappointed with its thin layer of coins, "on nicer days I make more money."

Strangers are both intrigued and repelled by this slight, black-clad figure, a pilled skullcap low on her forehead, who is slumped against a wall adorned with graffiti. Black dirt is caked under her fingernails and nestled in the crevices of her open palms.

A patch of sidewalk near the corner of 14th Street and University Place is Julie's regular spot to beg for spare change, to "spange," as she and her friends put it. This is where Julie spends most of her days, along with Whiskey, her tawny shepherd–pit bull mix, and Samantha, a pretty, 20-year-old brunette. Samantha, who goes by Sam and is from upstate New York, is dressed in baggy combat pants ripped at the crotch, and, like her companion, refuses to give her last name.

Along with "Dumpster diving"—scrounging for garbage outside restaurants—Julie and Sam meet their needs for food and shelter by using signs that advertise their plight. Sometimes Sam carries a sign that reads, "Trying to Get Home to My Mother's House." Julie's current sign, which is illustrated with paw prints, reads: "Homeless, Hungry and Broke. We are trying to get off the street tonight. Need @ $30 for a place to sleep. Please help. Thank you!!" The amount requested is her share of the approximately $65 that she and Sam will need to rent a cheap room for the night.

If they come up short, they will sleep on a side street, under scaffolding or an awning. Julie used to stay in squats on the Lower East Side, but more often than not, it's a cold, concrete bed for her.

> **FYI** Alison Stateman is an award-winning writer whose work has appeared in the *New York Times* and *The Washington Post*. As a former resident of NYC's East Village, she observed urban nomads' migration patterns firsthand, as they'd come and settle in each summer, sometimes right outside her front door. She wanted to explore their lives of perpetual motion and the often-angry responses their mere presence provoked among some of the neighborhood's residents.

For the last decade Julie has been part of a little-known segment of homeless youth often called urban nomads. Year in and year out they travel to a few select North American cities, living on little or no money on the fringes of a society they have grown disillusioned with or, like Julie, actively despise.

Like birds, they migrate according to the weather, spending the winter in the warmer parts of the South and West—San Francisco, New Orleans and Austin are favorites—before returning north as the weather grows milder. Manhattan is a prime destination, even though the life, never easy, is likely to get harder, given impending budget cuts that would affect the city's social services.

According to statistics provided by the Partnership for the Homeless, an advocacy group, an estimated 19,000 homeless and runaway youths live in New York's shelters or on its streets.

"New York is a place where people come for all reasons," said City Councilman Alan J. Gerson, who sponsored a conference at Pace University two weeks ago to explore the growing problem of homeless youth in the city. "That's the history of New York. So if a person is homeless on our streets, they are our problem and our imperative."

BASIC BLACK, AND TATTOOS

Urban nomads like Julie are a population that social scientists have only recently begun to study. Chief among those who focus on this group is Don C. Des Jarlais, research director at the Baron Edmond de Rothschild

Chemical Dependency Institute at Beth Israel Medical Center. The center has just issued preliminary findings from its Urban Nomad Study, now in its third year.

For the purposes of the study, urban nomads are defined as youths who have traveled to at least five different cities or towns in the past three years and at least three within the past year. After interviewing several hundred people who fit these criteria, the researchers are getting a feel for who they are, though hard statistics are elusive.

"We haven't really attempted to get a good estimate of the numbers, but I'd say it's probably in the thousands," said Dr. Des Jarlais. He estimates that nationally there may be 5,000 to 10,000 urban nomads, 1,000 of whom pass through New York each year.

Dr. Des Jarlais discovered urban nomads during an earlier study of drug users on the Lower East Side. "I was curious how they managed, how they survive," he said. "And the subtext was, 'Could I do that?'"

"This is a challenging lifestyle," he added. "But it's not as if they have totally given up on their lives."

Dr. Des Jarlais says that while urban nomads sometimes exaggerate or dramatize their pasts, they tend not to make up stories. Their parents are often ambivalent about their children leaving. "Some parents were probably very upset that they left, and some were probably very happy to see them go." Seventy to 80 percent of urban nomads said they stayed in touch with their parents, usually their mothers, but, he said, "when we asked, 'Could you go back home?' only 50 percent said they could."

While urban nomads and the city's traditional homeless youth often share a history of physical or sexual abuse, the two groups differ in many respects. Typically, New York's population of runaways and homeless youths is heavily minority and includes both girls and boys. By contrast, urban nomads tend to be white and largely male, with backgrounds that are typically working-class and occasionally middle-class. Many are children from homes where a parent's remarriage has produced family conflicts. Others are simply bored.

"In general, their home situations are not good, but it is not like they are in dire danger or anything like that," Dr. Des Jarlais said. "They are sort of not getting along well at home and they want to do something different, so they leave."

Unlike most of New York's runaways, who often pursue the dual street-survival occupations of drug-dealing and prostitution and hang out in places like Times Square, urban nomads tend to shun prostitution and heavy drug use and are drawn to the East Village and the Lower East Side.

The East Village holds a particular attraction because of its history of social and political unrest, its squatter tradition and its punk roots, typified by landmarks like CBGB's on the Bowery. The usual attire of combat or work clothes or basic black, set off by multiple piercings and tattoos, also mirrors the punk and workingman sympathies of the typical urban nomad.

But looking different can backfire. "From the moment they get into town, they're targeted by police because of the way they look," said John Welch, program director of Safe Horizon's Streetwork Project on the Lower East Side, a group that serves several hundred urban nomads each year. "They're more visible." As a result, they are often ticketed for minor offenses, like panhandling.

DRUG-FREE, BURNED OUT

Passers-by will tell Julie she doesn't need money if she has enough cash to pay for her tattoos and all that silver. In fact, she often wears long-sleeve shirts to hide her extensive network of tattoos, and she readily explains that she got them for free from friends who were budding tattoo artists and practiced on her.

It may, however, be the choice of artwork that makes people pause. A pentagram and a black skull with twisted horns are imprinted on her neck, and her hands and left upper arm are decorated with the phrases "Godless" and "What Life?"

"It's a scare tactic," she said. "I'm not in any way a holy person, but I'm also not satanic. It kind of reflects how I feel inside about people and life and the world and stuff. I'm not a happy, colorful, optimistic person, so a lot of my tattoos interpret the way I feel about everything."

Julie's physical condition also startles. Her front teeth, which arch out slightly, are yellowed, and she is rail-thin even for her petite frame. Julie hasn't been to a doctor or dentist in more than 10 years. However, she can recite the dates on which Whiskey was vaccinated and spayed and carries the paperwork to prove it in her army-green pack.

In fact, Whiskey seems to be the only being she doesn't seem to dislike, herself included. At one point, she grasped Whiskey's face and wept. "I love this dog, man," she said as Whiskey licked her tears before she could wipe them away.

Dogs play a big part in the urban nomad culture, providing their street-bound owners with companionship and protection. "A lot of people say, 'Oh, why don't you stay in a shelter?'" Julie said, mimicking their concerned tone. "Well, obviously it's because I have a dog. 'Well, why don't you give the dog away?' I love my dog. I'm not going to give my dog away so I can stay in a shelter. I'd rather sleep in the street."

Almost everyone who passes her stares. Some people grimace in disgust; a few cross the street. When a woman starts to take a picture of Julie, the action pushes her over the edge. "Can you not do that, please?" Julie asks.

"People think of us as some kind of New York landmark," she said later, her pale blue eyes glowering. "It's amusing to them. I am amusing to them. 'Oh, look at that, honey,'" she said in the mocking tone she adopts when impersonating strangers. "'That little creep with the dog begging for money.'"

Indeed, many passers-by are drawn less by her than by her pet, who this day rests a weary head upon Julie's thigh and shivers despite the red sweater wrapped tightly around her. Several people who drop change in Julie's cup announce, "This is for the dog."

This angers Julie. "They think I'm going to use it for drugs," she explained. She admits that she used heroin for four years, but said she has been drug-free since 2001.

Although Julie says she has been coming to the city every year since she was 17, making cross-country excursions to San Francisco and Portland when she can prevail on Sam to watch Whiskey, she is hard pressed to explain exactly why she is here.

"First of all, I'm kind of preoccupied with my financial situation," she said, "and No. 2, five or six years ago I might be able to speak really clearly about how I feel about things, but now I'm just so exhausted with having to explain myself all the time. Maybe it's just because I've had so much time to think, because I'm just sitting around thinking, that it's just like my brain is just burned out.

"I've become this kind of totally miserable, hateful person because I have to look at all these people every single day," she added. "But I put myself here, so I can't really blame anybody else. I guess I could have done things a little differently when I was younger, but I don't know."

Julie says she ran away from her home in New Hampshire at the age of 15. Asked why she left, she responds with an obscenity about her parents. According to her account of her early years, she spent time in a children's home and a year at Keene State College in New Hampshire before flunking out and hitting the road with like-minded friends.

She says she misses her father, who just turned 60 and used to work in computers. But the few times she has reached out to her parents, she said, by phone or through visits, she has been rejected. According to Julie, they are still angry at her for running away.

After so many years on the street, Julie doesn't seem to know what to make of generosity or choice. When a sailor in town for Fleet Week approached and peeled off a $5 bill, she asked awkwardly if he were really a sailor. Later on, when asked what she'd like for dinner, she had to think for several minutes, not wanting to blow a rare opportunity to choose her food. She opted for Taco Bell.

Despite evidence to the contrary, Julie doesn't think of herself as homeless.

"Homeless people to me are people who push around shopping carts and push strollers and they just sit around," she said. "Lazy and crazy is what I say."

The next day she's not so sure. "Once you do this for a while," she said, "it gets kind of exhausting and it's hard not to give in to those things that will make your life a little bit easier, such as getting a job and settling down and having security blankets and a nice place to live."

Could she ever lead that kind of life? "I hope so," she replied morosely, "because I don't want to be pushing a shopping cart around when I'm 50. If I make it to 50."

Dr. Des Jarlais has found that urban nomads seldom reach that age. "We've found almost nobody over 30," he said. "Some of them tend to move into conventional society and some of them, of course, develop health problems and die." Few find their way into organized programs, in part because programs that meet their needs are scarce.

THE "GRAPES OF WRATH" ROUTE

Urban nomad culture is built upon a patchwork of traditions that reflect its anti-establishment bent. Hopping freight trains, a practice that harkens back to the hobo of the Depression, is a favored mode of transportation. Many urban nomads find work sporadically as house painters or migrant laborers in the tradition chronicled in John Steinbeck's *Grapes of Wrath*.

Shane, 26, a soft-spoken friend of Julie's who travels to Maine each August to harvest the state's famed blueberries, matches the template perfectly.

Unlike Julie, who is all explosive energy, Shane is mellowness personified. Though coated in grime from the top of his once-beige Dewar's baseball cap to the tips of his work boots, though his backpacks emit the musky odor of too many nights spent sleeping in the rain and soot, he manages to maintain an air of dignity.

Even his choice of tattoos belies a gentler nature, from the character from his favorite comic book, *The Realm of Chaos*, etched on his forearm to the heart and scroll adorned with the names of his two former dogs, Sasha and Blue, on his bicep. Perhaps because of the shave he just finagled in a rest-room at Kmart on Astor Place, his angular face, punctuated by a strawberry-blond goatee, looks surprisingly youthful.

Shane, who is stationed across the street from Julie, is biding his time in the city before moving on to his next odd job.

"I follow the harvest," he said. "I do blueberries in Maine, then I do beets. I go down to Virginia and do apples. I go up to Alaska and work in the canneries. I don't like to stay in one place for too long. I love traveling. I don't like the whole 9-to-5 thing. I like to go to work for a couple of weeks, a couple of months at a time, and save up for whatever gear I need and go on to the next place."

Shane said he has a regular winter gig painting houses in Townsend, Wash., a job that provides a steady income and a trailer for shelter. Like the majority of older urban nomads, he eventually tired of the city circuit and began opting for odd jobs that took him to smaller towns; by contrast, younger nomads are usually drawn to the glitz that bigger urban environments offer.

Shane says he likes his life. But even if he wanted to get a conventional job, doing so without a permanent address would be nearly impossible.

"Some people tell you to get a job," he said. "They don't understand that I'd love to have a job, but it's kind of hard when you're homeless to walk into a place when you don't have an address or anything. To get a place to live, you have to have a job, but then again to get a job, you have to have a place to live where you can wake up every day to go to work. That's why I do the harvests. You can camp right there and go to work."

Shane, who said he was born and raised in Washington State, was not always the self-described laid-back person he presents himself as today. A decade ago, he was a rebellious, hard-partying teenager, with a tough Navy man as a stepfather. At one point, his mother gave him an ultimatum: Follow the house rules or get out.

"I was doing a lot of drinking, so I wasn't listening to my mother, so I ended up getting kicked out when I was 16, so I've been on my own since then," he said. "She told me if I couldn't follow her rules and my stepfather's rules, then I wasn't welcome to live there. And being the know-it-all that I was as a teenager, I just left."

He first came to New York at 17, drawn by a sense that this was his true place. His real father, who had left his mother around the time Shane was born, was originally from the city, and though Shane has never met his father, the city has not disappointed.

"When I was young, I used to picture New York a lot and see movies about it," he said from his curbside vantage point, surrounded by skeletons of umbrellas, abandoned cigarettes and clouds of bus exhaust. "I guess I just always wanted to see it.

"It was just like I thought it would be," he added. "It's just beautiful. The old brownstones and old buildings. It's such an old city and has such history. I like it here."

Shane recently earned his high school equivalency diploma and spends time in the main reading room of the New York Public Library, writing in his journal and reading books like *Last Exit to Brooklyn*.

His mother, a former teacher, is retired and lives with his stepfather in Spain. He calls and writes her regularly, and he gets her mail sent care of Streetwork's Lower East Side center. "Me and mom are really close," he said. "I talk to her a lot."

Reaching into a torn Duane Reade bag, he pulled out photographs of his mother's Chihuahua, dressed in a sweater, and a postcard she had sent him from Portugal. Does his mother worry about him? "I think she used to because I used to be into a lot of drugs," he said. "But she knows I've grown out of that."

CONSIDER

1. How do urban nomads compare to your preconceptions of homeless teens? Is it fair to say they choose to be homeless? Why or why not?

2. What are your thoughts about the lifestyle of urban nomads? Are there elements that appeal to you? What does their lifestyle say about more conventional ways of living?

ITEM 3.13 ■ **Jim Goldberg, Images from *Raised by Wolves*, 1995**

Often our personal stories seem dulled by the comfort and regularity of our daily routines. But for many, daily life holds no such comforts. Some forgo what many consider routine comforts as an experiment or a gesture of freedom, while others have little choice in the matter. The photographs of Jim Goldberg shed some light on these stories of life outside the safety of home and family.

122   3.1 | LIFE STORIES

> For my 12th B-DAY, MY OLDMAN grabbed me and gave me a carton of smokes and a sheet of acid. Looking back now I would have rather gotten a hug but the only time my father would put his hands on me would be to beat the shit out of me.
>
> The next day I went to school and dropped 5 hits in my teacher's coffee when she had turned her back. Few minutes later she started writing all stranger shapes and figures on the board and passed out. The nun was out for a week.

CONSIDER

1. Which of the figures in Goldberg's images do you identify with? How would you explain your identification with the figure?

2. What kinds of emotional responses do Goldberg's photographs evoke? How do you think Goldberg expects his viewers and readers to respond? Does he expect to prompt viewers to action?

COMPOSE

3. How would you compare the stories told by Goldberg's images from *Raised by Wolves* with the images evoked by the urban nomad stories in Alison Stateman's "Postcards from the Edge"? In a two- or three-page paper, explore the ways these works help us understand teen homelessness.

ITEM 3.14 ■ Harry Benson, *Jubilant Clay*, 1964

Sometimes a single event stands out as a landmark in our lives. Most of us will likely never win a world championship in sports or some other event, but still we will stake our claims to success and use these moments to mark our lives. The image here represents one of these exceptional moments that is both public and celebratory.

CONSIDER

1. Harry Benson's photo of Muhammad Ali may have several focal points. In addition to the boxer's hand, what other focal points can you identify? How do different focal points change your impression of Ali or the story this image might have to tell about him?

2. Where is Ali's gaze directed in this photo? What about the gaze of the other figures in the image? How do these elements influence the gaze of the viewer of the image? What does this photo teach you about using the gaze to interpret images?

COMPOSE

3. Write a two- or three-paragraph description of someone you know well, organizing your observations around one focal point—one characteristic, activity, or trait that reveals something about the person's identity.

124   3.1 | LIFE STORIES

Excerpt from
An American Childhood

Annie Dillard
(1987)

FYI Award-winning author Annie Dillard has written more than a dozen books ranging from poetry to fiction to literary criticism. In 1974, her *Pilgrim at Tinker Creek* established Dillard as a premier writer of nonfiction. In *An American Childhood*, published in 1987, Dillard applied her nonfiction skills toward reflections on her parents and life, among other subjects.

Some boys taught me to play football. This was a fine sport. You thought up a new strategy for every play and whispered it to the others. You went out for a pass, fooling everyone. Best, you got to throw yourself mightily at someone's running legs. Either you brought him down or you hit the ground flat out on your chin, with your arms empty before you. It was all or nothing. If you hesitated in fear, you would miss and get hurt: you would take a hard fall while the kid got away, or you would get kicked in the face while the kid got away. But if you flung yourself wholeheartedly at the back of his knees—if you gathered and joined body and soul and pointed them diving fearlessly—then you likely wouldn't get hurt, and you'd stop the ball. Your fate, and your team's score, depended on your concentration and courage. Nothing girls did could compare with it.

Boys welcomed me at baseball, too, for I had, through enthusiastic practice, what was weirdly known as a boy's arm. In winter, in the snow, there was neither baseball nor football, so the boys and I threw snowballs at passing cars. I got in trouble throwing snowballs, and have seldom been happier since.

> **I got in trouble throwing snowballs, and have seldom been happier since.**

On one weekday morning after Christmas, six inches of new snow had just fallen. We were standing up to our boot tops in snow on a front yard on trafficked Reynolds Street, waiting for cars. The cars traveled Reynolds Street slowly and evenly; they were targets all but wrapped in red ribbons, cream puffs. We couldn't miss.

I was seven; the boys were eight, nine, and ten. The oldest two Fahey boys were there—Mikey and Peter—polite blond boys who lived near me on Lloyd Street, and who already had four brothers and sisters. My parents approved of Mikey and Peter Fahey. Chickie McBride was there, a tough kid, and Billy Paul and Mackie Kean too, from across Reynolds, where the boys grew up dark and furious, grew up skinny, knowing, and skilled. We had all drifted from our houses that morning looking for action, and had found it here on Reynolds Street.

It was cloudy but cold. The cars' tires laid behind them on the snowy street a complex trail of beige chunks like crenellated castle walls. I had stepped on some earlier; they squeaked. We could have wished for more traffic. When a car came, we all popped it one. In the intervals between cars we reverted to the natural solitude of children.

I started making an iceball—a perfect iceball, from perfectly white snow, perfectly spherical, and squeezed perfectly translucent so no snow re-mained all the way through. (The Fahey boys and I considered it unfair actually to throw an iceball at somebody, but it had been known to happen.)

I had just embarked on the iceball project when we heard tire chains come clanking from afar. A black Buick was moving toward us down the street. We all spread out, banged together some regular snowballs, took aim, and, when the Buick drew nigh, fired.

> **Often, of course, we hit our target, but this time, the only time in all of life, the car pulled over and stopped. Its wide black door opened; a man got out of it, running. He didn't even close the car door.**

A soft snowball hit the driver's windshield right before the driver's face. It made a smashed star with a hump in the middle.

Often, of course, we hit our target, but this time, the only time in all of life, the car pulled over and stopped. Its wide black door opened; a man got out of it, running. He didn't even close the car door.

He ran after us, and we ran away from him, up the snowy Reynolds sidewalk. At the corner, I looked back; incredibly, he was still after us. He was in city clothes: a suit and tie, street shoes. Any normal adult would have quit, having sprung us into flight and made his point. This man was gaining on us. He was a thin man, all action. All of a sudden, we were running for our lives.

Wordless, we split up. We were on our turf; we could lose ourselves in the neighborhood backyards, everyone for himself. I paused and considered. Everyone had vanished except Mikey Fahey, who was just rounding the corner of a yellow brick house. Poor Mikey, I trailed him. The driver of the Buick sensibly picked the two of us to follow. The man apparently had all day.

He chased Mikey and me around the yellow house and up a backyard path we knew by heart: under a low tree, up a bank, through a hedge, down some snowy steps, and across the grocery store's delivery driveway. We smashed through a gap in another hedge, entered a scruffy backyard and ran around its back porch and right between houses to Edgerton Avenue; we ran across Edgerton to an alley and up our own sliding woodpile to the Halls' front yard; he kept coming. We ran up Lloyd Street and wound through mazy backyards toward the steep hilltop at Willard and Lang.

He chased us silently, block after block. He chased us silently over picket fences, through thorny hedges, between houses, around garbage cans, and across streets. Every time I glanced back, choking for breath, I expected he would have quit. He must have been as breathless as we were. His jacket strained over his body. It was an immense discovery, pounding into my hot head with every sliding, joyous step, that this ordinary adult evidently knew what I thought only children who trained at football knew: that you have to fling yourself at what you're doing, you have to point yourself, forget yourself, aim, dive.

Mikey and I had nowhere to go, in our own neighborhood or out of it, but away from this man who was chasing us. He impelled us forward; we compelled him to follow our route. The air was cold; every breath tore my throat. We kept running, block after block; we kept improvising, backyard after backyard, running a frantic course and choosing it simultaneously, failing always to find small places or hard places to slow him down, and discovering always, exhilarated, dismayed, that only bare speed could save us—for he would never give up, this man—and we were losing speed.

He chased us through the backyard labyrinths of ten blocks before he caught us by our jackets. He caught us and we all stopped.

We three stood staggering, half blinded, coughing, in an obscure hilltop backyard: a man in his twenties, a boy, a girl. He had released our jackets, our pursuer, our captor, our hero: he knew we weren't going anywhere. We all played by the rules. Mikey and I unzipped our jackets. I pulled off my sopping mittens. Our tracks multiplied in the backyard's new snow. We had been breaking new snow all morning. We didn't look at each other. I was cherishing my excitement. The man's lower pants legs were wet; his cuffs were full of snow, and there was a prow of snow beneath them on his shoes and socks. Some trees bordered the little flat backyard, some messy winter trees. There was no one around: a clearing in a grove, and we the only players.

It was a long time before he could speak. I had some difficulty at first recalling why we were there. My lips felt swollen; I couldn't see out of the sides of my eyes; I kept coughing.

"You stupid kids," he began perfunctorily.

We listened perfunctorily indeed, if we listened at all, for the chewing out was redundant, a mere formality, and beside the point. The point was that he had chased us passionately without giving up, and so he had caught us. Now he came down to earth. I wanted the glory to last forever.

But how could the glory have lasted forever? We could have run through every backyard in North America until we got to Panama. But when he trapped us at the lip of the Panama Canal, what precisely could he have done to prolong the drama of the chase and cap its glory? I brooded about this for the next few years. He could have fried Mikey Fahey and me in boiling oil, say, or dismembered us piecemeal, or staked us to anthills. None of which I really wanted, and none of which any adult was likely to do, even in the spirit of fun. He could only chew us out there in the Panamanian jungle, after months or years of exalting pursuit. He could only begin, "You stupid kids," and continue in his ordinary Pittsburgh accent with his normal righteous anger and the usual common sense.

If in that snowy backyard the driver of the black Buick had cut off our heads, Mikey's and mine, I would have died happy, for nothing has required so much of me since as being chased all over Pittsburgh in the middle of winter—running terrified, exhausted—by this sainted, skinny, furious red-headed man who wished to have a word with us. I don't know how he found his way back to his car.

CONSIDER

1. What details in the story make the event stand out? How easy is it to decide whether the episode related by Dillard (the snowball throwing and subsequent chase) is an exceptional or everyday event? How would you argue this point one way or the other?

2. Think about the statement at the end of Dillard's essay, "nothing has required so much of me since as being chased all over Pittsburgh in the middle of winter." Is Dillard really saying this was the most trying event in her life? How do you explain the statement?

Cluster 3.2
Bodies

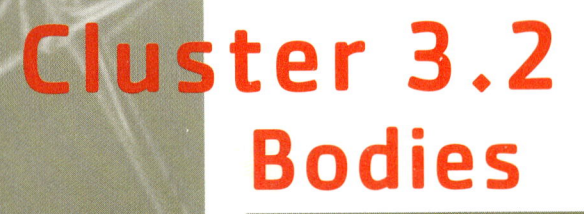

Recently, doctors performed the first face transplant. Medical innovations often raise questions, but the people protesting this procedure had a somewhat subtle argument, suggesting that replacing one person's face with that of another would lead to ethical concerns about identity. Would people receiving such transplants maintain their sense of self, or would they encounter troubling confusion about their identity when the bandages were removed and they met a new face in the mirror?

Of course, these questions play out daily as people turn to Botox, diet pills, and plastic surgery in search of a new and improved personal appearance. We inflict pain and suffering on ourselves in the name of our bodies, piercing, tattooing, and going under the knife to make ourselves feel better. Susan Bordo reflects on the ways media images distort our sense of identity in her essay "The Empire of Images in Our World of Bodies." Similarly, Josie Appleton argues in "The Body Piercing Project" that tattoos and piercings are not simply body decorations, but complex statements about identity.

To many Americans, the body represents a paradox. Advertisers bombard us with images of impossibly thin models that drive young people to anorexia and other eating disorders, and yet for the first time in our national history, the majority of American adults are seriously overweight. We also have some confusing ideas about identity, bodies, and culture. We celebrate actors and entertainers, but fixate on their clothes, makeup, or muscle tone rather than their talents or accomplishments. We've collected a series of *Rolling Stone* covers to help you explore these kinds of representations.

In this cluster we look also at the ways we define our identity in terms of physical selves. Henry Louis Gates's "In the Kitchen" explores relationships between hair and identity. Images of Bob Marley and Nat King Cole provide visual evidence of the ways physical features like hair or cultural expressions like hairstyles combine to become expressions of self. Identity, it turns out, is formed in a complex matrix that includes our mental and emotional makeup, our cultural surroundings, our affiliations with others, and our bodies.

The Empire of Images in Our World of Bodies

Susan Bordo
(2003)

> **FYI** Susan Bordo teaches philosophy at the University of Kentucky. Her book *Unbearable Weight* was named a Notable Book of 1993 by the *New York Times* and nominated for a Pulitzer Prize. It was among the first scholarly books to draw connections between images of the body and eating disorders.

In our Sunday news. With our morning coffee. On the bus, in the airport, at the checkout line. It may be a 5 a.m. addiction to the glittering promises of the infomercial: the latest in fat-dissolving pills, miracle hair restoration, makeup secrets of the stars. Or a glancing relationship while waiting at the dentist, trying to distract ourselves from the impending root canal. A teen magazine: tips on how to dress, how to wear your hair, how to make him want you. The endless commercials and advertisements that we believe we pay no attention to.

Constant, everywhere, no big deal. Like water in a goldfish bowl, barely noticed by its inhabitants. Or noticed, but dismissed: "eye candy"—a harmless indulgence. They go down so easily, in and out, digested and forgotten.

Just pictures.

Or perhaps, more accurately, perceptual pedagogy: "How to Interpret Your Body 101." It's become a global requirement; eventually, everyone must enroll. Fiji is just one example. Until television was introduced in 1995, the islands had no reported cases of eating disorders. In 1998, three years after programs from the United States and Britain began broadcasting there, 62 percent of the girls surveyed reported dieting. The anthropologist Anne Becker was surprised by the change; she had thought that Fijian aesthetics, which favor voluptuous bodies, would "withstand" the influence of media images. Becker hadn't yet understood that we live in an empire of images and that there are no protective borders.

I am not protected either. I was carded until I was 35. Even when I was 45, people were shocked to learn my age. Young men flirted with me even when I was 50. Having hated my appearance as a child—freckles, Jewish nose, bushy red hair—I was surprised to find myself fairly pleased with it as an adult. Then, suddenly, it all changed. Women at the makeup counter no longer compliment me on my skin. Men don't catch my eye with playful promise in theirs.

I'm 56. The magazines tell me that at this age, a woman can still be beautiful. But they don't mean me. They mean Cher, Goldie, Faye, Candace. Women whose jowls have disappeared as they've aged, whose eyes have become less droopy, lips grown plumper, foreheads smoother with the passing years. They mean Susan Sarandon, who looked older in 1991's *Thelma and Louise* than she does in her movies today. "Aging beautifully" used to mean wearing one's years with style, confidence, and vitality. Today, it means not appearing to age at all. And—like breasts that defy gravity—it's becoming a new bodily norm.

> "Aging beautifully" used to mean wearing one's years with style, confidence, and vitality. Today, it means not appearing to age at all.

In my 1993 book *Unbearable Weight*, I described the postmodern body, increasingly fed on "fantasies of rearranging, transforming, and correcting, limitless improvement and change, defying the historicity, the mortality, and, indeed, the very materiality of the body. In place of that materiality, we now have cultural plastic."

When I wrote those words, the most recent statistics, from 1989, listed 681,000 surgical procedures performed. In 2001, 8.5 million procedures were performed. They are cheaper than ever, safer than ever, and increasingly used not for correcting major defects but for "contouring" the face and body. Plastic surgeons seem to have no ethical problem with this. "I'm not here to play philosopher king," said Dr. Randal Haworth in a *Vogue* interview. "I don't have a problem with women who already look good who want to look perfect." Perfect. When did "perfection" become applicable to a human body? The word suggests a Platonic form of timeless beauty—appropriate for marble, perhaps, but not for living flesh.

Greta Van Susteren: former CNN legal analyst, 47 years old. When she had a face-lift, it was a real escalation in the stakes for ordinary women. She had a signature style: no bullshit, a down-to-earth lack of pretense. (During the O.J. trial, she was the only white reporter many black Americans trusted.) Always stylishly dressed and coiffed, she wasn't really pretty. No one could argue that her career was built on her looks. Perhaps quite the opposite. She sent out a subversive message: Brains and personality still count, even on television.

When Greta had her face lifted, another source of inspiration and hope bit the dust. The story was on the cover of *People*, and folks tuned in to her new show on Fox just to see the change—which was significant. But at least she was open about it. The beauties rarely admit they've had "work." Or if they do, it's vague, nonspecific, minimizing of the extent. Cher: "If I'd had as much plastic surgery as people say, there'd be another whole person left over!" OK, so how much have you had? The interviewers accept the silences and evasions. They even embellish the lie. How many interviews have you read that began: "She came into the restaurant looking at least 20 years younger than she is, fresh and relaxed, without a speck of makeup."

This collusion, this myth, that Cher or Goldie or Faye Dunaway, unaltered, is what 50-something looks like today has altered my face, however—without benefit of surgery. By comparison with theirs, it has become much older than it is.

My expression now appears more serious, too (just what a feminist needs), thanks to the widespread use of Botox. "It's now rare in certain social circles to see a woman over the age of 35 with the ability to look angry," a *New York Times* reporter observed recently. That has frustrated some film directors, like Baz Luhrmann, who directed *Moulin Rouge*. "Their faces can't really move properly," Luhrmann complained. Last week I saw a sign in the beauty parlor where I get my hair cut. "Botox Party! Sign Up!"

So my 56-year-old forehead will now be judged against my neighbor's, not just Goldie's, Cher's, and Faye's. On television, a commercial describes the product (which really is a toxin, a dilution of botulism) as "Botox cosmetic." No different from mascara and blush, it's just stuck in with a needle, and it makes your forehead numb.

To add insult to injury, the rhetoric of feminism has been adopted to help advance and justify the industries in anti-aging and body-alteration. Face-lifts, implants, and liposuction are advertised as empowerment, "taking charge" of one's life. "I'm doing it for me" goes the mantra of the talk shows. "Defy your age!" says Melanie Griffith, for Revlon. We're making a revolution, girls. Step right up and get your injections.

Am I immune? Of course not. My bathroom shelves are cluttered with the ridiculously expensive age-defying lotions and potions that beckon to me at the Lancôme and Dior counters. I want my lines, bags, and sags to disappear, and so do the women who can only afford to buy their alphahydroxies at Kmart. There's a limit, though, to what fruit acids can do. As surgeons develop ever more extensive and

> "When did "perfection" become applicable to a human body? The word suggests a Platonic form of timeless beauty—appropriate for marble, perhaps, but not for living flesh."

fine-tuned procedures to correct gravity and erase history from the faces of their patients, the difference between the cosmetically altered and the rest of us grows more and more dramatic.

"The rest of us" includes not only those who resist or are afraid of surgery but the many people who cannot afford basic health care, let alone aesthetic tinkering. As celebrity faces become increasingly more surreal in their wide-eyed, ever-bright agelessness, as *Time* and *Newsweek* (and *Discover* and *Psychology Today*) proclaim that we can now all "stay young forever," the poor continue to sag and wrinkle and lose their teeth. But in the empire of images, where even people in the news for stock scandals or producing septuplets are given instant digital dental work for magazine covers, that is a well-guarded secret. The celebrity testimonials, the advertisements, the beauty columns, all participate in the fiction that the required time, money, and technologies are available to all.

I've been lecturing about media images, eating problems, and our culture of body "enhancement" for nearly 20 years now. Undergraduates frequently make up a large share of my audiences, and they are the ones most likely to "get it." My generation (and older) still refers to "airbrushing." Many still believe it is possible to "just turn off the television." They are scornful, disdainful, sure of their own immunity to the world I talk about. No one really believes the ads, do they? Don't we all know those are just images, designed to sell products? Scholars in the audience may trot out theory about cultural resistance and "agency." Men may insist that they love fleshy women.

Fifteen years ago, I felt very alone when my own generation said these things; it seemed that they were living in a different world from the one I was tracking and that there was little hope of bridging the gap. Now, I simply catch the eyes of the 20-year-olds in the audience. They know. They understand that you can be as cynical as you want about the ads—and many of them are—and still feel powerless to resist their messages. They are aware that virtually every advertisement, every magazine cover, has been digitally modified and that very little of what they see is "real." That doesn't stop them from hating their own bodies for failing to live up to computer-generated standards. They know, no matter what their parents, teachers, and clergy are telling them, that "inner beauty" is a big laugh in this culture. If they come from communities that traditionally have celebrated voluptuous bodies and within which food represents love, safety, and home, they may feel isolation and guilt over the widening gap between the values they've grown up with and those tugging at them now.

In the world in which our children are growing up, there is a size zero, and it's a status symbol. The chronic dieters have been at it since they were 8 and 9 years old. They know all about eating disorders; being preached to about the dangers turns them right off. Their world is one in which anorexics swap starvation-diet tips on the Internet, participate in group fasts, offer advice on how to hide your "ana" from family members, and share inspirational photos of emaciated models. But full-blown anorexia has never been the norm among teenage girls; the real epidemic is among the girls with seemingly healthy eating habits, seemingly healthy bodies, who vomit or work their butts off as a regular form of anti-fat maintenance. These girls not only look "normal" but consider themselves normal. The new criterion circulating among teenage girls: If you get rid of it through exercise rather than purging or laxatives, you don't have a problem. Theirs is a world in which groups of dorm girls will plow voraciously through pizzas, chewing and then spitting out each mouthful. Do they have a disorder? Of course not—look, they're eating pizza.

Generations raised in the empire of images are both vulnerable and savvy. They snort when magazines periodically proclaim (about once every six months, the same frequency with which they run cover stories about "starving stars") that in the "new" Hollywood one can be "sexy at any size." They are literati, connoisseurs of the images; they pay close attention to the pounds coming and going—on J. Lo, Reese, Thora, Christina Aguilera, Beyoncé. They know that Kate Winslet, whom the director James Cameron called "Kate Weighs-a-lot" on the set of *Titanic*, was described by the tabloids as "packing on," "ballooning to," "swelling to," "shooting up to," "tipping the scales at" a "walloping," "staggering" weight—of 135 pounds. That slender Courtney Thorne-Smith, who played Calista Flockhart's friend and rival on *Ally McBeal*, quit the show because she could no longer keep up with the pressure to remain as thin as the series's creator, David E. Kelley, wanted them to be. That Missy Elliot and Queen Latifah are not on diets just for reasons of health.

I track the culture of young girls today with particular concern, because I'm a mother now. My 4-year-old daughter is a superb athlete with supreme confidence in her body, who prides herself on being able to do anything the boys can do—and better. When I see young girls being diminished and harassed by the culture it feels even more personal to me now. I'm grateful that there's a new generation of female athletes to inspire and support girls like my daughter, Cassie. That our icons are no longer just tiny gymnasts, but powerful soccer, softball, and tennis players, broad-shouldered track stars—Mia Hamm, Sarah Walden, Serena Williams, Marion Jones. During a recent visit to a high school, I saw how the eyes of a 14-year-old athlete shone as she talked about what Marion Jones means to her, and that fills me with hope.*

But then, I accidentally tune in to the Maury Povich show, and my heart is torn in two. The topic of the day is "back-to-girl" makeovers. One by one, five beautiful 12-, 13-, and 14-year-old "tomboys" (as Maury called them) are "brought back to their feminine side" (Maury again) through a fashion makeover. We first see them in sweatshirts and caps, insisting that they are as strong as any boy, that they want to dress for comfort, that they're tired of being badgered to look like girls. Why, then, are they submitting to this one-time, on-air transformation? To please their moms. And indeed, as each one is brought back on stage, in full makeup and glamour outfit, hair swinging (and, in the case of the black girls, straightened), striking vampy supermodel "power" poses, their mothers sob as if they had just learned their daughters' cancers were in remission. The moms are so overwhelmed they don't need more, but Maury is clearly bent on complete conversion: "Do you know how pretty you are?" "Look how gorgeous you look!" "Are you going to dress like this more often?" Most of the girls, unsurprisingly, say yes. It's been a frontal assault, there's no room for escape.

As jaded as I am, this Maury show really got to me. I wanted to fold each girl in my arms and get her out of there. Of course, what I really fear is that I won't be able to protect Cassie from the same assault. It's happening already. I watch public-television kids' shows with her and can rarely find fault with the gender-neutral world they portray. We go to Disney movies and see resourceful, spirited heroines. Some of them, like the Hawaiian girls in *Lilo and Stitch*, even have thick legs and solid bodies. But then, on the way home from the movies, we stop at McDonald's for a Happy Meal, and, despite the fact that Cassie insists she's a boy and wants the boy's toy—a hot-wheels car— she is given a box containing a mini-Barbie. Illustrating the box is Barbie's room, and my daughter is given the challenging task of finding all the matching pairs of shoes on the floor.

Later that day, I open a Pottery Barn catalog, browsing for ideas for Cassie's room. The designated boy's room is in primary colors, the bedspread dotted with balls, bats, catching mitts. The caption reads: "I play so many sports that it's hard to pick my favorites." Sounds like my daughter. On the opposite page, the girl's room is pictured, a pastel planetary design. The caption reads: "I like stars because they are shiny." That, too, sounds like my daughter. But Pottery Barn doesn't think a child can inhabit both worlds. If its catalogs were as segregated and stereotyped racially as they are by gender, people would boycott.

I rent a video—*Jimmy Neutron, Boy Genius*—for Cassie. It's marketed as a kids' movie, and the movie is OK for the most part. But then we get to the music video that follows the movie, unaccompanied by any warnings. A group I've never heard of sings a song called "Kids in America." Two of the girls are 13, two are 15, and one is 16—their ages are embla-

---

*Since the publication of this essay, Marion Jones has admitted to using steroids and subsequently lost her Olympic Medals.

zoned across the screen as each makes her appearance. They are in full vixen attire, with professionally undulating bodies and professionally made-up, come-hither eyes.

> **Can it really be that we now think dressing our daughters up like tiny prostitutes is cute?**

Why are we told their ages, I wonder? Are we supposed to be amazed at the illusion of womanhood created by their performance? Or is their youth supposed to make it all right to show this to little kids, a way of saying, "It's only make-believe, only a dress-up game"? It wasn't so long ago that people were outraged by news clips of JonBenet Ramsey performing in children's beauty pageants. In 2002, toddler versions of Britney Spears were walking the streets on Halloween night. Can it really be that we now think dressing our daughters up like tiny prostitutes is cute? That's what the psychologist Sharon Lamb, author of *The Secret Lives of Girls*, thinks. She advises mothers to chill out if their 9-year-old girls "play lovely little games in high heels, strip teasing, flouncing, and jutting their chests out," to relax if their 11-year-olds go out with "thick blue eye shadow, spaghetti straps and bra straps intertwined, long and leggy with short black dresses." They are "silly and adorable, sexy and marvelous all at once," she tells us, as they "celebrate their objectification," "playing out male fantasies . . . but without risk."

Without risk? I have nothing against girls playing dress-up. But flouncing is one thing; strip teasing is another. Thick blue eye shadow in mommy's bathroom is fine; an 11-year-old's night on the town is not. Reading those words "without risk," I want to remind Sharon Lamb that 22 to 29 percent of all rapes against girls occur when they are 11 and younger. We might like to think that those rapes are the work of deranged madmen, so disconnected from reality as to be oblivious to the culture around them. Or that all we need to do to protect our daughters is simply teach them not to take candy from or go into cars with strangers. The reality, however, is that young girls are much more likely to be raped by friends and family members than by strangers and that very few men, whether strangers or acquaintances, are unaffected by a visual culture of nymphets prancing before their eyes, exuding a sexual knowledge and experience that preteens don't really have. Feminists used to call this "rape culture." We never hear that phrase anymore.

Still, progressive forces are not entirely asleep in the empire of images. I think of *YM* teen magazine, for example. After conducting a survey that revealed that 86 percent of its young readers were dissatisfied with the way their bodies looked, *YM* openly declared war on eating disorders and body-image problems, instituting an editorial policy against the publishing of diet pieces and deliberately seeking out full-size models—without identifying them as such—for all its fashion spreads. A colleague suggested that this resistance to the hegemony of the fat-free body may have something to do with the fact that the editors are young enough to have studied feminism and cultural studies while they got their B.A.'s in English and journalism.

Most progressive developments in the media, of course, are driven by market considerations rather than social conscience. So, for example, the fact that 49 million women are size 12 or more is clearly the motive behind new, flesh-normalizing campaigns created by "Just My Size" and Lane Bryant. Ad campaigns for these lines of clothing proudly show off zaftig bodies in sexy underwear and, unlike older marketing to "plus size" women, refuse to use that term, insisting (accurately) that what has been called plus size is in fact average. It's a great strategy for making profits, but a species of resistance nonetheless. "I won't allow myself to be invisible anymore," these ads proclaim, on our behalf. "But I won't be made visible as a cultural oddity or a joke, either, because I'm not. I'm the norm."

The amorality of consumer capitalism, in its restless search for new markets and new ways to generate and feed desire, has also created a world of racial representations that are far more diverse now than when I wrote *Unbearable Weight*. This is another issue that has acquired special meaning for me, because my daughter is biracial, and I am acutely aware of the world that she sees and what it is telling her about herself. Leafing through current magazines, noting the variety of skin tones, noses, mouths depicted there, I'm glad, for the moment, that Cassie is growing up today rather than in the '70s, when Cheryl Tiegs ruled. It's always possible, of course, to find things that are still "wrong" with these representations; racist codes and aesthetics die hard. The Jezebels and geishas are still with us; and, although black male models and toddlers are allowed to have locks and "naturals," straight hair—straighter nowadays than I ever thought it was possible for anyone's hair to be—seems almost mandatory for young black women.

It's easy, too, to be cynical. Today's fashionable diversity is brought to us, after all, by the same people who brought us the hegemony of the blue-eyed blonde and who've made wrinkles and cellulite into diseases. It's easy to dismiss fashion's current love affair with full lips and biracial children as a shameless attempt to exploit ethnic markets while providing ethnic chic for white beauty tourists. Having a child, however, has given me another perspective, as I try to imagine how the models look through her eyes. Cassie knows nothing about the motives of the people who've produced the images. At her age, she can only take them at face value. And at face value, they present a world that includes and celebrates her, as the world that I grew up in did not include and celebrate me. For all my anger, cynicism, and frustration with our empire of images, I cannot help but be grateful for that.

And sometimes, surveying the plastic, digitalized world of bodies that are the norm now, I am convinced that our present state of enchantment is just a moment away from revulsion, or perhaps simply boredom. I see a 20-something woman dancing at a local outdoor swing party, her tummy softly protruding over the thick leather belt of her low-rider jeans. Not taut, not toned, not artfully camouflaged like some unsightly deformity, but proudly, sensuously displayed, reminding me of Madonna in the days before she became the sinewy dominatrix. Is it possible that we are beginning to rebel against the manufactured look of celebrity bodies, beginning to be repelled by their armored perfection?

> **Is it possible that we are beginning to rebel against the manufactured look of celebrity bodies, beginning to be repelled by their armored perfection?**

Such hopeful moments, I have to admit, are fleeting. Usually, I feel horrified. I am sharply aware that expressing my horror openly nowadays invites being thought of as a preachy prude, a relic of an outmoded feminism. At talks to young audiences, I try to lighten my touch, celebrate the positive, make sure that my criticisms of our culture are not confused with being anti-beauty, anti-fitness, or anti-sex. But I also know that when parents and teachers become fully one with the culture, children are abandoned to it. I don't tell them to love their bodies or turn off the television—useless admonitions today, and ones I cannot obey myself—but I do try to disrupt, if only temporarily, their everyday immersion in the culture. For just an hour or so, I won't let it pass itself off simply as "normalcy."

The lights go down, the slides go up. For just a moment, we confront how bizarre, how impossible, how contradictory the images are. We laugh together over Oprah's head digitally grafted to another woman's body, at the ad for breast implants in which the breasts stick straight up in the air. We gasp together as the before and after photos of Jennifer Lopez are placed side by side. We cheer for Marion Jones's shoulders, boo the fact that WNBA Barbie is just the same old Barbie, but with a basketball in her hand. For just a moment, we are in charge of the impact the faked images of "perfect" bodies have on us.

We look at them together and share—just for a moment—outrage.

CONSIDER

1. According to Bordo, we are routinely bombarded by so many idealized images of the human body that we may not even notice when or how they distort our sense of self. Make a list of where and when you encounter such images during a specific period of time (an hour, an afternoon, a day). Then use your evidence to evaluate Bordo's claim.

2. Bordo, as a feminist, is concerned primarily with the way images shape the perceptions of young women and girls. Are boys and young men similarly bombarded by unhealthy images? How do the popular media portray young men? Are 12- and 13-year-old boys, for example, sexualized in the same ways Bordo claims young girls are? Or are boys stereotyped in different ways? In a mixed group, discuss your findings and their implications.

COMPOSE

3. Why do people—particularly young women—admire or emulate bodies they know have been improved by surgery, impossible exercise regimens, chemicals, or photographic enhancements? (See Cluster 7.2, "Eye of the Beholder.") Why do we refuse to buy the claim that "one can be 'sexy at any size'"? In a brief essay, explore possible explanations for this phenomenon, perhaps focusing on the people and communities you know best.

4. "The Empire of Images in Our World of Bodies" ends with some hope that younger women are beginning to resist media images. Read Bordo's concluding paragraphs in context with the *Rolling Stone* covers that appear next (pages 136–137). Do the covers suggest any changes in the way younger people—one of the target audiences of *Rolling Stone*—think about beauty, physical perfection, and gender stereotypes? Which covers reinforce potentially hurtful stereotypes, and which undermine them? Offer your thoughts in a few detailed paragraphs.

FYI

ITEM 3.15 ■ **On the Cover of *Rolling Stone*: Photo Montage 2006–2007**

The profile essay is a staple of magazines because of our fascination with the lives of celebrities. Profiles highlight key aspects of people, helping us understand something about their identities. Essays employ thousands of words to capture the subject of the profile. These cover photographs try to accomplish something similar with a single image.

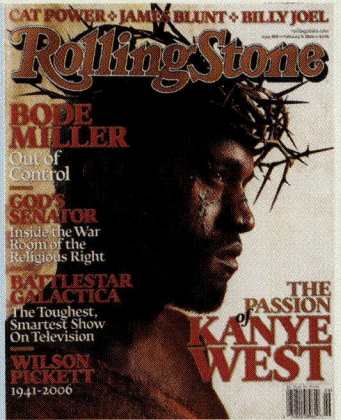

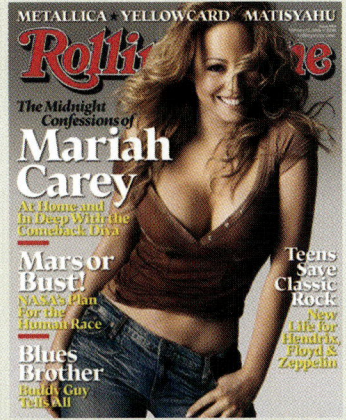

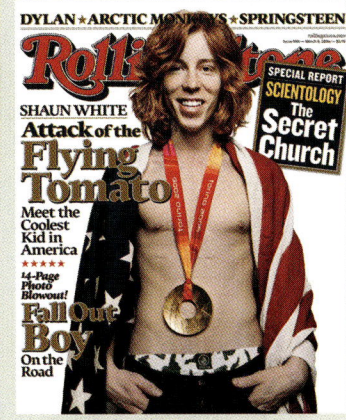

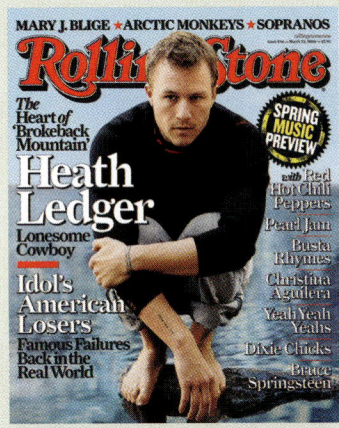

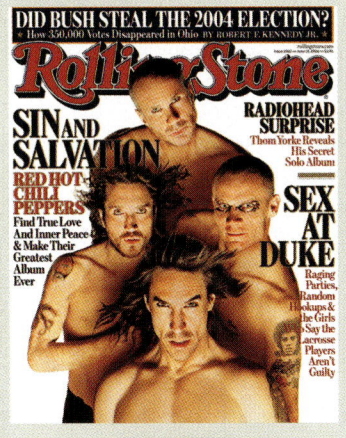

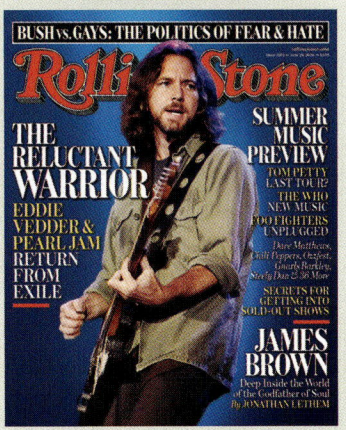

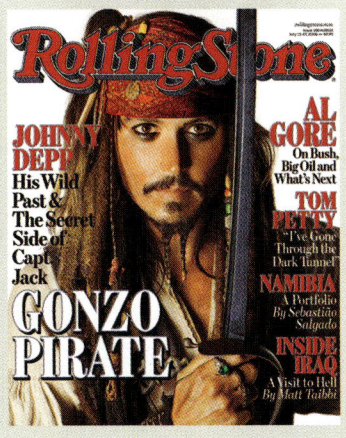

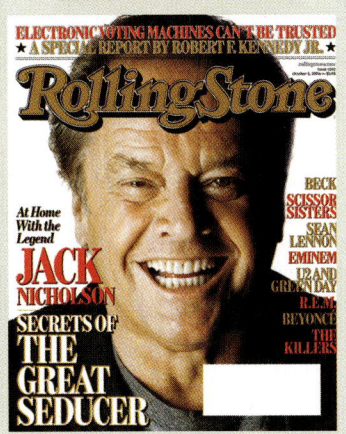

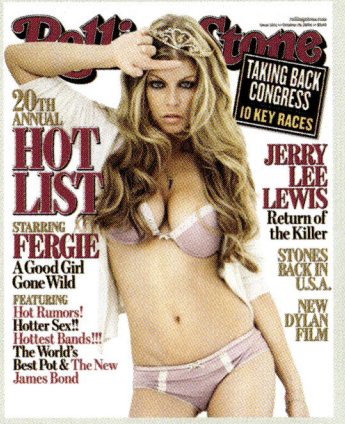

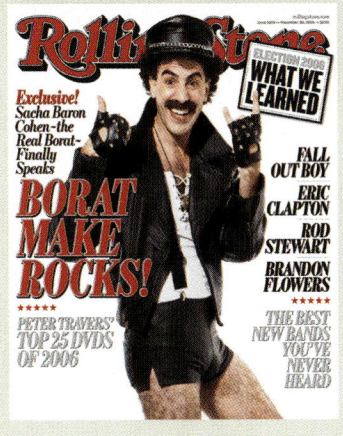

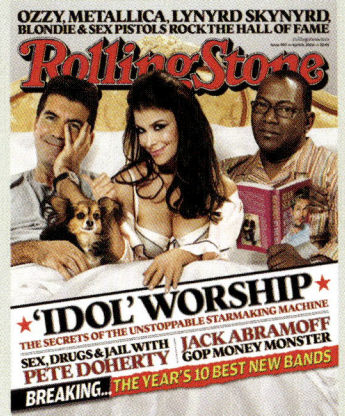

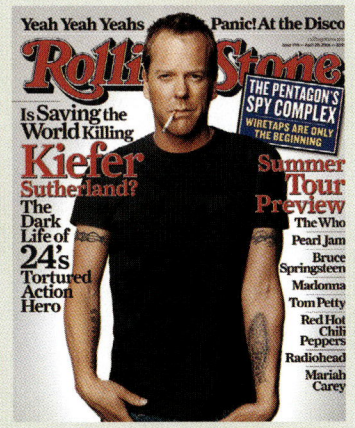

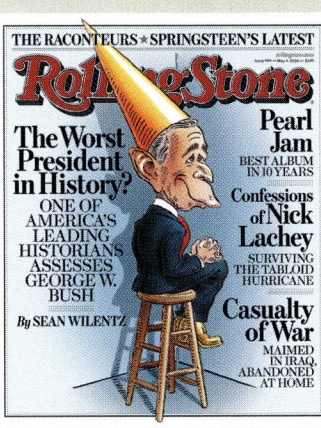

136   3.2 | BODIES

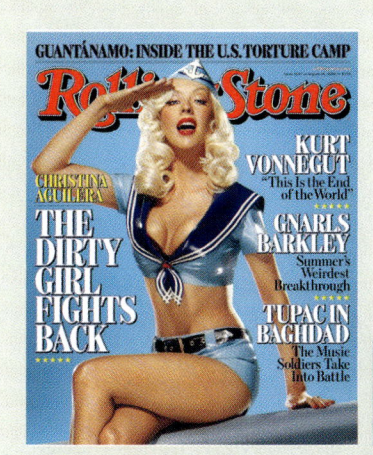

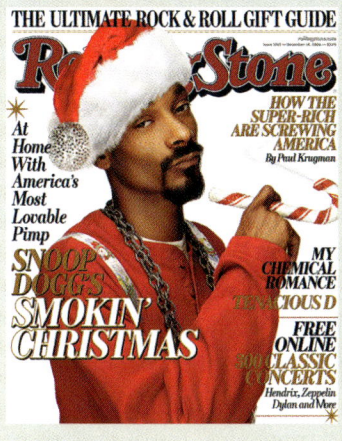

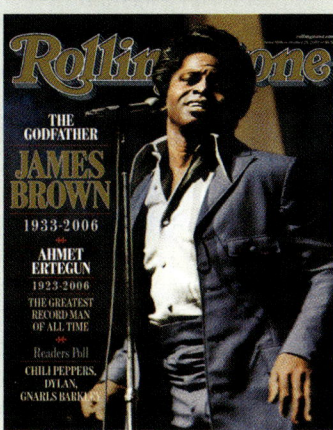

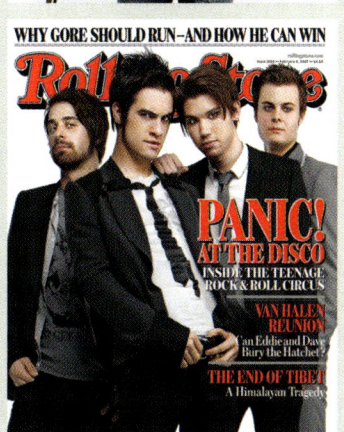

CONSIDER

1. You would ordinarily see a magazine on a newsstand or in your mailbox, separated in time and space from other issues. How does placing about a year's worth of *Rolling Stone* covers side by side change your perspective on the people portrayed in the images? (Not shown on these pages are covers that did not include portraits.)

2. Study the covers closely, and see if it is possible to cluster or group them in any revealing ways. What patterns do you see? If it helps, choose pairs of covers to read closely and compare.

3. What design elements in these covers are consistent, which of them vary, and how would you describe the organization and style of these covers? What makes a *Rolling Stone* cover a *Rolling Stone* cover? How does it attract its potential readers?

COMPOSE

4. Use the covers from *Rolling Stone* to prompt your thinking about gender and body issues as markers of identity. What might the covers suggest about the relative power of men and women in popular music? Are men and women presented differently? Why might most of the group shots focus on all-male bands? Why do we see only a head shot of certain artists? Use the covers to prompt an essay on gender in popular culture, but read or use other sources too.

137

The Body Piercing Project

Josie Appleton
(2003)

> **FYI** Josie Appleton writes about politics and culture for spiked.com, an online journal based in London. She is author of *Museums for 'The People'?*, and has contributed to publications including the *Spectator* and *BBC History Magazine*.

The opening of a tattoo and piercing section in the up-market London store Selfridges shows that body modification has lost its last trace of taboo.

"Metal Morphosis," nestled in the thick of the ladies' clothing section, is a world away from the backstreets of Soho—where the company has its other branch. Teenagers, middle-aged women, men in suits and young guys in jeans flock to peer at the rows of tastefully displayed rings and leaf through the tattoo brochures.

Tattooist Greg said that he had seen a "broad variety" of people: "everything from the girl who turned 18 to the two Philippino cousins who just turned 40." The piercer, Barry, said that a number of "Sloanies" come for piercings (the most expensive navel bar retails at £3000, and there is a broad selection that would set you back several hundred pounds). A handful of women have even asked to be tattooed with the label of their favourite bottle of wine.[1]

This is not just affecting London high-streets. According to current estimates, between 10 and 25 percent of American adolescents have some kind of piercing or tattoo.[2] And their mothers are taking it up, too—in the late 1990s, the fastest growing demographic group seeking tattoo services in America was middle-class suburban women.[3]

But while tattoos have been taken up by university students and ladies who lunch, more traditional wearers of tattoos—sailors, soldiers, bikers, gangs—find themselves increasingly censured.

In June 2003, the police rejected an applicant because his tattoos were deemed to have an "implication of racism, sexism or religious prejudice."[4] The U.S. Navy has banned "tattoos/body art/brands that are excessive, obscene, sexually explicit or advocate or symbolize sex, gender, racial, religious, ethnic or national origin discrimination" and "symbols denoting any gang affiliation, supremacist or extremist groups, or drug use."[5]

New-style tattoos are a very different ball-game to their frowned-upon forebears. While the tattoos of football supporters, sailors and gang-members tend to be symbols of camaraderie or group affiliation, the Selfridges brigade are seeking something much more individual.

For some, tattoos and piercing are a matter of personal taste or fashion. "It's purely aesthetic decoration," said 37-year-old Sarah, waiting to get her navel pierced at Metal Morphosis. The erosion of moral censure on tattooing, and the increasing hygiene of tattoo parlors, has meant that body modification has become a fashion option for a much wider group of people.

For others, tattooing seems to go more than skin-deep. Tattoo artist Greg thinks that many of those getting tattoos today are looking for "self-empowerment"—tattoos, he says, are about establishing an "identity for the self." As a permanent mark on your body that you choose for yourself, a tattoo is "something no one will ever be able to take away from you," that allows you to say *"this is mine."*

Seventeen-year-old Laura said that she got her piercings done because she "wanted to make a statement." When she turned 18, she planned to have "XXX"

---

[1] "Ladies who lunch get a tattoo for starters," *London Times*, 18 June 2003.
[2] "Body piercing, tattooing, self-esteem, and body investment in adolescent girls," *Adolescence*, Fall 2002.
[3] *The Changing Status of Tattoo Art*, by Hoag Levins.
[4] "Police reject tattooed applicant," BBC News, 16 June 2003.
[5] "Navy draws a line on some forms of body piercing, ornamentation, tattoos," *Stars and Stripes*, European edition, 29 January 2003.

tattooed on the base of her spine, symbolising her pledge not to drink, smoke or take drugs. "It's not to prove anything to anyone else," she said; "it's a pact with myself completely."

Sue said that she had her navel pierced on her fortieth birthday to mark a turning point in her life. Another young man planned to have his girlfriend's name, and the dates when they met, tattooed on his arm "to show her that I love her"—and to remind himself of this moment. "The tattoo will be there forever. Whether or not I feel that in the future, I will remember that I felt it at the time, that I felt strong enough to have the tattoo."

The tattoos of bikers, sailors and gang-members would be a kind of social symbol that would establish them as having a particular occupation or belonging to a particular cultural subgroup. By contrast, Laura's "XXX" symbol is a sign to herself of how she has chosen to live her life; Sue pierced her navel to mark her transition to middle-age. These are not symbols that could be interpreted by anyone else. Even the man who wanted to get tattooed with his girlfriend's name had a modern, personal twist to his tale: the tattoo was less a pact to stay with her forever than to remind himself of his feelings at this point.

Much new-style body modification is just another way to look good. But the trend also presents a more profound, and worrying, shift: the growing crisis in personal identity.

In his book *Modernity and Self-Identity* (1991), sociologist Anthony Giddens argues that it is the erosion of important sources of identity that helps to explain the growing focus on the body.[6] Body modification began to really take off and move into the mainstream in the late 1980s and early 1990s. At around this time, personal and community relationships that previously helped to provide people with an enduring sense of self could no longer be depended upon. The main ideological frameworks that provided a system to understand the world and the individual's place in it, such as class, religion, or the work ethic, began to erode.

These changes have left individuals at sea, trying to establish their own sense of who they are. In their piercing or tattooing, people are trying to construct a "narrative of self" on the last thing that remains solid and tangible: their physical bodies. While much about social experience is uncertain and insecure, the body at least retains a permanence and reliability. Making marks upon their bodies is an attempt by people to build a lasting story of who they are.

Many—including, to an extent, Giddens—celebrate modification as a liberating and creative act. "If you want to and it makes you feel good, you should do it," Greg tells me. Web sites such as the Body Modification Ezine (BMEzine)[7] are full of readers' stories about how their piercing has completely changed their life. One piercer said that getting a piercing "helped me know who I am." Another said that they felt "more complete . . . a better, more rounded and fuller person."[8] Others even talk about unlocking their soul, or finally discovering that "I AM."

> Much new-style body modification is just another way to look good. But the trend also presents a more profound, and worrying, shift: the growing crisis in personal identity.

But what these stories actually show is less the virtues of body piercing than the desperation of individuals' attempts to find a foothold for themselves. There is a notable contrast between the superlatives about discovering identity and Being and the ultimately banal act of sticking a piece of metal through your flesh.

Piercings and tattoos are used to plot out significant life moments, helping to lend a sense of continuity to experience. A first date, the birth of a child, moving house: each event can be marked out on the body, like the notches of time on a stick. One woman said that her piercings helped to give her memory, to "stop me forgetting who I

---

[6]*Modernity and Self-Identity: Self and Society in the Late Modern Age*, by Anthony Giddens, 1991.

[7]Body Modification Ezine, www.bmezine.com.
[8]Quoted in *Body Modification*, ed. by Mike Featherstone, 2000.

am." They work as a "diary" that "no one can take off you."[9]

This springs from the fact that there is a great deal of confusion about the stages of life today. Old turning points that marked adulthood—job, marriage, house, kids—have both stopped being compulsory and lost much of their significance. It is more difficult to see life in terms of a narrative, as a plot with key moments of transition and an overall aim. Piercings and tattoos are used to highlight formative experiences and link them together.

Some also claim that body modification helps them to feel "comfortable in my own skin" or proud of parts of their body of which they were previously ashamed. The whole process of piercing—which involves caring for the wound and paying special attention to bodily processes—is given great significance. By modifying a body part, some argue that you are taking possession of it, making it truly yours. "The nipple piercings have really changed my relationship to my breasts," one woman said.[10]

This is trying to resolve a sense of self-estrangement—the feeling of detachment from experiences, the feeling that your life doesn't really belong to you. One young woman says how she uses piercing: "[It's been] done at times when I felt like I needed to ground myself. Sometimes I feel like I'm not in my body—then it's time."[11]

But piercing is trying to deal with the problem at the most primitive and brutal level—in the manner of "I hurt, therefore I am." The experience of pain becomes one of the few authentic experiences. It also tries to resolve the crisis in individual identity in relation to my breasts or my navel, rather than in relation to other people or anything more meaningful in the world.

Many claims are made as to the transformative and creative potential of body modification. One girl, who had just had her tongue pierced, writes: "I've always been kind of quiet in school and very predictable. . . . I wanted to think of myself as original and creative, so I decided I wanted something pierced. . . . Now people don't think of me as shy and predictable, they respect me and the person I've become and call me crazily spontaneous."[12]

Others say they use modification to help master traumatic events. Transforming the body is seen as helping to re-establish a sense of self-control in the face of disrupting or degrading experiences. One woman carved out a Sagittarius symbol on her thigh to commemorate a lover who died. "It was my way of coming to terms with the grief I felt," she said. "It enabled me to always have him with me and to let him go."[13]

> **In the absence of obvious social outlets for creativity, the individual turns back on himself and to the transformation of his own flesh.**

Here the body being modified is a way of trying to effect change in people's lives. It is the way to express creativity, find a challenge, or put themselves through the hoops. "I was ecstatic. I did it!," writes one contributor to BMEzine. Instead of a life project, this is a "body project." In the absence of obvious social outlets for creativity, the individual turns back on himself and to the transformation of his own flesh.

Body piercing expresses the crisis of social identity—but it actually also makes it worse, too. Focusing on claiming control over my body amounts to making a declaration of independence from everybody else.

People with hidden piercings comment on how pleased they were they had something private. One says: "I get so happy just walking along and knowing that I have a secret that no one else could ever guess!" Another said that they now had "something that peo-

---

[9] Quoted in *Body Modification*.
[10] Quoted in *The Body Aesthetic*, ed. by Tobin A. Siebers, 2000.
[11] *Body Piercing in the West: A Sociological Inquiry*, by Susan Holtham.

[12] "My beautiful piercing," on BMEzine.
[13] *The Customized Body*, by Ted Polhemus and Housk Randall, 2000.

ple could not judge me for, and something that I could hide." Another said that her piercing made her realize that "what other people say or think doesn't matter. The only thing that mattered at that moment was that I was happy with this piercing; I felt beautiful and comfortable in my own skin. . . . They remind me that I'm beautiful to who it matters . . . **me**."[14]

Body modification encourages a turn away from trying to build personal identity through relationships with others and instead tries to resolve problems in relation to one's own body. When things are getting rough, or when somebody wants to change their lives, the answer could be a new piercing or a new tattoo. There is even an underlying element of self-hatred here, as individuals try to deal with their problems by doing violence to themselves. As 17-year-old Laura told me: "You push yourself to do more and more. . . . You want it to hurt."

This means that the biggest questions—of existence, self-identity, life progression, creativity—are being tackled with the flimsiest of solutions. A mark on the skin or a piercing through the tongue cannot genuinely resolve grief, increase creativity, or give a solid grounding to self-identity. For this reason, body modification can become an endless, unfulfilling quest, as one piercing only fuels a desire for another. All the contributions to BMEzine start by saying how much their life has been changed—but then promptly go on to plan their next series of piercings. "Piercing can be addictive!" they warn cheerily.

Body modification should be put back in the fashion box. As a way of improving personal appearance, piercing and tattooing are no better or worse than clothes, makeup or hair gel. It is when body modification is loaded with existential significance that the problems start.

[14]All from BMEzine.

CONSIDER

1. Early in "The Body Piercing Project," Appleton distinguishes between tattoos that affirm group identities (among bikers, sailors, gangs) and fashionable tattoos that are supposed to be expressions of individuality. Do you accept this distinction? Does it apply to you or to people you know with tattoos or piercings?

2. The people Appleton cites offer a full list of reasons for modifying their bodies to heighten their sense of identity or commitment. Which of their reasons, if any, do you find most convincing?

3. Examine the photos of tattoos and piercings in Items 3.16 and 3.17. Do these images reinforce Appleton's characterizations of people who practice body modification, or do the pictures suggest a different story? Explain your position.

COMPOSE

4. In most respects, "The Body Piercing Project" is an example of a causal analysis, a type of argument that attempts to explain a phenomenon—in this case, the growing popularity of body modifications. Try your hand at writing a similar analysis relating to another current fad that might really be about issues of group or personal identity. Topics might include anything from clothing fads to trends in gaming, sports, personal Web sites or blogs, or anything that people use to express an aspect of their identity.

ITEM 3.16 ■ A. Ramey, *Holding Cell, Maricopa County Jail*

The Maricopa County Jail is located in the heart of Phoenix, Arizona. This photograph, taken in a holding cell at the jail, contains several markers of identity. From the prison uniforms to the tattoos etched in the inmates' skin to the shapes formed by the hands of many of the figures, we discover signs that represent people and culture.

CONSIDER

1. How would you characterize the tattoos on the inmates in the Maricopa Jail? Is it fair to say these tattoos represent markers of affiliation with a group rather than body art? Why or why not?

2. How would you construct a reading of *Holding Cell, Maricopa County Jail*? What focal points in the image stand out? How would you discuss the relationships among the setting, the figures, their clothing, their tattoos, and their identity?

3.2 | BODIES

ITEM 3.17 ■ Uwe Krejci, *Teenagers with Facial Piercings*

No doubt, people of all ages pierce or decorate their bodies, but is there something about the teenage years that lends itself to experimentation with identity? The teenagers in Item 3.17 seem to be offering a challenge, looking to express their individuality—at least on the surface.

CONSIDER

1. Other than piercings, what markers of identity can you find in the image? Is it possible that the expressions of the individuals represent aspects of their identities? How would you characterize each of the individuals in the image?

2. Is it fair to say the individuals in *Teenagers with Facial Piercings* are more similar than different? Why or why not? How would you compare this image with *Holding Cell, Maricopa County Jail*?

In the Kitchen

Henry Louis Gates Jr.
(1994)

> **FYI** Henry Louis Gates Jr., chair of the W.E.B. Du Bois Institute for African and African-American Research at Harvard University, has written a number of scholarly and popular books, among them his memoir *Colored People*, from which "In the Kitchen" is excerpted.

We always had a gas stove in the kitchen, in our house in Piedmont, West Virginia, where I grew up. Never electric, though using electric became fashionable in Piedmont in the sixties, like using Crest toothpaste rather than Colgate, or watching Huntley and Brinkley rather than Walter Cronkite. But not us: gas, Colgate, and good ole Walter Cronkite, come what may. We used gas partly out of loyalty to Big Mom, Mama's Mama, because she was mostly blind and still loved to cook, and could feel her way more easily with gas than with electric. But the most important thing about our gas-equipped kitchen was that Mama used to do hair there. The "hot comb" was a fine-toothed iron instrument with a long wooden handle and a pair of iron curlers that opened and closed like scissors. Mama would put it in the gas fire until it glowed. You could smell those prongs heating up.

I liked that smell. Not the smell so much, I guess, as what the smell meant for the shape of my day. There was an intimate warmth in the women's tones as they talked with my Mama, doing their hair. I knew what the women had been through to get their hair ready to be "done," because I would watch Mama do it to herself. How that kink could be transformed through grease and fire into that magnificent head of wavy hair was a miracle to me, and still is.

Mama would wash her hair over the sink, a towel wrapped around her shoulders, wearing just her slip and her white bra. (We had no shower—just a galvanized tub that we stored in the kitchen—until we moved down Rat Tail Road into Doc Wolverton's house, in 1954.) After she dried it, she would grease her scalp thoroughly with blue Bergamot hair grease, which came in a short, fat jar with a picture of a beautiful colored lady on it. It's important to grease your scalp real good, my Mama would explain, to keep from burning yourself. Of course, her hair would return to its natural kink almost as soon as the hot water and shampoo hit it. To me, it was another miracle how hair so "straight" would so quickly become kinky again the second it even approached some water.

My Mama had only a few "clients" whose heads she "did"—did, I think, because she enjoyed it, rather than for the few pennies it brought in. They would sit on one of our red plastic kitchen chairs, the kind with the shiny metal legs, and brace themselves for the process. Mama would stroke that red-hot iron—which by this time had been in the gas fire for half an hour or more—slowly but firmly through their hair, from scalp to strand's end. It made a scorching, crinkly sound, the hot iron did, as it burned its way through kink, leaving in its wake straight strands of hair, standing long and tall but drooping over at the ends, their shape like the top of a heavy willow tree. Slowly, steadily, Mama's hands would transform a round mound of Odetta kink into a darkened swamp of everglades. The Bergamot made the hair shiny; the heat of the hot iron gave it a brownish-red cast. Once all the hair was as straight as God allows kink to get, Mama would take the well-heated curling iron and twirl the straightened strands into more or less loosely wrapped curls. She claimed that she owed her skill as a hairdresser to the strength in her wrists, and as she worked her little finger would poke out, the way it did when she sipped tea. Mama was a southpaw, and wrote upside down and backward to produce the cleanest, roundest letters you've ever seen.

The "kitchen" she would all but remove from sight with a handheld pair of shears, bought just for this purpose. Now, the kitchen was the room in which we were sitting—the room where Mama did hair and washed clothes, and where we all took a bath in that galvanized tub. But the word has another meaning, and the kitchen that I'm speaking of is the very kinky bit of hair at the back of your head, where your neck meets your shirt collar. If there was ever a part of our African past that resisted assimilation, it was the kitchen. No matter how hot the iron, no matter how powerful the chemical, no matter how stringent the mashed-potatoes-and-lye formula of a man's "process," neither God nor woman nor Sammy Davis, Jr., could straighten the kitchen. The kitchen was permanent, irredeemable, irresistible kink. Unassimilably African. No matter what you did, no matter how hard you tried, you couldn't de-kink a person's kitchen. So you trimmed it off as best you could.

When hair had begun to "turn," as they'd say—to return to its natural kinky glory—it was the kitchen that turned first (the kitchen around the back, and nappy edges at the temples). When the kitchen started creeping up the back of the neck, it was time to get your hair done again.

■ ■ ■

Sometimes, after dark, a man would come to have his hair done. It was Mr. Charlie Carroll. He was very light-complected and had a ruddy nose—it made me think of Edmund Gwenn, who played Kris Kringle in "Miracle on 34th Street." At first, Mama did him after my brother, Rocky, and I had gone to sleep. It was only later that we found out that he had come to our house so Mama could iron his hair—not with a hot comb or a curling iron but with our very own Proctor-Silex steam iron. For some reason I never understood, Mr. Charlie would conceal his Frederick Douglass–like mane under a big white Stetson hat. I never saw him take it off except when he came to our house, at night, to have his hair pressed. (Later, Daddy would tell us about Mr. Charlie's most prized piece of knowledge, something that the man would only confide after his hair had been pressed, as a token of intimacy. "Not many people know this," he'd say, in a tone of circumspection, "but George Washington was Abraham Lincoln's daddy." Nodding solemnly, he'd add the clincher: "A white man told me." Though he was in dead earnest, this became a humorous refrain around our house—"a white man told me"—which we used to punctuate especially preposterous assertions.)

> **She claimed that she owed her skill as a hairdresser to the strength in her wrists, and as she worked her little finger would poke out, the way it did when she sipped tea.**

My mother examined my daughters' kitchens whenever we went home to visit, in the early eighties. It became a game between us. I had told her not to do it, because I didn't like the politics it suggested—the notion of "good" and "bad" hair. "Good" hair was "straight," "bad" hair kinky. Even in the late sixties, at the height of Black Power, almost nobody could bring themselves to say "bad" for good and "good" for bad. People still said that hair like white people's hair was "good," even if they encapsulated it in a disclaimer, like "what we used to call 'good.'"

Maggie would be seated in her high chair, throwing food this way and that, and Mama would be cooing about how cute it all was, how I used to do just like Maggie was doing, and wondering whether her flinging her food with her left hand meant that she was going to be left-handed like Mama. When my daughter was just about covered with Chef Boyardee Spaghetti-O's, Mama would seize the opportunity: wiping her clean, she would tilt Maggie's head to one side and reach down the back of her neck. Sometimes Mama would even rub a curl between her fingers, just to make sure that her bifocals had not deceived her. Then she'd sigh with satisfaction and relief: No kink . . . yet. Mama! I'd shout, pretending to be angry. Every once in a while, if no one was looking, I'd peek, too.

I say "yet" because most black babies are born with soft, silken hair. But after a few months it begins to turn, as inevitably as do the seasons or the leaves on

3 | IDENTITIES

145

a tree. People once thought baby oil would stop it. They were wrong.

Everybody I knew as a child wanted to have good hair. You could be as ugly as homemade sin dipped in misery and still be thought attractive if you had good hair. "Jesus moss," the girls at Camp Lee, Virginia, had called Daddy's naturally "good" hair during the war. I know that he played that thick head of hair for all it was worth, too.

My own hair was "not a bad grade," as barbers would tell me when they cut it for the first time. It was like a doctor reporting the results of the first full physical he has given you. Like "You're in good shape" or "Blood pressure's kind of high—better cut down on salt."

I spent most of my childhood and adolescence messing with my hair. I definitely wanted straight hair. Like Pop's. When I was about three, I tried to stick a wad of Bazooka bubble gum to that straight hair of his. I suppose what fixed that memory for me is the spanking I got for doing so: he turned me upside down, holding me by my feet, the better to paddle my behind. Little *nigger*, he had shouted, walloping away. I started to laugh about it two days later, when my behind stopped hurting.

When black people say "straight," of course, they don't usually mean literally straight—they're not describing hair like, say, Peggy Lipton's (she was the white girl on "The Mod Squad"), or like Mary's of Peter, Paul & Mary fame; black people call that "stringy" hair. No, "straight" just means not kinky, no matter what contours the curl may take. I would have done *anything* to have straight hair—and I used to try everything, short of getting a process.

Of the wide variety of techniques and methods I came to master in the challenging prestidigitation of the follicle, almost all had two things in common: a heavy grease and the application of pressure. It's not an accident that some of the biggest black-owned companies in the fifties and sixties made hair products. And I tried them all, in search of that certain silken touch, the one that would leave neither the hand nor the pillow sullied by grease.

I always wondered what Frederick Douglass put on *his* hair, or what Phillis Wheatley put on hers. Or why Wheatley has that rag on her head in the little engraving in the frontispiece of her book. One thing is for sure: you can bet that when Phillis Wheatley went to England and saw the Countess of Huntingdon she did not stop by the Queen's coiffeur on her way there. So many black people still get their hair straightened that it's a wonder we don't have a national holiday for Madame C. J. Walker, the woman who invented the process of straightening kinky hair. Call it Jheri-Kurled or call it "relaxed," it's still fried hair.

I used all the greases, from sea-blue Bergamot and creamy vanilla Duke (in its clear jar with the orange-white-and-green label) to the godfather of grease, the formidable Murray's. Now, Murray's was some *serious* grease. Whereas Bergamot was like oily jello, and Duke was viscous and sickly sweet, Murray's was light brown and *hard*. Hard as lard and twice as greasy, Daddy used to say. Murray's came in an orange can with a press-on top. It was so hard that some people would put a match to the can, just to soften the stuff and make it more manageable. Then, in the late sixties, when Afros came into style, I used Afro Sheen. From Murray's to Duke to Afro Sheen: that was my progression in black consciousness.

We used to put hot towels or washrags over our Murray-coated heads, in order to melt the wax into the scalp and the follicles. Unfortunately, the wax also had the habit of running down your neck, ears, and forehead. Not to mention your pillowcase. Another problem was that if you put two palmfuls of Murray's on your head your hair turned white. (Duke did the same thing.) The challenge was to get rid of that white color. Because if you got rid of the white stuff you had a magnificent head of wavy hair. That was the beauty of it: Murray's was so hard that it froze your hair into the wavy style you

> "So many black people still get their hair straightened that it's a wonder we don't have a national holiday for Madame C. J. Walker, the woman who invented the process of straightening kinky hair."

brushed it into. It looked really good if you wore a part. A lot of guys had parts *cut* into their hair by a barber, either with the clippers or with a straight-edge razor. Especially if you had kinky hair—then you'd generally wear a short razor cut, or what we called a Quo Vadis.

We tried to be as innovative as possible. Everyone knew about using a stocking cap, because your father or your uncle wore one whenever something really big was about to happen, whether sacred or secular: a funeral or a dance, a wedding or a trip in which you confronted official white people. Any time you were trying to look really sharp, you wore a stocking cap in preparation. And if the event was really a big one, you made a new cap. You asked your mother for a pair of her hose, and cut it with scissors about six inches or so from the open end—the end with the elastic that goes up to the top of the thigh. Then you knotted the cut end, and it became a beehive-shaped hat, with an elastic band that you pulled down low on your forehead and down around your neck in the back. To work well, the cap had to fit tightly and snugly, like a press. And it had to fit that tightly because it was a press: it pressed your hair with the force of the hose's elastic. If you greased your hair down real good, and left the stocking cap on long enough, *voilà*: you got a head of pressed-against-the-scalp waves. (You also got a ring around your forehead when you woke up, but it went away.) And then you could enjoy your concrete do. Swore we were bad, too, with all that grease and those flat heads. My brother and I would brush it out a bit in the mornings, so that it looked—well, "natural." Grown men still wear stocking caps—especially older men, who generally keep their stocking caps in their top drawers, along with their cufflinks and their see-through silk socks, their "Maverick" ties, their silk handkerchiefs, and whatever else they prize the most.

A Murrayed-down stocking cap was the respectable version of the process, which, by contrast, was most definitely not a cool thing to have unless you were an entertainer by trade. Zeke and Keith and Poochie and a few other stars of the high-school basketball team all used to get a process once or twice a year. It was expensive, and you had to go somewhere like Pittsburgh or D.C. or Uniontown—somewhere where there were enough colored people to support a trade. The guys would disappear, then reappear a day or two later, strutting like peacocks, their hair burned slightly red from the lye base. They'd also wear "rags"—cloths or handkerchiefs—around their heads when they slept or played basketball. Do-rags, they were called. But the result was straight hair, with just a hint of wave. No curl. Do-it-yourselfers took their chances at home with a concoction of mashed potatoes and lye.

The most famous process of all, however, outside of the process Malcolm X describes in his "Autobiography," and maybe the process of Sammy Davis, Jr., was Nat King Cole's process. Nat King Cole had patent-leather hair. That man's got the finest process money can buy, or so Daddy said the night we saw Cole's TV show on NBC. It was November 5, 1956. I remember the date because everyone came to our house to watch it and to celebrate one of Daddy's buddies' birthdays. Yeah, Uncle Joe chimed in, they can do shit to his hair that the average Negro can't even *think* about—secret shit.

Nat King Cole was *clean.* I've had an ongoing argument with a Nigerian friend about Nat King Cole for twenty years now. Not about whether he could sing—any fool knows that he could—but about whether or not he was a handkerchief head for wearing that patent-leather process.

Sammy Davis, Jr.'s process was the one I detested. It didn't look good on him. Worse still, he liked to have a fried strand dangling down the middle of his forehead, so he could shake it out from the crown when he sang. But Nat King Cole's hair was a thing unto itself, a beautifully sculpted work of art that he and he alone had the right to wear. The only difference between a process and a stocking cap, really, was taste; but Nat King Cole, unlike, say, Michael Jackson, looked *good* in his. His head looked like Valentino's head in the twenties, and some say it was Valentino the process was imitating. But Nat King Cole wore a process because it suited his face, his demeanor, his name, his style. He was as clean as he wanted to be.

I had forgotten all about that patent-leather look until one day in 1971, when I was sitting in an

Arab restaurant on the island of Zanzibar surrounded by men in fezzes and white caftans, trying to learn how to eat curried goat and rice with the fingers of my right hand and feeling two million miles from home. All of a sudden, an old transistor radio sitting on top of a china cupboard stopped blaring out its Swahili music and started playing "Fly Me to the Moon," by Nat King Cole. The restaurant's din was not affected at all, but in my mind's eye I saw it: the King's magnificent sleek black tiara. I managed, barely, to blink back the tears.

CONSIDER

1. What meanings are associated with the "kitchen" in Gates's essay? What is the effect of the ambiguity he creates with these multiple associations?

2. Gates describes the transformative effects of his discoveries about hair. Gates says, "From Murray's to Duke to Afro Sheen: that was my progression in black consciousness." What do you think these comments mean?

Bob Marley Performing in Stockholm, Sweden

FYI

ITEM 3.18 ■ Images of Bob Marley and Nat King Cole

If you've ever gotten a really bad haircut, you surely appreciate the role your hair plays in building your self-confidence and your sense of personal style. But you might not often think about the ways in which your hair connects you to larger cultural, racial, political, and even religious traditions. The images of Nat King Cole and Bob Marley demonstrate how these different aspects of identity converge in hairstyles.

Nat King Cole

> **CONSIDER**
>
> 1. What elements do you find most striking in the image of Bob Marley? Is it fair to say that Marley will be forever associated with his hair? Why or why not?
>
> 2. What is most striking to you about the image of Nat King Cole? How would you discuss the image in terms of Gates's "In the Kitchen"?
>
> 3. What kind of comparison could you develop between the image of Marley and the image of Cole in terms of identity? What could you discuss about the images themselves? What themes and contexts would you refer to outside of the images? Would you argue that the figures are more similar or different? Why?

Cluster 3.3
Groups and Ethnicities

Identity is clearly wrapped up in our stories and in the physical selves we inhabit. But who we are is also influenced by the groups we belong to as a result of our nationality, upbringing, or education; the race or ethnicity we are born into; the religion we inherit or choose; or the gender we inhabit. We base shared identities not only on our own inside groups but also in relation to others who remain outside them. We may arbitrarily associate certain characteristics with another group as a way of strengthening our own group identity—perhaps construing the other group's members as exotic, savage, or primitive.

While many of these affiliations have become stable markers of identity—think of the five or six checkboxes on any form asking for our ethnicity—closer examination shows that even these groups are composed of sub-groups and that affiliations are much more murky than we might suppose. For instance, class cuts across ethnicities and complicates notions of identity, and few, if any, of us can trace our roots back to a single, stable, category. Lan Tran's "Lone Stars" reveals just how tricky it can be to define something like ethnicity.

Further, many groups have risen to the level of stereotype or mythology, idealized conceptions that have little in common with the real individuals who make up these groups today. "I Hated Tonto (Still Do)" by Sherman Alexie relates the pervasive ways that stereotypes shape our beliefs about identity. Images like *Damn!* By Hulleah J. Tsinhnahjinnie or nineteenth-century photographs of Native Americans also ask us to think more deeply about the ways group identities are constructed and critiqued.

Further, identities are also shaped by more personal or informal group structures. Alice Walker's "Everyday Use" treats identity in terms of family structures, ancestry, tradition, and ethnic heritage. It's not surprising that works like these call for critical reading and response as we inquire further into the relationships between groups and identity.

Lone Stars

Lan Tran
(2005)

I am dressed like Texas. It is past my bedtime but I am moonstruck with the idea of being a cowgirl—after all, we live in the Lone Star State. There I am, slant eyes and a longhorn drawl, bowl-cut hair and a ten-gallon hat. I have converted my jump rope into a lasso. It hangs awkwardly around my waist. I stomp my rodeo boots and sing at my father:

> The stars at night are big and bright,
> Deep in the heart of Texas!

I go for volume, not melody. He is silent, as if he does not recognize me. I evolve from rice paddy to cow patty with this entire campfire repertoire from school, which I trot out every evening. Though I push him to, my father does not sing along. Yellow is for skin, not roses.

"*Di ngu di*," ("Go to bed.") he says, turning away.

"Aren't you going to clap?"

This is our nightly ritual. We are more than an ocean apart.

One night when I am five, my father does acknowledge me, even though we have guests. My mother is still at work when he says, "Little One, bring out the *tra*, then you can go play." He gestures at a large teapot filled with a dark herbal drink. It smells of pretty blossoms and earthy roots, but I make a sour face because I am painfully shy around strangers. Our living room is packed with Vietnamese college students who have come to hear my father discuss politics.

"Go," my father says, handing me a tray. I walk into the living room first, but he quickly moves around me to go to his seat. Everyone is focused on my father's words when he begins to speak. Before them he is another person. Though dressed plainly, as always, in brown pants and a simple white shirt, there is a charisma about him I do not often see. "We are not economic immigrants," he tells his audience. "We are political refugees." The students nod, listening raptly. My movements are an intrusion, so I nervously set the tray down and scurry back to the warmth of the kitchen. Behind me, my father's voice echoes, "We must remember our history."

History, I nod to myself, thinking of my homework. At school, we are learning about our proud Texan heritage and our assignment is to draw pictures reflecting that pride. In addition, we have been promised extra-credit stars if we bring in special projects. I have already earned a spangling row next to my name. I am a shameless hoarder of stars.

The previous night, I folded a paper pony for class. My teacher was charmed, so tonight I am determined to outdo myself. I am going to make a chuck wagon!

I take out a white sheet of paper, making careful folds to ensure the creases are sharp and precise. Through the door, I hear my father say, "We have lost our homeland and are marooned in a foreign country."

I sit, assessing my wagon. It needs something more. In the other room, my father is saying, "Until there is no more communism, there is no home to return to." A murmur rises from the students, the significance of which escapes me. Whenever I have asked my mother, "Why do these people have to come over and listen to Dad?" I have been told he has very important ideas. But it is all vague to me; the only thing I know is that Vietnam is extremely important to my father.

Vietnam . . . yes! I have the perfect idea for my chuck wagon project! Something to please both my teacher and my dad. I grab the red and yellow markers nearby and with a few quick strokes, I color the wagon's covering so it looks like the Vietnamese flag in my classroom atlas.

FYI Lan Tran writes fiction, poetry, and nonfiction. She is also a performer of her work and has appeared at the Lincoln Theater, the Ford Theater, and numerous off-Broadway venues. Her nonfiction reflections on her Vietnamese-American childhood have appeared in the collection, *Waking Up American*, from which the essay below is taken.

Now, I know the mini nylon banner on my father's desk looks different than the flag in the atlas—his flag is yellow, like our coloring, with three red horizontal stripes representing the lifeblood of Vietnam's northern, central, and southern regions. But the nylon banner is old, and I learned at school that flags can change. We Texans haven't always flown our current colors: red, white, and blue with a single star. During the Texas revolution, a white cotton flag was unfurled, with a black cannon and the words COME AND TAKE IT painted beneath. Naturally, I want my project to have the most up-to-date emblem of my father's homeland. I want to make something unforgettable.

When I finish coloring my special project, I continue drawing more pictures for school. A little later, my father comes in for more *tra*. "Are you having a good talk, Daddy?" He grunts to indicate its acceptability. "What are you talking about?" I ask him.

"*Chinh tri ve dat nuoc. Con chua hieu duoc,*" ("Political matters, our national landscape. You're too young to understand.") he answers.

"I know landscape," I protest, then show him my drawing of a cactus in the sun. "And look," I find another picture, "this is Texas." I hand him a purple outline of my beloved land.

My father regards the dark lines meant to convey the edges and boundaries of my home state. "*Nhung con co biet ve Viet Nam khong?*" ("But can you draw Vietnam?") he asks. I hold an uncapped marker in my right hand, hesitant. Is he really asking me to draw it? Though I have memorized the shape of Texas, the borders of Vietnam are hazy.

"*Yeu nuoc nhu vay,*" ("You're quite a patriot.") my father chides.

"I am a patriot," I say.

My father shakes his head, a certain gesture of his disappointment.

"*Con nghi con hieu long ai quoc?*" ("You think you know patriotism?")

I nod vigorously at first, remembering a recent field trip to the Alamo—our tour around the famous mission, we children wide-eyed at the stone church, the wooden barracks. And oh, the gift shop with the armadillo toys!

"Davy Crockett was a patriot," I say.

"*Con dau co biet.*" ("You have no idea what it means.") "*Ong noi con yeu nuoc,*" ("Your grandfather was a patriot.") he corrects me. He wags his finger slowly and deliberately—a wiper that sweeps my confidence away. "*Con khong biet Vietnam.*" ("You don't know Vietnam.")

I clench my fists, steaming. This is my father, a man to whom I can never give the right answers, to whom I am wrong because I am not Vietnamese enough.

When he turns his back, my eye catches the colored wagon beneath the other drawings. Maybe this will please him. While he gets more hot water, I lift the top napkin from the tea tray and place my chuck wagon beneath it. Moments later, my father carries the tray into the other room. I listen for sounds of approval, but instead I hear the tray slamming down and my name being yelled.

I walk into the living room slowly. There is a pool of liquid on the table where the tea has spilled, but my father is focused on something else.

"Little One, did you draw this?"

He holds up the chuck wagon—two of its wheels are soggy but it has the blood red covering I colored and is emblazoned with a lone star: golden, big, and bright. Everywhere I look, unfriendly eyes stare at me. I nod.

"Why?"

"Because it's the flag of Vietnam." There is a dark mumbling among the visitors, and they look at each other.

My father slams his palm on the coffee table, then lifts the chuck wagon higher, shaking it. "*Day la co cong san, con ve co giet hai nuoc!*" ("This is the flag of communist Vietnam! You have drawn the flag that murdered our homeland!") He points to the golden star. "This is *not* our flag!"

My father rips my chuck wagon in half. I am dismissed. The meeting ends.

In the silence of my room, I kick the wall. My sharp-toed boots leave a faint mark, which I bend to wipe off and then decide not to. Though my father's words incite deep longing in others—a vision of Vietnam free from communists—what I hear incites anger and shame in me. I am an activist's daughter, but from that moment on, I actively remain ignorant of his causes. For many

> "This is my father, a man to whom I can never give the right answers, to whom I am wrong because I am not Vietnamese enough."

years, I care more about Sam Houston than Saigon. I remember the Alamo. My father remembers Vietnam.

Three words. Dien Bien Phu. I am a college student when these words come for me, a mouthful of reprimand. In the dorms to let off steam during midterms, we are playing "Jeopardy" in teams. There are five of us on each team and the tie-breaking answer is, "In 1954, the French lost a major battle here to the Viet Minh. This led to the north-south partition of Vietnam along the 17th parallel."

My teammates cannot believe our luck. A Vietnamese history question! They don't even bother conferring, just hand me a fat felt pen to write down our answer. Someone pats me on the back.

Across from us, the other team is deep in a huddle, whispering and glancing at me nervously. They think I am speechless because I know the answer. The only thing I know is that the northern part went to the communists. "Hurry," a teammate whispers, "we're gonna kick some ass!" I write down "What is the DMZ?" because I once heard a Vietnam vet say he traveled there.

The other team's card reads, "What is Dien Bien Phu?" The winners jump up and down. My teammates stare at me openmouthed in disbelief.

"What the hell's wrong with you?" one of them finally asks.

I want to say, "Hey, I'm American," but I don't know anything about the U.S. in Vietnam either, except what I've seen in movies.

"You were five years old when a *what* traumatized you?"

I'm with my roommate, who's an editor for our school's African American paper, trying to explain why I'm not as in touch with my roots as she is.

"A chuck wagon," I mumble.

"A what?"

I thought she would be understanding, but the more I try to explain to her—

"A chuck wagon."

"How old are you?"

—the more I'm beginning to realize how foolish it all seems.

"I'm twenty."

"Exactly. That happened almost fifteen years ago. Don't you think it's time to let it go?" I just fidget, so she says, "I mean, my parents piss me off, too, but you don't see me tryin' to stop being black." When I don't respond, she shakes her head. "A chuck wagon."

Perhaps my grievance is outweighed by my ignorance.

"Dad, what happened in Vietnam?" It is winter break, months later, and I am home for the holidays.

"Happened when?" We are eating dinner together, and he does not look at me as he reaches for pieces of stuffed bitter melon.

"I don't know," I shrug, "how about the twentieth century?" There, I've admitted my ignorance; now he will be really annoyed. But he looks up, stops chewing, and then points his chopsticks at me and says, "Come with me."

"But we're eating...."

"It's more important," my father taps his temple, "that you consume this."

I follow him into the family room and watch as he roots around inside a tall, dark cabinet to bring out an old map of Vietnam. It crinkles with history as he unfolds it. The map is so old, a colonial relic, that our country is labeled *Indochine*.

"Here," my father points at an ambiguous landmass. "This is where the Chinese invaded centuries ago. And here," he indicates another region, "is where the French came in centuries later."

As we sit on the wool rug, I am struck by my father's patience. I thought he would be appalled at my ignorance—there were all those times as a child when he dismissed me with condescension. But tonight, it is as if he's been expecting my questions—has been expecting them for quite some time. "During the French occupation, my family and I had to dig a tunnel under our property and live there. One day, they torched our house. We sat beneath in the darkness, listening to the sounds of our home burning down. It was incredibly hot." He speaks slowly, but my mind races to capture all the details.

My father then narrates a timeline and, as he progresses, the names of historical figures begin bleeding into names of family. With each major battle, my father also recounts the death of one of our kin. "In the 1954 campaign against the French, your great uncle died," he says, or, "During a battle in '67 they bombed my cousin's school, killing him." I have never met these people; they are brittle leaves on our family tree, so at the mention of each name I ask, "Did you know him well?" or, "Were you close to him?"

My father nods vaguely each time and continues to describe a litany of events, each tied to another name and another and another until the distance between the past and present dissolves as each death draws closer and closer to my dad. From ancestor to great-grandfather to grandfather to his generation, at times he must grit his teeth to continue handing me this history of Vietnam: a heartbreaking tally of men he has known and loved. There are moments when I do not recognize the quaver in his voice. When he finishes, I am speechless. We do not look at each other, just stare at the map—its intimate curves indicating landmasses and waterways. If we could cry together, there would be tears enough to wash all the borders between the Alamo and Dien Bien Phu.

"There is something you should know . . . about your grandfather's death."

"How he fell? The train? Mom said it was a horrible accident."

"Well, he did fall, but it was no accident."

"Someone pushed him? Mom said—"

"Little One, your mother doesn't know this. Your grandfather originally fought with the Viet Minh for a free Vietnam but wanted to leave them when they unveiled their communist agenda. He thought he'd be safe in Hanoi, but they still went after him for 'crimes against the people.'"

"Even though he once fought with them?"

My father nods. "Your grandfather knew the communists were determined to find him guilty—which would also condemn his children—so for our freedom, he chose to kill himself. But he couldn't commit suicide outright, since that would be admitting guilt, so he faked it. It looked accidental, but your grandfather jumped to his death for your aunts, your uncle . . . and for me."

> **When he finishes, I am speechless. We do not look at each other, just stare at the map— its intimate curves indicating landmasses and waterways.**

My father now tears openly. I do not ask, "Were you close to him?" Instead I watch his hand trace the 17th parallel on the map, and I think of the imaginary line my grandfather crossed when he stepped off the platform. Instinctively my hand trails my father's and we brush over mountains and rivers as our fingers sweep, mine following his, across the page. Suddenly, my father stops. Why, I am uncertain. But as my hand approaches his, he reaches for mine. And when I look at him, he squeezes.

They say, too, that at the Alamo, when they knew they were out-numbered, Colonel Travis drew a line in the sand and said, "Anyone who's willing to die, cross this line!"

CONSIDER

1 What are your thoughts on the relationship between the narrator and her father in "Lone Stars"? Is it fair to say their relationship reflects typical tensions between parents and children? Why or why not?

2 How does the use of the Vietnamese language in "Lone Stars" influence your reading of the story? What other details in the work shed light on the connections between nationality and identity?

3 What is your take on hyphenated identities? How many sub-identities would it take to accurately reflect the identity of a member of a group? Would you argue that we have moved beyond the need to attach ethnic labels to ourselves? Why or why not?

COMPOSE

4 How do you interpret the last paragraph of "Lone Stars"? How does the ending of the piece relate to the narrator's ambiguity about her heritage? Write a short analysis in which you use the ending of "Lone Stars" as a lens for discussing issues of identity.

FYI

ITEM 3.19 ■ Matthias Clamer, *Young Men Entering Cowboy Saloon*

What preconceptions do we have about Westerns? In old-time films, the stereotypes abound—good guys, white hats, black hats, cowboys, evil outlaws. Then there's the classic scene in which the hero (or the scoundrel) walks into the saloon. Matthias Clamer's photograph of two men entering a cowboy saloon resonates with these clichés. Or does it?

CONSIDER

1. What group in *Young Men Entering Cowboy Saloon* stands out? How might you interpret the image in terms of stereotypes?

2. How does the composition of *Young Men Entering Cowboy Saloon* relate to its themes? What caption might you write for the image and why?

155

Everyday Use

Alice Walker
(1973)

> **FYI** Winner of the Pulitzer Prize for her 1983 novel *The Color Purple*, Alice Walker has long been a champion of civil rights and women's issues. Since the 1970s she has been publishing novels, short stories, poetry, and essays exploring African American culture and identity. "Everyday Use" first appeared in the collection of short stories *In Love and Trouble*, in 1973.

I will wait for her in the yard that Maggie and I made so clean and wavy yesterday afternoon. A yard like this is more comfortable than most people know. It is not just a yard. It is like an extended living room. When the hard clay is swept clean as a floor and the fine sand around the edges lined with tiny, irregular grooves, anyone can come and sit and look up into the elm tree and wait for the breezes that never come inside the house.

Maggie will be nervous until after her sister goes: she will stand hopelessly in corners, homely and ashamed of the burn scars down her arms and legs, eyeing her sister with a mixture of envy and awe. She thinks her sister has held life always in the palm of one hand, that "no" is a word the world never learned to say to her.

You've no doubt seen those TV shows where the child who has "made it" is confronted, as a surprise, by her own mother and father, tottering in weakly from backstage. (A pleasant surprise, of course: What would they do if parent and child came on the show only to curse out and insult each other?) On TV mother and child embrace and smile into each other's faces. Sometimes the mother and father weep, the child wraps them in her arms and leans across the table to tell how she would not have made it without their help. I have seen these programs.

Sometimes I dream a dream in which Dee and I are suddenly brought together on a TV program of this sort. Out of a dark and soft-seated limousine I am ushered into a bright room filled with many people. There I meet a smiling, gray, sporty man like Johnny Carson who shakes my hand and tells me what a fine girl I have. Then we are on the stage and Dee is embracing me with tears in her eyes. She pins on my dress a large orchid, even though she has told me once that she thinks orchids are tacky flowers.

In real life I am a large, big-boned woman with rough, man-working hands. In the winter I wear flannel nightgowns to bed and overalls during the day. I can kill and clean a hog as mercilessly as a man. My fat keeps me hot in zero weather. I can work outside all day, breaking ice to get water for washing; I can eat pork liver cooked over the open fire minutes after it comes steaming from the hog. One winter I knocked a bull calf straight in the brain between the eyes with a sledge hammer and had the meat hung up to chill before nightfall. But of course all this does not show on television. I am the way my daughter would want me to be: a hundred pounds lighter, my skin like an uncooked barley pancake. My hair glistens in the hot bright lights. Johnny Carson has much to do to keep up with my quick and witty tongue.

But that is a mistake. I know even before I wake up. Who ever knew a Johnson with a quick tongue? Who can even imagine me looking a strange white man in the eye? It seems to me I have talked to them always with one foot raised in flight, with my head turned in whichever way is farthest from them. Dee, though. She would always look anyone in the eye. Hesitation was no part of her nature.

"How do I look, Mama?" Maggie says, showing just enough of her thin body enveloped in pink skirt and red blouse for me to know she's there, almost hidden by the door.

"Come out into the yard," I say.

Have you ever seen a lame animal, perhaps a dog run over by some careless person rich enough to own a car, sidle up to someone who is ignorant enough to be kind to him? That is the way my Maggie walks. She has been like this, chin on chest, eyes on ground, feet in shuffle, ever since the fire that burned the other house to the ground.

Dee is lighter than Maggie, with nicer hair and a fuller figure. She's a woman now, though sometimes I forget. How long ago was it that the other house burned? Ten, twelve years? Sometimes I can still hear the flames and feel Maggie's arms sticking to me, her hair smoking and her dress falling off her in little black papery flakes. Her eyes seemed stretched open, blazed open by the flames reflected in them. And Dee. I see her standing off under the sweet gum tree she used to dig gum out of; a look of concentration on her face as she watched the last dingy gray board of the house fall in toward the red-hot brick chimney. Why don't you do a dance around the ashes? I'd wanted to ask her. She had hated the house that much.

I used to think she hated Maggie, too. But that was before we raised money, the church and me, to send her to Augusta to school. She used to read to us without pity; forcing words, lies, other folks' habits, whole lives upon us two, sitting trapped and ignorant underneath her voice. She washed us in a river of make-believe, burned us with a lot of knowledge we didn't necessarily need to know. Pressed us to her with the serious way she read, to shove us away at just the moment, like dimwits, we seemed about to understand.

Dee wanted nice things. A yellow organdy dress to wear to her graduation from high school; black pumps to match a green suit she'd made from an old suit somebody gave me. She was determined to stare down any disaster in her efforts. Her eyelids would not flicker for minutes at a time. Often I fought off the temptation to shake her. At sixteen she had a style of her own: and knew what style was.

I never had an education myself. After second grade the school was closed down. Don't ask my why: in 1927 colored asked fewer questions than they do now. Sometimes Maggie reads to me. She stumbles along good-naturedly but can't see well. She knows she is not bright. Like good looks and money, quickness passes her by. She will marry John Thomas (who has mossy teeth in an earnest face) and then I'll be free to sit here and I guess just sing church songs to myself. Although I never was a good singer. Never could carry a tune. I was always better at a man's job. I used to love to milk till I was hooked in the side in '49. Cows are soothing and slow and don't bother you, unless you try to milk them the wrong way.

I have deliberately turned my back on the house. It is three rooms, just like the one that burned, except the roof is tin; they don't make shingle roofs any more. There are no real windows, just some holes cut in the sides, like the portholes in a ship, but not round and not square, with rawhide holding the shutters up on the outside. This house is in a pasture, too, like the other one. No doubt when Dee sees it she will want to tear it down. She wrote me once that no matter where we "choose" to live, she will manage to come see us. But she will never bring her friends. Maggie and I thought about this and Maggie asked me, "Mama, when did Dee ever *have* any friends?"

She had a few. Furtive boys in pink shirts hanging about on washday after school. Nervous girls who never laughed. Impressed with her they worshiped the well-turned phrase, the cute shape, the scalding humor that erupted like bubbles in lye. She read to them.

When she was courting Jimmy T she didn't have much time to pay to us, but turned all her faultfinding power on him. He *flew* to marry a cheap city girl from a family of ignorant flashy people. She hardly had time to recompose herself.

When she comes I will meet—but there they are!

Maggie attempts to make a dash for the house, in her shuffling way, but I stay her with my hand. "Come back here," I say. And she stops and tries to dig a well in the sand with her toe.

It is hard to see them clearly through the strong sun. But even the first glimpse of leg out of the car tells me it is Dee. Her feet were always neat-looking, as if God himself had shaped them with a certain style. From the other side of the car comes a short, stocky man. Hair is all over his head a foot long and hanging from his chin like a kinky mule tail. I hear Maggie suck in her breath. "Uhnnnh," is what it sounds like. Like when you see the wriggling end of a snake just in front of your foot on the road. "Uhnnnh."

Dee next. A dress down to the ground, in this hot weather. A dress so loud it hurts my eyes. There are yellows and oranges enough to throw back the light of the sun. I feel my whole face warming from the heat waves it throws out. Earrings gold, too, and hanging down to her shoulders. Bracelets dangling and making noises when she moves her arm up to shake the folds of the dress out of her armpits. The dress is loose and flows, and as she walks closer, I like it. I hear Maggie go "Uhnnnh" again. It is her sister's hair. It stands straight up like the wool on a sheep. It is black as night and around the edges are two long pigtails that rope about like small lizards disappearing behind her ears.

"Wa-su-zo Tean-o!" she says, coming on in that gliding way the dress makes her move. The short stocky fellow with the hair to his navel is all grinning and he follows up with "Asalamalakim, my mother and sister!" He moves to hug Maggie but she falls back, right up against the back of my chair. I feel her trembling there and when I look up I see the perspiration falling off her chin.

"Don't get up," says Dee. Since I am stout it takes something of a push. You can see me trying to move a second or two before I make it. She turns, showing white heels through her sandals, and goes back to the car. Out she peeks next with a Polaroid. She stoops down quickly and lines up picture after picture of me sitting there in front of the house with Maggie cowering behind me. She never takes a shot without making sure the house is included. When a cow comes nibbling around the edge of the yard she snaps it and me and Maggie and the house. Then she puts the Polaroid in the back seat of the car, and comes up and kisses me on the forehead.

Meanwhile Asalamalakim is going through motions with Maggie's hand. Maggie's hand is as limp as a fish, and probably as cold, despite the sweat, and she keeps trying to pull it back. It looks like Asalamalakim wants to shake hands but wants to do it fancy. Or maybe he don't know how people shake hands. Anyhow, he soon gives up on Maggie.

"Well," I say. "Dee."

"No, Mama," she says. "Not 'Dee,' Wangero Leewanika Kemanjo!"

"What happened to 'Dee'?" I wanted to know.

"She's dead," Wangero said. "I couldn't bear it any longer, being named after the people who oppress me."

"You know as well as me you was named after your aunt Dicie," I said. Dicie is my sister. She named Dee. We called her "Big Dee" after Dee was born.

"But who was *she* named after?" asked Wangero.

"I guess after Grandma Dee," I said.

"And who was she named after?" asked Wangero.

"Her mother," I said, and saw Wangero was getting tired. "That's about as far back as I can trace it," I said. Though, in fact, I probably could have carried it back beyond the Civil War through the branches.

"Well," said Asalamalakim, "there you are."

"Uhnnnh," I heard Maggie say.

"There I was not," I said, "before 'Dicie' cropped up in our family, so why should I try to trace it that far back?"

He just stood there grinning, looking down on me like somebody inspecting a Model A car. Every once in a while he and Wangero sent eye signals over my head.

"How do you pronounce this name?" I asked.

"You don't have to call me by it if you don't want to," said Wangero.

"Why shouldn't I?" I asked. "If that's what you want us to call you, we'll call you."

"I know it might sound awkward at first," said Wangero.

"I'll get used to it," I said. "Ream it out again."

Well, soon we got the name out of the way. Asalamalakim had a name twice as long and three times as hard. After I tripped over it two or three times he told me to just call him Hakim-a-barber. I wanted to ask him was he a barber, but I didn't really think he was, so I didn't ask.

"You must belong to those beef-cattle peoples down the road," I said. They said "Asalamalakim" when they met you, too, but they didn't shake hands. Always too busy: feeding the cattle, fixing the fences, putting up salt-lick shelters, throwing down hay. When the white folks poisoned some of the herd the men stayed up all night with rifles in their hands. I walked a mile and a half just to see the sight.

Hakim-a-barber said, "I accept some of their doctrines, but farming and raising cattle is not my style." (They didn't tell me, and I didn't ask, whether Wangero [Dee] had really gone and married him.)

We sat down to eat and right away he said he didn't eat collards and pork was unclean. Wangero, though, went on through the chitlins and corn bread, the greens and everything else. She talked a blue streak over the sweet potatoes. Everything delighted her. Even the fact that we still used the benches her daddy made for the table when we couldn't afford to buy chairs.

"Oh, Mama!" she cried. Then turned to Hakim-a-barber. "I never knew how lovely these benches are. You can feel the rump prints," she said, running her hands underneath her and along the bench. Then she gave a sigh and her hand closed over Grandma Dee's butter dish. "That's it!" she said. "I knew there was something I wanted to ask you if I could have." She jumped up from the table and went over in the corner where the churn stood, the milk in it clabber by now. She looked at the churn and looked at it.

"This churn top is what I need," she said. "Didn't Uncle Buddy whittle it out of a tree you all used to have?"

"Yes," I said.

"Un huh," she said happily. "And I want the dasher, too."

"Uncle Buddy whittle that, too?" asked the barber.

Dee (Wangero) looked up at me.

"Aunt Dee's first husband whittled the dash," said Maggie so low you almost couldn't hear her. "His name was Henry, but they called him Stash."

"Maggie's brain is like an elephant's," Wangero said, laughing. "I can use the churn top as a centerpiece for the alcove table," she said, sliding a plate over the churn, "and I'll think of something artistic to do with the dasher."

When she finished wrapping the dasher the handle stuck out. I took it for a moment in my hands. You didn't even have to look close to see where hands pushing the dasher up and down to make butter had left a kind of sink in the wood. In fact, there were a lot of small sinks; you could see where thumbs and fingers had sunk into the wood. It was beautiful light yellow wood, from a tree that grew in the yard where Big Dee and Stash had lived.

After dinner Dee (Wangero) went to the trunk at the foot of my bed and started rifling through it. Maggie hung back in the kitchen over the dishpan. Out came Wangero with two quilts. They had been pieced by Grandma Dee and then Big Dee and me had hung them on the quilt frames on the front porch and quilted them. One was in the Lone Star pattern. The other was Walk Around the Mountain. In both of them were scraps of dresses Grandma Dee had worn fifty and more years ago. Bits and pieces of Grandpa Jarrell's paisley shirts. And one teeny faded blue piece, about the size of a penny matchbox, that was from Great Grandpa Ezra's uniform that he wore in the Civil War.

"Mama," Wangro said sweet as a bird. "Can I have these old quilts?"

I heard something fall in the kitchen, and a minute later the kitchen door slammed.

"Why don't you take one or two of the others?" I asked. "These old things was just done by me and Big Dee from some tops your grandma pieced before she died."

"No," said Wangero. "I don't want those. They are stitched around the borders by machine."

"That'll make them last better," I said.

"That's not the point," said Wangero. "These are all pieces of dresses Grandma used to wear. She did all this stitching by hand. Imagine!" She held the quilts securely in her arms, stroking them.

"Some of the pieces, like those lavender ones, come from old clothes her mother handed down to her," I said, moving up to touch the quilts. Dee (Wangero) moved back just enough so that I couldn't reach the quilts. They already belonged to her.

"Imagine!" she breathed again, clutching them closely to her bosom.

"The truth is," I said, "I promised to give them quilts to Maggie, for when she marries John Thomas."

She gasped like a bee had stung her.

"Maggie can't appreciate these quilts!" she said. "She'd probably be backward enough to put them to everyday use."

"I reckon she would," I said. "God knows I been saving 'em for long enough with nobody using 'em. I hope she will!" I didn't want to bring up how I had offered Dee (Wangero) a quilt when she went away to college. Then she had told me they were old-fashioned, out of style.

"But they're *priceless*!" she was saying now, furiously; for she has a temper. "Maggie would put them on the bed and in five years they'd be in rags. Less than that!"

"She can always make some more," I said. "Maggie knows how to quilt."

Dee (Wangero) looked at me with hatred. "You just will not understand. The point is these quilts, *these* quilts!"

"Well," I said, stumped. "What would *you* do with them?"

"Hang them," she said. As if that was the only thing you *could* do with quilts.

Maggie by now was standing in the door. I could almost hear the sound her feet made as they scraped over each other.

"She can have them, Mama," she said, like somebody used to never winning anything, or having anything reserved for her. "I can 'member Grandma Dee without the quilts."

I looked at her hard. She had filled her bottom lip with checkerberry snuff and it gave her face a kind of dopey, hangdog look. It was Grandma Dee and Big Dee who taught her how to quilt herself. She stood there with her scarred hands hidden in the folds of her skirt. She looked at her sister with something like fear but she wasn't mad at her. This was Maggie's portion. This was the way she knew God to work.

When I looked at her like that something hit me in the top of my head and ran down to the soles of my feet. Just like when I'm in church and the spirit of God touches me and I get happy and shout. I did something I never done before: hugged Maggie to me, then dragged her on into the room, snatched the quilts out of Miss Wangero's hands and dumped them into Maggie's lap. Maggie just sat there on my bed with her mouth open.

"Take one or two of the others," I said to Dee.

But she turned without a word and went out to Hakim-a-barber.

"You just don't understand," she said, as Maggie and I came out to the car.

"What don't I understand?" I wanted to know.

"Your heritage," she said. And then she turned to Maggie, kissed her, and said, "You ought to try to make something of yourself, too, Maggie. It's really a new day for us. But from the way you and Mama still live you'd never know it."

She put on some sunglasses that hid everything above the tip of her nose and chin.

Maggie smiled; maybe at the sunglasses. But a real smile, not scared. After we watched the car dust settle I asked Maggie to bring me a dip of snuff. And then the two of us sat there just enjoying, until it was time to go in the house and go to bed.

CONSIDER

1. How do the quilts function as a symbol of identity in the story? Is it fair to say the quilts represent specific aspects of identity, or do they serve to illustrate larger motifs about family and ethnicity?

2. What role do names play in the story? Would you agree with Dee that names given to African Americans by slave owners are associated with oppression? Why or why not?

CHALLENGE

3. How do you interpret the mother's decision regarding the quilts at the end? Hold a discussion with classmates in which you debate the merits of the decision.

3 | IDENTITIES

FYI

ITEM 3.20 ■ AIDS Quilt, Washington, DC

The AIDS Quilt project started in 1987 in San Francisco as an effort to memorialize victims of AIDS. Since then, the project has expanded into an international effort focusing on education and prevention of HIV/AIDS. The project continues to celebrate the memory of AIDS victims, consisting in 2008 of over 44,000 panels, each commemorating a life.

CONSIDER

1. What focal points can you pick out in AIDS Quilt, Washington, DC? What strikes you about the camera angle or framing of the image? How does the composition of the image help deliver its message?

2. What can be said about the identities represented in the image? Is it fair to say the image is primarily about gay men with AIDS? Why or why not?

Edward Curtis, *A Navaho*, c. 1904

Gertrude Käsebier, *Zitkala-Sa*, c. 1898

Edward Curtis, *White Duck*, c. 1908

ITEM 3.21 ■ Photographs of Native Americans

When you think of Native Americans, what images come to mind? And where did these images come from—movies, history books, cartoons? If they don't come from personal experience, chances are that your impressions may be influenced by turn-of-the-twentieth-century representations of American Indians like those created by Edward Curtis (1868–1952) and Gertrude Käsebier (1852–1934).

CONSIDER

1. What do you notice about Curtis's and Käsebier's choices of subject, focal point, arrangement, design elements, or details? What might these details suggest about how Curtis and Käsebier perceived their subjects' identities and cultures?

2. Partly because of the technical limitations of his equipment, Curtis sometimes staged images—posing the subjects and adding or removing items in order to focus on the details that he believed to be most culturally authentic. Does knowing this fact affect how you see his portraits? Does it affect your sense of how "real" his representations might be?

I Hated Tonto (Still Do)

Sherman Alexie
(1998)

> **FYI** — Sherman Alexie, winner of a PEN/Hemingway Award for Best First Book in 1992, has written prolifically about his experiences growing up on a Spokane Indian reservation in Washington. His work uses several different genres, including poetry, short stories, novels, film, and stand-up comedy.

I was a little Spokane Indian boy who read every book and saw every movie about Indians, no matter how terrible. I'd read those historical romance novels about the stereotypical Indian warrior ravaging the virginal white schoolteacher.

I can still see the cover art.

The handsome, blue-eyed warrior (the Indians in romance novels are always blue-eyed because half-breeds are somehow sexier than full-blooded Indians) would be nuzzling (the Indians in romance novels are always performing acts that are described in animalistic terms) the impossibly pale neck of a white woman as she reared her head back in primitive ecstasy (the Indians in romance novels always inspire white women to commit acts of primitive ecstasy).

Of course, after reading such novels, I imagined myself to be a blue-eyed warrior nuzzling the necks of various random, primitive, and ecstatic white women.

And I just as often imagined myself to be a cinematic Indian, splattered with Day-Glo Hollywood war paint as I rode off into yet another battle against the latest actor to portray Gen. George Armstrong Custer.

But I never, not once, imagined myself to be Tonto.

I hated Tonto then and I hate him now.

However, despite my hatred of Tonto, I loved movies about Indians, loved them beyond all reasoning and saw no fault with any of them.

I loved John Ford's *The Searchers*.

I rooted for John Wayne as he searched for his niece for years and years. I rooted for John Wayne even though I knew he was going to kill his niece because she had been "soiled" by the Indians. Hell, I rooted for John Wayne because I understood why he wanted to kill his niece.

I hated those savage Indians just as much as John Wayne did.

I mean, jeez, they had kidnapped Natalie Wood, transcendent white beauty who certainly didn't deserve to be nuzzled, nibbled, or nipped by some Indian warrior, especially an Indian warrior who only spoke in monosyllables and whose every movement was accompanied by ominous music.

In the movies, Indians are always accompanied by ominous music. And I've seen so many Indian movies that I feel like I'm constantly accompanied by ominous music. I always feel that something bad is about to happen.

I am always aware of how my whole life is shaped by my hatred of Tonto. Whenever I think of Tonto, I hear ominous music.

I walk into shopping malls or family restaurants, as the ominous music drops a few octaves, and imagine that I am Billy Jack, the half-breed Indian and Vietnam vet turned flower-power pacifist (now there's a combination) who loses his temper now and again, takes off his shoes (while his opponents patiently wait for him to do so), and then kicks the red out of the necks of a few dozen racist white extras.

You have to remember Billy Jack, right?

Every Indian remembers Billy Jack. I mean, back in the day, Indians worshiped Billy Jack.

Whenever a new Billy Jack movie opened in Spokane, my entire tribe would climb into two or three vans like so many circus clowns and drive to the East Trent Drive-In for a long evening of greasy popcorn, flat soda pop, fossilized licorice rope, and interracial violence.

We Indians cheered as Billy Jack fought for us, for every single Indian.

Of course, we conveniently ignored the fact that Tom Laughlin, the actor who played Billy Jack, was definitely not Indian.

After all, such luminary white actors as Charles Bronson, Chuck Connors, Burt Reynolds, Burt Lancaster, Sal Mineo, Anthony Quinn, and Charlton Heston had already portrayed Indians, so who were we to argue?

I mean, Tom Laughlin did have a nice tan and he spoke in monosyllables and wore cowboy boots and a jean jacket just like Indians. And he did have a Cherokee grandmother or grandfather or butcher, so he was Indian by proximity, and that was good enough in 1972, when disco music was about to rear its ugly head and bell-bottom pants were just beginning to change the shape of our legs.

When it came to the movies, Indians had learned to be happy with less.

We didn't mind that cinematic Indians never had jobs.

We didn't mind that cinematic Indians were deadly serious.

We didn't mind that cinematic Indians were rarely played by Indian actors.

We made up excuses.

"Well, that Tom Laughlin may not be Indian, but he sure should be."

"Well, that movie wasn't so good, but Sal Mineo looked sort of like Uncle Stubby when he was still living out on the reservation."

"Well, I hear Burt Reynolds is a little bit Cherokee. Look at his cheekbones. He's got them Indian cheekbones."

"Well, it's better than nothing."

Yes, that became our battle cry.

"Sometimes, it's a good day to die. Sometimes, it's better than nothing."

We Indians became so numb to the possibility of dissent, so accepting of our own lowered expectations, that we canonized a film like *Powwow Highway*.

When it was first released, I loved *Powwow Highway*. I cried when I first saw it in the theater, then cried again when I stayed and watched it again a second time.

I mean, I loved that movie. I memorized whole passages of dialogue. But recently, I watched the film for the first time in many years and cringed in shame and embarrassment with every stereotypical scene.

I cringed when Philbert Bono climbed to the top of a sacred mountain and left a Hershey chocolate bar as an offering.

I cringed when Philbert and Buddy Red Bow waded into a stream and sang Indian songs to the moon.

I cringed when Buddy had a vision of himself as an Indian warrior throwing a tomahawk through the window of a police cruiser.

I mean, I don't know a single Indian who would leave a chocolate bar as an offering. I don't know any Indians who have ever climbed to the top of any mountain. I don't know any Indians who wade into streams and sing to the moon. I don't know of any Indians who imagine themselves to be Indian warriors.

> "We Indians became so numb to the possibility of dissent, so accepting of our own lowered expectations, that we canonized a film like *Powwow Highway*."

■ ■ ■

Wait—

I was wrong. I know of at least one Indian boy who always imagined himself to be a cinematic Indian warrior.

Me.

I watched the movies and saw the kind of Indian I was supposed to be.

A cinematic Indian is supposed to climb mountains.

I am afraid of heights.

A cinematic Indian is supposed to wade into streams and sing songs.

I don't know how to swim.

A cinematic Indian is supposed to be a warrior.

I haven't been in a fistfight since sixth grade and she beat the crap out of me.

I mean, I knew I could never be as brave, as strong, as wise a visionary, as white as the Indians in the movies.

I was just one little Indian boy who hated Tonto because Tonto was the only cinematic Indian who looked like me.

CONSIDER

1. Alexie draws a distinction between the "cinematic Indians" he saw at the movies and the Native Americans who lived in his community. What differences does he identify? What do you think he means when he says that the "cinematic Indians" were the "Indians we were supposed to be"?

2. Alexie talks of the ways his reactions changed over time upon watching media representations of Native Americans. How have your perceptions of ethnicities and identity shifted as you've aged?

ITEM 3.22 ■ Hulleah J. Tsinhnahjinnie, *Damn!*, 1998

Collage represents a powerful form of expression because it can bring iconic images into relationship with one another to create new meanings. An image that seems straightforward can become complex through combination and arrangement with other items—an Oscar Mayer Wienermobile speaks volumes when juxtaposed with an American Indian and a short quotation.

CONSIDER

1. Compare *Damn!* by Hulleah J. Tsinhnahjinnie with Sherman Alexie's "Why I Hated Tonto (Still Do)." How does your reading of one text influence your interpretation of the other?

2. What message(s) do you take from *Damn!*? How does the composition of the image contribute to its message? What does this message about Native American culture and life tell us about issues of identity?

CHALLENGE

3. How do you think others view some of the groups that you belong to? Think about a group that contributes to your identity: a nationality, a religion, a profession, a lifestyle. Has your group been depicted in television, films, or other popular media? If so, how accurate do you think these representations are? Can you imagine an outsider capturing your group adequately in words or images? Can you point to someone who has done so?

Writing About Identity

You might find that writing about identity is more enjoyable than you first imagined. Even if you're a reluctant writer, there is something about people that can be fascinating. We often love to gossip about one another. Why not take it to the next level by formally composing your thoughts and sharing them with others? And you'll have many options to consider when it comes to expressing your thoughts about identity.

Your first concern is likely to be your **audience**. In many cases, writing about identity turns out to be a personal affair. Writing Project 3.1, for instance, asks you to compose a personal memoir. It might be that looking within leads you to discoveries you'd rather not share with others. You'll get no argument from us, and you should give yourself permission to write for yourself at times. But most of the writing you do about identity will be focused outward, toward an audience. Writing about public figures, for instance, often aims at an audience of general readers interested in the person under discussion. A magazine piece on Johnny Depp assumes a broad range of readers probably familiar with the actor and his movies, but perhaps not aware of the details of his personality and background. So writing about identity can sometimes be very private but also highly public.

Your own writing projects will likely fall somewhere between these extremes, depending on other aspects of your **writing situation**. Your assignments and your own sense of **purpose** will no doubt determine a good deal about how you proceed. You might be asked to develop a cultural critique like that of Susan Bordo (pages 129–135). You probably will need to conduct a fair amount of research to draw conclusions about your topic. And you'll have to key in to the **contexts** surrounding the work you're taking up—you'd be hard pressed to think about online representations of identity without considering virtual environments like World of Warcraft or Second Life. But your own sense of identity and your status as an **author** will also shape the work you do. You might have personal experience with hyphenated ethnicities or an organization with a strong group identity. This background will inform your thinking and in some ways determine the avenues you pursue as you write about identity.

You'll also have many choices to make about **genre** and **medium**. Yes, you can compose essays about identity, but you can also express identity through the development of a Facebook or MySpace page. Indeed, the possibilities call for serious decision making and can lead to some interesting opportunities. An image like *Damn!* (page 165), for instance, uses some simple moves with an image editor to say something about identity. The figure of the Native American is cropped and pasted over the background image of the Oscar Mayer Wienermobile and then a caption is added with text. The possibilities for making statements about identity by using such juxtapositions are exciting—a Barbie in a homeless shelter, a preppie in a biker bar, Einstein judging *American Idol*. Other choices you make about genre

WRITING ABOUT IDENTITY

and media will be more specific. Billy Smith's essay (pages 173–178) integrates images into his discussion of photographer Gordon Parks. The essay calls for careful thinking about how words and images come together.

You'll also need to think about the **details** of how you develop your compositions about identity. In many instances, you'll want to think about how readers will move through the information you provide. Lan Tran's "Lone Stars" (pages 151–154), for instance, weaves together a number of episodes to give us a sense of her experiences with identity. In the process, she employs a number of narrative strategies. She creates a sense of setting and brings the figures in her essay to life through details and dialog that move the essay along and give us insight into the characters and their identity. By combining aspects of storytelling with strategies like providing careful descriptions, writing can bring into focus aspects of individuals.

And you'll need to employ strategies of **invention** and **revision** to create your compositions about identity. Before beginning, you can generate ideas and organize your thoughts (see Chapter 2). You'll want to share drafts of your work with others, collect feedback, and then revise based on their suggestions. You'll have to attend to the formal elements of your compositions, documenting sources, editing for clarity, and otherwise polishing what you create. All of this work should serve to help you and your readers think about concerns of identity. Your task is to explore the numerous questions about identity and the multiple facets and connections that come together to make us who we are.

Project 3.1

Composing a Personal Memoir

A memoir assignment can be both the good news and the bad news for a writer. Because the source for the writing is personal experience, anyone can compose a memoir, and you can get started right away. But, since you're charged with making aspects of your life interesting for others, you must translate your own experiences into writing that is meaningful on several levels. For this project, compose a three- to five-page essay in which you explore an event or experience. Concentrate on creating a personal reflection that speaks to larger concerns likely to be shared by your readers. For instance, rather than simply recounting an embarrassing second grade moment, use that moment to explore issues of insecurity, peer pressure, or teacher/student relationships. As you work, also be selective in the information you choose to include. Most memoir essays use a single event or a limited set of episodes, but include episodes that illustrate larger themes. You'll also want to be deliberate about including details and elements of narrative (see Chapter 2) to engage the interests of readers. You may want to also include relevant images to bring the memoir to life.

Before you begin, take a look at "Uncle Duane" on the following pages to see how student writer Allen Shannon approached this task.

STUDENT PROJECT
Allen Shannon, "Uncle Duane"

Shannon 1

Allen Shannon
Prof. Anderson
English 102
22 March 2008

Uncle Duane

First-person perspective reflects the personal nature of the memoir.

My mother always told and retold stories about her family. She had two brothers and two sisters. I, being an only child, loved the stories about my mother's large family. I knew all of my aunts and uncles except for one, my Uncle Duane. Mom seldom shared his story, I think because it broke her heart to do so. It seemed like I pestered her for years, but she would just say matter-of-factly that tragedies happen to people all the time and it's better to focus on the here and now.

Then one night during my senior year in high school, just as I was about to head out for my first college visit, Mom opened up about her brother. She sat across from me at Jade Garden, our favorite Chinese restaurant, as I babbled on about SAT scores and minimum GPAs. "Allen," she interrupted. "I want to tell you something about your Uncle Duane."

The use of dialogue helps move the narrative along.

"Okay, Mom." I knew enough to close my mouth and open my ears.

Mom went on, "I don't know if I can tell you his whole story." She lifted the lid from the ceramic tea pot on the table and lowered in two bags of green tea. "I really just have fragmented images myself."

***

She described it as a movie preview with short clips. Clips with no ending, no beginning, just snippets of unconscious maneuverings. The first swatch of thought is Uncle Duane buying his wife a car with a good transmission, one that would run from Wyoming to New Mexico. The second image is his dog, who he usually took on the road with him when he drove the 200 miles from Basin to Greenriver. The third fragment is Uncle Duane on the phone, trying to call his mom, my grandmother. He's just about to drive that 200 mile distance to go to work in a factory that makes diapers. My grandmother's not at home, so he leaves a message. That message would later be talked about and listened to by my mother

168 WRITING ABOUT IDENTITY

Shannon 2

and her siblings for many painful hours. Duane hops into his truck, sans the dog, and takes off on the last trip of his life.

Mom's brother was a simple guy. He loved to hunt, fish, and spend hours in his workshop creating beautiful things. He was also an inventor. He made a weird looking gadget that would extract metal posts from the ground. For those people who live in the east this won't make sense. But in the west, ranchers use metal posts to mark off their property, then they fence the area with barbed wire which is strung tight and connected to the post. Every now and then you have to move a fence and getting that metal post out of the ground can be a bugger. My mom's brother took an old car jack and invented and patented a device that can do the job in a few simple steps.

— The use of details brings the narrative to life.

When my mom was seventeen she moved to California and on one temperate summer day, Duane came to visit. He was also living in California, but more to the north. They had not seen each other in about a year. At one point in Duane's life he'd been a biker. Mom described his bushy beard and long hair, flying as he rode his motorcycle with extended forks that made his chopper look just like those guys on *Easy Rider*. Mom said it wasn't so much that Duane took to the road to find himself, but to free himself. He never quite fit with the "in" crowd. He was running away from a troubled childhood and the little hick town that never accepted him. My mom's parents had divorced and the entire family had fallen apart. She described it as a bomb that dropped, blowing the family apart, and scattering shattered little pieces all over the country. She and Duane landed in California. Their lunch together was semi-silent. They tried to fill the uneasy gaps with a few shared family moments, but they were both empty and vacant as the California desert. Neither could verbalize their loneliness nor bridge the vast chasm between them.

— Similes and metaphors engage the reader with the subject of the memoir.

On the way down from Bakersfield my uncle's tire had popped and he'd hitch-hiked all the way to Long Beach from the outskirts of LA. He'd gone to a motorcycle store and was able to get the tire patched, but he needed a ride back to where he'd stashed his bike. My mom had a friend with a car and they drove through LA. Mom marveled how her brother ever

Shannon 3

found the spot where his chopper was hidden. But in the dark on a non-descript freeway, her brother knew exactly where to go. The bike was hidden in some bushes along I-5. "For a guy who could barely read and transposed his numbers," mom said, "he whipped the tire back on in a matter of minutes and was ready to be on his way. He was like that though. He could study anything mechanical, take it apart, then, reassemble it without a hitch." Mom reaches across the table, picks up the tea pot and pours the steaming liquid into each of our cups. "When he rode off, his hair whipped behind him. No helmet, of course. Just the growl of his chopper fading into the night. I cried driving back into LA. I just ached inside for both of our empty souls. We had grown up in the same family, but really didn't know each another. We were still strangers."

> **The memoir uses specific episodes to offer broader insights.**

My mom quit California and moved back to New Mexico to go to college. She seldom heard from, or saw her brother. But one night out of nowhere Uncle Duane appeared on her doorstep. It was a visit much like the one in California, only this time her brother was in a cast from his waist to his neck. He'd been in a bad motorcycle accident. He and his girlfriend, Drifty, had gotten behind an old truck with a load of crap in the back. The truck had slowed and when Duane sped up to go around, the truck turned right in front of him. No blinker, no warning, just a quick turn to the left. The bike slid to the ground and he slid with it, but Drifty didn't make it. She slid under the truck and died instantly. My mom said the gulf between them was even wider and she didn't know how to talk to her brother about the death of his girlfriend. That same vacant and lost feeling invaded her heart, but between them there was more silence. Tears brimmed my mother's eyes as she whispered. "I had no idea how to comfort him in his pain."

Mom wipes the back of her thumb across one, and then the other eye. "Then things got better. Duane settled down and decided to get married. He'd bought a beautiful bit of acreage in Basin, Wyoming. When his son was born he became a new man. He took your cousin fishing, taught him how to whittle and gave him every bit of the love and affection that he himself had been denied by my father. He finally had gotten the things he deserved."

***

Shannon 4

I actually have my own memories of the next part of the story. My dad was going to graduate school in Texas. We had only lived there a few months and Mom and Dad had taken me out for a walk in the neighborhood. When we got back my mom had a message on the answering machine. It was her dad and it was urgent. She returned the call.

Duane had left Basin to drive to Greenriver—to go to work. Later, after speaking with his wife, he'd had a premonition, so his daily tasks took on a precautionary note. He bought the reliable car; a nice, "good runnin'" Buick. He wouldn't allow the dog along this one time. And ... he made one last call to his mom.

On the road to Greenriver my Uncle Duane followed a short distance behind another vehicle. They were traveling at a safe speed. Coming toward them, from the other direction, was a big welding truck, speeding. The truck in front of my uncle made it by the welding truck. The woman who was in that truck later said in court she noticed the welding truck weaving. As it passed them she turned and saw it cross into my uncle's lane. Welding trucks weigh anywhere from ten to twelve thousand pounds, and as this one swerved it hit the driver's side of Uncle Duane's Ford F-150 with such impact that the cab was blown apart and my uncle thrown out. My mother said Duane never wore a seat belt (because her father, with all of his *good* advice, convinced her brother and other members of the family they were useless). The guy in the welding truck was so drunk he never knew what happened. He barely got a scratch.

Mom fidgets with the edge of her tea cup, then looks up and smiles. "I'm not sure why I'm telling you this now." She reaches across the table and takes my hands in hers. "He didn't fit in, but I loved him regardless," she says. "I just wanted you to know that people, sometimes everything, is just hard to sort out."

Mom seems at a loss, but I understand. Uncle Duane was a fisherman, a hunter. He was rough around the edges, but deep down a good person with a good heart. Uncle Duane had come to know who he was, and he had finally found happiness. He'd grown into a person who lived for others—one who even with premonitions clouding his heart, provided the car, saved the dog, and, in the end, longed for one last conversation with his mother.

> **Memories maintain the personal focus and move the narrative along.**

Project 3.2

Researching and Profiling an Artist

This assignment asks you to create a researched portrait of a well-known artist, focused on explaining how his or her work responds to particular social issues. For example, when you encountered the photo *Drought Refugees. . . .* on page 97, perhaps you were curious about how it fit into photographer Dorothea Lange's larger body of work: Did she take other photographs related to the Great Depression? Do her photographs share common themes or design choices? What events in her life motivated her to document such scenes? What was the contribution of her work to public awareness of poverty? These are exactly the sorts of questions that can be asked about any artist's work—and they're the kinds of questions your project will address.

Depending on your instructor's preference, your profile may take the form either of a three- to five-page MLA-style essay or a multimedia exploration. (Ask your instructor for details.) Whichever form your project takes, you should strive to include at least two images or examples of your subject's work.

Before getting started, take a look at Billy Smith's paper (pages 173–178), which was produced in response to this assignment. You may also want to refer to the writing instruction in Chapter 2.

STUDENT PROJECT

Billy Smith, "Gordon Parks: Using Photographs to Spark Social Change"

While reading this paper, you can view many of the photographs Smith analyzes by visiting http:www.masters-of-photography.com/P/parks.html.

Smith 1

Billy Smith
Professor Strong
Composition 101
23 June 2008

Gordon Parks: Using Photographs to Spark Social Change

In America, it is quite possible to live in a cocoon, oblivious to the world around you. Confined living situations and close-knit social structures can prevent an individual from ever experiencing a reality outside of his or her own. Through an artistic medium such as photography, though, one can get a glimpse of a world far removed. Gordon Parks, photographer, artist, and writer, was a liaison between those Americans in one world and their fellow citizens who subsisted in a completely different one. Parks's work as an artist during the 1940s, '50s, and '60s revealed a population suffering from poverty, prejudice, and racism. Through his illustrative portrayals of Americans bearing the burdens of hardship, Parks opened the eyes of policymakers and voters alike and helped to jump-start a movement for improved social conditions.

Gordon Parks, an African American, was born in Fort Scott, Kansas, in 1912. Working at jobs ranging from dining car waiter to semiprofessional basketball player, Parks got his big break in 1942 when he began taking photographs for the Farm Security Administration. The move that brought him into the national spotlight, though, was his addition later that year to the staff of Life magazine. Parks would eventually find success as a novelist and poet, a musical composer, and a film director-producer (Shaft, The Learning Tree). However, it was during his tenure taking photographs for Life that Parks was really able to display his talent as an artist while simultaneously expanding cultural awareness of social ills.

From a historical standpoint, Gordon Parks found himself in a volatile period in American history. At the start of his professional career, the nation was consumed by World War II. After the war, much of the nation was enjoying the peace and prosperity of the 1950s. Parks, however, was examining the people who weren't reveling in postwar glory. Parks sought

Smith 2

out the laborers, the underpaid, underfed, underhoused, and underrepresented (see fig. 1). As the 1960s approached, the nation began to quiver with the tension of the civil rights movement. People like Malcolm X and Martin Luther King Jr. were constantly in the spotlight. Parks chose to exploit the abundance of prolific artistic material not so much to further his professional career. Rather, he also used his medium to portray the conflicts and struggles in American society during his lifetime, to tell the stories of people who were barely surviving in the boiler rooms and alleyways of America and of those whose faces were as recognizable as the flag itself.

Post–World War II America was a fascinating time to be shooting pictures. Before and during the war, most journalists focused on relaying news-related topics. Photographs were supplements to factual information, often grave war-related matters, to be printed in a news magazine or newspaper. After the war, though, people were less concerned with affairs of life or death and had the leisure time to become interested in their fellow Americans. Thus was born the human interest story. By highlighting a particular person or group, journalists could play on familiar and desirable themes such as heroics, love, hate, suffering, and triumph. Life magazine

Fig. 1. Sea Food Worker (Library of Congress, 1944).

was a significant member of this new guard of personal journalism. As a staff member of Life, Parks was trained in this new photographic style, and much of his work reflected this concentration on the human condition. At the time, it was important for photographers to distinguish their work along certain themes. Parks, not surprisingly, found his artistic passion in portraying social situations through American people, especially African Americans.

Possibly Parks's most memorable contribution to the artistic community was his piece titled American Gothic (see fig. 2). The image depicts a woman named Ella Watson, armed with a mop and a broom, staring directly at the camera with a large American flag in the background. Watson, a person Parks came to know through a colleague, had struggled through life while trying to support her children and grandchildren on a meager salary. The photograph conveys Watson's intensity and strength, and the viewer can see the suffering and determination in the woman's eyes. The shot mirrors a classic American painting by the same name, a choice Parks made in an effort to heighten the drama of the piece. With the flag behind her, Watson stands as a symbol of an America that is so foreign to the upper classes, an America that does not embrace all of its children.

Growing up as a black man in a ferociously segregated world, Parks's artwork served as an avenue for his feelings about race relations and the social circumstances of many blacks in America. Parks himself worked

Fig. 2. American Gothic (Library of Congress, 1944).

Smith 4

hard to overcome the barriers to his own success and ended up being financially comfortable. However, he focused a substantial part of his work on those African Americans who had not been so lucky, who were struggling just to make it to the next day. Such examples would be his pieces Muslim Schoolchildren (1963) and Family in Birmingham, Alabama (1956). Parks was torn by the poor conditions in which these people found themselves, but he also wrestled with how best he could help them. "I see some kid up there who cannot appreciate the distance that I have come. He is still poor. He's still cold. He's still hungry, and he's still being discriminated against" (Harris 64). Parks used his powers as a photographer to demonstrate the hardships of these people.

The "interest" in the human interest story was not limited to just those who were barely surviving. Parks also portrayed prominent figures in society, often African American, as another way to fight racial segregation and the poor conditions of many blacks at the time. For example, people like Duke Ellington (see fig. 3), Muhammad Ali, Malcolm X, and Pastor Ledbetter of Chicago were all successful black Americans. Parks wanted to use the fame of these people, as well as his own prominent status, to inspire younger African Americans to not settle for a poor start in life. As Parks was once quoted concerning his own accomplishments in a segregated world, "I could not be hampered by racism and what racism does to people. I refused to accept it. I ignored it. I walked around it" (Harris 69). Parks hoped that his tenacity and drive would be an example

Fig. 3. Duke Ellington (Library of Congress, 1944).

for other young people to not use race as a crutch but to work harder to overcome it.

    From high atop the mountain of wealth and comfort, it is difficult to see those who toil at the mountain's base. Gordon Parks made it his life's work to bridge that gap, to capture a moment in time on film and then display that moment to the rest of the nation, who undoubtedly weren't there to see it first hand. Being fortunate enough to publish in a well-read magazine like Life, Parks had access to an audience that was vast and varied, and his messages could be poignant and insightful. Though he was able to open the eyes of many Americans to the troubles of their compatriots, Parks was constantly torn by the idea that he could not do more. "Disillusionment sinks in when in the end you must leave the inhabitants of these places to their own fate, and that was always the case" (Bush 87). Ultimately, Gordon Parks felt that his role in advancing social change was to simply take the photographs. If he could bring to the attention of those with political power the nation's bruised and beaten, tired and hungry, abused and mistreated, perhaps the powerful could take the necessary initiatives to assist these people. And if Parks could bring to the attention of the poor and forgotten those figures who had risen from similar standing, despite racism and elitism, to take their own place at the top of the mountain, perhaps the poor would never give up hope of making it in America.

Smith 6

Works Cited

Bush, Martin H. The Photographs of Gordon Parks. Wichita: Wichita State UP, 1983.

"Gordon Parks" Masters of Photography. 2004. 10 June 2005 <http://www.masters-of-photography.com/P/parks/parks.html>.

Harris, Mark Edward. Faces of the Twentieth Century: Master Photographers and Their Work. New York: Abbeville, 1998.

Parks, Gordon. Half Past Autumn. Boston: Bullfinch, 1997.

Tausk, Peter. Photography in the 20th Century. London: Focal, 1980.

Project 3.3

Create a collage that combines words and images to express an aspect of your identity. Your collage should include at least four visual images of any kind—family photos, drawings, illustrations from books or magazines, images downloaded from the Web, and so on. It should also incorporate at least one word, but no more than one sentence, of text. Depending on your instructor's preference, you should either (1) turn in a hard copy of your collage or (2) post your collage on the Web. (Ask your instructor for details.)

Project 3.4

Create an online journal where you chronicle your experiences and share insights about your identity. Find an online blog hosting site (blogger and wordpress are good candidates), and create a personal blog. Select a name for your blog that reflects an aspect of your personality. Create an "About" page that tells readers something about yourself and your blog. Modify the appearance of your blog to reflect your tastes. Compose regular blog postings detailing your thoughts and experiences.

Project 3.5

Create a mock-up of an online profile page for a well-known individual. Imagine the page as a Facebook or MySpace profile with links to favorite applications, friends, wall postings, status messages, favorites, and so on. First, consider the identity of the subject of your profile. What adjectives might describe the individual? What activities might be associated with him or her? What episodes are significant in the person's life? What perspectives should guide your development of the profile? Next, using paper and drawing tools or an image editor, create a sketch of the profile page. As an alternative, compose a brief essay describing the profile page and explaining its elements.

CHAPTER 4

PLACES AND ENVIRONMENTS

ITEM 4.1 ■ Terry Falke, *Trail to Balanced Rock*, 1996

Browse a bookstore, and you'll usually find a counter near the front displaying coffee-table books full of eye-catching images. Terry Falke's *Trail to Balanced Rock* (Item 4.1) comes from just such a collection, a book of landscapes entitled *Observations in an Occupied Wilderness*. Similar anthologies record every imaginable spot on the planet, from the plains of the Serengeti to the ballparks of America.

But Falke is no casual observer: he brings a critical perspective to his presentation of iconic American places, as the title of his book suggests. Look at *Trail to Balanced Rock* carefully. Highlighted in golden sunlight, a spectacular rock formation from Arches National Park dominates the upper half of the image. People yearn for such open, untouched environments. Or do they? The lower and darker half of Falke's image offers a contrary point of view: fussy National Park signs and a smooth trail humble the startling monument. Nature seems defiled and lessened by these human impositions. As Falke presents it, the scene becomes ironic, even embarrassing.

How far can we go? Maybe we don't need nature at all. Item 4.2 displays the workings of an emerging technology called Photosynth, which can knit vast numbers of individual photographs of a scene into a coherent 3-D image, an alternative reality. Single shots disappear into a collective version of experience different from Falke's poignant take on Arches National Park. With Photosynth, any spot on the planet can be instantly reassembled and viewed. Why travel the globe when you can explore it with a computer?

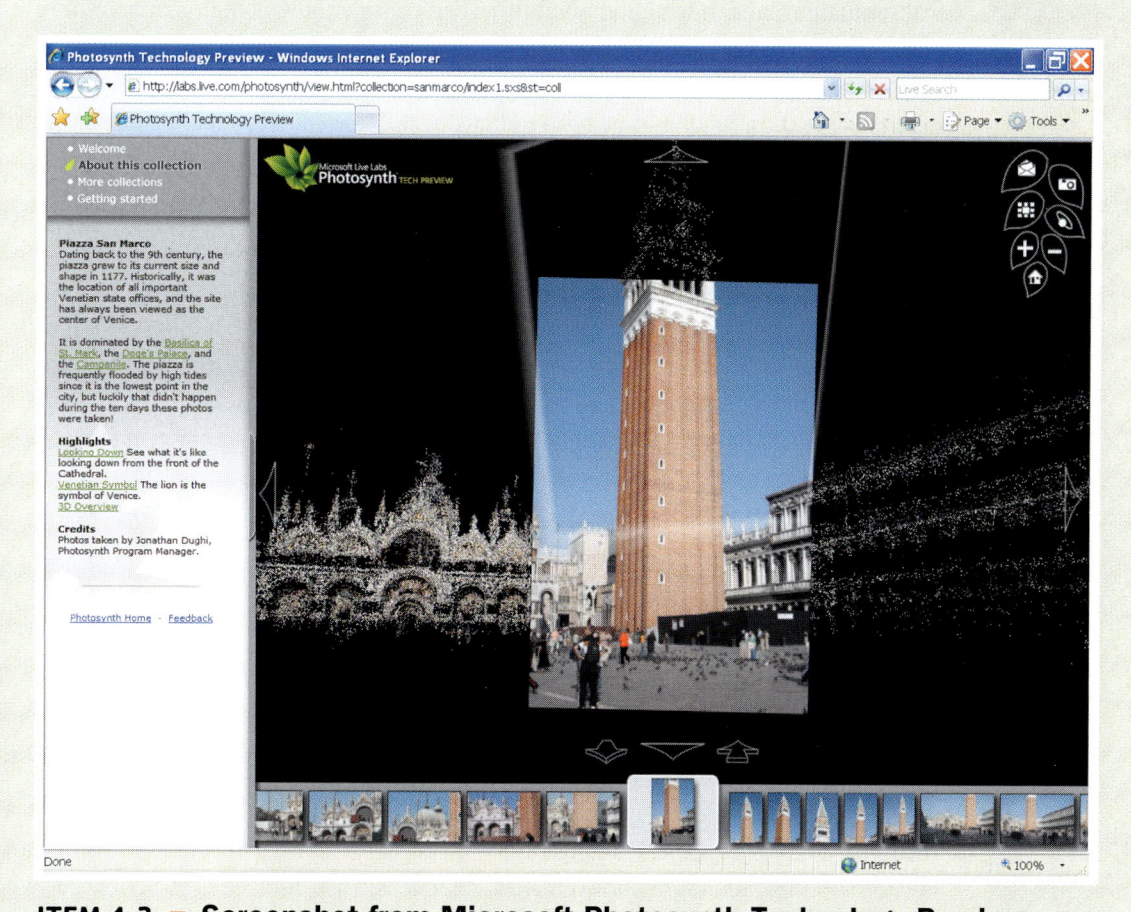

ITEM 4.2 ■ **Screenshot from Microsoft Photosynth Technology Preview**

Reading Texts About Places and Environments

In one way or another, places compose our lives. They are rich **subjects** to explore and write about. Yet it may be hard to imagine that the places *you* inhabit deserve serious scrutiny. Who cares about your home town or the music club where your band played its first gig? Doesn't it require really talented writers or photographers to make an **audience** appreciate special places? Sometimes it does. But almost anyone can learn to respond powerfully to the neighborhoods of the world. All it takes is identifying the details that make a place special.

It's easy, for example, to find cultural meanings and patterns in spectacular scenes or landscapes—Las Vegas's bizarre skyline clearly says something about American values (see Item 4.3), while gut-wrenching images from Hurricane Katrina tell an entirely different story (see Item 4.4). Yet the very skills that enable you to find meaning in conspicuous situations like these can help you detect patterns in less obvious locales. When you encounter a place, real or recreated, first ask, "Where am I?" and "What sort of place is this?" Then consider how you can give **purpose** and **structure** to your response to that environment.

In a *natural environment*, for instance, pay attention first to its features—terrain, climate, geological formations, and animal and plant life. Then consider how human marks or intrusions shape your own experience of nature (see Item 4.5). Put the place you are viewing or reading about into a physical or cultural **context** that helps to make sense of it, explaining, for example, how a desert shapes the structure of its native plants or why a wetland should be preserved.

In contrast to natural environments, *built environments* are those made, in whole or in part, by people. Whether these spaces have been casually assembled or formally designed, such human spaces serve functions you can describe and contemplate. One could just as easily learn from the relationships in a crowded diaper changing room (see Item 4.6) as from a soaring skyscraper (see Item 4.7) or virtual landscape such as Second Life. And, of course, writers, poets, and artists do exactly that, helping us to glimpse the layers of cultural experience embedded in built environments, from suburban homes to celebrated highways (see, for example, Item 4.8). Like these artists, you need to study the elements of an intriguing place, the people it attracts, the activities and events that occur there. Look for relationships and stories (see Item 4.9). All places have them.

Look, too, for the boundaries we put on places, if only to make them more manageable or give them **structure** in our minds. Some frontiers will seem natural—the rivers or mountains that mark regional or national borders. Other boundaries, you'll discover, are fashioned by people. An interstate highway, for instance, may be a *de facto* wall, sorting a town by race and class; ethnic groups may coalesce around schools, churches, and specialty stores (see Item 4.10). A writer or artist might discover such important cultural markers—or the task may fall to you.

To introduce audiences to environments you attach importance to, you must choose a **medium**. Writers typically compose essays, journals, or even travelogues; other artists may create paintings, photographs, Web sites, or videos. How a place is experienced—whether via the pages of a book or through the Plexiglas of a tour bus—makes a difference. Keep your options open.

Gallery: Places and Environments

ITEM 4.3 ■ **Paris Casino, The Strip, Las Vegas**

In the middle of the Nevada desert, the Las Vegas strip is a place that seems to represent an alternative reality. Here you see landmarks from Paris; elsewhere you might find a sphinx and pyramid, a pirate ship, a volcano, or Roman colonnades—as well as plenty of slot machines.

1. What does the photograph suggest about life and culture in Las Vegas? Why, for example, recreate the distinctive sights of Paris or ancient Rome in an American city? Does Las Vegas have a character of its own?

2. What sites or buildings in your current location would you photograph if you were trying to explain the place to viewers not familiar with it? Why?

The Water is Rising Pleas.

ITEM 4.5 ■ David Muench, *Grand Prismatic Spring, Yellowstone National Park, 1998*

Photographer David Muench captures the startling beauty of a hot springs pool at Yellowstone through a grid of trees scorched during a major wildfire in 1989. Parks like Yellowstone represent the government's attempts to preserve a natural environment while still making such places available to millions of tourists each year.

1. How would your reading of this natural image be different if either the pool or the burned trees were not competing for your attention?

2. There is a human presence in this image. Did you notice it immediately? Does it alter your sense of wilderness?

3. List three natural environments and three built environments you find especially interesting. Choose one and write about it—or photograph it, if that is an option.

ITEM 4.4 ■ Smiley N. Pool, Hurricane Katrina Photograph, *The Dallas Morning News*, September 5, 2005

The *Dallas Morning News* won a Pulitzer Prize for its coverage of Hurricane Katrina—a physical disaster that altered many people's sense of home, nation, and place. This image shows people on the roof of an apartment complex in New Orleans.

1. What elements of the photograph compete for your attention? What stories do they tell about this environment?

2. How does the news photo convey a sense of place? How do you react to the image now, several years after the hurricane?

ITEM 4.6 ■ **Melissa Ann Pinney,** *Disney World, Orlando, Florida,* **1998**

The diaper-changing room at Florida's Walt Disney World may not be your idea of a place worth pondering, but photographer Melissa Ann Pinney did: "Although I have always been drawn to what is hidden, especially concerning women's experiences, I couldn't say for certain that I would have recognized the secluded diaper-changing scene at Disney World as a possible subject until my daughter, Emma, was born."

1. What does Pinney's remark suggest about how we might learn to pay attention to new subjects and locales?

2. In looking at Pinney's photograph, do you wonder where the fathers are? Why is the space so crowded and poorly lit—at Disney World, no less? What types of questions about culture and society might an image of an environment of this kind raise?

3. If you were to describe or photograph a place as important and yet as mundane as the diaper-changing room at Disney World, what might it be and why?

GALLERY | PLACES AND ENVIRONMENTS

ITEM 4.7 ■ *Taipei 101*

Buildings are important places that influence how people live and think. Now, after a lull of several decades, cities and countries are again competing to see which can claim the tallest skyscraper. Completed in 2004 in the capital city of the Republic of China, Taipei 101 briefly claimed that title at 1670 feet (with spire) until displaced by Burj Dubai (at more than 2600 feet).

1. Why do you think communities strive to build the tallest structure in the world? What might such structures represent to a city or country?

2. What architectural features or characteristics do you see in Taipei 101 that suggest its ties to the culture and people of Taiwan? Would this skyscraper look out of place in London or Chicago? Why or why not?

3. Spend some time researching the current boom in the construction of skyscrapers. Where are these structures being built? How might you explain the trend?

Route 66

Well if you ever plan to motor west
Just take my way that's the highway that's the best
Get your kicks on Route 66

Well it winds from Chicago to L.A.
More than 2000 miles all the way
Get your kicks on Route 66

Well it goes from St. Louie down to Missouri
Oklahoma City looks oh so pretty
You'll see Amarillo and Gallup, New Mexico
Flagstaff, Arizona, don't forget Winona
Kingman, Barstow, San Bernadino

Would you get hip to this kindly tip
And go take that California trip
Get your kicks on Route 66

Well it goes from St. Louie down to Missouri
Oklahoma City looks oh so pretty
You'll see Amarillo and Gallup, New Mexico
Flagstaff, Arizona, don't forget Winona
Kingman, Barstow, San Bernadino

Would you get hip to this kindly tip
And go take that California trip
Get your kicks on Route 66

"Route 66" by Bobby Troup © 2002 Troup-London Music. Used by permission.

ITEM 4.8 ■ Bobby Troup, "Route 66," 1946

Can a road be a place? If so, US Highway 66 certainly qualifies. Sometimes called "the mother road," it was the first major east-west highway in the United States. Starting in Chicago, it snaked through eight states—Illinois, Missouri, Kansas, Oklahoma, Texas, New Mexico, Arizona, and California. Bobby Troup's upbeat song "Route 66" was an early rock 'n' roll anthem, but the storied highway itself and many of the small towns it visited faded with the building of the Interstates.

[1] How would you characterize the tone of Troup's lyrics? Where does Route 66 lead? Why is the destination significant to Americans?

[2] Are highways themselves really places or are they just the paths to a destination? What role do roads play in our lives, songs, stories, or myths?

ITEM 4.9 ■ Richard Harrod, *Café, Montmartre*, May 29, 2005

The street-side café, a rarity in the United States, is a public space common in France and other European countries, a place for people to relax, read, or merely observe life over food and drink. It is also a cultural tradition that may represent a different attitude toward life.

1. What elements must be in place to make a public space such as an outdoor café or restaurant work? Why do you think such places are *relatively* rare in American cities? In what sorts of places are you most likely to see them?

2. Would you guess that the people in this photograph are mainly tourists or Parisian locals? Point to details that support your case.

ITEM 4.10 ■ Alice Attie, from *Harlem in Transition*, 2000

Artist-writer Alice Attie spent a year documenting changes occurring in Harlem, a famous African American community in New York City. In her photographs, Attie directs viewers' attention to the neighborhood's people and storefronts, highlighting the contrasts between small, locally owned businesses—often boarded up or on the verge of going under—and the gleaming corporate chain stores currently moving into this New York City area. The stark differences suggest Attie's purpose: to document this older neighborhood culture before it vanishes entirely.

GALLERY | PLACES AND ENVIRONMENTS

1. Take a close look at Attie's photographs. What specific details of architecture, signage, décor, or other elements seem to distinguish the chain storefronts from the locally owned business? What social, cultural, or economic factors do you think might contribute to these different styles?

2. Why do you think Attie includes a human figure in the photos of the Starbucks and Disney Store franchises? Write a few sentences explaining what you think the man in the suit and the girl on the bicycle add to the images.

3. Harlem is a neighborhood with a rich heritage. Do some research in the library or on the Internet to learn about the history and culture of the area, and then look again at Attie's photographs. Write a paragraph discussing how these images fit into your overall impression of the place.

Cluster 4.1
Places We Inhabit

Ask a dozen assorted people to name the place that holds the most memories and emotional associations, and you'll likely get a single response: "Home." For many people across the world, "home" may refer to urban apartments, row houses, single-family farms, or small villages. But for many Americans, the term implies a big single-family house with a lawn and a garage in a residential neighborhood filled with similar dwellings—in other words, a suburb, the subject David Brooks explores in "Our Sprawling, Supersize Utopia."

We also inhabit places stored in our memories. Indeed, the very world *nostalgia* has as its root the Greek *nostos*, meaning "return home" and so it is not surprising that our longing for places that are either vanishing or distant and unreachable should evoke responses in writing, films, or music. Jenny Attiyeh provides such an account of a cherished spot in "My Ghost Town: A Vanishing Personal History."

But we don't just live in our homes or memories. We occupy dorm rooms, flock to stadiums, and cruise the malls, making various public places our own. In "The Comfy Chair Revolution," author Glenn Reynolds draws our attention to attempts by retail establishments to make themselves more livable environments where we'll want to spend time . . . and shop.

And, of course, a great many of us find ourselves inhabiting imaginary places these days, whether in the increasingly realistic realms of video games or in social environments like Facebook or MySpace. In "Where the Avatars Roam," Michael Gerson takes readers into Second Life, an online alternative world that has sparked much commentary and criticism. He examines it as a political experiment with lessons to teach about the real world.

CONSIDER

1. Examine the floor plan for "The Dover," a prefabricated home advertised to first-time buyers by Sears, Roebuck during the early 1950s. What sort of buyer would have considered this a "dream house"? How does this house's size and layout compare to the places you've lived? Is this a house you'd aspire to buy? Why or why not?

2. Think about the focal points and the point of view in the tiny sketch of the home buyers. What draws your attention: The couple? Their attire? The house? What do you think Sears wants you to focus on? Why?

COMPOSE

3. On the Web or in a newspaper, browse through some advertisements for new housing developments and compare them to the ad for "The Dover." What differences and similarities do you see? Write a paragraph or two reporting your findings.

THE DOVER
SIX ROOMS, BATH AND LAVATORY

THERE is a certain warmth and "hominess" about a wooden house—a readiness to receive the stamp of its owner's personality and an ability to adapt itself to its environment. It answers the needs of well-to-do or modest builder and holds its own in town or country.

The Dover is an Americanized English type Colonial story and a half cottage with a convenient floor plan. The massive chimney helps to "tie in" the front gable and the cowled roof lines help to give a compact appearance. The exterior walls are planned for clear bevel siding but will look equally attractive if shingles are used. In either case, we suggest light colors of paint or stain, in contrast to dark shutters, chimney and weathered roof.

The shutters on the front windows are batten type, to match the batten type circle head front door.

Our home building service will furnish every detail to help you have a home as attractive as the Dover. We guarantee quality and quantity, and our ready cut system of construction conserves your building dollars.

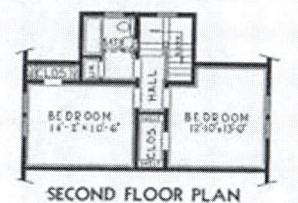

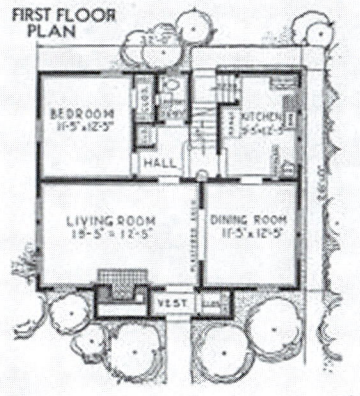

MODERN HOME No. 3262 ALREADY CUT AND FITTED

SECOND FLOOR PLAN

FIRST FLOOR PLAN

THE FLOOR PLANS

From the terrace, the front door opens into a vestibule which has a large coat closet for outer wraps. Handy for your guests. The living room and dining room extend across the entire front of the house and are connected with a plaster arch, also used from living room to vestibule and hall. Plenty of windows assure bright cheerful rooms and a pleasant outlook.

Most every family can use a first floor bedroom—if not for the family, a guest likes a little privacy from the Master bedrooms. Many have converted this room into a combination library and den and still have a "spare" bedroom available by putting a "rollaway" bed in the closet. Note that the semi-open stairs also open into the kitchen—a step-saving convenience. The kitchen will accommodate cabinets quoted in options. The second floor contains two large bedrooms and the bath is above the average size. Linen storage and good closets. Fill out blank for complete delivered price.

Sears, Roebuck and Co.   641 ▶ Page 33 ◀

ITEM 4.11 ■ Sears Catalog, *The Dover*, 1950s

At one time, Sears and other retailers sold prefabricated homes available through their catalogs. Such offers appealed especially to first-time buyers.

Our Sprawling, Supersize Utopia

David Brooks
(2004)

> **FYI** David Brooks is a columnist for the *New York Times*. His book, *On Paradise Drive: How We Live Now (and Always Have) in the Future Tense*, from which this essay is adapted, was published in 2004 by Simon & Schuster.

We're living in the age of the great dispersal. Americans continue to move from the Northeast and Midwest to the South and West. But the truly historic migration is from the inner suburbs to the outer suburbs, to the suburbs of suburbia. From New Hampshire down to Georgia, across Texas to Arizona and up through California, you now have the booming exurban sprawls that have broken free of the gravitational pull of the cities and now float in a new space far beyond them. For example, the population of metropolitan Pittsburgh has declined by 8 percent since 1980, but as people spread out, the amount of developed land in the Pittsburgh area increased by nearly 43 percent. The population of Atlanta increased by 22,000 during the 90's, but the expanding suburbs grew by 2.1 million.

The geography of work has been turned upside down. Jobs used to be concentrated in downtowns. But the suburbs now account for more rental office space than the cities in most of the major metro areas of the country except Chicago and New York. In the Bay Area in California, suburban Santa Clara County alone has five times as many of the region's larger public companies as San Francisco. Ninety percent of the office space built in America by the end of the 1990's was built in suburbia, much of it in far-flung office parks stretched along the interstates.

These new spaces are huge and hugely attractive to millions of people. Mesa, Ariz., a suburb of Phoenix, now has a larger population than Minneapolis, St. Louis, or Cincinnati. It's as if Zeus came down and started plopping vast developments in the middle of farmland and the desert overnight. Boom! A master planned community. Boom! A big-box mall. Boom! A rec center and 4,000 soccer fields. The food courts come and the people follow. How many times in American history have 300,000-person communities materialized practically out of nothing?

In these new, exploding suburbs, the geography, the very landscape of life, is new and unparalleled. In the first place, there are no centers, no recognizable borders to shape a sense of geographic identity. Throughout human history, most people have lived around some definable place—a tribal ring, an oasis, a river junction, a port, a town square. But in exurbia, each individual has his or her own polycentric nodes—the school, the church, and the office park. Life is different in ways big and small. When the New Jersey Devils won the Stanley Cup, they had their victory parade in a parking lot; no downtown street is central to the team's fans. Robert Lang, a demographer at Virginia Tech, compares these new sprawling exurbs to the dark matter in the universe: stuff that is very hard to define but somehow accounts for more mass than all the planets, stars, and moons put together.

We are having a hard time understanding the cultural implications of this new landscape because when it comes to suburbia, our imaginations are motionless. Many of us still live with the suburban stereotypes laid down by the first wave of suburban critics—that the suburbs are dull, white-bread kind of places where Ozzie and Harriet families go to raise their kids. But there are no people so conformist as those who fault the supposed conformity of the suburbs. They regurgitate the same critiques decade after decade, regardless of the suburban reality flowering around them.

The reality is that modern suburbia is merely the latest iteration of the American dream. Far from being dull, artificial, and spiritually vacuous, today's suburbs are the products of the same religious longings and the same deep tensions that produced the American identity from the start. The complex faith of Jonathan Edwards, the propelling ambition of Benjamin Franklin, the dark, meritocratic fatalism of Lincoln—all these inheritances have shaped the outer suburbs.

At the same time the suburbs were sprawling, they were getting more complicated and more interesting, and they were going quietly berserk. When you move through suburbia—from the old inner-ring suburbs out through the most distant exurbs—you see the most unexpected things: lesbian dentists, Iranian McMansions, Korean megachurches, outlaw-biker subdevelopments, Orthodox shtetls with Hasidic families walking past strip malls on their way to shul. When you actually live in suburbia, you see that radically different cultural zones are emerging, usually within a few miles of one another and in places that are as architecturally interesting as a piece of aluminum siding. That's because in the age of the great dispersal, it becomes much easier to search out and congregate with people who are basically like yourself. People are less tied down to a factory, a mine or a harbor. They have more choice over which sort of neighborhood to live in. Society becomes more segmented, and everything that was once hierarchical turns granular.

You don't have to travel very far in America to see radically different sorts of people, most of whom know very little about the communities and subcultures just down the highway. For example, if you are driving across the northern band of the country—especially in Vermont, Massachusetts, Wisconsin or Oregon—you are likely to stumble across a crunchy suburb. These are places with meat-free food co-ops, pottery galleries, sandal shops (because people with progressive politics have a strange penchant for toe exhibitionism). Not many people in these places know much about the for-profit sector of the economy, but they do build wonderful all-wood playgrounds for their kids, who tend to have names like Milo and Mandela. You know you're in a crunchy suburb because you see the anti-lawns, which declare just how fervently crunchy suburbanites reject the soul-destroying standards of conventional success. Anti-lawns look like regular lawns with eating disorders. Some are bare patches of dirt, others are scraggly spreads of ragged, weedlike vegetation, the horticultural version of a grunge rocker's face.

Then a few miles away, you might find yourself in an entirely different cultural zone, in an upscale suburban town center packed with restaurants—one of those communities that perform the neat trick of being clearly suburban while still making it nearly impossible to park. The people here tend to be lawyers, doctors, and professors, and they drive around in Volvos, Audis and Saabs because it is socially acceptable to buy a luxury car as long as it comes from a country hostile to U.S. foreign policy.

Here you can find your Trader Joe's grocery stores, where all the cashiers look as if they are on loan from Amnesty International and all the snack food is especially designed for kids who come home from school screaming, "Mom, I want a snack that will prevent colorectal cancer!" Here you've got newly renovated Arts and Crafts seven-bedroom homes whose owners have developed views on beveled granite; no dinner party in this clique has gone all the way to dessert without a conversational phase on the merits and demerits of Corian countertops. Bathroom tile is their cocaine: instead of white powder, they blow their life savings on handcrafted Italian wall coverings from Waterworks.

> **But there are no people so conformist as those who fault the supposed conformity of the suburbs.**

You travel a few miles from these upscale enclaves, and suddenly you're in yet another cultural milieu. You're in one of the suburban light-industry zones, and you start noting small Asian groceries offering live tilapia fish and premade bibimbap dishes. You see Indian video rental outlets with movies straight from Bollywood. You notice a Japanese bookstore, newspaper boxes offering the *Korea Central Daily News* and hair salons offering DynaSky phone cards to Peru.

One out of every nine people in America was born in a foreign country. Immigrants used to settle in cities and then migrate out, but now many head straight for suburbia, so today you see little Taiwanese girls in the figure skating clinics, Ukrainian boys learning to pitch and hints of cholo culture spreading across Nevada. People here develop their own customs and patterns that grow up largely unnoticed by the general culture. You go to a scraggly playing field on a Saturday morning, and there is a crowd of Nigerians playing soccer. You show up the next day, and it is all Mexicans kicking a ball around. No lifestyle magazine is geared to the people who live in these immigrant-heavy wholesale warehouse zones.

You drive farther out, and suddenly you're lost in the shapeless, mostly middle-class expanse of exurbia. (The inner-ring suburbs tend to have tremendous income inequality.) Those who live out here are very likely living in the cultural shadow of golf. It's not so much the game of golf that influences manners and morals; it's the Zenlike golf ideal. The perfect human being, defined by golf, is competitive and success-oriented, yet calm and neat while casually dressed. Everything he owns looks as if it is made of titanium, from his driver to his BlackBerry to his wife's Wonderbra. He has achieved mastery over the great dragons: hurry, anxiety and disorder.

His DVD collection is organized, as is his walk-in closet. His car is clean and vacuumed. His frequently dialed numbers are programmed into his phone, and his rate plan is well tailored to his needs. His casual slacks are well pressed, and he is so calm and together that next to him, Dick Cheney looks bipolar. The new suburbs appeal to him because everything is fresh and neat. The philosopher George Santayana once suggested that Americans don't solve problems; we just leave them behind. The exurbanite has left behind that exorbitant mortgage, that long commute, all those weird people who watch "My Daughter Is a Slut" on daytime TV talk shows. He has come to be surrounded by regular, friendly people who do not scoff at his daughter's competitive cheerleading obsession and whose wardrobes are as Lands' End–dependent as his is.

Exurban places have one ideal that soars above all others: ample parking. You can drive diagonally across acres of empty parking spaces on your way from Bed, Bath & Beyond to Linens 'n Things. These parking lots are so big that you could recreate the Battle of Gettysburg in the middle and nobody would notice at the stores on either end. Off on one side, partly obscured by the curvature of the earth, you will see a sneaker warehouse big enough to qualify for membership in the United Nations, and then at the other end there will be a Home Depot. Still, shoppers measure their suburban manliness by how close they can park to the Best Buy. So if a normal healthy American sees a family about to pull out of one of those treasured close-in spots just next to the maternity ones, he will put on his blinker and wait for the departing family to load up its minivan and apparently read a few chapters of "Ulysses" before it finally pulls out and lets him slide in.

> **Still, shoppers measure their suburban manliness by how close they can park to the Best Buy.**

You look out across this landscape, with its sprawling diversity of suburban types, and sometimes you can't help considering the possibility that we Americans may not be the most profound people on earth. You look out across the suburban landscape that is the essence of modern America, and you see the culture of Slurp & Gulps, McDonald's, Disney, breast enlargements and "The Bachelor." You see a country that gave us Prozac and Viagra, paper party hats, pinball machines, commercial jingles, expensive orthodontia, and Monster Truck rallies. You see a trashy consumer culture that has perfected parade floats, corporate-sponsorship deals, low-slung jeans, and frosted Cocoa Puffs; a culture that finds its quintessential means of self-expression through bumper stickers ("Rehab Is for Quitters").

Indeed, over the past half century, there has been an endless flow of novels, movies, anti-sprawl tracts, essays and pop songs all lamenting the shallow conformity of suburban life. If you scan these documents all at once, or even if, like the average person, you absorb them over the course of a lifetime, you find their depictions congeal into the same sorry scene. Suburban America as a comfortable but somewhat vacuous realm of unreality: consumerist, wasteful, complacent, materialistic, and self-absorbed.

Disneyfied Americans, in this view, have become too concerned with small and vulgar pleasures, pointless one-upmanship. Their lives are distracted by a buzz of trivial images, by relentless hurry instead of contemplation, information rather than wisdom and a profusion of unsatisfying lifestyle choices. Modern suburban Americans, it is argued, rarely sink to the level of depravity—they are too tepid for that—but they don't achieve the highest virtues or the most demanding excellences.

These criticisms don't get suburbia right. They don't get America right. The criticisms tend to come enshrouded in predictions of decline or cultural catastrophe. Yet somehow imperial decline never comes, and the social catastrophe never materializes. American standards of living surpassed those in Europe around 1740. For more than 260 years, in other words, Americans have been rich, money-mad, vulgar, materialistic and complacent people. And yet somehow America became and continues to be the most powerful nation on earth and the most productive. Religion flourishes. Universities flourish. Crime rates drop, teen pregnancy declines, teen-suicide rates fall, along with divorce rates. Despite all the problems that plague this country, social healing takes place. If we're so great, can we really be that shallow?

Nor do the standard critiques of suburbia really solve the mystery of motivation—the inability of many Americans to sit still, even when they sincerely want to simplify their lives. Americans are the hardest-working people on earth. The average American works 350 hours a year—nearly 10 weeks—more than the average Western European. Americans switch jobs more frequently than people from other nations. The average job tenure in the U.S. is 6.8 years, compared with more than a decade in France, Germany and Japan. What propels Americans to live so feverishly, even against their own self-interest? What energy source accounts for all this?

Finally, the critiques don't explain the dispersion. They don't explain why so many millions of Americans throw themselves into the unknown every year. In 2002, about 14.2 percent of Americans relocated. Compare that with the 4 percent of Dutch and Germans and the 8 percent of Britons who move in a typical year. According to one survey, only slightly more than a quarter of American teenagers expect to live in their hometowns as adults.

What sort of longing causes people to pick up and head out for the horizon? Why do people uproot their families from California, New York, Ohio and elsewhere and move into new developments in Arizona or Nevada or North Carolina, imagining their kids at high schools that haven't even been built yet, picturing themselves with new friends they haven't yet met, fantasizing about touch-football games on lawns that haven't been seeded? Millions of people every year leap out into the void, heading out to communities that don't exist, to office parks that are not yet finished, to places where everything is new. This mysterious longing is the root of the great dispersal.

To grasp that longing, you have to take seriously the central cliché of American life: the American dream. Albert Einstein once said that imagination is more important than knowledge, and when you actually look at modern mainstream America, you see what a huge role fantasy plays even in the seemingly dullest areas of life. The suburbs themselves are conservative utopias, where people go because they imagine orderly and perfect lives can be led there. This is the nation of Hollywood, Las Vegas, professional wrestling, Elvis impersonators, *Penthouse* letters, computer gamers, grown men in LeBron James basketball jerseys, faith healers, and the whole range of ampersand magazines (*Town & Country, Food & Wine*) that display perfect parties, perfect homes, perfect vacations, and perfect lives. This is the land of Rainforest Cafe theme restaurants, Ralph Lauren WASP-fantasy fashions, Civil War re-enactors, gated communities with names like Sherwood Forest and vehicles with names like Yukon, Durango, Expedition and Mustang, as if their accountant-owners were going to chase down some cattle rustlers on the way to the Piggly Wiggly. This is the land in which people dream of the most Walter Mitty-esque personal transformations as a result of the low-carb diet, cosmetic surgery, or their move to the Sun Belt.

Americans—seemingly bland, ordinary Americans—often have a remarkably tenuous grip on reality. Under the seeming superficiality of suburban American life, there is an imaginative fire that animates Americans and propels us to work so hard, move so much and leap so wantonly.

Ralph Waldo Emerson once wrote that those who "complain of the flatness of American life have no perception of its destiny. They are not Americans." They don't see that "here is man in the garden of Eden; here, the Genesis and the Exodus." And here, he concluded fervently, will come the final Revelation. Emerson was expressing the eschatological longing that is the essence of the American identity: the assumption that some culminating happiness is possible here, that history can be brought to a close here.

The historian Sacvan Bercovitch has observed that the United States is the example par excellence of a nation formed by collective fantasy. Despite all the claims that American culture is materialist and pragmatic, what is striking about this country is how material things are shot through with enchantment.

America, after all, was born in a frenzy of imagination. For the first European settlers and for all the subsequent immigrants, the new continent begs to be fantasized about. The early settlers were aware of and almost oppressed by the obvious potential of the land. They saw the possibility of plenty everywhere, yet at the start they lived in harsh conditions. Their lives took on a slingshot shape—they had to pull back in order to someday shoot forward. Through the temporary hardships they dwelt imaginatively in the grandeur that would inevitably mark their future.

This future-minded mentality deepened decade after decade, century after century. Each time the early settlers pushed West, they found what was to them virgin land, and they perceived it as paradise. Fantasy about the future lured them. Guides who led and sometimes exploited the 19th-century pioneers were shocked by how little the trekkers often knew about the surroundings they had thrown themselves into, or what would be involved in their new lives. As so often happens in American history, as happens every day in the newly sprawling areas, people leapt before they really looked.

Americans found themselves drawn to places where the possibilities seemed boundless and where there was no history. Francis Parkman, the great 19th-century historian, wrote of his youthful self, "His thoughts were always in the forest, whose features possessed his waking and sleeping dreams, filling him with vague cravings impossible to satisfy."

Our minds are still with Parkman's in the forest. Our imagination still tricks us into undertaking grand projects—starting a business, writing a book, raising a family, moving to a new place—by enchanting us with visions of future joys. When these tasks turn out to be more difficult than we dreamed, the necessary exertions bring out new skills and abilities and make us better than we planned on being.

> **If we're so great, can we really be that shallow?**

And so we see the distinctive American mentality, which explains the westward crossing as much as the suburban sprawl and the frenzied dot-com-style enthusiasms. It is the Paradise Spell: the tendency to see the present from the vantage point of the future. It starts with imagination—the ability to fantasize about what some imminent happiness will look like. Then the future-minded person leaps rashly toward that gauzy image. He or she is subtly more attached to the glorious future than to the temporary and unsatisfactory present. Time isn't pushed from the remembered past to the felt present to the mysterious future. It is pulled by the golden future from the unsatisfactory present and away from the dim past.

Born in abundance, inspired by opportunity, nurtured in imagination, spiritualized by a sense of God's blessing and call and realized in ordinary life day by day, this Paradise Spell is the controlling ideology of national life. Just out of reach, just beyond the next ridge, just in the farther-out suburb or with the next entrepreneurial scheme, just with the next diet plan or credit card purchase, the next true love or political hero, the next summer home or all-terrain vehicle, the next meditation schools, the right moral revival, the right beer and the right set of buddies; just with the next technology or after the next shopping spree—there is this spot you can get to where all tensions will melt, all time pressures will be relieved and happiness can be realized.

This Paradise Spell is at the root of our tendency to work so hard, consume so feverishly, to move so much. It inspires our illimitable faith in education, our frequent born-again experiences. It explains why, alone among developed nations, we have shaped our welfare system to encourage opportunity at the expense of support and security; and why, more than people in comparable nations, we wreck our families and move on. It is the call that makes us heedless of the past, disrespectful toward traditions, short on contemplation, wasteful in our use of the things around us, impious toward restraints, but consumed by hope, driven ineluctably to improve, fervently optimistic, relentlessly aspiring, spiritually alert, and, in this period of human history, the irresistible and discombobulating locomotive of the world.

CONSIDER

1. Brooks claims that "modern suburbia is merely the latest iteration of the American dream." What is your understanding of the term "American dream"? How does that dream relate to your personal notions of *home* and *environment*?

2. How does Brooks define the "Paradise Spell"? Do you agree with his explanation of why Americans historically have been so mobile a people?

3. Can you identify any "cultural zones," as David Brooks describes them, where you live?

COMPOSE

4. Using the resources of your campus library or the Web, explore the history and cultural impact of Levittown, Pennsylvania, a planned community built after World War II to provide single-family homes for returning GIs and their new families. Summarize your findings in a brief report, illustrated if possible.

5. David Brooks writes that "throughout human history, most people have lived around some definable place." Write a paragraph in which you describe the geographic center of your home town.

CHALLENGE

6. Reread "Our Sprawling, Supersize Utopia," published in 2004, in light of recent increases in energy prices and concerns about environmental degradation. Then write a paper arguing whether Americans will finally abandon the highly mobile suburban lifestyles that Brooks describes. Will American horizons contract or will the Paradise Spell once again triumph in the long run?

William Eggleston, *Memphis*, c. 1972

FYI

ITEM 4.12 ■ **Images from Suburban Life**

Artists and photographers over the years have been fascinated by images of suburban life. Here are some images that depict suburban scenes and mores, including a still from the 1998 film *Pleasantville*, which portrayed a black-and-white suburb sitcom world that gradually blossomed into a richer and more colorful version of life.

Still from *Pleasantville*, 1998

"We're really happy. Our kids are healthy, we eat good food, and we have a nice home," from Bill Owens, *Suburbia*, 1973.

1950s family room from *Life* Magazine

CONSIDER

1. Examine the depictions of suburban family life from the 1950s to the 1970s on these pages. (Released in 1998, *Pleasantville* depicts a 1950s suburb.) Which images seem the most positive, and which seem ambivalent or negative? In which of these places would you most like to live? Why?

2. In compiling *Suburbia*, Bill Owens asked the families he photographed to comment on the pictures and then used their words as captions. What does the caption of "We're really happy" reveal about the couple in the photograph above? Do you think the caption is an effective one? Why or why not?

3. Look closely at the placement of people in the photographs. Which arrangement do you find most effective? Most interesting? Why? Which is least interesting? Which seems most natural or authentic? Which seems least natural?

4. Think about the use of color film versus black and white in these images and about why the photographers made the choices they did. If you had to illustrate an essay on the American suburb, would you choose color or black-and-white images? Why do you think *Pleasantville* uses both black and white and color?

COMPOSE

5. Examine the photos for clues to the different eras they represent. Make a list of the specific features you find for each image, and then explain in a brief rhetorical analysis how these details affect the photos and the way you react to them.

201

My Ghost Town: A Vanishing Personal History

Jenny Attiyeh
(2001)

> **FYI** Jenny Attiyeh has been reporting on politics, the arts, and culture since 1987. She is currently a freelance reporter based in Boston, writing regularly for newspapers including the *Christian Science Monitor* and the *Boston Globe*.

GRAFTON, Utah—My grandfather liked to dare me to walk to the cemetery at night, up the mud road from our house, past the orchards, the looming cows, past the tumbledown barn into the open, empty fields. From there I could almost see the mounds rising against the bluff. Grampa urged me on. Early settlers were buried here in unmarked graves, and nearby lay the headstone of a young boy, killed by Indians. As I turned and headed rapidly for home, I could hear Grampa chuckling in the dark.

It was Grampa who had brought us to Grafton, this ghost town on the edge of Zion National Park. He was born and raised in Utah, and wanted us to take part, to learn to love it as he did. So we camped out in an old adobe brick house, without running water or electricity, on a few acres of land my parents had bought. I was a little girl in diapers when we first came here for long holidays, driving from Los Angeles in a tattered VW Bug. The town—a handful of abandoned buildings, apple trees, lizards and the Virgin River, carving too close to the bank—became mine.

Happiness for me was waking up from a nap to eat watermelon by the irrigation ditch that ran in front of our house. At least that's how it seems when I look at the photograph—my eyes are still sleepy, my white shirt a makeshift napkin, fingerprinted with a mixture of juice and red Utah dust. At night we slept on cots, with an applewood fire spitting out cinders onto our canvas sleeping bags. In the mornings, frost lined the windows, and it was so cold I was afraid to get out of bed.

But that was 30 years ago. Today, Grafton as I knew it is dying. There are no windows left in the old brick house, and the walls are scarred with graffiti. On the mantelpiece it reads, "Albert Loves Rhonda for Eternity and Mike." Deep cracks in the walls have encouraged passers-by to help themselves to the fired bricks. And down by the river, another empty house gapes, its front porch torn off by vandals. With its supports removed, the second story wall collapsed soon after, exposing adobe bricks to the melting rain.

We'd heard the rumors, of course. Grafton was falling apart, but we were far away. Now, we've finally come back to see what's left of our land.

I had no idea it was so beautiful. As a child, I had taken the place for granted—the still warmth of the afternoons, the slow brown river, the red sandstone cliffs poking into the sky. Down the road, I looked for the Indian chief my grandfather had drawn on the blackboard of the schoolhouse, but he was long gone.

As I stood and watched, a dozen teenagers climbed into the open face of a deserted house nearby, up the broken staircase to the second floor. They were laughing and shoving each other—giggling at the poetry sprayed on the plaster walls. I felt like a tight-faced schoolmarm, injured and entitled, and I told them to get down. "Can't you guys read the sign?" They did not answer, and moved off.

It became clear to me that I really didn't want to share this town with anyone—I just wanted to be left alone, to piece together the past. But my claims on Grafton were as nothing compared to those who came before me. Built by Mormons in 1859, the settlement was doomed from the start. Frequent flooding of the Virgin River washed away the crops and destroyed irrigation ditches, making life close to impossible. At one point, the entire town was relocated upstream, but to no avail. By the 1930s, Grafton had turned into a ghost town, gathering beer bottles and tumbleweeds.

I realize now that I, too, have abandoned Grafton—to the trash, the vandals, the deterioration. Perhaps I can make amends. Sheepishly, I begin to clean up. My father and I pick up loose boards from a collapsed shed and put them in a pile. A rusty nail grazes my palm. We make slow progress, but as the debris grows higher, I feel vaguely comforted.

Soon, the town will be busy with the sounds of restoration. In the past few years, a group of local townspeople and grassroots environmentalists has banded together to preserve what's left of Grafton. They plan to stabilize the old buildings and keep a close watch on the place to cut down on vandalism. There's already a shiny red gate blocking access to the adobe church, and a spanking-new sign explaining what is to come.

Grafton is soon to become a place of public purpose. But when I consider the pamphlets to be distributed at the information booth, I am sick at the thought—for Grafton is no longer mine. It has been appropriated.

For my part, I like Grafton best the way it used to be, but it is too late for that now. Already, too many tourists, drawn by the guidebooks, come to gawk at the town, leaving behind their lunch wrappers. I want the Grafton of my childhood, serene and apart. A place where I could commune with cows and watch the stinging red ants build their hills in the dirt. I would have liked my own daughter to play here someday, lost in daydreams.

It is almost dusk now, and the crickets buzz softly in the grass. As I stretch out on the front porch, I hear my parents' voices inside, low and reassuring. The red mountains fade to brown in the dying light. Gawkers pass by, making tracks in the dirt road. They call out, "No Trespassing!" and drive on by.

"We own the place," I tell them. But they probably don't believe me. And, in some way, it really isn't true. Slowly the dust resettles, and the crickets start up again. Slightly panicked, I look around at my old haunts. I'd like the sun to set quietly on Grafton, and its ghosts. At the cemetery up the road, there is no more room.

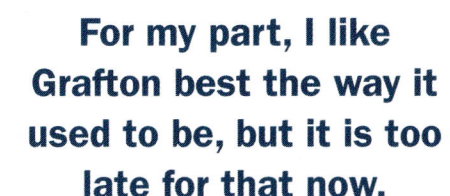

> "For my part, I like Grafton best the way it used to be, but it is too late for that now."

CONSIDER

1. Reread "My Ghost Town: A Vanishing Personal History," paying special attention to the specific details Attiyeh uses to describe Grafton. Which details are most effective in helping you "see" the town? Which particular words and phrases do you find most powerful?

2. Why do you think Attiyeh is annoyed when she encounters teenagers exploring the old schoolhouse? How, in her opinion, is their interest in Grafton different from hers? Do you agree that there is a difference? Why or why not?

COMPOSE

3. Make a list of ten places that are or have been important in your life. Then also list the events, experiences, and emotions you associate with each place. Have any of these "disappeared" from your life? If so, how? If not, why not?

CHALLENGE

4. Write an essay describing and eulogizing a place from your childhood that no longer exists. Consider sharing your work in an oral presentation, complete with images (if possible).

5. Nostalgia is a powerful feeling, one that shows up in nearly every aspect of our lives and influences fashion, art, architecture, film, and product design. More often than not, nostalgia is considered harmless. But might this relentless yearning for times past create problems for an individual or even a society? (For example, some Russians living now in a freer but more tumultuous society long for the stability of the Communist era.) Study manifestations of nostalgia in a specific group or segment of society, and then write a serious argument about the very human inclination to cherish things long gone.

ITEM 4.13 ■ Jonathan M. Levine, *Jelly! Austin*, January 23, 2008

Computers and the Web make it possible for more and more people to work at home. But what do they do when they get lonely or bored? They can now join Jelly, an "every-so-often casual working session" that typically takes place at a coffeehouse or restaurant. Jelly coworking meet-ups are scheduled events, the intellectual equivalent of a flash mob.

CONSIDER

1. Is Jelly an event or a place? Can it be both?

2. How would you define a workplace? What specifically might a communal workplace offer that a home office would not?

3. According to its Web site, Jelly encourages "casual coworking." But some entrepreneurs are building dedicated coworking facilities to serve the growing market of at-home workers who might long for communal experiences. Does the idea make sense to you? How might such a space differ from the communal workspace you're probably most familiar with—the library?

4.1 | PLACES WE INHABIT

The Comfy Chair Revolution

Glenn Reynolds
(2006)

> **FYI** Glenn Reynolds, a Professor of Law at the University of Tennessee, is the blogger responsible for the popular blog *Instapundit*. Describing his chief interest as "the intersection between advanced technologies and individual liberty," he is the author of *An Army of Davids: How Markets and Technology Empower Ordinary People to Beat Big Media, Big Government, and Other Goliaths*. "The Comfy Chair Revolution" is the first chapter of that book.

I've noticed a gradual change in public surroundings over the past few years. Unlike the hard, unappealing settings of traditional retail space (ground rule: "*get 'em in, get their money, get 'em out*"), more and more stores are being designed to encourage customers to linger.

Some of these transformations are obvious—the cozy coffee bars and cafés featured by many bookstores, for instance. But the phenomenon has spread to less obvious locales. In the mall near my house, for example, an Abercrombie spin-off called Hollister & Co. features comfortable leather chairs complete with end tables and stacks of magazines. The first time I was there I joked to a salesgirl that I might come back with my laptop and camp out. "People do," she responded. And when I went back a couple of weeks later, the circle of armchairs nearest the cash registers was completely occupied by teenagers with cell phones and PDAs. A conversation with a couple of staffers confirmed that the store was intentionally designed to serve as a "hangout."

And I think this shift in design may be the key to understanding how personal technology has changed us. In the old days, retailers knew that most people squeezed shopping in between the office and home. The goal was to sell as much as possible to people during the small amount of time available. Hence the keep 'em moving philosophy. But people live differently now. Lots of people work independently, or part-time, or as telecommuters. The lifestyle is more fluid, in part because technologies like cell phones, laptops, and PDAs allow people to work no matter where they are while also staying connected to family, friends, and colleagues. I see a lot of folks with that kind of personal tech hanging out wherever there's a pleasant setting, checking email, returning calls, or writing. It's work that doesn't quite feel like work.

THE APPEAL OF THE "THIRD PLACE"

This fluidity gives retailers and other businesses a different kind of opportunity. Retailers have always tried to sell the idea of a certain lifestyle along with their product: a sweater can become a symbol of social status. But if you become somebody's hangout, you don't just sell the suggestion of a kind of lifestyle, you're selling a particular way of life. If price and selection are the main basis for competition, people can always buy on the Internet; but everyone—especially teenagers—will still want a place to go. By becoming a place to hang out, a store can sell both the experience and the goods.

Does it work? Well, I'm writing this on a laptop in a Borders right now, comfortably ensconced upon a leather couch and waiting for the line to thin so I can order a latte. I do a lot of writing here, especially during the summers or on breaks when the university is closed. (And they sell me more books and CDs as a result.) A few years ago, in the pre-laptop, pre-Wi-Fi era, it would have been much more cumbersome and inconvenient to work and hang out simultaneously.

Examples of this trend are ubiquitous. A new public library in my area is breaking the old library taboo against food and installing a luxurious coffee bar of the sort normally found only in chain book superstores. Some malls provide a place for tired moms to chat on their cell phones while their kids romp in elaborate play areas. Health food stores provide welcoming spaces complete with live music and kitchen access. Even many churches in my area feature coffee bars with Wi-Fi.

As the trend has continued, we've started to see all sorts of amenities added: not just comfy chairs and beverage service, but wireless broadband Internet access, fireplaces, books and magazines (already begun at Hollister & Co.), and other furnishings and services designed to keep customers around, comfy, and receptive. Businesses reap rewards in the form of impulse buys and customer loyalty. But everyone enjoys the benefits of an abundance of safe, comfortable places to hang out, something that advocates of "community" were calling for just a few years ago.

People like to go out, and providing inexpensive hangouts may draw more business in a recession than when people are feeling flush. And it may be cheaper too, even when times are good. After all, you can buy a lot of comfy chairs for the price of a single Super Bowl ad slot.

Certainly the prevalence of comfy chairs and hangout-marketing bespeaks an attempt to meet an unfulfilled need for safe and comfortable public spaces. My Borders hangout is a good example—and it also illustrates how capitalism, combined with personal technology, can promote community.

I have an office with a nice computer, and I have a study at home with a nicer computer. But I often pack up my laptop, or a book that I'm reading, or student papers to grade, and relocate to this third place: somewhere more congenial than the office, less isolated than home.

Others must feel the same way because when I'm tapping away at my laptop, I find myself surrounded by people of all sorts. On a typical day, the place is hopping: tables are filled by students, alternately studying and flirting; a parent drilling a home-schooled child on Babylonian history; one or two road-warrior salespeople catching up on scheduling and messages; a gaggle of Bible-studiers arguing about Job; and a leather-clad cyberpunk youth sitting with his more conventional mother. By now, I know all the regulars by sight, and many by name. We keep up on each other's lives in a casual sort of way.

This third place, of course, is the "Third Place" that sociologist Ray Oldenburg called essential to civilization in his 1989 book *The Great Good Place*.[1] The third place, Oldenburg observes, must possess the following characteristics: it has to be free or inexpensive, offer food and drink, be accessible, draw enough people to feel social, and foster easy conversation. Oldenburg lamented that such places were disappearing.

Back in 1989, they were. Today, they're not—and you can thank the much-maligned chain book superstores for this. Certainly when I moved to my upscale Knoxville suburb some years ago there weren't many such places. Nor had there been many in Washington D.C.: the Afterwords Café at Kramerbooks was the closest thing, but it didn't really fit the bill. When I lived in New Haven, Connecticut, the famous Atticus Books was like a poor man's Borders: cozy, but no public restrooms. (They've since added them, in the face of competition from the palatial Barnes & Noble–operated Yale co-op down the street.)

> **Even many churches in my area feature coffee bars with Wi-Fi.**

Now, within about a mile of each other in my Knoxville suburb, stand three big bookstore/café complexes: Borders, Barnes & Noble, and Books-A-Million. All seem to be thriving.

They're doing well because they've identified a need and they're meeting it. You'd think that this would make a lot of people happy—and, of course, it does, as I can tell just by looking around. But you'd think it would make more than just the customers happy; you'd think that it would please the people who are always worrying about America's need for "community."

In that, however, you would mostly be mistaken. While hostility toward book superstores has receded from its late-1990s peak, it is still very real. Independent bookstores, we are told, are genuine; chain bookstores are all about marketing. Chain bookstores are bad for small presses, bad for communities, and—as Carol Anne Douglas writes in *Off Our Backs*—bad for feminists, whose books apparently can only be bought at "feminist bookstores."[2]

I don't know about the feminists, but small-press sales appear to be up thanks to chain bookstores' larger selection of titles. Communities are surely benefiting from the introduction of pleasant third places

---

[1] Ray Oldenburg, *The Great Good Place: Cafes, Coffee Shops, Bookstores, Bars, Hair Salons, and Other Hangouts at the Heart of a Community* (Marlowe & Co., 1999).

[2] Carol Anne Douglas, "Support Feminist Bookstores!" *Off Our Backs*, 31 December 2000, 1.

where they didn't exist before. And what's more, with the exception of a handful of independents, chain bookstores are better at being third places.

Perhaps this is because independent bookstores traditionally have been run by people who like books. These people generally aren't interested in offering the other amenities that Oldenburg names as important and that superstores provide: coffee shops, big chairs, and live music performances. At many independent bookstores, employees like books better than people and want you to know it—the bookish version of the music geeks in the book (and movie) *High Fidelity*.[3] (Small bookstores may not have the money for these amenities, either, though they're not terribly expensive.)

The chains, however, aren't in business for personal gratification. They just want to keep customers coming back.

Want coffee? *Got it!*

Want a triple mocha latte and handmade fresh sandwiches and salads? *Got it!*

And, interestingly, the extra traffic that these amenities produce means that chain stores typically can afford a better selection of books than the independents, which is why small presses are benefiting right along with latte-lovers.

Well, no surprise there. That's what capitalism is all about. Funny that it's a dirty word to some people. But put technology and capitalism together, and what we often get is an updated version of the good old days; the changes we associated with technology and capitalism—fast-food-style uniformity, alienation, and lowest-common-denominator treatment—were actually products of a particular, and transitional, stage in technology. Now that the technology has changed, so have the economics, and so has the response from business. And it goes way beyond Borders.

As a believer in markets, I think that this trend will eventually find an equilibrium point. As an observer of the current direction of technological change, I think that equilibrium point will be a lot closer to where things were in the eighteenth century than to where they were just a few years ago. And this will be on account of many forces both pushing and pulling the change along, Let's look at these "pushes" and "pulls."

[3] Nick Hornby, *High Fidelity* (Riverhead, 1996).

FORWARD MY MAIL TO STARBUCKS, PLEASE

The "push" comes from the office environment. You have almost certainly read *Dilbert*, and I'm tempted to simply cite the comic strip and say, "Case closed." But there's more to it than that.

Yes, the office environment can be unpleasant, and the commute can be nasty and time-consuming and expensive—just a few reasons people like to work at home. But working at home has its own problems. It can be hard to maintain the work/non-work boundaries. And who wants to meet with clients in your den?

On the other hand, offices are expensive. I've noticed a lot of small business people in my area giving up their offices and having meetings in public places—Starbucks, Borders, the public library, and so on. In fact, a real estate agent recently told me that the small-office commercial real estate market is actually suffering as a result of so many people making this kind of move.

The "push" comes from people wanting to get out of offices. But the "pull" comes from the technology that makes it possible, and from businesses' desire to cash in. The existence of personal tech like laptops, PDAs, and cell phones, coupled with Wi-Fi and other technologies that allow Internet access from all over means that you don't need to be at the office nearly as much anymore.

If a home is, in Le Corbusier's words, a "machine for living," then an office is a "machine for working." But nowadays, the machinery is looking a bit obsolete. The traditional office took shape in the nineteenth century, largely due to new technology. People needed to be close to each other to communicate and make use of services like telegraphs, telephones, and messengers (and later copy and fax machines and elaborate computer equipment). You can pretty much carry all that stuff with you now. And people are doing just that.

Consequently, a market has arisen for places that cater to this more fluid workstyle. Right now we're seeing the early phase of that, with amenities that focus on Wi-Fi and lattes. In time, we're likely to see much more than that. A recent article in *Salon* by Linda Baker finds that many urban-design types are looking beyond connectivity to interconnectivity. For example, she points to pervasive urban networks that let people access the Web, determine whether their friends are in the area via a tool called FriendFinder, and arrange meetings:

> "I can come into downtown Athens [Georgia] with a PDA, send a text message that I'm going to be in Blue Sky Coffee for two hours, then turn it off and put it in my pocket," explains Shamp. "Then when one of my buddies comes into downtown, he can use the WAG zone to find out where his friends are."[4]

> **If a home is, in Le Corbusier's words, a "machine for living," then an office is a "machine for working."**

Various target groups will get different amenities; business users might like readily available Internet printing, for example, more than friend-finding—or maybe not. But my guess is that the end result will look more like the eighteenth-century coffee-houses, in which so many of that day conducted their business (Lloyd's of London started in Lloyd's coffee-house), than like the office towers where the twentieth century's men in the gray flannel suits encamped.

In the eighteenth century, the coffee-house was a hotbed of activity. "There," according to British newsweekly *The Economist*, "for the price of a cup of coffee, you could read the latest pamphlets, catch up on news and gossip, attend scientific lectures, strike business deals, or chat with like-minded people about literature or politics." These coffee-houses even served as offices—Richard Steele, editor of London's popular periodical, the *Tatler*, requested that his mail be delivered to his favorite coffee haunt. Londoners would drop in at several coffee-houses to participate in all kinds of conversation. "Regulars could pop in once or twice a day, hear the latest news, and check to see if any post awaited them.... [M]ost people frequented several coffee-houses, the choice of which reflected their range of interests."[5]

THE GENIUS OF BUILD-A-BEAR

I believe this is part of a larger phenomenon. Nineteenth- and twentieth-century technology seemed to favor aggregation, uniformity, and large size. Twenty-first-century technology seems to favor diversity, variety, and small size—along with a much higher degree of interconnection. From politics to work, from factories to malls, I think there are quite a few revolutions along these lines yet to come, and I think they'll go well beyond comfy chairs.

In fact, they're moving the factories into the malls. Build-A-Bear, a place where I've spent a lot of time, is a good example. My daughter had her birthday recently, and during her party I experienced what I'll call a Virginia Postrel moment. The party was at Build-A-Bear, a place that I thought was sure to go out of business when it first opened. *Why put a factory in a mall?* Who, I asked, would pay top dollar to assemble their own teddy bear or other stuffed animal when you could buy perfectly good ones off the shelf? Well, that was before I had a daughter, and now I know the answer: lots of little girls!

During the party it was interesting to watch the girls picking out animals with the help of the friendly salespeople. (Note: The phrase "Would you like me to stuff your monkey?" sounds, somehow, *er*, inappropriate.) As my wife pointed out, the animal-and-clothing combinations that the girls put together reflected their own personalities and styles.

The girls were very happy, but I couldn't help thinking that quite a few bluenoses would have disapproved. Customized bears (or monkeys!) that you put together yourself? An endless array of bear-pants, bear-glasses, bear-hats, bear-dresses, bear-briefcases, and even bear-roller skates to go with them? Who needs it? Rotten kids, spoiled rotten!

---

[4] Linda Baker, "Urban Renewal: The Wireless Way," *Salon*, 29 November 2004. Available online at http://www.salon.com/tech/feature/2004/11/29/digital_metropolis/index_np.html.

[5] "The Internet in a Cup," *The Economist*, 18 December 2003. Available online at http://www.economist.com/World/europe/displayStory.cfm?story_id=2281736.

Except that actually they're rather nice girls, who with no prompting spent considerably less than the party budget allowed for, and who cooperated sweetly in picking things out and complimenting each others' choices. So as I was paying the bill (the cashier was an Albanian Kosovar refugee, who seems to have settled in rather well in that most inclusive and most American of institutions: the shopping mall), I had a Postrel moment: I realized why I was so thoroughly wrong about the prospects for Build-A-Bear.

Virginia Postrel has argued in her book, *The Substance of Style*,[6] that aesthetic values are becoming a major driver—perhaps the major new driver—of economic activity. It's easy to scoff at this because aesthetics seem divorced from function: an ugly car gets you where you're going just as quickly and reliably as a pretty one, an ugly coat keeps you just as warm as a handsome one, and an ugly house keeps the rain off just as well as a showplace.

Nonetheless, attractiveness matters. We all know that an ugly spouse can be just as faithful and loving as a gorgeous one—even, if popular legend is to be believed, more so—but we nonetheless tend to choose mates whose looks we like. To my daughter and her friends, it's natural to spend a lot of time thinking about what looks good. And, judging by the attention that my nephews pay to the subjects of their interests (automobiles, airplanes, and other vehicles, mostly), looks matter there too.

So does customization. What the folks at Build-A-Bear figured out, and what I missed entirely when I scoffed at their business plan, is that people don't just want things to look good. They want them to look good *their way*. That's what makes Build-A-Bear work.

Other stores have stuffed animals that are just as attractive, but the buyers don't feel that they are *unique*. So where will this lead? People talk about "customizing" outfits with accessories, but how long before on-the-spot manufacturing of clothing lets people design clothing themselves, or download designs from the Internet and produce truly one-of-a-kind outfits? People are already experimenting, and I suspect that a "Build-An-Outfit" will be coming soon to a mall near you.

I also suspect that it's just the beginning. (Design your own car? Why not?) But I also have another suspicion that verges on certainty: when it happens, people will complain. Just as people complained about the enforced conformity of old-style mass-production, people (often the same people) will complain about the multiplicity of choices offered by new technologies.

But then, complaining is an aesthetic style too, of a sort—though it's one that, for better and worse, may not fit in as well at malls as it does elsewhere. And as malls develop (beyond comfy chairs and Build-A-Bear) that may become much more significant.

Reportedly, the new trend is toward a different kind of mall, the "lifestyle center," which fits the beyond-comfy-chairs description pretty well. Changes in shopping habits and an increased competitiveness due to the Internet and other local specialized boutiques have motivated retailers in shopping centers to be more imaginative in order to keep bringing in customers.[7] And people are specifically invoking the "third place" point in pitching these facilities, as this account of one such venture makes clear.

> His idea for Camano Commons, a 3.3-acre gathering place, is to try to capture that European spirit of places where private commerce and public leisure mix readily, said the project's marketing director, Theresa Metzger.
>
> "In Paris, you have the sidewalk cafe. In England, you have the neighborhood pub," Metzger said. . . .
>
> "Americans are so unfamiliar with third places, so I always like to describe it this way: Remember the TV show, 'Cheers'? They didn't always get along, but when somebody was missing, they got concerned," Ericson said.[8]

I think we'll see more of that. In my local mall, blue-haired Goths with multiple piercings cluster in one area, while Dungeons & Dragons-playing teens stake out their territory in another spot. All the while, senior citizens and families stroll around them. It seems to me that the traditional downtown is being replaced by commercial spaces. And that has its ups, its downs, and its lessons.

---

[6] Virginia Postrel, *The Substance of Style: How the Rise of Aesthetic Value Is Remaking Commerce, Culture, and Consciousness* (HarperCollins, 2003).

[7] Beth Mattson, "Where Town Square Meets the Mall," *Minneapolis-St. Paul Business Journal*, 27 August 1999. Available online at http://www.bizjournals.com/twincities/stories/1999/08/30/focus3.html?page=1.

[8] Scott Morris, "A Third Place for Camano," *Daily Herald* (Everett, WA), 5 September 2003. Available online at http://www.heraldnet.com/Stories/03/9/5/17437484.cfm.

The "up" is that Americans are getting the kind of safe, diverse, and communal public space that critics of suburbanization have long called for. Rather than being locked in their tract homes, watching television and not knowing their neighbors, Americans are increasingly spending their time in public spaces surrounded by all sorts of other people.

Another upside is that—unlike the cumbersome white-elephant "downtown revitalization" projects envisioned by urban planners and funded by massive quantities of taxpayers' money—these public spaces are market-driven and actually generate tax dollars rather than consume them. And, because it's market-driven, the comfy-chair revolution can turn on a dime to meet consumer needs and interests.

FREEDOM OF…SHOPPING?

The downside is that the traditional downtown has been replaced by corporate-controlled space. What's wrong with that? Well, in the traditional downtown, things like the First Amendment's guarantee of free speech apply. In malls, they generally don't. (One of my former students has written an interesting law review article on this subject.[9]) But that's where the people are, meaning that First Amendment guarantees of the right to protest downtown are increasingly meaningless when nobody goes downtown. Indeed, here in Knoxville the antiwar protests, such as they were, were held on the sidewalk in front of West Town Mall when the protest organizers realized that a weekend protest downtown would be the proverbial tree falling unheard in the forest. Malls often have such offensive characteristics as omni-present security cameras coupled with draconian bans on picture taking. It's not like Singapore, exactly, but it's not your old-fashioned downtown square either.

But there's a lesson too. One reason why people go to malls instead of downtown is that they feel safe. Part of this is physical safety. Though that's partly an illusion. Mall crime doesn't get reported much—all those advertisers make it easy to persuade local media to keep it quiet—but there's lots more of it than you'd think.

Makes sense: criminals go where the money is, and a mugger would starve to death in most downtowns.

But more important than the desire for physical safety, I think, is the desire to go un-hassled by unpleasant people. Vagrants (relatively safe from prosecution in light of Supreme Court decisions), panhandlers, and accosters of pedestrians ranging from Bible-thumping street preachers to various political activists are free to express themselves in downtowns, thanks to the expansive First Amendment jurisprudence of the past half-century. But, except in a few states where the state constitution has been interpreted to treat malls as public space, they're barred from these spaces. And, in a curious coincidence, that's where people tend to go. (How do people really feel about this? I've observed that in the movie *Airplane*, the audience always cheers when the airport solicitors get beaten up.)

So what's the lesson? Free speech absolutists (and I'm pretty much one myself) may tell people that being hassled by loudmouths is part of democracy. And people may even agree—but they'll still choose the mall over downtown if the hassle-factor gets very high. What that means, among other things, is that public-sector rules are always subject to private-sector competition. It also suggests that you can enact rules that promote free speech at the cost of people being hassled—but if you go too far, people will vote with their feet by choosing a controlled environment with fewer hassles.

This sort of market-constrained approach to rights may trouble some people, though it's really just a public-private version of the sort of competition among states that federalists have always supported. Either way, it's a reality worth keeping in mind when planning rules and regulations for public and quasi-public spaces—especially since we are likely to see the latter increase as a result of the comfy-chair revolution.

The upside, though, is that the traditional lonely orator, trying to get his (it was almost always "his") message across in the public square, isn't so important as a symbol of free speech anymore. The Supreme Court once wrote, "The liberty of the press is the right of the lonely pamphleteer who uses carbon paper or a mimeograph just as much as of the large metropolitan publisher who uses the latest photocomposition methods."[10] But more recently, the Court noted, "Through the use of Web

---

[9] For much more on the subject of malls, private property, and free speech, see Jennifer Niles Coffin, "The United Mall of America: Free Speech, State Constitutions, and the Growing Fortress of Private Property," Volume 33, University of Michigan J.L., Reform 615 (2000).

[10] *Branzburg v. Hayes*, 408 U.S. 665, 794 (1972).

pages, mail exploders, and newsgroups, the same individual can become a pamphleteer."[11]

But, actually, technology has made it possible for individuals to become not merely pamphleteers, but vital sources of news and opinion that rival large metropolitan publishers in audience and influence. Since these independent sources are both *less* expensive and usually less annoying, perhaps First Amendment doctrine will take the difference into account.

Charles Black once wrote of "the plight of the captive auditor," who is subjected to messages that "he cannot choose but hear."[12] Limits to technology may have required us to overlook the captive auditor's plight in the past in the name of free speech—causing many people to vote with their feet in favor of controlled private space. But newer technologies may justify a different approach today: the First Amendment often requires the government to pursue the least restrictive means in regulating speech. Perhaps there should be at least an implicit requirement that speakers use the least *annoying* means of speaking too, or at least abide by limits when choosing the most annoying. This doesn't strike me as a bad thing. While the Internet makes publishing—and hence a free press—easier and cheaper, technologies like The Cloud and FriendFinder should make free speech, and public orations, easier and cheaper too, without the need to annoy. They'd better, anyway, because people's willingness to put up with annoyance is limited, while people's choices are, thanks to technology and the market, growing all the time.

What makes this issue difficult is that the tidy division between public and private spaces that we've taken for granted in recent years is breaking down. Traditional public spaces, like town squares, usually lack amenities. Even public restrooms are often hard to find. Private-public spaces like bookstores and coffee-houses have amenities and are open to everyone; but people tend to develop a proprietary interest in the places they frequent most. (No surprise to anyone who has ever heard a Londoner refer to "my pub.") Likewise, as people develop more control over their environments, they tend to have less tolerance for things that threaten that control. Americans tolerate TV commercials but hate popup ads, accept junk mail but despise spam, and, I suspect, will respond even less favorably to interruptions by strangers in public places once they become accustomed to meeting mostly with people they know or have something in common with. The "third place" may be a partial remedy to that, but as with the pub, we're likely to see people who don't fit in get a somewhat chillier reception. Determining the boundaries for acceptable public conduct, especially in private-public places, may prove a challenge in the future.

Working it out won't be easy, but then all revolutions have their difficulties.

---

[11]*Reno v. American Civil Liberties Union*, 521 U.S. 844, 870 (1997).
[12]Charles L. Black Jr., "He Cannot Choose but Hear: The Plight of the Captive Auditor," Volume 53, *Columbia Law Review* (1953), 960.

CONSIDER

1. Reynolds describes his local Hollister & Co. store—with its comfortable lounging areas—as a "hangout" for teens. Describe a local spot to which you would apply the term. What makes a place a hangout? Is it an environment, as Reynolds suggests, that represents a particular lifestyle?

2. Reynolds describes a need for "safe and comfortable public spaces." What social functions might such places promote and what might their absence do to a community?

3. Reynolds argues that the concept of a "third place" is more common in Europe than in the United States. What is a "third place"? Do you have a third place or would you want one?

COMPOSE

4. Spend a few hours in a local hangout examining the environment and observing the people and activities there. Then write a description of what you have experienced.

CHALLENGE

5. Reynolds defends big chain retailers such as Barnes & Noble against those who prefer smaller, independent bookstores. Analyze his argument and then try to apply it critically to other kinds of retail operations. Is a Wal-Mart Superstore better for a town than many mom-and-pop stores?

Where the Avatars Roam

Michael Gerson
(2007)

> **FYI** Michael Gerson, a graduate of Wheaton College, is a member of the Council on Foreign Relations. A Republican, he served as speechwriter for President George W. Bush (2001–06). His article on Second Life originally appeared in the *Washington Post*.

I am not usually found at bars during the day, though the state of the Republican Party would justify it. But here I was at a bar talking to this fox—I mean an actual fox, with fluffy tail and whiskers. It turns out that, in the online world of Second Life, many people prefer to take the shape of anthropomorphic animals called "furries," and this one is in a virtual bar talking about her frustrating job at a New York publishing house. But for all I know, she could be a man in outback Montana with a computer, a satellite dish and a vivid imagination.

For a columnist, this is called "research." For millions of Americans, it is an addictive form of entertainment called MMORPGs—massively multiplayer online role-playing games. In this entirely new form of social interaction, people create computer-generated bodies called avatars and mingle with other players in 3-D fantasy worlds.

Some of these worlds parallel a form of literature that J.R.R. Tolkien called "sub-creation"—the Godlike construction of a complex, alternative reality, sometimes with its own mythology and languages. I subscribe along with my two sons (an elf and a dwarf) to The Lord of the Rings Online, based on Tolkien's epic novels, which sends its participants on a series of heroic quests. I'm told that World of Warcraft, which has more than 8 million subscribers, takes a similar approach. Some of the appeal of these games is the controlled release of aggression—cheerful orc killing. But they also represent a conservative longing for medieval ideals of chivalry—for a recovery of honor and adventure in an age dominated by choice and consumption.

Second Life, however, is a different animal. Instead of showing the guiding hand of an author, this universe is created by the choices of its participants, or "residents." They can build, buy, trade and talk in a world entirely without rules or laws; a pure market where choice and consumption are the highest values. Online entrepreneurs make real money selling virtual clothing, cars and "skins"—the photorealistic faces and bodies of avatars. Companies such as Dell, IBM and Toyota market aggressively within Second Life.

The site has gotten some recent attention for its moral lapses. A few of its residents have a disturbing preference for "age play"—fantasy sex with underage avatars—which has attracted the attention of prosecutors in several countries.

But Second Life is more consequential than its moral failures. It is, in fact, a large-scale experiment in libertarianism. Its residents can do and be anything they wish. There are no binding forms of community, no responsibilities that aren't freely chosen and no lasting consequences of human actions. In Second Life, there is no human nature at all, just human choices.

And what do people choose? Well, there is some good live music, philanthropic fundraising, even a few virtual churches and synagogues. But the main result is the breakdown of inhibition. Second Life, as you'd expect, is highly sexualized in ways that have little to do with respect or romance. There are frequent outbreaks of terrorism, committed by online anarchists who interrupt events, assassinate speakers (who quickly reboot from the dead) and vandalize buildings. There are strip malls everywhere, pushing a relentless consumerism. And there seems to be an inordinate number of vampires, generally not a sign of community health.

Libertarians hold to a theory of "spontaneous order"— that society should be the product of uncoordinated

Source: Michael Gerson, "Where the Avatars Roam." From *The Washington Post*, July 6, 2007, p. A15, © 2007 The Washington Post. All rights reserved. Used by permission and protected by the Copyright Laws of the United States. The printing, copying, redistribution, or retransmission of the material without express written permission is prohibited.

human choices instead of human design. Well, Second Life has plenty of spontaneity, and not much genuine order. This experiment suggests that a world that is only a market is not a utopia. It more closely resembles a seedy, derelict carnival—the triumph of amusement and distraction over meaning and purpose.

Columnists, like frontier trackers, are expected to determine cultural directions from faint scents in the wind. So maybe there is a reason that *The Lord of the Rings* is ultimately more interesting than Second Life. Only in a created world, filled with moral rules, social obligations and heroic quests, do our free choices seem to matter. And even fictional honor fills a need deeper than consumption.

G.K. Chesterton wrote that when people are "really wild with freedom and invention" they create institutions, such as marriages and constitutions; but "when men are weary they fall into anarchy." In that anarchy, life tends to be nasty, brutish, short—and furry.

CONSIDER

1. Gerson makes a critical distinction between the ethical structure of fantasy games such as The Lord of the Rings Online and Second Life. Define that difference in your own words and expound upon Gerson's claim. Do you agree that it would explain why behavior within the two types of communities might differ?

2. Gerson mentions that prosecutors in some areas have been concerned by activity in Second Life that would be illegal in the real world. Under what circumstances (if any) should the laws and mores of the real world apply to a fantasy space?

FYI

ITEM 4.14 ■ **Ryan Bretag, Welcome to the Texas State University Second Life Campus, March 26, 2007**

Real places are often recreated in Second Life's virtual world. Here, for example, is a photograph from Second Life of "Old Main" at Texas State University—a signature building on that campus.

CONSIDER

1. Even at a quick glance, you likely recognize that this shot represents a virtual rather than a real place. But what exactly about the image tells you that? What's absent from the image?

2. At what point might a virtual environment like Second Life (see the accompanying article by Michael Gerson) become a real place? How would you describe the nature or terms of that reality?

Cluster 4.2
Borderlands

Borderlands are geographical regions where people, separated by political or geographical boundaries, nonetheless meet and merge, sometimes in a hybrid culture. They are rarely settled or comfortable places, especially when they must parley stark differences among people divided by language, traditions, values, religion, and political systems. Such border regions can be found all along the divide between Mexico—a Spanish-speaking, Catholic, oligarchic, third-world nation—and the United States, an English-speaking, Protestant, first-world superpower. As the editorial cartoons in Item 4.15 suggest, waves of immigrants heading north to seek better jobs and opportunity have made these regions a political flashpoint. The rationale for immigration, often illegal, seems simple: America needs workers, and Mexicans need jobs. But the sheer number of immigrants has weighed heavily on American border communities and states who see their makeup and characters changing. Mexico has been affected no less.

Charles Bowden's "Our Wall" takes a close-up look at what happens when miles of fence suddenly divide communities that have long shared a cultural symbiosis. Benjamin Alire Sáenz, a resident of El Paso, Texas, offers a more personal look at the problem in his poem "War," describing what life feels like in a divided city. And Randal C. Archibold reports on how the musical tradition of the *corrido* gives Mexican immigrants throughout the United States a vehicle for staying connected to their homeland.

CONSIDER

1. Can you find a common theme in these editorial cartoons? What do the borderlands in these cartoons have in common?

2. Border enforcement has increased since 2003, the date of Kevin Tuma's cartoon questioning the integrity of the United States' Immigration and Naturalization Service (INS). But what problems are inevitable in enforcing immigration regulations along a political boundary that stretches more than 1900 miles?

3. How might these cartoons be different if they tried to depict those border regions where Mexican and Americans cities and towns abut? What cultural complications occur in these heavily populated areas?

COMPOSE

4. All three cartoons reflect the point of view of American editorial cartoonists. In a brief comparison/contrast essay, explain how a Mexican cartoonist might depict the borderland.

FYI

ITEM 4.15 ■ Editorial Cartoons on Immigration

Any set of editorial cartoons about Mexican immigration to the United States will reflect a range of opinions and ironies. As these images suggest, while the border itself may be only an arbitrary line or diminutive stream, it carries weighty implications—political, cultural, and economic.

Kevin Tuma

Rex Babin

Signe Wilkinson

Our Wall

Charles Bowden
(2007)

> **FYI** Writer Charles Bowden, a correspondent for *GQ*, has written books and articles about the Mexican/American border, including *Down by the River: Drugs, Money, Murder, and Family* (2004). "Our Wall" appeared in *National Geographic* in May of 2007.

In the spring of 1929, a man named Patrick Murphy left a bar in Bisbee, Arizona, to bomb the Mexican border town of Naco, a bunny hop of about ten miles (16 kilometers). He stuffed dynamite, scrap iron, nails, and bolts into suitcases and dropped the weapons off the side of his crop duster as part of a deal with Mexican rebels battling for control of Naco, Sonora. When his flight ended, it turned out he'd hit the wrong Naco, managing to destroy property mainly on the U.S. side, including a garage and a local mining company. Some say he was drunk, some say he was sober, but everyone agrees he was one of the first people to bomb the United States from the air.

Borders everywhere attract violence, violence prompts fences, and eventually fences can mutate into walls. Then everyone pays attention because a wall turns a legal distinction into a visual slap in the face. We seem to love walls, but are embarrassed by them because they say something unpleasant about the neighbors—and us. They flow from two sources: fear and the desire for control. Just as our houses have doors and locks, so do borders call forth garrisons, customs officials, and, now and then, big walls. They give us divided feelings because we do not like to admit we need them.

Now as the United States debates fortifying its border with Mexico, walls have a new vogue. At various spots along the dusty, 1,952-mile (3,141 kilometers) boundary, fences, walls, and vehicle barriers have been constructed since the 1990s to slow the surge in illegal immigration. In San Diego, nine miles (14 kilometers) of a double-layered fence have been erected. In Arizona, the state most overrun with illegal crossings, 65 miles (105 kilometers) of barriers have been constructed already. Depending on the direction of the ongoing immigration debate, there may soon be hundreds more miles of walls.

The 800 or so residents of Naco, Arizona, where Patrick Murphy is part of the local lore, have been living in the shadow of a 14-foot-high (four meters) steel wall for the past decade. National Guard units are helping to extend the 4.6-mile (7.4 kilometers) barrier 25 miles (40 kilometers) deeper into the desert. The Border Patrol station is the biggest building in the tiny town; the copper roof glistens under the blistering sun. In 2005, a pioneering bit of guerrilla theater took place here when the Minutemen, a citizen group devoted to securing the border, staked out 20 miles (32 kilometers) of the line and patrolled it. Today about 8,000 people live in Naco, Sonora, on the Mexican side of the metal wall that slashes the two communities.

Only a dirt parking lot separates the Gay 90s bar from the Naco wall. Inside, the patrons are largely bilingual and have family ties on both sides of the line. Janet Warner, one of the bartenders, has lived here for years and is one of those fortunate souls who has found her place in the sun. But thanks to the racks of stadium lights along the wall, she has lost her nights, and laments the erasure of the brilliant stars that once hung over her life. She notes that sometimes Mexicans jump the new steel wall, come in for a beer, then jump back into Mexico. The bar began in the late 1920s as a casino and with the end of Prohibition added alcohol. The gambling continued until 1961, when a new county sheriff decided to clean up things. On the back wall are photographs of Ronald and Nancy Reagan when they'd stop by on their way to a nearby Mexican ranch.

The bar is one of only a handful of businesses left. The commercial street leading to the border is lined with defunct establishments, all dead because the U.S. government sealed the entry to Mexico after 9/11 and rerouted it to the east. Leonel Urcadez, 54, a handsome man who has owned the bar for decades, has mixed feelings about the wall. "You get used to it," he says. "When they first built it, it was not a bad idea—cars were crossing illegally from Mexico and the Border Patrol would chase them. But it's so ugly."

The two Nacos came into being in 1897 around a border crossing that connected copper mines in both nations. By 1901 a railroad linked the mines. A big miners' strike in 1906, one cherished by Mexicans as foreshadowing the revolution in 1910, saw troops from both nations facing each other down at the line. The town of Naco on the Mexican side changed hands many times during the actual revolution—at first the prize was revenue from the customs house. Later, when Arizona voted itself dry in 1915, the income came from the saloons. Almost every old house in Naco, Arizona, has holes from the gun battles. The Naco Hotel, with its three-foot (one meter) mud walls, advertised its bulletproof rooms.

The boundary between Mexico and the United States has always been zealously insisted upon by both countries. But initially Mexicans moved north at will. The U.S. patrols of the border that began in 1904 were mainly to keep out illegal Asian immigrants. Almost 900,000 Mexicans legally entered the United States to flee the violence of the revolution. Low population in both nations and the need for labor in the American Southwest made this migration a non-event for decades. The flow of illegal immigrants exploded after the passage of the North American Free Trade Agreement in the early 1990s, a pact that was supposed to end illegal immigration but wound up dislocating millions of Mexican peasant farmers and many small-industrial workers.

The result: Naco was overrun by immigrants on their way north. At night, dozens, sometimes hundreds, of immigrants would crowd into motel rooms and storage rental sheds along the highway. The local desert was stomped into a powder of dust. Naco residents found their homes broken into by desperate migrants. Then came the wall in 1996, and the flow of people spread into the high desert outside the town.

The Border Patrol credits the wall, along with better surveillance technology, with cutting the number of illegal immigrants captured near Naco's 33-mile (53 kilometers) border by half in the past year. Before this new heightening of enforcement, the number caught each week, hiding in arroyos thick with mesquite and yucca, often exceeded the town's population. At the moment, the area is relatively quiet as "coyotes," or people smugglers, pause to feel out the new reality, and the National Guard has been sent in to assist the Border Patrol. At the nearby abandoned U.S. Army camp, the roofs are collapsing and the adobe bricks dribble mud onto the floor. Scattered about are Mexican water bottles—illegals still hole up here after climbing the wall.

Residents register a hodgepodge of feelings about the wall. Even those who have let passing illegal immigrants use their phones or given them a ride say the exodus has to stop. And even those sick of finding trash in their yards understand why the immigrants keep coming.

"Sometimes I feel sorry for the Mexicans," says Bryan Tomlinson, 45, a custodial engineer for the Bisbee school district. His brother Don chimes in, "But the wall's a good thing."

A border wall seems to violate a deep sense of identity most Americans cherish. We see ourselves as a nation of immigrants with our own goddess, the Statue of Liberty, a symbol so potent that dissident Chinese students fabricated a version of it in 1989 in Tiananmen Square as the visual representation of their yearning for freedom.

> **A border wall seems to violate a deep sense of identity most Americans cherish.**

Walls are curious statements of human needs. Sometimes they are built to keep restive populations from fleeing. The Berlin Wall was designed to keep citizens from escaping from communist East Germany. But most walls are for keeping people out. They all work for a while, until human appetites or sheer numbers overwhelm them. The Great Wall of China, built mostly after the mid-14th century, kept northern tribes at bay until the Manchu conquered China in the 17th century. Hadrian's Wall, standing about 15 feet (5 meters) high, 9 feet (3 meters) wide, and 73 miles (117 kilometers) long, kept the crazed tribes of what is now Scotland from running amok in Roman Britain—from A.D. 122 until it was overrun in 367. Then you have the Maginot Line, a series of connected forts built by France after World War I to keep the German army from invading. It was a success, except for one flaw: The troops of the Third Reich simply went around its northwestern end and invaded France through the Netherlands and Belgium.

Now tourists visit its labyrinth of tunnels and underground barracks.

In 1859 a rancher named Thomas Austin released 24 rabbits in Australia because, he noted, "the introduction of a few rabbits could do little harm and might provide a touch of home, in addition to a spot of hunting." By that simple act, he launched one of the most extensive barriers ever erected by human beings: the rabbit fences of Australia, which eventually reached 2,023 miles (3,256 kilometers). Within 35 years, the rabbits had overrun the continent, a place lacking sufficient and dedicated rabbit predators. For a century and a half, the Australian government has tried various solutions: imported fleas, poisons, trappers. Nothing has dented the new immigrants. The fences themselves failed almost instantly—rabbits expanded faster than the barriers could be built, careless people left gates open, holes appeared, and, of course, the rabbits simply dug under them.

In Naco all the walls of the world are present in one compact bundle. You have Hadrian's Wall or the Great Wall of China because the barrier is intended to keep people out. You have the Maginot Line because a 15-minute walk takes you to the end of the existing steel wall. You have the rabbit fences of Australia because people still come north illegally, as do the drugs.

Perhaps the closest thing to the wall going up on the U.S.-Mexico border is the separation wall being built by Israel in the West Bank. Like the new American wall, it is designed to control the movement of people, but it faces the problem of all walls—rockets can go over it, tunnels can go under it. It offends people, it comforts people, it fails to deliver security. And it keeps expanding.

Rodolfo Santos Esquer puts out *El Mirador*, a weekly newspaper in Naco, Sonora, and he finds the wall hateful. He stands in his cramped office—a space he shares with a small shop peddling underwear—and says, "It looks like the Berlin Wall. It is horrible. It is ugly. You feel more racism now. It is a racist wall. If people get close to the wall, the Border Patrol calls the Mexican police, and they go and question people."

And then he lightens up because he is a sunny man, and he says it actually hasn't changed his life or the lives of most people in town. Except that the coyotes now drive to the end of the wall before crossing. And as the wall grows in length, the coyotes raise their rates. Santos figures half the town is living off migrants going north—either feeding them and housing them or guiding them into the U.S. Passage to Phoenix, about 200 miles (320 kilometers) away, is now $1,500 and rising. He notes that after the wall went up in 1996, the migration mushroomed. He wonders if there is a connection, if the wall magically beckons migrants. Besides, he says, people just climb over it with ropes.

> **We think of walls as statements of foreign policy, and we forget the intricate lives of the people we wall in and out.**

Santos fires up his computer and shows an image he snapped in the cemetery of a nearby town. There, there, he points as he enlarges a section of the photo. Slowly a skull-shaped blur floats into view against the black of the night—a ghost, he believes. The border is haunted by ghosts—the hundreds who die each year from heat and cold, the ones killed in car wrecks as the packed vans of migrants flee the Border Patrol, and the increasing violence erupting between smugglers and the agents of Homeland Security. Whenever heat is applied to one part of the border, the migration simply moves to another part. The walls in southern California drove immigrants into the Arizona desert and, in some cases, to their deaths. We think of walls as statements of foreign policy, and we forget the intricate lives of the people we wall in and out.

Emanuel Castillo Erúnez, 23, takes crime and car wreck photos for *El Mirador*. He went north illegally when he was 17, walked a few days, then was picked up and returned to Mexico. He sits on a bench in the plaza, shielded by a New York Yankees cap, and sums up the local feeling about the wall simply: "Some are fine with it, some are not." He thinks of going north again, but then he thinks of getting caught again. And so he waits.

There is a small-town languor about Naco, Sonora, and the wall becomes unnoticeable in this calm. The Minutemen and National Guard terrify people. At the Hospedaje Santa María, four people wait for a chance to go over the wall and illegally enter the wealth of the United States. It is a run-down, two-story building, one of many boarding houses for migrants in Naco. Salvador Rivera, a solid man in his early 30s, has been here about a year. He worked in Washington State, but, when his mother fell ill, he returned home to Nayarit, Mexico, and is now having trouble getting past the increased security. He left behind an American girlfriend he can no longer reach.

"For so many years, we Mexicans have gone to the U.S. to work. I don't understand why they put up a wall to turn us away. It's not like we're robbing anybody over there, and they don't pay us very much."

But talk of the wall almost has to be prompted. Except for those engaged in smuggling drugs or people, border crossers in Naco, Sonora, continue to enter through the main gate, as they always have. They visit relatives on the other side, as they always have. What has changed is this physical statement, a big wall lined with bright lights, that says, yes, we are two nations.

Jesús Gastelum Ramírez lives next door to the wall, makes neon signs, and looks like Willie Nelson. He watches people climb the wall and he understands a reality forgotten by most U.S. lawmakers—that simply to go through the wire instantly raises a person's income tenfold. Gastelum knows many of his neighbors smuggle people, and he understands.

Until recently, a volleyball team from the Mexican Naco and a team from the U.S. Naco used to meet once a year at the point where the wall ends on the west side of town, put up a net on the line, bring kegs of beer, and play a volleyball game. People from both Nacos would stream out to the site and watch. And then the wall would no longer exist for a spell. But it always confronts the eye.

Dan Duley, 50, operates heavy equipment and is a native of the Naco area. He was living in Germany after serving in the Air Force when the Berlin Wall came down, and he thought that was a fine thing. But here he figures something has to be done. "We need help," he says. "We're being invaded. They've taken away our jobs, our security. I'm just a blue-collar man living in a small town. And I just wish the government cared about a man who was blue."

But then, as in many conversations on the border, the rhetoric calms down. Duley, along with many other Naco residents, believes the real solution has to be economic, that jobs must be created in Mexico. There is an iron law on this border: The closer one gets to the line, the more rational the talk becomes because everyone has personal ties to people on the other side. Everyone realizes the wall is a police solution to an economic problem. The Mexicans will go over it, under it, or try to tear holes in it. Or, as is often the case, enter legally with temporary visiting papers and then melt into American communities. Of the millions of illegal immigrants living in the United States, few would have come if there wasn't a job waiting for them.

Over in Naco, Sonora, the final night of a fiesta is in full roar. Men drinking beer move by on horseback, groups of girls in high heels prance past. Nearby, folks play bingo, and in the band shell a group does a sound check for the big dance. Looming over the whole party is a giant statue of Father Hidalgo with his bald head and wild eyes. He launched the Mexican Wars of Independence in 1810. Two blocks away, the steel wall glows under a battery of lights.

In the Gay 90s bar in Naco, Arizona, a quinceañera, the 15th-birthday celebration that introduces a young girl to the world, is firing up. There are 200 people in the saloon's back room, half from Mexico and half from the U.S. The boys wear rented tuxedo vests, the girls are dressed like goddesses. One man walks in with a baby in a black polka-dot dress with pink trim.

The birthday girl, Alyssa, stands with her family for an official portrait.

Walls come and go, but quinceañeras are forever, I say to the man with the baby. He nods his head and smiles.

The steel barrier is maybe a hundred feet (30 meters) away. Outside in the darkness, Mexicans are moving north, and Border Patrol agents are hunting them down. Tomorrow, work will continue on the construction of the wall as it slowly creeps east and west from the town. Tourists already come to look at it.

I have no doubt someday archaeologists will do excavations here and write learned treatises about the Great Wall of the United States. Perhaps one of them will be the descendant of a Mexican stealing north at this moment in the midnight hour.

CONSIDER

1. Bowden describes a wall as "a visual slap in the face." Thinking of the walls you encounter, what is your reaction to his claim? Is it accurate for Bowden to suggest that walls stem from "fear and the desire for control"?

2. What does Bowden's short historical account of the two Nacos (of Sonora and Arizona) suggest about relationships between border towns? How are borderland dwellers affected by their proximity to people from a neighboring country?

3. Bowden suggests that over time, most walls fail to keep people out. Is his claim persuasive, given the evidence he presents—especially the fact that the income of Mexican immigrants increases tenfold when they cross north into the United States?

COMPOSE

4. The wall between the two Nacos, Bowden suggests, has only enforced the notion that "yes, we are two nations." Write either a comparison/contrast or a proposal essay that examines the implications of his claim. Can a region ever successfully meld two distinct national cultures?

CHALLENGE

5. Write a rhetorical analysis of "Our Wall" to assess Bowden's effort to offer a balanced perspective on the issue of a border fence between Mexico and the United States. Does he take a side in the article for or against the divide? Or is his approach more even-handed?

ITEM 4.16 ■ Diane Cook and Len Jenshel, *Tijuana, Mexico*, 2006

Diane Cook and Len Jenshel's photograph, with its simple, factual title, conveys the tension that marks the boundary between the United States and Mexico, one fraught with social and political implications. The cross marks the spot where an unidentified Mexican ("no identificado") died while attempting to cross into the United States.

CONSIDER

1. How would you characterize this photograph: Does it present information or make an argument? How does it resemble or differ from the editorial cartoons depicting the border in Item 4.15?

2. What information might you need to understand the photograph? Use the Web to explore the controversies embedded in the image.

3. The natural environment here is represented entirely by a blue sky. What is the human contribution to the environment? What feelings does the image evoke?

COMPOSE

4. *Tijuana, Mexico* was one of several photographs taken by Diane Cook and Len Jenshel to accompany Charles Bowden's *National Geographic* article "Our Wall." In a short report or argument, explore the way an image like this one might affect your reading of such a text. Would such emotive images color your perceptions before you read a piece, simply make you more interested in reading it, or influence you in some other way?

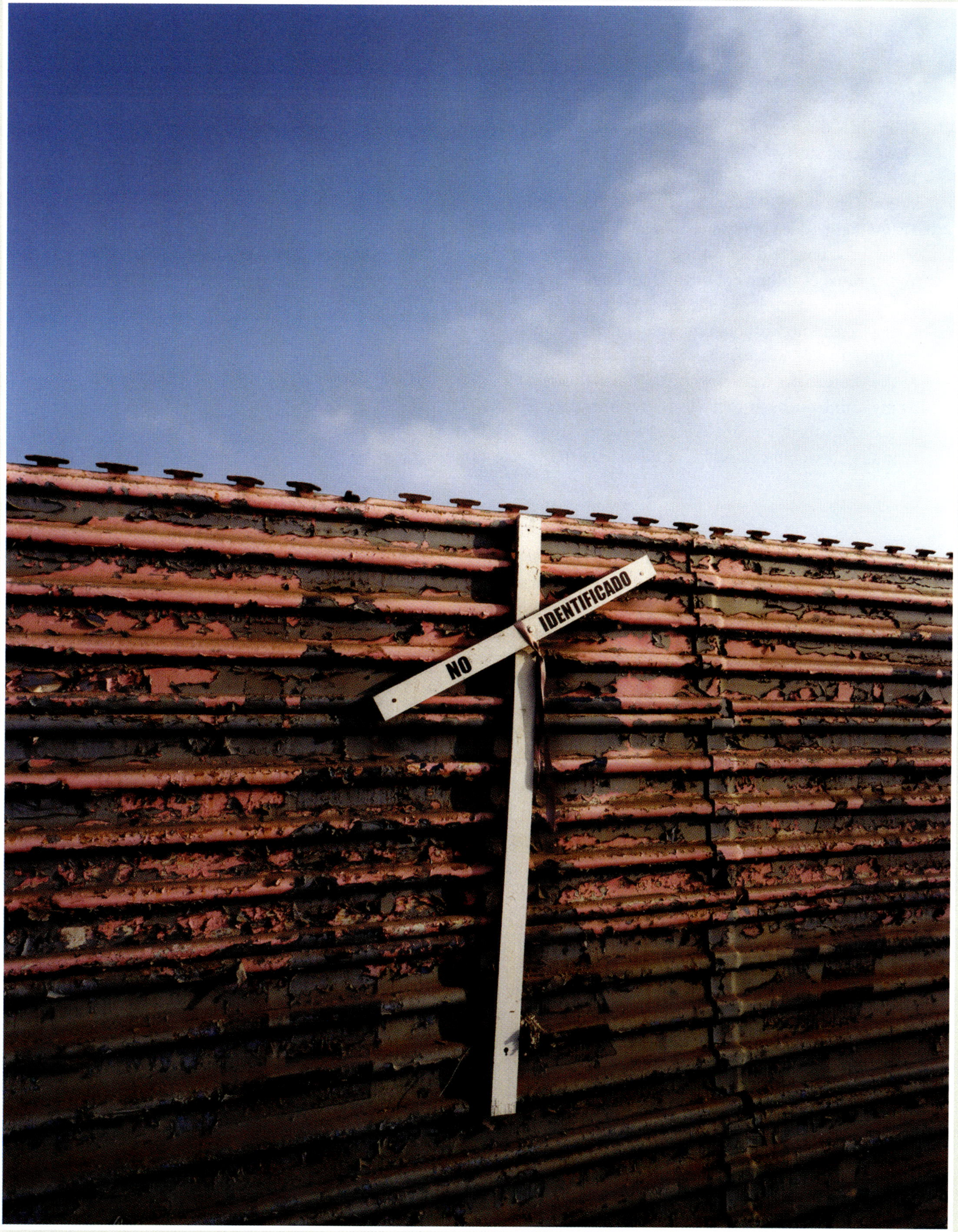
NO
IDENTIFICADO

War (in the City in Which I Live)

Benjamin Alire Sáenz
(2006)

> All my life—let me say this so you understand—*all my life*
> I have heard stories of the river and how people were willing
> To die to cross it. To die just to get to other side. The other
> Side was the side I lived on. "And people die to get here?"
> 5 My mother nodded at my question in that way that told me
> She was too busy to discuss the matter and went back
> To her ritual of rolling out tortillas for her seven children, some
> Of whom asked questions she had no answers for. We were
> Poor as a summer without rain, an outhouse and a pipe
> 10 Bringing in cold water from a well that was unreliable
> As the white man's treaties with the Indians, unreliable
> As my drunk uncles, unreliable as my father's Studebaker
> Truck. I was six. It was impossible for me to fathom
> Why anyone would risk death for the chance to live like us.

■ ■ ■

> 15   I have heard people laugh when
> They see the Río Grande for the first time. *That is the river?*
> But that river has claimed a thousand lives, Mexicans caught
> In its currents mistaking the river as something tame, and in
> One second devouring them whole. The survivors
> 20 Have handed down this lesson: Nothing in the desert is
> Tame. Not the people, not the sand, not the winds, not
> The sun, not even the river that resembles a large ditch
> And laughed at by visitors and locals alike. Nothing
> In the desert has ever had anything resembling mercy
> 25 On Mexicans attempting to leave their land, to become
> Something they weren't meant to be.

■ ■ ■

>   People are still crossing. People are still dying. Some have
> Died suffocating in box cars. Some have drowned. Some
> Have been killed by vigilantes who protect us in the name
> 30 Of all that is white. Some have died in a desert larger than
> their dreams. Some were found, no hint of their names
> On their remains. In the city that is my home, Border Patrol
> Vans are as ubiquitous as taxi cabs in New York. Green Vans
> Are a part of my landscape, a part of my imagination, no less
> 35 Than the sky or the river or the ocotillos blooming in spring.
> The West is made of things that make you bleed. I no longer
> Hang images of summer clouds or Indians carrying pots on their
> Talented heads or Mexican peasants working the land with magic
> Hands. On my walls, I no longer hang paintings of the Holy Poor.

FYI Born in New Mexico (1954), award-winning novelist, essayist, and poet Benjamin Alire Sáenz lives in El Paso, Texas, where he writes about the experiences of living in a borderland city. "War" is from his collection of poetry *Dreaming the End of War*, 2006.

■ ■ ■

We have been fighting a war on this border
For hundreds of years. We have been fighting the war so long
That the war has become as invisible as the desert sands we
Trample on.

I do not know how long all this will continue. Peace
Is like the horizon. We can see it in the distance
But it is always far and we can never touch it.

■ ■ ■

Every day
In what passes for a newspaper in the city in which
I live, someone writes a letter ranting against the use
Of the Spanish language because this is America and I can
Taste the hate in the letter, can almost feel the spit
In the letter writer's mouth and I know we could not
Ever speak about this without one of us wanting to hurt
The other in the city in which I live.

■ ■ ■

I will tell you a sad story: White people are moving away
From this city that has claimed my heart. They are running away
From my people. They are running away from all that keeps
Us poor. I want them to stay and fight. I want them
To stay and live with my people. *We have chased them
Away.* I want them to love the people who make the food
They love. *We have chased them away—are you happy? Are you
Happy?* And there are people waiting in line, spending
Their fortunes just for a chance to enter, waiting, just blocks
Away from where I sit, waiting to come over, waiting in Juárez
Just to cross the river, from China and India and all the nations
Of Africa and Central America and Asia. No poet, no engineer, no
Politician, no philosopher no artist, no novelist has ever
Dreamed a solution. I am tired of living in exile. I am tired
Of chasing others off the land.

Let me say this again. Again. Again.
I want, I want this war to end. To end.

CONSIDER

1. As a child, how does Sáenz experience his life in the United States? Why do people even "from China and India and all the nations" want to come here?

2. What details throughout the poem convey Sáenz's sense of the West as he has experienced it? What kind of territory is it that people are fighting over in this borderland? Why might it still have claimed his heart?

CHALLENGE

3. Sáenz writes that he is "tired of living in exile" and "tired / Of chasing others off the land." In an argument, try to reconcile those seemingly contradictory perspectives. What does it mean to be an exile from a place? Who in his poem are among the exiles? What would need to happen for the war he describes to end?

ITEM 4.17 ■ Joe Grossinger, from *El Paso Street Art*, 2007

Included among the *El Paso Street Art* photographs Joe Grossinger has posted on his Flickr site are a series of shots like these of decorated overpasses on I-10—which cuts through the Texas city.

224   4.2 | BORDERLANDS

CONSIDER

1. Search for the name *Ruben Salazar* on the Web if you don't recognize it. Why would he be celebrated in a Texas border city?

2. How would you characterize the overpass art representing the United States of America? What is its theme?

3. What function does street art like this—wall murals and other public art—have in a community? How does the community represent and reconcile various points of view?

COMPOSE

4. Find and describe two of more examples of street art in your local community. What types of images are depicted? To whom might the images appeal?

225

Far From Home, Mexicans Sing Age-Old Ballads of a New Life

Randal C. Archibold
(2007)

> **FYI** Shortly after the U.S. Congress failed to pass a comprehensive reform of immigration policies, this feature story about the *corrido* appeared in the *New York Times* (July 6, 2007). The *corrido* is a popular form of Spanish-language folk ballad that now records the experiences of Mexicans in the United States. Randal C. Archibold is a reporter for the *Times* who has written extensively about immigration issues.

NAMPA, Idaho — Watching television coverage of immigration marches, Jose F. Garcia got mad. He got frustrated. He got his button accordion.

In short order, Mr. Garcia squeezed out the beginnings of a corrido, a kind of Mexican folk ballad that tells a story, often with a moral, and sang out the lyrics that came to him.

> Now they are putting up barriers in front of us so we don't return;
> but that is not going to block us from crossing into the United States,
> We leap them like deer, we go under them like moles.

Mr. Garcia, accompanied by his young son Benjamin on a snare drum, recently belted out the song, "Latinos Unidos," in an onion field for the benefit of researchers from the Western Folklife Center, a nonprofit cultural organization in Elko, Nev., that has begun a project to document Mexican influences and folklore in the ranching West.

Corridos have long telegraphed the melancholy of Mexico's northern frontier. Heroes die. Lovers are crossed. And, in the controversial narco-corrido form, drug dealers are celebrated.

But as migrants moved north, modern corridos have also been inspired by everyday occurrences and current events, with some written about the Kennedys, crops, floods and truck stops.

Mr. Garcia has recorded a corrido about the Sept. 11 terrorist attacks, "Tragedia en Nueva York," complete with a jet sound whining through the guitars, horns and accordion.

> It was Sept. 11 when the world woke up
> in the year 2001 when it was reported
> that in the twin towers two airplanes crashed

(In Spanish, the lyrics rhyme.)

The Western Folklife Center intends to build an archive of such material, recording for posterity the Mexican presence far from the border and turning some of it into segments for public television and radio.

Although the project was conceived before the immigration debate intensified, Hal Cannon, the founding director of the center and its popular offshoot, the annual Cowboy Poetry Gathering, said it could serve as a reminder that, come what may, the Latino influence has already taken root.

"I think that's an important song," Mr. Cannon told his colleagues after listening to a few verses of Mr. Garcia's corrido, which Mr. Garcia plans to perform with his band and may play as part of a corrido competition the folklife center is organizing here on July 15.

Through the project, Mr. Cannon said later, "Relationships will be built, understanding will be

ITEM 4.18 ■ Chad Chase, *Jose F. Garcia and His Son Benjamin at a Benefit Near Nampa, Idaho, for the Western Folklife Center,* July 6, 2007

built and we will be documenting something that is quite ephemeral."

Musicians and scholars debate what qualifies as a corrido. To purists, Mr. Garcia's immigration song, though sung in the style of a corrido and with instruments common to the form, does not make the cut.

"I believe somebody has to die," said Juan Dies, an ethnomusicologist who is based in Chicago and is working with the center on the project. "But some people don't feel that way."

"The community defines what a corrido is, not a scholar from Chicago," added Mr. Dies, who specializes in Mexican music. "It is, basically, a musical news story."

Mr. Garcia's repertory, apart from immigration and terrorism, includes songs of desperate lovers and other more traditional corrido themes, which he and other musicians have found the crowds here, ever nostalgic, tend to favor.

"To me, a corrido is a song with a message," said Mr. Garcia, who recently opened a dance club but is hoping for a big break some day for his band. "I don't like the ones about drug traffickers that are popular on the radio and that the young kids these days like. But as long as it is telling a story with a message to me it is a corrido."

Some of the older corridos here speak of the beauty of the valley—one, a romantic ballad called "Nampa," extols the virtues of its women and "silvery moon nights"—or bar fights long forgotten. But the longing for home, and the difficulty of going back, are more popular themes among the current crop of local musicians.

"If I write one about my friend over there the people would say, hey, who wants to hear about him?" said Gerardo Barca, a musician known by his nickname, Lalo. "People want to be transported home, to time and events there."

So Mr. Barca wrote the bittersweet "Lindos Recuerdos," or "Beautiful Memories," about the loss of his family's ranch in Michoacan to development after he left 15 years ago and his inability to ever return.

> "These are just beautiful memories of times that won't come back;
> Since the times have changed,
> and where there was that little ranch now there is a city."

"Everybody here can relate to that, to that idea of wanting to go home but never really making it," he said.

Latino immigrants, primarily from Mexico and Texas, came to the Treasure Valley here in three waves. The first arrived in the 1800s to work in mines and build railroads, another came to work in agriculture in the postwar boom of the 1940s and 1950s and a third in the past couple of decades as Boise and its suburbs have swollen over farmland.

From 1990 to 2000, the Hispanic population of Idaho grew 92 percent, to 101,690, with most of that growth in the Treasure Valley.

Alfredo Paz, a local musician, laments that the younger generation prefers narco-corridos, a rough equivalent to gangsta rap and something he and his band members refuse to perform.

"We don't want to sing about drugs or rape or anything like that," said Mr. Paz, who does perform corridos about double-crossed lovers and his signature, "Le Quedan Plumas Al Gallo," or "The Rooster Still Has His Feathers." The song is about a man defeated in love but still the cock of the walk.

Mr. Garcia, who has been in the United States for more than 20 years, said he was carrying on a musical tradition handed down from his father and practiced in the small village where he grew up.

"I always wanted to be somebody so I composed music," he said.

While watching the immigration marches that day, Mr. Garcia said he felt compelled to put "our story" to music, scratching out the words over several weeks, right up to the day the folklife center researchers came calling.

"I feel we need to write out stories and this was a big part of our story here," he said. "Corridos used to be like newspapers. Well, maybe, they still should be."

> "Corridos used to be like newspapers. Well, maybe, they still should be."

CONSIDER

1. Though *corridos* have many subjects, in what way is the genre of song tied to issues of home, homeland, and migration? What role does nostalgia play in performing and listening to such music? Might the forms of the *corridos* Mr. Garcia prefers be compared to traditional country music?

2. Does the political context for "Far From Home"—appearing shortly after the failure to pass immigration reform in the United States—impact your reading of the story? Why or why not?

3. The photograph in Item 4.18 accompanied the *New York Times* feature. It shows Jose Garcia and his son performing his *corrido* "Latinos Unidos" in an Idaho onion field. Why might that location be both surprising and unremarkable, depending on one's familiarity with the Latino presence in the United States? What statement does the photograph make?

COMPOSE

4. Write a short report examining the way music and songs sometimes connect us to places. You might consider, for example, the way a particular song evokes a personal memory of a place or time. Or find songs that resonate more widely among people of specific groups or generations, making particular places significant for any number of reasons—Shenendoah, Haight-Ashbury, Harlem.

Cluster 4.3
Roads We Travel

Can the road be a place? It certainly seems so in the United States, where every rock and country band worth a nickel has at least one ode to the highway in its song list. Since the middle of the twentieth century, the road trip has served as a rite of passage for many college-aged men and women, some who head south for their spring-break bacchanals while others steer for national parks or venture to cross the continent, sea to shining sea. Hollywood versions of such road trips are often tawdry, erotic, and comic—and perhaps not so far off the mark.

But in this section, we also look at some other versions. The grandest account of the American road may belong to John Steinbeck in *The Grapes of Wrath* (1939), chronicling the Depression-era trek of desperate Okies to California, looking for a better life and repeating a journey made almost a century earlier by Americans on a gold rush. Jack Kerouac published his ground-breaking novel *On the Road* (1957) in more prosperous times and thereby claimed the highway for an evolving youth culture. But Holland Cotter looks at Kerouac's account differently fifty years later, thinking about his own more troubling experiences with the realities of a racially divided country in "On My Road." Like any place, the road shapes who we are but does so as part of a process, a movement from here to there. These journeys evoke endless responses in every medium. And the *here* and *there* matter.

CONSIDER

1. How many additional films, TV shows, or books can you identify that are about the road—either in the modern era or in times prior to the internal combustion engine? In these works, how does the road (or journey) function as a place? What happens to people there? What is it they might be seeking?

2. What stereotypes does the movie poster for *Road Trip* employ? Who or what is not included in the picture? Why?

COMPOSE

3. Papers about personal road trips tend to fill up quickly with clichés—flat tires, missed turns, and cheap hotels. Write a description of a significant road trip you have experienced that is actually about *the road*, not what happened to you there. Focus on the places you have seen.

4. Write a paper describing your most clichéd road trip adventure. Keep it brief.

FYI

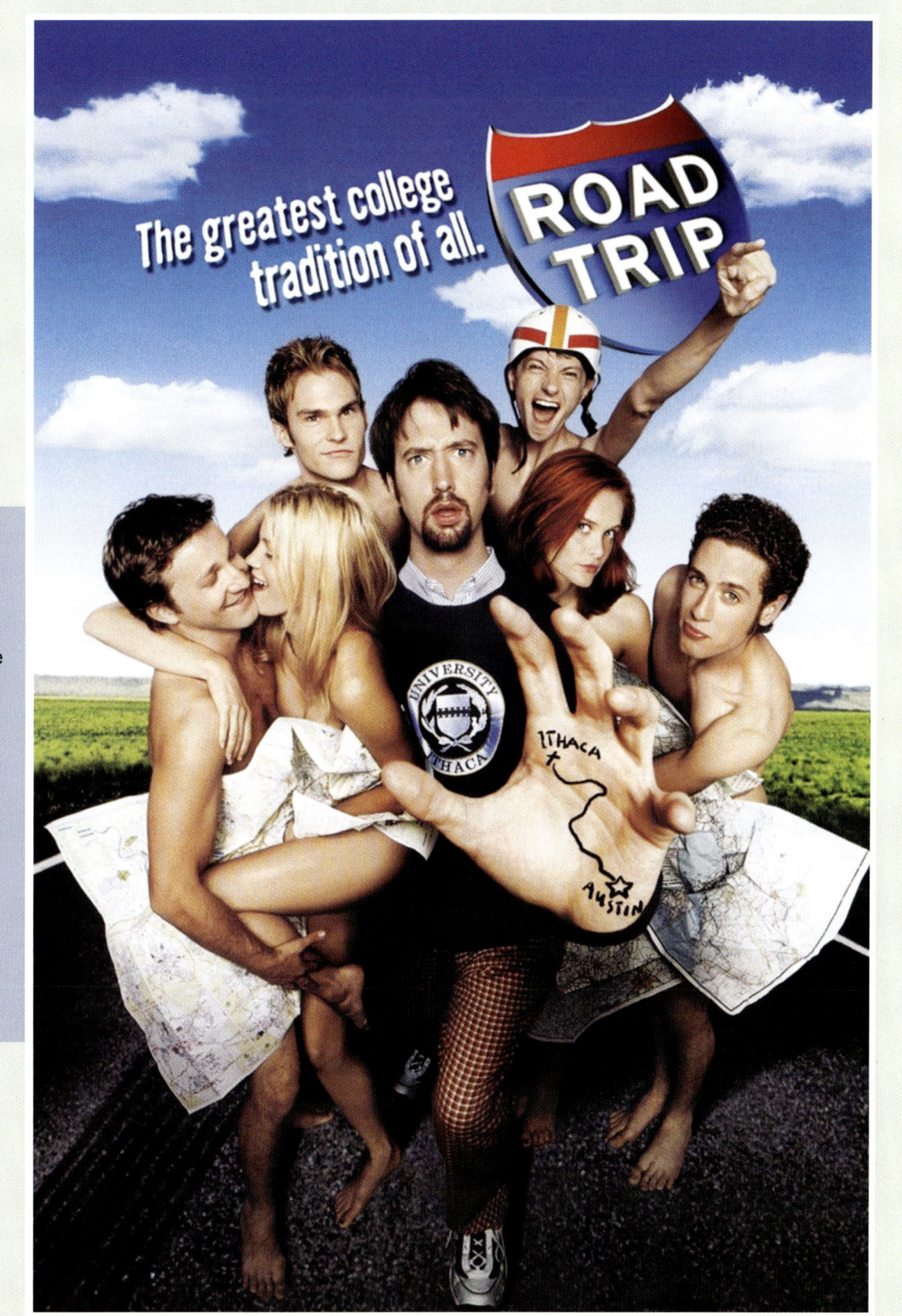

ITEM 4.19 ■ *Road Trip* Movie Poster, 2000

Heroes have been on the road since Homer's *Odyssey*. But the twentieth century brought two new inventions: motor vehicles and films. Their marriage produced travel narratives of varying quality, from the road pictures of Bob Hope and Bing Crosby (1940–52) to films like *The Long Long Trailer* (1954), *Easy Rider* (1969), *Badlands* (1973), *Thelma and Louise* (1991), and *Y tu mamá también* (2001). And, of course, that epochal quest, *Road Trip* (2000).

From *The Grapes of Wrath*

John Steinbeck
(1939)

> **FYI** Nobel-prize-winning novelist John Steinbeck published *The Grapes of Wrath* in 1939, immortalizing the migration west of thousands of Americans displaced by drought and poverty during the Great Depression. The novel follows the Joad family as it joins the procession of desperate people heading west on Route 66, at the time the main road to Los Angeles. They were fleeing the Dust Bowl that had destroyed farms and livelihoods throughout the Midwest.

CHAPTER 12

Highway 66 is the main migrant road. 66—the long concrete path across the country, waving gently up and down on the map, from the Mississippi to Bakersfield—over the red lands and the gray lands, twisting up into the mountains, crossing the divide and down into the bright and terrible desert, and across the desert to the mountains again, and into the rich California valleys.

66 is the path of a people in flight, refugees from dust and shrinking land, from the thunder of tractors and shrinking ownership, from the desert's slow northward invasion, from the twisting winds that howl up out of Texas, from the floods that bring no richness to the land and steal what little richness is there. From all of these the people are in flight, and they come into 66 from the tributary side roads, from the wagon tracks and the rutted country roads. 66 is the mother road, the road of flight.

Clarksville and Ozark and Van Buren and Fort Smith on 64, and there's an end of Arkansas. And all the roads into Oklahoma City, 66 down from Tulsa, 270 up from McAlester. 81 from Wichita Falls south, from Enid north. Edmond, McLoud, Purcell. 66 out of Oklahoma City; El Reno and Clinton, going west on 66. Hydro, Elk City, and Texola; and there's an end to Oklahoma. 66 across the Panhandle of Texas. Shamrock and McLean, Conway and Amarillo, the yellow. Wildorado and Vega and Boise, and there's an end of Texas. Tucumcari and Santa Rosa and into the New Mexican mountains to Albuquerque, where the road comes down from Santa Fe. Then down the gorged Rio Grande to Las Lunas and west again on 66 to Gallup, and there's the border of New Mexico.

And now the high mountains. Holbrook and Winslow and Flagstaff in the high mountains of Arizona. Then the great plateau rolling like a ground swell. Ashfork and Kingman and stone mountains again, where water must be hauled and sold. Then out of the broken sun-rotted mountains of Arizona to the Colorado, with green reeds on its banks, and that's the end of Arizona. There's California just over the river, and a pretty town to start it. Needles, on the river. But the river is a stranger in this place. Up from Needles and over a burned range, and there's the desert. And 66 goes on over the terrible desert, where the distance shimmers and the black center mountains hang unbearably in the distance. At last there's Barstow, and more desert until at last the mountains rise up again, the good mountains, and 66 winds through them. Then suddenly a pass, and below the beautiful valley, below orchards and vineyards and little houses, and in the distance a city. And, oh, my God, it's over.

The people in flight streamed out on 66, sometimes a single car, sometimes a little caravan. All day they rolled slowly along the road, and at night they stopped near water. In the day ancient leaky radiators sent up columns of steam, loose connecting rods hammered and pounded. And the men driving the trucks and the overloaded cars listened apprehensively. How far between towns? It is a terror between towns. If something breaks—well, if something breaks we camp right here while Jim walks to town and gets a part and walks back and—how much food we got?

Listen to the motor. Listen to the wheels. Listen with your ears and with your hands on the steering wheel; listen with the palm of your hand on the gearshift lever; listen with your feet on the floor boards. Listen to the pounding old jalopy with all your senses, for a change of tone, a variation of rhythm may mean—a week here? That rattle—that's tappets. Don't hurt a bit. Tappets can rattle till Jesus comes again without no harm. But that thudding as the car moves along—can't hear that—just kind of feel it. Maybe oil isn't gettin' someplace. Maybe a bearin's startin' to go. Jesus, if it's a bearing, what'll we do? Money's goin' fast. And why's the son-of-a-bitch heat up so hot today? This ain't no climb. Le's look. God Almighty, the fan belt's gone! Here, make a belt outa this little piece a rope. Le's see how long—there. I'll splice the ends. Now take her slow—slow, till we can get to a town. That rope belt won't last long.

'F we can on'y get to California where the oranges grow before this here ol' jug blows up. 'F we on'y can.

And the tires—two layers of fabric worn through. On'y a four-ply tire. Might get a hundred miles more outa her if we don't hit a rock an' blow her. Which'll we take—a hunderd, maybe, miles, or maybe spoil the tubes? Which? A hunderd miles. Well, that's somepin you got to think about. We got tube patches. Maybe when she goes she'll only spring a leak. How about makin' a boot? Might get five hunderd more miles. Le's go on till she blows.

We got to get a tire, but, Jesus, they want a lot for a ol' tire. They look a fella over. They know he got to go on. They know he can't wait. And the price goes up.

Take it or leave it. I ain't in business for my health. I'm here a-sellin' tires. I ain't givin' 'em away. I can't help what happens to you. I got to think what happens to me.

How far's the nex' town?

I seen forty-two cars a you fellas go by yesterday. Where you all come from? Where all of you goin'?

Well, California's a big state.

It ain't that big. The whole United States ain't that big. It ain't that big. It ain't big enough. There ain't room enough for you an' me, for your kind an' my kind, for rich and poor together all in one country, for thieves and honest men. For hunger and fat. Whyn't you go back where you come from?

This is a free country. Fella can go where he wants.

That's what *you* think! Ever hear of the border patrol on the California line? Police from Los Angeles—stopped you bastards, turned you back. Says, if you can't buy no real estate we don't want you. Says, got a driver's license'? Le's see it. Tore it up. Says you can't come in without no driver's license.

It's a free country.

Well, try to get some freedom to do. Fella says you're jus' as free as you got jack to pay for it.

In California they got high wages. I got a han'bill here tells about it.

Baloney! I seen folks comin' back. Somebody's kiddin' you. You want that tire or don't ya'?

Got to take it, but, Jesus, mister, it cuts into our money! We ain't got much left.

Well, I ain't no charity. Take her along.

Got to, I guess. Let's look her over. Open her up, look a' the casing—you son-of-a-bitch, you said the casing was good. She's broke damn near through.

> **Fella says you're jus' as free as you got jack to pay for it.**

The hell she is. Well—by George! How come I didn' see that?

You did see it, you son-of-a-bitch. You wanta charge us four bucks for a busted casing. I'd like to take a sock at you.

Now keep your shirt on! I didn' see it, I tell you. Here—tell ya what I'll do. I'll give ya this one for three-fifty.

You'll take a flying jump at the moon! We'll try to make the nex' town.

Think we can make it on that tire? Got to. I'll go on the rim before I'd give that son-of-a-bitch a dime.

What do ya think a guy in business is? Like he says, he ain't in it for his health. That's what business is. What'd you think it was? Fella's got—See that sign 'longside the road there? Service Club. Luncheon Tuesday, Colmado Hotel? Welcome, brother. That's a Service Club. Fella had a story. Went to one of them meetings an' told the story to all them business men. Says, when I was a kid my ol' man give me a haltered heifer an' says take her down an' git her serviced. Ant the fella says, I done it, an' ever' time since then when I hear a business man talkin' about service, I wonder who's gettin' screwed. Fella in business got to lie an cheat, but he calls it somepin else. That's what's important. You go steal that tire an' you're a thief, but he tried to steal your four dollars for a busted tire. They call that sound business.

Danny in the back seat wants a cup a water. Have to wait. Got no water here.

Listen—that the rear end? Can't tell.

Sound telegraphs through the frame. There goes a gasket. Got to go on. Listen to her whistle. Find a nice place to camp an' I'll jerk the head off. But, God Almighty, the food's gettin' low, the money's gettin' low. When we can't buy no more gas—what then?

Danny in the back seat wants a cup a water. Little fella's thirsty.

Listen to that gasket whistle. Chee-rist! There she went. Blowed tube an' casing all to hell. Have to fix her. Save that casing to make boots; cut 'em out an' stick 'em inside a weak place.

Cars pulled up beside the road, engine heads off, tires mended. Cars limping along 66 like wounded things, panting and struggling. Too hot, loose connections, loose bearings, rattling bodies.

Danny wants a cup a water.

People in flight along 66. And the concrete road shone like a mirror under the sun, and in the distance the heat made it seem that there were pools of water in the road.

Danny wants a cup a water.

He'll have to wait, poor little fella. He's hot. Nex' service station. *Service* station, like the fella says.

> **Where does the courage come from? Where does the terrible faith come from?**

Two hundred and fifty thousand people over the road. Fifty thousand old cars—wounded, steaming. Wrecks along the road, abandoned. Well, what happened to them? What happened to the folks in that car? Did they walk? Where are they? Where does the courage come from? Where does the terrible faith come from?

And here's a story you can hardly believe, but it's true, and it's funny and it's beautiful. There was a family of twelve and they were forced off the land. They had no car. They built a trailer out of junk and loaded it with their possessions. They pulled it to the side of 66 and waited. And pretty soon a sedan picked them up. Five of them rode in the sedan and seven on the trailer, and a dog on the trailer. They got to California in two jumps. The man who pulled them fed them. And that's true. But how can such courage be, and such faith in their own species? Very few things would teach such faith.

The people in flight from the terror behind—strange things happen to them, some bitterly cruel and some so beautiful that the faith is refired forever.

CONSIDER

1. What is the effect of Steinbeck's use of so many place names in his description of Highway 66 and the people traveling on it? Are you familiar with any of them? Does this matter?

2. How have the physical challenges of the road changed since the 1930s? Does the world described here have anything in common with that of the typical middle-class American today? With that of more recent immigrants heading to America (see Cluster 4.2 "Borderlands")?

3. Compare Steinbeck's "mother road" to the highway Bobby Troup sings about in "Route 66," composed in 1946 (see Gallery Item 4.8). How can the same highway have changed so much in the popular imagination? What does Route 66 mean today?

COMPOSE

4. Steinbeck describes hard times on the road—much tougher than most Americans ever experience today. Can someone in your generation understand the hardships of the Joad family? Write an argument based on a claim you develop in response to that question.

CHALLENGE

5. Do a detailed rhetorical analysis of this selection from *The Grapes of Wrath* to describe and explain how readers might be influenced by some of the many devices of language Steinbeck uses, from parallelism and repetition to the listing of place names and imaginative use of a spoken voice. Here's a tip: Try reading the chapter aloud to *hear* how the prose feels. Who is the speaker?

ITEM 4.20 ■ *Cadillac Ranch*, 2007

Some have argued that Stanley Marsh 3's *Cadillac Ranch* (1974) is the most famous piece of "sculpture" in the state of Texas. Commissioned by Marsh and executed by a group of artists called The Ant Farm, the work consists of ten Cadillacs from that marque's glory years (1943–63) buried nose down west of Amarillo along Interstate 40, near what's left of old Route 66. The bold graffiti sprayed on the vehicles is the not unwelcome contribution of visitors and vandals.

CONSIDER

1. Use the Internet or library to research Amarillo's eccentric and creative philanthropist, Stanley Marsh 3. What other creative works has he commissioned? What was his rationale for creating *Cadillac Ranch*?

2. Why might the placement of the *Cadillac Ranch* along Route 66 be significant? How might a member of the Joad family (see the selection from Steinbeck's *Grapes of Wrath*) react to this odd piece of art?

COMPOSE

3. If *Cadillac Ranch* were recreated today along a highway near you, what would you suggest be planted in the ground? Write a proposal paper in which you explain your rationale for this new piece of public art.

From On the Road

Jack Kerouac
(1951)

In no time at all we were back on the main highway and that night I saw the entire state of Nebraska unroll before my eyes. A hundred and ten miles an hour straight through, an arrow road, sleeping towns, no traffic, and the Union Pacific streamliner falling behind us in the moonlight. I wasn't frightened at all that night; it was perfectly legitimate to go 110 and talk and have all the Nebraska towns—Ogallala, Gothenburg, Kearney, Grand Island, Columbus—unreel with dreamlike rapidity as we roared ahead and talked. It was a magnificent car; it could hold the road like a boat holds on water. Gradual curves were its singing ease. "Ah, man, what a dreamboat," sighed Dean. "Think if you and I had a car like this what we could do. Do you know there's a road that goes down Mexico and all the way to Panama?—and maybe all the way to the bottom of South America where the Indians are seven feet tall and eat cocaine on the mountainside? Yes! You and I, Sal, we'd dig the whole world with a car like this because, man, the road must eventually lead to the whole world. Ain't nowhere else it can go—right? Oh, and are we going to cut around old Chi with this thing! Think of it, Sal, I've never been to Chicago in all my life, never stopped."

"We'll come in there like gangsters in this Cadillac!"

"Yes! And girls! We can pick up girls, in fact, Sal, I've decided to make extra-special fast time so we can have an entire evening to cut around in this thing. Now you just relax and I'll ball the jack all the way."

"Well, how fast are you going now?"

"A steady one-ten I figure—you wouldn't notice it. We've still got all Iowa in the daytime and then I'll make that old Illinois in nothing flat." The boys fell asleep and we talked and talked all night.

It was remarkable how Dean could go mad and then suddenly continue with his soul—which I think is wrapped up in a fast car, a coast to reach, and a woman at the end of the road—calmly and sanely as though nothing had happened. "I get like that every time in Denver now—I can't make that town any more. Gookly, gooky, Dean's a spooky.

> **FYI** Jack Kerouac's novel *On the Road* is itself the stuff of legends. Typed on a single continuous scroll of paper in 1951, the rambling narrative was rejected by publishers. But when *On the Road* did finally appear in 1957, it became a sensation, one of those rare works that supposedly speaks for an entire generation, in this case, the Beats—whose anti-establishment attitudes and celebration of youth culture set the stage for the Age of Aquarius. In the selection reprinted here, the novel's hero, Dean Moriarity, and Kerouac's alter ego, Sal Paradise, deliver a Cadillac they've driven across the country for a travel bureau to Chicago, with two other college boys also along for the ride.

Zoom!" I told him I had been over this Nebraska road before in '47. He had too. "Sal, when I was working for the New Era Laundry in Los Angeles, nineteen forty-four, falsifying my age, I made a trip to Indianapolis Speedway for the express purpose of seeing the Memorial Day classic hitch hiking by day and stealing cars by night to make time. Also I had a twenty-dollar Buick back in LA, my first car, it couldn't pass the brake and light inspection so I decided I needed an out-of-state license to operate the car without arrest so went through here to get the license. As I was hitchhiking through one of these very towns, with the plates concealed under my coat, a nosy sheriff who thought I was pretty young to be hitchhiking accosted me on the main drag. He found the plates and threw me in the two-cell jail with a county delinquent who should have been in the home for the old since he couldn't feed himself (the sheriff's wife fed him) and sat through the day drooling and slobbering. After investigation, which included corny things like a fatherly quiz, then an abrupt turnabout to frighten me with threats, a comparison of my handwriting, et cetera, and after I made the most magnificent speech of my life to get out of it, concluding with the confession that I was lying about my car-stealing past and was only looking for my paw who was a farmhand hereabouts, he let me go. Of course I missed the races. The following fall I did the same thing again to see the Notre Dame–California game in South Bend, Indiana—trouble none this time and, Sal, I had just the money for the ticket and not an extra cent and didn't eat anything all up and back except for what I could panhandle from all kinds of crazy cats I met on the road and at the same time gun gals. Only guy in the United States of America that ever went to so much trouble to see a ballgame."

I asked him the circumstances of his being in LA in 1944. "I was arrested in Arizona, the joint absolutely the worst joint I've ever been in. I had to escape and pulled the greatest escape in my life, speaking of escapes, you see, in a general way. In the woods, you know, and crawling, and swamps—up around that mountain country. Rubber hoses and the works and accidental so-called death facing me I had to cut out of those woods along the ridge so as to keep away from trails and paths and roads. Had to get rid of my joint clothes and sneaked the neatest theft of a shirt and pants from a gas station outside Flagstaff, arriving LA two days later clad as gas attendant and walked to the first station I saw and got hired and got myself a room and changed name (Lee Buliay) and spent an exciting year in LA, including a whole gang of new friends and some really great girls, that season ending when we were all driving on Hollywood Boulevard one night and I told my buddy to steer the car while I kissed my girl—I was at the wheel, see—and *he didn't hear me* and we ran smack into a post but only going twenty and I broke my nose. You've seen before my nose—the crooked Grecian curve up here. After that I went to Denver and met Marylou in a soda fountain that spring. Oh, man, she was only fifteen and wearing jeans and just waiting for someone to pick her up. Three days three nights of talk in the Ace Hotel, third floor, southeast corner room, holy memento room and sacred scene of my days—she was so sweet then, so *young*, hmm, ahh! But hey, look down there in the night thar, hup, hup, a buncha old bums by a fire by the rail, damn me." He almost slowed down. "You see, I never know whether my father's there or not." There were some figures by the tracks, reeling in front of a woodfire. "I never know whether to ask. He might be anywhere." We drove on. Somewhere behind us or in front of us in the huge night his father lay drunk under a bush, and no doubt about it—spittle on his chin, water on his pants, molasses in his ears, scabs on his nose, maybe blood in his hair and the moon shining down on him.

I took Dean's arm. "Ah, man, we're sure going home now." New York was going to be his permanent home for the first time. He jiggled all over; he couldn't wait.

> **When there was a chance he shot ahead and passed cars by the half-dozen and left them behind in a cloud of dust.**

"And think. Sal, when we get to Pennsy we'll start hearing that gone Eastern bop on the disk jockeys. Geeyah, roll, old boat, roll!" The magnificent car made the wind roar; it made the plains unfold like a roll of paper; it cast hot tar from itself with deference—an imperial boat. I opened my eyes to a fanning dawn; we were hurling up to it. Dean's rocky dogged face as ever bent over the dashlight with a bony purpose of its own.

"What are you thinking, Pops?"

"Ah-ha, ah-ha, same old thing, y'know—gurls gurls gurls."

I went to sleep and woke up to the dry, hot atmosphere of July Sunday morning in Iowa, and still Dean was driving and driving and had not slackened his speed; he took the curvy corndales of Iowa at a minimum of eighty and the straightaway 110 as usual, unless both-ways traffic forced him to fall in line at a crawling and miserable sixty. When there was a chance he shot ahead and passed cars by the half-dozen and left them behind in a cloud of dust. A mad guy in a brand-new Buick saw all this on the road and decided to race us. When Dean was just about to pass a passel the guy shot by us without warning and howled and tooted his horn and flashed the tail lights for challenge. We took off after him like a big bird. "Now wait," laughed Dean, "I'm going to tease that sonofabitch for a dozen miles or so. Watch." He let the Buick go way ahead and then accelerated and caught up with it most impolitely. Mad Buick went out of his mind; he gunned up to a hundred. We had a chance to see who he was. He seemed to be some kind of Chicago hipster traveling with a woman old enough to be— and probably actually was—his mother. God knows if she was complaining, but he raced. His hair was dark and wild, an Italian from old Chi; he wore a sports shirt. Maybe there was an idea in his mind that we were a new gang from LA invading Chicago, maybe some of Mickey Cohen's men, because the limousine looked every bit the part and the license plates were California. Mainly it was just road kicks. He took terrible chances to stay ahead of us; he passed cars on curves and barely got back in line as a truck wobbled into view and loomed up huge. Eighty miles of Iowa we unreeled in this fashion, and the race was so interesting that I had no opportunity to be frightened. Then the mad guy gave up, pulled up at a gas station, probably on orders from the old lady, and as we roared by he waved gleefully. On we sped, Dean barechested, I with my feet on the dashboard, and the college boys sleeping in the back. We stopped to eat breakfast at a diner run by a white-haired lady who gave us extra-large portions of potatoes as churchbells rang in the nearby town. Then off again.

"Dean, don't drive so fast in the daytime."

"Don't worry, man, I know what I'm doing." I began to flinch. Dean came up on lines of cars like the Angel of Terror. He almost rammed them along as he looked for an opening. He teased their bumpers, he eased and pushed and craned around to see the curve, then the huge car leaped to his touch and passed, and always by a hair we made it back to our side as other lines filed by in the opposite direction and I shuddered. I couldn't take it any more. It is only seldom that you find a long Nebraskan straightaway in Iowa, and when we finally hit one Dean made his usual 110 and I saw flashing by outside several scenes that I remembered from 1947—a long stretch where Eddie and I had been stranded two hours. All that old road of the past unreeling dizzily as if the cup of life had been overturned and everything gone mad. My eyes ached in nightmare day.

"Ah hell, Dean, I'm going in the back seat, I can't stand it any more, I can't look."

"Hee-hee-hee!" tittered Dean and he passed a car on a narrow bridge and swerved in dust and roared on. I jumped in the back seat and curled up to sleep. One of the boys jumped in front for the fun. Great horrors that we were going to crash this very morning took hold of me and I got down on the floor and closed my eyes and tried to go to sleep. As a seaman I used to think of the waves rushing beneath the shell of the ship and the bottomless deeps thereunder—now I could feel the road some twenty inches beneath me, unfurling and flying and hissing at incredible speeds across the groaning continent with that mad Ahab at the wheel. When I closed my eyes all I could see was the road unwinding into me. When I opened them I saw flashing shadows of trees vibrating on the floor of the car. There was no escaping it. I resigned myself to all. And still Dean drove, he had no thought of sleeping till we got to Chicago. In the afternoon we crossed old Des Moines again. Here of course we got snarled in traffic and had to go slow and I got back in the front seat. A strange pathetic accident took place. A fat colored man was driving with his entire family in a sedan in front of us; on the rear bumper hung one of those canvas desert waterbags they sell tourists in the desert. He pulled up sharp, Dean was talking to the boys in the back and didn't notice, and we rammed him at five miles an hour smack on the waterbag, which burst like a boil and squirted water in the air. No other damage except a bent bumper. Dean and I got out to talk to him. The upshot of it was an exchange of addresses and some talk, and Dean not taking his eyes off the man's wife whose beautiful brown breasts were barely concealed inside a floppy cotton blouse. "Yass, yass." We gave him the address of our Chicago baron and went on.

The other side of Des Moines a cruising car came after us with the siren growling, with orders to pull over. "Now what?"

The cop came out. "Were you in an accident coming in?"

"Accident? We broke a guy's waterbag at the junction."

"He says he was hit and run by a bunch in a stolen car." This was one of the few instances Dean and I knew of a Negro's acting like a suspicious old fool. It so surprised us we laughed. We had to follow the patrolman to the station and there spent an hour waiting in the grass while they telephoned Chicago to get the owner of the Cadillac and verify our position as hired drivers. Mr. Baron said, according to the cop, "Yes, that is my car but I can't vouch for anything else those boys might have done."

"They were in minor accident here in Des Moines."

"Yes, you've already told me that—what I meant was, I can't vouch for anything they might have done in the past."

Everything was straightened out and we roared on. Newton, Iowa, it was, where I'd taken that dawn walk in 1947. In the afternoon we crossed drowsy old Davenport again and the low-lying Mississippi in her sawdust bed; then Rock Island, a few minutes of traffic, the sun reddening, and sudden sights of lovely little tributary rivers flowing softly among the magic trees and greeneries of mid-American Illinois. It was beginning to look like the soft sweet East again; the great dry West was accomplished and done. The state of Illinois unfolded before my eyes in one vast movement that lasted a matter of hours as Dean balled straight across at the same speed. In his tiredness he was taking greater chances than ever. At a narrow bridge that crossed one of these lovely little rivers he shot precipitately into an almost impossible situation. Two slow cars ahead of us were bumping over the bridge; coming the other way was a huge truck-trailer with a driver who was making a close estimate of how long it would take the slow cars to negotiate the bridge, and his estimate was that by the time he got there they'd be over. There was absolutely no room on the bridge for the truck and any cars going the other direction. Behind the truck cars pulled out and peeked for a chance to get by it. In front of the slow cars other slow cars were pushing along. The road was crowded and everyone exploding to pass. Dean came down on all this at 110 miles an hour and never hesitated. He passed the slow cars, swerved, and almost hit the left rail of the bridge, went head-on into the shadow of the unslowing truck, cut right sharply, just missed the truck's left front wheel, almost hit the first slow car, pulled out to pass, and then had to cut back in line when another car came out from behind the truck to look, all in a matter of two seconds, flashing by and leaving nothing more than a cloud of dust instead of a horrible five-way crash with cars lurching in every direction and the great truck humping its back in the fatal red afternoon of Illinois with its dreaming fields. I couldn't get it out of my mind, also, that a famous bop clarinetist had died in an Illinois car-crash recently, probably on a day like this. I went to the back seat again.

The boys stayed in the back too now. Dean was bent on Chicago before nightfall. At a road-rail junction we picked up two hobos who rounded up a half-buck between them for gas. A moment before sitting around piles of railroad ties, polishing off the last of some wine, now they found themselves in a muddy but unbowed and splendid Cadillac limousine headed for Chicago in precipitous haste. In fact the old boy up front who sat next to Dean never took his eyes off the road and prayed his poor bum prayers, I tell you. "Well," they said, "we never knew we'd get to Chicaga sa fast." As we passed drowsy Illinois towns where the people are so conscious of Chicago gangs that pass like this in limousines every day, we were a strange sight: all of us unshaven, the driver barechested, two bums, myself in the back seat, holding on to a strap and my head leaned back on the cushion looking at the countryside with an imperious eye—just like a new California gang come to contest the spoils of Chicago, a band of desperados escaped from the prisons of the Utah moon. When we stopped for Cokes and gas at a small-town station people came out to stare at us but they never said a word and I think

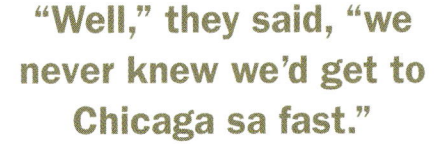

> "Well," they said, "we never knew we'd get to Chicaga sa fast."

4.3 | ROADS WE TRAVEL

made mental notes of our descriptions and heights in case of future need. To transact business with the girl who ran the gas-pump Dean merely threw on his T-shirt like a scarf and was curt and abrupt as usual and got back in the car and off we roared again. Pretty soon the redness turned purple, the last of the enchanted rivers flashed by, and we saw distant smokes of Chicago beyond the drive. We had come from Denver to Chicago via Ed Wall's ranch, 1180 miles, in exactly seventeen hours, not counting the two hours in the ditch and three at the ranch and two with the police in Newton, Iowa, for a mean average of seventy miles per hour across the land, with one driver. Which is a kind of crazy record.

CONSIDER

1. What might Dean Moriarity mean when he declares "the road must eventually lead to the whole world"? In this chapter, does the road mean different things to Dean and Sal? What might the Cadillac represent?

2. Fifty years ago in the heart of the Cold War, what would the appeal of a narrative as freewheeling as *On the Road* have been? What attraction—if any—does it have today? Do events in this chapter ring true? Why or why not?

3. How would you describe the style of this selection from Keroauc's novel? How does it differ from the language of other novels you have read? Point to features you admire or dislike.

COMPOSE

4. In the final paragraph of the selection, the boys in the car imagine themselves as outsiders in a strange environment—desperados from Utah or California gangsters cruising into Chicago. If you've ever similarly assumed an alter ego on a road trip, write a brief description of that experience.

COMPOSE

1. Using resources of the library and Web, explore the ideas of the Beat Generation, inspired by artists such as Jack Kerouac, Allen Ginsberg, Gregory Corso, and William S. Burroughs. With what activities, attitudes, and gathering places did they become associated in the late 1950s and early 1960s in the United States?

2. Members of the Beat Generation were quickly stereotyped as "beatniks" just as counter-culture figures in the 1960s were branded "hippies." Who might be considered members of the counter-culture today, and where would you find them?

ITEM 4.21 ■ **Jack Kerouac**

Jack Kerouac (1922–1969) became one of the voices of the Beat generation, a group of novelists, poets, and artists who shaped an American counter-culture in the 1950s. Kerouac's books include *The Subterraneans*, *Desolation Angels*, and *The Dharma Bums*.

On My Road

Holland Cotter
(2007)

> **FYI** Holland Cotter is a critic for the *New York Times* who ordinarily writes about the art scene. But the hoopla in 2007 over the fiftieth anniversary of *On the Road*'s publication inspired him to write this memoir, casting the novel in a less flattering light and putting a different spin on what people learn (or don't learn) from the places they visit. The piece appeared in the *Times* on September 2, 2007.

A high school friend—I'll call him Raymond—was in trouble. He'd been breaking into houses for thrills in our rich little white suburb of Boston. The police finally nabbed him; he was charged as a delinquent and shipped off to reform school in Austin, Tex., from which he sent back fearsome reports. In June of 1964, with school done for the year, I decided, in solidarity, to visit him.

Greyhound had a deal: an all-purpose, go-anywhere, good-for-a-year bus ticket for $100. I scraped the money together, bought the ticket, then told my parents. Fireworks. But I went anyway, with a promise that I'd check in with family en route. The next day I was on a bus out of Park Square station, with a way-too-big suitcase and a bag of books, headed south.

The books: Thoreau's "Walden," Dickinson's poems, Whitman's "Specimen Days" and Jack Kerouac's "On the Road." It was the Kerouac novel, first published 50 years ago this Wednesday, that inspired the trip. A drop-in on Raymond, though it held a certain lunatic appeal, was a pretext for a larger plan: to make the great American pilgrimage on Kerouac's "holy road."

Americans have, or at least once had, a thing for quest-journeys. You find evidence in 19th-century paintings of wilderness to the horizon. In literature John Bunyan's "Pilgrim's Progress" was a national best seller before the Civil War, second only to the Bible. Its redemptivist impulse powers Thoreau's perambulations. Kerouac, a confessed religionist, used Bunyan's dream trip from the City of Destruction to the Gates of Heaven as his literary model.

In the 1950s a cult of the frontier enjoyed a popular revival. Davy Crockett and the space race provided safe, secular options to two kids, two cars and 9 to 5. The stage-savvy Beats, with their motorbike saints, were part of the getaway package. Then in the early '60s the poetics of travel turned political, with civil rights marches, Freedom Rides and songs about all the roads a man must walk down before you call him a man. It was around this time, post-Beat, pre-hippie, when I was catching a bus south.

For some reason I had a romantic view of bus travel, maybe because Neal Cassady, Kerouac's buddy-hero, came to New York City for the first time by Greyhound with his teenage wife. What I quickly learned was that buses were the way poor people traveled long distance, people who couldn't afford planes, trains or cars. Many of my fellow passengers, and more and more the farther south I went, were African-American.

When I was growing up, the color line was firm in ways hard to imagine today, in both the North and the South. Racism was a dirty bomb ready to detonate. I knew no African-Americans—Negro was the term then—personally. None lived in my town; there was only one black student in my school, and he didn't stay.

Yet I was immersed in African America. It came to me through pop culture: the calypso craze, Xavier Cugat's mambo, the gumbo in Campbell's chicken gumbo soup, Desi Arnaz's "Babalu." It came in the evening news, with the image of Patrice Lumumba of Congo, earnest and articulate in his dark suit and glasses. He wasn't a National Geographic African, but an urbane modern politician. Adults around me clearly viewed him with hostility, as they did Malcolm X.

My father, like Kerouac, was a jazz fanatic, and he listened to it all: Charlie Parker, Count Basie, Dizzy Gillespie, Fats Waller, Miles Davis, Jelly Roll Morton, Billie Holiday, Dinah Washington. And blues and gospel. Mahalia Jackson's "Standing Here Wondering Which Way to Go" was the first road song I learned by heart. I was 10.

I had all this cultural information with me as I traveled from Boston to Baltimore, to Washington and on to Raleigh, N.C., Atlanta and Birmingham, Ala. But in some way, I was learning, it had always been abstract, imported into my life, from some source kept at a distance. Now I had a sense of that distance, and I wanted to ask questions. Why was Lumumba killed? Does Malcolm X truly hate us? What is it like to be in a church when Mahalia Jackson sings?

But I was a bookish kid, shy before I was bold, who looked even younger than he was. I felt vulnerable. I had never traveled alone so far from home, from my world. Still, there were hesitant conversations with people beside me, or across the aisles, or in bus terminals, and the trip took on a theme; it was about learning what it meant to be white in America, and how strange the very idea was.

In Washington I stayed with my great-uncle Sampson. I'd met him only a few times, and he never seemed to change: affable, energetic, with a shock of gray hair shooting out behind his head, like a Fragonard portrait. He had long ago moved out of the family loop, ever since he had finished Harvard Business School and gone into vaudeville as a songwriter and piano man. Later he married Tessa, a singer, settled in Washington and went into business. When I visited, they were sharing their house with Tessa's two divorced sisters, a tiny, adored white dog and back-to-back twin baby grands.

"We live each as he or she pleases," Sampson announced when I got there. "We eat when we're hungry, sleep till noon or get up before dawn, as we like. While you're with us, we hope you'll observe the house rules."

I did, and with the domestic anarchy we all spent a lot of time together, mostly visiting museums: Chinese scrolls at the Freer, the Shakespeare folios at the Folger, the National Gallery Vermeers. In the evenings we listened to music and read. I felt right at home. Safe.

On my last night they took me to a concert in Rock Creek Park. Harry Belafonte was introducing the singer Miriam Makeba. Tessa explained that she was in political exile from South Africa. She also explained what apartheid meant, a word I didn't know. On the way back in the cab she said that something was wrong in the country since Kennedy's assassination. Do you really have to go on with this trip? I thought: No, I don't. I said: Yes, I do.

> **Do you really have to go on with this trip? I thought: No, I don't. I said: Yes, I do.**

Next I crashed with a cousin, John, a young professor at the University of North Carolina at Chapel Hill. Smart, tense, busy with summer school, he gave me a tour of the neat, green campus, then said, "I want to show you another part of town." He drove me a short distance from the university to a road lined with falling-down houses, where African-Americans lived. I had never seen such poverty.

He asked to look at my Greyhound map, and he traced with his finger the route I was taking to Texas. "Look," he said, "when you get to Mississippi, stay on the bus. Don't get off. Go straight through." Just a few days earlier three civil-rights workers, two of them white and from the North, had disappeared near Meridian. The word was that they'd been murdered. This was Freedom Summer in Mississippi. Bad things were happening, beatings, burnings. John was afraid the South was going to blow.

After North Carolina the trip was different because I was different, on the alert. In Atlanta, on Peachtree Street—a name I knew from "Gone With the Wind"—I saw a restaurant with a side window for serving blacks and drinking fountains" labeled "black" and "white." I lost my wallet there and slept overnight in the bus station and then later in a park in Montgomery, Ala. A recruiting street preacher found me there, brought me to a soup kitchen breakfast, then gave me the third degree: "Have you found the Lord? Are you saved?" I honestly didn't know.

243

Of course I got off the bus in Mississippi, more than once. In Jackson I wanted to find Eudora Welty, but her name wasn't in the phone book. By this time lack of sleep, combined with hot weather, gave the days a kind of hallucinatory looseness. I was at ease on the road for the first time.

In a bus terminal farther south, I met a scared teenage soldier on his way from a home leave back to his base, then on to Vietnam. Americans still didn't know anything real about this war. He'd learn about it fast when he landed in Saigon. The country would learn about it when a quarter of a million protesters marched on Washington in 1965. Meanwhile Jackson was the biggest place he'd ever seen, and Asia meant nothing. I stayed with him because he said he felt sick, too sick to get on a bus. His side hurt, then it hurt much more. When he started crying, someone called a doctor. Another passenger came over. "Appendix, I expect."

Late at night, on the bus, I woke to find that I was resting my head on the shoulder of the sleeping woman in the seat beside me. When I woke again, she was still sleeping, but with her head on my shoulder. When we got where we were going—I can't remember where now—we went our separate ways.

There were other rides and stops and more complicated meetings, some offers of rooms and meals. I was reading intensely now, trying to center myself, gain focus.

"On the Road," which had started everything for me, ended up being of little help. Its excitations felt forced; its descriptions of Americans, particularly of African-Americans, seemed cartoonish, false, often mean. Were Kerouac and I traveling the same country? Why had I ever thought of him as bravehearted and generous? He was just another scared white boy, like me.

I finally reached Austin and was told that I couldn't see Raymond. He had been misbehaving and wasn't allowed visitors. It didn't matter. That had never been the point. I stayed in town a few days. After Sampson wired me some money, I started back by a different route, on another trip, in some ways a much stranger one, but a different story.

The bodies of the three civil rights workers—James Chaney, Andrew Goodman, Michael Schwerner—were unearthed in Mississippi early in August. By that time I was back home, catching up on news. There were uprisings in Harlem. The autobiography of Malcolm X was in stores. Home looked different; I was only half there. America, which had felt like a foreign place seen from bus windows a few months before, looked familiar, smaller.

> **America, which had felt like a foreign place seen from bus windows a few months before, looked familiar, smaller.**

I couldn't know that within the year Malcolm would be dead; that the bombing of North Vietnam, and the anger in response to it, would begin; that Kerouac's Beat would become a period artifact, replaced temporarily by something called Flower Power. Or that in a new century Americans would stop making quest-journeys, would spiritually stay put, put on weight, wait for the world to come to them. But I did sense where I might stand in relation to all of this. I didn't have to wonder which way I'd go.

After the summer I found myself reading a little less, and differently, and looking around me more. Thoreau—loner, sojourner, abolitionist—still made sense. Dickinson is forever. But "Specimen Days," Whitman's diaristic account of nursing Civil War soldiers, boys dying far from home, was a revelation, as if I'd never seen it before.

Then came college, where I majored in literature, but, half by chance, my first class was on African art. I loved it, went on to Chinese, then to Vermeer, then to India, where I stayed a long time. Actually I'm still there. Art ended up being my thing, not a thing just to look at, but to read like a map or a book; not just something to feel safe with, but something to get lost in, confused by; a world with lines and colors but no color lines—none.

And maybe it's just another stop on a long trip, one marked by the sight of Patrice Lumumba's face on TV, the voice of Miriam Makeba in a Washington park and by leaning-together slumbers on buses through the night.

CONSIDER

1. Cotter places both his bus trip and *On the Road* within a long American literary tradition of quests and journeys. Can you identify other works that fit into this tradition? What is its appeal? What have been the goals of journeys and quests in the past?

2. Cotter says his trip south from Boston proved to be "about learning what it meant to be white in America." How did the trip make it possible for him to come to this realization? In what ways has a change in place or environment altered your own sense of reality?

3. Cotter claims that Americans no longer explore the world: "in a new century Americans would stop making quest-journeys, would spiritually stay put, put on weight, wait for the world to come to them." Do you find his assessment convincing? Why or why not?

COMPOSE

4. Have you visited a place or series of places that changed your life? Write an essay modeled on Cotter's that describes your experience—although it need not be as significant or shattering an event. Your discovery may be on a smaller scale and considerably less serious. Remember, too, that not all shifts in perspective necessarily make a person wiser.

CHALLENGE

5. In a brief essay, specifically contrast the America Kerouac describes in *On the Road* with the country Holland Cotter experiences in his essay. Pay attention to differences in tone, language, and point of view. Does it matter that Cotter is looking back on his experiences more than forty years after the fact?

FYI

ITEM 4.22 ■ **Photographs of Signs Enforcing Racial Discrimination**

The images by Ben Shahn and Russell Lee shown here are only two of many on a Library of Congress Web page entitled "Photographs of Signs Enforcing Racial Discrimination: Documentation by Farm Security Administration–Office of War Information Photographers." Separate facilities for whites and blacks embody an aspect of American life still very much in place when Holland Cotter took his bus trip in 1964.

Ben Shahn, *Sign on a Restaurant, Lancaster, Ohio*, 1938

Russell Lee, *Man Drinking at a Water Cooler in the Street Car Terminal*, Oklahoma City, Oklahoma, July 1939

CONSIDER

1. What is your gut reaction to these images? In your travels or local environment today, are there any sites that you think might seem equivalently deplorable decades from now?

2. What is familiar about a place can often become invisible and seem normal to natives. What does travel do to such assumptions? Can you describe any times when, in the aftermath of travel, you looked differently at the place you call home?

CHALLENGE

3. Shahn's and Lee's photographs of ordinary locations—like those of Alice Attie in Gallery Item 4.10—are *documentary*, that is, they preserve a record of a place for future times. Take some photographs or videos of sites (or sights) in your local community that you expect people fifty or a hundred years from now might find important or intriguing. Write a brief description of your documentary project, providing a rationale for your choices.

Writing About Places and Environments

You can respond to a place or environment many ways, but always start with a **subject** that moves or intrigues you. (If you don't identify with or care about a place, you probably won't be sufficiently motivated to say much about it.) Write, too, from your own experiences or expertise. You know your neighborhood, a favorite restaurant, or a virtual environment far better than people who have never visited it. But you also need to find a revealing angle for your analysis, a way to give your commentary on a place a claim that both reflects your thinking and intrigues readers. In a paper, that perspective might be signalled through an introductory paragraph or thesis statement; in a photograph, the elements you choose to focus on might signal your subject.

Naturally, you'll need to consider how to engage an **audience**, deciding first who they might be and then considering how you might reach them. For instance, you would probably write about Fenway Park in Boston differently for an audience of Red Sox fans than you would for a New York readership. And what could you write about the legendary ballpark that would be fresh and new enough to attract a reader's attention? You might find your answer by looking where others haven't, narrowing your subject to cover a specific feature in the ballpark, whether in the architecture, the grounds, the concessions, or the fans. Or you might take a contrary or unexpected stance—the way Terry Falke's photograph of a familiar rock formation in Arches National Park (Item 4.1) becomes fresh because of what *else* he includes in his image. In either case, choosing a **focal point** gets you started.

It also raises the question of **purpose**. Audiences should see some rationale for your response to a place. Maybe you want to capture the vitality of a local bookstore or celebrate the beauty of Paris at night or critique the narrow view that people have of suburban culture—as David Brooks does in "Our Sprawling, Supersize Utopia." But you should have some goal in writing about a locale. You might have a story to tell about a place; you may simply want to report accurately about what you saw; you may wish to make an argument, perhaps for preserving the community against forces seeking to alter it. Or you might argue for change. But be certain to write for reasons audiences might appreciate. They'll respond more powerfully if you do.

You may have to supply background so that readers understand the **context** for your writing. That paper on Fenway Park, for example, might include at least a paragraph explaining to readers who don't follow the sport the mystique of this baseball shrine. Context may be harder to manage in other media, but then you might use an existing issue or problem to frame your project, as Diane Cook and Len Jenshel did in Item 4.16 when they photographed a portion of border fence between the United States and Mexico. If you prepare a photo essay showing human encroachments on wilderness spaces or decaying main streets in rural American towns, your work will likely make sense to most observers because they understand at least some of the cultural issues you are addressing. But be sure your projects supply enough signals for readers to see your point. Provide answers to basic questions such as *who, what, where, when,* and *why.*

As you can appreciate, your choice of a **genre** and **medium** will be crucial to reaching audiences and achieving your aims. Fortunately, you can write about places and environments in many ways, even combining media to make your point. You might use a narrative to tell a story about a place (as Jenny Attiyeh does with Grafton, Utah on pages 202–203) and incorporate photographs to underscore your points. Or you could take a more journalistic and academic approach, looking at a place analytically and making claims about it supported by evidence. An image then might become a part of the evidence—as it is in the essay by Jenna Williamson in Project 4.1. It's only a step further to making an argument, in which you push a particular point of view onto the place you are investigating. That strong assertion might be expressed directly through words in an essay or indirectly through the elements of composition in a photograph, for example, or the music and narrative accompanying a video.

The medium you choose may also determine your **structure**. In a paper, you will need to signal your intentions to writers clearly. A description of a place will still require a clear focal point and some a sense of direction: think about leading readers through a scene the same way they might look at a photograph, identifying strong subjects, developing them, and offering memorable details (see Michael Gerson's account of Second Life on pages 212–213). Reports and arguments will likely need more formal patterns of development, focusing on claims and evidence. You'd probably use a comparison/contrast structure (see pages 68–69) if you wanted to examine several different or related places. Or you could proceed more deliberately with an informative piece, anticipating the questions a reader might have and answering them. In some cases, you might even explore an idea through an interview with someone knowledgeable about a place or concept. In an argument about a place, you'd have to find ways of mustering logical and emotional appeals, sequencing them to build momentum for your claim—as Holland Cotter does in "On My Road" (see pages 242–245). In all these cases, you might want to use scratch outlines to try out various approaches. But do have some specific structure in mind. Don't just hope all the parts will hang together.

Readers will find your analysis or response to a place most engaging if they learn something new or unexpected from it. Look for a text that reveals an unusual point of view or conflicts in interesting ways with your own experiences—and that might generate a strong response from your readers. An essay merely explaining that "this postcard view of old Euclid Beach Park in Cleveland is completely cool" doesn't give your audience much to think about. But an analysis that helps readers think about the role of amusement parks in contemporary culture might have a broader appeal.

Then be sure to provide the **evidence** and **details** for your writing about a place or environment—and expect to do some research, no matter what kind of project you intend to create. Use the library and Internet to discover as much as you can about your subject so that you won't make the kinds of factual or contextual blunders that might discredit your entire effort. But don't limit your explorations to just what you can find in the library and online. Writing about places requires various forms of field research (see pages 86–87), whether that means a trip to interview people in a neighborhood or hours browsing a virtual environment to get a feel for its places and denizens (again, see Michael Gerson on role-playing games on pages 212–213). You have to develop a level of credibility with audiences. Naturally, for academic projects, you need to keep track of your sources and be prepared to document them. You also have to show respect for any images or other media you might want to incorporate into a project.

Finally, be sure to edit your project in all the appropriate ways. In a paper about places, pay particular attention to using and spelling names and proper nouns correctly—especially foreign words or expressions. Be conscientious too about your descriptions (see pages 67–68), keeping them lean and specific. Don't be afraid to be descriptive when you need to be, but avoid the tendency to pile on the adjectives and adverbs: *less* is often *more* when you want to convey a sense of place. In multimedia projects, learn how to use the technical tools available to you, whether it's a digital camera or specialized software. Take the time to read the instructions or Help menus.

Project 4.1

Analyzing a Representation of a Place

Describing a place, whether in words or in images, is always a rhetorical process: what a writer or artist "sees" in an environment reflects his or her particular context and point of view. For this project, find a textual or visual representation of a place you know well, and then compose a three- to five-page essay analyzing this representation. Think about the kind of portrait the text or image creates; how it uses words, images, or design elements to convey an impression; and how well it reflects your own sense of what the place is like. For example, you might compare a brochure describing dormitories at your campus to your own experience living in them or evaluate a Web site advertising the restaurant where you waited tables last summer. Or perhaps you recently visited the city where your favorite television show is set. Whatever place you choose, your task is to examine the representation in light of your own experience there.

Because this is an essay assignment, your primary medium will be words. However, if you're analyzing a visual representation of a place, you may decide to include that image or portions of it to support your analysis. Remember to discuss, cite, and document appropriately any outside text or images that appear in your paper.

Before you begin, take a look at "Gainesville: Selling Small-Town America" to see how student writer Jenna Williamson approached this task.

STUDENT PROJECT

Jenna Williamson, "Gainesville: Selling Small-Town America"

Williamson 1

Jenna Williamson
Prof. Ruszkiewicz
RHE 315
26 March 2007

Gainesville: Selling Small-Town America

Gainesville, Texas, is a pleasant town at the crossroads of Interstate 35 and Highway 82 founded during a nineteenth-century railroad boom. According to the town's website, "The city captures the essence of small-town America." Gainesville's current population is 16,250 residents, and city officials are eager for more. In contrast to the massive American urbanization of the twentieth century, there is a currently a migration back to small towns. Via the Internet, Gainesville's leaders are capitalizing on this trend. The website offers prospective residents the hope that they can have it all: a family-friendly, value-rich community coupled with the promise of flourishing economic opportunities. Gainesville is my mother's home, so it is where I have spent every major holiday for the last nineteen years. From my experience, there are many more layers to Gainesville than the website leads surfers to believe.

I am actually amazed that Gainesville even has a functioning website. The only place where I can get wireless in the town is at Starbucks off of Interstate 35. This new addition to the highway landscape is "ridiculous," according to my grandmother, a lifelong resident of Gainesville. Personally, coming from a generation raised in cities and suburbia, I have always felt suffocated by the stagnant, interpersonal environment that a small town offers. But after I asked my mother about the perks of small-town life, my attitude changed.

The intent of Gainesville's website is to attract potential visitors and residents. However, the images on the website's head banner (see <http://www.gainesville.tx.us/>) that supposedly represent Gainesville do not necessarily hold emotional value for the citizens: the pictures include Gainesville's unique attractions: giraffes from the Frank Buck Zoo

Opening ¶ provides important background information and concludes with a thesis that contrasts a town and its Web site.

Banner from the Web site functions as important evidence in this paper.

Williamson 2

and the marquee of the antique State Theater. The collage includes a plane as part of the city's economic promotion, alluding to the Gainesville Municipal Airport. It also highlights the railroad station and the courthouse, buildings that form the historical backbone of the city. In contrast, I asked my mom what images come to mind when she pictures her hometown. Of course, she mentioned her house, but she also said the church she grew up in and the town square, where she and her mom used to "go to town." She told me about California Street, where she would "make the drag" with her friends on Friday nights. The heart of the Gainesville community is in the neighborhoods where people actually know their neighbors. The richness of the town is found in the Waffle House restaurant where retired men gather for coffee and company, and it's found in the downtown stores where, as my mom says, "sure, the owners want you to spend your money . . . but they want you to come back in there and talk." Unlike the banner, the latter images might not help "sell" Gainesville, but they are certainly a more personal and accurate description of the town.

The site also tries to "sell" the economic opportunities in Gainesville, which undermines the spirit of the town. The website emphasizes the city's new Economic Development Corporation, which is "your partner" in beginning a business in Gainesville. After all, as a promotional clip states, Gainesville is "*the* ideal place for your business." The video describes Gainesville as "a congestion-free setting . . . [with] open roads, no lines at the post office, and a pollution-free environment." It gives the impression that the city leaders are trying to appeal to a young, ambitious, environmentally-conscious generation. While economic stability should certainly be a priority for the community, portraying Gainesville this way somewhat contradicts the mindset of "small-town America." My mom describes it this way: unlike larger places, in Gainesville, your worth "doesn't have anything to do with how much money your house costs or what street you live on." Ironically, the website is attempting to draw new residents via business opportunities, when in reality there is very limited availability for high-paying jobs. A 2004 study found that the median household income was $33,000 and the per capita income $17,000. Although Gainesville can provide only limited opportunity for job

Williamson 3

advancement, my mom actually sees that as a good thing. People put family and personal time on a more important level than their jobs. In a town like Gainesville, people realize that they might never have a six-digit salary. But salary isn't something that consumes Gainesville's residents; as my mom says, "the job part doesn't define success." By creating such an emphasis on economic development, Gainesville's website attempts to tailor to the individualism and self-advancement that mainstream society values. These characteristics are de-emphasized in a small town. The challenge for the city is to promote healthy economic growth while maintaining its definition of meaningful success. If the website strove to present this vision of Gainesville, it might actually be more appealing to a younger generation jaded by corporate America and lacking in community.

    I didn't realize how elemental this sense of community is in Gainesville until my grandfather died last year. The day after he passed away, someone put "God Bless Ed Alexander" on the State Theater Marquee downtown (see fig. 1). That blew my mind. People in a small town like Gainesville truly recognize the worth of a human being and his contributions to the community. Before my Nana came home from the hospital in Fort Worth, the whole town already knew about Papa. My Nana is an eighty-year-old

Fig. 1. State Theater Marquee acknowledging Ed Alexander.

The photograph is an emotional piece of evidence.

only child with no family left in town. But because she lives in a small town, she has a sense of family that many urban and suburban Americans cannot even fathom. Her neighbors brought her food, but they did not stop at that. She had to take her phone off the hook every once in a while because people were constantly calling to check in on her. When she went to the bank to straighten out her finances, people in the office stood up and walked around their desks to give her a hug. She was hugged in the grocery store and hugged at the gas station. If she had moved to Houston with my family, she would never have the sense of family she had in Gainesville. Through the way the community came together for Nana, I was able to see how a small town truly provides people with a foot to stand on.

On the homepage of the website, the mayor states that "Gainesville is a community that everyday reinforces those values that make small town life so attractive: the bond of family, lifelong friendships and a community spirit." From my knowledge of the town, this statement rings true; my mom claims that Gainesville is "where I got my values from." She has a unique perspective on small-town influence: "If you don't adhere to [these values] you disappoint so many people besides yourself. Some people would think that's a downside. But people love you and care about you--they truly do. You hold you head up and be the person you want to be, for yourself and for the community." My mother also shed a positive light on the infamous small town gossip that comes along with any type of close-knit community. When my Nana talks about someone, there are "some things she doesn't agree with, or wouldn't do the same way, but that doesn't mean she doesn't care about them." In a way, the community is seen as an extension of family.

Gainesville's website urges visitors to "come to Gainesville to start your family or business!" After exploring the town on a deeper level than the website offers, it is evident that Gainesville does have much to offer. In the context of industrialized, globalized, suburbanized America, a small town offers a richness that is difficult to convey through a website. My mom said, "I feel like if I leave Houston tomorrow, no one would really care. Neighborhood bunko is the closest thing to a small town atmosphere we have. I guess a small town is like a big bunko group." That "sense of having a place where you belong" is perhaps Gainesville's most appealing aspect.

Project 4.2

Observing and Analyzing a Public Space

Many of the writers and artists featured in this chapter are fascinated with documenting how the physical characteristics of places influence (and are influenced by) the people who inhabit them. For this project, you'll engage in a similar process of observation. You'll visit a public place, then write a three- to five-page paper that carefully describes and analyzes it in order to identify the connections among the physical space, the people in it, and the activities that go on there. The following questions for composing can help you begin developing ideas, collecting material, and writing your draft.

- Begin by selecting your subject—the place you'll visit and describe. Your site can be a building such as a restaurant or museum; a small cluster of related buildings, like a strip mall; a portion of a building, such as the lobby of your apartment complex; or an open area such as a park, graffiti wall, or cemetery. Whatever your focus, keep the following points in mind:

  - Choose a space that interests you. Your analysis may be more balanced and objective if you begin with a place that's not too familiar. However, there's a case to be made for using cultural experiences and expertise you may have in order to introduce readers to environments they may not have experienced themselves.
  - Check the accessibility of your site. Is it nearby and open to the public? A state prison, hard-hat construction site, or a monastery, no matter how intriguing, probably won't allow easy access, for example. Reflect too on potential ethical considerations. Will the presence of an observer alarm or embarrass people using the space? A lone male observer sitting in a parking garage after dark would almost certainly startle women en route to their cars. Also avoid sites where you're likely to intrude on private conversations or activities—as you might in the locker room at a fitness center.

- While it's important that you provide detailed descriptions of the place you've selected, details alone aren't enough. A key part of your purpose is to analyze what these details say about the relationship between the physical features of the space and the people and activities you observe there. You'll need to look for interesting social or cultural patterns and connections in the information you've collected and use them to focus your discussion:

  - What catches your eye? Does this space look similar to or different from places that serve similar functions?

- - Who is here? What are they wearing, doing, and saying? Do they appear comfortable, excited, impatient, tired? Who is *not* here, and why? Is the space designed to interest particular groups?
  - How do people use this space? Where do they sit, stand, or gather? What is a "normal" activity here? How can you tell?
  - How do people interact in this space? Who talks to whom? Who seems to be in charge? How can you tell?
  - Do you see anything that surprises you? Does anyone use the space in an unexpected way?
- It's likely that the audience for your paper won't have visited your site, so you'll need to describe it thoroughly and vividly (see pages 67–68) and to provide specific examples to illustrate the patterns you see. Strive to engage your readers by bringing the sights, sounds, and activities of the place to life, and then by helping your audience see the significance of these details.
- Although you'll gather most of the content for this project through direct observation, you may first need to do some background research: Who owns this space? When was it built, and has it been renovated or changed since that time? Has the space ever been used for something other than its current purpose? Find the answers to these questions by asking owners or employees, consulting local historical societies, checking the archives of local newspapers, or conducting research in the library or online.

  You may need to spend time systematically recording what you see, especially if the locale is new to you. Social scientists use the term *field observation* to refer to this process of collecting information. You'll find guidelines in Chapter 2 on pages 86–87.
- Think about the structure or arrangement of your paper in two parts. First you'll introduce readers to your site, providing relevant background information and a thorough description of it based on your field observation. Then you'll conclude with analysis, drawing readers' attention to one or more ways in which the physical layout of the place seems to influence the ways in which people use or inhabit it. As with all analytical writing, you'll need to provide supporting examples and details to illustrate the major points you make in your analysis.
- Considerations of style—the choices you make about word selection and tone—are especially important in descriptive writing. Concrete details and precise, vivid language will give readers a clear sense of the place and enhance your credibility by showing that you know your subject well.
- Although the primary medium for this project is words, keep in mind that drawings, maps, diagrams, or photographs can introduce readers to your site and provide powerful evidence to support your analysis. Remember that any visual materials you didn't create yourself must be appropriately cited and documented.
- Start your paper early enough so that you'll have time to return to the site if needed to check facts or fill gaps in your observations. Once you've completed a draft, review it or have a classmate or friend do so, suggesting areas for revision and editing. Don't be surprised if the project heads off into directions you haven't anticipated or reveals more about a place than you had expected.

STUDENT PROJECT
Kruti Parekh, "India: A Culinary Experience"

Parekh 1

Kruti Parekh
Dr. Ruszkiewicz
RHE 315M
October 30, 2006

India: A Culinary Perspective

It is often said that food has the ability to transport the soul to any location at any time. A trip to Italy can come in the form of chicken marsala and tiramisu, a vacation to Tokyo by way of miso soup and sashimi. Similarly, many a diner makes a short visit to Bombay over tandoori chicken and biryani. But restaurateurs know that the experience of cuisine comes from much more than the food. For many, the Indian restaurant in America (see fig. 1) portrays a romanticized version of India, a country renowned for its complex culture. Rather than represent the modern intricacies of the Asian subcontinent, Indian restaurants in

Fig. 1. Indian Restaurant, New York City.

Parekh 2

America use spices as a foundation for an atmosphere of ancient exotic luxury. The created ambience is a diluted portrait of the Indian landscape which, surprisingly, is to the taste of Indian and non-Indian diners alike.

Many restaurants start with a majestic color palate consisting of jewel tones and antique gold, a sharp contrast from the modern minimalist steel hues of office life. Immediately, the restaurant creates a sense of escape with the shades and textures of palatial India. Bronze religious statues of many armed gods and goddesses serve as elegant showpieces atop dark cherrywood bars heavily stocked with Bombay Sapphire. Wooden or antique metal elephants stand tall throughout the dining area to heighten the sense of an exotic, mystic India. Walls display folk art tapestries featuring the gaiety of Indian villagers, heavily gilded mirrors, or paintings of ancient figures from cultural or religious texts. All elements are highly nostalgic of a time far before the American ethnic restaurant. In a sense, the colors and shapes inside the Indian restaurant are the colors and shapes of what the American diner wants to think India looks like: colorful saris, intriguing mysticism, beautiful temples, the Taj Mahal.

The cuisine in an American Indian restaurant also complements the Western ideal of India. Serving traditional curries with a much higher ratio of meat, turning tropical native fruits into cocktails, and using an object of millions' worship as a centerpiece are just a few ways that Indian food becomes an Indian-American restaurant. Ironically, many will choose to eat at an Indian restaurant thinking themselves cultured, while the essence of India fades away around them. Behind the American notion of trendy Eastern themes, authentic Indian food, in fact, reflects the values of the culture. The cuisine demonstrates modesty by using meat sparingly, decency by abstaining from alcohol, and piety by respecting religion. All of this is dissolved to create the experience of the restaurant pleasurable for the American diner. In a way, the adaptations made for American tastes are colonialism all over again—a complex history and culture reduced to cocktails and statues. And yet, even the most culturally sensitive must applaud Indian restaurants for going beyond food and creating an ambience that generates awareness and interest in the Indian culture, albeit a distilled one.

Curiously, Indian patrons make up a significant number of satisfied diners at Indian restaurants. The forged exotic is the same but the effect is different on these diners. For Indian parents there is a sense of nostalgia mingled with pride because this is also the India they desire to remember. For them, this is a representation of their beloved culture, where the last remnants of glorious royalty stand tall, where a whole city woke to the fragrance of incense from morning worship, where the monsoon rain brought luscious mangos. The décor of the restaurant embodies the culture that first generation immigrants cling to. Dinner menus alone demonstrate this with their heavy emphasis on vegetarianism, regionalism and history. Dishes such as lamb curry are described according to spices, but also with a note of 16th century Mogul influence. Under the "South Indian" portion of the menu, there is a deliberate shift from Arabic-named entrées to more Sanskritic sounding ones, for example the word "korma" instead of "kabob." To the Indian diner, the vegetarian sections of the menu are a reminder of Gandhi's political stance and Vedic teachings of "ahimsa" (nonviolence). The Mogul empire, Sanskrit tradition, Gandhi's ethics, and Vedic knowledge are roots that run deep in the Indian cultural landscape, all modestly illustrated on a dinner menu. There on the glossy laminated pages laden with dinner selections exists a microcosm of language, culture, and history.

The dynamics of the restaurant's diners and employees in restaurants add an entirely new dimension to the material. The owner, as well as the chefs and the head of the wait staff, will almost always be Indian. For Indian diners the restaurant's employees are a reflection of the work ethic in modern times, and for non-Indian diners they are a reassurance of authenticity. The Indian diners in the restaurant also validate the authenticity of the restaurant, a notion spawned from "you know a Chinese restaurant is good when you see Chinese people there." An Indian restaurant's patrons range from parents providing a cultural experience for their American born children to trendy young professionals claiming their own cultural sophistication. Conversely, for the Indian customer the non-Indians enjoying the food and atmosphere of the restaurant reassure them of cultural acceptance of their proud heritage.

Parekh 4

    Indian restaurants in America are ultimately a blend of polar opposites. The food and décor of the restaurant portray a blend of Eastern and Western cultures, business and art, the old and new, progressive and nostalgic. Any element of design, food, or atmosphere can elicit a different reaction from any given diner. People come to Indian restaurants with intentions as varied as the cuisine, whether it be for a comforting piece of home, a new experience, an attempt at vegetarianism, an escape from the cubicle, or just good food.

Project 4.3

Write either a description or a report on a place that means a great deal to you. It can be a school, a gym, a store, a corner of the library, a café, your dorm room, a road, a church, your hometown, a favorite national park monument, and so on. For a personal space, such as a dorm room or library carrel, a description might work best; a place with more history and cultural connections—such as a church or national monument—might require the background information more characteristic of a report.

Project 4.4

Imagine that you have been asked to create a documentary to preserve a place you know well—the way Alice Attie does in her photographs from *Harlem in Transition* (Item 4.10, pages 190-191). In a short paper, explain what place you would choose and what your photo essay or documentary would certainly include. Provide an explanation for each of your choices.

Project 4.5

Choose an image of a place that you especially like: it might be a painting, a movie still, or a famous photograph or mural. Then do research in the library or on the Internet to discover what you can about the biographical, social, and historical contexts in which the image was created. Write a short paper summarizing your findings. Be sure to comment on whether and how this information changes your response to the image.

CHAPTER 5

MEDIA

ITEM 5.1 ■ Iraqi Mural Depicting Abu Ghraib, Sadr City, Iraq, 2004

Think of the usual suspects that come up in discussions of contemporary problems and you're likely to encounter, front and center, the media. But just what do people mean when they trot out a term like *the media*? To consider such a question, you'll need to explore the relationships between media as entities that spread information (like CNN) and mediums as the source materials and means of transmitting information (like clay as the source material for sculptures).

Consider Item 5.1 depicting a mural in Sadr City, Iraq. The image recalls one of the most disturbing photographs to emerge from the Abu Ghraib scandal, in which U.S. forces tortured Iraqi detainees. The author of the Abu Ghraib mural likely never attended journalism school and the mural contains no slick graphics, yet the painting transmits a message with more authority in Sadr City than a Western news report. Media items like these raise questions about how information is presented, controlled, and disseminated.

Thinking about media evokes concerns linking every dimension of society—from business to entertainment to community to politics. Consider the media relationships that can be "pulled out" of Item 5.2. The television episode of *South Park* takes on the online video game World of Warcraft (WOW). The episode includes game footage or *machinima* in which the characters enter the virtual world of WOW. Later, the entire episode is added to the iTunes music store, where it can be downloaded and played on a computer. Pulling apart these strands puts you on a path of exploration in which you'll untangle relationships among commerce, information, entertainment, politics, and social interactions, to name just some of the possibilities.

ITEM 5.2 ■ "**Make Love Not Warcraft,**" *South Park*, 2007

Reading Texts About the Media

Your first step in thinking about media texts is to determine the scope of their **subject**, what they are about. Media texts range from popular pieces meant for entertainment to hard-hitting news exposés designed to inform, with a slew of items falling somewhere in between. Consider the *Got Milk?* ad in Item 5.3. We might recognize the ad's spokesman, world champion Dave Mirra, and assume the image is about BMX bicycling. However, by looking closer we uncover the sponsor: America's Dairy Farmers and Processors. We can also explore the **contexts** related to media elements we're reading. For instance, we tend to think of television as a Western phenomenon, but Item 5.4 challenges those assumptions with its clear depiction of a captivated television audience juxtaposed with an undeveloped rural setting.

We can also think about the multiple **rhetorical situations** represented in a text. Consider Item 5.5, an image capturing the first YouTube Democratic primary debate in 2007. What **purposes** might CNN have for teaming up with YouTube? And what about the **speakers** and **audiences** represented in the image? The YouTube messages are created and received by citizens, candidates, news organizations, and the public at large using the Internet and television. As we read such texts, we'll inevitably ask questions about how media outlets and mediums influence communication. Playing cards (Item 5.6) seem an unlikely form of political propaganda, but the "Most Wanted" decks developed during the early days of the Iraq War became a conduit for political messages and spawned alternative decks representing competing positions.

Clearly, media messages can both document and shape society. Consider Lewis Hine's photograph of a girl in a cotton mill (see Item 5.7). *Girl Worker* was taken in 1908, the year Hine began working for the National Child Labor Committee, a nonprofit organization established in 1904 to put an end to child labor. At the time, child labor was viewed often as an economic opportunity for immigrants and poor families. Hine used his photography to challenge this assumption and document the problem. Other forms of media reveal aspects of society in more playful ways. Thinking about the constraints of **genres** and **mediums** can help us understand these messages. A toy car with a product name (see Item 5.8) can't deliver a very nuanced message. But it can plant a thought—sex—in the minds of model builders or viewers of a photograph. And if the message is part of a larger media landscape—stock cars, radio, television—it can sell a good deal of Viagra. And some media items present hybrid genres and use multiple mediums. The Human Rights Watch Web site (Item 5.9) relies on Web design and audio, text, images, and video to deliver a multimedia message.

You'll also need to think about the **structure** of the media messages you encounter. Movies such as *Princess Mononoke*, the Japanese anime film now distributed by Disney (Item 5.10), present a complex structure that tells a story—a film is divided into scenes, which are further divided into sequences or shots. And any given shot can be read for its structure and arrangement: In the film still, the large shape of the wolf dominates the foreground, Mononoke fills the center of the frame, and the forest in soft focus recedes into the background.

Finally, you'll want to consider how the items you're examining fit into a large media landscape. Films today come complete with complementary video games, talk show appearances, T-shirts and action figures, even fast food promotions. This kind of saturation across multiple forms of media has become a hallmark of contemporary entertainment and advertising, so you'll need to learn to draw connections and move fluidly from medium to medium.

Gallery: Messages in the Media

ITEM 5.3 ■ *Got Milk?*, 2004

It's easy to miss the tiny print at the bottom of the *Got Milk?* ad that tells us its sponsor: America's Dairy Farmers and Milk Processors. Similarly, we might not instantly recognize the ad's spokesman, world-champion BMX bicyclist Dave Mirra. However, the more we examine the image, the more we discover about its subject, the creator of the image, its intended audience, possible purposes behind the message, and strategies used to appeal to its viewers.

Miracle maker.

They call me Miracle Boy. Not for my gold medals, but because I've survived double back flips, getting hit by a car, and the mega ramp. What makes me so indestructible? Milk. It helps prevent broken bones. So you can concentrate on breaking records.

got milk?

DAVE MIRRA ©2004 AMERICA'S DAIRY FARMERS AND MILK PROCESSORS

1. What are your thoughts on the use of spokespeople to sell products? Do you find the strategy effective? Why or why not?

2. How do you interpret the message implied by the caption? Is it fair to say the message is encouraging reckless behavior? How might this message square with other messages in the ad?

3. Visit the Web site at *www.bodybymilk.com*. Based on the media elements on the Web site, what can you say about the audience the site is trying to reach? Why do you think the dairy industry might target this audience?

ITEM 5.4 ■ **Crowd Gathered Around an Outdoor TV Set in India, 1996**

Television has a way of bringing people together—as this image from a village in rural India suggests. Often those connections are made through the medium of the television itself; we might watch from our homes, more or less isolated, and then gather the next day with others to share insights about what we've seen. Item 5.4, however, depicts a different kind of connection facilitated through television, a connection that brings people together in physical space.

1. What do you find most striking about the image? How important is the setting? Is the subject matter more important than the visual composition of the image? Why or why not?

2. What are your thoughts about the crowd that has gathered to watch the television? Do you have similar experiences with television bringing people together? If you were to write an essay on television and community, what would you talk about and why?

3. What kind of show do you imagine the crowd is watching? How would your interpretation of the image change if the crowd were watching CNN? The Super Bowl? A Bollywood movie?

ITEM 5.5 ■ CNN/YouTube Democratic Presidential Debate, 2007

In 2007, *Time* magazine put on the cover of its person-of-the-year edition a mirrored image of a computer screen emblazoned with the word *YOU* in large letters. Later that year, CNN sponsored the YouTube Presidential debates. Item 5.5 depicts the first YouTube debate, held on July 23, 2007, among candidates in the Democratic primary. Both gestures suggest that everyday citizens now contribute to the media landscape in ways never before thought possible. Of course, it didn't take long for people to question the assumptions behind those gestures. Just how much reach does the individual have in a culture dominated by *Time* or CNN?

1. How many examples of speakers and audiences can you discover in Item 5.5? Can you make an argument that one speaker or audience is more central than the others in the rhetorical situation depicted in the image? What kinds of evidence would you use to support your position?

2. How much impact do you think citizens' voices on the Internet have on the political process? What would you say to someone who argued that the YouTube debates were just gimmicks?

3. Visit the Web site for the YouTube debates at *http://www.youtube.com/youchoose*. How would you compare the coverage offered through YouTube to what you might find in other media? What form of coverage do you favor and why?

ITEM 5.6 ■ Personality Identification Playing Cards, U.S. Army, 2003

It's no secret that wars play out in more spaces than on the battlefield. In 2003, an Army psychological operations group in Iraq announced the development of a set of playing cards depicting the most wanted members of Saddam Hussein's regime. The cards were to be distributed to soldiers where they might be used as portable "most wanted" posters, or for poker, blackjack, or other card games. The decks, then, served as resources for information and recreation and, no doubt, a host of other purposes.

1. What do you think about the relationship between the choice of the medium (playing cards) and the message(s) delivered by the cards? Is it fair to say the cards merely document the identities of Iraqis wanted by the U.S. military? What other messages might be conveyed by the cards?

2. Search the Internet for alternative "most wanted" cards. Do you find their messages to be as effective as the cards issued by the military? Why or why not?

3. What would you say to someone who argued that the cards trivialize the casualties and deaths suffered on both sides during the Iraq War? Do you believe the military crossed an ethical line in producing the cards? Why or why not?

268 GALLERY | MESSAGES IN THE MEDIA

ITEM 5.7 ■ Lewis Hine, *Girl Worker in Cotton Mill*, 1908

The photography of Lewis Hine has long been linked to child advocacy. His images depicting child labor are some of the best examples of photography that has been put to use to enact social change. Hine published countless photographs depicting the work of children in abusive situations. Images like *Girl Worker in Cotton Mill* represent historical documents depicting real concerns and contexts, and they raise questions about the relationships between art and society.

1. What strikes you about the composition of the image in *Girl Worker in Cotton Mill*? What can you say about the setting? What about the use of lighting or the camera angle? How does the photograph deliver its message?

2. Is it possible for an image to document social problems and still be artistic? Can we take pleasure from images that depict suffering or tragedies? What points might you make in a discussion about these concerns?

3. Search the Internet for additional images by Lewis Hine and information about his work documenting child labor. How does knowing the historical context of the photograph affect your reading of the image?

ITEM 5.8 ■ Philip Greenberg, Viagra Model Car

Nowhere are media intersections more evident than in NASCAR. Certainly, the cars are branded by sponsors ranging from M&Ms to Miller Lite. The drivers themselves are linked to their products. (Mark Martin regularly pilots the Viagra car and appears in television advertisements for the little blue pill.) Even toy models and figurines are pressed into service to deliver a sponsor's message. Philip Greenberg documents this phenomenon in his photograph.

1. What can you say about the arrangement of all of the elements in the photograph in item 5.8? What is the significance of substituting scantily clad women for the usual NASCAR pit crew? What message might the creator of the arrangement be sending?

2. What are the consequences of a race driver or athlete becoming closely associated with a product? Do you believe there is a difference between a golfer advertising for Nike and a race driver advertising laundry detergent or Viagra? Why or why not?

3. How far can we go in expanding the definition of what counts as a medium? Are designer clothes different from a Viagra car? Are cell phones? What other unexpected items might qualify as mediums through which messages are delivered?

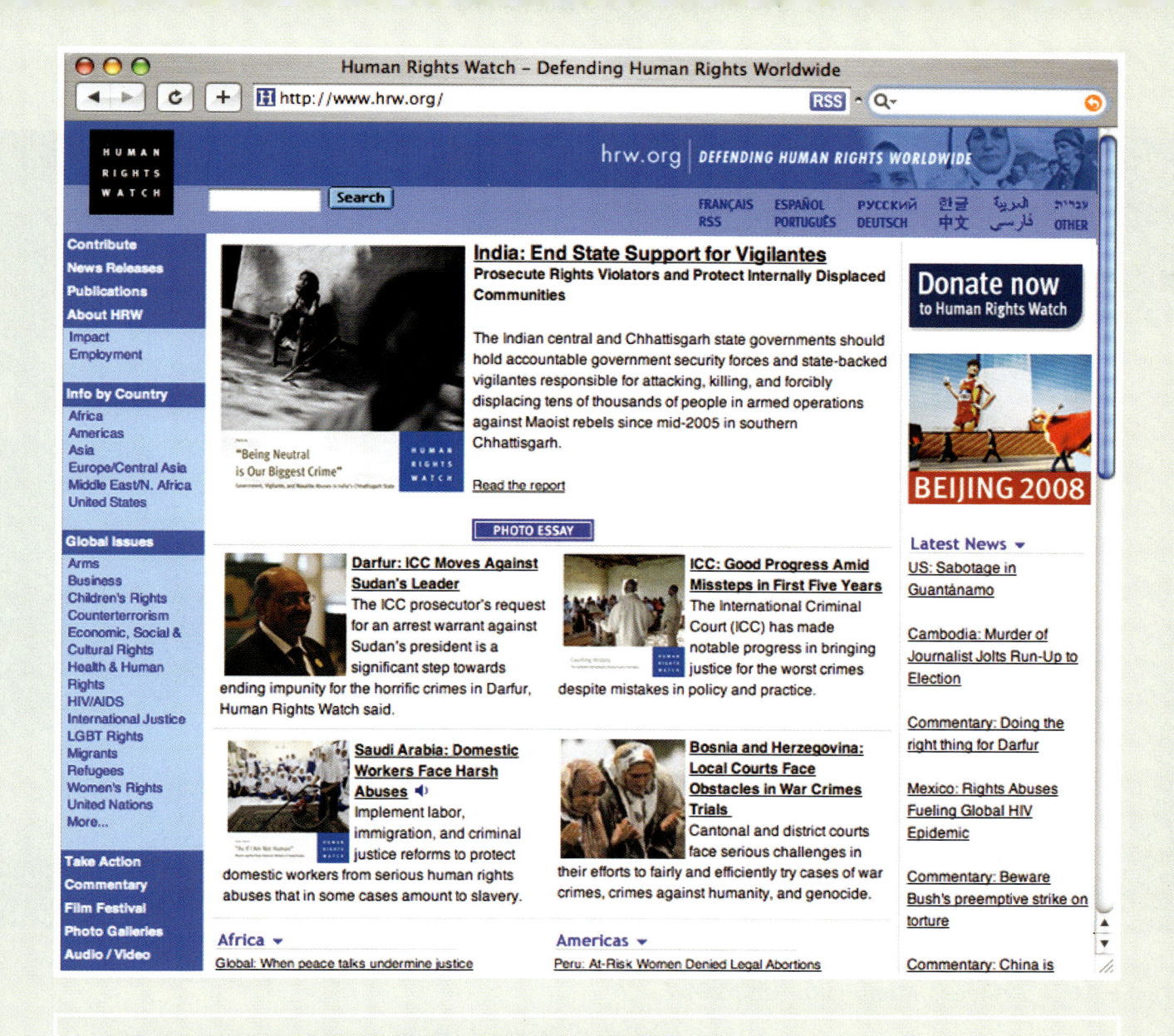

ITEM 5.9 ■ Human Rights Watch Web Site, 2008

Although the Web is roughly fifteen years old, it has already undergone tremendous changes. What began as a medium for sharing texts is now a platform for delivering animations, audio, and video. Further, what started out as an efficient means to link and deliver documents has evolved into a social space where individuals interact to conduct business, to relax, or to promote concerns about which they care deeply. The Human Rights Watch Web site demonstrates these changes in its structure and design. The menus on the left show media items ranging from photos to audio to video. They also reveal the complex ways Web sites engage global audiences.

1. What are your thoughts on the multiple language options at the top of the Human Rights Watch Web site? Is it possible that having too broad a reach might limit the effectiveness of the messages delivered by the site? What other strategies can you think of for addressing the site's multiple audiences?

2. How effective do you find the design of the Human Rights Watch Web site? How does the design of the site relate to its purpose and audience? If you could give the designers one recommendation for revising the site, what would you say?

3. Go to the Human Rights Watch Web site at *www.hrw.org*, and explore the resources in more detail. How well do you think the site uses audio and video? What about the presentation of articles or the interactive elements of the site? How would you evaluate the site in terms of its ability to integrate multiple forms of media into a single resource?

ITEM 5.10 ■ *Princess Mononoke* Still, 1997

Princess Mononoke is a full length anime film created by Hayao Miyazaki. You may have overheard or taken part in a debate about the merits of emerging genres like anime or graphic novels. Some argue that the over-the-top cartoonishness of anime has taken animation backwards, forgoing art for quick and unrealistic sketches. Others might question the impact of graphic novels on literacy, quarrelling with the cartoon-bubble model of reading. But advocates might argue that these forms enact new kinds of storytelling and provide literacy opportunities for people who might not otherwise read at all.

1. What are your thoughts on animated films? Is it possible to deliver a serious message in the medium of animation? If not, why? If so, what strategies must authors employ to present such a message?

2. *Princess Mononoke* was created by Japanese animator Hayao Miyazaki, but distributed in the United States by Disney. Is it fair to say that the Disney distribution channel affects the message of the film? Why or why not?

3. Search the Internet for information about Japanese anime. What roles do the mediums of graphic novels and animated films play in the development of anime? How would you evaluate anime as an artistic endeavor as opposed to a cultural phenomenon?

ITEM 5.11 ■ Filming an Episode of *Survivor*

Although not the first example of reality television, when *Survivor* appeared on American television screens in 2000, it became a media phenomenon. The show began with the premise of stranding a group of strangers on an isolated island with no creature comforts, and then folded in the scheming and competition that accompanies the quest for the show's million-dollar prize payoff. Viewers tuned in regularly, and then went back to their workplaces, schools, and neighborhoods to debate the merits of who got voted off the island.

1. How critically do you view reality TV? Do you believe Item 5.11 gives an accurate portrayal of the kind of behind-the-scenes activities that take place on shows like *Survivor*? Is there any way in which this image is staged?

2. What are your views on reality TV and culture? Is it fair to say that reality TV has a negative impact on culture? Does it mirror culture? What arguments would you make about the role of reality TV in society?

3. Search on the Web to learn more about the *Survivor* spoiler phenomenon. How does the phenomenon reflect changing relationships between producers and consumers of media?

Cluster 5.1
Stories of War

The coverage of war we find in the media, from CNN to C-SPAN to military blogs, might lead us to believe that documenting conflicts is a modern phenomenon. But war stories have been a part of the public consciousness since even before Homer put into epic form the details of a jealous rivalry, a wooden horse, and the fall of the city of Troy. The need to capture the conflicts that seem to define every generation stems in part from a fascination with the human elements that surface during war. Stories of heroism, personal trials, and suffering compel our attention, despite the tragic nature of the circumstances that surround them. The media has a long history of covering conflicts, a history in which film, radio, television, even reporters in the field have delivered messages both critiquing and supporting wars. Sometimes the motive behind these stories is the need to simply record historic events—events the public has a keen interest in, events deeply connected to our politics and public policies. Filmmaker Ken Burns, in an interview with Gene Santoro, discusses the challenges that arise when documenting stories of war.

But war coverage quickly raises additional questions. Recall the controversies surrounding the Pentagon's decision to forbid the photographing of caskets returning from the Iraq War. Or, consider the role of the news in exposing the torture of prisoners at Abu Ghraib prison. Since information itself is another weapon in contemporary war, the role of the media is more powerful than we might think, and editors, documentarians, and reporters must constantly make choices about how to tell their stories, as David Carr relates in "Telling War's Story at Just Enough Distance." Susan Sontag reflects as well on the power images have in conveying the realities of war. In "Regarding the Pain of Others," she explains that photographs tell us "what war does." Indeed, images like *Vietnam Napalm* and *Iraqi Prisoner Consoles His Son* convey a visual punch that shatters our complacency regarding war. As wars recede in time, there is always a worry that they will similarly fade from memory. Perhaps the concern is best captured in the well-recognized formulation of George Santayana that those who cannot remember history are doomed to repeat it. Telling stories about wars is one way of responding to this fear.

A Conversation with Ken Burns

Gene Santoro

> **FYI** With the debut of *The Civil War* in 1990, Ken Burns established himself as a premier documentary filmmaker. Using archival photographs and a technique of panning and zooming, Burns was able to take historical materials and bring them to life in the medium of film. His subsequent works include *Baseball*, *Jazz*, and the 2007 film discussed below, *The War*.

Seventeen years after *The Civil War* copped dozens of awards, including two Emmys and a Peabody, Ken Burns has gone back to war—World War II—with *The War*. Born in Brooklyn, the son of a cultural anthropologist, Burns dreamed of becoming a Hollywood director in the mold of John Ford or Howard Hawks, but the major influences on his own work include photographers Walker Evans and Dorothea Lange, who captured indelible images of ordinary men and women in the Depression, and documentary filmmakers like D. A. Pennebaker, who pioneered an intimate and direct style. Over his thirty-year career since *Brooklyn Bridge*, Burns has rarely revisited a topic, roving over the likes of baseball, jazz, Lewis and Clark, and Frank Lloyd Wright. After *The Civil War*, Burns vowed never to tackle the subject of war again, yet his Florentine Films spent nearly six years assembling *The War*. The fourteen-hour survey follows events through the eyes of a few dozen people.

Gene Santoro: Why does World War II still matter?

Ken Burns: I can't imagine a time it won't. It is the greatest cataclysm in human history, killing more human beings, engaging more human effort, than any other event. Right now is a particularly fruitful period for the war in popular culture because the young men who fought are now old men, and many of them have finally begun to tell their stories. It's a bittersweet intersection we find ourselves at: the rich memories of these men and the realization that they're at the end of their lives. We're losing a thousand veterans a day. The film I made would not be possible five years from now.

Gene Santoro: There are so many movies and documentaries already about World War II.

Ken Burns: Well, there are excellent films that put me in the moment but didn't show me the context. There are documentaries that gave me the context but were sort of soulless, didn't tell me what it was like to be in that war.

None of them seemed able to understand the simultaneity of the two theaters. And so we try to tell an entirely bottom-up, intimate story of the war that gives you a sense of what it meant to be in battle but at the same time communicate the largeness of it. The overarching story is chronologically anchored in these four regular American towns, so that we would have a sense of home, a place to return to, while showing both theaters.

Gene Santoro: Putting it all together must have been quite a logistical challenge.

Ken Burns: It was the most complicated production we've ever had. We were trying to do two things that seemed mutually exclusive: tell an intimate story and at the same time a history of the war. The film is very much like *War and Peace*, where you get to know fifty or so individuals intimately. They're the foreground. The background is this epic struggle. The incredibly complex artistic effort came in merging these two seemingly disparate aspects.

Gene Santoro: A lot of original picture research forms the basis of the film.

Ken Burns: We went through tens of thousands of stills and thousands of hours of footage. That was

> *The central characters are the young men who did the fighting and the dying, whose stories are told not just in a specific moment, which has been done, but across the arc of the war, which has not been done.*

the monster task. We visited archives all around the world: Tokyo, Moscow, Berlin, London, hundreds in the United States. The National Archives was our single most important repository. But with this film we've merged all those materials with the home movies and graduation pictures of the towns and people we met there.

So it's at once intimate and general. Famous shots like the men falling at Omaha Beach are alongside things no one has ever seen before, not just from private archives but the National Archives. Because we had the privilege and luxury to spend years on this project, we did not only get familiar stories that play again and again in World War II documentaries.

Gene Santoro: There's loads of film, even color film, of the war.

Ken Burns: And it's very potent stuff. After we got over the excitement and shock of how much color footage there was, we figured out how to use it effectively to make the battles come alive. That was one of the most exciting parts of the production. That footage combined with the presence of these men, who are our fathers and grandfathers, is what makes this so special. It has an emotional immediacy for us that increases the challenge of using the photos and footage to bring it alive, to make it as real as we feel it to be—to make you feel like you're in the battle.

Gene Santoro: Did you see yourself working in the tradition of famous war correspondents Ernie Pyle and Bill Mauldin?

Ken Burns: In the sense that there's a kind of impossibility to communicating what happens in war. Oliver Wendell Holmes Jr., who was wounded six times in the Civil War, said, "We have shared the incommunicable experience of war. We have felt, we still feel, the passion of life at its top. In our youths, our hearts were touched with fire." So we used intermediaries, like Pyle and Mauldin, to try to describe the indescribable, explain the unexplainable, and fathom the unfathomable.

Gene Santoro: Which means adopting the soldier's viewpoint.

Ken Burns: Our understanding of the war is distracted and mediated by an unnecessary interest in celebrity generals and politicians, by the continual focus on strategy and tactics, on armaments and weaponry, and by the demonization of evil, all things Nazi, for instance.

We try to remove that. Those generals are players on our stage, but the central characters are the young men who did the fighting and the dying, whose stories are told not just in a specific moment, which has been done, but across the arc of the war, which has not been done.

Gene Santoro: Your arc's midpoint is June 6, 1944.

Ken Burns: The parallels between the Civil War and the Second World War were affecting us. After Gettysburg, some said the war would be over, but the worst killing was yet to come. The same was true of D-Day. Patton, I think, said, "All plans change the minute the fighting starts." So you have the improvisation that takes place continually in war, and how much of it goes wrong. Like Peleliu—an island of no strate-

dead. But as photography evolved toward lightweight cameras and higher-speed films, the dead became less visible.

The images of the victims of American wars past—the villagers of My Lai, the charred head of an Iraqi soldier from the Persian Gulf War—created significant controversy when they were published. Some editors and photographers say war photography is edited with a heavier hand because of its ability not just to offend the viewer, but to implicate him or her as well.

"The distinction with war photography is that we have willed that person dead," said Harold Evans, author of *Pictures on a Page*, adding, "We have willed it by sending the soldier there to do that dirty work for us."

Mr. Evans was a vocal defender of publication of the picture of the Iraqi soldier immolated in his vehicle, which created an outcry when it appeared in the *Observer* of London. Daniel Okrent, then managing editor of a weekly version of *Life*, declined to publish the picture.

"It was too horrible, but then I remember thinking, how can it be too horrible to depict war?" Mr. Okrent said. "I don't know if we did the right thing."

Mr. Kelly of *Time* is in the midst of wondering about similar things. As a way to communicate the costs of the war, he chose a photograph of an Iraqi boy being tended to by his aunt who had been severely burned in a firefight near Baghdad, in addition to losing both his arms and his family.

"You don't want to give the reader a sanitized war, but there has to be some judgment and taste," he said.

Ms. Sontag wondered whom such standards actually protect. "The friends I have all over the world are seeing horrifying images of what is happening when those bombs drop," she said. "I am always suspicious when institutions talk about good taste. Taste belongs to individuals."

John Gaps III, photography director of the *Des Moines Register*, agreed to a point. "Any time you start applying the word *taste* to war, you minimize and trivialize what is happening on the battlefield," said Mr. Gaps, a former Associated Press combat photographer.

Arab news executives said their Western counterparts were misleading viewers and readers by showing a war without death and pain.

"What happens in Iraq is not covered honestly on CNN, BBC," an Al-Jazeera news executive said in a telephone interview from Doha, Qatar. "We don't see any of those killed by the American forces." It also explains, he said, why the rest of the world feels so differently about this war than most Americans do.

Network news executives gave various reasons for their limited tolerance of gore compared with their Arab colleagues. For one, they said, there are more Arab reporters roving around the towns and villages of the country on their own, while many Western journalists travel with military units that fight and move on. "I don't think people have been walking around body-littered fields," said Jim Murphy, executive producer of the *CBS Evening News*.

Steve Capus, executive producer of the *NBC Nightly News*, said his program is able to communicate the reality of war without reveling in death or injury. "You watch some Arab coverage and you get a sense that there is a bloodbath at the hands of the U.S. military," he said. "That is not my take on it."

Ted Koppel, the anchor of *Nightline*, who is traveling with the Third Infantry Division in Iraq, said the conflict might seem bloodless to viewers at home because it sometimes even seems sanitized to troops who rely on long-range weapons.

"This war is fought in many respects at arm's length," Mr. Koppel said. "The damage is done, people are killed, but without the people who do the killing seeing very much of the consequences until hours or days later, when they advance."

By then, he said, Iraqis have often removed their dead soldiers' bodies. *Nightline* has focused its cam-

> "Some editors and photographers say war photography is edited with a heavier hand because of its ability not just to offend the viewer, but to implicate him or her as well."

eras on bombing victims more than perhaps any other American news program. One recent night, the program focused on civilians mistakenly hit by fire from the Third Infantry Division. One man's chest was bloody, and the camera did not shy away. Another man's left eye was gouged; it showed that, too.

"The fact that people get killed in a war is precisely what people need to be reminded of," Mr. Koppel said.

Ephemeral American standards—no one seems to know where the line is, yet very few transgress it—seem consistent for still and motion photography. The objective, said Howell Raines, executive editor of the *New York Times*, is "to try to capture the true nature of an event, whether it's a disaster like the World Trade Center or a war, but also to do so with restraint and an avoidance of the gratuitous use of images simply for shock value."

Sometimes the shock value of particularly gruesome imagery can have a practical effect. The last time Saddam Hussein was backed into a corner by the United States—in 1991—broadcast reports showed the "highway of death," seeming to indicate an assault on fleeing Iraqis that had turned into mass killing. By some accounts, the administration's fear of the negative publicity led top United States officials to declare a cease-fire without a move first to capture Baghdad or to destroy Republican Guard units. Saddam Hussein lived to fight another day.

John Szarkowski, former director of photography at the Museum of Modern Art and author of several books on photography, said that the scarcity of truly horrific images of war preserves their power when they eventually appear.

"I don't think that editors should feel an obligation to print every bloody picture that comes in," he said. "After a while, people get in-ured to the suffering in the photograph, and that is not good for anyone. In that sense, each successive image has less impact than the one that came before it."

> **Arab news executives said their Western counterparts were misleading viewers and readers by showing a war without death and pain.**

CONSIDER

1. Do you believe that coverage of wars has the ability to influence public opinion? If so, what obligation does the news media have to remain objective? What would you say to someone who argued that reporters shouldn't try to be objective at all?

2. Use the Internet to investigate coverage of the Iraq War in other countries. How would you compare what you found to coverage of the war in the United States?

3. What are your thoughts on the coverage of the Iraq War? Do you feel like the news media has sanitized the war? Why or why not?

FYI

ITEM 5.13 ■ George Bush Meeting with Burned Soldier

Advances in armor and medical technology have translated into a much higher survival rate for soldiers injured in the Iraq War. With these advances, however, come new challenges as soldiers return home scarred and disabled. While much controversy has been raised about the treatment these soldiers receive, it is clear that the challenges are not only medical but also emotional.

CONSIDER

1. The photograph shown above is one of dozens taken during a visit President George W. Bush paid to recovering soldiers. Do you think that the news media is intruding on a private moment by documenting such visits? Why or why not?

2. What is the significance of this photograph in relation to David Carr's "Telling War's Deadly Story with Just Enough Distance"? What are your thoughts on the decision by Reuters to distribute the image over the Internet?

3. The authors and editors of this book have had to make decisions about images included in these sections. Do you think the criteria for making such decisions shift depending on whether the images will be included in a news report or a textbook? Are there images in this section you would remove? Are there other images from the Iraq War that you would include?

From Regarding the Pain of Others

Susan Sontag
(2003)

In June 1938 Virginia Woolf published *Three Guineas*, her brave, unwelcomed reflections on the roots of war. Written during the preceding two years, while she and most of her intimates and fellow writers were rapt by the advancing fascist insurrection in Spain, the book was couched as the very tardy reply to a letter from an eminent lawyer in London who had asked, "How in your opinion are we to prevent war?" Woolf begins by observing tartly that a truthful dialogue between them may not be possible. For though they belong to the same class, "the educated class," a vast gulf separates them: the lawyer is a man and she is a woman. Men make war. Men (most men) like war, since for men there is "some glory, some necessity, some satisfaction in fighting" that women (most women) do not feel or enjoy. What does an educated—read: privileged, well-off—woman like her know of war? Can her recoil from its allure be like his? Let us test this "difficulty of communication," Woolf proposes, by looking together at images of war. The images are some of the photographs the beleaguered Spanish government has been sending out twice a week; she footnotes: "Written in the winter of 1936–37." Let's see, Woolf writes, "whether when we look at the same photographs we feel the same things." She continues:

> This morning's collection contains the photograph of what might be a man's body, or a woman's; it is so mutilated that it might, on the other hand, be the body of a pig. But those certainly are dead children, and that undoubtedly is the section of a house. A bomb has torn open the side; there is still a bird-cage hanging in what was presumably the sitting room....

> **FYI** The late Susan Sontag, an essayist, novelist, theater director, and antiwar activist, had an abiding interest in photography and culture. Her 1978 book *On Photography* is often cited as groundbreaking in its analysis of the role of photographs in the media and society. Sontag applied a background in literature to critique photographs in terms of their status both as art objects and as forces that shape belief and culture. In *Regarding the Pain of Others*, from which this essay is taken, she updates her position on the power of images to change the ways we think about violence. The excerpt reprinted here reflects Sontag's thinking about images and war, although it was written before the war in Iraq began.

The quickest, driest way to convey the inner commotion caused by these photographs is by noting that one can't always make out the subject, so thorough is the ruin of flesh and stone they depict. And from there Woolf speeds to her conclusion. We do have the same responses, "however different the education, the traditions behind us," she says to the lawyer. Her evidence: both "we"—here women are the "we"—and you might well respond in the same words.

> You, Sir, call them "horror and disgust." We also call them horror and disgust. . . . War, you say, is an abomination; a barbarity; war must be stopped at whatever cost. And we echo your words. War is an abomination; a barbarity; war must be stopped.

Who believes today that war can be abolished? No one, not even pacifists. We hope only (so far in vain) to stop genocide and to bring to justice those who commit gross violations of the laws of war (for there are laws of war, to which combatants should be held), and to be able to stop specific wars by imposing negotiated alternatives to armed conflict. It may be hard to credit the desperate resolve produced by the aftershock of the First World War, when the realization of the ruin Europe had brought on itself took hold. Condemning war as such did not seem so futile or irrelevant in the wake of the paper fantasies of the Kellogg-Briand Pact of 1928, in which fifteen leading nations, including the United States, France, Great Britain, Germany, Italy, and Japan, solemnly renounced war as an instrument of national policy; even Freud and Einstein were drawn into the debate with a public exchange of letters in 1932 titled "Why War?" Woolf's *Three Guineas*, appearing toward the close of nearly two decades of plangent denunciations of war, offered the originality (which made this the least well received of all her books) of focusing on what was regarded as too obvious or inapposite to be mentioned, much less brooded over: that war is a man's game—that the killing machine has a gender, and it is male. Nevertheless, the temerity of Woolf's version of "Why War?" does not make her revulsion against war any less conventional in its rhetoric, in its summations, rich in repeated phrases. And photographs of the victims of war are themselves a species of rhetoric. They reiterate. They simplify. They agitate. They create the illusion of consensus.

Invoking this hypothetical shared experience ("we are seeing with you the same dead bodies, the same ruined houses"), Woolf professes to believe that the shock of such pictures cannot fail to unite people of good will. Does it? To be sure, Woolf and the unnamed addressee of this book-length letter are not any two people. Although they are separated by the age-old affinities of feeling and practice of their respective sexes, as Woolf has reminded him, the lawyer is hardly a standard-issue bellicose male. His antiwar opinions are no more in doubt than are hers. After all, his question was not, What are your thoughts about preventing war? It was, How in your opinion are we to prevent war?

It is this "we" that Woolf challenges at the start of her book: she refuses to allow her interlocutor to take a "we" for granted. But into this "we," after the pages devoted to the feminist point, she then subsides. No "we" should be taken for granted when the subject is looking at other people's pain.

Who are the "we" at whom such shock-pictures are

> **Photographs of the victims of war are themselves a species of rhetoric. They reiterate. They simplify. They agitate. They create the illusion of consensus.**

aimed? That "we" would include not just the sympathizers of a smallish nation or a stateless people fighting for its life, but—a far larger constituency—those only nominally concerned about some nasty war taking place in another country. The photographs are a means of making "real" (or "more real") matters that the privileged and the merely safe might prefer to ignore.

"Here then on the table before us are photographs," Woolf writes of the thought experiment she is proposing to the reader as well as to the spectral lawyer, who is eminent enough, as she mentions, to have K.C., King's Counsel, after his name and may or may not be a real person. Imagine then a spread of loose photographs extracted from an envelope that arrived in the morning post. They show the mangled bodies of adults and children. They show how war evacuates, shatters, breaks apart, levels the built world. "A bomb has torn open the side," Woolf writes of the house in one of the pictures. To be sure, a cityscape is not made of flesh. Still, sheared-off buildings are almost as eloquent as bodies in the street. (Kabul, Sarajevo, East Mostar, Grozny, sixteen acres of lower Manhattan after September 11, 2001, the refugee camp in Jenin. . . .) Look, the photographs say, *this* is what it's like. This is what war does. And *that*, that is what it does, too. War tears, rends. War rips open, eviscerates. War scorches. War dismembers. War ruins.

Not to be pained by these pictures, not to recoil from them, not to strive to abolish what causes this havoc, this carnage—these, for Woolf, would be the reactions of a moral monster. And, she is saying, we are not monsters, we are members of the educated class. Our failure is one of imagination, of empathy: we have failed to hold this reality in mind.

But is it true that these photographs, documenting the slaughter of noncombatants rather than the clash of armies, could only stimulate the repudiation of war? Surely they could also foster greater militancy on behalf of the Republic. Isn't this what they were meant to do? The agreement between Woolf and the lawyer seems entirely presumptive, with the grisly photographs confirming an opinion already held in common. Had the question been, How can we best contribute to the defense of the Spanish Republic against the forces of militarist and clerical fascism? the photographs might instead have reinforced their belief in the justness of that struggle.

The pictures Woolf has conjured up do not in fact show what war, war as such, does. They show a particular way of waging war, a way at that time routinely described as "barbaric," in which civilians are the target. General Franco was using the same tactics of bombardment, massacre, torture, and the killing and mutilation of prisoners that he had perfected as a commanding officer in Morocco in the 1920s. Then, more acceptably to ruling powers, his victims had been Spain's colonial subjects, darker-hued and infidels to boot; now his victims were compatriots. To read in the pictures, as Woolf does, only what confirms a general abhorrence of war is to stand back from an engagement with Spain as a country with a history. It is to dismiss politics.

For Woolf, as for many antiwar polemicists, war is generic, and the images she describes are of anonymous, generic victims. The pictures sent out by the government in Madrid seem, improbably, not to have been labeled. (Or perhaps Woolf is simply assuming that a photograph should speak for itself.) But the case against war does not rely on information about who and when and where; the arbitrariness of the relentless slaughter is evidence enough. To those who are sure that right is on one side, oppression and injustice on the other, and that the fighting must go on, what matters is precisely who is killed and by whom. To an Israeli Jew, a photograph of a child torn apart in the attack on the Sbarro pizzeria in downtown Jerusalem is first of all a photograph of a Jewish child killed by a Palestinian suicide-bomber. To a Palestinian, a photograph of a child torn apart by a tank round in Gaza is first of all a photograph of a Palestinian child killed by Israeli ordnance. To the militant, identity is everything. And all photographs wait to be explained or falsified by their captions. During the fighting between Serbs and Croats at the beginning of the recent Balkan wars, the same photographs of children killed in the shelling of a village were passed around at both Serb and Croat propaganda briefings. Alter the caption, and the children's deaths could be used and reused.

Images of dead civilians and smashed houses may serve to quicken hatred of the foe, as did the hourly reruns by Al-Jazeera, the Arab satellite television network based in Qatar, of the destruction in the Jenin refugee camp in April 2002. Incendiary as that footage was to the many who watch Al-Jazeera throughout the world, it did not tell them anything about the Israeli army they were not already primed to believe. In contrast, images offering evidence that contradicts cherished pieties are invariably dismissed as having been staged for the camera. To photographic corroboration of the atrocities committed by one's own side, the standard response is that the pictures are a fabrication, that no such atrocity ever took place, those were bodies the other side had brought in trucks from the city morgue

> "Look, the photographs say, *this* is what it's like. This is what war does. And *that*, that is what it does, too. War tears, rends. War rips open, eviscerates. War scorches. War dismembers. War ruins."

and placed about the street, or that, yes, it happened and it was the other side who did it, to themselves. Thus the chief of propaganda for Franco's Nationalist rebellion maintained that it was the Basques who had destroyed their own ancient town and former capital, Guernica, on April 26, 1937, by placing dynamite in the sewers (in a later version, by dropping bombs manufactured in Basque territory) in order to inspire indignation abroad and reinforce the Republican resistance. And thus a majority of Serbs living in Serbia or abroad maintained right to the end of the Serb siege of Sarajevo, and even after, that the Bosnians themselves perpetrated the horrific "breadline massacre" in May 1992 and "market massacre" in February 1994, lobbing large-caliber shells into the center of their capital or planting mines in order to create some exceptionally gruesome sights for the foreign journalists' cameras and rally more international support for the Bosnian side.

> **During the fighting between Serbs and Croats at the beginning of the recent Balkan wars, the same photographs of children killed in the shelling of a village were passed around at both Serb and Croat propaganda briefings. Alter the caption, and the children's deaths could be used and reused.**

Photographs of mutilated bodies certainly can be used the way Woolf does, to vivify the condemnation of war, and may bring home, for a spell, a portion of its reality to those who have no experience of war at all. However, someone who accepts that in the world as currently divided war can become inevitable, and even just, might reply that the photographs supply no evidence, none at all, for renouncing war—except to those for whom the notions of valor and sacrifice have been emptied of meaning and credibility. The destructiveness of war—short of total destruction, which is not war but suicide—is not in itself an argument against waging war unless one thinks (as few people actually do think) that violence is always unjustifiable, that force is always and in all circumstances wrong—wrong because, as Simone Weil affirms in her sublime essay on war, "The Iliad, or The Poem of Force" (1940), violence turns anybody subjected to it into a thing. No, retort those who in a given situation see no alternative to armed struggle, violence can exalt someone subjected to it into a martyr or a hero. In fact, there are many uses of the innumerable opportunities a modern life supplies for regarding—at a distance, through the medium of photography—other people's pain. Photographs of an atrocity may give rise to opposing responses. A call for peace. A cry for revenge. Or simply the bemused awareness, continually restocked by photographic information, that terrible things happen. Who can forget the three color pictures by Tyler Hicks that the *New York Times* ran across the upper half of the first page of its daily section devoted to America's new war, "A Nation Challenged," on November 13, 2001? The triptych depicted the fate of a wounded Taliban soldier in uniform who had been found in a ditch by Northern Alliance soldiers advancing toward Kabul. First panel: being dragged on his back by two of his captors—one has grabbed an arm, the other a leg—along a rocky road. Second panel (the camera is very near): surrounded, gazing up in terror as he is being pulled to his feet. Third panel: at the moment of death, supine with arms outstretched and knees bent, naked and bloodied from the waist down, being finished off by the military mob that has gathered to butcher him. An ample reservoir of stoicism is needed to get through the great newspaper of record each morning, given the likelihood of seeing photographs that could make you cry. And the pity and disgust that pictures like Hicks's inspire should not distract you from asking what pictures, whose cruelties, whose deaths are *not* being shown.

For a long time some people believed that if the horror could be made vivid enough, most people would finally take in the outrageousness, the insanity of war.

Fourteen years before Woolf published *Three Guineas*—in 1924, on the tenth anniversary of the national mobilization in Germany for the First World War—the conscientious objector Ernst Friedrich published his *Krieg dem Kriege! (War Against War!)*. This is photography as shock therapy: an album of more than one hundred and eighty photographs mostly drawn from German military and medical archives, many of which were deemed unpublishable by government censors while the war was on. The book starts with pictures of toy soldiers, toy cannons, and other delights of male children everywhere, and concludes with pictures taken in military cemeteries. Between the toys and the graves, the reader has an excruciating photo-tour of four years of ruin, slaughter, and degradation: pages of wrecked and plundered churches and castles, obliterated villages, ravaged forests, torpedoed passenger steamers, shattered vehicles, hanged conscientious objectors, half-naked prostitutes in military brothels, soldiers in death agonies after a poison-gas attack, skeletal Armenian children. Almost all the sequences in *War Against War!* are difficult to look at, notably the pictures of dead soldiers belonging to the various armies putrefying in heaps on fields and roads and in the front-line trenches. But surely the most unbearable pages in this book, the whole of which was designed to horrify and demoralize, are in the section titled "The Face of War," twenty-four close-ups of soldiers with huge facial wounds. And Friedrich did not make the mistake of supposing that heartrending, stomach-turning pictures would simply speak for themselves. Each photograph has an impassioned caption in four languages (German, French, Dutch, and English), and the wickedness of militarist ideology is excoriated and mocked on every page. Immediately denounced by the government and by veterans' and other patriotic organizations—in some cities the police raided bookstores, and lawsuits were brought against the public display of the photographs—Friedrich's declaration of war against war was acclaimed by left-wing writers, artists, and intellectuals, as well as by the constituencies of the numerous antiwar leagues, who predicted that the book would have a decisive influence on public opinion. By 1930, *War Against War!* had gone through ten editions in Germany and been translated into many languages.

> "For a long time some people believed that if the horror could be made vivid enough, most people would finally take in the outrageousness, the insanity of war."

In 1938, the year of Woolf's *Three Guineas*, the great French director Abel Gance featured in close-up some of the mostly hidden population of hideously disfigured excombatants—*les gueules cassées* ("the broken mugs") they were nicknamed in French at the climax of his new *J'accuse*. (Gance had made an earlier, primitive version of his incomparable antiwar film, with the same hallowed title, in 1918.) As in the final section of Friedrich's book, Gance's film ends in a new military cemetery, not just to remind us of how many millions of young men were sacrificed to militarism and ineptitude between 1914 and 1918 in the war cheered on as "the war to end all wars," but to advance the sacred judgment these dead would surely bring against Europe's politicians and generals could they know that, twenty years later, another war was imminent. "*Morts de Verdun, levez-vous!*" (Rise, dead of Verdun!), cries the deranged veteran who is the protagonist of the film, and he repeats his summons in German and in English: "Your sacrifices were in vain!" And the vast mortuary plain disgorges its multitudes, an army of shambling ghosts in rotted uniforms with mutilated faces, who rise from their graves and set out in all directions, causing mass panic among the populace already mobilized for a new pan-European war. "Fill your eyes with this horror! It is the only thing that can stop you!" the madman cries to the fleeing multitudes of the living, who reward him with a martyr's death, after which he joins his dead comrades: a sea of impassive ghosts overrunning the cowering future combatants and victims of *la guerre de demain*. War beaten back by apocalypse.

And the following year the war came.

CONSIDER

1. What point does Susan Sontag make about men, women, and war? Do you agree? Why or why not?

2. Has the public become desensitized to images of war and violence now that newspapers, television news, and the Web bring combat and terror incidents directly into our homes? What would we gain in sensitivity—if anything—by restricting the number of graphic images presented?

CHALLENGE

3. The embedding of journalists and photographers with coalition combat troops during the Iraq War has been the subject of much controversy. The public receives battlefield reports and films of combat almost instantly. Some analysts argue that the objectivity and independence of the journalists is compromised by the close relationships they develop with coalition troops, as well as the restrictions placed on them by the need to conceal troop movements, numbers, and strategies. Use library and Web resources to explore the issues raised by embedded coverage of the Iraq War, and then write a paper evaluating the strategy from the point of view of the public. Does it help citizens understand the war better?

ITEM 5.14 ■ Nick Ut, *Vietnam Napalm*, 1972

Nick Ut's photograph of villagers fleeing a napalm attack stands as one of the most recognizable depictions of the atrocities of the Vietnam War. After taking the picture, Ut hurried the young girl, Phan Thi Kim Phuc, into a car and rushed her to the hospital. Years later, Kim Phuc credited the photographer with saving her life.

CONSIDER

1. The image in Item 5.14 won the Pulitzer Prize for photographer Nick Ut. Is it fair to say the subject matter is more important than the composition of the photograph? Why or why not?

2. Can you think of any reasons why it might have been wrong to take the picture? What kinds of decisions might a photographer make when taking a picture like this?

3. The photograph of fleeing South Vietnamese children is perhaps the most recognized image of the Vietnam War. Why do you think this photograph has been reproduced so many times? Can you think of any problems with such a horrific image becoming iconic?

5.1 | STORIES OF WAR

ITEM 5.15 ■ *Iraqi Prisoner Consoles his Son,* March 31, 2003

We often associate war with violence, with the wounds of battle demonstrated in graphic images of flesh and blood. But the effects of war reach far beyond the physical damage of wounded soldiers and civilians. Item 5.15 was taken during the early days of the Iraq War. It depicts a father and his four-year-old son held at a U.S. camp for prisoners of war.

Source: Associated Press.

CONSIDER

1. What are your reactions to the image shown above? What about the composition of the image makes it powerful?

2. Although the image appeals to the emotions, it does not demonstrate the violence of war explicitly. How would you respond to someone who argued that the photograph of the Iraqi father is a sanitized image from the war?

CHALLENGE

3. In what ways are the images in this cluster biased? What images might provide alternative messages? How might one argue that the impacts of war can be seen in a positive light? Hold a discussion with classmates regarding the disagreements that might arise when it comes to supporting or critiquing wars.

Cluster 5.2
Film Stories over the Years

Step into any video store, and where do you find most people? The new releases section, of course. We've come to expect the latest and greatest visual effects. We flock to *The Dark Knight* and anticipate trailers chock full of computer-generated mummies and transforming robot cars and trucks. Ironically, though, movies represent a form of narrative that relies on a strong connection with films that have come before, often decades earlier, that established the techniques and motifs we take for granted in the latest stream of DVD releases. Films teach us how media often take up political messages or document their historical contexts. *Casablanca*, for instance, evokes a threatening Nazi presence that speaks to the wartime concerns of its 1942 audience.

Films also reveal how media evolve and respond to technical changes. Some older films seem almost comic in their sentiments and crude in their production, but they represent the state of the art of filmmaking and storytelling of the past. Alfred Hitchcock's films may pale next to recent thrillers, but in their time they changed the way people viewed movies and kept viewers on the edge of their seats. *North by Northwest*, for instance, dazzled audiences in 1959 with the use of sound and the editing of its famous crop-dusting sequence.

Finally, films show us the ways that media reflect and shape cultural concerns. Spike Lee's *Do the Right Thing* explores inner-city race relations. *Crash* and *Brokeback Mountain* take up concerns of race and sexuality. These films all sparked vigorous public debate about their controversial topics.

5 | MEDIA

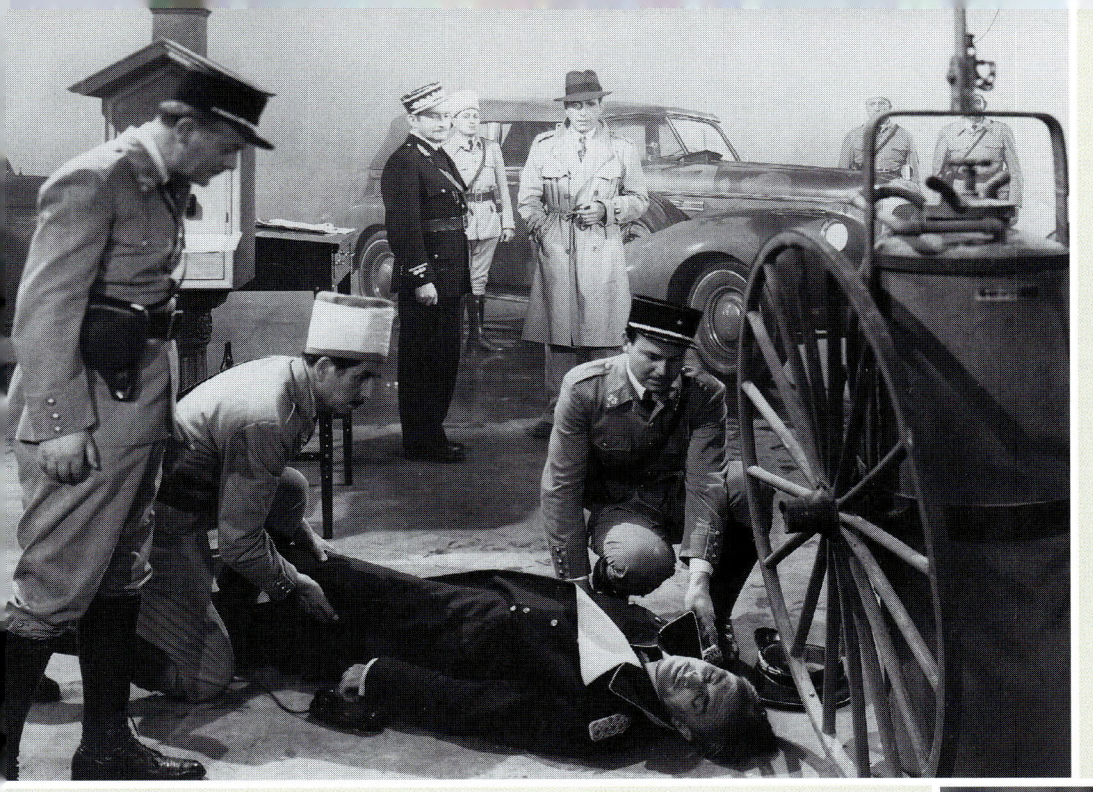

ITEM 5.16 ■ Still Images from *Casablanca*, Directed by Michael Curtiz, 1942

CONSIDER

View *Casablanca*; then respond to the following questions:

1. Decide whether you could best interpret the film in terms of its romantic story or its historical context. How would you explain your choice?

2. Do you think the still images from *Casablanca* in Item 5.16 capture the relationships between the characters? What about the images most clearly demonstrates their state of mind?

3. How does viewing the political intrigues of World War II through the medium of film differ from learning about it through documentaries or textbooks?

293

ITEM 5.17 ■ Still Images from *North by Northwest*, Directed by Alfred Hitchcock, 1959

Alfred Hitchcock may be the filmmaker most often associated with mystery and suspense. Films like *The Birds*, *Psycho*, *Rear Window*, and *Vertigo* demonstrate the innovations Hitchcock undertook. By pushing the boundaries for effects and plot development, Hitchcock introduced elements of intrigue and realistic terror into his movies. *North by Northwest* exemplifies the filmmaking invention and themes of suspense that are hallmark Hitchcock. From the famous car chase, crop-dusting, and cliff-hanging scenes to the motif of the innocent man wrongfully accused, the film represents a storytelling classic that filmmakers have followed and elaborated on in numerous films up to the present day.

Cary Grant, pursued by a crop-duster in *North by Northwest*, 1959

Eva Marie Saint and Cary Grant hanging on the face of Mount Rushmore in *North by Northwest*

CONSIDER

View *North by Northwest*; then respond to the following questions:

1. The crop-dusting scene from *North by Northwest* is one of the best known in film. What makes chase scenes so appealing to filmgoers? Based on elements of suspense like chases and cliff-hangers, how would you compare films to other forms of storytelling such as novels or plays?

2. How does a medium like film depend on stars like Eva Marie Saint or Cary Grant? Can you think of contemporary actors who have a shaping influence on films?

3. How aware of filmmaking techniques are you when you watch movies? How aware should you be? Discuss these questions in a group, drawing on recent films you have seen or classics from the past. Is a technique that draws attention to itself—the amazing slow-motion shots in the *Matrix* trilogy, for example—distracting or riveting (or both)? At what point does a technique become a cliché?

CHALLENGE

4. View one or two Hitchcock films in addition to *North by Northwest*, and then think through all of the films you have seen that present echoes of the themes and scenes found in Hitchcock's movies. How do spy movies relate to Hitchcock's work? What about action or suspense films? Slasher movies? Choose one or two later movies, and write a paper exploring how they emulate and extend the earlier films.

Fear of a Black Cinema

Amy Taubin
(2002)

> **FYI** Amy Taubin has been a film critic for the *Village Voice* since 1987 and is contributing editor of *Sight and Sound*. In addition to writing about film, Taubin has also acted on stage and in film. She has appeared in avant-garde films, among them Michael Snow's *Wavelength* (1967) and Andy Warhol's *Couch* and *The Thirteen Most Beautiful Women* (1964).

Top-ten lists: fun to read, painful to write. Always sucker myself into doing them on the grounds it would be cowardly not to. It's not the fear that colleagues and readers will mock my choices that makes the task so fraught with anxiety. ("They're all gonna laugh at you," as Carrie's mother warned her; and shouldn't it give me pause that *Carrie* gets shut out year after year from my list and everyone else's?) No, it's being limited to ten—the eternal frustrating ten. Ten might have been reasonable 50 years ago when cinema had been around for only half a century and few critics had access to film cultures other than those of the U.S., Western Europe and occasionally the Soviet Union. But even those early lists were possible only with the tacit agreement to exclude entire categories of cinema—no avant-garde films, perhaps a token documentary, and, of course, forget about the tawdry glories of exploitation.

Now, however, with the vast increase in production and with films from virtually every country on the globe available in specialized theaters, ten is out of the question. This time around, shall I bump Chantal Akerman's *Jeanne Dielman 23, quai du Commerce, 1080 Bruxelles*, a formally stringent harbinger of a feminist cinema that is still slow in coming, in order to accommodate Zacharias Kunuk's *The Fast Runner* (*Atanarjuat*), the first-ever Inuit theatrical feature, which employs digital video, the medium of the future, to record a myth of origins set in a primal white-on-white landscape far stranger and more ravishing than that of *Star Wars*? Completed in 2001, the first year of the new millennium, *The Fast Runner* suggests that cinema has not lost its capacity for radical renewal. But alas, the list is filled, and so I rationalize the omission with a new rule—no films that have not stood the test of time for at least 25 years—which I impulsively break with the last-minute addition of David Cronenberg's as yet unreleased *Spider*. What can I say? Cronenberg's ingenious deployment of first-person narrative in a medium that's characteristically resistant to subjectivity seems a greater—and more perverse—achievement than Kunuk's epic action-adventure. (Since list-making is a perverse endeavor, perversity has the advantage.) My other even more bizarre rules: I categorically exclude silent cinema except for its last stand in Dziga Vertov's *The Man with a Movie Camera*, comedy (thus slighting pleasure at its most direct) and any film not produced in Europe or North America (thus reinforcing a hegemony I claim to despise). It's a contortionist's nightmare, which could be solved by increasing the number to a plausible 25.

In which case, Spike Lee's *Do the Right Thing* is guaranteed a place. How could it not be, since it established Lee as the most dedicated resistance fighter to infiltrate the Hollywood system—the filmmaker who put the fraught and disavowed issues of race and racism at the center of his films and refused to be ghettoized for doing so? Released in 1989, *Do the Right Thing* was Lee's third feature and the first to deal with the relationships between black characters (the residents of a single block in the Brooklyn neighborhood of [Bedford-Stuyvesant]) and white characters (the owner of the local pizzeria and his two sons, and the police).

Made after eight years of Reaganism had rolled back the gains of the Civil Rights movement and during the summer that the first George Bush was making his bid for the presidency with the help of the blatantly racist Willie Horton ads, *Do the Right Thing* was directly inspired by a series of incidents of racial violence and police brutality. There was Eleanor Bumpers, a very large, very likely psychotic black woman who was shot to death when she waved a knife at cops who'd come to arrest her. The cops claimed they acted in self-defense, but considering that the first bullet tore off Bumpers' hand, it was hard to understand why they felt obliged to keep firing. There was also Michael Stewart, a graffiti artist who was arrested for defacing subway property and strangled to death in a police chokehold. (The cops maintained he had a heart attack.)

> **Made after eight years of Reaganism had rolled back the gains of the Civil Rights movement and during the summer that the first George Bush was making his bid for the presidency with the help of the blatantly racist Willie Horton ads, *Do the Right Thing* was directly inspired by a series of incidents of racial violence and police brutality.**

At the climax of *Do the Right Thing* one of the neighborhood teenagers is similarly strangled while struggling with police. His death precipitates a riot that ends with the pizzeria burnt to the ground. To say the film struck a nerve would be an understatement. Lee was attacked for inciting black youth to riot in the streets, for sabotaging the upcoming mayoral campaign of David Dinkins, the African-American opponent of 12-year incumbent Ed Koch, and for single-handedly turning back the clock to the fiery racial confrontations of the 1960s. It was not only members of the white establishment press who were outraged; Lee caught heat from black intellectuals including conservative black writer Stanley Crouch, who accused him of "proto-fascism." The racism inherent in the attacks on *Do the Right Thing* is evidenced in the fact that most of the critics were more horrified by the destruction of white-owned property than by the death of the black teenager, which was almost never mentioned. As Lee has frequently noted, none of the critics who attacked him apologized when Dinkins, indeed, defeated Koch and New York did not go up in flames. It was, rather, South Central L.A. which, a few years later, was burnt and looted; the cause, however, was not a movie but the acquittal of the cops in the Rodney King case. And, of course, police brutality continues unabated (witness the killing of Amadou Diallo and the torture of Abner Louima at the hands of the NYPD).

The noise surrounding *Do the Right Thing* propelled Lee on to the covers of *Time*, *Newsweek* and various other mainstream media showcases (a neither unwelcome nor, one imagines, entirely unstrategized development), but it also obscured the brilliance of the film itself: its bold, ingenious formal hybridity, its unforced emotional range from exuberance to despair, the way its individual images and actions are packed with contradictory meanings. The setting is a single 24-hour day—the hottest day of the summer—on a single street in one of Brooklyn's poor, black neighborhoods. The title sequence—Rosie Perez dancing to Public Enemy's "Fight the Power"—encapsulates the theatrical style and confrontational strategy of the whole. Perez is part prize-fighter and part hootchy-kootchy dancer, but even when she's bumping and grinding, she's too fierce and self-contained to be read as a seductress. The dance is more political than sexual provocation, as if Lee were baiting the feminist critics, who dismissed his first feature *She's Gotta Have It* (1986) as male fantasy, to have another go at him.

In a series of fast-cut vignettes we're introduced to the residents of the block. Mister Señor Love Daddy (Samuel L. Jackson), the local-radio DJ, watches over the neighborhood like an angelic referee as he spins records and issues advice. The narrative is framed between his morning wake-up call and his final admonition to "register to vote." The film has more than its share of caustic observers. Da Mayor (Ossie Davis), an elderly drunk, stumbles up and down the street and romantically yearns for Mother-Sister (Ruby Dee), perpetually glaring down at him from her upper-floor window. At the end of the block, just past the Korean-owned grocery store and the Italian-owned pizzeria, sit three beer-bellied middle-aged men whose sole purpose in life is to provide a running commentary on their own bodily functions and everyone else's problems, particularly those of their busier, although not necessarily more purposeful, neighbors. There's a trio of young men with fragile, stunted identities—Buggin' Out (Giancarlo Esposito), Smiley (Roger Guenveur Smith) and Radio Raheem (Bill Nunn), the designated martyr who looks as menacing as NBA player Patrick Ewing in the post but clings to his outsized boom-box as his only hedge against invisibility. Their inchoate anger and frustrated desire for agency eventually focuses, with tragic consequences, on Sal (Danny Aiello), the paternalistic proprietor of the pizzeria, and his two sons (John Turturro and Richard Edson).

"Always do the right thing," says Da Mayor, buttonholing Mookie (Spike Lee), who's on his way to deliver a pizza and can't believe Da Mayor has interrupted him mid-stride with such an obvious piece of advice. "Mookie does not have heroic stature" was Wim Wenders' lame explanation of why the Cannes jury decided to award the Palme d'Or to Steven Soderbergh's *sex, lies, and videotape* rather than to *Do the Right Thing* (as if James Spader's impotent video freak did). There are no heroes in *Do the Right Thing*, but Mookie and Sal are more realist constructions than the film's other characters, who are so markedly one-dimensional they seem to have been lifted from a medieval morality play. The passive-aggressive Mookie has two women in his life—his beautiful, introspective sister Jackie (Joie Lee) and his girlfriend Tina, who's even more pugilistic in her speech than in her dancing. (She's the woman in the opening sequence.) But it's Mookie's father-son relationship with Sal, complicated by race and economic dependence, that becomes intolerable for him. When Mookie, in a

> **There are no heroes in *Do the Right Thing*, but Mookie and Sal are more realist constructions than the film's other characters, who are so markedly one-dimensional they seem to have been lifted from a medieval morality play.**

rage at Sal for being instrumental in Radio Raheem's death, hurls a garbage can through the pizzeria's plate-glass facade, thus precipitating the riot, it's an act of liberation and destruction—overdetermined all around.

But it's also a futile act, since it has no political context. Anyone who thinks this film could inspire violence is seeing their own paranoia and not what's on screen. Watching Mookie sitting shellshocked on the curb as the pizzeria burns, and Smiley tip-toeing through the embers to paste his fetishised Xeroxed image of Malcolm X and Martin Luther King on the skeleton of the wall which Sal had dedicated to curling stock photos of Italian-American celebrities, one feels overwhelmingly sadness—that the moment of a political movement with visionary, charismatic leaders and an organized strategy to "fight the power" is past and nothing has replaced it. Lee says he's been asked many times—although never by an African-

American—if Mookie did the right thing. The more interesting question is, where does he go from here? On the depressing morning after, Mookie and Sal forge an uneasy truce based on their mutual knowledge that they'll never see each other again. Sal asks Mookie what he's going to do, and Mookie, who was introduced counting his cash, answers as he walks away, "Get paid." Even as one finds relief in the open ending, one has to wonder if Mookie is going to follow the path of Spike Lee, who may have final cut on his films, but also has learned to make strategic accommodations to the "powers that be." Or will he choose a more vampiristic form of black entrepreneurship? In Lee's *Clockers* (1995) Delroy Lindo's neighborhood drug honcho Rodney, when asked why he sells crack to kids, answers, just as flatly as Mookie, "to get paid."

Part hip-hop musical, *Do the Right Thing* has deeper roots in the agit-prop theater of the 1930s and 1940s. "Fight the Power" is the film's anthem, but the soundtrack is dominated by William J. E. Lee's orchestral jazz score, its harmonies, rhythms and textures echoing the stage-musical scores of Marc Blitzstein and Aaron Copland. Lee may have fond memories of the film version of *Bye Bye Birdie* (1963), but *Do the Right Thing* is a lot closer to Blitzstein's *The Cradle Will Rock*, the 1938 musical about organized labor that Orson Welles directed on Broadway. And it's Welles' combination of theatrical showmanship and cinematic confidence that Lee seems to have absorbed here. Even the swooping, gliding crane shots have a theatrical feel, the sensation you get when you're so riveted by something on stage that it's as if you've been physically transported from your balcony seat into the middle of the action.

Do the Right Thing was shot on a real Brooklyn street, and the buildings have a solidity no set could provide. On the other hand, the action is choreographed as if the street were a stage. Performers zip on and off as they would in a vaudeville revue. Lee juxtaposes fragments of scenes, isolating the revealing glance, gesture, word. Differing wildly in tone and style, the fragments are hung on a single thread of mounting tension. A trio of characters—one black, one white, one Asian—look straight into the camera as they read off a list of ethnic and racial slurs, enunciating every syllable as in a spelling contest. Mookie and Pino, Sal's overtly racist son, watch the ever so slightly flirtatious interplay between Sal and Mookie's sister from opposite angles and with mirrored emotions.

Had the space not been so theatricalized, the conceit that this one street is a microcosm of the social order (and specifically of race relations) would have frayed. We would have wondered why no one ventured outside its confines or how a dozen brownstones could house enough hungry pizza eaters to keep Mookie on the run for an entire day. The fusion of realism and theatricality not only generates aesthetic sparks, it suggests the complicated interplay between race as the bedrock of everyday life and race as a spectacle (the passing parade). As Mister See or Love Daddy is wont to say: "And that's the triple truth, Ruth."

FYI

ITEM 5.18 ■ **Still Images from *Do the Right Thing*, Directed by Spike Lee, 1989**

Do the Right Thing does not always make it to the top of critics' lists of favorites, but the 1989 film is striking for its allusions to historical events as it prompts us to ask how we might respond to problems with race relations in the world. The film also marks the emergence of director Spike Lee as a force in Hollywood filmmaking. The film uses music and a plot that encapsulates the events of a single day to focus on concerns of race and violence.

CONSIDER

1. What are your thoughts on political messages and entertainment in films? Should films be political? Must they entertain? What happens when they try to do both?

2. How accurately must a film represent the social issues it comments on? Does limiting the scope of the action to a single block in *Do the Right Thing* affect the film's ability to represent race relations?

COMPOSE

3. Watch *Do the Right Thing*; then answer the question asked of Spike Lee: Does Mookie do the right thing at the end of the movie? Consider alternative perspectives as you develop an answer, and then develop a list of reasons that might be used to support your position. Report your stance in a brief presentation to a group of classmates.

The Collateral Damage of Crash

Brian D. Johnson
(2006)

> **FYI** Brian D. Johnson, a senior editor for *Macleans* magazine, has written on topics ranging from politics to art to travel. He is also the film critic for *Macleans* and author of the book *Brave Films, Wild Nights: 25 Years of Festival Fever*. "The Collateral Damage of *Crash*" first appeared in *Macleans* in April of 2006.

It's finally settling down, the *Brokeback*-lash against *Crash* winning best picture at the Academy Awards. But what was it all about? It's hard to remember an Oscar vote that has produced such bitter acrimony. Annie E. Proulx, who wrote the story on which *Brokeback Mountain* is based, moaned that the Oscar went to Trash. David Cronenberg—miffed that fellow Canadian Paul Haggis had stolen his own *Crash* title, and robbed a nomination from *A History of Violence*—called the Academy decision "stupid." The Academy is famous for stupidity. This, after all, is the group that preferred *Rocky* to *Taxi Driver* and *Forrest Gump* to *Pulp Fiction*. But its latest decision wasn't another triumph of dumb sentiment over smart drama.

Everyone has been quick to point out that those conservative liberals of the Academy chose a safe movie about racism over a daring homosexual romance. Gay rights activists cried foul. And critic Roger Ebert, who believed *Crash* actually was the best picture of 2005, scurried to defend himself against charges of homophobia. Others pointed out that Hollywood, in its parochial wisdom, chose a movie shot in Los Angeles over a runaway production filmed in Alberta. It's true that *Crash*, as a self-portrait of Los Angeles, appeals to Hollywood narcissism. The pivotal scene—of a bigoted white cop molesting a black woman in front of her husband—occurs as the couple is driving home from an awards ceremony.

But no matter what motivated the choice, its most disturbing consequence has nothing to do with racism or homophobia. In selecting *Crash* over *Brokeback*, the Academy of Motion Picture Arts and Sciences has voted against its own interests—by honouring the science of television over the art of cinema. *Crash* is a pretty good movie, well-acted and well-shot, but it looks like it belongs on TV. And that's how most of the Oscar voters would have seen it. Shortly before the ballot deadline, Lionsgate Entertainment sent *Crash* DVDs to all of the Academy's members—some 6,000. Many would have also seen *Brokeback* on DVD, and—missing the detail of the big screen—found it strangely slow.

Crash was made by a man who's spent most of his career writing for the small screen. And Haggis lends it the high-octane, episodic style of series drama. Much of it is shot in TV-style close-ups or medium shots. The telegraphic dialogue tells us exactly how its characters feel, and what we should think of them. *Brokeback Mountain* is a slow, subtle movie full of open space and awkward silence. Its characters don't say much, and what they do say is often not what they mean:

Ennis: This is a one-shot thing we got goin' on here.
Jack: It's nobody's business but ours.
Ennis: You know I ain't queer.
Jack: Me neither.

Compare that terse exchange to this stretch of edifying reflection from Graham, the black cop played by Don Cheadle in *Crash*:

> In L.A., nobody touches you. We're always behind this metal and glass. I think we miss that touch so much, that we crash into each other, just so we can feel something.

If that sounds more like a screenwriter than a cop, it's because Haggis likes to use his characters to spell out his themes in boldface. The movie is an outlet mall of racial stereotypes—white, black, Hispanic, Iranian,

Korean—which all implode with ironic twists. The message rings loud and clear: racial intolerance is a two-way street of road rage, an accident waiting to happen, and if we could only see past the displaced anger to embrace our common hopes and fears, we'd find there's not much separating us.

Brokeback may have become the butt of talk show jokes as that gay cowboy picture, but no one could mistake it for a message movie. It's a canvas of emotion, not ideas. And what's exemplary about this film is not that it's sexually transgressive, but that it's so stubbornly old-fashioned. In a movie culture that thrives on fast cuts and special effects, *Brokeback Mountain* is an oasis of calm. It reminds us that the big screen should be a place to get lost in, not a wall of unrelenting stimulus.

Watching a movie with an audience in the dark is fundamentally different than viewing it on TV. Cinema holds us hostage. It requires us to submit to the screen, to "go under," and ideally it's a dream-like experience. TV lets us keep our distance. While it fights for our attention, the medium is in our control—literally under our thumb. We're always conscious of the room beyond the frame, and it's easy to leave, or simply change the channel.

Brokeback owes its pacing to the western, in which the screen is a place, an open range where silence carries as much weight as words. But the same can be said of *Capote*. I saw both movies on the same day, at packed world premieres during the Toronto International Film Festival. What amazed me was how they both cast such a quiet spell over the audience. That's partly due to the civility of festival-goers. But it also demonstrated the subtle power of these pictures, which leave viewers space for their own imaginings.

You might argue that the styles of *Crash* and *Brokeback* just reflect their subject matter. One is a contemporary drama with half a dozen storylines colliding in the streets of L.A., the other a period piece about two men living a secret life in the wild. The action in *Crash* is jammed into two days; *Brokeback* sprawls over two decades. And cowboys, by nature, are less talkative than cops and carjackers.

But these movies have opposite goals for tragedy. As Ennis fondles the denim shirt once worn by his partner, his anguish comes to us unfiltered. *Crash*, which treats L.A. as a Middle East of American misunderstanding, can't stop replicating irony and coincidence. In the end, as all the narrative lanes merge, its multi-track mix of racism, revenge, violence and pathos is compressed into a soft-rock aria of redemption. The movie has been compared to Robert Altman's *Short Cuts*, but Altman is ragged, not smooth. Like television, *Crash* tries to synthesize the world.

> "TV and video are changing the grammar of cinema. From the ads and trailers to the movies themselves, Hollywood bombards us with sound and image."

TV and video are changing the grammar of cinema. From the ads and trailers to the movies themselves, Hollywood bombards us with sound and image. Movie-going etiquette disintegrates as viewers eat and talk. The megaplex, the food court of film, is the architectural equivalent of the remote, offering the illusion of infinite choice.

Meanwhile, the gap between popcorn movies and the art house has never been wider. It's inspiring to see *Brokeback* and *Capote* seduce a mainstream audience without pandering to TV attention spans. But long, uncut, real-time shots are becoming as rare as unfenced prairie. Some directors have made an avant garde fetish of slow cinema, notably Gus Van Sant in *Gerry*, *Elephant* and *Last Days*—yet all those titles were, paradoxically, made for TV by HBO. While movies become more TV-like, specialty TV strains to be more cinematic.

One final irony. At the Oscar ceremony, *Brokeback* star Jake Gyllenhaal, serving as a pitchman to boost declining theatre attendance, introduced a montage of spectacular movie clips by saying "there's no place to see them like the big screen." So why show them on television? By the same logic, in honouring *Crash*, the Academy only proved that its own industry—the business of filling theatres—is surrendering to home entertainment.

FYI

ITEM 5.19 ■ **Still Images from *Crash*, directed by Paul Haggis, 2004, and *Brokeback Mountain*, directed by Ang Lee, 2005**

In 2006 the Academy of Motion Picture Arts and Sciences awarded *Crash* its Oscar for best film. Some argued that the choice lacked courage because Academy voters were afraid of the controversial content of *Brokeback Mountain*, also a best picture nominee. Others felt that *Crash* warranted the selection with its clever weaving together of episodes to tackle an equally tough topic.

CONSIDER

View *Crash*; then answer the following questions:

1. Is it fair to characterize the film as small-screen entertainment as Brian D. Johnson argues in "The Collateral Damage of *Crash*"? Would you say that television as a medium is not as capable of telling compelling stories or exploring issues in depth as film is? Why or why not? (Consider reading Steven Johnson's "Watching TV Makes You Smarter," pages 50–53, as you take up the question.)

2. How does the filmmaking contribute to the story told in the film? What techniques stand out, and what insights do they offer?

3. What is your position on the way *Crash* addresses racism? Does the film reinforce stereotypes? What issues come into play when crafting a message about racism, and how does the film tackle these issues?

304   5.2 | FILM STORIES OVER THE YEARS

COMPOSE

4 View *Brokeback Mountain*; then write a one-page review arguing whether the film should or shouldn't have won the 2006 best picture award. Consider the stories and messages in the film, the characters and acting, and the filmmaking as you put together your argument.

CHALLENGE

5 Think about the films you have seen in the last five or so years, and select the movie that you feel deserves to be counted as one of the best of all time. Begin with your gut reactions, and then think about criteria that might underlie your judgment. You must move past opinion and toward arguing a position that others can agree or disagree with based on a rationale related to aspects of the filmmaking or the story told by the movie. Compose a paper in which you argue for your selection.

Cluster 5.3
Citizens Making Media

When YouTube first bubbled up as a popular site on the Internet, many people lumped it together with other "I'm bored" Web sites—sites where you might waste half an hour of water cooler time looking for a shrug or a chuckle. But quickly things began to change; one day YouTube was hosting videos like the short spoof *Lazy Sunday*, and soon after the site became a launching pad for presidential candidates like Barack Obama (see page 34). It didn't take long for people to realize there was something revolutionary about the nature of Web sites where users, not corporations or paid publishers, provided the content. As Henry Jenkins explains in "From YouTube to YouNiversity," sites like YouTube or Flickr prompt us to reevaluate the relationships between producers and consumers of media.

These sites also completely reshuffle questions concerning authorship and mediums of composition. A site that uses Web 2.0 software allows multiple users to edit an article. A site like OhmyNews serves as a conduit for disseminating the reports from tens of thousands of journalists. Scott Adams reflects on these developments from a cartoonist's perspective in "Giving Stuff Away on the Internet" and in his *Dilbert* comic.

Further, Web sites now serve as social hubs where people interact not only with media but also with one another: The sites are part of a larger movement toward making the Web a place both for delivering information and for socializing, as seen in the concurrent development of sites like MySpace and Facebook. In "MySpace Data Mining," Brad Stone considers the implications that come from posting private information to public spaces online. It's no wonder these latest media developments on the Web are now the subject of serious study.

From YouTube to YouNiversity

Henry Jenkins
(2007)

FYI Henry Jenkins is a professor at MIT and directs the MIT Comparative Culture and Media Studies Program. He has written a number of books on fan fiction and online culture including *Fans, Bloggers and Gamers: Exploring Participatory Culture*, and *Convergence Culture: Where Old and New Media Collide*. "From YouTube to YouNiversity" first appeared in the *Chronicle for Higher Education* in February of 2007.

Consider these developments: At the end of last year, *Time* named "You" its Person of the Year "for seizing the reins of the global media, for founding and framing the new digital democracy, for working for nothing and beating the pros at their own game." Earlier in the year, *Newsweek* described such sites as Flickr, MySpace, Craigslist, Digg, and YouTube as "putting the 'We' in the Web." The business "thought leader" Tim O'Reilly has termed these new social-network sites "Web 2.0," suggesting that they represent the next phase in the digital revolution—no longer about the technologies per se but about the communities that have grown up around them. Some are even describing immersive online game worlds such as Second Life as the beginnings of Web 3.0. All of this talk reflects changes that cut across culture and commerce, technology and social organization.

Over the past few years, we have also seen a series of books (both journalistic and academic) that analyze and interpret these new configurations of media power. In his recent book *The Wealth of Networks*, Yochai Benkler describes the reconfiguration of power and knowledge that occurs from the ever more complex interplay between commercial, public, educational, nonprofit, and amateur media producers. Grant McCracken's *Plenitude* talks about the "generativeness" of this cultural churn. Chris Anderson (*The Long Tail*) shows how these shifts are giving rise to niche media markets, and Thomas W. Malone (*The Future of Work*) analyzes how such changes are reshaping the management of major companies. My own book, *Convergence Culture: Where Old and New Media Collide*, describes a world where every story, image, sound, brand, and relationship plays itself out across the widest possible array of media platforms, and where the flow of media content is shaped as much by decisions made in teenagers' bedrooms as it is by decisions made in corporate boardrooms.

These writers come from very different disciplinary perspectives—business, law, anthropology, and cultural studies—and they write in very different styles. We can't really call this work an intellectual movement: Most of us didn't know of one another's existence until our books started to hit the shelves. Yet taken together, these books can be read as a paradigm shift in our understanding of media, culture, and society. This work embodies an ecological perspective on media, one that refuses to concentrate on only one medium at a time but insists that we take it all in at once and try to understand how different layers of media production affect one another. As such, these books represent a new route around the ideological and methodological impasses between political economy (with its focus on media concentration) and cultural studies (with its focus on resistant audiences). And these books represent a new way of thinking about how power operates within an informational economy, describing how media shifts are changing education, politics, religion, business, and the press.

Many of these books share the insight that a networked culture is enabling a new form of bottom-up power, as diverse groups of dispersed people pool their expertise and confront problems that are much more complex than they could handle individually. They are able to do so because of the ways that new media platforms support the emergence of temporary social networks that exist only as long as they are needed to face specific challenges or respond to the immediate needs of their members. Witness, for example, the coalition of diverse ideological interests that came together last year to fight for the principle of network neutrality on the Web.

The science-fiction writer and Internet activist Cory Doctorow has called such groups "adhocracies." An adhocracy is a form of social and political organization with few fixed structures or established relationships between players and with minimum hierarchy and maximum diversity. In other words, an adhocracy is more or less the polar opposite of the contemporary university (which preserves often rigid borders between disciplines and departments and even constructs a series of legal obstacles that make it difficult to collaborate even within the same organization). Now try to imagine what would happen if academic departments operated more like YouTube or Wikipedia, allowing for the rapid deployment of scattered expertise and the dynamic reconfiguration of fields. Let's call this new form of academic unit a "YouNiversity."

How might media studies, the field most committed to mapping these changes as they affect modern life, be taught in a YouNiversity?

First, media studies needs to become comparative, teaching critics to think across multiple media systems and teaching media makers to produce across multiple media systems. The modern university has inherited a set of fields and disciplines structured around individual media—photography, cinema, digital culture, literature, theater, and painting are studied in different departments using different disciplinary perspectives. Programs have taken shape through an additive logic (with members of each new generation fighting for the right to study the new medium that affects their lives the most). For a long time, my institution, the Massachusetts Institute of Technology, had a program in film and media studies, a redundant term that strikes me as the rough equivalent of calling the English department the books-and-literature department. For a long time at MIT, books about film were in the architecture library, and those on television were in the humanities library—unless they were about gender, in which case they were in the women's-studies library, or they took a Marxist perspective, in which case they were in the economics library. Such fragmentation does a disservice to students, so that when we ask journalism students to decide whether they want to go into print or broadcasting, or when we ask business students to choose between marketing, advertising, or public relations, we don't reflect the integrated contexts within which media are produced, marketed, and consumed.

> **The modern university has inherited a set of fields and disciplines structured around individual media—photography, cinema, digital culture, literature, theater, and painting are studied in different departments using different disciplinary perspectives.**

A conceptual shift took place eight years ago at MIT when the program in film and media studies recast itself as the program in comparative media studies—inspired in part by the models of comparative literature and comparative religion. The word "comparative" serves multiple functions for the program, encouraging faculty members to think and teach across different media, historical periods, national borders, and disciplinary boundaries, and to bridge the divide between theory and practice as well as that separating academic life from other institutions also confronting profound media change.

This comparative approach has allowed the program to respond more fully to the needs of students with different career goals, disciplinary backgrounds, and professional experiences. By design, about a third of our master's students will go into Ph.D. programs and pursue careers in higher education; the rest will take jobs as advertising executives, game designers, educational-technology specialists, policy makers, museum curators, and journalists. Many are returning to graduate school after the first phases of their careers, coming with a new urgency and determination to master the "big picture" issues shaping the spaces where they have worked.

To educate such students, we don't so much need a faculty as we need an intellectual network. The program has a large pool of loosely affiliated faculty members who participate in an ad hoc manner depending on the needs and interests of individual students: Sometimes they may contribute nothing to the program for several years and then get drawn into a research or thesis project that requires their particular expertise. Our students' thesis advisers come not only from other universities around the world but also from industry; they include Bollywood choreographers, game designers, soap-opera writers, and journalists. We encourage our students to network broadly and draw on the best thinking about their topic, wherever they can find it.

Second, media studies needs to reflect the ways that the contemporary media landscape is blurring the lines between media consumption and production, between making media and thinking about media. A recent study from the Pew Internet & American Life Project found that 57 percent of teens online have created their own media content. As our culture becomes more participatory, these young people are creating their own blogs and podcasts; they are recording their lives on LiveJournal and developing their own profiles on MySpace; they are producing their own YouTube videos and Flickr photos; they are writing and posting fan fiction or contributing to Wikipedia; they are mashing up music and modding games. Much as engineering students learn by taking apart machines and putting them back together, many of these teens learned how media work by taking their culture apart and remixing it.

In such a world, the structural and historical schisms separating media production and critical-studies classes no longer seem relevant. Students around the country are pushing to translate their analytic insights about media into some form of media production. And they are correctly arguing that you cannot really understand how these new media work if you don't use them yourself. Integrating theory and practice won't be simple. Some students in the entering classes in the program in comparative media studies have had little or no access to digital tools, and others have been designing their own computer games since elementary school. Even among those who have media-production experience, they have worked with very different production tools or produced very different forms of media content in very different contexts.

Responding to these wildly divergent backgrounds and expectations requires us to constantly redesign and renegotiate course expectations as we try to give students what they need to push themselves to the next level of personal and professional development. We have encouraged faculty members to incorporate production opportunities in their courses so that students in a children's-media class, for example, are asked to apply the theories they have learned to the design of an artifact for a child (medium unspecified), then write a paper explaining the assumptions behind their design choices. We may have students composing their own children's books, building and programming their own interactive toys, shooting photo essays, producing pilots for children's shows, or designing simple video games or Web sites.

Before we started our master's program, I went on the road to talk with representatives of more than 50 companies and organizations. They told me that they value the flexibility, creativity, and social and cultural insights liberal-arts majors bring to their operations. They also shared a devastating list of concerns—liberal-arts students fall behind other majors in terms of teamwork, leadership, project completion, and problem solving. In other words, they were describing the gap between academic fields focused on fostering autonomous learners and professional contexts demanding continuing collaborations. Those desired skills were regularly fostered in other disciplines that have laboratory-based cultures that test new theories and research findings through real-world applications. At a university with strong traditions of applied physics or applied mathematics, we needed to embrace the ideal of applied humanities. And as a result, we have created a context where our students put their social and cultural knowledge to work through real-world applications such as designing educational games, developing media-literacy materials, or consulting with media companies about consumer relations.

Third, media studies needs to respond to the enormous hunger for public knowledge about our present moment of profound and persistent media change. Given this context, it is nothing short of criminal that so much of contemporary media theory and analysis remains locked away in an academic ghetto, cut off from larger conversations. Media scholars have much to contribute to—and much to learn from—the discussions occurring among designers, industry leaders, policy makers, artists, activists, journalists, and educators about the direction of our culture.

At such a moment, we need to move beyond preparing our students for future roles as media scholars, wrapped up in their own disciplinary discourses, and instead encourage them to acquire skills and experiences as public intellectuals, sharing their insights with a larger public from wherever they happen to be situated. They need to be taught how to translate the often challenging formulations of academic theory into a more public discourse.

Academic programs are only starting to explore how they might deploy these new media platforms—blogs and podcasts especially—to expand the visibility of their research and scholarship. Consider, for example, the case of *Flow*, an online journal edited at the University of Texas at Austin. *Flow* brings together leading media scholars from around the world to write short, accessible, and timely responses to contemporary media developments: In contrast with the increasingly sluggish timetable of academic publishing, which makes any meaningful response to the changing media environment almost impossible, a new issue of *Flow* appears every two weeks.

Blogs represent a powerful tool for engaging in these larger public conversations. At my university, we noticed that a growing number of students were developing blogs focused on their thesis research. Many of them were making valuable professional contacts; some had developed real visibility while working on their master's degrees; and a few received high-level job offers based on the professional connections they made on their blogs. Blogging has also deepened their research, providing feedback on their arguments, connecting them to previously unknown authorities, and pushing them forward in ways that no thesis committee could match. Now all of our research teams are blogging not only about their own work but also about key developments in their fields. We have redesigned the program's home page, allowing feeds from these blogs to regularly update our content and capture more of the continuing conversations in and around our program. We have also started offering regular podcasts of our departmental colloquia and are experimenting with various forms of remote access to our conferences and other events.

We make a mistake, though, if we understand such efforts purely in terms of distance learning or community outreach, as if all expertise resides within universities and needs simply to be transmitted to the world. Rather, we should see these efforts as opportunities for us to learn from other sectors equally committed to mapping and mastering the current media change.

> **The modern university should work not by defining fields of study but by removing obstacles so that knowledge can circulate and be reconfigured in new ways.**

Each media-studies program will need to reinvent itself to reflect the specifics of its institutional setting and existing resources, and what works today will need to be rethought tomorrow as we deal with further shifts in the information landscape. That's the whole point of an adhocracy: It's built to tap current opportunities, but, like ice sculpture, it isn't made to last. The modern university should work not by defining fields of study but by removing obstacles so that knowledge can circulate and be reconfigured in new ways. For media studies, that means taking down walls that separate the study of different media, that block off full collaboration between students, that make it difficult to combine theory and practice, and that isolate academic research from the larger public conversations about media change.

Until we make these changes, the best thinking (whether evaluated in terms of process or outcome) is likely to take place outside academic institutions—through the informal social organizations that are emerging on the Web. We may or may not see the emergence of YouNiversities, but YouTube already exists. And its participants are learning plenty about how media power operates in a networked society.

CONSIDER

1. Jenkins suggests that media decisions are now being made not only in boardrooms, but also in "teenagers' bedrooms." Do you agree that consumers have such power when it comes to media decisions? Why or why not?

2. What are your thoughts on the kinds of remix writing that Jenkins describes? What concerns are there with moving toward writing based on mixing existing pieces of media?

3. Would you appreciate the kind of educational program advocated by Jenkins? If you could customize your own education, what people would you recruit from your school to help you? What kinds of projects would you select?

ITEM 5.20 ■ Openlogue, *A Newbie's Guide to Literary Theory*, 2008

People have sometimes compared the Internet to a huge photocopy machine—users place documents online; other users find the documents, and then download copies to their own computers. New forms of Internet media, however, have dramatically extended the kinds of publication that take place online. With the click of an Edit link, a reader can access the text of an article, make changes, add links to additional resources, and even embed images and media into the page. These editable Web sites raise numerous questions about how we produce and consume knowledge.

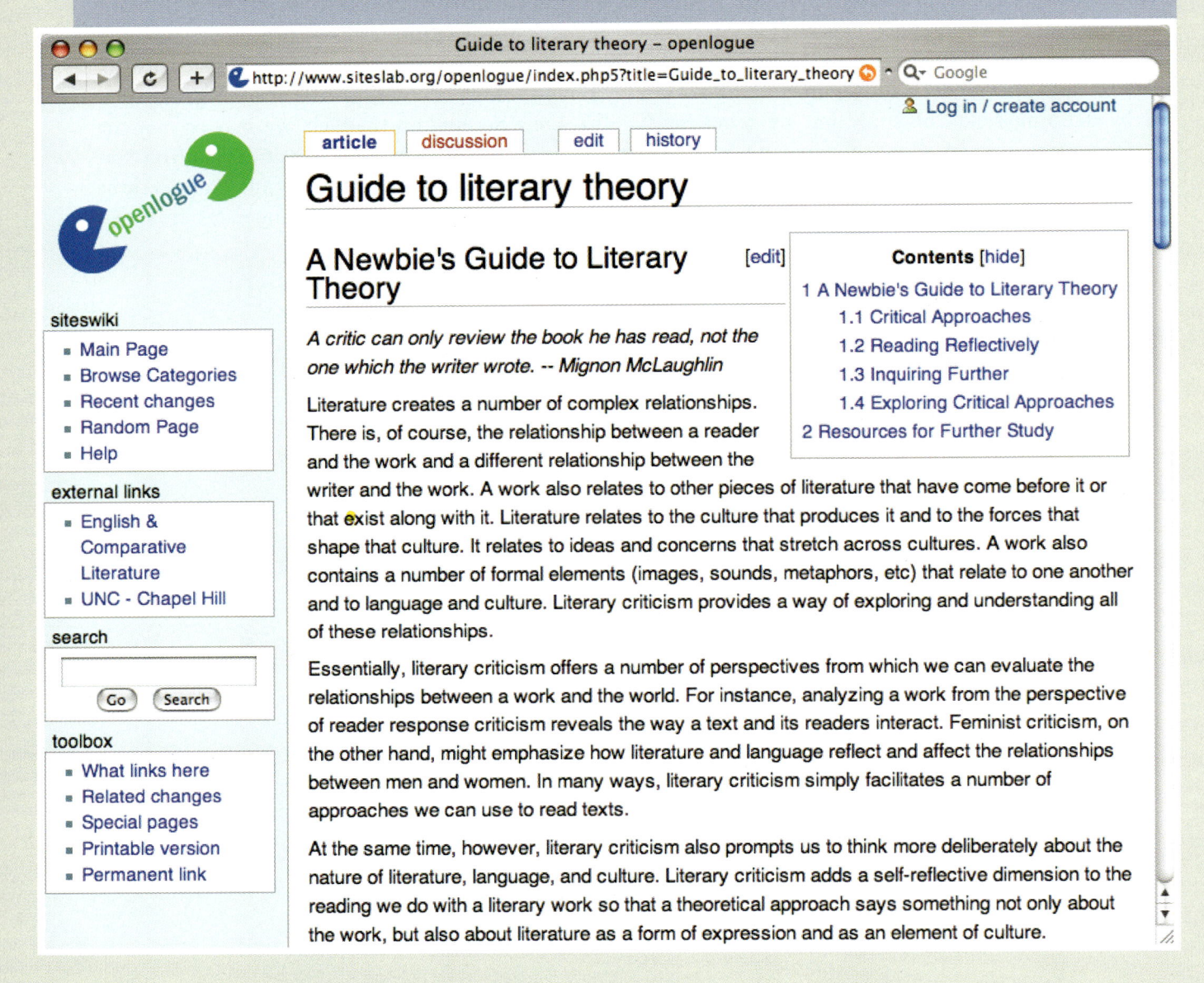

Guide to literary theory – openlogue

http://www.siteslab.org/openlogue/index.php5?title=Guide_to_literary_theory

Log in / create account

openlogue

article | discussion | edit | history

Guide to literary theory

A Newbie's Guide to Literary Theory [edit]

A critic can only review the book he has read, not the one which the writer wrote. -- Mignon McLaughlin

Contents [hide]
1 A Newbie's Guide to Literary Theory
 1.1 Critical Approaches
 1.2 Reading Reflectively
 1.3 Inquiring Further
 1.4 Exploring Critical Approaches
2 Resources for Further Study

Literature creates a number of complex relationships. There is, of course, the relationship between a reader and the work and a different relationship between the writer and the work. A work also relates to other pieces of literature that have come before it or that exist along with it. Literature relates to the culture that produces it and to the forces that shape that culture. It relates to ideas and concerns that stretch across cultures. A work also contains a number of formal elements (images, sounds, metaphors, etc) that relate to one another and to language and culture. Literary criticism provides a way of exploring and understanding all of these relationships.

Essentially, literary criticism offers a number of perspectives from which we can evaluate the relationships between a work and the world. For instance, analyzing a work from the perspective of reader response criticism reveals the way a text and its readers interact. Feminist criticism, on the other hand, might emphasize how literature and language reflect and affect the relationships between men and women. In many ways, literary criticism simply facilitates a number of approaches we can use to read texts.

At the same time, however, literary criticism also prompts us to think more deliberately about the nature of literature, language, and culture. Literary criticism adds a self-reflective dimension to the reading we do with a literary work so that a theoretical approach says something not only about the work, but also about literature as a form of expression and as an element of culture.

siteswiki
- Main Page
- Browse Categories
- Recent changes
- Random Page
- Help

external links
- English & Comparative Literature
- UNC - Chapel Hill

search
[Go] [Search]

toolbox
- What links here
- Related changes
- Special pages
- Printable version
- Permanent link

CONSIDER

1 Visit Wikipedia or another Web site that allows users to edit its content. Explore the options for revising existing materials or adding new articles. How easy is it to create materials at the site? What issues are raised by opening authorship to readers?

2 What are the potential benefits of adding audio, video, or animations to articles? What about the drawbacks? Which subjects are best suited for including these kinds of media?

3 Early Web articles offered electronic versions of printed texts, with perhaps a few images. Later, Web publications allowed commentary from readers and links to media. Today, Web sites enable readers to take on the role of authors. What do you imagine online publication will look like in five years? How about in twenty-five years?

ITEM 5.21 ■ Oh Yeon-ho, founder and editor of OhmyNews

Oh Yeon-ho is considered one of the pioneers of citizen journalism. His OhmyNews service, based in Seoul, Korea, began as an Internet experiment in 2000, but now draws upon as many as 60,000 citizen journalists for its worldwide coverage of news, politics, sports, and culture. Like more conventional agencies, OhmyNews sets high standards for its contributors and requires that they adhere to a strict code of ethics. In particular, contributors must support the principle that "all citizens are reporters," and that they will not engage in personal attacks or use any duplicitous means of gathering information. Contributors to OhmyNews are also expected to apologize for their mistakes "fully and promptly," a lesson many mainstream news organizations might take to heart.

CONSIDER

1. For what types of news and information might you trust a Web site such as OhmyNews, which relies on citizen journalists for much of its reporting? How would you expect its news coverage to differ from that of mainstream news sites such as CNN or the *New York Times*? Provide examples of articles you might find on OhmyNews.

2. In 2007, OhmyNews founder Oh Yeon-ho received the prestigious Honor Medal for Distinguished Service in Journalism from the Missouri School of Journalism "in recognition of his pioneering work in engaging citizens as journalists for democracy." Are there any potential dangers in opening up "the press"—sometimes described as the Fourth Estate of government—to writers and citizens from outside of the traditional ranks of journalists?

3. What other forms of communication or activity have been democratized by their appearance on the Web? Has the Web genuinely encouraged citizens to play a greater role in politics, government, and culture? Or have we seen mostly an increase in chatter?

MySpace Data Mining

Brad Stone
(2007)

> **FYI** Brad Stone has been an online author for the past two decades as well as a technology correspondent for *Newsweek*. He currently writes about the Internet and consumer culture for the *New York Times*. "My Space Data Mining" first appeared in the *New York Times* in September of 2007.

Members of the booming social network Web sites treat their individual profile pages as a creative canvas for personal expression. The social networking companies see those pages as a lush target for advertisers—if only they could customize the ads. Although Internet companies have talked about specifically aiming their ads since the inception of the Web, so far advertising on social networks has been characterized by mass-marketed pitches for mortgages and online dating sites.

But MySpace, the Web's largest social network and one of the most trafficked sites on the Internet, says that after experimenting with technology over the last six months it can tailor ads to the personal information that its 110 million active users leave on their profile pages.

Executives at Fox Interactive Media, the News Corporation unit that owns MySpace, will begin speaking about the results of that program this week. They say the tailoring technology has improved the likelihood that members will click on an ad by 80 percent on average.

"We are blessed with a phenomenal amount of information about the likes, dislikes and life's passions of our users," said Peter Levinsohn, president of Fox Interactive Media, who will talk about the program at an address to investors and analysts at a Merrill Lynch conference in Los Angeles on Tuesday. "We have an opportunity to provide advertisers with a completely new paradigm."

MySpace's rival, Facebook, also says it is experimenting with ad customization with the help of Microsoft, which signed with the up-and-coming social network last year to provide display ads on the service. To the consternation of privacy advocates, who say Internet users are unaware of such activity, the social networks regard these detail-stocked profile pages as a kind of "digital gold," as one Fox executive put it last year.

The companies hope that customizing ads to their members' stated enthusiasms will improve the effectiveness of the ads and recruit new advertisers who want to pitch their messages to refined slices of the online audience. Fox executives also hope the technology can help MySpace recapture some of the momentum and attention that has recently gone to Facebook.

Richard Greenfield, the managing director of Pali Research, predicts that MySpace's fledgling program will help increase MySpace's current revenue to $70 million a month from $40 million a month by next year.

"This is a critical evolution of the MySpace business model envisioned from the day News Corporation bought it," Mr. Greenfield said.

A 100-employee team inside the Fox Interactive Media offices in Beverly Hills, called the "monetization technology group," has designed computer algorithms to scour MySpace pages. In the first phase of the program, which the company calls "interest-based targeting," the algorithms assigned members to one of 10 categories that represents their primary interest, like sports, fashion, finance, video games, autos and health.

The algorithms make their judgments partly on certain keywords in the profile. A member might be obvious by describing himself as a financial information enthusiast, for example. But more than likely the clues are more subtle. He might qualify for that category by listing Donald Trump as a hero, *Fortune* magazine as a favorite publication or "Wall Street" as a favorite movie.

The system also looks at the groups members belong to, who their friends are, their age and gender, and what ads they have responded to in the past. "Our targeting is a balance of what users say, what they do and what they say they do," said Adam Bain, the chief technology officer at Fox Interactive.

MySpace evidently does not completely trust the technology. Every two weeks, 200 temporary workers, which the company calls "relevance testers," come to

Fox Interactive's offices to manually check member profiles against the categories they have been assigned to.

The company said that several national advertisers are trying out the service, though they declined to name them. Fox Interactive executives say that some kinds of ads benefited more than others. Clicks on tailored auto ads more than doubled and clicks on music ads jumped by 70 percent.

For the last two months, Fox Interactive has also experimented with the second phase of its targeting program, called "hyper targeting," in which it further divides the 10 enthusiast categories into hundreds of subcategories. For example, sports fans are divided into subgroups like basketball, college football and skiing, while film enthusiasts are further classified by their interest in genres like comedies, dramas and independent films, and even particular actors and actresses.

For now, Fox's advertising sales representatives are selling the new kinds of ad abilities. In November, according to Michael Barrett, Fox Interactive Media's chief revenue officer, the company will set up an automated online system to allow smaller companies to aim at MySpace users with their ads without ever talking to a human being at Fox.

A punk band performing in Seattle, for example, could publicize a performance by looking up all the people on MySpace who live in that area who are punk fans.

MySpace also plans to give its advertisers information about what kind of people its ads have attracted. "We want them to leave knowing more about their audience than when they came into the door," said Arnie Gullov-Singh, a senior director at Fox Interactive.

That is precisely the goal that worries some privacy advocates. They argue that users of social networks like MySpace and Facebook are not aware they are being monitored and that current ad-targeting is only the first step in what has become a huge arms race to collect revealing data on Internet users.

"People should be able to congregate online with their friends without thinking that big brother, whether it is Rupert Murdoch or Mark Zuckerberg, are stealthily peering in," said Jeff Chester, executive director at the Center for Digital Democracy in Washington.

His organization will ask the Federal Trade Commission, during a planned hearing on Internet privacy in November, to investigate social networks for unfair and deceptive practices, he said.

MySpace and Facebook executives argue that they are harming no one. They say that they are using information their members make publicly available, and contrast their ad targeting with efforts by Yahoo, America Online and Microsoft, whose advertising technologies follow people around the Web and try to deduce what they are interested in based on what sites they are looking at.

Fox executives also say they are planning on letting users opt-out of the ad-targeting program on MySpace, though it means those members will see fewer relevant ads.

At least one MySpace member has no problems with the new technology. Mark Gong, a 26-year old photojournalist from Washington, runs the 3,000-member Wanderlust group on MySpace and on his profile expresses an interest for foreign films like "Lost in Translation" and "The Spanish Apartment." Not surprisingly, that has defined him as a prime target for travel ads on MySpace from companies like ShermansTravel.com, a travel deal site. "I'm not opposed to advertising," Mr. Gong said. "They have got to make money."

But he also says he hopes MySpace spends the extra cash on making the site more reliable and fending off the Facebook threat. He says many members of his group have flocked to Facebook in the last two months and that even he is logging into Facebook more often. "Everybody I know is switching to Facebook," he said. "MySpace has its work cut out for it."

CONSIDER

1. How do you feel about ads on social networking sites? Are you willing to suffer through ads to have free access to social networks? Do you like the ads? Are you fed up? At what point might you consider leaving a social network because of its ads?

2. Do you feel like the postings you make to a social network belong to you? To the owners of the network? To the public domain? What changes might you make in your online behavior depending on your answers to these questions?

Giving Stuff Away on the Internet

Scott Adams
(November 1, 2007)

> **FYI** Scott Adams has been publishing *Dilbert* since 1989. He regularly releases episodes to the public at dilbert.com. He also blogs about comics and other issues at dilbertblog.typepad.com.

I spend about a third of my workday blogging. Thanks to the miracle of online advertising, that increases my income by 1%. I balance that by hoping no one asks me why I do it.

As with most of my life decisions, my impulse to blog was a puzzling little soup of miscellaneous causes that bubbled and simmered until one day I noticed I was doing something. I figured I needed a rationalization in case anyone asked. My rationalization for blogging was especially hard to concoct. I was giving away my product for free and hoping something good came of it.

I did have a few "artist" reasons for blogging. After 18 years of writing "Dilbert" comics, I was itching to slip the leash and just once write "turd" without getting an email from my editor. It might not seem like a big deal to you, but when you aren't allowed to write in the way you talk, it's like using the wrong end of the shovel to pick up, for example, a turd.

Over time, I noticed something unexpected and wonderful was happening with the blog. I had an army of volunteer editors, and they never slept. The readers were changing the course of my writing in real time. I would post my thoughts on a topic, and the masses told me what they thought of the day's offering without holding anything back. Often they'd correct my grammar or facts and I'd fix it in minutes. They were in turns brutal and encouraging. They wanted more posts on some topics and less of others. It was like the old marketing saying, "Your customers tell you what business you're in."

At some point I realized we were collectively writing a book, or at least the guts of one. I compiled the most popular (mostly the funniest) posts and pitched it to a publisher. I got a six-figure advance, and picked a title indirectly suggested by my legion of accidental collaborators: "Stick to Drawing Comics, Monkey-Brain!"

As part of the book deal, my publisher asked me to delete the parts of my blog archive that would be included in the book. The archives didn't get much traffic, so I didn't think much about deleting them. This turned out to be a major blunder in the "how people think" category.

A surprising number of my readers were personally offended that I would remove material from the Internet that had once been free, even after they read it. It was as if I had broken into their homes and ripped the books off their shelves. They felt violated. And boy, I heard about it.

Some left negative reviews on Amazon.com to protest my crass commercialization. While no one has given the book a bad review for its content, a full half of the people who comment trash it for having once been free, as if that somehow mattered to the people who only read books on paper. In the end, the bad feeling I caused by not giving away my material for free forever will have a negative impact on book sales.

I've had mixed results with giving away content on the Internet. I was the first syndicated cartoon-ist to offer a comic on the Internet without charge (www.dilbert.com). That gave a huge boost to the newspaper sales and licensing. The ad income was good too. Giving away the "Dilbert" comic for free continues to work well, although it cannibalizes my reprint book sales to some extent, and a fast-growing percentage of readers bypass the online ads with widgets, unauthorized RSS feeds and other workarounds.

A few years ago I tried an experiment where I put the entire text of my book, "God's Debris," on the Internet for free, after sales of the hard copy and its sequel, "The Religion War" slowed. My hope was that the people who liked the free e-book would buy the sequel. According to my fan mail, people loved the free book. I know they loved it because they emailed to ask when the sequel would also be available for free. For readers of my non-Dilbert books, I inadvertently set the market value for my work at zero. Oops.

So I've been watching with great interest as the band "Radiohead" pursues its experiment with pay-what-you-want downloads on the Internet. In the near term, the goodwill has inspired lots of people to pay. But I suspect many of them are placing a bet that paying a few bucks now will inspire all of their favorite bands to offer similar deals. That's when the market value of music will approach zero.

That's my guess. Free is more complicated than you'd think.

ITEM 5.22 ■ Scott Adams, *Dilbert* "Web 2.0" Cartoon, September 9, 2007

Scott Adams has a background in business and began his cartooning career by doodling during meetings. His work often speaks to issues of media and technology but also gives him an opportunity to reflect on the office personalities and politics that have become a staple of his *Dilbert* cartoons.

CONSIDER

1. Compare "MySpace Data Mining" with "Giving Stuff Away on the Internet." Is it fair to say the pieces offer similar depictions of the Internet? Why or why not?

2. What are your thoughts about the relationships between new media like the Internet and old media like newspaper cartoons or music on CDs? Do you believe that new media will eventually replace older media? Will they coexist? Explain your position.

COMPOSE

3. Explore the Web to find examples of people giving stuff away. Look beneath the surface to discover any monetary connections with the "free stuff." Are there ads that might be earning a Web site money? Might an item be available "free"—with a charge for shipping and handling equal to the value of the item? What other financial tendrils can you discover among the free things online? Write a one- to two-page analysis in which you explore the relationships between free stuff and economics.

Writing About Media

We're surrounded by media messages all the time, so it makes sense that we're struck by the urge to interpret them. The best method for sorting through competing messages is often to write about them. Writing allows you to stop to reflect (a helpful approach, given the rate of media bombardment in our worlds). And writing may even enable you to resist some of the influences of media messages—you'll most likely not end the practice of pop stars pushing products, but you may find an awareness that defuses many of the appeals of these pitches. Further, you have many opportunities to participate in the media world by choosing your own **subject** (pages 56–59) and sharing your work with others. Like never before, you too can become a creator of media messages through blogs, videos, podcasts, or even simple Web sites that let you tell your own story.

With so many options, you'll first need to consider your **audience** (pages 60–63). If you are writing about media for a school assignment, your audience may well be your classmates or your instructor. As with any writing, consider how you might adjust the project based on the knowledge and beliefs of these readers. In "From YouTube to YouNiversity," for instance, Henry Jenkins aims his composition at an audience familiar with the educational concerns of universities. In other cases, you can write about media for an unknown and often broad audience. The nice (and challenging) thing about contemporary media is their limitless potential to reach people. You can post a media composition that might be viewed by thousands of people around the globe. If you are aiming to reach a wide range of people on the Internet, you may need to adjust your composition—perhaps offering more contextual information or revising decisions about how to use materials in your composition.

These choices will be directly connected to your **purpose** (pages 64–66). Analysis is a staple of compositions about media. When writing analytical pieces, you'll need to use some specialized vocabularies to develop your discussion—perhaps talking about emphasis or arrangement in a magazine ad or camera angles in a film, much as Brian D. Johnson discusses film dialog and editing in "The Collateral Damage of *Crash*." You'll also want to learn how to integrate media elements into your composition. Your composition can integrate media examples, and then unpack them with your analysis. You may find that you want to take other approaches to media—perhaps moving from analysis to critique or argument. If, for instance, you want to offer a proposal regarding privacy and the media, you will rely less on integrating pieces into the composition and more on developing the logic of your argument.

Perhaps one of the most exciting decisions you will make is what **medium** (pages 77–83) to use as you compose. In a print essay you can insert images into your composition—perhaps downloading example images or taking screen captures from a film to discuss them. Capturing television shows can be more tricky (unless you can download a version to your computer). Still, you can bring these pieces into a paper for discussion. If you want to work with music or audio files, though, you'll probably need to move to electronic forms. You can work with Web pages or a blog to gain more flexibility—you can embed or link to videos, images, and sound files easily on the Web. If you want to work with even more flexibility, you may need to employ a multimedia form for your composition. You can use a video editor to weave together samples from films or television. And you can use audio editors to discuss music or speeches. All of these options will require some technical learning, but will also open new possibilities for your writing.

And, as with all your writing, you'll want to allow ample opportunities to **invent** ideas (pages 88–89). If you are writing analytical essays, freewrite, create outlines, conduct research, compose maps, and use other familiar strategies to develop ideas. If you are working in an electronic medium, spend time learning the steps involved in composing in that medium. As you learn about the technology, refine your thinking—what new ideas about the project spring to mind as you learn to use a new feature of a program? Similarly, be sure to share drafts of your essays as you **revise** your writing. For media projects, share versions of your work as well—perhaps asking peers or your instructor to look over your projects as you compose or posting versions online for critique. Always save the original project files so you can make changes based on feedback.

Project 5.1

Exploring a Filmmaker

We often hear about someone having a particular style of writing, but can the same thing be said about other forms of media? At least for films it can. In fact, students of film use the French term *auteur* to describe the ways a director approaches her art. Like it sounds, *auteur* suggests a kind of authorship role for the creators of films. Figuring out just how much influence a director has over films, though, is a bit tricky. Films are one of the truly collaborative forms of art—think of the people behind the scenes: set makers, makeup artists, sound and lighting designers, not to mention the actors. Still, there are elements of films that can be traced to their directors and that allow us to talk about their style.

In this assignment, you will analyze two or more films created by the same director(s). Look for common elements that give these films a unique style—cinematography, locations, sets, soundtracks. Think about themes that recur in the films. Consider the use of actors as well—often directors have favorite actors that appear in many of their films. Compose a four- or more page paper in which you argue whether or not the filmmaker has a unique style. Use evidence from the films to support your claim. As you discuss the films, be sure to provide detailed analysis of the elements that allow you to talk about the filmmaker as an auteur. (You may want to use images from the films to further support your points.)

STUDENT PROJECT
Virginia Wooten, *North by Northwest* and *Spellbound*: Identifiably Hitchcock

Wooten 1

Virginia Wooten
Professor Anderson
English 49
11 April 2006

North by Northwest and Spellbound: Identifiably Hitchcock

With over fifty films to his name, Alfred Hitchcock is known far and wide as the master of suspense. In his works, he utilizes many of the same film techniques and develops many similar themes, which culminate into an identifiable style that is all his own. In the 1945 film, *Spellbound*, Hitchcock employs varying creative point of view shots and extensive use of metaphor to elaborate a mystery plot. Nineteen years later, in what is widely regarded as one of his best films, *North by Northwest*, he employs the same techniques to create suspense, intrigue, and even humor. The films resonate thematically as well; Hitchcock uses the classic plot device of mistaken identity in both films. The works also share the theme of professional women in love, but portray distinct perspectives about these women. While *Spellbound* belongs to the era of black and white film and *North by Northwest* was produced much later in Hitchcock's life, the two films, like all of the products of his illustrious career, are markedly "Hitchcock."

Hitchcock uses camera angles and creative sequences to create unique perspectives for the viewer. One perspective especially effective in creating suspense is to film from the protagonist's viewpoint so that the viewer experiences exactly what the character experiences. This subjective "first person" point of view is used to great effect in *North by Northwest*'s famous crop-duster scene (Dirks). Hitchcock switches back and forth between the subjective shot to shots showing Roger Thornhill in the isolated expanse of country. As Thornhill looks in every direction around him, the viewer shares his point of view and experiences the emptiness of the land. Thus, the viewer also feels the sense of isolation, creating a nervous atmosphere. Later, once the action begins, Hitchcock couples the subjective shots with reaction shots. The viewer sees the

(margin note: The opening forecasts elements to be compared and offers a thesis for the paper.)

plane coming toward her through the eyes of Thornhill. After this shot, the viewer sees Thornhill racing through the field (fig. 1), and then the viewer is once again taken back to Thornhill's perspective of the killer plane. These subjective shots are enhanced by the subjective audio; the viewer experiences the complete silence of the fields, and then hears the droning of cars, bus, and plane grow louder and fade as they approach and pass by.

Analysis of scene describes film techniques with details.

The subjective shot is distinctively used in two scenes in Spellbound. In the first scene, the protagonist, John Ballantine (who at this point is really only known as J.B.), walks down the stairs in the midst of his amnesiac mind's reverie. Dr. Brulov (unknown to the viewer) slyly makes him a drink of milk mixed with something to put him to sleep. The viewer sees Dr. Brulov pass Ballantine the glass, and then the point of view switches to that of Ballantine. The horizontally tilted milk glass takes up

The ¶ draws a comparison as it discusses the second film in terms of the viewer.

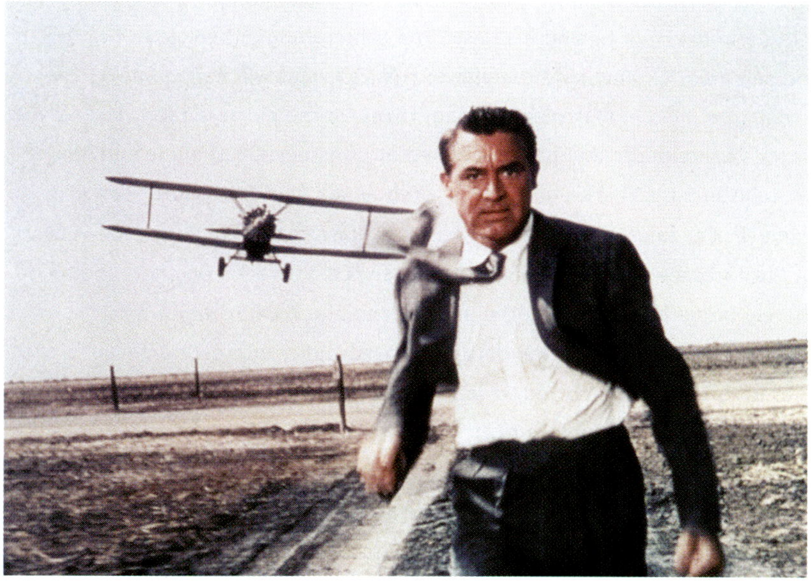

Fig. 1. Geometry, angles, compositions: the crop-duster sequence (The Kobal Collection, 2008).

the entire screen with its circular outline, and the viewer watches the milk steadily leave the glass as Ballantine drinks the liquid. As the milk disappears, the room comes blurrily into view, seen from the perspective of the bottom of the clear glass. The blurred vision of the room through the glass also indicates Ballantine's mind growing hazy with the potion in the milk (even though at this point the viewer is not aware of Dr. Brulov's scheme). Then, the shot moves to the next morning. Once Dr. Brulov explains his trick, the significance of the drawn-out milk shot makes sense. During the scene, the viewer is led to naively believe that Ballantine is merely drinking a glass of milk, making the viewer as unsuspecting as Ballantine himself.

The second shot occurs at the climax of the film, after Dr. Constance Peterson uncovers the identity of the murderer as the former head psychologist of Green Manor, Dr. Murchison. When he draws the gun that he used for the first murder, she expertly convinces him not to shoot as she slowly walks toward the door and slides out of danger. Murchison is left sitting in his chair behind his desk. The camera angle then takes the first person point of view, and the viewer realizes what will happen next. The small gun, held in Murchison's hand, takes up the entire screen. It slowly moves from its original position aimed at Constance, turning left toward Murchison himself. The gun is then fired at the viewer as Murchison kills himself. For this scene, Hitchcock uses a "flash frame" to shock the viewer. A flash frame is a "single clear frame inserted between two shots that can barely be perceived, giving the appearance of a flash of white when viewed." This use of the flash frame is particularly interesting because two frames are hand-tinted red, in what is Hitchcock's first use of color (Dirks).

Both Spellbound and North by Northwest employ the use of metaphor, "a filmic device in which a scene, character, object, and/or action may be associated, identified, or interpreted as an implied representation of something else that is unrelated" (Dirks). In Spellbound the image of doors opening is very significant. Taking into account the plot based upon elements of Freud's practice of

Wooten 4

psychoanalysis, the opening doors represent the "opening" of the character's mind. When Ballantine and Dr. Peterson first kiss, the shot moves from a close-up of Dr. Peterson to a shot of a door opening upon another door, which opens upon another door, and so on. Dr. Peterson had previously shut herself off to the concept of love, but in this scene she allows her mind to accept these impulses. The presence of opening doors also signifies Ballantine rejecting the guilt of his brother's death in his childhood and allowing his mind to function without reserve. Another metaphor exists in the famous dream sequence designed by surrealist Salvador Dalí. As Ballantine recounts his dream to Dr. Brulov and Dr. Peterson, the viewer enters the eerie world of his dream. The backdrop of the dream is made up of a drapery of huge, staring eyes (fig. 2). In the sequence of bizarre events that unfolds in the dream, a man cuts the drapes with a large pair of scissors. The eyes can simply represent the truth, or can hold any number of meanings. They can represent the

Fig. 2. Expressionism in art (The Kobal Collection, 2008).

Wooten 5

revealing nature of dreams, Ballantine's consciousness, or his memory. As the man cuts the eyeball, the significance ranges from the destruction of memory through the guilt complex, the distortion of perspective, the inability to discover the truth, manipulation of the mind, or the representation of psychoanalysis itself.

In North by Northwest, Hitchcock uses metaphor to produce an underhanded comic effect. In the final scene, he transitions from Thornhill pulling Kendall up the cliff on Mount Rushmore to Thornhill pulling her up onto the bed in the train. The final shot of the film is the train entering into a dark tunnel. Viewers could innocently view this parting shot as the train moving on, signifying the movement of the characters into the future and whatever it might hold. The discerning viewer would pick up on the sexual nature of the train entering the tunnel, and recognize the metaphor alluding to the acts taking place on the train (Dirks). Also, this scene shows the continued use of Freudian themes in Hitchcock's later movies, though much less explicit than in Spellbound.

The two films are characteristically Hitchcock not only in their stylistics, but also thematically. The classic mistaken identity plot is the foundation for both films, though Spellbound puts a new twist on the action by making even the protagonist himself unaware of his true identity. Ballantine is an amnesiac with a guilt complex, according to the diagnosis of his doctor and lover, Constance Peterson. He assumes the identity of Dr. Edwardes, whom it is suspected he murdered. In North by Northwest, Thornhill is mistaken for the spy George Kaplan, who does not really exist. Both movies shake up the characters' and viewers' perceptions of reality and allow Hitchcock to address questions of sanity and trust. Another shared theme that perhaps carries more cultural and societal significance is that of the role of women in the two films. Both films portray confident, beautiful, professional, and independent women. In Spellbound, Ingrid Bergman plays Dr. Peterson, a highly intelligent woman distinguished in her career. She rejects the notion of love, deeming it merely a reaction to physical appearances resembling one's parents and as something blown out of proportion by romance literature. Eva

Wooten 6

Marie Saint plays the crafty Eve Kendall in North by Northwest. After unsuspectingly falling for a criminal, she is employed by the FBI as a secret agent to expose him. While both are originally strong characters, the films portray different scenarios and characterizations of women in love.

Spellbound portrays love as an engulfing, weakening force. Dr. Peterson's entire character transforms as she "loosens up" and falls in love with Ballantine. She loses her objective view of her patient as their psychoanalysis sessions turn into make-out sessions. The film might be said to be antifeminist in that it portrays intellect and emotion in females as mutually exclusive; the intelligent female doctor who exudes masculine level-headedness is incapable of emotional attachment, while the feminine woman consumed by love is incapable of rational thought. Dr. Brulov makes two sexist, though admittedly humorous, comments. "Women make the best psychoanalysts until they fall in love. After that they make the best patients," he remarks. Later, after Dr. Peterson's passionate plea for his cooperation, he warns her, "We both know that the mind of a woman in love is operating on the lowest level of intellect." In North by Northwest, the female character seems more restrained, and therefore, more powerful. Eve Kendall acts as seductress and slyly lures Thornhill into her snare. Though her interests do become confused as the plot progresses, she holds out against her feelings in the end. She returns to bad-guy Vandamm and her duty as a spy, rejecting the option to remain with Thornhill. Fortunately, she has such a hold on Thornhill that he follows her and eventually helps her win her freedom from the set-up. Hitchcock presents two scenarios of women forced to choose between their profession (psychologist and spy) and their love for a man. Perhaps the portrayal of Kendall as the stronger, more independent female character reflects the 1959 production date, set in the beginning of the "sexual revolution" and the liberated woman. The loyal Dr. Peterson could reflect the culture of domesticity surrounding the earlier (1945) Spellbound.

At first glance, North by Northwest, the story of an advertising man mistaken for a spy, and Spellbound, a surreal film heavy on the psychoanalysis, seem to share little in common. But the stamp of Hitchcock becomes evident

The author compares films to bring out similarities and differences.

Wooten 7

The conclusion completes the comparison and reiterates the thesis.

when one looks at the stylistic and thematic connections. Both films use similar techniques to manipulate the points of view from which the story is told, drawing viewers in with subjective shots. Both films feature themes of mistaken identity and explore relationships between women and men. The films even share some locales. In both movies, a scene takes place at the ticket window in Grand Central Station, as well as on the dining car of a train. While these similarities are obvious, the film techniques and thematic connections are more subtle. Still, once we become familiar with Hitchcock's directorial nuances and favorite themes, it becomes easy to spot them in his works and to appreciate his ability to craft works of suspense that are uniquely Hitchcock.

Wooten 8

Works Cited

"Alfred Hitchcock." Wikipedia. 12 April 06 <http://en.wikipedia.org/wiki/ Alfred_Hitchcock>.

Dirks, Tim. "Cinematic Terms: A Film-Making Glossary." 2006. 10 April 06 <http://www.filmsite.org/filmterms18.html>.

"Expressionism in Art." 9 April 06 <http://faculty.cua.edu/johnsong/ hitchcock/ pages/expressionism/expressionism.html>.

North by Northwest. DVD. Dir. Alfred Hitchcock. MGM. 1959.

"North by Northwest: Geometry, Angles, Compositions: The Crop-duster Sequence." 9 April 06 <http://faculty.cua.edu/johnsong/hitchcock/ pages/stills-NxNW/ geometry-2.html>.

"North by Northwest." Internet Movie Database. 9 April 06 <http://www .imdb.com/title/tt0053125/>. 2006.

"Spellbound." Internet Movie Database. 9 April 06 <http://www.imdb. com/title/ tt0038109/>. 2006.

Spellbound. VHS. Dir. Alfred Hitchcock. Vanguard Films Inc. 1945.

Project 5.2

Composing a Photo Essay

Earlier in this chapter, we discussed the ways in which multimedia genres like videos and Web pages are creating new kinds of texts. In this project, we invite you to create a photo essay designed to instruct an audience about a moment in history or an aspect of contemporary culture. Inform your essay with research conducted using the Internet, the library, or interviews. Select at least eight images that allow you to convey important information about your topic, and then incorporate those images into Web pages and add captions and explanations that allow you to tell a story about your topic.

OPTION 1: RESEARCH A HISTORICAL MOMENT OR EVENT

Select a time in the past that will provide ample opportunities for locating images. You might research the Vietnam War, the Great Depression, World War II, the Civil Rights movement, or some other major episode in history.

OPTION 2: RESEARCH AN ASPECT OF CULTURE

Consider some element of contemporary culture. You might look at a group or activity, like NASCAR fans or disc golf; explore a cultural issue such as teen pregnancy; or examine a cultural phenomenon such as vacations or exercise.

Whichever option you select, you'll need to conduct more extensive research. You might begin by exploring the online resources of your library. You can also conduct keyword searches on the Internet. You may also want to conduct interviews. Take careful notes, and be sure to tell the subject that you will be using the interview for your essay. (For more on interview techniques see page 86.) You may use any or all of these options. Just be sure to have a wide array of research sources to support your project. You may find that your composing process for this project is more complicated than for a traditional essay. If you compose your project using stand-alone Web pages, you will need to use a Web editor to create an opening page, pages for each of the images, and a page for a conclusion. You'll also need to create a navigational and design scheme for the pages. If you use an online service to create your slideshow (e.g., Flickr or Photobucket), you can use the slideshow tools on their Web site. In either case, you will need to locate, sequence, and caption images to make points about your topic.

STUDENT PROJECT

Michael Lee, "Images of History: The Hmong"

Michael Lee composed this photo essay, excerpts of which follow, partly as a way of exploring his own heritage as a Hmong American. His family immigrated to the United States shortly after the Vietnam War, and, as he reports, the Hmong culture native to Vietnam has since been dispersed as communists in Laos have retaliated for the Hmong's assistance of U.S. troops during the war. Lee worries that "the Hmong traditions and the Hmong language itself are quickly diminishing and may be even inevitably dying off." He hopes that the essay will serve to preserve some of his personal and cultural history.

Images of History: The Hmong

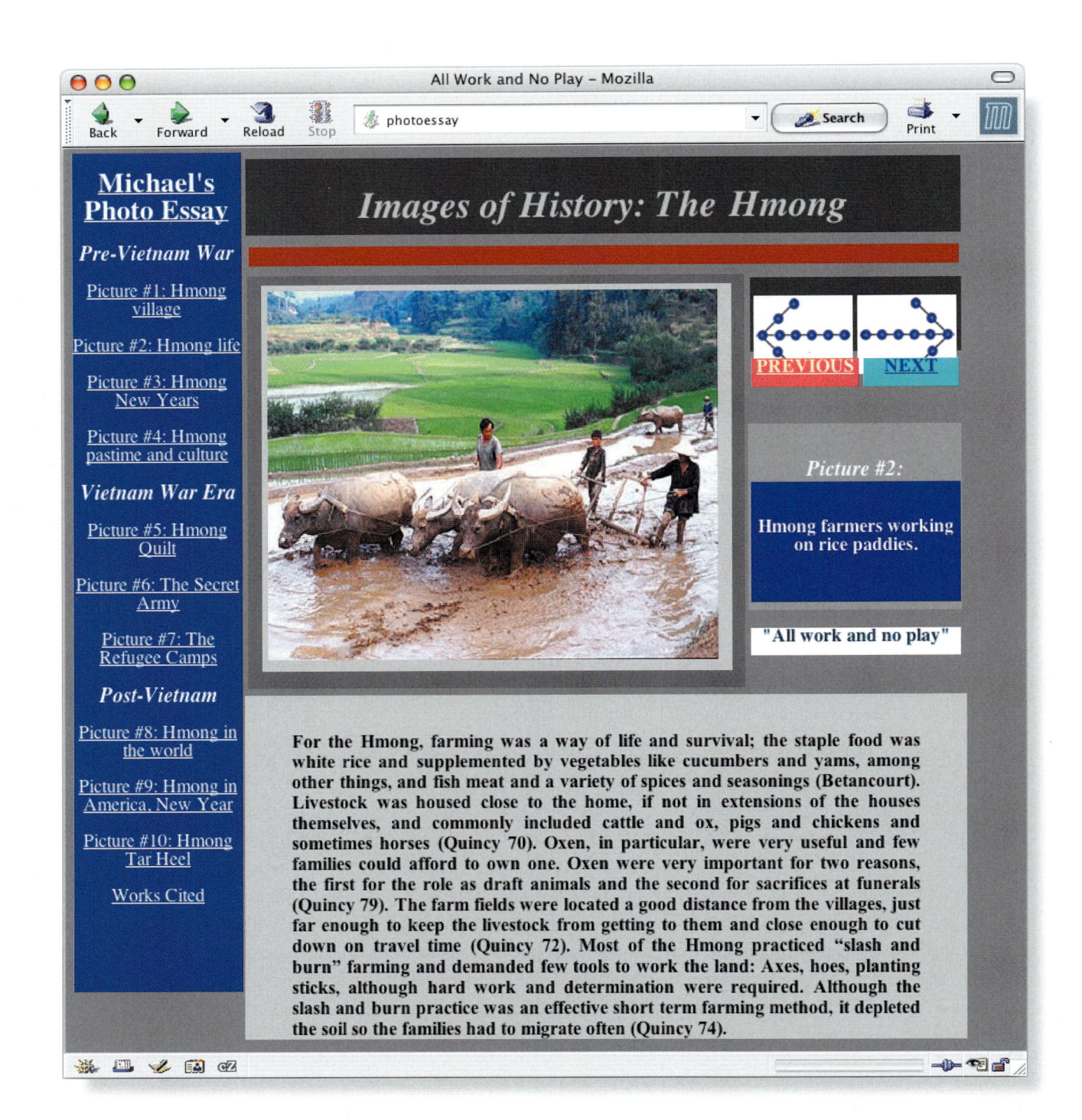

Michael's Photo Essay

Pre-Vietnam War

Picture #1: Hmong village

Picture #2: Hmong life

Picture #3: Hmong New Years

Picture #4: Hmong pastime and culture

Vietnam War Era

Picture #5: Hmong Quilt

Picture #6: The Secret Army

Picture #7: The Refugee Camps

Post-Vietnam

Picture #8: Hmong in the world

Picture #9: Hmong in America, New Year

Picture #10: Hmong Tar Heel

Works Cited

PREVIOUS   NEXT

Picture #2:

Hmong farmers working on rice paddies.

"All work and no play"

For the Hmong, farming was a way of life and survival; the staple food was white rice and supplemented by vegetables like cucumbers and yams, among other things, and fish meat and a variety of spices and seasonings (Betancourt). Livestock was housed close to the home, if not in extensions of the houses themselves, and commonly included cattle and ox, pigs and chickens and sometimes horses (Quincy 70). Oxen, in particular, were very useful and few families could afford to own one. Oxen were very important for two reasons, the first for the role as draft animals and the second for sacrifices at funerals (Quincy 79). The farm fields were located a good distance from the villages, just far enough to keep the livestock from getting to them and close enough to cut down on travel time (Quincy 72). Most of the Hmong practiced "slash and burn" farming and demanded few tools to work the land: Axes, hoes, planting sticks, although hard work and determination were required. Although the slash and burn practice was an effective short term farming method, it depleted the soil so the families had to migrate often (Quincy 74).

Images of History: The Hmong

Michael's Photo Essay

Pre-Vietnam War

Picture #1: Hmong village

Picture #2: Hmong life

Picture #3: Hmong New Years

Picture #4: Hmong pastime and culture

Vietnam War Era

Picture #5: Hmong Quilt

Picture #6: The Secret Army

Picture #7: The Refugee Camps

Post-Vietnam

Picture #8: Hmong in the world

Picture #9: Hmong in America, New Year

Picture #10: Hmong Tar Heel

Works Cited

Picture #7: Hmong leaving a refugee camp, as well as family members.

"Family means no one is forgotten."

After America withdrew from the war in 1975 and the communist Pathet Lao took over the country, the Hmong had to endure the hatred and revenge of the communist. Keith Quincy, author of *Hmong: History of a People*, writes that "On May 9th the Pathet Lao paper, Khao Xane Pathet Lao, intimated the party's position [concerning the Hmong]: 'It is necessary to extirpate, down to the root, the 'Hmong' minority'" (76). When America evacuated, many of the Hmong were either killed in mysterious ways, sent to "reeducation camps" to never be seen again, abandoned in the mountain wilderness, returned to their barren and bombarded villages and homes, or simply murdered by communist soldiers. Since 1975 and 1992, about 100,000 Laotian Hmong have crossed the Mekong River into Thailand to take refuge in refugee camps, while approximately 200,000 Hmong remained in Laos in order to rebuild their homes and essentially their lives (Pfaff). The refugee camps were not exactly the safest and most welcoming places for the Hmong who fled to Thailand, but when the alternative was facing prosecution and precarious futures in communist Laos, many Hmong understandably chose to begin life over again.

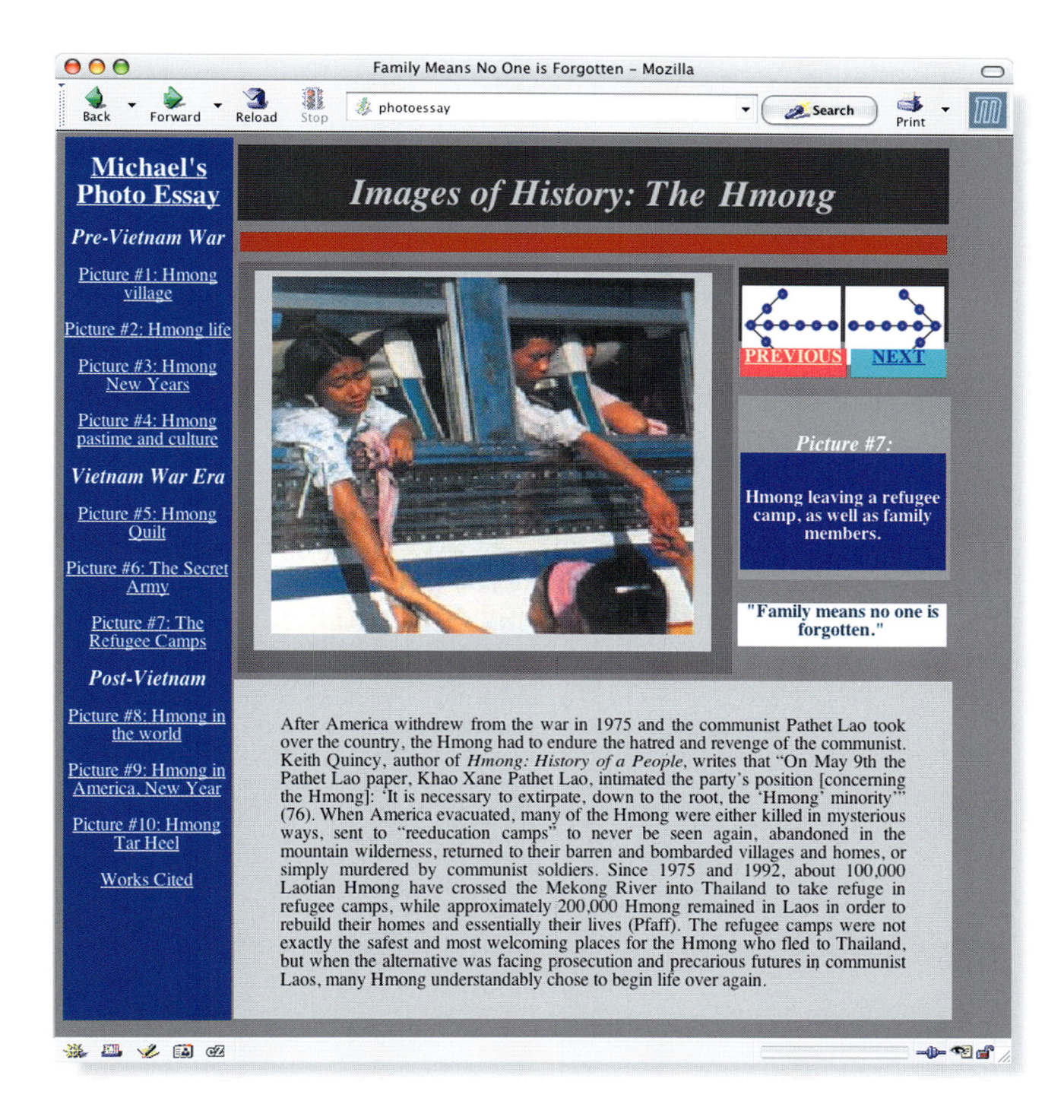

In the photo essay, Michael Lee does a good job of surrounding his photographs with explanatory text that relates the history of the Hmong people and lays out the issues inherent in their treatment during and after the war. In addition to textual explanations and captions, he incorporates a brief quotation or catch-phrase into each page of the essay. The structure of his essay includes both *next* and *previous* links on every page and a standardized menu on the left that places the images in a chronological sequence.

Project 5.3

This assignment asks you to develop a detailed assessment of a film you've recently seen by writing a two- to three-page review essay. Consult magazines that regularly publish extended film reviews, such as the *New Yorker* or *Atlantic Monthly*, to get a sense of how writers typically structure their commentary. Many reviews start with background information and a summary, and then move on to evaluate technical and artistic elements and the major concerns treated in the movie. If the film touches on controversies, spell them out and explain for your readers how the film addresses these issues. For major themes developed by the film, consider how sophisticated the film is in treating these motifs and comment on the strengths or weaknesses of the thematic elements. Finally, offer an overall judgment about the movie. What one or two things should readers who are thinking about viewing the film know? Is there a particular group who would appreciate the film more than others? Would you recommend the movie? How strongly?

Project 5.4

Newspaper design has undergone many changes over the years. Early papers consisted of mainly text, perhaps divided into a few columns. The addition of the multi-column layout changed the ways newspapers presented information. Color and the development of newspaper layout software further changed the design of papers. Conduct research into the evolution of newspaper design, and then develop a mock-up or redesign of a paper. You can use publishing software for your mock-up, or just use paper and drawing tools. Think about the rationales behind design changes that you might make. After you have developed a mock-up, write a page or so discussing your revisions.

Project 5.5

Create a video mashup that offers commentary on an aspect of culture. Use a video editor to modify audio and video files to create a video with a new meaning. There are two possibilities for creating the mashup. You can take an existing video, and then add new audio to change its meaning. Or you can take a piece of audio—e.g., a song or speech with a clear message—and then add images that deliver your commentary. To generate your message, rely on strategies of juxtaposition. If the audio you use promotes a concept like equality or fair play, you'll want to layer images over the audio that help viewers see it in a new light—for instance, images of poverty layered over messages of equality will create a juxtaposition that delivers the mashup message. When finished, share your mashup with classmates, or post it to a video-sharing Web site.

CHAPTER 6
TECHNOLOGY AND SCIENCE

ITEM 6.1 ■ **The Hobo-Dyer Equal Area Projection Map of the World**

If you look quickly at the two views of the world that open this chapter, it might appear that someone has simply rotated a map 180 degrees. But when you examine the images more carefully, you'll see that the labels on the "upside-down" map are correctly placed and printed left to right, just as we would expect. The real change is simply that what we ordinarily think of as the Southern Hemisphere now appears at the top—where we expect the familiar powers of Asia, Europe, and North America to be.

What might be the point behind flipping the image? Shouldn't north be the apex of any map? Well, maybe not if you live in Australia. When we look at the upside-down map, the focal point becomes Australia, followed by South America and Africa. As a way of explaining the geographical makeup of the world, the two maps provide startlingly different views: they prompt us to consider who gets to be on top—and why. It turns out that *North* and *South* are human inventions, essential to the science of mapmaking, but conventions nonetheless.

Choosing to emphasize the Northern or Southern Hemisphere changes the way information is presented in maps. And these choices help us think about other decisions we make when we translate ideas about our world into texts and artifacts that we can share. Objectivity may be the goal of science, but when we convey information through writing or other media, we are refashioning the data to reflect our perspectives and experiences.

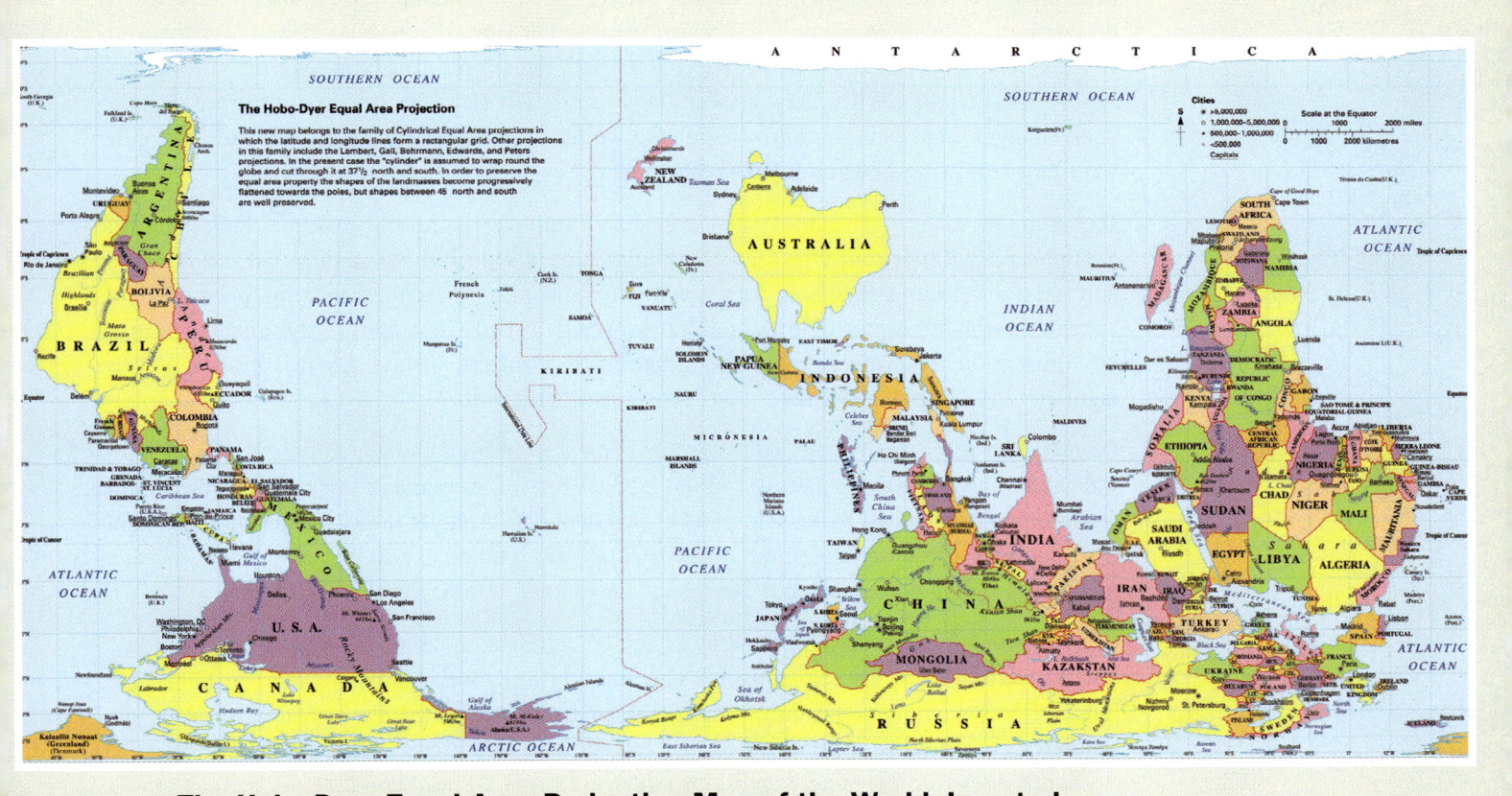

ITEM 6.2 ■ **The Hobo-Dyer Equal Area Projection Map of the World, Inverted**

333

Reading Texts About Technology and Science

Texts that convey technical or scientific information must be read with care, in part because the subjects they address are often unfamiliar or complex. Most of us have had the experience of being frustrated by a technical manual accompanying the new digital camera or printer we have purchased. Most technical manuals these days try to convey instructions through both words and images, and many offer variations of instructions in multiple languages (see Item 6.3). Technologies themselves even become texts to be read—just look at the dashboard controls and displays in your car (see Item 6.4).

However, even texts that offer explanations of technological or scientific information are tailored for specific **audiences** and **purposes**. A bar graph depicting statistics can seem straightforward enough, but by massaging the scale, the creator of the graph can easily distort the data to emphasize one category over another (see Item 6.5). Similarly, an item as simple as a health poster may report basic medical facts, but do so in a way that also sends messages about awareness and prevention—consider the typical anti-drug or alcohol abuse poster (see Item 6.6).

Mediums also shape technical or scientific texts. Medical imaging, for instance, relies heavily on computer-generated images that reveal microscopic, genetic, or internal parts of the body never before visible to the naked eye (see Item 6.7). Such a new medium requires a whole new set of expert reading skills. Even a technology as familiar as a GPS device in your car or backpack changes what you can know about the world, as it eliminates the mystery of unfamiliar terrain or confusing neighborhood streets.

Technologies also impact the ways we share and distribute information. Following the September 11, 2001, terror attacks, activity immediately spiked in online news sites, chat rooms, and message forums—but still low-tech communication thrived as missing persons flyers appeared on mailboxes, buildings, and kiosks (see Item 6.8). Such ad hoc and amateur sources of information require readers to pay attention to **context**, always asking questions: "Who made it?" "When was it created?" and "Who was it written for?"

Even ancient technologies respond to specific audiences and situational contexts. Today we know little about the anonymous petroglyphs dating back tens of thousands of years, found around the world in areas inhabited by ancient peoples (see Item 6.9). And yet these images of people, animals, tools, or astronomical features seem strikingly informational. Will our own images reveal as much information about us to our descendants millennia from now (see Item 6.10)?

Of course, technical information and ideas can be organized in almost endless ways. Be alert to how **structural** elements help convey and explain information. A Web site like EarthPulse (see Item 6.11) uses columns, headings, and white space to control the flow of ideas on its pages. Similarly, conventions of **genre** affect the arrangement and presentation of material in a text. A scientific report on weather conditions might use common print conventions such as headers and figure captions, combined with graphs, tables, and charts. A newspaper report might emphasize eyewitness accounts and photographs while relying on conventions of newspaper **design** such as headline size and the use of columns (see Item 6.12). We have to look critically at how such devices serve the purpose of someone presenting or seeking information.

Gallery: Technology and Science

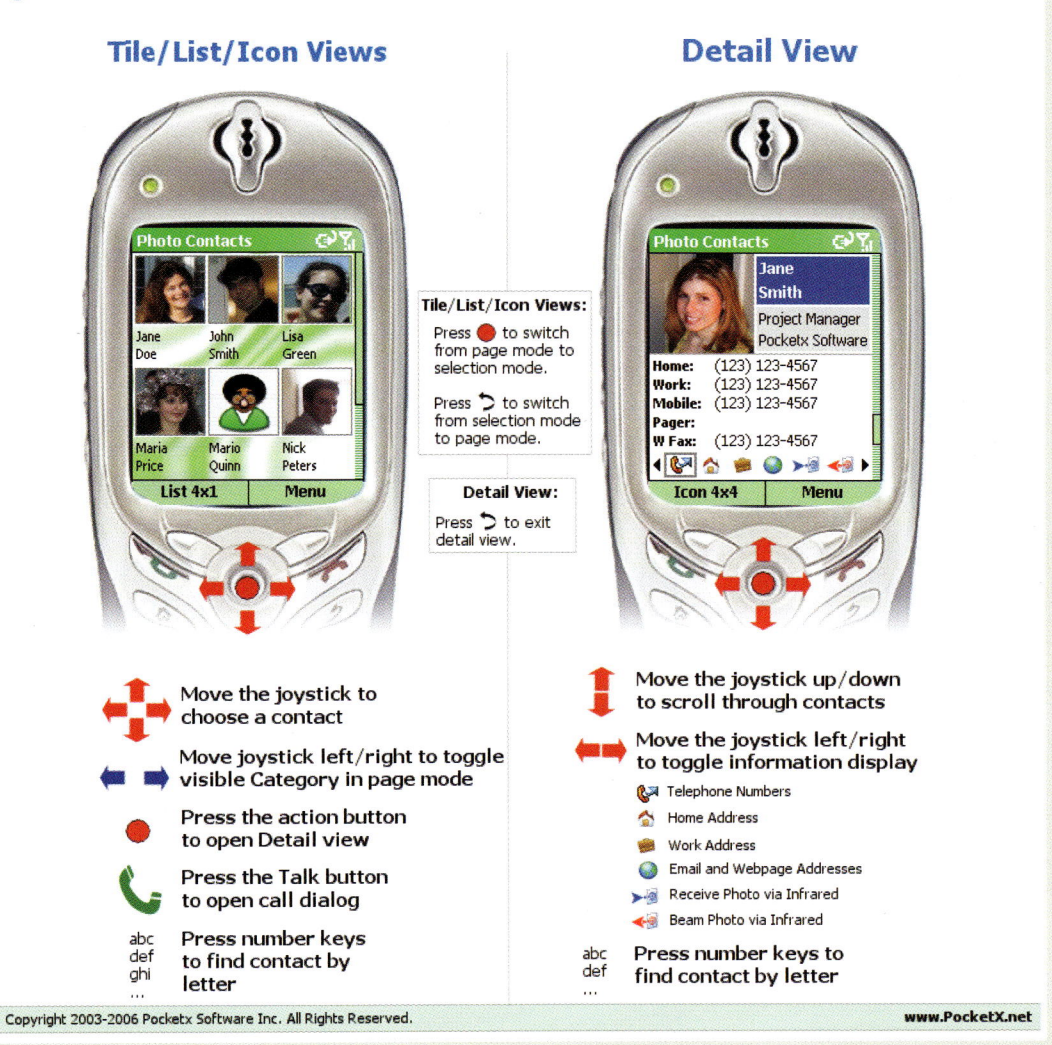

Photo Contacts Smartphone Edition
Quick View Guide

PocketX Software

Tile/List/Icon Views

Tile/List/Icon Views:
Press ● to switch from page mode to selection mode.

Press ↰ to switch from selection mode to page mode.

Detail View:
Press ↰ to exit detail view.

- Move the joystick to choose a contact
- Move joystick left/right to toggle visible Category in page mode
- Press the action button to open Detail view
- Press the Talk button to open call dialog
- abc def ghi … Press number keys to find contact by letter

Detail View

- Move the joystick up/down to scroll through contacts
- Move the joystick left/right to toggle information display
  - Telephone Numbers
  - Home Address
  - Work Address
  - Email and Webpage Addresses
  - Receive Photo via Infrared
  - Beam Photo via Infrared
- abc def … Press number keys to find contact by letter

Copyright 2003-2006 Pocketx Software Inc. All Rights Reserved.   www.PocketX.net

---

ITEM 6.3 ■ PocketX Software, Cell Phone Instructions

When creating technical descriptions, such as those in a cell phone manual, writers must think carefully about the sequencing of steps, provide clear iconic images that show how to perform the individual tasks that make up the process, and offer concise written text that complements the visual instructions—no small matter.

1 Describe the devices the technical writers for PocketX use to convey information nonverbally in the instructions. Which work especially well? Do you find yourself confused at any point?

2 At what points in the instructions do the writers use words? Why do you think they might have chosen words versus images or other nonverbal means of communicating the information? How do the written text and visual representations work together?

3 If the writers of the manual asked you to evaluate these instructions, how would you rate them? Do you think you could easily use the photo contacts feature? What suggestions could you make for improvement?

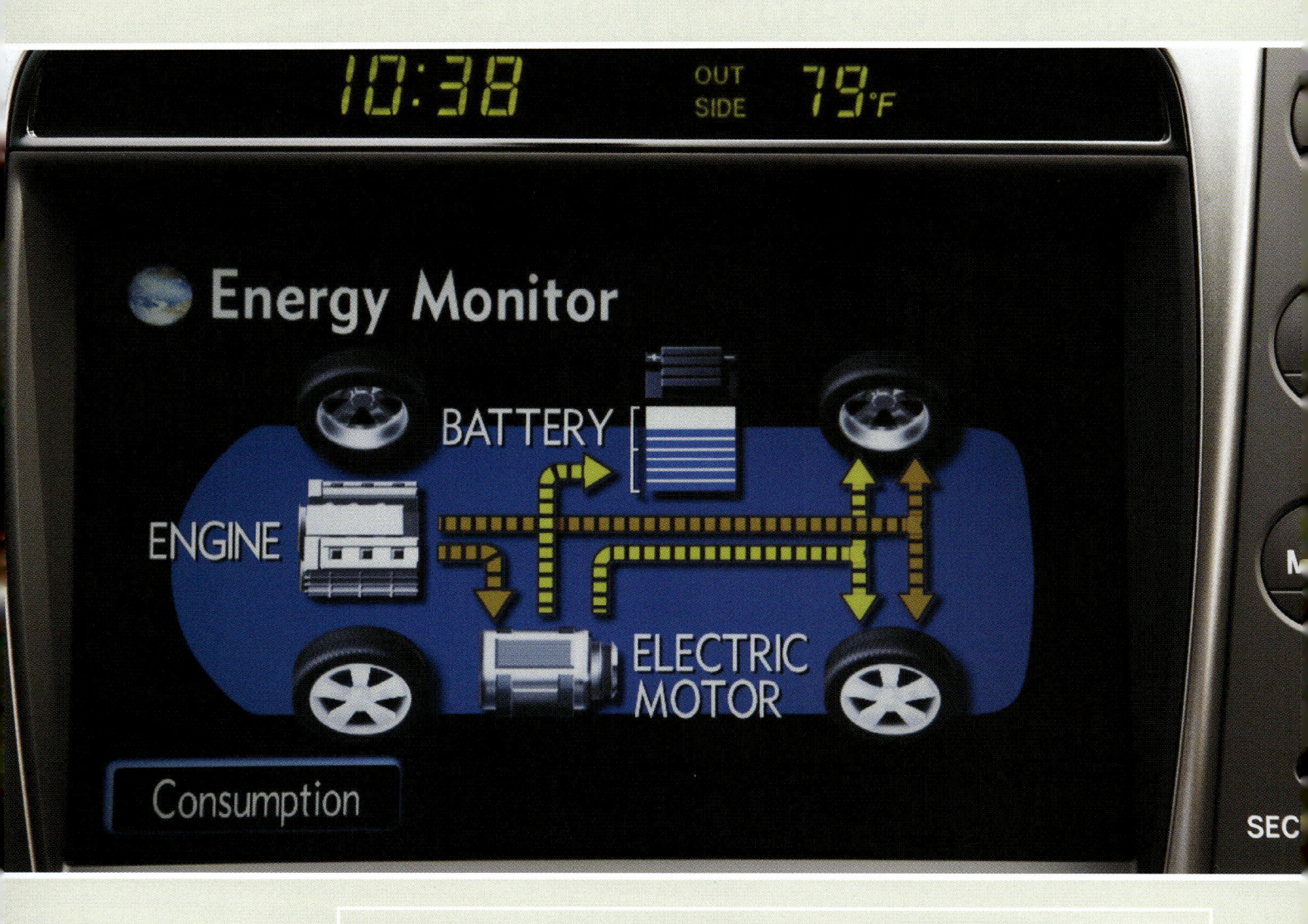

ITEM 6.4 ■ Lexus, LCD Screen on a Lexus GS 450h, 2008

As automobile manufacturers add more and more features to new models, it becomes a challenge to design controls that make sense and are easy to operate. Drivers are also now developing new relationships with the technologies of their vehicles, changing their driving habits as information feeds update them about fuel consumption, engine load, and even tire pressure. This display on a 2008 Lexus GS 450h hybrid informs drivers about which engine (gas or electric) is in use and to what degree, as well as about how power is being transferred to the wheels.

1. The screen here uses images to convey much of its information. Can you tell what each icon means? Which item makes the least sense to you? Which icon makes the most sense?

2. What audience might have difficulty understanding this display? What audience might find it easiest to navigate? Why?

3. Is it obvious to you from the screen what "consumption" means? Can you tell immediately if the car is using battery or gas power (or both)? What icons or words would you add to this screen to help drivers monitor their fuel use quickly without taking their attention from the road?

336   GALLERY | TECHNOLOGY AND SCIENCE

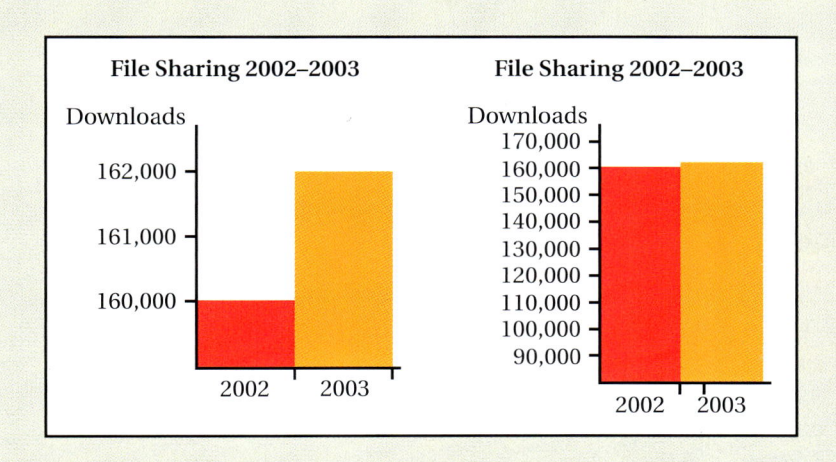

Table 1 - The Geography of File Sharing (numbers in %)

Country	Share of users	Share of downloads	Share World Population	Share World GDP	Share World Internet Users	Software Piracy Rate
United States	30.9	35.7	4.6	21.2	27.4	23
Germany	13.5	14.1	1.3	4.5	5.3	32
Italy	11.1	9.9	0.9	2.9	3.2	47
Japan	8.4	2.8	2.0	7.2	9.3	35
France	6.9	6.9	1.0	3.1	2.8	43
Canada	5.4	6.1	0.5	1.9	2.8	39
United Kingdom	4.1	4.0	1.0	3.1	5.7	26
Spain	2.5	2.6	0.6	1.7	1.3	47
Netherlands	2.1	2.1	0.3	0.9	1.6	36
Australia	1.6	1.9	0.3	1.1	1.8	32
Sweden	1.5	1.7	0.1	0.5	1.0	29
Switzerland	1.4	1.5	0.1	0.5	0.6	32
Brazil	1.3	1.4	2.9	2.7	2.3	55
Belgium	0.9	1.2	0.2	0.6	0.6	31
Austria	0.8	0.6	0.1	0.5	0.6	30
Poland	0.5	0.7	0.6	0.8	1.1	54

Notes on country covariates:
Shares of users and downloads is from the file sharing dataset described in the text. All other statistics are from *The CIA World Factbook* (2002, 2003), except the software piracy rates which are from the *Eighth Annual BSA Global Software Piracy Study* (2003). All values are world shares, except the piracy rates are the fractions of business application software installed without a license in the country. All non-file sharing data are for 2002 except population which is for 2003.

ITEM 6.5 ■ Bar Graphs and Table Representing File Sharing, 2002–2003

Visual representations of data such as tables, charts, and graphs are powerful ways of representing patterns and trends—but they need to be designed and presented with care. The two bar graphs illustrating the number of music downloads in 2002 and 2003 convey the same information, but manipulate their data. In reality, the numbers in Table 1 provide a better explanation of the changes during the period. And one would need to look at more recent years' figures to determine whether these downloading patterns continue today.

1. Examine the information presented in Table 1. Then, look again at the two bar graphs. In what ways might each of the graphs mislead readers? What information is distorted or hidden by each graph?

2. How carefully do you consider the statistics behind the graphs that you see in publications or ads? In what circumstances might the creators of graphs deliberately manipulate their presentations? Cite some examples.

3. What kinds of information do you expect to be most honestly presented? For example, are genres like technical documentation manuals, baseball statistics, or cookbooks subject to manipulation? Why or why not? Are weather maps skewed? Poll numbers?

Girlie Drinks...
women's diseases.

brain damage

STDs

heart problems

liver disease

menstrual disorders

A third of all girls older than 12 have tried a popular new alcoholic beverage. Known as "girlie drinks" or "alcopops," their sweet fruity flavor can't conceal the negative health consequences. Companies market these "starter drinks" to appeal to girls and young women. Don't be taken in.

American Medical Association
Physicians dedicated to the health of America

www.AlcoholPolicyMD.com

ITEM 6.6 ■ **American Medical Association,** *Girlie Drinks . . . Women's Diseases Poster*, 2004

Public health posters provide readers with basic information, yet they may also carry deeper messages. Behind the facts presented might be warnings about behavior risks that wouldn't be quite as powerful if stated directly. This poster was published by the American Medical Association in response to concerns about rising consumption of "alcopop" among adolescents and young women.

---

1 How does this poster present factual information about "girlie drinks"? Do you think that a reader unfamiliar with the issue could adequately grasp the problem after reading the poster? Why or why not?

2 How would you characterize the target audience for the poster? How can you tell? How do you think that group would respond to the information presented on the poster and to the behavioral warning it implies? What other groups might also be targeted by this poster?

3 How successful do you think informational public health advertising campaigns are in changing people's attitudes and behavior? What kinds of health warnings are most and least effective, in your opinion? Cite examples of particular slogans, advertisements, posters, or campaigns to support your observations.

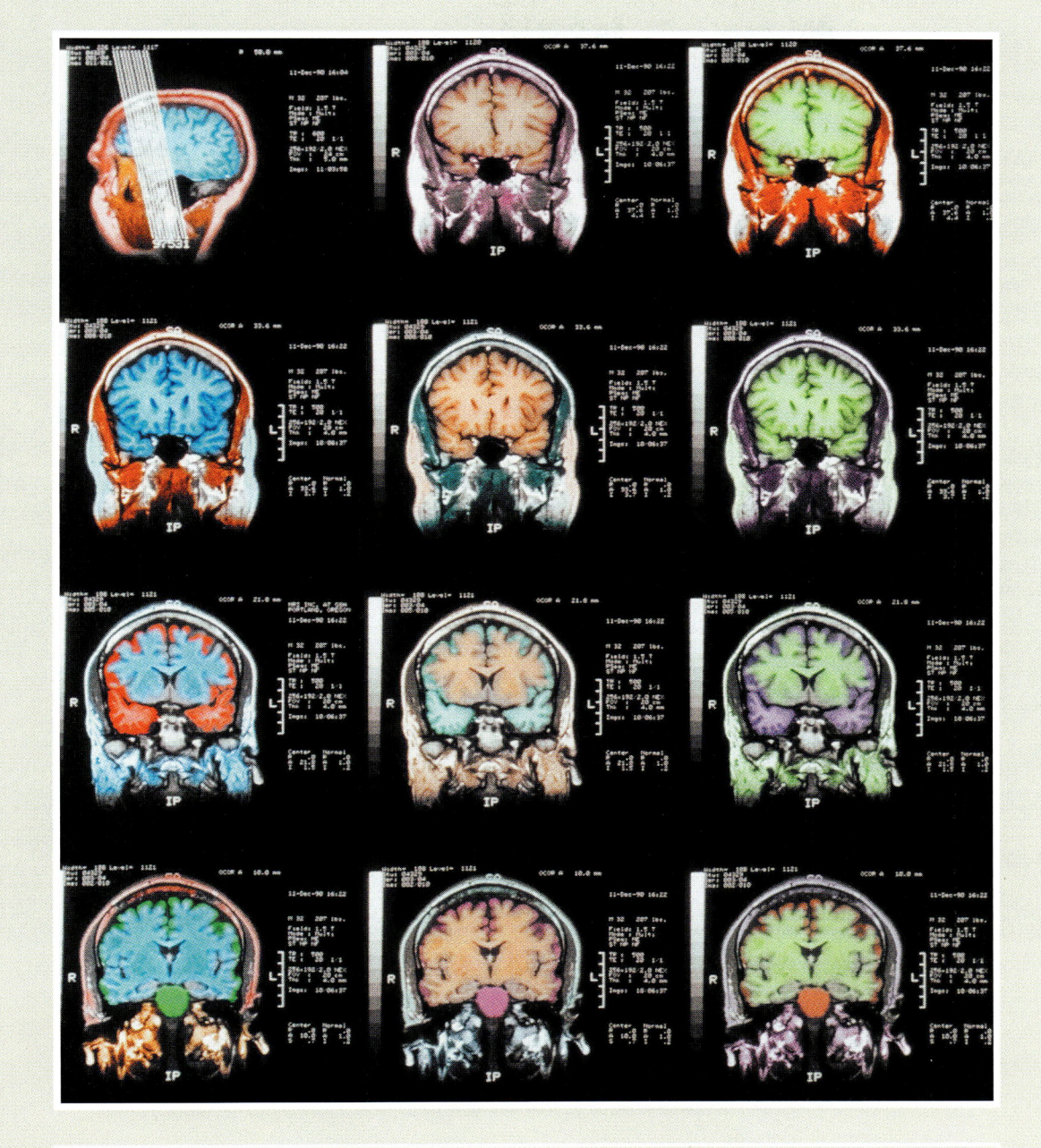

ITEM 6.7 ■ MRI Brain Images

Magnetic Resonance Imagery (MRI) has quickly gone from a cutting-edge medical technology to a normal diagnostic procedure. It gives doctors a way of seeing into parts of the body previously invisible without surgery. Radioactive dyes also enhance the procedure, enabling technicians to pinpoint specific areas of the body.

1. Vivid as these images are, they still have to be read by a skilled technician to reveal their data. What do you suspect that a doctor or technician would need to learn in order to interpret such data?

2. What kinds of information about a patient's health might *not* be adequately conveyed by MRI images? When might medical professionals need to rely on other kinds of information?

3. Can you imagine any downsides to high-tech medical tools such as MRI? For instance, do they drive up the cost of medical insurance? Might they be used too often? Might the cost of using them be out of reach for some patients?

ITEM 6.8 ■ Kiosk with Informational Flyers

Today, we think of information technology chiefly in electronic terms. But in busy public spaces such as college campuses, printed flyers are still an efficient way to display information, as on this kiosk at the University of Michigan.

1. In your experience, what are the most common kinds of information displayed on kiosks and similar public posting sites? What are some of the advantages and limitations of this venue? What kinds of information do you think are best and least suited to this kind of posting?

2. Consider the flyer as a genre. What kinds of content and design features do readers expect to see in this sort of document? What does it take for one flyer to stand out from the others?

3. What digital equivalents can you think of to poster boards or kiosks? How would you describe writings on a Facebook wall or other online postings in terms of information sharing? How are new technologies reshaping our sense of flyers and notes posted in public places?

ITEM 6.9 ■ **Newspaper Rock, Utah, 2007**

Few of the images we produce today are likely to endure as long as these petroglyphs in Utah. Clearly, the images meant more to the ancient peoples than they do to us today: we struggle to interpret the symbols, animal signs, and human representations because we lack the contexts within which they were interpreted.

1. Look at the rock carefully. Which of the images intrigue you the most? Why? What might the function of these images be?

2. What can you infer about the ancient culture that created these images? Do the images remind you of any modes of communication we use today (for example, graphic novels or the cell phone instructions on page 335)?

3. Information technologies change rapidly. Videotapes and photo film have seen their best days and will likely go the way of the vinyl record—a curiosity sought by enthusiasts. What contemporary information technologies or media are most likely to be accessible in five hundred or a thousand years? Why?

4. If you become aware of an unusual or suspicious release of an unknown substance nearby, it doesn't hurt to protect yourself.

5. Get away from the substance as quickly as possible.

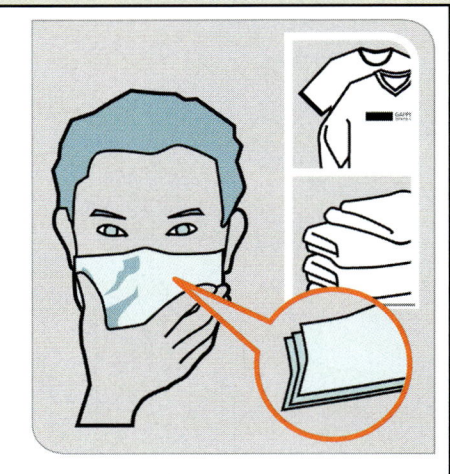

6. Cover your mouth and nose with layers of fabric that can filter the air but still allow breathing.

> **ITEM 6.10** ■ **Ready.gov Images**
>
> These ready.gov images were developed to offer guidance to citizens in the event of a terrorist attack. The panels are meant to convey pure information, clearly and simply. Without knowing their context, however, readers might be hard pressed to discern exactly what kind of advice the images convey.

1. The sequence of images represented by panels #4–6 certainly offers reasonable advice in context. But do they make sense to you without the captions? Should they?

2. How seriously do you take government warnings about safety or other concerns? What kinds of communication problems arise when it comes to distributing safety information? How might ready.gov messages be improved?

3. Log on to the ready.gov Web site and explore the warning information. Then look at some of the parodies of ready.gov. (Do a Web search on "ready.gov parody.") What do the spoof images have in common with the real thing? What do they tell us about the challenges involved in using images to convey information?

GALLERY | TECHNOLOGY AND SCIENCE

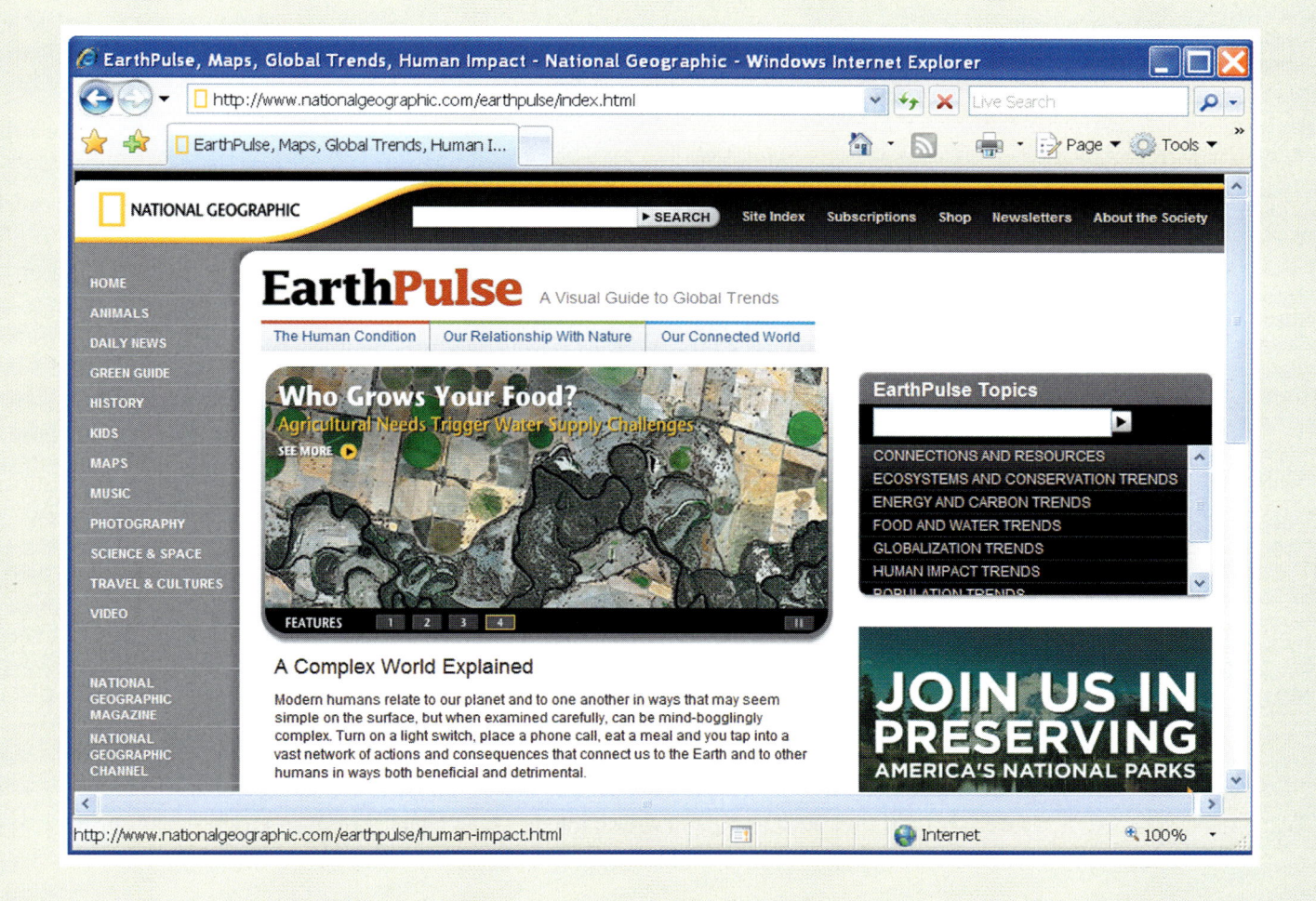

ITEM 6.11 ■ National Geographic, *EarthPulse* Web Site

National Geographic's *EarthPulse* Web site presents data about global trends through interactive maps that allow viewers to focus in on particular phenomena or locales. In addition to the navigational and design features built into the maps, the site uses repetition (lists of key trends and thumbnail-sized maps are repeated at the bottom of the page), and white space to create appealing arrangements. It combines images, animations, and text to provide a comprehensive picture of geographical and human phenomena affecting the planet.

1. Visit the *EarthPulse* Web site and browse through its features. In addition to repetition and arrangement, what other structural and design elements can you recognize in the Web site? How many of these strategies could be applied to other forms of writing?

2. Are you part of the intended audience for this site? How do you know? If so, how effectively have the designers tailored the site to your needs? If not, how would the site need to change for you to visit and use it?

3. How important do you think design strategies are to informative writing? Is it fair to say that design is more important when it comes to informative versus other kinds of writing?

343

Cluster 6.1
Mapping Knowledge

When we think of science, we often picture physical acts of experimentation—the lowering of the slide cover, the lifting of the dissection scalpel, even the smell of formaldehyde. But today much scientific work bears little resemblance to what we might remember from our high school biology lab. In disciplines ranging from the earth sciences to neurobiology, scientists are more likely to spend hours testing data models on their office PC than measuring rock formations or mixing chemicals in test tubes.

The maturation of computing and the growth of digitized information have strongly affected the sciences: researchers now process data at rates that would have been impossible even ten years ago. Similarly, networks now facilitate the sharing of both information and computing power, helping scientists to build on one another's work. Finally, innovative modes of representing information have launched new fields and transformed others by harnessing scientific data and mapping them through two- or three-dimensional images.

The texts and images in this cluster emphasize these changes. Specifically, they consider how the study of mapping is undergoing revolutionary change as geographers grapple with the impact of technology on their field. The first astronauts to see the Earth from space remarked on how the view utterly changed their perspectives on the political maps we have come to think of as a natural part of our geographical landscape: from space, no colors or borders divide the planet. We examine the famous *Blue Marble* photo taken during one of those early space missions, then look at how new technologies now enable NASA to create images of the earth that expand on what the original Apollo missions saw.

Then, we consider the ways in which viewing the world from numerous global and mapped perspectives is fast becoming an everyday activity, thanks to software that empowers ordinary citizens to become mapmakers. Evan Ratliff's "Google Maps is Changing the Way We See the World" and *The Denver Post* Editorial Board's "Now on Google Maps: You" survey some of the possibilities, risks, and ethical dilemmas these new tools create.

Finally, two literary pieces—Elizabeth Bishop's "The Map" and Susan Neville's essay on visiting a factory that manufactures globes, "On Maps and Globes," invite you to reflect on how making and reading maps are interpretive acts that define us in relationship to others and to the world.

In addition to the texts and images in this section, see Chapter 4, "Places and Environments" for other readings that raise issues about how we imagine and represent physical spaces.

ITEM 6.12 ■ NASA, *Blue Marble*, 1972

The *Blue Marble* photo, taken by Apollo 17 astronauts on December 7, 1972, is one of the most widely recognized photographs ever taken. Because the astronauts had the sun behind them when they took the photograph, it shows a brightly lit Earth shot through with colors reminiscent of a child's marble.

ITEM 6.13 ■ Images from *Blue Marble: Next Generation*, 2005

In 2005, NASA produced *Blue Marble: Next Generation*, the most recent installment of an ongoing project named after the original 1972 photo. According to NASA's Web site, this project aimed to create "the most detailed true-color image of the Earth's surface ever produced." From data collected using state-of-the-art sensors on NASA satellites, scientists stitched together 12 months of observations of the land surface, coastal oceans, sea ice, and clouds into a seamless, photo-like mosaic of every square kilometer of our planet. In addition to providing more detailed still images than ever before, *Blue Marble: Next Generation* made it possible for images and data to be viewed in interactive formats. More information about the project is available at http://earthobservatory.nasa.gov.

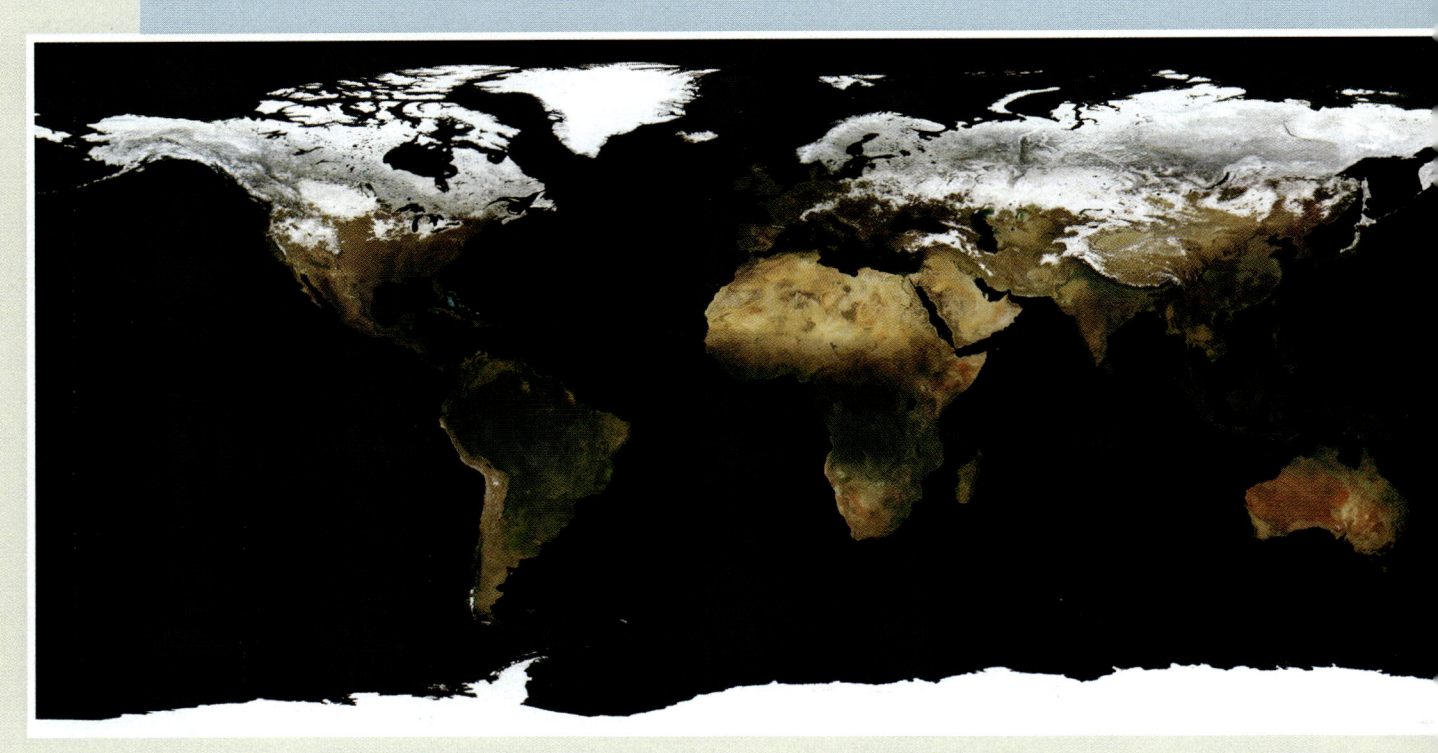

Blue Marble: Next Generation global monthly composite image for January 2004.

Still image of *Blue Marble: Next Generation* time animation, a 3-dimensional global image which rotates 360 degrees

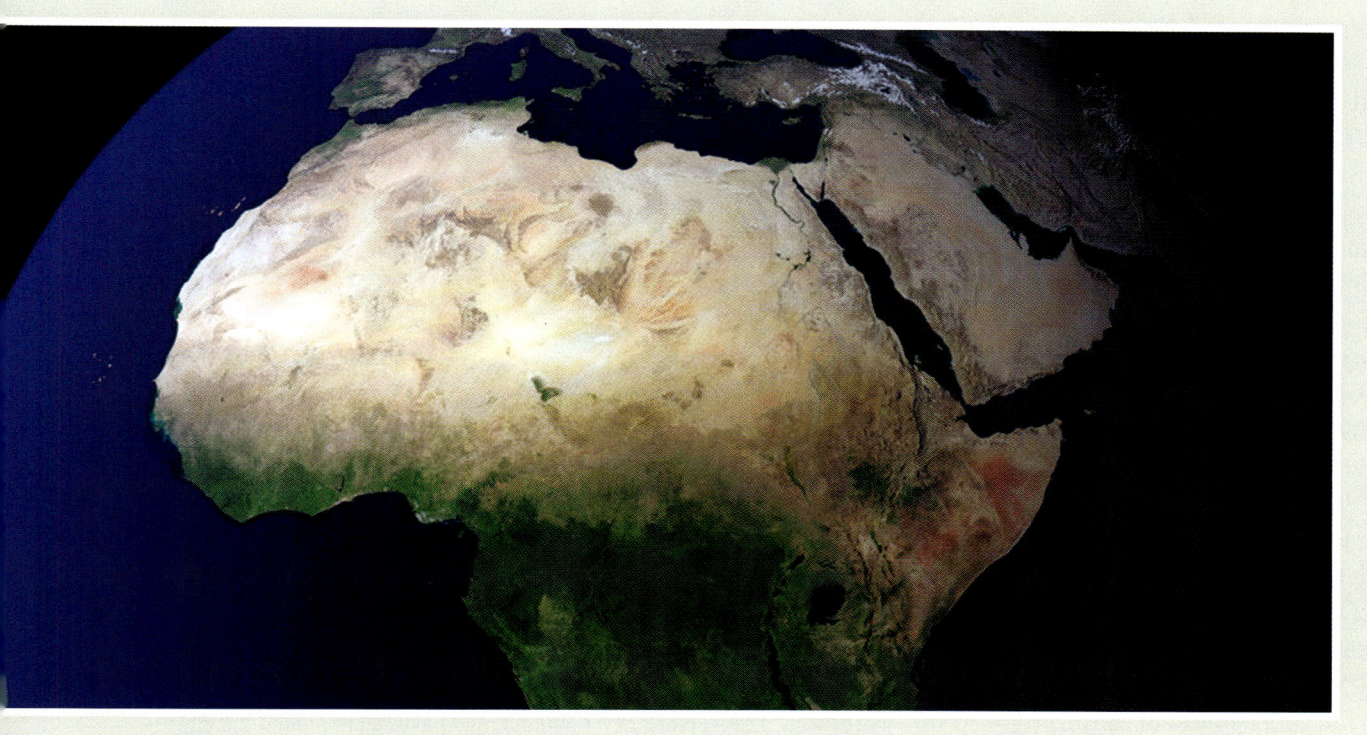

Blue Marble: Next Generation **high resolution land surface image showing Northern and Central Africa**

CONSIDER

1. The original 1972 *Blue Marble* photograph was included in Life Books' volume of *100 Photos that Changed the World* (2003). It has also been credited with inspiring increased environmental awareness and opposition to nuclear weapons. Why do you think the photo might have had such a powerful effect on a 1970s audience? Do you think the photo has an equally strong impact on viewers today? Why or why not?

2. Compare the *Blue Marble: Next Generation* images (visit http://earthobservatory.nasa.gov/Newsroom/BlueMarble/ to see more samples from the project) with the original 1972 photo. What kinds of knowledge do the different images make possible?

COMPOSE

3. Astronauts who view the earth from space remark both on the absence of visible political dividing lines and on how fragile the planet looks when seen from a vast distance. Do you think that a photograph—or any other visual representation—can replicate this experience? Write a paragraph exploring your thoughts on this question.

Google Maps Is Changing the Way We See the World

Evan Ratliff
(2007)

> **FYI** — Evan Ratliff is the co-author of *Safe: The Race to Protect Ourselves in a Newly Dangerous World* (HarperCollins, 2005), as well as a contributing editor for *Wired* magazine, where the following piece appeared on June 26, 2007.

In 1765, a 22-year-old British naval officer named James Rennell set out to map the entire Indian subcontinent. Traveling with a small party of soldiers, he used the advanced technologies of the day: a compass and a distance-measuring wheel called a perambulator. During the six-year journey, one soldier was killed by a tiger, five were mauled by a leopard, and Rennell was wounded in an attack by angry locals. He survived, and his detailed maps and atlas, published in the 1780s, defined British understanding of India for generations. Years later, a British geographer wrote that, to Rennell, "blanks on the map of the world were eyesores." More than two centuries later, within the decidedly safer confines of Building 45 on Google's Mountain View, California campus, John Hanke clicks the 3-foot image of Earth projected on his office wall and spins it around to India. Hanke, the director of Google Earth and Google Maps, zooms in for a closer look at Bangalore. At first, the city appeared in Google Earth as little more than a hi-res satellite photo. "Bangalore wasn't mapped on Google's products," he says, "and it really wasn't very well mapped, period."

Now, however, hundreds of small icons pop up on the screen. Pointing at one brings up a text bubble identifying a location of interest: a university, a racetrack, a library. An icon hovering over the Karnataka High Court calls up a photo of its bright red exterior and a link to an account of its long, distinguished history. Another, atop M. Chinnaswamy Stadium, links to a Wikipedia entry about the legendary cricket matches played there. "As you can see, it's very well mapped now," Hanke says, pulling up a photo of a Hindu temple.

The annotations weren't created by Google, nor by some official mapping agency. Instead, they are the products of a volunteer army of amateur cartographers. "It didn't take sophisticated software," Hanke says. "What it took was a substrate—the satellite imagery of Earth—in an accessible form and a simple authoring language for people to create and share stuff. Once that software existed, the urge to describe and annotate just took off."

Discovering the New World
7 glimpses into the hyperlocal future.

The Internet of Things
What if you could walk down an unfamiliar street, use your camera phone to take a picture of a building, and instantly know everything about it, from the architect to the list of tenants. The technology to make common objects clickable, like hyperlinked words on a Web site, is available today in the form of 2-D barcodes. These digital tags look like empty crossword puzzles. Users create them online, print them out, and paste them around the city. Then anyone with a phonecam can "click" on them. A program on the phone decodes the pattern and redirects the curious pedestrian to a Web page. One project, called Smartpox, is using these barcodes to build online communities that center around, for example, scavenger hunts and restaurant reviews. Members slap a barcode on a given establishment, and in-the-know passersby can get the dirt on its crème anglaise. At Semapedia.com, you can drop in any Wikipedia URL to instantly generate a 2-D barcode pointing to the corresponding entry.

A career in cartography used to be the prerogative of well-funded adventurers—men like Rennell or Lewis and Clark—with full government backup. Even after the advent of commercial satellite and aerial photography, the ability to make maps remained largely in the hands of specialists. Now, suddenly, mapmaking power is within the grasp of a 12-year-old. In the past two years, map providers like Google, Microsoft, and Yahoo have created tools that let anyone with an Internet connection layer their own geographic obsessions on top of ever-more-detailed road maps and satellite images. A host of collaborative annotation projects have appeared—not to mention tens of thousands of personal map mashups—that plot text, links, data, and even sounds onto every available blank space on the digital globe. It's become a sprawling, networked atlas—a "geoweb" that's expanding so quickly its outer edges are impossible to pin down.

There are the narrowly focused maps, like hidden mountain-biking trails, local restaurant favorites, and annotated travel guides. Then there are the more elaborate efforts, all of which "give people the power to create their own ground truth," says Mike Liebhold, a senior researcher specializing in geospatial technology at Silicon Valley's Institute for the Future. When a large fire broke out in Georgia in April, a resident quickly built a regularly updated map showing the burn areas. In Indonesia, for which Google still has no underlying road map, someone is tracing routes over satellite photos to create his own. The US Holocaust Memorial Museum recently released an annotated layer in Google Earth that displays the Darfur genocide in horrifying geographic detail, showing burned villages and linking to photos and videos.

Whether it's citizens appearing at local zoning-board meetings with elaborate Google Earth presentations or the Air Force using the app to reach victims during Hurricane Katrina, the new mapmaking is about much more than spotting your house in a satellite photo. "This is about individuals as local observers, creating their own map data," says Michael Goodchild, a professor of geography at UC Santa Barbara. "It's 6 billion pairs of eyes."

The idea of providing digital maps for the masses is not new. Xerox Parc launched its first online mapping application a year before Netscape produced its first browser in the early '90s, and online driving directions of varying reliability have been ubiquitous for nearly a decade. Google released the first version of Google Maps in January 2005, followed by the more intricate 3-D world of Google Earth five months later. (Those two applications—along with Google Maps for Mobile, which calls up maps and local search results on mobile devices—are overlapping views of the same underlying data.)

At first, the data all flowed one way, from the mapper to the user. But Paul Rademacher, a DreamWorks Animation programmer, changed that when he invented the map mashup. In the fall of 2004 he was looking for an apartment in the Bay Area. Driving the streets with a pile of craigslist ads and pages of maps balanced on his lap, he thought, "Wouldn't it be better to have one map with all the listings on it?" When Google released the first version of Google Maps a couple of months later, Rademacher took a close look at the source code, written in JavaScript.

The New World

Traffic Tracker

When a gasoline tanker crash destroyed a freeway overpass near San Francisco this spring, Seattle-based Inrix knew right away that something big had gone down. The company scooped the news choppers because its Smart Dust Network, analyzing data from more than 625,000 commercial vehicles and 13,000 road sensors, saw the chaos unfold. Currently, coverage is limited. But in the future, personal GPS systems will likely know the location of each stitch of gridlock, thanks to communication with every other vehicle on the road.

Eight weeks later, he had a demo that linked craigslist housing ads to pins he'd added to a Google map. One Thursday night, he posted a link to the demo on craigslist, and by the next day thousands of people had already taken it for a spin. "I had no idea how big it would be," he says. "I just wanted to write something that was useful."

Rademacher's HousingMaps was an even bigger hit inside Google. The company hired him and opened up the Google Maps code so anyone could work with it. Microsoft and Yahoo followed suit, and before long the Web was awash in map mashups.

"Someday, there will be the Paul Rademacher statue in front of the Googleplex," says Greg Sterling, an analyst at Sterling Market Intelligence. Today, the number of mashed-up Google Maps exceeds 50,000. (Google Maps itself is now the second-most-trafficked mapping site, after MapQuest.) Practically overnight, new companies were formed to meet the demand for Web sites and software tools to help people create and distribute their maps. Platial features thousands of user-generated maps of favorite bookstores, bar crawls, and road trips. Panoramio lets users peg their personal photos to Google maps, and it has already logged more than a million pics.

This April, Google launched its own mashup software, My Maps, which allows users to personalize their Google maps by attaching images, text, and video. They can either save them privately or publish them for strangers to find. My Maps wasn't revolutionary: Microsoft added a similar feature to Live Search Maps back in 2005, and Yahoo-owned Flickr allows users to geo-tag photos. The difference was that Google also announced plans to add another dimension to the mapping universe by making the entire geoweb—not just Google Maps—searchable.

"We are approaching it as a problem that's not unlike page rank and the Web," Hanke says. "Now that you've got a lot of stuff out there, it will become important to sift the wheat from the chaff."

Building 45 can be found in Google Earth just southeast of the company's main campus. (Employees put a 3-D rendering of the building at the proper coordinates. Look for the bland box with blue siding and a pyramid-topped column over the entrance.) When I visited the real thing, there was nothing to signal that this was the headquarters of a cartographic revolution except a few plastic globes and the occasional map pinned to a cubicle wall. But make no mistake: On the second floor, Hanke, 40, and his engineers are laying the groundwork for just that. In Mountain View and at companion offices in New York, Bangalore, Hyderabad, São Paulo, Sydney, and Zurich, they take terabytes of raw satellite imagery, aerial photography, and road map data that Google buys from commercial providers, stitch them together, then send them back out as the base maps for Google Earth and Google Maps.

Hanke grew up in Cross Plains, Texas, a town of just over 1,000 people, about 120 miles southwest of Fort Worth. Google Earth's satellite view of Cross Plains reveals a compact grid of two dozen streets surrounded by open farmland. "There was a blinking red light and a Dairy Queen and a few stores downtown," Hanke recalls. "Like a lot of other kids, I wanted to see what else was out there." After college, he spent four years working in Washington, DC, and in Burma on what he will describe only as "foreign policy type of stuff" for the US government before eventually joining a video game startup.

In 2001, Hanke cofounded a company named Keyhole. Inspired in part by the Neal Stephenson novel *Snow Crash*—the protagonist uses a software program called Earth, created by the "Central Intelligence Corporation" and containing "a perfectly detailed rendition of Planet Earth"—Hanke and a collection of programmers used their game design experience to create an online 3-D globe by streaming in commercial satellite images stored on the Keyhole servers. They called it Earth Viewer.

In 2003, echoing the *Snow Crash* plot, Hanke signed a deal with the government venture arm In-Q-Tel (partially funded by the CIA) that put Earth Viewer in the hands of the National Geospatial-Intelligence Agency, the department that handles maps and satellite imagery for US military and intelligence units, and which remains one of Google Earth's largest customers. "At the time, what was on the globe was fairly lo-res, widely available commercial imagery," says Gregg Black, director of the agency's eGeoint Management Office. "But immediately we said, 'Wow, this is going to be powerful.'" Black loved how easy it was to use. "We could do these mashups and expose existing legacy data sources"—intelligence data overlaid on the latest hi-res satellite imagery—"in a matter of hours, rather than weeks, months, or years."

Among civilians, Earth Viewer became a cult hit. People delighted in tilting the planet in all directions and zooming down to their homes. Particularly popular was a feature allowing users to mark and save locations. The original idea, Hanke says, "was that if I wanted to meet you at the Stanford game, I would be able to find a spot outside the stadium." But enthusiasts began finding and marking oddities like planes in mid flight and blurred-out military installations. To take advantage of the phenomenon, the company created a descriptive language called keyhole markup language, or KML, which lets anyone annotate maps, not only with their own place markers but also with lines, icons, and three-dimensional shapes. Users could save their annotations as KML files, which anyone could then open as a layer in Earth Viewer.

In 2004, not long after Sergey Brin downloaded a copy of Earth Viewer and interrupted a Google meeting to "fly" to the house of each executive in the room, the company bought Keyhole for an undisclosed amount, renamed it Google Earth, and moved Hanke's team into Building 45.

Since Google relaunched the software in June 2005, the stand-alone Google Earth program has been down-

The New World

Pinpointed Photography

Organizing vacation pics would be so much easier if you could remember exactly where you took each one. The Ricoh 500SE can help: This 8-megapixel digicam comes with a built-in GPS receiver that notes longitude and latitude in the file every time you fire up the shutter. (Programs like Google Maps can decode them.) Not ready to drop $1,100? Try a lower-tech workaround: Follow your photos with snapshots of the readout from a cheap GPS unit and type in the coordinates later as tags on Flickr. As GPS becomes more of a must-have feature, you'll see this kind of kung fu embedded in all your gadgets. Imagine checking your computer to see exactly where you left your glasses.

loaded more than 250 million times. The program's seamless zoom-in feature has become ubiquitous on television news shows. And there are dedicated sites—such as Google Sightseeing and Virtual Globetrotting—built for scouring and saving odd and interesting finds from not only Google Earth but also competing 3-D globes like NASA's World Wind and Microsoft's Live Search Maps. Scientists, students, and government agencies use Google Earth layers to display their data to the public—the migration of a tagged whale shark in the Atlantic, say, or the latest earthquake activity in the Hayward fault zone. Google provides extras, like photographs from *National Geographic* and restaurant reviews from Yelp. Or you can turn on third-party layers that monitor commercial US planes in flight or that mark the world's best surf spots, complete with webcam video. "It's always been the case that maps have value because they show one subset of data and hide the rest," says David Weinberger, author of *Everything Is Miscellaneous*, a new book about the value of disorder in the information age. Given the infinite data that can be layered into Google Earth, however, we can now "include everything, then sort and draw the maps on the fly."

In the midst of all this cacophony, Google is discovering that a smart, effective search engine is once again the key. Google Earth and Google Maps have long had search boxes, but you couldn't find much. Typing in "pizza New York," for example, brought up links to sites that Google itself had generated, usually by buying up Yellow Pages listings or crawling the Web for pizza mentions that had New York addresses.

But with the launch of My Maps, Google is anchoring its new search strategy to KML. The company is indexing *all* KML files on the Web—it has cataloged several million so far—and is working with the Open Geospatial Consortium to make KML the standard. "Right now, Google Maps is mostly about searching for businesses," says Jessica Lee, a Google product manager. "But what we don't have is the sort of niche, long-tail content. We don't know where all the endangered species or the pandas in China live, or where the best places to go bird-watching are. By providing the tools, we can let other people create it."

The underlying digital imagery, meanwhile, is constantly reflecting more of the real world. In late May, Google announced Street View, an ambitious project that incorporates street-level photography into Google Maps for the San Francisco Bay Area, New York, Las Vegas, Denver, and Miami. (Microsoft's mapping products already contained street-level photographs for a few cities.) It's not hard to imagine a cell phone that pinpoints your location and then shows you a digital version of the city block in front of you, just as you see it, but annotated with all of the geoweb's information you need to find nearby a store, office, or restaurant. In essence, as Mike Liebhold at the Institute for the Future puts it, "you'll be able to click on the real world."

The New World

Going Off the Grid

For smartcard-carrying citizens of the 21st century, leaving home without an RFID-safe wallet is the equivalent of wearing a T-shirt with your Social Security number silk-screened on it. That's why, about a year ago, Difrwear began offering billfolds with a built-in mesh Faraday cage to block RFID scanners. (Think of it as a tinfoil hat for your bank account.) In a completely wired world, radio-proof accessories, buildings, and even entire neighborhoods will serve as disconnected oases, the only ways to go offline.

Online maps are clearly no longer just useful toys for finding your way to the stadium. During Hurricane Katrina, the Air Force used Google Earth to map out hundreds of rooftop rescues in New Orleans. Later, though, a user noticed that some of Google's satellite images of the city had been replaced with ones that predated Katrina. After reading press reports, congressmember Brad Miller (D-North Carolina) wrote to CEO Eric Schmidt complaining that the company "appears to be doing the victims of Hurricane Katrina a great injustice by airbrushing history." Google quickly replaced the images—which it said had been added automatically because their resolution was higher—with post-storm satellite photos.

"It was a surprise," says Chikai Ohazama, a Keyhole founder who now manages Google's constant updating of satellite and road map data. The incident, he says, "has definitely given me an appreciation that the database has become so much a part of people's lives."

And part of people's politics. Countries like Morocco and Bahrain have tried to block Google Earth, only to have residents smuggle in PDF files of the data. The BBC recently reported that Iraqi residents have been using the software to plot escape routes that avoid insurgent hot spots. And Hanke's team was accused of censorship when it swapped in alternate imagery of Basra after Britain said insurgents were using Google Earth to target its soldiers.

Censorship is only one part of a broader issue: Who controls the maps we use, and how much can we trust them? "Mapping has always been a tool of dominance," says Michael Goodchild, the UC Santa Barbara geographer. "There is no such thing as an objective map." It's no coincidence, he says, that the last golden age of mapmaking was the colonial era, when cartographers were dispatched to catalog western Europe's conquests around the world. James Rennell's maps weren't just an effort to understand India; they were a means to show, as he once said, "the advantages that may be derived from our territorial acquisitions."

Today the power still lies in the hands of the map makers. The only difference is that we're all mapmakers now, which means geography has entered the complex free-for-all of the information age, where ever-more-sophisticated technology is better able to reflect the world's rich, chaotic complexity. "Once you express location in human terms, you get multiple places with the same name, or political issues over where boundaries are, or local differences," says David Weinberger. "As soon as you leave the latitude/longitude substrate, you get lost in the ambiguous jumble of meaning. It's as close to Babel as we get."

ITEM 6.14 ■ Aerial Streetview Photo

This high-resolution photo, which captures a moment on a busy city street, is similar to kinds of moment-by-moment images of places available to users of Google's "Street View" maps.

Now on Google Maps: You

The Denver Post
(2007)

> **FYI** This editorial was published in *The Denver Post* on June 9, 2007. Editorial pieces signed by the Editorial Board are a regular feature of most newspapers in the United States. The fact that the board signs an opinion piece means that it is the consensus opinion of the entire editorial staff rather than just one writer.

Google's new pavement-level photographic maps remind us a little of "Candid Camera," the long-ago TV show that caught people in the act of being themselves.

Unlike "Candid Camera," a product of times before the Internet, Google's high-resolution street maps, called "Street View," are available 24/7 worldwide, packed with images taken at a moment in time. For some unwitting subjects, that moment in time was less than auspicious.

In San Francisco, Google's cameras caught a man picking his nose on a street corner. In Miami, protesters are seen picketing outside an abortion clinic. In other cities, men are seen entering adult book stores or leaving strip clubs.

Such embarrassing or compromising images are raising questions of privacy and whether Google has gone too far in trying to make the world more accessible. Those are legitimate concerns, even in an era of cellphone cameras and police surveillance eyes, like those that line sections of East Colfax Avenue.

While the Google images catch fleeting moments in time, they really aren't so fleeting, given that they're displayed on the Internet's leading search engine.

Denver is one of five cities—along with the San Francisco Bay area, New York, Las Vegas and Miami—that Google has chosen for its first run of Street View.

In some of Denver's downtown photos, the sky is overcast and the images of people are dark and blurry. At the corner of University Boulevard and East Alameda Avenue, last fall's pumpkin patch is visible.

Only parts of Denver have been mapped so far. But eventually, we can imagine that one of us will spot ourselves or someone we know in an unflattering or far-too-personal posture, like the lady in Oakland who found her street on Google's map. When she zoomed in on her apartment building, she was startled to see her cat staring out the living room window.

While such images are no different from what everyone can capture or see walking down the street, in a free society we expect some level of anonymity. Beyond embarrassing moments, there's also the issue of personal security.

Amazon.com abandoned its photographic maps last year after privacy concerns were raised. Its cameras photographed women walking into domestic violence shelters. For now, Google seems to be taking the concerns seriously, and that's the responsible thing to do. It says it will update the photos periodically, and is offering a "help" button on Street View so users can request removal of an objectionable image. Google also hopes to avoid an Amazon.com-type situation by not displaying images of shelters.

Smile. You're on Candid Google.

CONSIDER

1. Evan Ratliff traces complicated developments in mapping technologies for the readers of *Wired*, a magazine aimed at nonspecialists. How successful do you think he is in making the material clear and understandable? What strategies does he use to make technical information accessible?

2. In the concluding paragraph of Ratliff's article, David Weinberger compares the current state of mapmaking to the Tower of Babel. What do you think he means by this analogy? Do you agree that the democratic, easy-to-access nature of new mapping technologies has led to a chaotic "jumble" of meaning? Why or why not?

3. Which of the developments described in Ratliff's article and the *Denver Post* editorial do you find most intriguing? Which do you find troubling or potentially problematic? Why?

4. What limits should be placed on companies' ability to capture and display images of the Earth? When those images contain private homes, cars, or other structures—or people—should companies be required to obtain permission to use them? Who should have access to and be responsible for controlling such information?

The Map

Elizabeth Bishop
(1946)

Land lies in water; it is shadowed green.
Shadows, or are they they shallows, at its edges
showing the line of long sea-weeded ledges
where weeds hang to the simple blue from green.
Or does the land lean down to lift the sea from under,
drawing it unperturbed around itself?
Along the fine tan sandy shelf
is the land tugging at the sea from under?

The shadow of Newfoundland lies flat and still
Labrador's yellow, where the moony Eskimo
has oiled it. We can stroke these lovely bays,
under a glass as if they were expected to blossom,
or as if to provide a clean cage for invisible fish.
The names of seashore towns run out to sea,
the names of cities cross the neighboring mountains
—the printer here experiencing the same excitement
as when emotion too far exceeds its cause.
These peninsulas take the water between thumb and finger
like women feeling for the smoothness of hard-goods.

Mapped waters are more quiet than the land is,
Lending the land their waves' own conformation:
and Norway's hare runs south in agitation,
profiles investigate the sea, where land is.
Are they assigned, or can the countries pick their colors?
—What suits the character or the native waters best.
Topography displays no favorites; North's as near as West.
More delicate than the historians' are the map-makers' colors.

> **FYI** Elizabeth Bishop (1911–1979) wrote numerous poems concerned with travel and places. She was known for the meticulous methods she used in composing and revising her poems. She would often work on a poem for months, even years, polishing the language until it conveyed the ideas exactly as she wished. "The Map" first appeared in her collection *North and South* in 1946.

CONSIDER

1. What details do you notice in "The Map"? Do these details tell us more about geography or about human activities?

2. How do you interpret Bishop's claim in the final lines that "more delicate than the historians' are the map-makers' colors"? In what ways can maps be thought of as history?

COMPOSE

3. Find a map of an area you have an interest in, and compose either a poem or a one- or two-paragraph description telling what the map expresses about its subject. Consider the geographical features covered by the map as well as design elements used by the mapmakers as you explain how the map can be regarded as an interpretation of the place.

On Maps and Globes

Susan Neville
(2001)

> **FYI** Susan Neville is the author of four works of creative nonfiction: *Indiana Winter; Fabrication: Essays on Making Things and Making Meaning; Twilight in Arcadia;* and *Iconography: A Writer's Meditation.* Her prize-winning collections of short fiction include *In the House of Blue Lights,* and *Invention of Flight.* She teaches writing at Butler University and in the Warren Wilson MFA Program for Writers. The essay that follows is taken from *Fabrication* (2001), a series of pieces inspired by visits Neville made to factories throughout the Midwest to observe how everyday products are manufactured.

My daughter spins a globe and asks me questions.

Who put these lines, she asks, across the continents? And how much blood was used to draw them? And who keeps the record of the bridges and the lanes on this connecting road? And who decided on the color of this county?

And what's the distance between here where I'm living out my life, and there, where you live yours?

And if we took the places where we're standing, and we pinned them both together, behind the point where we were joined, would there always be a fold or pleat of shadow?

And if the stars are rushing out toward some edge, is the distance between each molecule increasing?

Of course I tell her I don't know.

And I ask myself about the distance between a real and a made-up place, between this hill and that abstraction, between this word and understanding, between transgression and forgiveness.

I try to find some answers to these questions, but most days the evidence seems inconclusive.

Every day this week a globe has risen orange and tangled itself in the branches of the eastern oak tree. Every day this week the globe has disappeared and left a brief vermilion cloud in the branches of the western sycamore. In between, the blue between the earth and stars was so unseasonably intense it shattered windows. What do I know that I can count on knowing again tomorrow? The sun rises, the sun sets, but from what I can observe it might as well be pulled by chariots. The earth might as well drop off to nothing at the edge right there behind my neighbor's.

I need someone who's been someplace to tell me where I am and how to get to someplace else.

He hovers over a light table, North Carolina spread beneath his fingers. A negative made of something like cellophane, as red as cherry Jell-O, covers the entire table. He moves a jeweler's glass from one place to another. All the other lights are off. Even the shadows in the room are red, and the round lens of his glasses, and the steel of the X-acto blade's reflecting red, and he's cutting and peeling the red plastic negative to get a perfect line.

It's these hands that scribe the microscopic lines that tell you whether the road you want to travel has two or four lanes and where the exits are. He cuts the parallel lines between one highway shoulder and another so cleanly on the red negative that the printer's ink will be trapped between the lines, a good clean fill. If he cuts a jagged line, it will look like hell, and you're liable to think there's a jog in the road ahead, when there isn't one.

He's done this job for his entire working life.

On a good day, the cartographer will focus so completely on the line that the world outside the light table completely disappears or, rather, the world becomes that line and he lets himself fall into it. This is the zen of cartography. If the blade is dull or the red too brittle, or if his concentration slips, he has to begin again at the beginning. If he focuses on the entire project, he says, the trip is overwhelming. If he focuses on the point where the blade meets the negative, time disappears. North Carolina, Australia, Greenland, New York City: it's always the same trip.

And it always begins where someone else left off. Like poetry, a map is an attempt to bring the whole of the physical universe into one point where you can see it, an attempt to bring what seems like chaos into something meaningful on a human scale. We map the ocean, and we map what we see of the stars. The question is always what metaphor to use, what shape to scatter these disparate points across, what shape will most closely resemble the mystery of the thing itself. Like journalism, a modern map is always an attempt at objectivity, yet always somehow subjective, always an attempt to bring wildness under control.

This cartographer alone in this red-lit glowing heart of a room in Indianapolis could easily get us lost. He could confuse us, but he won't. A cartographer draws a line between here and there so that we can find "there" when we want to. The line shows that someone's been there. It shows that we can get there. This room is devoted to accuracy, to being as correct as human beings can be, which is to say that in certain ways we are deluded. Greenland is not that big. The sharper your focus, the more the map has the shape of the land it's abstracting, the more it resembles the thing itself.

And once, the cartographer explains, despite all the edits each map goes through, the company sold a map of the United States for fifteen years before a little girl in Tucson, Arizona, discovered that the name of her city was misspelled. The final edit.

Mapmakers steal whatever they're allowed to. The content comes from the place itself; they can copyright a certain combination of font and color. Now and then a cartographer will insert a mythical place to foil potential plagiarists—a town named after your company, the name of your girlfriend's mother—and the cartographer can choose a color for the land or ocean and you can choose the font, but for the most part you're not allowed to be creative. You don't add flourishes, you don't draw gargoyles in uncharted lands; a modern map doesn't call attention to its fabricated nature.

But it is fabricated. It's an illusion of realism. Someone in Australia called last week and wants to put that continent in North America, and why not? Who says that North is up and South is down? You can't just make a world, you have to think about these things and what they mean.

And then there are the changes in fashion. Wrought iron's a big deal now. Everything used to be mahogany, then along came distressed maple. Colors begin to look like last season's colors, the continents wearing old-fashioned, worn-out clothes.

So how is the world made?

It's made in two hemispheres, and in the shape of a flower.

Each hemisphere is drawn with twelve petals. The ocean is the color of the sky, the lettering is black, and the continents are shades of green and orange and purple. The rosettes are broken in odd places. A tip of New South Wales floats with New Zealand. Half of Zimbabwe floats with Angola and half with Madagascar. The Galapagos Islands are cut in two and there's an entire blue petal with nothing but the South Atlantic Ocean. Look at your globe closely, and you'll see that it's printed on paper in the shape of orange slices.

> **Like journalism, a modern map is always an attempt at objectivity, yet always somehow subjective, always an attempt to bring wildness under control.**

The world is made in nine and twelve and sixteen inches. The world is made in blue and antique. The world is made in paper and in plastic. The world is made in standard shades and in colors like kiwi and in inks like cobalt and gold that look expensive for those places that need to be filled with conservative, expensive-looking globes. The world can talk, the world can be flat or bumpy. The world can be lit from without or within.

And here's the painful truth:

The world is made on an assembly line. Every day, hundreds are created.

There are so many of them made. How could each one possibly be special?

And how could there possibly be exploding stars, my daughter asks, and were they ever for one second important in some cosmic scheme, and is our sun really going to burn itself out and when it does, are there other worlds being born somewhere to take our place?

And when they take our place, if they do, what will happen to, among other things, Shakespeare? Will God keep *Romeo and Juliet* up there with His collected works? How will *King Lear* hold up alongside the classics of some backwater near Alpha Centauri or some part of the sky we haven't even mapped yet?

My daughter overhears the teenage siblings of her friends. Oh yes, you are the special one, my only love, dame Juliet, dear Romeo, and without you I couldn't live one more second. All day long I think of you.

Here in the globe factory, there are stacks and stacks of flattened worlds and hundreds of spinning globes suspended from the ceiling. There are hundreds of them all rolling down parallel tracks, all constantly moving from here to there, from one side of the universe of this warehouse to the other until they're folded into boxes.

How was the morning after the big bang? my daughter asks. Did worlds explode like this and was there someone there to hang them up in space exactly where they should go, to find the best possible place for that candle sconce, that chandelier, the proper setting for this whole experiment.

The universe where the worlds are made, I said, smells oddly like a bowling alley.

And how was it formed, this world?

Sexually.

After the rosette is cut, the scrap discarded, it's joined to cardboard and formed into two half shells by machinery that comes, again like flowers, in genders. The female part is a metal mold engraved with mountains. The male part is a pole that pushes the cardboard down into the mold and allows the petals of the earth to come together into a half sphere. When the male and female parts have joined together, the mountains swell up on the earth's surface, and the hemispheres are hot to the touch.

They're so hot it takes a while to cool.

Once they do, they move to the drill press, where they dance and spin with joy, off-center like hula hoops; the rough edges are trimmed, and it begins again, this sexual process, this paper mating. A bead of glue is placed on a diaphragm hoop and inserted partway into one hemisphere and then the other hemisphere slides down onto the cardboard hoop until they're joined finally in marriage, the north and south, the up and down, the yin and yang, and then the balls roll down a track like the tracks where they store bowling balls—that metaphor again.

> **The world is made on an assembly line. Every day, hundreds are created. There are so many of them made. How could each one possibly be special?**

But even after marriage, there's still a crack, as there is in any human system, and something could insert itself and split the two asunder if it weren't for the woman whose job is to put a thin strip of self-adhesive equator tape around the belly. Globe after globe, she affixes equators, the thinnest tape. There can't be a wrinkle; it has to cover the crack completely and it's a tape the size of a line you'd draw with a felt-tipped marker. She's done this for ten years, eight hours a day. If she makes a mistake, that entire world is ruined.

So she pays attention to each and every one. Some days she tapes two thousand globes on one shift. Thirty-five people work each day in the globe department. The sparrow falls, they see it. The equator woman is good at what she does. She hardly ever makes mistakes.

Of course the plastic worlds are something else entirely. The human skill is entirely in the speed you work and in your ability to stay out of the way of the machinery.

There's one large machine that heats the printed plastic and then a gust of air sucks the plastic down into a hemisphere. Over and over, a woman places the plastic on a machine, the machine sucks, the woman places the plastic, the machine sucks. She takes the plastic hemisphere and places it on a stack of other hemispheres like a stack of helmets. OK, I admit it. I hate plastic. The machine sucks. I love the paper globes.

Remember the part in *West Side Story* where Maria spins before a mirror and sings? The sight of one thousand worlds hanging from the ceiling takes your breath away like good music, it does, but my favorite thing in all of creation is the moment when the globes move one by one, like teenagers, in front of something like three showerheads, three blow-dryers, and they twirl around like Maria while they're covered from head to toe with shining lacquer. They go into this room all preteen dull and they come out sixteen years old with shining hair and singing "I Feel Pretty."

There used to be a man here spraying the top, then the middle, and then the bottom all day long, but now this is one area where the globes are all alone, without the parents, and they dance for joy and come out of the ballroom with glazed and shining secret faces.

And I dearly love the spinning lathes and the dark unglobed room where two men stand and fabricate the metal bases and meridians from coins of blank steel. There's no brilliant color here, but without the base, the world's globes would roll off tables, back behind living room sofas.

On a lathe it only takes five seconds to take a flat coin and spin it into the shape you want. Like the lacquer room, you get this rush somehow from your eye feeling the surface of the metal spin into folds and waves, like the earth's crust. The men hold two poles, in the shape of hedge clippers, their arms out like they're pushing a wheelbarrow, and the lathe spins and they push the metal coins against the chuck and voilà, it's a rounded base. Then they cuff the small edges on another spinning wheel.

Of course the base they're spinning could literally be stamped in some more automated process, but these two men would lose their jobs, and for now the capital investment would be greater than the salaries and benefits paid to them. So this is a process on its eventual way out, unfortunately. Because there's something in the way these men work the lathe, like a potter at the wheel or a weaver spinning yarn, where you can see the shape taking form because of the rapid turning that echoes the way a teacher uses a flashlight and a finished globe to show the spinning of the still unfinished earth. It's a kinetic and at the same time metaphorical knowledge of the way the universe was formed. We felt it long before we knew it, that is, if we know anything at all. The lathe, on the other hand, feels true and sturdy, the way you feel some hand against your shoulder when you wobble too far one way or another.

There's no substitute for this kind of knowledge. You have to feel it.

And why is the world still made like this when all the maps you need are on computer programs? In addition to the globes, there are more than ten thousand maps in stacks against the wall or being rolled and cut on tables. Political maps, physical maps, historical maps: a map of the Colonial Possessions of World Powers in 1914, another of Europe in 1648, still another showing Voyages and Discoveries to 1610, and another of Western Land Claims and the Ordinance of 1787. Why all these anachronistic objects? Why are all these people working? Why the postal service shipping these boxes? Why is all this necessary?

> **And why is the world still made like this when all the maps you need are on computer programs?**

I know the answer to that one, my daughter says. It's because, she says, they're pretty things. And when someone is talking with real children in a class and someone asks where is Romania, the teacher can take minutes to go to the computer and call something up upon the screen or she can pull a map down from the ceiling or send the globe on one more rotation around the classroom, passed hand to hand, right there.

And it only takes a split second. And your hand might brush against your teacher's hand, or your best friend's, or some boy you like. It's the way it is, she says, when you pass those plates of glass cups at church.

I run my hand across a globe. You feel the body of the earth when you do this. You feel the roll of mountains, the smooth surface of plateaus. You feel the ocean. You sense the children who have gone before you. You think of the mysteries of travel and return. You think of gravity. Your body remembers a particular basketball and hoop, a particular car trip to Florida, the love that binds you to one place and not another one. And through that one place, if you love it deeply, to every other place there is, to every possibility.

Everything you need to know, my daughter says, the answer to every single question you could think to ask your teachers. For that one moment, you can sense the answers. For that one moment only, it's right there in your hand.

CONSIDER

1. At the beginning of this essay, Susan Neville's daughter spins a globe and asks her mother questions—questions that continue throughout the piece. What kinds of things do the maps inspire Neville's daughter to wonder about? What might Neville be suggesting about the functions and importance of maps?

2. Why do you think Neville describes the manufacturing process at the globe factory in such exhaustive detail? What might her purpose be?

3. At one point, Neville asks why people still bother to make maps "when all the maps you need are on computer programs." What answer(s) does she give to this question? Do you agree?

COMPOSE

4. Neville says, that "a modern map is always an attempt at objectivity, yet always somehow subjective, always an attempt to bring wildness under control." Do you agree? Write two or three paragraphs exploring your response to this claim, drawing on material from other readings and images in this chapter to support your ideas.

CHALLENGE

5. Create a map of a place that is important to you, choosing a format and medium that allows you to record the kinds of information you most want to convey. Review the different kinds of maps presented in this cluster to help you make your selections.

Cluster 6.2
Life Science

We often think about the biological and genetic sciences in paradoxical ways. Recent advances in technology have dramatically expanded knowledge in these fields beyond what scientists even twenty years ago could have imagined. Developments in medical imaging enable scientists to map physiological processes not visible to the human eye, and the Human Genome Project took advantage of advances in computing to construct a complete map of human DNA. Knowledge in these fields is now so sophisticated and advanced that it seems as though there's not much else to discover. Yet we all recognize that life is an infinitely complex and mysterious process—that no matter how sophisticated our research, we are, after all, dealing with a phenomenon that we will never fully understand.

This tension between scientific knowledge and life's mysteries probably explains why issues surrounding genetic research capture our public imagination, sparking both excitement and fear. Cautionary tales about genetic experiments run amok have been the stuff of popular entertainment for centuries: *Frankenstein* and *Brave New World* are still among the most widely read novels, and Ridley Scott's cult classic film *Blade Runner* retains a huge fan following nearly 25 years after its release (see the movie posters on page 361). Such dystopic visions tell just part of the story, however. Many people, like writer Nicholas Wade in "Genetic Engineers Who Don't Just Tinker" see immense positive potential in biological research, envisioning a time when scientists can cure diseases before they start, create non-polluting fuels, or even alter the genes of an acorn so that it grows into a house rather than a tree.

The texts and images in this cluster explore exactly these kinds of advances, looking at new knowledge in the sciences, including advances in cloning and genetic modification of animals such as glow-in-the-dark cats and fish. We consider how these rapid advances put scientists into new roles—as creators who "write" new DNA codes and "build" new organisms—that go beyond traditional collection and reporting of data. The complexity of these new roles is explored in Natalie Angier's "Pursuing Synthetic Life, Dazzled by Reality" and the artworks from the *Gene(sis)* exhibit. Finally, we consider how new developments in biology and genetics are reported to and interpreted by the public in Max Houck's "*CSI*: Reality," examining how these texts help us to understand this work and its larger implications.

FYI

ITEM 6.15 ■ **Movie Posters for *Frankenstein*, 1931; *Blade Runner: The Final Cut*, 2007 (recut of 1982 original film); and *Gattaca*, 1997.**

Widely regarded as classics of the genre, *Frankenstein*, *Blade Runner*, and *Gattaca* explore the perils of using science and technology to manipulate human life: The 1931 adaptation of Mary Shelley's novel features Boris Karloff as Dr. Frankenstein's ill-fated creation; *Blade Runner* stars Harrison Ford as a futuristic bounty hunter who falls in love with a cloned "replicant"; and *Gattaca* portrays a genetically engineered society in which "inferiors" are euthanized at age thirty.

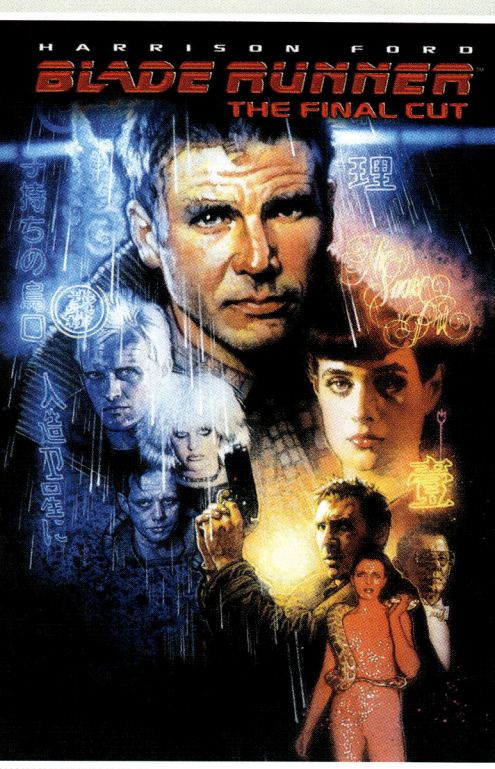

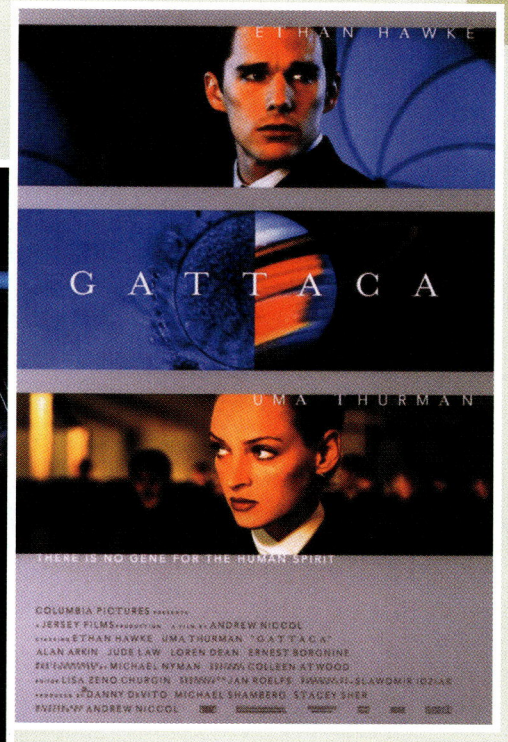

CONSIDER

1. What do the images in the posters suggest about our anxieties about scientific interventions into human life? What ethical, political, or social questions can you infer? Point to specific details and design features to support your responses.

2. If you didn't know when each of these movies was released, would you be able to make an accurate guess by looking at the posters? How could you tell? Point to specific details of content and design that provide clues. Do you see any evidence that attitudes about science and technology have changed over the years?

COMPOSE

3. To what degree have your own perceptions of the limits and possibilities of science been influenced by popular culture? Write a few paragraphs exploring this question, citing particular examples of books, movies, television, or other popular texts that have made a strong impression on you.

4. View one of these films and write a review of it, following the assignment on page 330.

Genetic Engineers Who Don't Just Tinker

Nicholas Wade
(2007)

> **FYI** Nicholas Wade is the author of numerous books, the most recent of which is *Before the Dawn: Recovering the Lost History of Our Earliest Ancestors* (2006). He is also a longtime science reporter for the *New York Times*, where the following article appeared on July 8, 2007.

Forget genetic engineering. The new idea is synthetic biology, an effort by engineers to rewire the genetic circuitry of living organisms.

The ambitious undertaking includes genetic engineering, the now routine insertion of one or two genes into a bacterium or crop plant. But synthetic biologists aim to rearrange genes on a much wider scale, that of a genome, or an organism's entire genetic code. Their plans include microbes modified to generate cheap petroleum out of plant waste, and, further down the line, designing whole organisms from scratch.

Synthetic biologists can identify a network of useful genes on their computer screens by downloading the gene sequences filed in DNA data banks. But a DNA molecule containing these various genes and their control elements would be a chain of hundreds of thousands of DNA units in length. Though human cells effortlessly duplicate a genome of three billion units, the longest piece of DNA synthesized so far is just 35,000 units long.

Scientists at the J. Craig Venter Institute in Rockville, Md., hope to take a giant stride in synthetic biology by creating a piece of DNA 580,076 units in length from simple chemicals, chiefly the material that constitutes DNA's four-letter chemical alphabet. This molecule would be an exact copy of the genome of a small bacterium. Dr. Venter says he then plans to insert it into a bacterial cell. If this man-made genome can take over the cell's functions, Dr. Venter should be able to claim he has made the first synthetic cell.

Such an achievement could suggest some new plateau has been reached in human control of life and evolution. But Dr. Venter's synthetic genome will probably be seen to represent a feat of copying evolution's genetic programming, not of creating new life itself.

Synthetic biologists, as they survey all the new genes and control elements whose DNA sequences are now accumulating in data bases, seem to feel extraordinary power is almost within their grasp.

"Biology will never be the same," Thomas F. Knight of M.I.T.'s Computer Science and Artificial Intelligence Laboratory wrote recently in describing the new engineering discipline he sees as emerging from it.

Adherents of the new discipline held their third annual conference last month in Zurich but their creations are still at the toy rocket stage. A dish of bacteria that generates a bull's eye pattern in response to the chemicals in its environment. A network of genes that synthesizes the precursor chemical to artemisin, an anti-malaria drug. "The understanding of networks and pathways is really in its infancy and will be a challenge for decades," says James J. Collins, a biomedical engineer at Boston University.

That hasn't stopped synthetic biologists from dreaming. "Grow a house" is on the to-do list of the M.I.T. Synthetic Biology Working Group, presumably meaning that an acorn might be reprogrammed to generate walls, oak floors and a roof instead of the usual trunk and branches. "Take over Mars. And then Venus. And then Earth"—the last items on this modest agenda.

Most people in synthetic biology are engineers who have invaded genetics. They have brought with them a vocabulary derived from circuit design and software development that they seek to impose on the softer substance of biology. They talk of modules—meaning networks of genes assembled to perform some standard function—and of "booting up" a cell with new DNA-based instructions, much the way someone gets a computer going.

The first practical applications of synthetic biology may not be so far off. "The real killer app for this field has become bioenergy," Dr. Collins says. Under the stimulus of high gas prices, synthetic biologists are re-engineering microbes to generate the components of natural gas and petroleum. Whether this can be done economically remains to be seen. But one company, LS9 of San Carlos, Calif., says it is close to that goal. Its re-engineered microbe "produces hydrocarbons that look, smell and function" very similarly to those in petroleum, said Stephen del Cardayre, the company's vice president for research.

> 'Grow a house' is on the to-do list of the M.I.T. Synthetic Biology Working Group, presumably meaning that an acorn might be reprogrammed to generate walls, oak floors and a roof instead of the usual trunk and branches.

Synthetic biologists are well aware that, like any new technology, theirs can be used for good or ill, and they have encouraged open discussion of possible risks at their annual meetings.

One possible danger is bioterrorism. According to a report in *Science*, Blue Heron Biotechnology, a DNA synthesis company, has already received requests, which it rejected, for DNA sequences encoding a plant toxin and part of the smallpox virus. Synthetic biologists hope that self-regulation will head off government supervision that could be expected to come in a field that has such potential for mischief.

Evolution continually refines its creations by means of the naturally occurring mutations in DNA that are the raw material of natural selection. This propensity to innovate may not be so welcome to synthetic biologists, who seek stable systems. But they hope to spot mutations with error-detection algorithms and then go back to the original cells. "You can think of it as a reboot," said Ron Weiss, a synthetic biologist at Princeton.

Even if the mutation problem can be squelched, it remains to be seen how far synthetic biologists can wrest evolution's strange system to entirely different purposes and whether the human organism is one they will propose to debug and upgrade.

CONSIDER

1. What are the key differences, according to this article, between synthetic biology and the more traditional research in genetic engineering? Summarize these differences in a few sentences.

2. Nicholas Wade observes that in the near future, synthetic biology will enable scientists to design "whole organisms from scratch." Would it be fair to say that synthetic biology is a creative activity, analogous to writing, art, or composing music?

3. Which of the projects or project ideas mentioned in the article intrigue you the most? Why?

COMPOSE

4. Wade ends the article by asking whether scientists will use the new developments in biology to "debug" and "upgrade" the "human organism." What kinds of human applications can you imagine for synthetic biology? What ethical considerations might such applications raise? Write two or three paragraphs exploring your thoughts on this issue.

FYI

ITEM 6.16 ■ Photos of Genetically Engineered Animals

In the above photo, the cat on the left is one of three created by a South Korean team of scientists using a synthetically produced gene that makes it glow red when exposed to ultraviolet light. (The cat on the right is an unaltered cat seen under the same ultraviolet light.) "Glowing" RFP genes are used by researchers to mark changes made in an organism's genome. The scientists say they created the cats in the hope of using altered felines to develop treatments for human genetic diseases.

Taikong Corporation of Taiwan, using a fluorescent protein extracted from jellyfish, created these genetically modified glow-in-the-dark fish shown in the photo on the right, which are now being sold as pets. In a *Wall Street Journal* interview, Taikong manager Bill Kuo said, "Imagine you come home from work, turn out the lights and look at these. It's very relaxing."

CONSIDER

1. What is your reaction to these photographs? Does seeing photos of the animals affect your opinion of the scientific developments that created them? Explain your response.

2. Would you consider buying a genetically engineered pet? Why or why not?

364   6.2 | LIFE SCIENCE

Edourdo Kac, *GFP Bunny*

FYI

ITEM 6.17 ■ **Art Works from *Gene(sis)*: Contemporary Art Explores Human Genomics**

In 2002, the Henry Art Gallery at the University of Washington opened an exhibition featuring art created in response to human genetics research. We reproduce three of the submissions here: Edourdo Kac's *GFP Bunny*, a genetically altered rabbit created in collaboration with geneticists; one of Bill Scanga's series *Eighteen Frogs with Pants Categorized by Color*, a comic critique that uses taxidermy to look at human attempts to manipulate animals; and Daniel Lee's *Juror No. 6*, a digitally manipulated photograph exploring the combination of human and animal forms.

Bill Scanga, from the series *Eighteen Frogs with Pants Categorized by Color*

Daniel Lee, *Juror No. 6*

CONSIDER

1. Which of the three works above makes the strongest statement, in your opinion? What details would you discuss to explain your choice?

2. These three works all use different media. How would you relate the different media to the topic of genetics? How does each piece's medium relate to its message?

CHALLENGE

3. Would you say that it is ethical to alter an animal for the purposes of art or entertainment (for example, for the purpose of creating trendy pets such as glow-in-the-dark fish)? How would you explain the ethical difference between altering an animal for art versus for science? What might make one more acceptable than the other? Hold a discussion with classmates, and debate these questions.

Pursuing Synthetic Life, Dazzled by Reality

Natalie Angier
(2008)

> **FYI** — Natalie Angier is a Pulitzer Prize-winning science writer for the *New York Times*, where this piece originally appeared on February 5, 2008. She is also the author of *Natural Obsessions; The Beauty of the Beastly* (1988); *Woman: An Intimate Geography*; and *The Canon: A Whirligig Tour of the Beautiful Basics of Science* (2004).

When scientists announced on Jan. 24 that they had reconstituted the complete set of genes for a microbe using just a few bottles of chemicals, the feat was hailed as a kind of shining Nike moment in the field of synthetic biology, the attempt to piece together living organisms from inert scratch.

Reporting in the journal *Science*, Dr. J. Craig Venter and his colleagues at the J. Craig Venter Institute said they had fabricated the entire DNA chain of a microbial parasite called *Mycoplasma genitalium*, exceeding previous records of sustained DNA synthesis by some 18-fold. Any day now, the researchers say, they will pop that manufactured mortal coil into a cellular shell, where the genomic code will "boot up," as Dr. Venter puts it, and the entire construct will begin acting like a natural-born *M. genitalium*—minus the capacity, the researchers promise, to infect the delicate tissues that explain the parasite's surname.

Yet even as researchers rhapsodize about gaining the power to custom-design organisms that will supply us with rivers of cheap gasoline, better chemotherapeutic agents or—here's my latest fantasy—a year-round supply of fresh eggnog, the most profound insights to emerge from the pursuit of synthetic life just may be about real life.

Scientists who seek to imitate living cells say they can't help but be perpetually dazzled by the genuine articles, their flexibility, their versatility, their childlike grandiosity. No matter what outrageous or fattening things we may ask our synthetic cells to do, scientists say, it's nothing compared with what cells already have done of their own accord, usually in the format of bacteria. Microbes have been found to survive and even thrive in places where if they had any sense they would freeze, melt, explode, disintegrate, starve, suffocate, or at the very least file a very poor customer review.

"We have micro-organisms that live in such strong acid or base solutions that if you put your finger in, the skin would dissolve almost instantly," Dr. Venter said in an interview. "There's another organism that can take three million rads of radiation and not be killed." How can a microbe withstand a blast of radioactivity that is a good 1,500 times greater than what would kill any of us virtually on the spot? "Its chromosome gets blown apart," Dr. Venter said, "but it stitches everything back together and just starts replicating again."

Given the wealth of biological and metabolic templates that nature has invented over nearly four billion years of evolutionary tinkering, scientists say, any sane program to synthesize new life forms must go hand in hand with a sustained sampling of the old. "My view is that we know less than 1 percent of what's out there in the biological universe," Dr. Venter said.

Last year, he and his colleagues went prospecting for new organisms in the deep midocean, long thought to be one of earth's least animate regions. Sure, life evolved in the seas, but shallow seas, where sunlight can penetrate, were considered the preferred site for biodiversity. Even with the startling discovery in the 1980s of life on the ocean floor, around the hydrothermal vents, the midocean waters couldn't shake their reputation as an impoverished piece of real estate: too far down for *solar energy*, too high up for its geothermal equivalent.

Yet when the Venter team began sampling the waters for the most basic evidence of life, the presence of genetic material, they found themselves practically awash in novel DNA. "From our random sequencing in the ocean, we uncovered six million new genes," he said, genes, that is, unlike any yet seen in any of the mammals, reptiles, worms, fish, insects, fungi, microbes or narcissists that have been genetically analyzed so far. With just that first-pass act of nautical sequencing, Dr. Venter said, "we doubled the number of all genes characterized to date."

> Given the wealth of biological and metabolic templates that nature has invented over nearly four billion years of evolutionary tinkering, scientists say, any sane program to synthesize new life forms must go hand in hand with a sustained sampling of the old.

Researchers assume that most of the novel DNA is microbial in origin, but they have yet to identify the organisms or see what they can do, because most microbes are notoriously difficult to cultivate in the lab. Bacteria may happily swim through toxic waste, but when it comes to confinement on an agar plate, thank you, they'd rather be dead.

Technical challenges notwithstanding, scientists have made some progress in investigating preposterous life forms and tallying the biochemical tools that such extremophiles use. Thermophilic microbes, for example, which can withstand temperatures of 238 degrees Fahrenheit, well above the boiling point of water, have stiffening agents in their membranes to keep them from melting away, and they build their cell proteins with a different assortment of amino acids than our cells do, allowing the construction of strongly bonded protein chains that won't collapse in the heat.

By contrast, said Steven K. Schmidt, a microbiologist at the University of Colorado in Boulder, when you look at organisms that thrive in subzero conditions, "their membranes are really loosey-goosey, very fluid," and so resist stiffening and freezing. It turns out there are a lot of these loosey-gooses around. Dr. Schmidt and his colleagues study the fridgophile life forms that make their home in glacial debris high in the Andes Mountains, 20,000 feet above sea level, where the scene may look bleak, beyond posthumous, but where, he said, "we've been pretty amazed at the extreme diversity of things we've found." The complexity of the Andean microbial ecosystem, he said, "is greater than what you'd find in your garden."

Yes, microbes were here first, and they've done everything first, and synthetic lifers are happy to scavenge for parts and ideas. Drew Endy, an assistant professor in the biological engineering department at the Massachusetts Institute of Technology, and his colleagues are putting together a registry of standardized biological parts, which they call BioBrick parts. The registry consists of the DNA code for different biological modules, interchangeable protein parts that they hope may someday be pieced together into a wide variety of biological devices to perform any task a bioengineer may have in mind, rather like the way nuts, bolts, gears, pulleys, circuits and the like are assembled into the machines of our civilization. Numbering some 2,000 parts and growing, the registry contains many recipes for clever protein modules invented by bacteria. One sequence engineered by researchers in Melbourne, Australia, encodes the instructions for a little protein balloon, for example. "It's based on a natural part found in a marine micro-organism that controls the buoyancy of the cell," Dr. Endy said.

Invisible though it may be, the microbial community ever keeps us afloat.

CONSIDER

1. How persuasive do you find Natalie Angier's claim that synthetically engineered life can never match the diversity and magnificence of nature? What evidence and examples does she cite to support this idea?

2. Angier's amazement focuses on the extraordinary diversity and adaptability of microbes. Why might she have chosen this focus? Can you think of other examples in the plant or animal world that she could have cited to support her claim?

CSI: Reality

Max M. Houck
(2005)

> **FYI** Max M. Houck is director of West Virginia University's Forensic Science Initiative, a program that develops research and professional training for forensic scientists. A trace evidence expert and forensic anthropologist, he was assigned to the Trace Evidence Unit at the FBI Laboratory from 1992 to 2001. He wrote this article for *Scientific American*, where it appeared in June 2005.

Attorneys, investigators and educators have felt the impact of television's popular forensics programs.

Forensic science has been the backbone of mystery stories from Edgar Allan Poe's Dupin adventures to Sir Arthur Conan Doyle's Sherlock Holmes tales to Jack Klugman's *Quincy* television series to today's wildly successful forensics shows. Holmes's methods presaged many actual techniques for linking physical evidence to the perpetrator of a crime, such as blood testing. Forensic science was codified as a profession in the early 1900s and exploded into the public consciousness in the 1990s with the advent of DNA analysis.

Forensics has never been more popular or popularized: eight crime dramas, including *CSI: Crime Scene Investigation* and its sibling programs, made it into the top 20 shows last October. On one Thursday that month, 27 percent of all American televisions that were turned on were tuned to *CSI*. On cable, CourtTV's *Forensic Files*, a documentary-style series featuring real crimes and real scientists, airs four days a week. Such programs give the impression that forensic laboratories are fully staffed with highly trained personnel, stocked with a full complement of state-of-the-art instrumentation and rolling in the resources to close every case in a timely fashion.

The gap between public perception and reality, however, is vast. And the popularity of these shows has led to complaints of a "*CSI* effect": at least some lawyers and judges have the impression that jurors schooled on *CSI*, which has been on the air since 2000, now demand unreasonable levels of physical evidence in trials. Whether the *CSI* effect truly exists as a quantifiable influence on courtroom behavior is still a subject of debate. Of no debate, though, is the effect that the *CSI* programs have had on the activities of police, who now collect more pieces of physical evidence than ever before; in academia, where some forensics programs are growing exponentially; and in overburdened working laboratories, which are a far cry from the glitzy, blue-lit analysis palaces of TV.

THE EFFECT IN THE COURTROOM

In one of this season's episodes of *CSI*, the plot included a television crew recording the activities of the fictional crime scene investigators. Lead researcher Gil Grissom rebuffs the TV crew's attempts, saying, "There's too many forensics shows on TV." Numerous attorneys and judges who believe that jurors are afflicted with the *CSI* effect would agree. But to what extent do *CSI* and its relatives influence the expectations that jurors bring to trials?

The press started to pay attention to the issue in 2003, collecting anecdotes from attorneys and judges about what appeared to be a change in the behavior of jurors. In 2005 Oregon district attorney Josh Marquis, vice president of the National District Attorneys Association, told CBS News, "Jurors now expect us to have a DNA test for just about every case. They expect us to have the most advanced technology possible, and they expect it to look like it does on television." Indeed, jurors in a Los Angeles murder case complained that a bloody coat had not been tested for DNA, even though such tests were unnecessary: the defendant had already admitted to having been at the crime scene. The judge noted that TV had taught jurors about DNA tests but not about when they should be used. In a study in Delaware of how juries deal with evidence, one juror tangling with a complex DNA case complained that these kinds of problems did not happen "on *CSI*."

> "Jurors now expect us to have a DNA test for just about every case. They expect us to have the most advanced technology possible, and they expect it to look like it does on television."

Attorneys blamed the *CSI* effect when a Baltimore jury acquitted a man of murder—testimony from two eyewitnesses was trumped by a lack of physical evidence. "I've seen a big change in jurors and what they expect over the last five years," defense attorney Joseph Levin of Atlantic City, N.J., told a local newspaper. "Jurors can ask questions of the judge while in deliberations, and they're asking about what they see as missing evidence. They want to know where the fingerprints are or the DNA. If it's not there, they want to know why." In the California murder trial of actor Robert Blake, prosecutors tried to persuade the jury by establishing Blake's motive and opportunity, and they presented witnesses who testified that Blake asked them to kill his wife. But no gunshot residue or blood spatter evidence was presented, and Blake was acquitted. A juror was quoted as saying that if the prosecutor "had all that information, that would have meant [Blake] was guilty." The defeat was the prosecutor's first in 50 murder cases.

Before *CSI* became popular, attorneys mostly worried about whether a jury was going to understand the complexity of DNA evidence. Now, though, many spend time clarifying the difference between television and reality—it is common for lawyers to ask prospective jurors about their exposure to forensics-themed TV programs. And some prosecutors are attempting to preempt any potential fallout from the *CSI* effect. In trials in Arizona, Illinois and California, they have put so-called negative evidence witnesses on the stand to alert jurors to the fact that real-life detectives often fail to find physical evidence, such as DNA or fingerprints, at crime scenes.

Several legal experts have argued, however, that the *CSI* effect may be illusory. The newspaper that quoted Atlantic City lawyer Levin also noted that Superior Court Judge Albert Garofolo said, "My initial reaction might have been 'Yes, there is a *CSI* effect.' But I think this may be more of a suspicion than anything else. There's a feeling this could be real, but in truth I can't recall a situation where I've heard a jury say they were expecting more."

In 2005 in the *Wall Street Journal*, Simon Cole of the department of criminology, law and society at the University of California, Irvine, and his student Rachel Dioso wrote: "That television might have an effect on courtrooms is not implausible.... But to argue that '*C.S.I.*' and similar shows are actually raising the number of acquittals is a staggering claim, and the remarkable thing is that, speaking forensically, there is not a shred of evidence to back it up. There is a robust field of research on jury decision-making but no study finding any *C.S.I.* effect. There is only anecdotal evidence."

What appears to be the first study of the *CSI* effect was published in February by Kimberlianne Podlas, an attorney and assistant professor of media law and ethics at the University of North Carolina at Greensboro. Podlas concluded that the chalices of, and reasoning for, acquittals were the same for frequent *CSI* viewers as for prospective jurors who did not watch the show—she saw no *CSI* effect. Several participants, however, said that a lack of forensic testing was an issue, despite the fact that physical evidence would not have resolved the hypothetical charges. Studies of real juries have been advocated, and at least five graduate students (three in the U.S. and two in England) are preparing theses examining the effect.

WHAT IS REAL?

Whether or not forensics shows are measurably influencing the demands and decisions of juries, television is unquestionably giving the public a distorted view of how forensic science is carried out and what it can and cannot do. The actors playing forensic personnel portrayed on television, for instance, are an amalgam of police officer/detective/forensic scientist—this job description does not exist in the real world. Law enforcement, investigations and forensic science are each sufficiently complex that they demand their own education, training and methods. And specialization within forensic laboratories has been the norm since the late 1980s. Every forensic scientist needs to know the capabilities of the other subdisciplines, but no scientist is an expert in every area of crime scene investigation.

In addition, laboratories frequently do not perform all types of analyses, whether because of cost, insufficient resources or rare demand. And television shows incorrectly portray forensic scientists as having ample time for every case; several TV detectives, technicians and scientists often devote their full attention to one investigation. In reality, individual scientists will have many cases assigned to them. Most forensics labs find backlogs to be a major problem, and dealing with them often accounts for most requests for bigger budgets.

> **Whether or not forensics shows are measurably influencing the demands and decisions of juries, television is unquestionably giving the public a distorted view of how forensic science is carried out and what it can and cannot do.**

Fictional forensics programs also diverge from the real world in their portrayal of scientific techniques: University of Maryland forensic scientist Thomas Mauriello estimates that about 40 percent of the forensic science shown on *CSI* does not exist. Carol Henderson, director of the National Clearinghouse for Science, Technology and the Law at Stetson University College of Law, told a publication of that institution that jurors are "sometimes disappointed if some of the new technologies that they think exist are not used." Similarly, working investigators cannot be quite as precise as their counterparts on the screen. A TV character may analyze an unknown sample on an instrument with flashing screens and blinking lights and get the result "Maybelline lipstick, Color 42, Batch A-439." The same character may then interrogate a witness and declare, "We know the victim was with you because we identified her lipstick on your collar." In real life, answers are seldom that definite, and the forensic investigator probably would not confront a suspect directly. This mismatch between fiction and reality can have bizarre consequences: A Knoxville, Tenn., police officer reported, "I had a victim of a car robbery, and he saw a red fiber in the back of his car. He said he wanted me to run tests to find out what it was from, what retail store that object was purchased at, and what credit card was used."

GROANING UNDER THE LOAD

Despite not having all the tools of television's *CSI* teams, forensic scientists do have advanced technologies that are getting more sophisticated all the time. Initial DNA-testing methods in the late 1980s required samples the size of a quarter; current methods analyze nanograms. The news routinely reports the solution of a cold case, a suspect excluded or a wrongful conviction overturned through advanced forensic technology. Databases of DNA, fingerprints and firearms ammunition have become important resources that can link offenders to multiple crimes.

Nevertheless, far from being freed to work telegenic miracles, many labs are struggling under the in-creasing demands they face. As police investigators gain appreciation for the advantages of science and also feel pressure to collect increasing amounts of evidence, they are submitting more material from more cases for forensic analysis. Police detectives who at one time might have gathered five pieces of evidence from a crime scene say they are collecting 50 to 400 today. In 1989 Virginia labs processed only a few dozen cases. The number of cases being submitted this year has ballooned into the thousands. Of course, not every item at a crime scene can or should be collected for testing. The remote chance of an item being significant has to be weighed against the burden of backlogged cases. But social, professional and political pressures based on unrealistic expectations engendered by television mean that if an officer brings in a bag filled with cigarette butts, fast-food wrappers and other trash, chances are good that most of the items will be scheduled for analysis.

And all that work will have to be done, in many cases, by already overloaded staffs. For example, the state of Massachusetts has 6.3 million people outside of Boston and eight DNA analysts for that region. (Boston has three analysts of its own.) New York City has eight million people and 80 DNA analysts. But Massachusetts and New York City have similar rates of violent crime (469.4 versus 483.3 per 100,000), which is the kind of crime most likely to involve DNA evidence. Massachusetts, like many other states, thus appears to be woefully understaffed. Thankfully, the state has recognized this imbalance and has authorized the hiring of more forensic DNA analysts.

A consequence of the new trends, then, is exacerbation of the already disturbing backlog problem. A study recently published by the Department of Justice's Bureau of Justice Statistics found that at the end of 2002 (the latest available data), more than half a million cases were backlogged in forensic labs, despite the fact that tests were being processed at or above 90 percent of the expected completion rate. To achieve a 30-day turnaround time for the requests of that year, the study estimated a need for another 1,900 full-time employees. Another Justice Department study showed that the 50 largest forensic laboratories received more than 1.2 million requests for services in 2002: the backlog of cases for these facilities had doubled in the course of one year. And these increases have happened even though crime rates have fallen since 1994.

Another side effect of the increased gathering of physical evidence is the need to store it for various lengths of time, depending on local, state or federal laws. Challenges for storing evidence include having the computers, software and personnel to track the evidence; having the equipment to safely stow biological evidence, such as DNA; and having adequate warehouse space for physical evidence. In many jurisdictions, evidence held past a certain length of time may be destroyed or returned. Storage can be a critical issue in old or cold cases—the Innocence Project at the Benjamin N. Cardozo Law School in New York City has found that the evidence no longer exists in 75 percent of its investigations into potentially wrongful convictions.

Just keeping track of the evidence that does exist can be problematic: a 2003 study by the American Society of Crime Laboratory Directors indicated that more than a quarter of American forensic laboratories did not have the computers they needed to track evidence. Mark Dale, director of the Northeast Regional Forensic Institute at the University at Albany and former director of the New York Police Department Laboratory, estimates that more than 10,000 additional forensic scientists will be needed over the next decade to address these various issues. In addition, appropriate modernization of facilities will cost $1.3 billion, and new instruments will require an investment of greater than $285 million.

THE EFFECT ON CAMPUS

On the positive side, through *CSI* and its siblings, the public has developed a fascination with and respect for science as an exciting and important profession unseen since the Apollo space program. Enrollment in forensic science educational programs across the U.S. is exploding. For example, the forensic program at Honolulu's Chaminade University went from 15 students to 100 in four years. At my institution, West Virginia University, the forensic and investigative sciences program has grown from four graduates in 2000 to currently being the third largest major on campus, with more than 500 students in the program.

The growth of existing programs and the advent of new ones have been such that the National Institute of Justice, in collaboration with West Virginia University, produced a special report, *Education and Training in Forensic Science: A Guide for Forensic Science Laboratories, Educational Institutions and Students*. The report formed the basis for an accreditation commission under the American Academy of Forensic Sciences. As of this past January, 11 programs had received provisional, conditional or full accreditation.

CSI's popularity may have also affected the demographics of forensic science. In the 1990s women and minorities were underrepresented as leads in television series with a scientific theme; the current slate of *CSI* dramas, however, has generally improved this representation. Women are now in the majority in forensic science educational programs in the U.S. and in much of the profession. Two thirds of forensic science laboratory management personnel are currently male, a figure sure to decrease as the newer women workers advance.

The best result of public interest in forensics, though, would be increased investment in forensics research. In the past, most research was conducted in police laboratories working on specific, case-related questions. But for technologies to advance markedly, testing is needed in the controlled environment of the academic laboratory. Such labs could investigate questions that clearly require more research. For example, recent legal challenges have called into question the long-held assumption of the absolute uniqueness of fingerprints, tool marks, bite marks, bullet striations and handwriting matches.

As forensic science is increasingly relied on, it must become more reliable: a recent National Institute of Justice report to Congress stated that basic research is needed into the scientific underpinning of impression evidence, such as tire marks or footprints; standards for document authentication; and firearms and tool-mark examination. The report also recommended that the federal government sponsor research to validate forensic science disciplines, addressing basic principles, error rates and standards of procedure. Clearly, more funding for such research would be beneficial: one must wonder why the U.S. spent a mere $7 million this fiscal year for basic forensic science research through the National Institute of Justice when $123 million was spent on alternative medicine through the National Institutes of Health.

One of the most fundamental obligations of any democratic government to its citizens is to ensure public safety in a just manner. Forensic science is an integral and critical part of the criminal justice process. In the 21st century properly educated, well-equipped, fully staffed forensic science laboratories are essential to the fulfillment of that obligation. The popular interest in forensic science is at an all-time high, as are the challenges to the veracity of forensic science methods and capacities. Even if no so-called *CSI* effect exists in the courtroom, the real effect is the realization of the need for the advancement of forensic science laboratories and research.

CONSIDER

1. Houck's article is an example of a causal argument: he first argues that the "*CSI* effect" exists, then traces some key effects of that trend. Write a brief summary of the article. How difficult did you find it to identify the major parts of the argument? How does Houck use structure, phrasing, and/or format to signal key points?

2. What evidence does Houck present to demonstrate that the "*CSI* effect" exists? Do you find his case convincing? Why or why not?

CHALLENGE

3. Watch an episode of a crime drama such as *CSI* or a movie whose plot relies significantly on science or technology. Take careful notes on the scientific concepts, developments, or procedures depicted, and then do research to investigate the show's accuracy. Write a short essay describing your findings.

ITEM 6.18 ■ Still from *CSI: Miami*

One of the most practical developments to result from recent findings in genetic science is the widespread use of DNA evidence in the court system, which has not only changed the ways in which crimes are investigated and prosecuted but has also captured the public's fascination, as the popularity of "scientific" crime dramas such as *CSI* illustrates.

CONSIDER

1. Examine the still from *CSI: Miami* in light of Max Houck's analysis in "*CSI*: Reality." What details in the image can you cite to support, refute, or complicate Houck's claims?

CHALLENGE

2. Conduct research on representations of criminal investigation in popular culture. What can you discover about the relationships between stories about crime fighting and technology over time? Write an essay detailing your findings.

Cluster 6.3
Living in Virtual Worlds

The Tyrian landscape depicted in the image below exists only in the collective imagination of the online inhabitants of ArenaNet's online role-playing game Guild Wars. Massively multiplayer online role-playing games (MMORPGs), which enable thousands of gamers to participate simultaneously in a virtual world through the Internet, are no longer the exclusive realms of the technological elite and the socially inept. Millions of players now "inhabit" the virtual worlds of games such as Guild Wars, World of Warcraft, Ultima Online, and others. These online communities have become a second life for many users, a virtual world forged by technology that exists only in cyberspace.

Science fiction writer William Gibson popularized the concept of "cyberspace" in his 1984 novel *Neuromancer*. For Gibson, the virtual world of cyberspace could best be understood as a "consensual hallucination." As the readings in this section show, however, the effects of cyberspace on the psychology, economics, ethics, and laws of humans in the "real world" can be quite profound. How do we respond to virtual information? Andrea L. Foster's "The Avatars of Research" addresses this issue, as do images of Second Life environments created by Boise State and Ohio State Universities. How are attachments to virtual selves different from real-life relationships? Alan Sipress offers some thoughts in "Does Virtual Reality Need a Sheriff?" Kevin Spivey's "Baby, You Mean the World of Warcraft to Me" offers a humorous take on this question. What legal principles govern behavior in a virtual world? Finally, Stephen Johnson makes a provocative case for the cognitive value of virtual literacy in "This Is Your Brain on Video Games."

ITEM 6.19 ■ **ArenaNet, Screenshot of Tyrian Landscape, Guild Wars**
Source: GuildWars.com screenshot. Copyright © ArenaNet, Inc. 2003–2008. Used by permission of ArenaNet, Inc.

The Avatars of Research

Andrea L. Foster
(2005)

> **FYI** Andrea L. Foster writes about technology issues for *The Chronicle of Higher Education*. This article first appeared in the September 30, 2005, issue of that publication.

At a recent instructional workshop at Elon University, a group of eight professors and staff members take their first steps in a virtual world called Second Life. Seated around computers, they tap their keyboards and move their mice so that their online characters walk around a virtual swimming pool.

The digital scene looks like a pool party attended by the world's clumsiest guests, as one after another stumbles into the water.

"I'm drowning!" cries Gerald Gibson, an assistant professor of communications, as he watches his online character go down in several feet of water.

"Hit page up and then control-c," advises Karen Marsh-Lovvorn, an instructional technologist at Elon, who led the summer workshop for professors, hoping to entice them to use Second Life in their classes. Mr. Gibson complies, and his character shoots up out of the water and lands poolside.

Though all this online frolicking may seem frivolous, the professors' interest in virtual worlds is strictly professional. These cartoonlike environments—called massively multiplayer online games—which can be played from anywhere in the world, have become popular laboratories for scholars to study individual and group behavior or test their entrepreneurial skills. Other virtual worlds studied by researchers include World of Warcraft and Everquest.

Second Life, in particular, has become a magnet for researchers because the world places few constraints on them. And Linden Lab, the San Francisco-based company that created the game two years ago, allows college students and scholars free entry to its make-believe world of 50,000 players worldwide. Other people paid a one-time fee of $10 to explore the world until this month, when Linden Lab announced free entry for everyone. Nonacademics who want to own "land" on which to build such things as virtual homes and entertainment areas must pay $10 a month for the rights. Participants mask their identities, taking on the roles of animated characters, known as avatars. They socialize, build neighborhoods, form groups of friends, and, in some cases, even marry. The connections and tensions that develop among avatars speak volumes about the behavior of people and organizations in real life, which is intriguing to sociologists, psychologists, and anthropologists, among other social scientists.

Business professors are interested in Second Life because subscribers create, buy, and sell the colorful characters, costumes, virtual belongings, buildings, and neighborhoods that populate the cyberuniverse. The digital inventions are purchased with a virtual currency called "Linden dollars," which can be exchanged for real money. Indeed, a few people make a living by selling real estate in Second Life for real money. Virtual goods worth an actual $18-million are sold among Second Life participants each year, according to Linden Lab.

"Going up and setting up a business in Second Life is fundamentally not that different from setting up a business in the real world," says Kevin Werbach, an assistant professor of legal studies and business ethics at the University of Pennsylvania's Wharton School. "You have to have a core set of skills in defining an idea, implementing it, selling it, and managing the processes, which is really the essence of being an entrepreneur."

RICH ENVIRONMENTS

Students, too, are drawn to this new world of research. Jon Maggio, a senior here at Elon, is fascinated by sociology and virtual worlds. So when a sociology professor suggested that he combine his two passions into a research project, he jumped at the opportunity.

Over the summer, Mr. Maggio followed a blog about goings-on in Second Life and was intrigued by what he read: Participants in the community strive for social acceptance, hire private investigators to spy on virtual spouses, hurl harassment charges at each other, and debate whether a virtual marriage ceremony performed by a minister's avatar is—well, real. In one scandalous case, two virtual characters reportedly developed such a strong connection that their human operators ditched their respective spouses and moved in together.

"There's so much here," says Mr. Maggio. "I could spend the rest of my life studying this thing."

He originally planned to center his sociology research project on Second Life. But he has recently expanded it to include two more popular virtual environments—World of Warcraft and Final Fantasy 11, which are more action-oriented than Second Life and offer the chance to slay dragons and monsters.

Mr. Maggio's research focuses on the intersection between virtual and real worlds, more specifically on the potential for abuse in the buying and selling of digital objects. Some allege that entrepreneurs have set up small offices crammed with computers where workers in developing countries, such as China, spend all day in virtual worlds in order to create and acquire the digital goods therein, which their bosses then trade for real money on sites like eBay. The bosses take most of the money and pay the workers less than a dollar an hour, according to reports, including a February column by Tom Loftus on msnbc.com.

Eventually Mr. Maggio plans to do graduate work in the budding field of cyberculture studies, studying the sociological aspects of virtual worlds.

He was introduced to Second Life by some students of Megan S. Conklin, an assistant professor of computer science at Elon, who is a self-described campus "evangelist" for Second Life.

She has asked her students to use the virtual community as a laboratory to explore issues concerning marriage, gender identity, social status, religion, and monetary policy, among other topics.

"I can get my students to understand in five minutes what I would normally have to lecture about for five hours," Ms. Conklin tells her colleagues at the Second Life workshop, which she leads along with Ms. Marsh-Lovvorn.

Ms. Conklin shows the Elon professors her avatar, named Professor Radiks. Dressed in a Victorian-era bustle and wide-brimmed hat, she moves around online amid the professors' avatars. These include Tatsui, a woman in a skintight red outfit; Liniope, a large, muscular man with a creepy gaze; and Ms. Marsh-Lovvorn's own avatar, Echinacea. (A gardener, the technologist named her characters after herbs.) The character looks like its creator, dressed in a purple shirt and black sweater-and-pants set, the same outfit worn by Ms. Marsh-Lovvorn during the workshop.

GROWING ATTRACTION

Computer scientists are not the only scholars making use of Second Life.

Architecture students at the University of Texas at Austin and at the University of California at Berkeley have used Second Life to create virtual buildings and public spaces to see what they might be like to inhabit. At the Wharton School, students are interested in testing their entrepreneurial and marketing techniques by setting up businesses in Second Life to bring in virtual cash.

Aaron Delwiche, an assistant professor of communication at Trinity University in San Antonio, had his students use Second Life in the spring of 2004 to study game design. They took advantage of object-creating tools in the virtual world to develop games that could familiarize new players with the software. Mr. Delwiche also had an expert on virtual worlds who lives in Copenhagen deliver a guest lecture to his class remotely, using the Second Life environment.

This month Linden Lab announced to Second Life participants that students from eight colleges would roam the virtual world during the fall semester. The students are enrolled in architecture, computer science, international business, sociology, and urban-planning courses, among others. In each class, the last name of the students' avatars is the same, so other avatars can easily spot which players are doing research.

Participants in Second Life don't always take kindly to being the subject of researchers' fascination, however. Some have complained that students are coy about their research or ask repetitive and inane questions.

Students in Ms. Conklin's class, all of whom are known in Second Life by the surname Radiks, were taken aback by some of the angry messages they received.

"I'm afraid I've had just about enough of these questions from Radiks," one avatar wrote in an online forum. "I'm not some kind of strange subject, here to be analyzed and questioned and interviewed and watched and photographed for a scientific or anthropological study at whatever rubbish uni they're from. I'm a person and I'm sick of this."

Ms. Conklin defended her students in the same online forum, saying they were abiding by Second Life's research-ethics policy, which requires researchers to identify themselves and to get the permission of a participant before publishing his or her comments.

WELCOMING STUDENTS

Linden Lab never anticipated that its environment would be widely used by college students, says Robin D. Harper, vice president for community development. But once professors began encouraging students to explore the online community, company executives put policies in place to entice college classes to the site.

Before the company began offering free access to Second Life this month, only students and professors in a class could explore the virtual world at no charge. Each class gets a parcel of virtual land on which to build housing, public parks, or casinos, for example, to test students' design skills and to attract other participants. For classroom use, the company waives its monthly "maintenance fee" of $25 for one acre. After the course ends, students can keep their avatars and continue using Second Life free.

Linden Lab has found that students and professors give the company useful advice on how to improve the virtual world, says Ms. Harper. Three years ago students in a class in architecture and urban planning at the University of Texas at Austin recommended that the company allow Second Life participants to join multiple groups in order to create closer social networks. The advice was taken.

"The challenge is for new teachers, who aren't that familiar with Second Life," to find the tools to create things, says Ms. Harper. "So our focus is more on helping them locate the resources they need."

Ms. Marsh-Lovvorn assumes that role at Elon. During the workshop, she shows the professors that by clicking on the "edit" and "appearance" menus in Second Life, they can modify their avatars' bodies, facial features, or race. They can make themselves as ordinary or freakish as they want, giving themselves oversize heads, long torsos, or fluorescent eyes. One character, Araiya Bomazi, appears to be part-human, part-squirrel.

Mr. Gibson, the communications professor, decided to change the gender of his avatar. "I'm tired of being in touch with my feminine side," he declared.

Ms. Conklin also presents the professors with a list of possible assignments for their students. Among them: Interview Second Life participants to determine why the avatars have a certain appearance or dress; investigate how the community's economy works; and discuss whether class hierarchies have emerged, and if so, how they work.

Ms. Conklin's students were able to experience firsthand the effects of tinkering with Second Life's internal economy.

In a popular activity within the community, participants spend Linden dollars to rate other avatars on their appearance and behavior, an activity that determines avatars' social status. (All Second Life participants are given a small sum of Linden dollars upon entering the world.)

In the middle of Ms. Conklin's three-week course in the winter term, Linden Lab raised the cost of rating an avatar from one to 25 Linden dollars, in order to tighten the money supply. "Some economics students immediately were able to start doing graphs and thinking about supply and demand and talking about monetary-policy issues," said Ms. Conklin. "It was really great."

Along with their online explorations, Ms. Conklin's students viewed the movie *The Matrix* and read *Snow Crash*, a 1992 science-fiction novel by Neal Stephenson that explores an alternative social world in cyberspace. (The avatars' surname, Radiks, is a reference to Radikal Kourier Systems, a company in the book.)

Second Life mimics much of what goes on in real life, but not everything. A player can change night to day at any time, an upheaval that registers only on his or her own computer screen. And Ms. Marsh-Lovvorn shows the professors that by clicking on the "fly" tab, at the bottom of the screen, they can take off like birds.

The professors do so and soar to Forcythia's Fantasy, a maze of walls, caverns, and greenery that includes animals in a stable, tents in a recreation area, and a castle.

Not every professor who has been introduced to Second Life is sold on it as a teaching tool.

Barth Strempek, an associate professor of business administration at Elon, says he is skeptical about using the software to teach business skills. "If I want to teach my students how to sell, I'm not sure this is the right place," he says. "I want them meeting people face to face." He also worries that the virtual environments could cut into young people's outdoor activities, like playing sports.

Ms. Conklin responds that because students are going to play around in virtual worlds anyway, they should be able to think critically about what is happening in the emerging social spaces. When students visit virtual worlds for class, she says, "at least they're doing homework in them."

ITEM 6.20 ■ Images of Academic Environments in Second Life

At Idaho State University, students studying public health train in Second Life to respond to virtual disasters such as this one.

Minerva Island, a research and teaching space developed by Dr. Sharon Collingwood for the Department of Women's Studies at the Ohio State University. It houses courses, discussion groups, and lectures, some conducted by avatars designed to represent famous women throughout history.

CONSIDER

1. Whether you have experience with virtual environments or not, how do you react to the notion that activities within these spaces can be seriously studied for insight into human behavior?

2. Both virtual academic environments such as Minerva Island and gaming environments such as Guild Wars are constructed to seem "real" in some way to their users. What is it about each imaginary spot that helps to make it a functional space? What does a virtual place have to do to be an appealing environment?

COMPOSE

3. "Going up and setting up a business in Second Life is fundamentally not that different from setting up a business in the real world," says Professor Kevin Werbach in Foster's article. Write an essay exploring that claim or one about any equivalent activity in a virtual environment. Is this a locale where issues such as "marriage, gender identity, social status, religion, and monetary policy" can be legitimately explored?

CHALLENGE

4. If you had the opportunity to buy land and "build" in Second Life, what would the landscape and any structures you created look like? Describe or draw them.

Does Virtual Reality Need a Sheriff?

Reach of Law Enforcement Is Tested When Online Fantasy Games Turn Sordid

Alan Sipress
(2007)

FYI — Alan Sipress is a staff writer for *The Washington Post*, where he has written dozens of articles on technology and the business of technology. This article first appeared in the *Post* on June 2, 2007.

Earlier this year, one animated character in Second Life, a popular online fantasy world, allegedly raped another character.

Some Internet bloggers dismissed the simulated attack as nothing more than digital fiction. But police in Belgium, according to newspapers there, opened an investigation into whether a crime had been committed. No one has yet been charged.

Then last month, authorities in Germany announced that they were looking into a separate incident involving virtual abuse in Second Life after receiving pictures of an animated child character engaging in simulated sex with an animated adult figure. Though both characters were created by adults, the activity could run afoul of German laws against child pornography, prosecutors said.

As recent advances in Internet technology have spurred millions of users to build and explore new digital worlds, the creations have imported not only their users' dreams but also their vices. These alternative realms are testing the long-held notions of what is criminal and whether law enforcement should patrol the digital frontier.

"People have an interest in their property and the integrity of their person. But in virtual reality, these interests are not tangible but built from intangible data and software," said Greg Lastowka, a professor at the Rutgers School of Law at Camden in New Jersey.

Some virtual activities clearly violate the law, like trafficking in stolen credit card numbers, he said. Others, like virtual muggings and sex crimes, are harder to define, though they may cause real-life anguish for users.

Simulated violence and thievery have long been a part of virtual reality, especially in the computer games that pioneered online digital role-playing. At times, however, this conduct has crossed the lines of what even seasoned game players consider acceptable.

In World of Warcraft, the most popular online game, with an estimated 8 million participants worldwide, some regions of this fantasy domain have grown so lawless that players said they fear to brave them alone. Gangs of animated characters have repeatedly preyed upon lone travelers, killing them and making off with their virtual belongings.

Two years ago, Japanese authorities arrested a man for carrying out a series of virtual muggings in another popular game, Lineage II, by using software to beat up and rob characters in the game and then sell the virtual loot for real money.

Julian Dibbell, a prominent commentator on digital culture, chronicled the first known case of sexual assault in cyberspace in 1993, when virtual reality was still in its infancy. A participant in LambdaMOO, a community of users who congregated in a virtual California house, had used a computer program called a "voodoo doll" to force another player's character to act out being raped. Though this virtual world was rudimentary and the assault simulated, Dibbell recounted that the trauma was jarringly real. The woman whose character was attacked later wept—"post-traumatic tears were streaming down her face"—as she vented her outrage and demand for revenge in an online posting, he wrote.

Since then, advances in high-speed Internet, user interfaces and graphic design have rendered virtual reality more real, allowing users to endow their characters with greater humanity and identify ever more closely with their creations.

Nowhere is this truer than in Second Life, where more than 6 million people have registered to create characters called avatars, cartoon human figures that respond to keyboard commands and socialize with others' characters. The breadth of creativity and interaction in Second Life is greater than on nearly any other virtual-reality Web site because there is no game or other objective; it is just an open-ended, lifelike digital environment.

Moreover, Linden Labs, which operates Second Life, has given users the software tools to design their characters and online setting as they see fit; some avatars look like their real-life alter egos, while others are fantastical creations.

This virtual frontier has attracted a stunning array of immigrants. Former senator John Edwards of North Carolina, a candidate for the [2008] Democratic presidential nomination, has opened a virtual campaign headquarters.[1] Reuters and other news agencies have set up virtual bureaus. IBM has developed office space for employee avatars. On May 22, Maldives became the first country to open an embassy in Second Life, with Sweden following this week.

Second Life is intended only for adults, and about 15 percent of the properties on the site—in essence, space on computer servers that appear as parcels of land—have been voluntarily flagged by their residents as having mature material. Though some is relatively innocent, in some locations avatars act out drug use, child abuse, rape and various forms of sadomasochism.

"This is the double-edged sword of the wonderful creativity in Second Life," Dibbell said in an interview.

One user found herself the unwilling neighbor of an especially sordid underage sex club. "Tons of men would drop in looking for sex with little girls and boys. I abhorred the club," wrote the user on a Second Life blog under the avatar name Anna Valeeva. She even tried to evict the club by buying their land, she wrote.

The question of what is criminal in virtual reality is complicated by disagreements among countries over what is legal even in real life. For example, virtual renderings of child abuse are not a crime in the United States but are considered illegal pornography in some European countries, including Germany.

After German authorities began their investigation, Linden Labs issued a statement on its official blog condemning the virtual depictions of child pornography. Linden Labs said it was cooperating with law enforcement and had banned two participants in the incident, a 54-year-old man and a 27-year-old woman, from Second Life.

Some Second Life users objected on the blog that Linden Labs had gone too far.

"Excuse me. You banned two residents, both mature, who did a little role-playing? No children, I repeat no children, were harmed or even involved in that act," protested another user on the Second Life blog. "Since when is fantasy against the fricking law?"

Philip Rosedale, the founder and chief executive of Linden Labs, said in an interview that Second Life activities should be governed by real-life laws for the time being. He recounted, for example, that his company has called in the FBI several times, most recently this spring to ensure that Second Life's virtual casinos complied with U.S. law. Federal investigators created their own avatars and toured the site, he said.

In coming months, his company plans to disperse tens of thousands of computer servers from California and Texas to countries around the world in order to improve the site's performance. Also, he said, this will make activities on those servers subject to laws of the host countries.

Rosedale said he hopes participants in Second Life eventually develop their own virtual legal code and justice system.

"In the ideal case, the people who are in Second Life should think of themselves as citizens of this new place and not citizens of their countries," he said.

[1] Edwards dropped out of the campaign in April 2007 and later endorsed Democratic nominee Barack Obama.

CONSIDER

1. Why do you think people commit virtual crimes? What might motivate such acts? Do you think that virtual crimes are ethically comparable to real crimes? Why or why not?

2. How do you react to the fact that Second Life has not evolved into a peaceful and harmonious utopia? Would you expect activities in a virtual world to differ significantly from those in the real one?

3. What is the implication when a story about crime in Second Life appears in *The Washington Post*, a major national newspaper? Are we taking fantasy role playing too seriously, or does it make sense to consider events in virtual worlds as newsworthy?

COMPOSE

4. Choose a mainstream product or corporation and then write an argument to its corporate board of directors urging that it either buy an island in Second Life or avoid the environment entirely.

This Is Your Brain on Video Games
Gaming sharpens thinking, social skills, and perception.

Steven Johnson
(2007)

FYI Steven Johnson writes the "Emerging Technology" column for *Discover* magazine. His work has also appeared in *Wired*, *Slate*, and *The New York Times Magazine*. He is the author of the 2000 book *Everything Bad Is Good for You: How Today's Popular Culture Is Actually Making Us Smarter*. Johnson's "Watching TV Makes You Smarter" appears in Chapter 1 (pages 50–53).

James Gee, a professor of learning sciences at the University of Wisconsin, was profoundly humbled when he first played a video game for preschool-age kids called *Pajama Sam: No Need to Hide When It's Dark Outside*. Gee's son Sam, then 6, had been clamoring to play the game, which features a little boy who dresses up like his favorite action hero, Pajama Man, and sets off on adventures in a virtual world ruled by the dastardly villain Darkness. So Gee brought *Pajama Sam* home and tried it himself. "I figured I could play it and finish it so I could help Sam," says Gee. "Instead, I had to go and ask him to help me."

Gee had so much fun playing *Pajama Sam* that he subsequently decided to try his hand at an adult video game he picked at random off a store shelf—an H. G. Wells-inspired sci-fi quest called *The New Adventures of the Time Machine*. "I was just blown away when I brought it home at how hard it was," he says.

Gee's scholarly interest was also piqued. He sensed instantly that something provocative was happening in his mind as he struggled to complete the puzzles of the time machine. "I hadn't done that kind of new learning since graduate school. You know, as you get older, you kind of rest on your laurels."

Gee's epiphany led him to the forefront of a wave of research into how video games affect cognition. Bolstered by the results of laboratory experiments, Gee and other researchers dared to suggest that gaming might be mentally enriching. These scholars are the first to admit that games can be addictive, and indeed part of their research explores how games connect to the reward circuits of the human brain. But they now recognize the cognitive benefits of playing video games: pattern recognition, system thinking, even patience. Lurking in this research is the idea that gaming can exercise the mind the way physical activity exercises the body: It may be addictive because it's challenging.

All of this, of course, flies in the face of the classic stereotype of gamers as attention deficit–crazed stimulus junkies, easily distracted by flashy graphics and on-screen carnage. Instead, successful gamers must focus, have patience, develop a willingness to delay gratification, and prioritize scarce resources. In other words, they think.

The video game Tetris, among the earliest games to launch the industry, involves falling tile-like tetraminoes that a player must quickly maneuver so they fit into space at the bottom of the screen. In the early 1990s, Richard Haier, a professor of psychology at the University of California at Irvine, tracked cerebral glucose metabolic rates in the brains of Tetris players using positron-emission tomography (PET) scanners. The glucose rates show how much energy the brain is consuming, and thus serve as a rough estimate of how much work the brain is doing. Haier determined the glucose levels of novice Tetris players as their brains labored to usher the falling blocks into correct locations. Then he took their levels again after a month of regular play. Even though the test subjects had improved their game performance by a factor of seven, Haier found that their glucose levels had decreased. It appeared that the escalating difficulty of the game trained the test subjects to manipulate the Tetris blocks mentally with such skill that they barely broke a cognitive sweat completing levels that would have utterly confounded them a month earlier.

Nearly a decade after Haier's study, Gee hit upon an explanation. He found that even escapist fantasy games are embedded with one of the core principles of learning—students prosper when the subject matter challenges them right at the edge of their abilities. Make the lessons too difficult and the students get frustrated. Make them too easy and they get bored. Cognitive psychologists call this the "regime of competence" principle. Gee's insight was to recognize that the principle is central to video games: As players progress, puzzles become more complex, enemies swifter and more numerous, and underlying patterns more subtle. Most games don't allow progress until you've reached a certain level of expertise.

To understand why games might be good for the mind, begin by shedding the cliché that they are about improving hand-eye coordination and firing virtual weapons. More than 70 percent of video games contain no more bloodshed than a game of Risk, and are popular because they challenge mental dexterity. Among the best-selling game franchises, *The Sims* involves almost no hand-eye coordination or quick reflexes. One manages a household of characters, each endowed with distinct drives and personality traits, each cycling through an endless series of short-term needs (companionship, say, or food), each enmeshed in a network of relationships with other characters. Playing the game is a nonstop balancing act. Even a violent game like *Grand Theft Auto* involves networks of characters that the player must navigate and master, picking up clues and detecting patterns.

> **'Basically, how we think is through running perceptual simulations in our heads that prepare us for the actions we're going to take,' he says. 'By modeling those simulations, video games externalize how the mind works.'**

Gee contends that the way gamers explore virtual worlds mirrors the way the brain processes multiple, but interconnected, streams of information in the real world. "Basically, how we think is through running perceptual simulations in our heads that prepare us for the actions we're going to take," he says. "By modeling those simulations, video games externalize how the mind works."

Even if Gee is right and video games are learning machines, one question remains: Do the skills learned in the virtual world translate into the real one?

The answer comes from a slew of recent studies, one of which began when then cognitive sciences research assistant and ardent gamer Shawn Green worked with University of Rochester cognitive sciences professor Daphne Bavelier on a project investigating visual perception in video game players. On standard tests that measure attention span and information-processing time, Green found that gamers consistently outperformed nongamers. When Green tweaked the tests to make them challenging enough so the gamers wouldn't have perfect scores, the nongamers sometimes performed so poorly that their answers might as well have been random guesses. The researchers addressed an admitted weakness of the study—that visually intelligent people were more likely to be attracted to video games in the first place—by immersing a group of nonplayers for a week in the World War II game *Medal of Honor*. They found that the group's skills on the standard visual tests improved as well.

Green did the initial research as part of his honors thesis, and after graduation, he and Bavelier continued the study. *Nature* published the results in May 2003. Since then the pair has also found that gamers can visually track more objects simultaneously than nongamers and that playing video games improves this ability. Their latest research on the visual precision of gamers is forthcoming in *Psychological Science and the Journal of Experimental Psychology*. Green says his main interest is the brain's plasticity, but cautiously concedes there may be practical applications to playing video games. "Strong peripheral vision is useful to law enforcement, firefighters, and the military. They need those enhanced skills," he adds.

The notion that video games can develop abilities that apply to real-world situations has been expressed by many and is increasingly being put to the test. In October 2006 the Federation of American Scientists (FAS) endorsed video games as a potential means for teaching "higher-order thinking skills, such as strategic thinking, interpretive analysis, problem solving, plan formulation and execution, and adaptation to rapid change." They cited "owners mode," a component of the video football game *Madden*, which lets players manage an NFL team, as teaching basic business skills. Team games, such as *EverQuest* and *World of Warcraft*, develop cooperation and communication skills that the FAS says are useful in business settings.

A prime example of gaming that tangibly improves professional technique comes from James Rosser, director of the Advanced Medical Technology Institute at Beth Israel Medical Center in New York City. He found that laparoscopic surgeons who played games for more than three hours a week made 37 percent fewer errors than their nongaming peers, thanks to improved hand-eye coordination and depth perception. The Harvard Business School Press published a new book in November 2006 by John Beck, who has looked at three distinct groups of white-collar professionals: hard-core gamers, occasional gamers, and nongamers. The findings contradict nearly all the preconceived ideas about the impact of games. The gaming population turned out to be consistently more social, more confident, and more comfortable solving problems creatively. They also showed no evidence of reduced attention spans compared with nongamers. "It wasn't surprising that gamers were more competitive, or more strategic, but the social and leadership skills that they exhibit don't fit the stereotype of a loner in the basement," Beck says.

The U.S. military has long supported the premise that learning through games can prepare soldiers for the complex, rapid-fire decision making of combat. Since 2002, they have offered new versions of their own game, *America's Army*, which lets potential recruits play at everything from boot camp to Special Forces missions. According to the gamemakers at West Point, the purpose of *America's Army* is to "give the player an idea of what it's like for real U.S. Army soldiers to train for duty." More than 4-and-a-half million registered players have completed the game's basic training.

In the fall of 2003 two media researchers at the University of Southern California set up a study to look at the patterns of brain activity triggered by violent video games. Peter Vorderer and René Weber booked time on an fMRI machine, loaded a popular game called *Tactical Ops* on an adjoining computer console, and watched one test subject after another pretend to be part of a Special Forces team trying to prevent a terrorist attack.

Before Vorderer and Weber even looked at any of the brain scans, they were surprised by the behavior of the dozen or so adults who volunteered for the test. Participating in an fMRI study involves lying for extended periods of time in an extremely confined and loud space. Even a mild claustrophobic will invariably find the experience intolerable, and most people need a break after 20 minutes. But most of the *Tactical Ops* players happily stayed in the machine for at least an hour, oblivious to the discomfort and noise because they were so entranced by the game.

The genesis of this reaction may lie in the neurotransmitter dopamine. A number of studies have revealed that game playing triggers dopamine release in the brain, a finding that makes sense, given the instrumental role that dopamine plays in how the brain handles both reward and exploration. Jaak Panksepp, a neuroscientist collaborating with the Falk Center for Molecular Therapeutics at Northwestern University, calls the dopamine system the brain's "seeking" circuitry, which propels us to explore new avenues for reward in our environment. The game world is teeming with objects that deliver clearly articulated rewards: more life, access to new levels, new equipment, new spells. Most of the crucial work in game interface design revolves around keeping players notified of potential rewards available to them and how much those rewards are needed.

If you create a system in which rewards are both clearly defined and achieved by exploring an environment, you'll find human brains drawn to those systems, even if they're made up of virtual characters and simulated sidewalks. It's likely those Tactical Ops players in an fMRI machine were able to tolerate the physical discomfort of the machine because the game environment so powerfully stimulated the brain's dopamine system.

Of course, dopamine is also involved in the addictiveness of drugs. "The thing to remember about dopamine is that it's not at all the same thing as pleasure," says Gregory Berns, a neuroscientist at Emory University School of Medicine in Atlanta, who looks at dopamine in a cultural context in his book, *Satisfaction*. "Dopamine is not the reward; it's what lets you go out and explore in the first place. Without dopamine, you wouldn't be able to learn properly."

What kind of cognitive skills should we expect to find in the Pokémon generation? Not surprisingly,

> **If you create a system in which rewards are both clearly defined and achieved by exploring an environment, you'll find human brains drawn to those systems, even if they're made up of virtual characters and simulated sidewalks.**

Gee has got a list. "They're going to think well about systems; they're going to be good at exploring; they're going to be good at reconceptualizing their goals based on their experience; they're not going to judge people's intelligence just by how fast and efficient they are; and they're going to think nonlaterally. In our current world with its complex systems that are quite dangerous, those are damn good ways to think."

Gee's remarks remind me of an experience I had a few years earlier, introducing my 7-year-old nephew to *SimCity 2000*, the best-selling urban simulator that lets you create a virtual metropolis on your computer, build highways and bridges, zone areas for development, and raise or lower taxes. Based on the player's decisions, neighborhoods thrive or decline, streets get overrun with traffic or remain wastelands, and criminals prosper or disappear. When I walked my nephew through the game, I gave him only the most cursory overview of the rules; I was mostly just giving him a tour of the city I'd built. But he was absorbing the rules nonetheless. At one point, I showed him a block of rusted, crime-ridden factories that lay abandoned and explained that I'd had difficulty getting this part of my city to come back to life. He turned to me and said, "I think you need to lower your industrial tax rates." He said it as calmly and as confidently as if he were saying, "I think we need to shoot the bad guy."

In a 20-minute tour of *SimCity*, my nephew had learned a fundamental principle of urban economics: Some areas zoned for specific uses can falter if the zone-specific taxes are too high. Of course, if you sat my 7-year-old nephew down in an urban studies classroom, he would be asleep in 10 seconds. But just like those *Tactical Ops* players happily trapped for an hour in an fMRI, something in the game world had pulled at him. He was learning in spite of himself.

CONSIDER

1. According to Johnson, what skills and capacities do video games teach? Do his arguments ring true? How do your experiences—either of playing video games yourself or of knowing others who do—reinforce or problematize Johnson's claims?

2. Can you think of other activities that build the qualities that Johnson attributes to video games—for example, sports or board games such as chess—or do you think the video gaming environment is unique? What arguments and evidence might you use to explain your thoughts on this question?

CHALLENGE

3. Read Steven Johnson's "Watching TV Makes You Smarter" on pages 50-53 and compare his conclusions in that essay with the arguments he makes in "This Is Your Brain on Video Games." Considering his thoughts, write an argument of your own either extending his claims about the positive effects of popular culture or challenging them.

Baby, You Mean the World of Warcraft to Me

Kevin Spivey
(2006)

> **FYI** *The Onion* is a satirical newspaper founded in 1988 by students at the University of Wisconsin. They publish fictional news and opinion pieces that poke fun at the news media. In addition to the original newspaper, *The Onion* also produces parodies of television and radio news broadcasts on their website at *www.theonion.com*. World of Warcraft is currently the most popular online video game worldwide, with more than 8.5 million active players.

Come on, honey, why do you have to be like that? You know that you're my Elven princess. My one and only. I would dare say that there is no one in all the realm who doesn't know of our love. I have sung your praises from the mouth of the Shadowthread Cave to the Stranglethorn Vale of the Eastern Kingdoms. I've introduced you to my comrades-in-arms in the Ulster guild, and they all accept you as kin.

And now you want to dissolve the greatest love ever to brighten my basement?

When we met, I was looking for a group fit to take the Zul'Gurub instance. But as I stocked up on provisions at the convenience store before my quest, and our eyes locked, I realized that I was not looking for a group, I was looking for love, and I found it in you. You are the sun, the moon, the Cinderhide Armsplints of the Monkey. There is so much we have to offer one another. Unfailing loyalty, a Strength of 250, someone who can go out for snacks in the heat of battle. Can't you see we're made for each other?

Darling, no orc can keep me from you. I would make my way into the heart of Moonglade and fight an army of trolls just to be by your side. I would go up against Varimathras, the ruler of the Undead himself, if he so much as hinted that he was a danger to you. Make no mistake, I would get aggro on anyone who would threaten you.

This is, of course, provided the system is not down due to a faulty patch.

Don't you see that I did it all for you? My love for you exceeds Level 60, higher than anyone thought possible in this fantastic computer universe. My spirit soars when you are near. You restore my mana with a kiss. I even named my epic mount after you. Her name is Helen, and her hair shimmers in the sunlight, and together we ride forward into destiny.

I would climb the highest peak of Mount Hyjal to toil for 100 days and 100 nights in the mines in order to extract the precious ore so that I may fashion you a necklace of the finest thorium. My warrior, Hamm-uster, devoted his game's life to the professions of mining and smithing just so that I might accomplish that very thing. All you need do is join me in the WoW and hold the necklace up to the virtual sun. Then you may see the efforts I have expended to create this thing of beauty for you. The dishes can wait until tomorrow.

Helen, my mage, when I was ganked by a lowly rogue from Tennessee in the Caverns of Time and stripped of my treasured belongings, I rose from the grave with one purpose in mind. I had to be resurrected, not to seek revenge, but to return to you.

There is no other way to put it: You take my breath bar away.

Why do we need to go out to have fun? Everything we could possibly want is right in WoW. Fine dining, theater, romantic sunsets—they're all there. The outside world just costs money, and I don't have a magic breastplate to protect me from people's stares. Come with me so I can treat you like the princess you are.

Please, baby, if you leave, you will increase by 32 percent the chance of doing direct damage to my heart. Please reconsider.

Source: "Baby, You Mean the World of Warcraft to Me" by Kevin Spivey from *The Onion*, 42:16, April 19, 2006. Reprinted with permission of *The Onion*. Copyright © 2008 by ONION, INC. www.theonion.com.

CONSIDER

1. This piece makes frequent use of World of Warcraft terminology. Do you think it's necessary to be familiar with this game to find the piece funny? Why or why not?

2. What does the piece suggest about how players of this and similar games approach relationships? How do the implied claims in this piece connect to or refute Steven Johnson's claims in "This Is Your Brain on Video Games"?

Writing About Technology and Science

Writing about technological and scientific topics often involves conveying complex information in a clear, accurate way. If you're composing an assignment for a college course or a work-related project, you often won't have much choice about your topic. When you have a choice, however, find a **subject** that interests you—preferably one that you already know something about and about which you're motivated to learn more. Perhaps a family member or friend struggles with a disease and you want to research the newest treatment options. Or you've noticed a new technological development related to one of your interests, as Beau Faulkner did when he noticed that alternative reality games (ARGs) were being used to market new music releases (see his paper on pages 389–394). For more tips on finding a subject, see pages 56–59.

While most scientific and technical writing is often informative in nature, you'll still need to spend some time thinking about your **purpose**. Will you be presenting the results of your own original research on a topic? Reporting on a new development within a field? Providing step-by-step instructions that show readers how to perform a process or correctly use a technical device? Each of these purposes suggests different choices about content, structure, and design. As you think about your project's purpose, keep some general guidelines in mind: first, any technical or scientific project should address an authentic, current concern in the field or serve a genuine need for your audience. If your research question is too broad ("Is medical imaging changing society?") to be pressing or useful, you need to refine your approach so that you can investigate with more focus ("How is fMRI influencing consumerism?"). See pages 64–65 for more on identifying and refining your purpose in a writing project.

Once you know you have an engaging topic and a clear purpose, begin pulling together information for your project. In some cases, you'll have prior expertise or direct experiences or observations to draw upon. However, most scientific and technical writing requires substantial **research** (see pages 84–87 for detailed advice). If you're not an expert on your topic, try these strategies: begin by browsing through background sources such as encyclopedias or postings to online groups to get a sense of current conversations and hot topics within a field. Next, use library databases to find academic journals written by specialists on your topic and general-interest publications intended for the wider public. As you read, pay attention to the main ideas and to the ways that the articles convey information. Take careful notes and keep an eye out for images, factual data, or quotations you might want to incorporate into your project. And remember to keep track of source information so that you can cite and document everything appropriately.

As you work on your project, you will likely become much better informed about your topic than your **audience** is (see pages 60–63). So you'll want to consider what kinds of background information they'll require to understand your discussion and what key terms you'll have to define. Depending on how much your audience knows, you may need to translate specialized terminology and jargon into laypersons' terms, or use familiar examples, visuals, or analogies to illustrate unfamiliar concepts, as Max Houck does in "*CSI*: Reality" (pages 368–373).

Your audience's needs will also help you determine how to **structure** your project. Much scientific and technical writing fits within clearly defined **genres**—lab report, technical instructions, abstract, research report, etc.—that carry specific expectations for content, structure, and formatting. While these genres don't generally leave much room for creative disgression, they have the advantage of predictability—if you can find a few examples of the genre, you'll have a rough blueprint for organizing your own document. Whatever genre your project fits, strive to present your material in a reasonably straightforward, accessible way. Use headings when needed to point out major areas of information. Incorporate images and other visuals that will help you explain your topic. Avoid flashy or distracting **design elements**; let the information be your focus. (For more details about structure and genres, see pages 67–76.)

In choosing a **medium**, consider your genre and audience and—perhaps most importantly—your own technical skills. If you feel comfortable with new technologies, an online video, Web-based photo essay, or podcast will showcase your strengths. Yet remember that low-tech tools are often equally effective. Both Beau Faulkner and Hannah Bailey create successful papers using only a word-processing program and a digital camera (see pages 389–394 and 395–398).

Don't wait until your draft is complete to begin assessing your work. Careful, ongoing **revision** nearly always produces a stronger final product. As you research and draft, think about how your focus might be adjusted. Solicit feedback about your draft, and think about your writing in terms of how well it conveys its information to readers. Make any needed adjustments, then test the revised draft on readers again. Once you're generally pleased with the project, **edit** and **proofread** carefully, paying special attention to whether outside sources are cited and documented appropriately (see pages 88 and 89 for more on revision and editing strategies and page 87 for more on documenting sources).

Project 6.1

Explaining a New Development in Technology or Science

This assignment requires you to bridge the distance between the ways in which information is conveyed in specialized disciplines and the ways in which the general public learns about developments in technology or the natural or social sciences. You will identify a new trend or development in one of these fields, conduct research to gain a thorough understanding of that development, then compose an essay aimed at a general audience that explains the topic in an easy-to-understand format.

Begin your project by thinking about a field that you are curious about or that you see yourself pursuing one day. Conduct initial research to see what issues or trends currently occupy the field—you might find that astronomers are interested in the privatization of space or that geologists are preoccupied with new developments in climatology. Once you've developed some of the hot topics for the field, select one that strikes your interest. Next, conduct research to find both academic journal articles and general-interest publications on your topic. When you have a good general grasp of the issue, you're ready to begin drafting.

Here are some tips to consider as you compose:

- Consider how readers who may not have experience with your topic will respond to the information you supply. It may be necessary to include illustrations or definitions of unfamiliar concepts—think about when the communication of material is likely to trip readers up and how you can adjust your writing to help the audience understand key ideas.
- Structure your explanations carefully to help readers move logically through the information. Provide specific examples or illustrative images to assist readers' understanding of complicated ideas.
- Use straightforward, concise, and objective language to communicate your points. In this kind of writing, let the information be the main focus.
- When you have a full draft, print it out and review it carefully, looking for areas that need revision and editing. If possible, have a friend who is unfamiliar with your topic read your draft, pointing out any areas of confusion.

STUDENT PROJECT

Beau Faulkner, "Year Zero: A Viral Marketing Promotion"

Beau Faulkner wrote this paper as a way of exploring his interest in a cutting-edge advertising campaign he saw marketers using to promote a new album by musician Trent Reznor of the band Nine Inch Nails. Because Reznor's album was among the first to use this kind of marketing, Faulkner discusses it at length as he explains how alternate reality game (ARG) marketing works.

Faulkner 1

Beau Faulkner
RHE 315
Professor Ruszkiewicz
29 April 2007

Year Zero: A Viral Marketing Promotion

With the advent of the Internet a new term has been coined in advertising: viral marketing. Viral marketing describes any strategy relying on individuals to pass on a marketing message to others, creating an exponential growth in the message's exposure and influence. Before the Internet, similar strategies had been referred to as "word-of-mouth," "creating a buzz," or "network marketing." Hotmail is one of the original services that employed viral marketing by including information on getting a free hotmail account at the bottom of all e-mails sent from hotmail addresses. Using the free e-mail service was the incentive for passing on the advertising message. One of the newer strategies in the realm of viral marketing is to use alternate reality games (ARGs).

An alternate reality game is an interactive narrative using the real world as a platform to tell a story that may be affected by participants' ideas or actions. As a viral marketing strategy, ARGs rely on participants passing their message to others for its entertainment value. ARGs generally use multiple media (such as telephone, fax, e-mail, and mail) but rely on the Internet as the central binding medium. The television series Lost and the video game Halo 2 are two of the most prominent products that employed ARGs to drum up interest in their plots. Year Zero, the new concept album by Trent Reznor of Nine Inch Nails (NIN), is the first music album to employ an ARG campaign. ARGs are still in their infancy at this stage, and the rules of an ARG are not entirely set. The idea is to have the fictitious alternate reality bleed into the consumers' reality as thoroughly as

> The opening ¶ provides background information and defines terms that may be unfamiliar to readers.

> This sentence introduces the example the writer will use to explain how ARGs work.

Faulkner 2

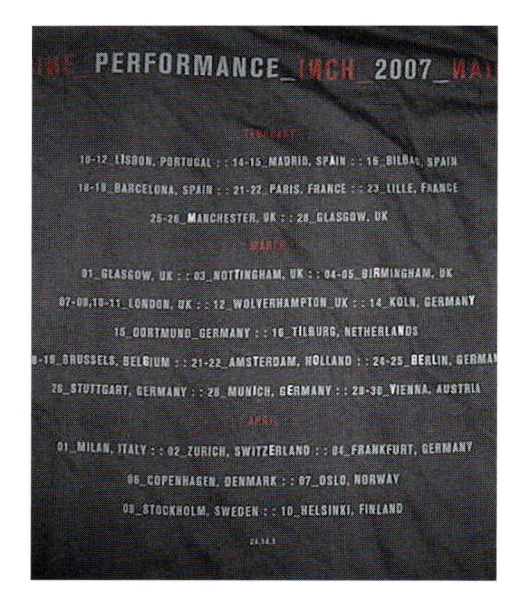

Fig. 1. Tour shirt with highlighted letters.

possible to accomplish two things: to deeply involve individuals with the plot and to generate a buzz for a product by piquing interest in the innovation of the strategy itself. To quote the title of a track from the band's previous album, "The Line Begins to Blur" when following such a complex ARG.

A good place to start the story of this campaign is the same place you would open any story, in the beginning. It all started with a new European NIN tour t-shirt in February. Highlighted letters on the back of the shirt spelled out the phrase, "I am trying to believe" (see fig. 1). Googling this phrase, fans discovered iamtryingtobelieve.com, which provides clues to a plethora of other Web sites all acting as puzzle pieces for the concept of Year Zero. The pieces paint a fragmented picture of a harsh totalitarian reality in the year 2022, in which freedom means nothing and citizens are under constant surveillance by a corrupt government. Each Web site raises more questions than answers, which motivated fans to want to find the next piece of the puzzle. Throughout Reznor's European tour in February 2007, fans found a total of four USB drives in bathroom stalls at Nine Inch Nails shows in Portugal, Spain and England. There were high-quality MP3s on the drives of unreleased NIN songs from

Fig. 1 shows readers this complicated pattern of letters, eliminating the need for lengthy explanation within the paragraph.

Faulkner 3

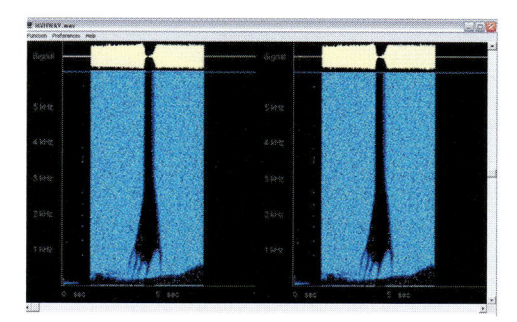

Fig. 2. Spectrographic image from MP3.

Year Zero. The drives also housed static MP3 files. The static tracks each had different coded characteristics deciphered through means such as Morse code or spectrograph analysis. One track revealed a phone number (which plays a fictitious wiretapped phone conversation) and another had spectrograph imagery of a hand reaching down from the sky (see fig. 2). Each picture, phone audio message, and Web site contains within it clues to yet another piece in the Year Zero story and Internet forums have been the venue for piecing it all together. So far deciphering messages from the viral campaign has required knowledge of computer graphics, audio recording, chemistry, and the Spanish language. The necessity for group participation to decode the narrative is clear since no one person is knowledgeable in all these subjects. Internet forums not only enable fans to discuss the album and work together to uncover the plot, they also further the viral reach of Year Zero.

    Artistic interest and spreading awareness of societal dangers are the focal points of the campaign, according to Reznor. In an exclusive interview with Gigwise, Reznor states, "I decided to write an essay about where the world might be if we continue down the path that we're on with a neoconesque government doing whatever it pleases, which seems to be the way it works over here (America)." Reznor found a message that he could really get behind in his art and knew his music alone could not capture that message fully. As an artist that thrives on creation, the desire to make something influential is difficult to deny. Reznor wants more than to just sell records. He wants to make an impression on his audience. He wants to stimulate thought, conversation, and questioning minds. The dystopian society he projects with his vision is a warning for what

> At this point, the paper shifts from explaining how the ARG works to exploring its effects.

Faulkner 4

Fig. 3. Fictitious articles on the Web site (iamtryingtobelieve.com).

the future may bring, and he wants his fans to wake up to current trends leading in that direction. Reznor expressed delight with the fact that he has seen forum posts on the Internet of fans drawing parallels between the plot of his story and our current state of affairs (see fig. 3). I found posts on Year Zero threads that linked to articles about current legal issues such as martial law and the separation of church and state. The effect his campaign has had on the activities and topics of conversation for fans overshadows any change accomplished by the record alone.

 Commercial interest, although downplayed by Reznor himself, is obviously a factor in the construction of this reality. On his official fan-club web site (http://www.nin-thespiral.com/), Reznor posted a blog entry stating, "The term 'marketing' sure is a frustrating one for me at the moment. What you are now starting to experience IS 'year zero.' It's not some kind of gimmick to get you to buy a record -- it IS the art form." According to Reznor, Year Zero is not about the money. Still, you have to be a paying member of Reznor's fan-club "The Spiral" to even view such postings. Clearly the campaign is about more than just the money, but dollars and cents factor in. Numerous Web sites and music magazines, such as Rolling Stone and Spin, have done articles focused on the complexity of this inventive campaign. Trent Reznor gets maximum publicity through what amounts to free

Faulkner 5

advertising from such articles about his viral marketing promotion. The media hype from the mere innovation of the campaign is bound to boost sales. The fans that have followed the campaign will definitely buy the album, but they also increase exposure by discussing the promotion with others. Those that hear about the campaign get their interest piqued and tell others, and the virus is spread at an exponential rate. Search engine optimization specialist Matt Cutts even applauded Reznor for Web site design because googling keywords leaked from each puzzle piece provides the intended "next puzzle" Web site. Exposure for Reznor and his product, the album Year Zero, explodes at a minimal financial cost for him. Increased notoriety will certainly correlate with an increase in sales.

    The success of the campaign on album sales has yet to be established since Year Zero is not going to be released until April 17th, but if the buzz is any indicator, the campaign will prove profitable. Reznor is likely to see the campaign as a success on an artistic level regardless of sales. He has become the god of an alternate reality and has influenced people in a manner that may lead to positive changes in this reality as well. If sales reflect a successful campaign, the music industry will surely take note and the art of promotion and advertising could be revolutionized. Blatant advertisements are easy to ignore or even avoid these days, but the subtlety of promotion masked in entertainment is effective by enticing consumers to seek out ads.

Faulkner 6

Works Cited

Cutts, Matt. "Nice Piece of Viral Marketing: NIN." Blog posting. 10 March 2007 Matt Cutts: Gadget, Google, and SEO. 10 April 2007 <http://www.mattcutts.com/blog/nice-piece-of-viral-marketing-nin/>.

Echoing the Sound: A Forum for NIN Discussion. 31 March 2008 <http://www.echoingthesound.org/>

IamTryingToBelieve. 22 April 2007 <www.iamtryingtobelieve.com>.

>
> Faulkner 7
>
> MP3 Spectrograph Image. 25 April 2007
> <http://individual.utoronto.ca/botley/2432.mp3>.
>
> "Nine Inch Nails: The Rezurrection." Interview with Trent Reznor. 31 March 2008 <http://www.gigwise.com/contents.asp?contentid=29738>.
>
> "Year Zero (game)." Wikipedia. 22 April 2007
> <http://en.wikipedia.org/wiki/Year_Zero_(alternate_reality_game)>.

Publisher's Note: Alternate Reality Games (ARGs) are widely credited to 42 Entertainment as the inventor and innovator of the genre. Ilovebees, the award-winning campaign for Halo 2, was created by 42 Entertainment in 2004. Year Zero, for NIN's 2007 album release, was created by 42 Entertainment in 2007, and went on to win the Cyber Grand Prix award in Cannes Lions 2008. 42 Entertainment also created the ground-breaking, 15-month experience Why So Serious? alternate reality experience for *The Dark Knight* in 2008. For more on this case study, go to www.42entertainment.com/yearzero.

Project 6.2

Composing a Set of Instructions

As a student you frequently find yourself reading instructions, and after you graduate and enter the workforce, you may well be called upon occasionally to write instructions to explain procedures and processes to others. Writing instructions for others requires you to slow down and carefully think through how to convey specialized knowledge in a way that's accessible and understandable to readers. It requires you to be aware of your audience, and to put yourself in the audience's place as you anticipate the most important things for your readers to know, questions they might have, and places where they are likely to become confused. Drafting instructions also gives you the opportunity to present information using both text and visual images in order to engage readers on multiple levels.

This assignment asks you write a set of step-by-step instructions explaining how to use a particular device or perform a specialized procedure that you know well. Assume that your audience does not know about the process you're explaining, and that you want them to be able to perform it successfully after reading the instructions once. Your instructions should incorporate both words and visual elements, and they should be concise but clear.

Here are some tips to keep in mind:

- Choose your visual images carefully. They should supplement and reinforce the textual information—not distract from it. Make sure that the visuals you include are clear and legible and that they are the most crucial in helping your audience understand what to do.

- Pay special attention to layout. Readers should be able to easily follow the order of steps and to see how images and visuals relate to accompanying text.

- Before you turn in this project, have a friend who is not familiar with your chosen process read the draft and ask any questions he or she has about the way you have described the process. And don't be surprised if you learn something new about your process as you work on these instructions.

STUDENT PROJECT

Hannah Bailey, "Fitting and Preparing Pointe Shoes"

Hannah Bailey, a serious ballet student who dances as a part-time apprentice with a professional dance company, developed these instructions for an audience of less advanced dance students who have questions about choosing, fitting, and preparing pointe shoes. While pointe shoes are fairly low-tech—most are still made by hand of cloth, wood products, and glue—they are an essential piece of equipment for a ballet dancer, and using them requires specialized instruction and expertise.

Bailey 1

Hannah Bailey
Professor Friend
English Composition
17 February 2008

Fitting and Preparing Pointe Shoes

Every young ballerina is intrigued by pointe shoes. It excites every little girl to watch the advanced dancers turn and jump so gracefully on the tips of their toes, knowing that one day she will do the same. But although pointe shoes look pretty, they are not simply decorative. They are in fact a dancer's most important piece of technical equipment, providing a tiny platform on which her full weight can be perfectly balanced during hundreds of different steps and combinations. Pointe shoe design is so complex and precise that the shoes are made only by trained craftsmen, who can spend hours constructing a single pair by hand. In order to work properly, each shoe must also be carefully customized by the dancer who wears it, a process that takes know-how and practice. The following instructions are a step-by-step guide for dancers preparing for their first class on pointe.

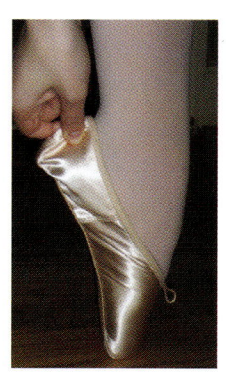

Fig. 1. Getting the right fit.

Bailey 2

For your first pair of shoes, don't shop online. Go to a local dance supply store and get help from the employees to find the right size, both in length and width. Things to look for:

1) The shoes should be snug, not baggy on the sides. Pulling the drawstring that runs around the top of the shoe and tying it will help, but if you see wrinkles or bulges, there is too much fabric.

2) The vamp (the top part over your toes) should not be too short or too long; it should go all the way to the base of the toes—but no further.

3) There should be no more than half a pinch of extra fabric on the heel when you stand on pointe (see fig. 1).

Don't rush the process of trying on shoes; you need to try different brands to see which look and feel best on your feet.

Sewing the Shoes

When you buy your pointe shoes they won't be ready to wear. It is the job of the dancer to sew on the ribbons and elastic because they need to be custom-fitted:

1) Cut the long piece of ribbon that comes with the shoes into four equal pieces. (Note: ribbons may need to be trimmed later if they are too long).

2) Use matches or a lighter to burn the ends of the ribbons so they do not fray (see fig. 2).

3) Decide whether to sew the ribbons shiny side in or out to be consistent; don't end up with unmatched shoes!

4) Now comes the sewing part. You will need a needle and thread. Many dancers purchase Stitch Kits specifically designed for sewing pointe shoes. (Stitch Kits can be bought in any dance store.) Line up one ribbon on the inner seam on the arch side of the shoe and another along the inner seam on the

Fig. 2. Burning the ends of the ribbons.

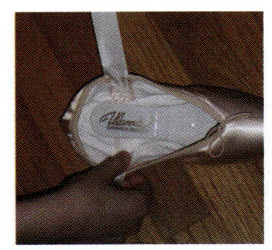

Fig. 3. Sewing the ribbons.

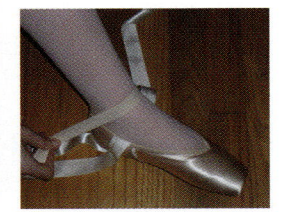

Fig. 4. Measuring the elastic.

Bailey 3

outer side of the shoe, placing the ribbon all the way down to the shank, or bottom, of the shoe (see fig. 3). Once you have it all lined up, sew a box around the ribbon, leaving the top part of the box unsewn so the ribbon can move.

    5) Cut the elastic to fit tightly around your ankle. To measure, take the elastic and pull it tight from where the top of the heel is in your shoe, around the front, and to the back where you started. Remember to pull it tight because you do not want your shoes to slip off the heels (see fig. 4).

    6) Burn the edges of the elastic with matches or a lighter so that they will not fray. (*See* step 2, above.)

    7) Then line up the elastic an equal distance apart from the back center of the heel on the inside and sew a square on the inside.

Lacing up the Shoes

    The last step in putting on pointe shoes is lacing them up; this may sound easy, but it is actually more complicated than it looks.

    1) Slide your foot through the elastic and into one shoe, making sure the drawstring is tucked inside the shoe.

    2) Take the inside ribbon (on the arch) with your right hand and wrap it across the front and around the back two times, ending with the extra ribbon on the inside in your left hand (see fig. 5).

    3) Take the outer ribbon in your right hand and wrap it across the front and around the back one and a half times, ending with the extra ribbon on the inside (see fig. 6).

    4) Tie a knot with the two pieces and tuck it under the layers of ribbon to hide it. Trim off any dangling ends (see fig. 7).

    5) Repeat steps 1–4 for the other shoe.

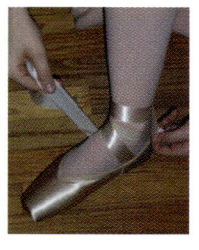

Fig. 5. Wrapping the inside ribbon.

Fig. 6. Wrapping the outer ribbon.

Fig. 7. Securing the ribbon.

Bailey 4

Knowing how to choose the correct pointe shoes for your feet, how to sew your shoes, and how to wear pointe shoes correctly, are all keys to a dancer's success. Going on pointe for the first time is exciting, and knowing how to properly fit, sew, and lace up the shoes makes the process a lot less stressful (see fig. 8).

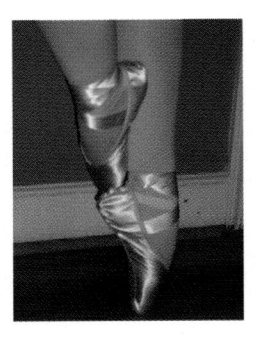

Fig. 8. Going on pointe.

Project 6.3

Write an essay that explores an ethical controversy related to new developments in technology or the sciences (for example, debates over the ethical dimensions of cloning, "designer babies," genetically engineered foods, etc.). Conduct research to explore a range of viewpoints, then write a paper that stakes out and defends one position on the debate.

Project 6.4

Read an academic journal article on a scientific or technical topic that interests you. Then, write summaries of the article aimed at two different audiences—for example, students taking an introductory-level college course in the field, specialists in the field, laypeople, or a classroom of elementary-school students. Be sure that the content, style, and structure of your summaries reflect the particular needs of each audience.

CHAPTER 7

STYLE, DESIGN, AND CULTURE

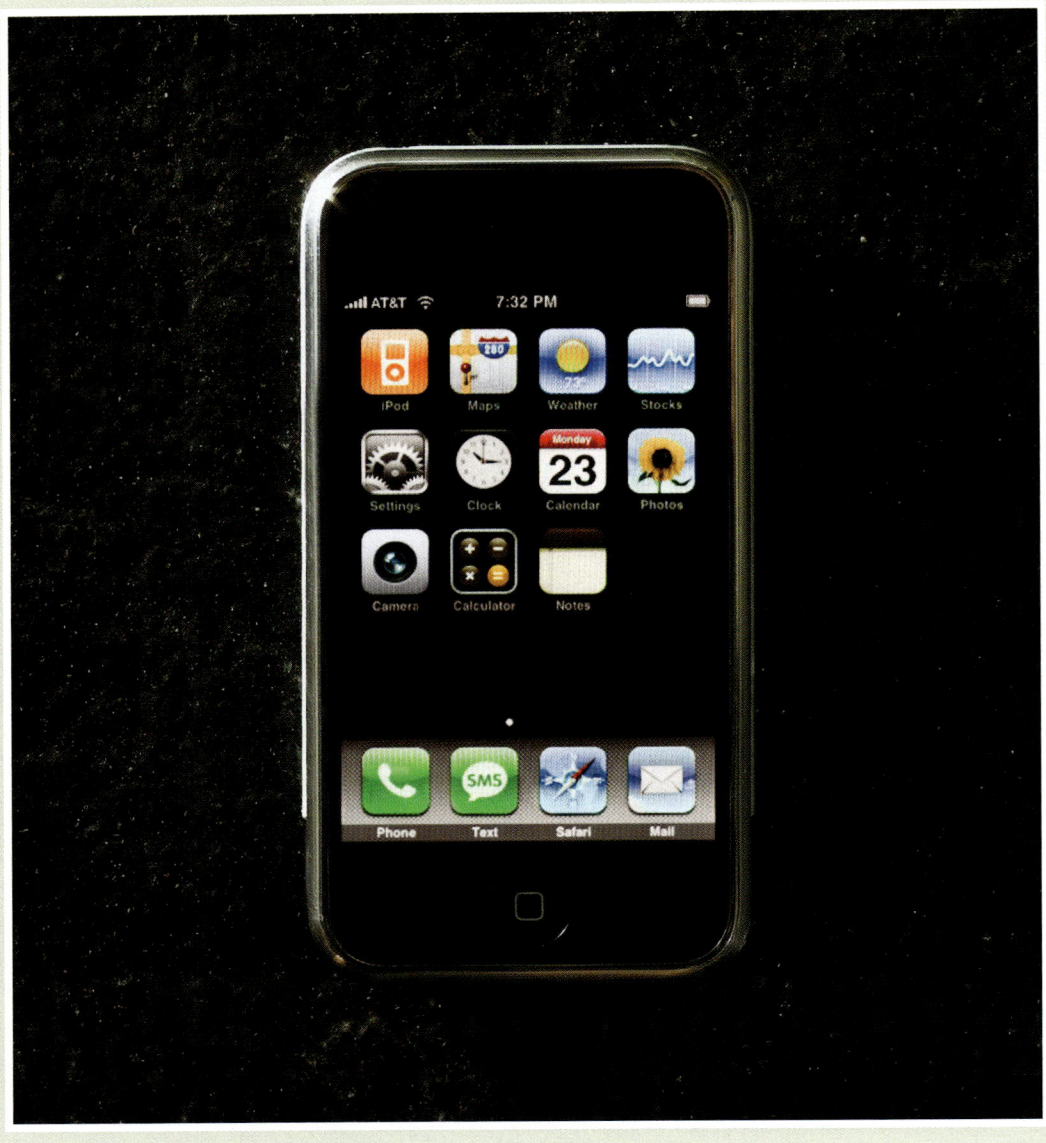

ITEM 7.1 ■ **First generation iPhone, 2007**

400

Why did Apple's iPhone find almost half a million buyers during its first weeks on the market? A great many of those customers simply wanted to own the next cool tool—a technical wonder that would change the way the ubiquitous cell phone looked and worked. The iPhone seemed like a triumph of design. The device's home screen presented colorful icons highlighted by black borders and chrome (see Item 7.1). Flip the phone from vertical to horizontal and a video playing onscreen magically assumed proper HDTV proportions. Downloaded music was presented via a virtual Rolodex of album art. The Internet, photographs, and maps were handled just as deftly. And how cool was that—a cell phone, PDA, and MP3 player that was intuitive and fun?

But if we are living, as Virginia Postrel asserts, in an age when more and more people have come to value and demand brilliant design, we've also become alert to its ironies and limitations. Consider then the Hispter PDA (see Item 7.2), an ingenious invention of Web author Merlin Mann. This "fully extensible system for coordinating incoming and outgoing data" gently reminds us how easy it is to design and decorate beyond our needs. So if the iPhone represents one end of the design spectrum, at the other we find a stack of notecards joined by a binder clip as a humbler response to the need to keep track of appointments and ideas. The Hipster PDA is, in fact, a three-dimensional piece of criticism, a provocative cultural commentary on how we can respond to issues of style and design. And the Hipster PDA doesn't cost $200.

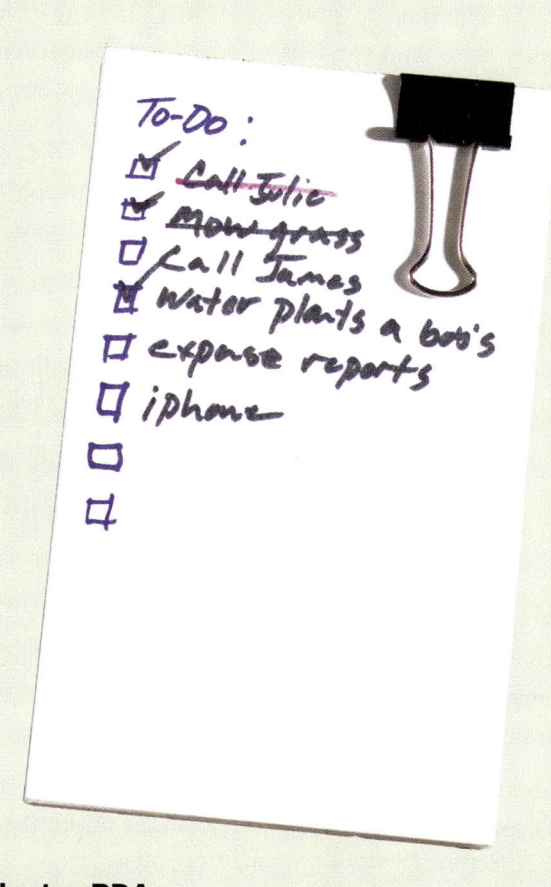

ITEM 7.2 ■ **Hipster PDA**

Reading Texts About Style, Design, and Culture

The human impulse to make and decorate objects seems planted in our genes. And the designs we give to buildings, books, furniture, jewelry, household goods, and clothes all have intriguing stories to tell, if we can figure out how to analyze and write about them.

We can learn a lot about design simply by paying attention to what others find intriguing, so potential **subjects** for design analyses are just about limitless. For instance, the entire fashion industry seems obsessed with ever-changing colors, shapes, and materials—and their fads and obsessions invite responses of all kinds (see Item 7.3). There's plenty of unabashed design, too, in more mundane consumer products (see Item 7.4)—or in the ads that promote them.

A key to understanding design is found in the choices someone made in creating this style or that object. Such choices often depend upon the intended **audience** for a design: Who will use this object, buy this product, or interact with this advertising campaign? Quite often, too, designers set out deliberately to seduce us, to make the objects they fashion irresistible, cool, and desirable, thereby creating our needs as much as serving them (see Item 7.5). Sometimes they explore ethical boundaries too: expect to find intriguing problems at the intersection between the **purposes** of a design or product and the motives of both its designers and users (see Item 7.6).

And that's why it is important to study issues of style in their **context**: much about style and design is tied to the tastes and passions of a given moment. For instance, you might ask what designers were thinking when they created leisure suits or hot pants. And that's precisely the question to ask: What *were* they thinking? What about the particular times and cultural surroundings encouraged or explained such choices? What societal forces explain the status or popularity of some designs (see Item 7.7)?

Of course, designs can also be examined as responses to quite practical needs defined by a **genre** or **medium**. Auto companies will build experimental concept cars to wow audiences with their hunkered-down rooflines and experimental materials. But the vehicles rolling off their assembly lines must meet thousands of mundane criteria: people have to fit inside and there had better be room for some luggage too. Such specifications represent the realities of the genre.

You'll discover, too, that objects designed by an individual or company often share similar characteristics, patterns, and features that convey a message and create a distinctive style—we can call these repeated patterns and characteristics a *design language*. (see Item 7.8). Once you detect a design language you'll likely be intrigued by the way it operates—and, perhaps, by the psychological cravings it satisfies.

But how do you get a handle on a particular design or detect the patterns that distinguish objects that might, at first glance, seem quite similar? You look for distinguishing characteristics. Consider how in high school you may have "read" nuances in the clothing, language, gestures, and behavior of your fellow students to slot them into groups—the nerds, geeks, Goths, preppies, and emos (see Item 7.9).

With similar attention to detail, couldn't you also recognize the specific people, places, and styles of your world? You could probably push such analyses still further, to consider how these patterns came together to reflect the needs of the people creating them or living within them. When you do, you're on your way to understanding and writing about style.

Gallery: Style, Design, and Culture

ITEM 7.3 ■ **Twentieth Century Fox,** *The Devil Wears Prada,* **Screensaver, 2006**

What role does fashion design play in our daily lives? In the 2006 film version of Lauren Weisberger's 2003 novel *The Devil Wears Prada*, Meryl Streep (left), in the role of arrogant and dictatorial magazine editor Miranda Priestly, schools a naïve and skeptical assistant played by Anne Hathaway about the power and influence of the fashion industry.

1. Initially, Miranda's assistant Andy does not take the fashion industry seriously, but she is soon seduced by its glamour, sway, and competitiveness. Are there any ways that your own life intersects with fashion and style? How important is this industry in shaping taste, design, and even behavior?

2. Do men and women respond differently to fashion or perhaps have different concepts of what clothing should be designed to do?

3. What does the image of Miranda's outer office convey about the world of fashion and design? What items, other than clothes, make fashion statements?

4. Designer or label-branded products are now routinely available at mass-market stores such as Kmart and Target. What is the appeal of having these high-profile (in some circles) names appear on relatively low-budget items: clothes, appliances, housewares?

5. Fashions change seasonally, as do tastes in clothes and accessories. Do such rapid and regular variations in style inspire or hinder excellence in design? Offer good reasons for your opinions.

ITEM 7.4 ■ **Greg Marting, Giro Atmos Bicycle Helmet, 2003**

Can well-designed consumer products actually be works of art? The Museum of Modern Art (MoMA) in New York places many everyday items in its collection, including this aerodynamic bike helmet made of polystyrene, polycarbonate, carbon composite, and nylon. Pretty as an Easter bonnet.

1. Why do you think this helmet was selected for inclusion in the collection of a major museum of art? Do you see any correlation between its function as a helmet and its eye-catching appearance?

2. Does the design strike you as contemporary or might it be mistaken for an object from an earlier period? What features of the helmet might help you to date it if you didn't know it was produced in 2003?

3. Could you imagine this product fabricated from natural materials: metal, leather, wood, cloth? Cite examples of products whose design is at least partially determined by the materials used in its construction.

4. Do consumer products as mundane as a bike helmet really belong in museums? Why or why not?

ITEM 7.5 ■ Nintendo Wii Controller, 2006

Nintendo changed video gaming in 2006 when it introduced its award-winning Wii, with a new and innovative controller it calls a Wiimote. A gamer manipulates the sophisticated controller as if it were a real object, pointing it like a gun or swinging it like a golf club or baseball bat—the motion, feel, and sound of the device enhancing the video experience.

1. Why do so many video gamers find the Wii's unique controller irresistible? What is your reaction to the Wii device?

2. Many first-time gamers find the Wiimote especially *intuitive*. What does that term mean when applied to an object of design? What recent technologies or products strike you as intuitive? Which require a steeper learning curve?

3. Can you imagine other uses for the technology operating in the Wii controller? What are some of these possible applications?

MARY J. BLIGE
GAP (PRODUCT) RED™ TANK TOP

EMPOWE(RED)

(GAP) RED

CAN AN INDIVIDUAL CHANGE THE WORLD?   YES YOU CAN.
ALL GAP (PRODUCT) RED™ CLOTHING IS DESIGNED TO HELP ELIMINATE AIDS IN AFRICA.

DO THE (RED) THING™   TO FIND OUT MORE, GO TO GAP.COM/RED   GAP IS A PROUD PARTNER OF (PRODUCT) RED™

ITEM 7.6 ■ **Mary J. Blige Gap (PRODUCT) RED Collection Ad, 2006**

In 2006, Gap joined other manufacturers in offering products in support of the worldwide (PRODUCT) RED initiative designed to provide financial support for economic development in Africa. Companies dedicate a percentage of the profits from the sale of (PRODUCT) RED merchandise directly to a campaign to fight malaria, tuberculosis, and AIDS. In addition to hip hop, soul singer Blige, Gap ads featured Jennifer Garner, Chris Rock, and Apolo Ohno, among others.

[1] What adjectives might you use to describe the style of the ad: for example, sophisticated, subtle, comical, thought-provoking, pretentious? Defend your choices.

[2] How does the word EMPOWE(RED) function in the ad? How is it connected to Blige and the overall (RED) campaign itself?

[3] Do you believe that ads such as this one with social or political themes actually help to sell a product or idea? How do you find yourself responding to them? Might many people miss the point entirely?

[4] Design your own version of the Gap (PRODUCT) RED campaign, focusing on a different but appropriate celebrity. Or parody the concept of politically conscious ads.

406   GALLERY | STYLE, DESIGN, AND CULTURE

ITEM 7.7 ■ Still from *King Kong*, 1933; Poster for *King Kong*, 1976

Time marches on and contexts change. The Empire State Building (1930–1931), still New York City's most famous skyscraper, was, for instance, very much a product of its age. The United States may have been in a deepening depression in the early 1930s, but Americans wanted to believe in progress—and the Empire State Building fulfilled their need for a symbol of that faith. So it is no accident that a giant ape chose to climb the Empire State Building in the movie *King Kong* (1933). But in producer Dino De Laurentiis's 1976 remake, Kong straddles the twin towers of the World Trade Center, completed in 1973. Even the ape looks different.

1. How do the Empire State Building and the World Trade Center towers differ in their visual presence or impact in these images?

2. Can you identify a structure today that might represent what these buildings did in 1933 and 1976? How does the destruction of the World Trade Center in 2001 change the way you might read the 1976 poster?

3. In recent years, nations have jockeyed to design the world's tallest building. Research one of these structures and describe what its design may represent to the country or city constructing it. Buildings to examine might include Taipei 101 (see Item 4.7), Burj Dubai, or the Freedom Tower.

ITEM 7.8 ■ Jeep Design Language, 1940–Present Day

A design language (or style) is the themes, elements, and patterns that come together to define a particular look or idea. To grasp the elements of a particular style, try placing items that share a design language side by side, and then observe what changes from one to the other. For example, the original Jeep was hurriedly cobbled together at the outset of World War II to provide GIs with a rugged, all-terrain vehicle. Looks didn't matter. Yet the original design became so recognized that it still provides the inspiration for Jeep products almost seventy years later.

[1] Study these photographs carefully and then try to describe the elements essential to defining the design language of a Jeep. What features must a Jeep have? How far from these core elements might a designer stray and still create a recognizable product?

[2] To what audiences does Jeep appeal? What elements can you point to in the design language that give you clues about Jeep's intended market?

[3] In a drug or grocery store, compare the design language used in the packaging of a particular brand-name medication or product with that of a store-brand equivalent. What design features and elements (color, fonts, package, shape, etc.) does the lower-priced store brand mimic? Is such packaging helpful or deceptive?

GALLERY | STYLE, DESIGN, AND CULTURE

ITEM 7.9 ■ Jay B. Sauceda, *Let Me Learn Ya Somethin'*, **2008**

Emo is both a genre of rock music and a self-conscious style. According to *Wikipedia*, the markers of emo fashion include tight jeans, T-shirts and sweaters, straight bangs falling over the eyes, studded belts, black shoes or sneakers, and an "emotional, sensitive, shy, introverted, or angsty" attitude. Think Peter Parker in *Spider-Man 3,* or the fellow artfully posed in this photograph. Emo is, of course, only one of many cultural styles that have been cultivated by young people over the years.

1. What details do you notice in the photograph? How do these elements shape your interpretation of the character in it?

2. Do you think students in high school and college consciously design their identities or do they simply fall into them, naturally gravitating toward others who most resemble them in style and deportment? Does it make a difference whether people choose a group or find themselves slotted into one?

3. Using the resources of the Web, describe the style associated with a particular stereotypical teen depicted in films and TV shows. It might be the jock, the cheerleader, the nerd, the Goth, the stereotyped minority student, the preppie, or even a character who tries to resist stereotypes.

Cluster 7.1
The Design of Everyday Things

The most difficult objects to design well may be the simplest, such as the items in this cluster. If a design is working well, be it for a building, an electronic gizmo, or a newspaper front page, you may barely notice it. But its appearance isn't accidental: people have made choices about its function, shape, and materials. So it makes sense, at least occasionally, to think about such objects and how they influence us. The images and readings in this section explore the not-so-rudimentary principles behind items as common as chairs, suburban houses, and irritating commercials.

You may find it intriguing to listen to designers such as Michael Bierut and Niels Diffrient explain what it is that they do: their principles of their craft seem sensible and accessible. But, as Cathleen McGuigan demonstrates in "The McMansion Next Door," the homes many of us live in are often untouched by modern aesthetics. Why does design seem to count for so little in the most expensive objects we purchase? Could it be that bad design might even be good for commerce? That's *Salon* media critic Seth Stevenson's take on the advertising campaign no one can seem to forget: *"HeadOn: Apply directly to the forehead."* What was it designed to accomplish?

CONSIDER

1. Is the F-16 pictured in Item 7.10 (or any aircraft) an everyday object? Do you consider it "beautiful"? Why or why not?

2. It is sometimes argued that form should follow function. Can you identify items not designed specifically to please the eye that might nonetheless be attractive? Can you think of exceptions to the principle—that is, purely practical objects without any special visual appeal?

3. Do you find any political or ethical problems in celebrating the beauty of objects designed for war such as the F-16? Explain your position, citing examples.

ITEM 7.10 ■ F-16 Fighting Falcon

Designer Niels Diffrient describes the F-16 fighter jet, used by the United States Air Force and Navy, as "a beautiful object that does its job." Yet at first glance, it appears that all of its design decisions have been based on function, rather than appearance or aesthetics.

To Hell With the Simple Paper Clip

Michael Bierut
(2004)

> **FYI** Michael Bierut is a graphic designer whose clients range from Princeton University to Walt Disney. In addition, he has written extensively about design and is a commentator on Public Radio International's "Studio 360." Bierut is also one of the founding writers of DesignObserver.com, a blog for contemporary designers, where this short essay appeared on July 14, 2004.

If there's one design cliché that has come to really irritate me, it's this one: answering the question "What's your favorite design?" with an answer like "The simple paper clip." Or the rubber band. Or the stop sign. Or the Post-It Note. Or any other humble, unauthored object from everyday life.

To me, this is like answering the question "What's your favorite song?" with "You know, is there any song as beautiful as the laughter of a child?" It's corny. It's lazy. It's a cop-out.

I do admit, it's a tempting cop-out. We've all done it at one time or another. In the *New York Times Magazine*'s design issue five years ago, they put the question to a bunch of well-known people, some designers, some not. A few people named objects that were actually designed, although, oddly, the designer was not always named: the Pie Watch (named by Leon Wieseltier, not credited to M&Co.), the Braun Travel Alarm Clock (named by Martha Stewart, not credited to Dieter Rams). And, okay, even I myself went on the record for the Beatles's "White Album" without crediting Richard Hamilton.

But more frequent were the hymns to those damned anonymous objects, sometimes industrial in origin like the Sylvania half-frosted light bulb (chosen by Richard Gluckman), or something humble like chopsticks (chosen by Frogdesign's Hartmut Esslinger). Or how about . . . beads? That's right, just beads. "Beads focus and concentrate esthetic attention," we learned from Nest's Joseph Holtzman. "One becomes supremely aware of color, shape and especially surface."

Ah, the humble bead! On some level, I do see why designers in particular like to dodge this question. On one hand, you can be honest, select as your favorite something that you yourself designed, and look like an egomaniac, which you probably are. The alternative is to pick something someone else designed, and thus give aid and comfort to a competitor. Tough choice. Wait, how about . . . the humble white t-shirt, designed by absolutely no one? Perfect!

The white t-shirt and 121 other objects are currently on view at New York's Museum of Modern Art, in an exhibition that will either be the last word on the subject or start a new orgy of paper clip fetishization. "Humble Masterpieces," on view through September 27th [2004], was organized by the first-rate curator (and unrepentant Post-It Note fan) Paola Antonelli, and includes the Bic Pen, the whisk broom, the tennis ball, and bubble wrap. "Although modest in size and price, "Antonelli observes, "some of these objects are true masterpieces of the art of design and deserving of our admiration." And now, thanks to MoMA, so are many of their designers: Antonelli and her staff have diligently researched the names of the creators of these seemingly authorless objects. So we learn that Scotch tape was—what, designed? invented? discovered?—in 1930 by Richard G. Drew (American, 1886–1956). And it's all sparked a lively discussion on the Speak Up website where people are posting their own nominations.

Antonelli points out that MoMA's commitment to finding the sublime in the everyday has a long history. The museum's landmark "Machine Art" show in 1934 exhibited industrial objects like springs and ball bearings. The undeniable beauty of these objects must have been a revelation to audiences used to

> **But what is the effect on the 21st-Century museumgoer who is confronted with a display of Legos, Slinkys, soy sauce dispensers and M&Ms? I wonder.**

Victoriana and ersatz Streamline. The intention, I think, was to create a bracing demonstration of how form following function could lead to enduring, honest solutions, unencumbered by the fussy hand of the stylist. But what is the effect on the 21st-Century museumgoer who is confronted with a display of Legos, Slinkys, soy sauce dispensers and M&Ms? I wonder.

At any rate, now that MoMA's put its imprimatur on the whole idea, perhaps we can finally move on. All these things have now gotten their rightful due, and it's time to turn our attention to other worthy subjects. So if one of these days you're challenged to come up with your own favorite design and you just can't come up with one, take the easy way out: just pick something designed by me.

CONSIDER

1. If you were asked to identify your favorite design, how might you respond? Would you find it difficult to single out an object for admiration solely on the basis of style or design?

2. In his essay, Bierut mentions a wide range of designed objects, from the Pie Watch, Braun Travel Alarm Clock, and Beatles's *White Album* to beads, T-shirts, and whiskbrooms. Which of these items might *not* have occurred to you to consider as an object of design? Why not?

COMPOSE

3. Using Bierut's essay as a starting point, how would you characterize the difference between the lead items in this chapter—the Apple iPhone and the Hipster PDA—as objects of design (see Items 7.1 and 7.2). Would either, neither, or both of these objects deserve a place in MoMA's "Humble Masterpieces" exhibition? Why or why not?

4. Bierut seems willing to salute the objects of simple design in the MoMA show, but he is also eager to move "our attention to other worthy objects." Why might a designer lose patience with so much attention to humble objects?

CHALLENGE

5. Bierut seems to suggest that the 2004 collection of "Humble Masterpieces" at MoMA differs in important ways from the 1934 exhibition of "Machine Art." Use the Internet to research the 1934 show, and then try to answer the question Bierut poses in his second to last paragraph: "What is the effect on the 21st-century museumgoer who is confronted with a display of Legos, Slinkys, soy sauce dispensers and M&Ms [at the 2004 "Humble Masterpieces" show]"? Might museumgoers find the more recent show less illuminating than audiences found the 1934 exhibition?

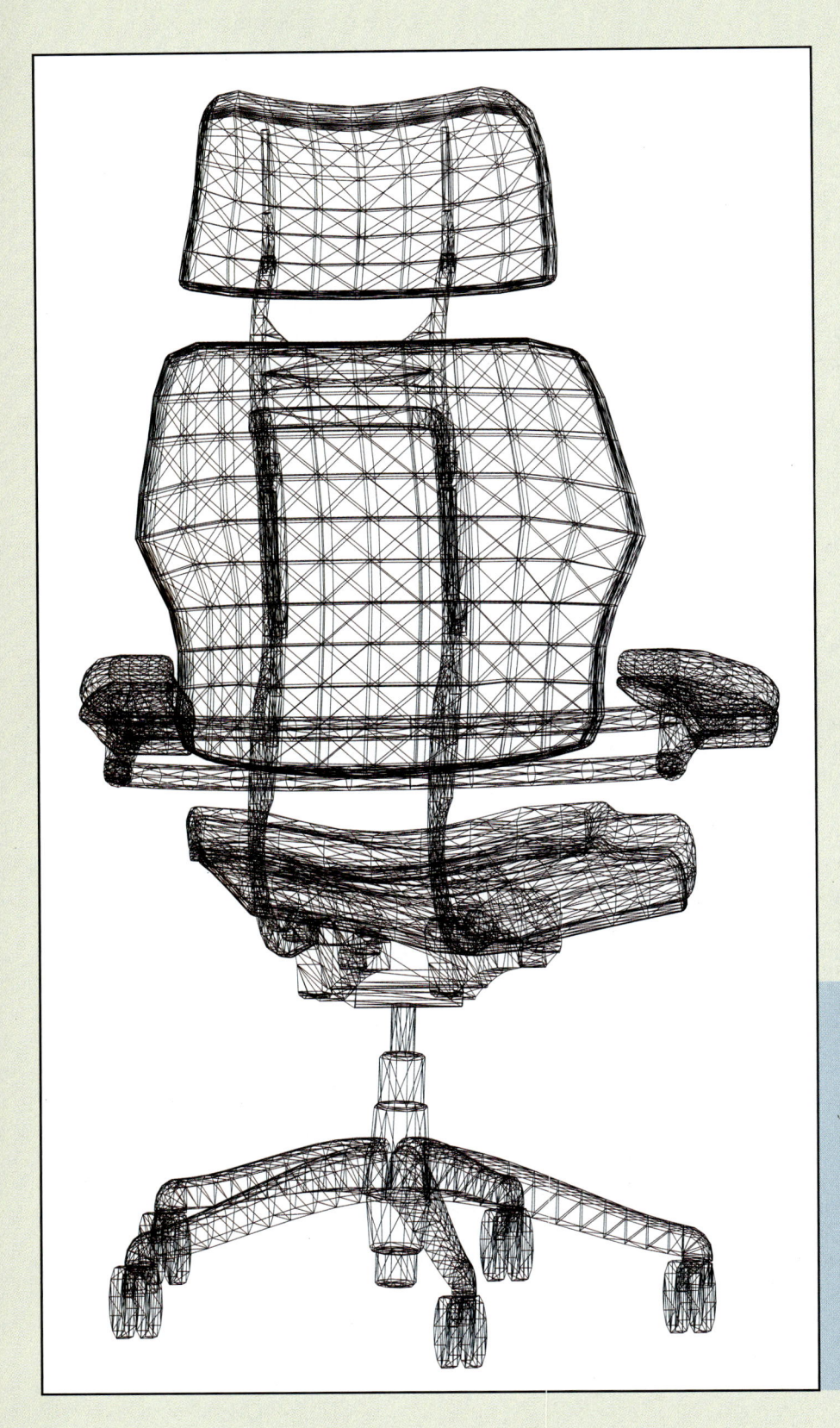

ITEM 7.11 ■ The Freedom Chair, 1999

Niels Diffrient designed the Freedom chair shown here to be *elegant* in the mathematical sense of the term—a simple solution to a complex problem. Existing chairs had too many knobs and adjustments. Diffrient wanted to create seating that would adapt itself to the human frame, as he explains in an interview on pages 415–416. The result is a chair that is not only simple and comfortable, but also quite beautiful.

7.1 | THE DESIGN OF EVERYDAY THINGS

Questions for Niels Diffrient

A Machine for Sitting

Interview by Pilar Viladas
(2003)

> **FYI** Niels Diffrient is a renowned industrial designer famously attuned to the human factor in the design of things. Among the best known of his numerous creations is the "Freedom" series of office chairs modeled on the way people actually use them. The interview with Niels Diffrient appeared in the *New York Times Magazine* on November 30, 2003. Pilar Viladas, the design editor of that magazine, has also served as an editor at *Progressive Architecture, Home and Garden,* and *Architectural Digest*.

In your 50 years as a designer, what have you wanted to accomplish?

It's my intent to make design a more consequential endeavor, not a decorative endeavor. I decided the best field to work in would be commercial furniture. [Industrial designer] Henry Dreyfuss introduced me to "human-factors engineering" in 1955—it's now called ergonomics. We worked on making the machines fit people. I had worked in [architect] Eero Saarinen's office on furniture. I learned a lot from Eero. We didn't know a lot about ergonomics then. We learned it, pardon the pun, by the seat of our pants.

For something as technical as ergonomics, where does the inspiration come from?

The nature of inspiration includes the understanding of all the factors necessary to design. It's like a physicist trying to bring together a comprehensive theory of the universe. You can't leave anything out. Academics in human-factors engineering are only interested in the data. I'm looking to find out how the data may be used to improve a situation. Why would you design something if it didn't improve the human condition?

How does this apply to the Freedom Chair, one of the designs you're most known for?

The problem with many ergonomically designed office chairs is they have all these knobs and levers—to adjust the seat height, recline of the backrest, height of the armrests, the headrest and so on. But most people never use them. The things that this chair does to address that problem are: When you recline, you don't have to adjust the chair—it adapts to your body weight. When you decide that the armrests are not where you want them to be, you grab one or both arms and move them up or down. They're coordinated, so if you pull one up, the other follows.

What's an example of an everyday object that you think is well designed?

One of my favorites is the umbrella. I also like the titanium-and-carbon-fiber tennis rackets. They're light, strong and never warp. The umbrella, the bicycle, the pencil, the tennis racket—these are immensely efficient. The Post-it note—most of us take it for granted, but it's a design. The F-16 fighter jet—it's a beautiful object that does its job.

What about things that don't work?

The New York City taxicab is one of the worst-adapted products for its purpose. Also, those entrancing, simple chairs that people love to look at. A good deal of the Bauhaus falls into that category of what I call functional style. I'm a sucker for this stuff, too, like everyone else—I have Breuer and Mies bent-tube furniture in my living room, but I hardly ever sit in them. I sit in a comfortable chair and look at them. I saw a photo of Ettore Sottsass, who designs all this way-out stuff, in his studio. That's not design to be used. I have tremendous respect for Ettore because his competence at form-giving is extraordinary. So is Michael Graves's, and so is Philippe Starck's. That's their strength. You can't blame them—they look upon themselves as poets and artists. Sottsass did things for Olivetti—typewriters, adding machines. When someone of his caliber moves into accepting constraints of performance and function, he does extraordinary design.

Do you agree with the notion that people are more savvy about design these days?

Yes, with qualifiers. There is a class of person who is educated enough and sensitive to elements of aesthetic refinement. You could almost directly design for these people because they're discriminating. But the whole nature of my profession is design for the masses. They're [attuned] to certain things—price, availability, distribution, functionality. If it does something obviously better, they'll buy it. You want to use function as a door-opener. After that, it would be nice if the product were well styled.

Is there anything you haven't designed but would like to?

Clothing. I carry a pocketknife, and when I sit down, it slides out of my pocket. If men's trousers had just a little "step" in the pocket, things wouldn't slide out. It could be a major marketing advantage to address functional issues in clothing.

CONSIDER

1. Diffrient describes designs that he particularly admires: umbrellas, pencils, tennis rackets, and bicycles. Consider these objects closely, and then try to list the design qualities they might have in common. Why might a designer like Diffrient admire a pencil? How might he respond to Michael Bierut's impatience with simple designs, as expressed in "To Hell With the Simple Paper Clip"?

2. Do a Web search for "Marcel Breuer furniture" to see what kind of chairs Diffrient looks at in his living room. What might the rationale be for either designing or owning such furniture?

CHALLENGE

3. Diffrient points out that an object as ordinary as a Post-it® note can embody great design. Working in a group, try to come up with an alternative design for the Post-it note or, perhaps, the umbrella. What effect does an existing design have on our ability to imagine alternatives?

ITEM 7.12 ■ Le Corbusier, Villa Savoye at Poissy, France, 1928–29

Le Corbusier (1887–1965) was a French architect who applied principles of modern architecture to the private home—which he famously argued should be regarded as "a machine." He hoped to build practical housing for the urban masses.

CONSIDER

1. Villa Savoye was built more than eighty years ago. Does it look dated or contemporary?

2. Contrast the style of the Villa Savoye with that of typical homes in American suburbs. Would Le Corbusier's home fit into such neighborhoods?

3. Do you find Villa Savoye effective as a design? Would you want to live in a modernist structure of this kind? Why or why not?

The McMansion Next Door: Why the American House Needs a Makeover

Cathleen McGuigan
(2003)

> **FYI** Cathleeen McGuigan is Senior Editor for the Arts and serves as the architecture critic for *Newsweek* magazine. Her articles on film and visual culture have also appeared in the *New York Times Magazine*, *Harper's*, and *Rolling Stone*.

Design is everywhere, right? Your toothbrush, your running shoes, your cool-looking couch, your latte machine, your laptop. OK, no one would mistake Indiana for Italy, but you can finally buy good design almost anywhere, from the mall to the Internet. But there's one big-ticket item in this country that is virtually untouched by the hand of a good designer: your house.

Most new off-the-rack houses aren't so much designed as themed: Mediterranean, French country, faux Tudor, neo-Colonial. These houses may offer—on the high end—every option money can buy, from a media room to a separate shower for the dog. But the market actually gives consumers little true choice: the developer house, in most price ranges, is amazingly similar from coast to coast, across different climate zones and topographies.

If you ripped off the roofs—and the turrets and gables and fake widow's walks—or peered into the windows—double-hung, round, Palladian, picture (often in the same house!)—you'd find essentially the same thing: a vast foyer with chandelier; formal living and dining rooms (rarely used); open-plan kitchen/family room; master suite and bedrooms; many bathrooms; at least a three-car garage. It makes me wonder whatever happened to the modern house, and why the core idea of modernism—that through mass production, ordinary people could afford the best design—never caught on when it came to houses.

Le Corbusier called the house "a machine for living in"—which meant, notes New York architect Deborah Gans, that the house is a tool people control, not the other way round.

The brilliance of the modern house was in the flexible spaces that flowed one to the next, and in the simplicity and toughness of the materials. Postwar America saw a few great experiments, most famously in L.A.'s Case Study Houses in the late 1940s and '50s. Occasionally, a visionary developer, such as Joseph Eichler in California, used good modern architects to design his subdivisions. Today they're high-priced collectibles.

Modernist houses, custom-designed for an elite clientele, are still built, of course. But when I recently asked Barbara Neski, who, with her husband, Julian, designed such houses in the 1960s and beyond, why modern never went mainstream, she replied, "What happens when you ask a child to draw a house?" You get a box with a triangle on top. A little gabled house still says "home."

Yet the cozy warmth of that iconic image doesn't explain the market for neotraditional houses today. Not all these houses are ugly and shoddy: though most are badly proportioned pastiches of different styles, some are built with attention to detail and materials. But, as the epithet *McMansion* suggests, they're just too big—for their lots, for their neighborhoods and for the number of people who actually live in them. And why do they keep getting bigger, when families are getting smaller? In 1970, the average new single-family house was 1,400 square feet; today it's 2,300.

The housing industry says that we want bigger and bigger houses. But I think they're not taking credit for their marketing skills. Last year's annual report for Pulte

Source: C. McGuigan, "The McMansion Next Door." From *Newsweek*, October 27, 2003. © 2003 Newsweek, Inc. All rights reserved. Used by permission and protected by the Copyright Laws of the United States. The printing, copying, redistribution, or retransmission of the material without express permission is prohibited.

Homes, one of the nation's biggest builders, contains an astonishing fact: if you adjust for inflation, houses of the same size and comparable features are the same price today as they were in the 1970s. That means that if business is going to grow, the industry has to sell more product—not just more houses but more square footage. It's like the junk-food-marketing genius who figured out that people wouldn't go back for seconds but they'd pay more upfront to get, say, the 32-ounce Big Gulp.

This year, Pulte predicts, the number of houses built will be only slightly higher than last year's. "More and more of the same might not sound particularly exciting, but it is," the report says. "That's because houses ... will continue to get bigger and better, ensuring that real inflation-adjusted spending on residential construction will continue to rise." Bully for them—and for the folks in the real-estate and financing industries who base value on size not quality.

But finally some people are saying "Enough already." Sarah Susanka, a Minnesota architect, started a mini-movement with her best-selling 1998 book, *The Not So Big House*. Susanka argues that a good architect understands the importance of human scale. Under the dome of St. Peter's, you're meant to feel awe. But if your bedroom's the size of a barn, how cozy can you get?

The eco-conscious hate big houses, too, with the energy cost of heating and cooling all those big empty rooms. And now that McMansions not only are the staple of new suburbs but are invading older, leafy neighborhoods, built in place of tear-downs and overpowering the smaller vintage houses nearby, communities from Greenwich, Conn., to Miami Beach are beginning to take action.

> **But if your bedroom's the size of a barn, how cozy can you get?**

Some middle-class people who care about design have opted out of the new-house market. They'll re-model an old house, one with an honest patina of history that all the money in the world can't reproduce. And some architects are hatching low-cost plans for the mainstream market. Prefab is hot right now: designs that use factory-built modules are assembled on-site. It's much cheaper than conventional construction, and if it's done well, it can look great—and modern.

"We have this concept about design and mass culture in America, with Target, Banana Republic, Design Within Reach," says Joseph Tanney of Resolution: 4 Architecture, which won a *Dwell* magazine competition to design a cool house in North Carolina for only $80 a square foot (a custom house would be $200 to $400 per). The house is prefab, and the firm has half a doz-en more in the works. Seattle architect James Cutler (who designed Bill Gates's Xanadu) is working with Lindal Cedar Homes, a national build-er, to adapt a wood-and-glass modernist house for modular construction.

"I think there's a return to an interest in modernism," says New York architect Deborah Berke, "and I would call it warm modernism, not sleek minimalism." She argues that a younger generation, steeped in a love of cool design and loft living and ready for a first house, isn't going to buy a mini-McMansion. "That's where the industry is not reading the social signs yet."

As more people get into design—even starting with a toothbrush—the more they'll want their houses to reflect what they value. Flat roof? Peaked roof? It doesn't really matter: the best design reflects who we are and the time in which we live. Who knows what our grandchildren might come up with if someone hands them a crayon and says "Draw a house"?

CONSIDER

1. Do you agree with McGuigan's contention that the American house needs a makeover? Why or why not?
2. How would you account for the fondness people have for traditional design elements in the homes they buy? Why don't homes evolve the way other consumer products do—like cars, video equipment, or cell phones?

COMPOSE

3. Cathleen McGuigan writes that "the best design reflects who we are and the time in which we live." Using words and images, design a home that reflects who you are and the time in which you live. (You might want to review Cluster 4.1, "Places We Inhabit" on pages 192-213 for more ideas. See especially "Our Sprawling, Supersize Utopia" on page 194-199.)

ITEM 7.13 ■ "HeadOn: Apply directly to the forehead."

If you watched television during summer 2006, you probably recall the first time you saw the original advertisement for headache product HeadOn. The pitch was simple, direct, and, most people thought, a bit crude.

CONSIDER

1. How would you describe the style of the famous HeadOn product advertisement? Does it remind you of any other television commercials?

2. What doesn't the TV ad say about the product? What don't you know about HeadOn from its original TV spot?

COMPOSE

3. Many advertisements today take a soft-sell approach, soothing potential customers with lots of style and corporate image building and often making no direct allusions to specific products. Which approach do you regard as more effective for general audiences—the soft sell or HeadOn's direct messaging? Why? Explain your reasoning in a brief paper.

Head Case

The Mesmerizing Ad for Headache Gel

Seth Stevenson
(2006)

FYI We're accustomed to movie, restaurant, and product reviews, so why not reviews of commercials? They are, after all, carefully crafted appeals to our minds and pocketbooks—and often more stylish than the products they represent. In a nod to their cultural significance, Slate.com runs a regular feature called "Ad Report Card" analyzing some of the more popular or controversial television advertisements. Here, media critic Seth Stevenson examines what some regard as the mind-numbing TV spots for a product called HeadOn. The review appeared on Slate.com on July 24, 2006.

The Spot: *A woman rubs what appears to be a glue stick across her forehead. The voice-over repeats one sentence in triplicate: "HeadOn: Apply directly to the forehead. HeadOn: Apply directly to the forehead. HeadOn: Apply directly to the forehead." We cut to an image of the product in its packaging, while the voice-over tells us that "HeadOn is available without a prescription at retailers nationwide."*

When I first saw this ad, I was convinced it was a viral prank. Everything about it—the woman serenely rubbing stuff on her forehead; the lack of explanation as to what this stuff is; and, of course, the mind-numbing repetition of that weird catchphrase—just seemed too bizarre to be an actual commercial for an actual product. When I logged on to HeadOn.com, I expected a jokey Web site that would eventually redirect me to a promotion for Burger King or Axe deodorant or something.

But no, it turns out HeadOn is for real. (That is, the product does exist. I'm not sure I can use the word "real" in any reference to a topical homeopathic health remedy.) HeadOn is meant to treat headaches and is a gel suffused with various plant extracts that you apply—say it with me—directly to the forehead. I am told that doing so creates a cooling sensation. HeadOn is available at Wal-Mart for $5.24 if you care to check it out for yourself. Caveat emptor.

As for this ad campaign, it is utter genius. With this one 10-second spot, the makers of HeadOn have torn down all the pretenses that have gummed up the advertising industry for years. Production values? Persuasion? Emotion? Humor (of the intentional kind)? These are stalwarts of the old, outmoded advertising paradigm. The new, head-on (or HeadOn) approach holds that advertising is about blunt force.

It really is sad when you think about the hard work that gets done inside advertising agencies. All the writing and rewriting, the late-night brainstorming, the mining of creativity from the deepest recesses of one's cortex. And then there's the casting, the directing, the high-budget locations. The question we must now ask is: Why bother with any of this? The HeadOn ad is more effective at reaching its goals than 99 percent of the ads on television. And it succeeds on the strength of a few, bare-bones tactics that most advertisers carefully shun:

Repetition: According to Dan Charron, VP of sales and marketing for HeadOn, the company used focus groups to test all sorts of marketing tacks. One experimental approach maxed out on repetition, and the results were incredible. The focus groups' recollection of the ad, and of the product, was light-years better than with any other method. Which, of course, seems completely obvious—how can we forget something when it's being jammed into our brains? And yet I've never seen an ad embrace this insight with so much gusto.

I suspect most advertisers avoid the broken-record technique out of fear that it will annoy people. Which it does. But so what? Maybe a small percentage of us will snootily refrain from buying HeadOn—as an act of protest against an ad we find irritating—but this is a small price to pay when millions of other folks are now familiar with HeadOn, curious about it, and unlikely ever to forget its name. The repetition method serves no purpose for a well-established brand ("Coca-Cola: Pour it down your esophagus. Coca-Cola: Pour it down your esophagus"), but for a new product fighting to get noticed, it makes a lot of sense.

> **It's mesmerizing in its cheesiness and also eye-catching because it looks and sounds like nothing else on television.**

Kitsch: This ad was made in-house by HeadOn, and it boasts production values so bad they may seem intentional. (They're not.) That green, graph-paper background. The way the volume fades and surges on the voice-over loop. The big, yellow-arrow graphic in the middle of the screen. And above all, the very image of this chick rubbing goop back and forth across her noggin. It's mesmerizing in its cheesiness and also eye-catching because it looks and sounds like nothing else on television. (Though a past ad for Overstock.com similarly benefited from low production values.)

Mystery: We all know how to use the product. (My understanding is that it's meant to be applied to the forehead. In a direct manner.) But the ad never tells us just what HeadOn is for. I had assumed this was in compliance with some kind of FDA regulation, the way pharmaceutical ads never say just what a pill does. But in fact, according to Charron, HeadOn (being an over-the-counter product) is not even subject to these regulations. The omission of a key detail here is a purposeful marketing technique.

"A good way to get attention," says Charron, "is to not say what the product does. It touches on people's curiosity." Indeed—curiosity is what sent me to the HeadOn Web site, and it no doubt sent millions of other people there, as well. If some percentage of those people are headache sufferers, and also gullible, they might well be moved to buy some HeadOn.

Ubiquity: Charron says they've spent "tens of millions of dollars" on this HeadOn campaign. "If you watch any TV at all," he says, "chances are you've seen the ad in the last three weeks." It's airing on networks, on cable, and in syndication. During the day, prime time, and late night. It won't stop airing until mid-August, so you'd better get used to it.

If repetition within the ad is effective, why not extend this insight to repetition of the ad? Just keep airing it so often that it can't be escaped and can't be ignored. The ad is already generating tons of talk on the Web and has inspired a parody involving rapper Lil Jon. It's everywhere.

Grade: A+. And I haven't even touched on yet another powerful theory: These ads give viewers headaches, thus spurring demand.

CONSIDER

1. Stevenson's analysis of the HeadOn ad is highly subjective and personal, given from a first-person or "I" point of view. What are the advantages and risks of using this strategy in an evaluation?

2. Stevenson's first impression of a HeadOn ad is that it must be a "viral prank." Searching the term on the Internet or drawing on your own experiences (perhaps at a concert), define "viral marketing." How does it differ from traditional marketing approaches? (For more about viral marketing, see Beau Faulkner's essay "*Year Zero*: A Viral Marketing Promotion" on pages 389–393.)

3. Does Stevenson provide sufficient evidence to convince you of his claim that the HeadOn spots are "utter genius"? How seriously do you take such a claim? What was your own reaction to the campaign?

COMPOSE

4. Stevenson claims that most advertisers shun the four tactics that he believes account for the success of the HeadOn advertisements: repetition, kitsch, mystery, and ubiquity. In a short essay, try to apply these principles to other advertising campaigns that you regard as successful. Are these techniques as rare as Stevenson claims?

5. Pick a television commercial and analyze it, modeling your evaluation directly on the formula "Ad Report Card" uses. Be sure that you describe the ad briefly ("The Spot") and then conclude the analysis with a grade for the ad and a few pithy remarks. For assistance, see "Writing an Ad Analysis" on pages 72–73.

Cluster 7.2
The Eyes of the Beholder

Perhaps the first object of design was the human body—and the desire to beautify the human form marked the beginning of art and culture. We know that the craft of adorning the skin with pigment reaches back at least 10,000 years in Japan and other parts of Asia. Western seafarers brought the process of tattooing from Polynesia back to England, Europe, and the Americas, making this form of body decoration a worldwide art form that still thrives today. We know, too, that the ancient Egyptians and Romans used cosmetics; hair has been styled probably since Eve met Adam, and punk rockers in the 1970s weren't the first to pierce every available human appendage.

But how much transformation of the human form is too much? In an era when cosmetic surgery for teenagers is routine and when idealized images of the human form are a staple of art and advertising, have we undercut what it means to be human by trading our indisputable diversity for a universal definition of beauty? Some argue that this oppressive standard—one that almost no one can attain—has undermined the health and well-being of people worldwide, especially the young. In this cluster, a press release for Dove's "Campaign for Real Beauty" expresses this point of view and outlines a campaign to broaden accepted standards of beauty. But Virginia Postrel pushes back, arguing in "The Truth About Beauty" that universal standards, in fact, guide the judgments people make about each other's looks. Daniel Aksts probes the issue even more deeply in "Looks *Do* Matter," asking how Americans can simultaneously worship physically perfect celebrities and yet care so little about their own physical appearance. The implications of his analysis reach well beyond matters of style: our health and well-being may be at stake.

Clearly, whatever *beauty* means matters.

FYI

ITEM 7.14 ■ Still from Dove's Campaign for Real Beauty

As part of its "Campaign for Real Beauty" (see next entry), Dove, a Unilever brand that makes beauty bars, body washes, face care, anti-perspirant/deodorants, body mists, and hair care and styling aids, designed a campaign to challenge beauty stereotypes and invite women to join in a discussion about real beauty. The campaign focuses on real women, including the six women shown here, who do not fit the traditional and unrealistic standards of beauty portrayed in the media.

Do you believe that real beauty comes in many shapes and sizes?

Join the campaign   campaignforrealbeauty.com   Dove

CONSIDER

1. What is your initial reaction to the image and the question it poses? Do you think most people would answer the question honestly?

2. Would you pay more or less attention to advertisements (or even films and other entertainments) if they featured more people who looked like those you see every day, perhaps sitting in your classroom?

3. Notice that the Dove image includes a call to "Join the campaign." How seriously would you and your friends respond to such a call? What action could you take to support such a campaign?

The Campaign for Real Beauty Background

CAMPAIGN FOR REAL BEAUTY MISSION

The Dove Campaign for Real Beauty is a global effort launched in 2004 to serve as a starting point for societal change and act as a catalyst for widening the definition and discussion of beauty. The campaign supports the Dove mission: to make more women feel beautiful every day by widening stereotypical views of beauty.

The brand's commitment to the mission starts with using real women, not professional models, of various ages, shapes and sizes to provoke discussion and debate about today's typecast beauty images. Employing various communication vehicles including advertising, a Web site, billboards, events, a Self-Esteem Fund and more—the campaign invites women to join in a discussion about beauty and share their views with women around the world.

LISTENING TO WOMEN

The Dove Campaign for Real Beauty was inspired by a major global study—The Real Truth About Beauty: A Global Report. The study validated the hypothesis that the definition of beauty had become limiting and unattainable, as if only thin, young and blond were beautiful. Dove found the current, narrow definition of beauty was having a profound effect on the self-esteem of women:

- Only 2% of women around the world describe themselves as beautiful.
- 81% of women in the U.S. strongly agree that "the media and advertising set an unrealistic standard of beauty that most women can't ever achieve."

DEBUNKING STEREOTYPES

The Dove Campaign for Real Beauty was created to provoke discussion and encourage debate. Based on the global study findings, Dove started a series of communication campaigns to challenge beauty stereotypes and invite women to join in a discussion about beauty.

The campaign launched in September 2004 with a much-talked-about ad campaign featuring real women whose appearances are outside the stereotypical norms of beauty. The ads asked viewers to judge the women's looks (*Oversized? Outstanding?* or *Wrinkled? Wonderful?*) and invited them to cast their votes at www.campaignforrealbeauty.com. As part of the launch campaign, Dove invited women to rediscover the beauty in their own hair. Television advertising challenged society's narrow vision that "one size fits all" hair is for everyone.

In June 2005, Dove kicked off the second phase of the Campaign for Real Beauty with advertising featuring six real women with real bodies and real curves. This phase of the campaign was created to debunk the stereotype that only thin is beautiful and it once again drove thousands of women to campaignforrealbeauty.com to discuss beauty issues.

Continuing its ongoing commitment to widen the narrow definition of beauty, Dove launched the third phase of the Campaign for Real Beauty in February 2007. The Dove global study, "Beauty Comes of Age," revealed 91% of women ages 50–64 believe it is time for society to change its views about women and aging. Pro•age boldly challenges the "only young-is-beautiful" stereotype. The campaign celebrates the essence of women 50+—wrinkles, age spots, grey hair and all. It was brought to life through a communications campaign created with internationally renowned photographer Annie Leibovitz.

FYI Dove, a global marketer of beauty products, created the Campaign for Real Beauty in 2004 to serve as a starting point for societal change and act as a catalyst for widening the definition and discussion of beauty. A form of viral marketing, the Campaign for Real Beauty spread its message through online videos, various public initiatives, and a strong presence on the Web, inviting women to participate in a discussion to redefine real beauty to include people of more diverse sizes, shapes, and ages. The press information reprinted here explains the mission and methodology of the Campaign. More information on the campaign is available at www.Dove.com.

The Campaign for Real Beauty is currently focused on how girls today are bombarded with unrealistic, unattainable messages and images of beauty that impact their self-esteem. Dove has teamed up with the entertainment industry to provide girls with a reality check on what is real vs. Hollywood magic by hosting self-esteem workshops and providing new online self-esteem tools for moms and girls. The campaign was developed to help girls realize what they see in movies and magazines represents an unrealistic standard of beauty, not an everyday achievable look. As part of this effort, Dove also released "Onslaught," an online film dramatizing the barrage of beauty images girls face.

DOVE VIRAL FILMS

In September 2006, a news and media furor erupted when Spain banned overly thin models from its fashion runways. The debate spoke to the heart of the Dove Campaign for Real Beauty mission. In response, Dove produced a compelling short film, "Evolution," which depicts the transformation of a real woman into a model and promotes awareness of how unrealistic perceptions of beauty are created.

"Onslaught" is a new viral film that dramatically depicts the constant barrage of beauty images that girls absorb every day. Both visually and emotionally powerful, the film is a wake-up call for anyone concerned about the factors that impact self-esteem in young girls.

DOVE SUPPORTS SELF-ESTEEM

The current focus of the Campaign for Real Beauty is aimed at raising the self-esteem of girls and young women through the Dove Self-Esteem Fund. In the U.S., the Fund supports uniquely ME!, a program of the Girl Scouts of the USA. The program is designed to build self-confidence in girls ages 8–17 with education resources and hands-on activities.

Additionally, the Dove Self-Esteem Fund is sponsoring self-esteem building workshops with inspirational celebrities and new online tools in an effort to educate moms, mentors and girls. Dove is working toward the goal of truly making a difference in the lives of 5 million young people globally by 2010.

JOIN THE DEBATE AND HELP MAKE A DIFFERENCE

The Campaign for Real Beauty site at www.Dove.com houses a variety of tools for improving self-esteem in girls. Visitors can access new self-esteem building tools, take part in interactive self-esteem activities and join self-esteem discussion boards. They can also learn how to lead self-esteem workshops and read articles by leading self-esteem experts.

Since launching, nearly 4.5 million people have logged onto the Campaign's Web site. Thousands have shared words of encouragement, learned about self-esteem tips and joined Dove in encouraging a wider definition of beauty.

CONSIDER

1. Is physical beauty, whether entirely natural or enhanced by makeup, clothes, and accessories, a concept that can be altered by discussion and ad campaigns? Or do you suspect that Dove may run up against resistance at some points? What might those points of resistance be?

COMPOSE

2. Dove is proud that images in its ad campaign featuring real women are not altered or distorted to create an unrealistic or unattainable view of beauty. Write a short paper exploring the value of such authenticity in a world where even amateur photographers can digitally alter their shots and many films feature CGI (computer generated imagery) sequences. Is the preservation of reality more important in some circumstances than others?

3. Is the notion that design and fashion should feature "real" people idealistic and inspiring? Or do you feel manipulated by a company using so many commercial resources—magazine ads, billboards, foundation money, essay contests—to appeal to populist sentiments? Is everything truly beautiful, in its own way? Or does Dove simply expect to profit if more women think so?

FYI

ITEM 7.15 ■ Nikki Blonsky

Not every actress is thin. At age seventeen, Nikki Blonsky was cast in the lead role of Tracy Turnblad in the offbeat 2007 movie musical *Hairspray*. Tracy is an outgoing, popular, and plump teenager who wins the affection of Link, played in the film by Zac Efron.

CONSIDER

1. Is Nikki Blonsky only the exception that proves the rule that Americans prefer their celebrities thin-to-skeletal? Or can you point to other full-figured pop stars?

2. In "The Truth About Beauty," Virginia Postrel asserts that "Everyone falls short of perfection, but some are luckier than others." Does Blonsky fall into that *luckier* category? In what ways?

3. Might aesthetic standards vary by age, race, and gender? Is a black singer or actor less stigmatized by an ample figure? Can a man succeed more readily in Hollywood without being a perfect ten?

The Truth About Beauty

It's the same in the eye of every beholder

Virginia Postrel
(2007)

> **FYI**
> Virginia Postrel writes widely about culture, commerce, and design. She is the author of *The Substance of Style* (2003), which explores the increasing role that aesthetics and design are playing in a consumer society. Postrel has also written on economics for the *New York Times* and culture for *Atlantic Monthly*. In "The Truth About Beauty," an essay that appeared in *Atlantic Monthly* in March 2007, Postrel raises serious questions about the consequences of Dove's much-admired Campaign for Real Beauty described in a press release on pages 426–427.

Cosmetics makers have always sold "hope in a jar"—creams and potions that promise youth, beauty, sex appeal, and even love for the women who use them. Over the last few years, the marketers at Dove have added some new-and-improved enticements. They're now promising self-esteem and cultural transformation. Dove's "Campaign for Real Beauty," declares a press release, is "a global effort that is intended to serve as a starting point for societal change and act as a catalyst for widening the definition and discussion of beauty." Along with its thigh-firming creams, self-tanners, and hair conditioners, Dove is peddling the crowd-pleasing notions that beauty is a media creation, that recognizing plural forms of beauty is the same as declaring every woman beautiful, and that self-esteem means ignoring imperfections.

Dove won widespread acclaim in June 2005 when it rolled out its thigh-firming cream with billboards of attractive but variously sized "real women" frolicking in their underwear. It advertised its hair-care products by showing hundreds of women in identical platinum-blonde wigs—described as "the kind of hair found in magazines"—tossing off those artificial manes and celebrating their real (perfectly styled, colored, and conditioned) hair. It ran print ads that featured atypical models, including a plump brunette and a ninety-five-year-old, and invited readers to choose between pejorative and complimentary adjectives: "Wrinkled or wonderful?" "Oversized or outstanding?" The public and press got the point, and Dove got attention. Oprah covered the story, and so did the *Today* show. Dove's campaign, wrote *Advertising Age*, "undermines the basic proposition of decades of beauty-care advertising by telling women—and young girls—they're beautiful just the way they are."

Last fall, Dove extended its image building with a successful bit of viral marketing: a seventy-five-second online video called *Evolution*. Created by Ogilvy & Mather, the video is a close-up of a seemingly ordinary woman, shot in harsh lighting that calls attention to her uneven skin tone, slightly lopsided eyes, and dull, flat hair. In twenty seconds of time-lapse video, makeup artists and hair stylists turn her into a wide-eyed, big-haired beauty with sculpted cheeks and perfect skin. It's *Extreme Makeover* without the surgical gore.

But that's only the beginning. Next comes the digital transformation, as a designer points-and-clicks on the model's photo, giving her a longer, slimmer neck, a slightly narrower upper face, fuller lips, bigger eyes, and more space between her eyebrows and eyes. The perfected image rises to fill a billboard advertising a fictitious line of makeup. Fade to black, with the message "No wonder our perception of beauty is distorted." The video has attracted more than 3 million YouTube views. It also appears on Dove's campaignforrealbeauty.com Web site, where it concludes, "Every girl deserves to feel beautiful just the way she is."

Every girl certainly wants to, which explains the popularity of Dove's campaign. There's only one problem: Beauty exists, and it's unevenly distributed. Our eyes and brains pretty consistently like some human forms better than others. Shown photos of strangers, even babies look longer at the faces adults rank the best-looking. Whether you prefer Nicole Kidman to Angelina Jolie, Jennifer Lopez to Halle Berry, or Queen Latifah to Kate Moss may be a matter of taste, but rare is the beholder who would declare Holly Hunter or Whoopi Goldberg—neither of whom is homely—more beautiful than any of these women.

For similar reasons, we still thrill to the centuries-old bust of Nefertiti, the Venus de Milo, and the exquisite faces painted by Leonardo and Botticelli. Greta Garbo's acting style seems stilted today, but her face transcends time. We know beauty when we see it, and our reactions are remarkably consistent. Beauty is not just a social construct, and not every girl is beautiful just the way she is.

Take Dove's *Evolution* video. The digital transformation is fascinating because it magically makes a beautiful woman more striking. Her face's new geometry triggers an immediate, visceral response—and the video's storytelling impact is dependent on that predictable reaction. The video makes its point about artifice only because most people find the manipulated face more beautiful than the natural one.

In *Survival of the Prettiest: The Science of Beauty*, Nancy Etcoff, a psychologist at Harvard Medical School, reported on experiments that let people rate faces and digitally "breed" ever-more-attractive composite generations. The results for female faces look a lot like the finished product in the Dove video: "thinner jaws, larger eyes relative to the size of their faces, and shorter distances between their mouths and chins" in one case, and "fuller lips, a less robust jaw, a smaller nose and smaller chin than the population average" in another. These features, wrote Etcoff, "exaggerate the ways that adult female faces differ from adult male faces. They also exaggerate the youthfulness of the face." More than youth, the full lips and small jaws of beautiful women reflect relatively high levels of female hormones and low levels of male hormones—indicating greater fertility—according to psychologist Victor Johnston, who did some of these experiments.

More generally, evolutionary psychologists suggest that the features we see as beautiful—including indicators of good health like smooth skin and symmetry—have been rewarded through countless generations of competition for mates. The same evolutionary pressures, this research suggests, have biologically programmed human minds to perceive these features as beautiful. "Some scientists believe that our beauty detectors are really detectors for the combination of youth and femininity," wrote Etcoff. Whether the beauty we detect arises from nature or artifice doesn't change that visceral reflex.

Perhaps surprisingly, Etcoff herself advised Dove on several rounds of survey research and helped the company create workshops for girls. Dove touts her involvement (and her doctorate and Harvard affiliation) in its publicity materials. She sees the campaign as a useful corrective. Media images, Etcoff notes in an e-mail, are often so rarefied that "they change our ideas about what people look like and what normal looks like . . . Our brains did not evolve with media, and many people see more media images of women than actual women. The contrast effect makes even the most beautiful non-model look less attractive; it produces a new 'normal.'"

> "The current focus of the Campaign for Real Beauty is aimed at raising the self-esteem of girls and young women through the Dove Self-Esteem Fund."

Dove began its campaign by recognizing the diverse manifestations of universally beautiful patterns. The "real women" pictured in the thigh-cream billboards may not have looked like supermodels, but they were all young, with symmetrical faces, feminine features, great skin, white teeth, and hourglass shapes. Even the most zaftig had relatively flat stomachs and clearly defined waists. These pretty women were not a random sample of the population. Dove diversified the portrait of beauty without abandoning the concept altogether.

But the campaign didn't stop there. Dove is defining itself as the brand that loves regular women—and regular women, by definition, are not extraordinarily beautiful. The company can't afford a precise definition of *real beauty* that might exclude half the population—not a good strategy for selling mass-market consumer products. So the campaign leaves real beauty ambiguous, enabling the viewers to fill in the concept with their own desires. Some take real beauty to mean "nature unretouched" and interpret the *Evolution* video as suggesting that uncannily beautiful faces are not merely rare but nonexistent. Others emphasize the importance of character and personality: Real beauty comes from the inside, not physical appearance. And *Advertising Age's* interpretation is common: that Dove is reminding women that "they're beautiful just the way they are."

Another Dove ad, focusing on girls' insecurities about their looks, concludes, "Every girl deserves to feel good about herself and see how beautiful she really is." Here, Dove is encouraging the myth that physical beauty is a false concept, and, at the same time, falsely equating beauty with goodness and self-worth. If you don't see perfection in the mirror, it suggests, you've been duped by the media and suffer from low self-esteem.

But adult women have a more realistic view. "Only two percent of women describe themselves as beautiful" trumpets the headline of Dove's press release. Contrary to what the company wants readers to believe, however, that statistic doesn't necessarily represent a crisis of confidence; it may simply reflect the power of the word *beautiful*. Dove's surveys don't ask women if they think they're unattractive or ugly, so it's hard to differentiate between knowing you have flaws, believing you're acceptably but unimpressively plain, and feeling worthlessly hideous. In another Dove survey, 88 percent of the American women polled said they're at least somewhat satisfied with their face, while 76 percent said they're at least somewhat satisfied with their body. But dissatisfaction is not the same as unhappiness or insecurity.

Like the rest of the genetic lottery, beauty is unfair. Everyone falls short of perfection, but some are luckier than others. Real confidence requires self-knowledge, which includes recognizing one's shortcomings as well as one's strengths. At a recent conference on biological manipulations, I heard a philosopher declare during lunch that she'd never have plastic surgery or even dye her hair. But, she confessed, she'd pay just about anything for fifteen more IQ points. This woman is not insecure about her intelligence, which is far above average; she'd just like to be smarter. Asking women to say they're beautiful is like asking intellectuals to say they're geniuses. Most know they simply don't qualify.

CONSIDER

1. Read Postrel's opening paragraphs carefully. What specific words and phrases signal to you that she may have doubts about Dove's Campaign for Real Beauty? Does Postrel echo any reservations you might have had about the Dove marketing strategy?

2. What evidence does Postrel offer for her central claim that beauty exists? Are you convinced by her arguments and citations that there is, indeed, a common and shared concept of beauty? Or do you agree with the Dove campaign that such notions can be broadened and redefined? Discuss the questions with colleagues, drawing on examples beyond those cited in the article.

3. Postrel notes that even the so-called "real" women Dove presents exhibit traits commonly associated with traditional notions of beauty: symmetry, feminine features, hourglass shapes, good teeth, and so on. Is Dove's definition of beauty really more inclusive than those it criticizes?

COMPOSE

4. In "The Truth About Beauty," Postrel concludes that adult women may not be as insecure or unsatisfied with their looks as the Dove campaign assumes. But what effects might unrealistic advertising images (or idealized faces and bodies) have on younger women or children? In a short essay, explore the question, drawing on the Dove campaign, Postrel's essay, or other materials you may be familiar with.

5. What, if any, consequences might the Dove campaign and Postrel's response have for *men*? Write a short essay to sort out any gender differences (or similarities) when it comes to definitions of physical beauty. For instance, might men react one way to the Dove Campaign for Real Beauty in public and another way in private?

FYI

ITEM 7.16 ■ Christo Komarnitski, *Obesity Planet*, March 18, 2005

Although Americans aren't the only people growing in size, the image of the ugly American has taken on new proportions, as this political cartoon from Eastern Europe suggests. It originally appeared in the Bulgarian newspaper, *Sega*.

CONSIDER

1. What elements of American culture does the cartoon present? What claim does artist Christo Komarnitski make?

2. How would you describe the visual style of Komarnitski? Do you find it appealing?

3. How might you editorialize about America's weight problems? Either describe a cartoon you might draw or, if you have the talent, translate your critique of American eating habits into an actual cartoon or poster.

Looks *Do* Matter

Daniel Akst
(2005)

Everyone knows looks shouldn't matter. Beauty, after all, is only skin deep, and no right-thinking person would admit to taking much account of how someone looks outside the realm of courtship, that romantic free-trade zone traditionally exempted from the usual tariffs of rationality. Even in that tender kingdom, where love at first sight is still readily indulged, it would be impolitic, if not immature, to admit giving too much weight to a factor as shallow as looks. Yet perhaps it's time to say what we all secretly know, which is that looks do matter, maybe even more than most of us think.

We infer a great deal from people's looks—not just when it comes to mating (where looks matter profoundly), but in almost every other aspect of life as well, including careers and social status. It may not be true that blondes have more fun, but it's highly likely that attractive people do, and they start early. Mothers pay more attention to good-looking babies, for example, but, by the same token, babies pay more attention to prettier adults who wander into their field of vision. Attractive people are paid more on the job, marry more desirable spouses, and are likelier to get help from others when in evident need. Nor is this all sheer, baseless prejudice. Human beings appear to be hard-wired to respond to how people and objects look, an adaptation without which the species might not have made it this far. The unpleasant truth is that, far from being only skin deep, our looks reflect all kinds of truths about difference and desire—truths we are, in all likelihood, biologically programmed to detect.

Sensitivity to the signals of human appearances would naturally lead to successful reproductive decisions, and several factors suggest that this sensitivity may be bred in the bone. Beauty may even be addictive. Researchers at London's University College have found that human beauty stimulates a section of the brain called the ventral striatum, the same region activated in drug and gambling addicts when they're about to indulge their habit. Photos of faces rated unattractive had no effect on the volunteers to whom they were shown, but the ventral striatum did show activity if the picture was of an attractive person, especially one looking straight at the viewer. And the responses occurred even when the viewer and the subject of the photo were of the same sex. Good-looking people just do something to us, whether we like it or not.

People's looks speak to us, sometimes in a whisper and sometimes in a shout, of health, reproductive fitness, agreeableness, social standing, and intelligence. Although looks in mating still matter much more to men than to women, the importance of appearance appears to be rising on both sides of the gender divide. In a fascinating cross-generational study of mating preferences, every 10 years different groups of men and women were asked to rank 18 characteristics they might want enhanced in a mate. The importance of good looks rose "dramatically" for both men and women from 1939 to 1989, the period of the study, according to David M. Buss, an evolutionary psychologist at the University of Texas. On a scale of 1 to 3, the importance men gave to good looks rose from 1.50 to 2.11. But for women, the importance of good looks in men rose from 0.94 to 1.67. In other words, women in 1989 considered a man's looks even more important than men considered women's looks 50 years earlier. Since the 1930s, Buss writes, "physical appearance has

---

FYI "Looks *Do* Matter" is a more detailed and demanding examination of the issues raised by both the Dove Campaign for Real Beauty and Virginia Postrel's rebuttal of its core assumptions. Author Daniel Akst puzzles at length over the contradictions he perceives in an American society obsessed with beauty and fashion and yet increasingly slovenly in appearance and behavior. Akst writes a monthly business column for the *New York Times* and has several novels to his credit, including *The Webster Chronicle* (2001) and *St. Burl's Obituary* (1996). "Looks *Do* Matter" originally appeared in *Wilson Quarterly*, Summer 2005.

gone up in importance for men and women about equally, corresponding with the rise in television, fashion magazines, advertising, and other media depictions of attractive models."

In all likelihood this trend will continue, driven by social and technological changes that are unlikely to be reversed anytime soon—changes such as the new ubiquity of media images, the growing financial independence of women, and the worldwide weakening of the institution of marriage. For better or worse, we live now in an age of appearances. It looks like looks are here to stay.

■ ■ ■

The paradox, in such an age, is that the more important appearances become, the worse most of us seem to look—and not just by comparison with the godlike images alternately taunting and bewitching us from every billboard and TV screen. While popular culture is obsessed with fashion and style, and our prevailing psychological infirmity is said to be narcissism, fully two-thirds of American adults have abandoned conventional ideas of attractiveness by becoming overweight. Nearly half of this group is downright obese. Given their obsession with dieting—a $40 billion-plus industry in the United States—it's not news to these people that they're sending an unhelpful message with their inflated bodies, but it's worth noting here nonetheless.

Social scientists have established what most of us already know in this regard, which is that heavy people are perceived less favorably in a variety of ways. Across cultures—even in places such as Fiji, where fat is the norm—people express a preference for others who are neither too slim nor too heavy. In studies by University of Texas psychologist Devendra Singh, people guessed that the heaviest figures in photos were eight to 10 years older than the slimmer ones, even though the faces were identical. (As the nation's bill for hair dye and facelifts attests, looking older is rarely desirable, unless you happen to be an underage drinker.)

America's weight problem is one dimension of what seems to be a broader-based national flight from presentability, a flight that manifests itself unmistakably in the relentless casualness of our attire. Contrary to the desperate contentions of some men's clothiers, for example, the suit really is dying. Walk around midtown Manhattan, and these garments are striking by their absence. Consumer spending reflects this. In 2004, according to NPD Group, a marketing information firm, sales of "active sportswear," a category that includes such apparel as warm-up suits, were $39 billion, nearly double what was spent on business suits and other tailored clothing. The irony is that the more athletic gear we wear, from plum-colored velour track suits to high-tech sneakers, the less athletic we become.

> **The irony is that the more athletic gear we wear, from plum-colored velour track suits to high-tech sneakers, the less athletic we become.**

The overall change in our attire did not happen overnight. America's clothes, like America itself, have been getting more casual for decades, in a trend that predates even Nehru jackets and the "full Cleveland" look of a pastel leisure suit with white shoes and belt, but the phenomenon reaches something like an apotheosis in the vogue for low-riding pajama bottoms and flip-flops outside the home. Visit any shopping mall in summer—or many deep-Sunbelt malls year round—and you'll find people of all sizes, ages, and weights clomping through the climate-controlled spaces in tank tops, T-shirts, and running shorts. Tops—and nowadays often bottoms—emblazoned with the names of companies, schools, and places make many of these shoppers into walking billboards. Bulbous athletic shoes, typically immaculate on adults who go everywhere by car, are the functional equivalent of SUVs for the feet. Anne

Hollander, an observant student of clothing whose books include *Sex and Suits* (1994), has complained that we've settled on "a sandbox aesthetic" of sloppy comfort; the new classics—sweats, sneakers, and jeans—persist year after year, transcending fashion altogether.

We've come to this pass despite our seeming obsession with how we look. Consider these 2004 numbers from the American Society of Plastic Surgeons: 9.2 million cosmetic surgeries (up 24 percent from 2000) at a cost of $8.4 billion, and that doesn't count 7.5 million "minimally invasive" procedures, such as skin peels and Botox injections (collectively up 36 percent). Cosmetic dentistry is also booming, as is weight-loss surgery. Although most of this spending is by women, men are focusing more and more on their appearance as well, which is obvious if you look at the evolution of men's magazines over the years. Further reflecting our concern with both looks and rapid self-transformation is a somewhat grisly new genre of reality TV: the extreme makeover show, which plays on the audience's presumed desire to somehow look a whole lot better fast.

But appearances in this case are deceiving. The evidence suggests that a great many of us do not care nearly enough about how we look, and that even those who care very much indeed still end up looking terrible. In understanding why, it's worth remembering that people look the way they do for two basic reasons—on purpose and by accident—and both can be as revealing as a neon tube top.

Let's start with the purposeful. Extremes in casual clothing have several important functions. A big one nowadays is camouflage. Tent-like T-shirts and sweatsuits cover a lot of sins, and the change in our bodies over time is borne out by the sizes stores find themselves selling. In 1985, for example, the top-selling women's size was eight. Today, when, as a result of size inflation, an eight (and every other size) is larger than it used to be, NPD Group reports that the top-selling women's size is 14. Camouflage may also account for the popularity of black, which is widely perceived as slimming as well as cool.

That brings us to another motive for dressing down—way down—which is status. Dressing to manifest disregard for society—think of the loose, baggy hipsters in American high schools—broadcasts self-determination by flaunting the needlessness of having to impress anybody else. We all like to pretend we're immune to "what people think," but reaching for status on this basis is itself a particularly perverse—and egregious—form of status seeking. For grownups, it's also a way of pretending to be young, or at least youthful, since people know instinctively that looking young often means looking good. Among the truly young, dressing down is a way to avoid any embarrassing lapses in self-defining rebelliousness. And for the young and fit, sexy casual clothing can honestly signal a desire for short-term rather than long-term relationships. Indeed, researchers have shown that men respond more readily to sexy clothing when seeking a short-term relationship, perhaps because more modest attire is a more effective signal of sexual fidelity, a top priority for men in the marriage market, regardless of nation or tribe.

Purposeful slovenliness can have its reasons, then, but what about carelessness? One possible justification is that, for many people, paying attention to their own looks is just too expensive. Clothes are cheap, thanks to imports, but looking good can be costly for humans, just as it is for other species. A signal such as beauty, after all, is valuable in reproductive terms only if it has credibility, and it's been suggested that such signals are credible indicators of fitness precisely because in evolutionary terms they're so expensive. The peacock's gaudy tail, for example, attracts mates in part because it signals that the strutting bird is robust enough not only to sustain his fancy plumage but to fend off the predators it also attracts. Modern humans who want to strut their evolutionary stuff have to worry about their tails too: They have to work them off. Since most of us are no longer paid to perform physical labor, getting exercise requires valuable time and energy, to say nothing of a costly gym membership. And then there is the opportunity cost—the pleasure lost by forgoing fried chicken and Devil Dogs. Eating junk food, especially fast food, is probably also cheaper, in terms of time, than preparing a low-calorie vegetarian feast at home.

These costs apparently strike many Americans as too high, which may be why we as a culture have engaged in a kind of aesthetic outsourcing, transferring the job of looking good—of providing the desired supply of physical beauty—to the specialists known as "celebrities," who can afford to devote much more time and energy to the task. Offloading the chore of looking great onto a small, gifted corps of professionals saves the rest of us a lot of trouble and expense, even if it has opened a yawning aesthetic gulf between the average person (who is fat) and the average model or movie star (who is lean and toned within an inch of his or her life).

Although the popularity of Botox and other such innovations suggests that many people do want to look better, it seems fair to conclude that they are not willing to pay any significant price to do so, since the great majority do not in fact have cosmetic surgery, exercise regularly, or maintain anything like their ideal body weight. Like so much in our society, physical attractiveness is produced by those with the greatest comparative advantage, and consumed vicariously by the rest of us—purchased, in a sense, ready made.

Whether our appearance is purposeful or accidental, the outcome is the same, which is that a great many of us look awful most of the time, and as a consequence of actions or inactions that are at least substantially the result of free will.

■ ■ ■

Men dressed liked boys? Flip-flops at the office? Health care workers who never get near an operating room but nevertheless dress in shapeless green scrubs? These sartorial statements are not just casual. They're also of a piece with the general disrepute into which looking good seems to have fallen. On its face, so to speak, beauty presents some serious ideological problems in the modern world. If beauty were a brand, any focus group that we convened would describe it as shallow and fleeting or perhaps as a kind of eye candy that is at once delicious and bad for you. As a society, we consume an awful lot of it, and we feel darn guilty about it.

Why should this be so? For one thing, beauty strikes most of us as a natural endowment, and as a people we dislike endowments. We tax inheritances, after all, on the premise that they are unearned by their recipients and might produce something like a hereditary aristocracy, not unlike the one produced by the competition to mate with beauty. Money plays a role in that competition; there's no denying that looks and income are traditionally awfully comfortable with each other, and today affluent Americans are the ones least likely to be overweight. By almost any standard, then, looks are a seemingly unfair way of distinguishing oneself, discriminating as they do on the basis of age and generally running afoul of what the late political scientist Aaron Wildavsky called "the rise of radical egalitarianism," which was at the very least suspicious of distinction and advantage, especially a distinction as capricious and as powerful as appearance.

Appearance can be a source of inequality, and achieving some kind of egalitarianism in this arena is a long-standing and probably laudable American concern. The Puritans eschewed fancy garb, after all, and Thoreau warned us to beware of enterprises that require new clothes. Nowadays, at a time of increased income inequality, our clothes paradoxically confer less distinction than ever. Gender distinctions in clothing, for instance, have been blurred in favor of much greater sartorial androgyny, to the extent that nobody would any longer ask who wears the pants in any particular household (because the correct answer would be, "everybody"). The same goes for age distinctions (short pants long ago lost their role as uniform of the young), class distinctions (the rich wear jeans too), and even distinctions between occasions such as school and play, work and leisure, or public and private. Who among us hasn't noticed sneakers, for

> "Offloading the chore of looking great onto a small, gifted corps of professionals saves the rest of us a lot of trouble and expense..."

example, at a wedding, in a courtroom, or at a concert, where you spot them sometimes even on the stage?

> "Who among us hasn't noticed sneakers, for example, at a wedding, in a courtroom, or at a concert, where you spot them sometimes even on the stage?"

The problem is that, if anything, looks matter even more than we think, not just because we're all hopelessly superficial, but because looks have always told us a great deal of what we want to know. Looks matter for good reason, in other words, and delegating favorable appearances to an affluent elite for reasons of cost or convenience is a mistake, both for the individuals who make it and for the rest of us as well. The slovenliness of our attire is one of the things that impoverish the public sphere, and the stunning rise in our weight (in just 25 years) is one of the things that impoverish our health. Besides, it's not as if we're evolving anytime soon into a species that's immune to appearances. Looks seem to matter to all cultures, not just our image-besotted one, suggesting that efforts to stamp out looksism (which have yet to result in hiring quotas on behalf of the homely) are bucking millions of years of evolutionary development.

The degree of cross-cultural consistency in this whole area is surprising. Contrary to the notion that beauty is in the eye of the beholder, or at the very least in the eye of the culture, studies across nations and tribal societies have found that people almost everywhere have similar ideas about what's attractive, especially as regards the face (tastes in bodies seem to vary a bit more, perhaps allowing for differing local evolutionary ecologies). Men everywhere, even those few still beyond the reach of Hollywood and Madison Avenue, are more concerned about women's looks than women are about men's, and their general preference for women who look young and healthy is probably the result of evolutionary adaptation.

The evidence for this comes from the field of evolutionary psychology. Whatever one's view of this burgeoning branch of science, one thing it has produced (besides controversy) is an avalanche of disconcerting research about how we look. Psychologists Michael R. Cunningham, of the University of Louisville, and Stephen R. Shamblen cite evidence that babies as young as two or three months old look longer at more attractive faces. New mothers of less attractive offspring, meanwhile, have been found to pay more attention to other people (say, hospital room visitors) than do new mothers of better-looking babies. This may have some basis in biological necessity, if you bear in mind that the evolutionary environment, free as it was of antibiotics and pediatricians, might have made it worthwhile indeed for mothers to invest themselves most in the offspring likeliest to survive and thrive.

The environment today, of course, is very different, but it may only amplify the seeming ruthlessness of the feelings and judgments we make. "In one study," reports David M. Buss, the evolutionary psychologist who reported on the multi-generational study of mating preferences, "after groups of men looked at photographs of either highly attractive women or women of average attractiveness, they were asked to evaluate their commitment to their current romantic partner. Disturbingly, the men who had viewed pictures of attractive women thereafter judged their actual partners to be less attractive than did the men who had viewed analogous pictures of women who were average in attractiveness. Perhaps more important, the men who had viewed attractive women thereafter rated themselves as less committed, less satisfied, less serious, and less close to their actual partners." In another study, men who viewed attractive nude centerfolds promptly rated themselves as less attracted to their own partners.

Even if a man doesn't personally care much what a woman looks like, he knows that others do. Research suggests that being with an attractive woman raises a man's status significantly, while dating a physically unattractive woman moderately lowers a man's status. (The effect for women is quite different; dating an attractive man raises a woman's status only somewhat, while dating an unattractive man lowers her status only nominally.) And status matters. In the well-known "Whitehall studies" of British civil servants after World War II, for example, occupational grade was strongly correlated with longevity: The higher the bureaucrat's ranking, the longer the life. And it turns out that Academy Award-winning actors and actresses outlive other movie performers by about four years, at least according to a study published in the Annals of Internal Medicine in 2001. "The results," write authors Donald A. Redelmeier and Sheldon M. Singh, "suggest that success confers a survival advantage." So if an attractive mate raises a man's status, is it really such a wonder that men covet trophy wives?

In fact, people's idea of what's attractive is influenced by the body types that are associated with status in a given time and place (which suggests that culture plays at least some role in ideas of attractiveness). As any museumgoer can tell you, the big variation in male preferences across time and place is in plumpness, and Buss contends that this is a status issue: In places where food is plentiful, such as the United States, high-status people distinguish themselves by being thin.

There are reasons besides sex and status to worry about how we look. For example, economists Daniel S. Hamermesh, of the University of Texas, and Jeff E. Biddle, of Michigan State University, have produced a study suggesting that better-looking people make more money. "Holding constant demographic and labor-market characteristics," they wrote in a well-known 1993 paper, "plain people earn less than people of average looks, who earn less than the good-looking. The penalty for plainness is five to 10 percent, slightly larger than the premium for beauty." A 1998 study of attorneys (by the same duo) found that some lawyers also benefit by looking better. Yet another study found that better-looking college instructors—especially men—receive higher ratings from their students.

Hamermesh and some Chinese researchers also looked into whether primping pays, based on a survey of Shanghai residents. They found that beauty raises women's earnings (and, to a lesser extent, men's), but that spending on clothing and cosmetics helps only a little. Several studies have even found associations between appearance preferences and economic cycles. Psychologists Terry F. Pettijohn II, of Ohio State University, and Abraham Tesser, of the University of Georgia, for example, obtained a list of the Hollywood actresses with top box-office appeal in each year from 1932 to 1995. The researchers scanned the actresses' photos into a computer, did various measurements, and determined that, lo and behold, the ones who were the most popular during social and economic good times had more "neoteny"—more childlike features, including bigger eyes, smaller chins, and rounder cheeks. During economic downturns, stronger and more rectangular female faces—in other words, faces that were more mature—were preferred.

> **Several studies have even found associations between appearance preferences and economic cycles.**

It's not clear whether this is the case for political candidates as well, but looks matter in this arena too. In a study that appeared recently in *Science*, psychologist Alexander Todorov and colleagues at Princeton University showed photographs of political candidates to more than 800 students, who were asked to say who had won and why based solely on looks. The students chose correctly an amazing 69 percent of the time, consistently picking candidates they judged to look the most competent, meaning those who looked more mature. The losers were more likely to have babyfaces, meaning some combination of a round face, big eyes, small nose, high forehead and small chin. Those candidates apparently have a hard time winning elections.

To scientists, a convenient marker for physical attractiveness in people is symmetry, as measured by taking calipers to body parts as wrists, elbows, and feet to see how closely the pairs match. The findings of this research can be startling. As summarized by biologist Randy Thornhill and psychologist Steven W. Gangestad, both of the University of New Mexico, "In both sexes, relatively low asymmetry seems to be associated with increased genetic, physical, and mental health, including cognitive skill and IQ. Also, symmetric men appear to be more muscular and vigorous, have a lower basal metabolic rate, and may be larger in body size than asymmetric men.... Symmetry is a major component of developmental health and overall condition and appears to be heritable." The researchers add that more symmetrical men have handsomer faces, more sex partners, and their first sexual experience at an earlier age, and they get to sex more quickly with a new romantic partner. "Moreover," they tell us, "men's symmetry predicts a relatively high frequency of their sexual partners' copulatory orgasms."

Those orgasms are sperm retaining, suggesting that symmetric men may have a greater chance of getting a woman pregnant. It doesn't hurt that the handsomest men may have the best sperm, at least according to a study at Spain's University of Valencia, which found that men with the healthiest, fastest sperm were those whose faces were rated most attractive by women. There's evidence that women care more about men's looks for short-term relationships than for marriage, and that as women get closer to the most fertile point of the menstrual cycle, their preference for "symmetrical" men grows stronger, according to Thornhill and Gangestad. Ovulating women prefer more rugged, masculinized faces, whereas the rest of the time they prefer less masculinized or even slightly feminized male faces. Perhaps predictably, more-symmetrical men are likelier to be unfaithful and tend to invest less in a relationship.

Asymmetric people may have some idea that they're behind the eight ball here. William Brown and his then-colleagues at Dalhousie University in Halifax, Nova Scotia, looked at 50 people in heterosexual relationships, measuring such features as hands, ears, and feet, and then asked about jealousy. The researchers found a strong correlation between asymmetry and romantic jealousy, suggesting that asymmetrical lovers may suspect they're somehow less desirable. Brown's explanation: "If jealousy is a strategy to retain your mate, then the individual more likely to be philandered on is more likely to be jealous."

In general, how we look communicates something about how healthy we are, how fertile, and probably how useful in the evolutionary environment. This may be why, across a range of cultures, women prefer tall, broad-shouldered men who seem like good reproductive specimens, in addition to offering the possibility of physical protection. Men, meanwhile, like pretty women who appear young. Women's looks seem to vary depending on where they happen to be in the monthly fertility cycle. The University of Liverpool biologist John Manning measured women's ears and fingers and had the timing of their ovulation confirmed by pelvic exams. He found a 30 percent decline in asymmetries in the 24 hours before ovulation—perhaps more perceptible to our sexual antennae than to the conscious mind. In general, symmetrical women have more sex partners, suggesting that greater symmetry makes women more attractive to men.

To evolutionary biologists, it makes sense that men should care more about the way women look than vice versa, because youth and fitness matter so much more in female fertility. And while male preferences do vary with time and place there's also some remarkable underlying consistency. Devendra Singh, for instance, found that the waist-to-hip ratio was the most important factor in women's attractiveness to men in 18 cultures he studied. Regardless of whether lean or voluptuous women happen to be in fashion, the favored shape involves a waist/hip ratio of about

> "It doesn't hurt that the handsomest men may have the best sperm..."

0.7. "Audrey Hepburn and Marilyn Monroe represented two very different images of beauty to filmgoers in the 1950s," writes Nancy Etcoff, who is a psychologist at Massachusetts General Hospital. "Yet the 36-24-34 Marilyn and the 31.5-22-31 Audrey both had versions of the hourglass shape and waist-to-hip ratios of 0.7." Even Twiggy, in her 92-pound heyday, had a waist/hip ratio of 0.73.

■ ■ ■

Is it cause for despair that looks are so important? The bloom of youth is fleeting, after all, and the bad news that our appearance will inevitably broadcast about us cannot be kept under wraps forever. Besides, who could live up to the impossible standards propagated by our powerful aesthetic-industrial complex? It's possible that the images of models and actresses and even TV newscasters, most of them preternaturally youthful and all selected for physical fitness, have driven most Americans to quit the game, insisting that they still care about how they look even as they retire from the playing field to console themselves with knife and fork.

> **If the pressure of all these images has caused us to opt out of caring about how we look, that's a shame, because we're slaves of neither genes nor fashion in this matter.**

If the pressure of all these images has caused us to opt out of caring about how we look, that's a shame, because we're slaves of neither genes nor fashion in this matter. By losing weight and exercising, simply by making ourselves healthier, we can change the underlying data our looks report. The advantages are almost too obvious to mention, including lower medical costs, greater confidence, and a better quality of life in virtually every way.

There's no need to look like Brad Pitt or Jennifer Lopez, and no reason for women to pursue Olive Oyl thinness (a body type men do not especially prefer). Researchers, in fact, have found that people of both sexes tend to prefer averageness in members of the opposite sex: The greater the number of faces poured (by computer) into a composite, the higher it's scored in attractiveness by viewers. That's in part because "bad" features tend to be averaged out. But the implication is clear: You don't need to look like a movie star to benefit from a favorable appearance, unless, of course, you're planning a career in movies.

To a bizarre extent, looking good in America has become the province of an appearance aristocracy—an elect we revere for their seemingly unattainable endowment of good looks. Physical attractiveness has become too much associated with affluence and privilege for a country as democratically inclined as ours. We can be proud at least that these lucky lookers no longer have to be white or even young. Etcoff notes that, in tracking cosmetic surgery since the 1950s, the American Academy of Facial Plastic and Reconstructive Surgery reports a change in styles toward wider, fuller-tipped noses and narrower eyelids, while makeup styles have tended toward fuller lips and less pale skin shades. She attributes these changes to the recalibration of beauty norms as the result of the presence of more Asian, African, and Hispanic features in society.

But what's needed is a much more radical democratization of physical beauty, a democratization we can achieve not by changing the definition of beauty but by changing ourselves. Looking nice is something we need to take back from the elites and make once again a broadly shared, everyday attribute, as it once was when people were much less likely to be fat and much more likely to dress decently in public. Good looks are not just an endowment, and the un-American attitude that looks are immune to self-improvement only breeds the kind of fatalism that is blessedly out of character in America.

As a first step, maybe we can stop pretending that our appearance doesn't—or shouldn't—matter. A little more looksism, if it gets people to shape up, would probably save some lives, to say nothing of some marriages. Let's face it. To a greater extent than most of us are comfortable with, looks tell us something, and right now what they say about our health, our discipline, and our mutual regard isn't pretty.

CONSIDER

1. How do you react to the evidence Akst presents suggesting that we may be biologically programmed to respond favorably to attractive people? In what ways does society seem to reward good looks? Point to specific examples.

2. Akst also makes it clear that people are influenced in their perceptions by the prevalence of thin and beautiful people in the media. Yet, personally, more and more Americans seem to care less about their weight and appearance. How does Akst account for this contradiction? What alternative explanations might you offer?

3. If you are fond of dressing casually, how would you defend your choices of apparel, given Akst's generally unflattering catalog of reasons for such behavior? If you prefer a more formal style of dress in public environments, offer a rationale for your personal sense of style and design.

COMPOSE

4. Spend time at some local gathering spot—such as a mall, campus, airport, or church—and systematically observe the modes of dress you see there. Use your field observations (see pages 86–87) to suggest the topic of an essay you might publish as an op-ed in a local paper or, perhaps, on a blog. Are the modes of dress you see more casual than would seem appropriate for the locale? Do some people or groups stand out for their distinctive dress or style? Do you see problems in the way the people you observed choose to present themselves or, perhaps, something else entirely? Your paper should respond in some way to "Looks *Do* Matter."

Cluster 7.3
The Culture and Politics of Design

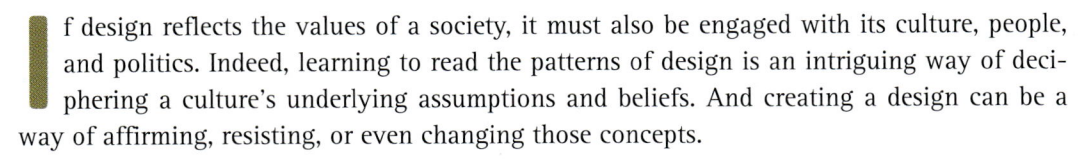

If design reflects the values of a society, it must also be engaged with its culture, people, and politics. Indeed, learning to read the patterns of design is an intriguing way of deciphering a culture's underlying assumptions and beliefs. And creating a design can be a way of affirming, resisting, or even changing those concepts.

Just how seriously designers take their work is evident within the diverse texts in this cluster. We begin with a manifesto by a group of designers seeking to distance their profession from the hype and exploitation that surrounds it—the "First Things First Manifesto." This statement is followed by two case studies of items reshaped, at least in part, by a need to make people see something familiar—sneakers and vending machines (in Japan)—differently.

ITEM 7.17 ■ GMC Yukon Hybrid Logo, 2008

With the climate changing and oil prices soaring, designers are applying their talents to products designed for a new era. This handsome badge, for example, announces that the 5800 lb GMC Yukon to which it is attached is a hybrid SUV capable of 20 mpg in the city. But some argue that it makes no sense to continue to design oversized and overweight products that only encourage Americans to indulge in their desires for big vehicles.

CONSIDER

1. What does the Yukon's badge convey to you? What adjectives would you apply to it?

2. Designers made the Yukon hybrid more aerodynamic than the standard-model SUV on which it is based. What responsibility do designers have today in shaping products? How much control might they actually have over such decisions?

3. If you drove a hybrid, would you want its design to contain elements that make it clear you have selected a green vehicle? Why or why not?

First Things First Manifesto 2000

Thirty-Three Designers

> **FYI** The original "First Things First Manifesto" appeared in 1964 in Britain at a time when people in many professions were reacting to upheaval and social change, some of it spurred by a critique of market capitalism. Those who wrote and signed that statement were affirming that their work as designers was, at its core, a political activity. In 1999, *Adbusters Magazine*, which encourages an ongoing critique of consumerism called "culture jamming," decided that an updated statement would be timely. Designers from around the world agreed and the result was the "First Things First Manifesto 2000."

We, the undersigned, are graphic designers, art directors and visual communicators who have been raised in a world in which the techniques and apparatus of advertising have persistently been presented to us as the most lucrative, effective and desirable use of our talents. Many design teachers and mentors promote this belief; the market rewards it; a tide of books and publications reinforces it.

Encouraged in this direction, designers then apply their skill and imagination to sell dog biscuits, designer coffee, diamonds, detergents, hair gel, cigarettes, credit cards, sneakers, butt toners, light beer and heavy-duty recreational vehicles. Commercial work has always paid the bills, but many graphic designers have now let it become, in large measure, what graphic designers do. This, in turn, is how the world perceives design. The profession's time and energy [are] used up manufacturing demand for things that are inessential at best.

Many of us have grown increasingly uncomfortable with this view of design. Designers who devote their efforts primarily to advertising, marketing and brand development are supporting, and implicitly endorsing, a mental environment so saturated with commercial messages that it is changing the very way citizen-consumers speak, think, feel, respond and interact. To some extent we are all helping draft a reductive and immeasurably harmful code of public discourse.

There are pursuits more worthy of our problem-solving skills. Unprecedented environmental, social and cultural crises demand our attention. Many cultural interventions, social marketing campaigns, books, magazines, exhibitions, educational tools, television programs, films, charitable causes and other information design projects urgently require our expertise and help.

We propose a reversal of priorities in favor of more useful, lasting and democratic forms of communication—a mindshift away from product marketing and toward the exploration and production of a new kind of meaning. The scope of debate is shrinking; it must expand. Consumerism is running uncontested; it must be challenged by other perspectives expressed, in part, through the visual languages and resources of design.

In 1964, 22 visual communicators signed the original call for our skills to be put to worthwhile use. With the explosive growth of global commercial culture, their message has only grown more urgent. Today, we

> "The profession's time and energy [are] used up manufacturing demand for things that are inessential at best."

renew their manifesto in expectation that no more decades will pass before it is taken to heart.

(Signed)

Jonathan Barnbrook, Nick Bell, Andrew Blauvelt, Hans Bockting, Irma Boom, Sheila Levrant de Bretteville, Max Bruinsma, Siân Cook, Linda van Deursen, Chris Dixon, William Drenttel, Gert Dumbar, Simon Esterson, Vince Frost, Ken Garland, Milton Glaser, Jessica Helfand, Steven Heller, Andrew Howard, Tibor Kalman, Jeffery Keedy, Zuzana Licko, Ellen Lupton, Katherine McCoy, Armand Mevis, J. Abbott Miller, Rick Poynor, Lucienne Roberts, Erik Spiekermann, Jan von Toorn, Teal Triggs, Rudy Vanderlans, Bob Wilkinson

CONSIDER

1. The designers who signed the manifesto want an alternative to consumer culture (one that produces objects for the purpose of selling them for profit). What role might designers have in a society without a consumer culture?

2. The designers list a variety of objects and "democratic" projects more worthy of their attention than the consumer products with which design is typically associated. What do designers imply about themselves and their work when they admit that "[c]ommercial work has always paid the bills." How likely is it that people in general (or designers, for that matter) will abandon Prada bags and Tumi luggage for nobler causes?

COMPOSE

3. Use the Web to explore the notion of "culture jamming." Define the concept, and look for particular examples of the phenomenon in your town or on your campus. Sources of information might include articles in alternative newspapers or magazines, riffs on radio talk shows or late-night TV programs, or even graffiti on buses or subways. In a brief essay, assess the impact you have seen, if any, of culture jamming.

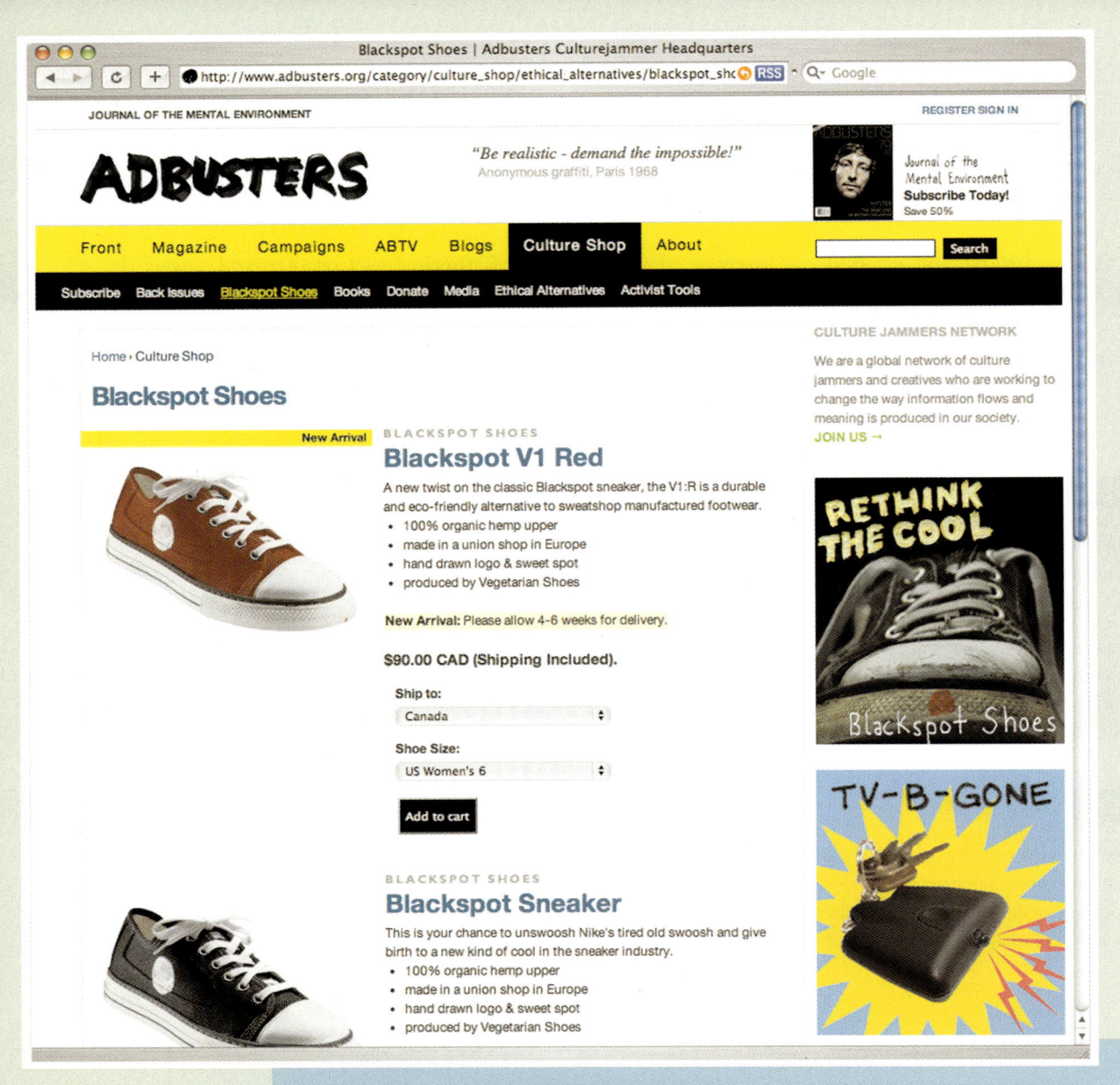

ITEM 7.18 ■ **Adbusters Web site, Blackspot Sneakers, 2007**

What can designers actually do to shape attitudes through their work? If you are as critical of duplicity in design and marketing as the people at Adbusters, you create your own brand of athletic shoes to show how to do things right.

CONSIDER

1. Examine the ad copy above for both Blackspot shoes carefully. With what specific political causes are these items linked?

2. To whom might these shoes appeal? Would wearers likely identify with particular political and social values? With particular parties or professions?

3. Can you identify products across the political spectrum whose designs make political or cultural statements? How do the statements of these products differ? How do their designs convey such differences?

Salon.com asks "Are you ready for some 'unswooshing'?"

Linda Baker
(2003)

> **FYI** Linda Baker is a freelance journalist based in Portland, Oregon. Her work focuses on the changing status of the American family, land use, and transportation planning and the environment. Baker's essays have appeared in *Sierra*, *E*, *The Progressive*, *Utne Reader*, and many other publications. This essay appeared on Salon.com in October 2003.

Kalle Lasn isn't scared of the U.S. PATRIOT Act. "America has become a bit of a monster," says the punchy, 60-something founder of Adbusters, the anti-consumption magazine based in Vancouver, B.C. "Some of the things the U.S. is doing, in Israel, in Cancún with the WTO, I just can't take it any longer. It's gotten to the point where I almost think I've become a terrorist."

But Lasn is no Osama bin Laden. The author of "Culture Jam: How to Reverse America's Suicidal Binge," Lasn is one of the leading figures in the "culture jamming" movement, an international grassroots effort that uses the logic of commercial images to critique corporate hegemony and rampant consumerism. Under his leadership, Adbusters' preferred method of culture jamming has been to publish ad parodies, such as "Absolute Impotence," a photo of the familiar bottle drifting in spilled vodka, or a Nike satire that morphs Tiger Woods' smile into a Swoosh.

Last month, Adbusters announced a new phase in state-of-the-art meme warfare. ("Memes" refer to the core images, slogans or ideas that culture jammers manipulate: e.g., a swoosh, or "Just Do It.") Although the campaign's targets, Nike and CEO Phil Knight, appear frequently in the magazine's culture jams, the latest strategy moves Adbusters out of the realm of parody and into the competitive world of global marketing and production.

More specifically, the Adbusters Media Foundation, the nonprofit that brought the world Buy Nothing Day and TV Turnoff Week, has decided to go into the sneaker manufacturing business. According to Lasn, the plan is to market a "Black Spot sneaker, a shoe that will resemble the retro-style Converse but with one crucial difference." In place of the ubiquitous Nike swoosh, the Adbusters shoe will display a prominent anti-logo "black spot," the magazine's anti-corporate trademark.

> "In place of the ubiquitous Nike swoosh, the Adbusters shoe will display a prominent anti-logo "black spot," the magazine's anti-corporate trademark."

"Phil Knight had a dream," reads the, well, ad for the "Unswoosher," located on the back cover of Adbusters' October issue. "He'd sell shoes. He'd sell dreams. He'd get rich. He'd use sweatshops if he had to. Then along came a new shoe. Plain. Simple. Cheap. Fair. Designed for only one thing: kicking Phil's ass."

By January, the magazine plans to manufacture an initial line of 10,000 sneakers, which will retail globally for about $65 a pair. The release will follow a $500,000 marketing campaign, hyping the sneakers on CNN, in the *New York Times*, and on the major networks. "One of the many reasons I really love this campaign," said Lasn, "is that we are selling a product, not an idea or advocacy. We are selling a sneaker. So those stations that have systematically refused to sell us air time over the past 10 years for our ideas will now have no choice but to sell us air time."

Since the nonprofit broke the news of the Black Spot late last August, Nike hasn't exactly been shaking in its shoes. "As a global leader, it doesn't surprise us that we occasionally get targeted by groups who use the strength of our brand to leverage their agenda," said Caitlin Morris, senior manager of Nike corporate communications.

Reaction on the anti-corporate-globalization front has been mixed. Some question the wisdom of an anti-advertising magazine going into the advertising business, while others think Lasn would be better off targeting clothing manufacturers that don't receive as much international scrutiny. But for some heavy hitters in the no-sweatshop movement, the Black Spot couldn't have come at a more propitious time—just days after the Converse brand sold out the "Chuck Taylor" shoe to Nike. For years, that was the sneaker of choice for millions opposed to megabrands churning out sneakers in Third World factories.

"The anti-sweatshop forces need a few alternatives in the marketplace," says Jeff Ballinger, author of the original *Harpers' Magazine* 1993 exposé on Nike's labor practices, and now vice president for policy and sourcing at No Sweat. "Kalle's right to see that. I've given 'sweatshop' talks to a wide variety of groups for over a decade and one of the first questions is: 'What can we buy?'"

Lasn admits the "ethical sneaker" may not succeed. Still, employing what appears to be a signature combination of brashness and nostalgia, Lasn said the time has come for a change in how activists deal with "rogue companies."

"We got tired of all the lefty whining and the boycotting. It wasn't making any difference," he said. "Quite apart from how many percentage points in market share the Black Spot sneaker can take away from Phil Knight—that's of course the ultimate goal but may be a long time coming—in the meantime, we can go a long way toward uncooling the Swoosh, which is losing momentum fast."

"I have a grandiose plan," Lasn said. "My dream as a culture jammer is that a small group of people with a limited budget could have the power to choose a megabrand we don't like for valid reasons and uncool that brand, to show that we the people as a civil society have the power to keep a corporation honest. Now that would be something that would actually redefine capitalism."

Adbusters, which has a circulation of 120,000, bills itself as the "Journal of the Mental Environment." The magazine's philosophy is that advertising encourages people to see themselves primarily as consumers, and its parodies reveal the "truth" behind slick corporate logos: the environmental and human costs of consumption, the abuses of corporate power, and private monopolization of public airwaves.

Lasn, whose descriptions of Knight [. . .] bear a certain resemblance to the "axis of evil" rhetoric coming out of Washington, D.C., is the former head of a market research company in Tokyo. As a culture critic, his diatribes against Nike don't focus on the athletic footwear corporation's labor practices per se, but on the notion of branding in general and the "pseudoempowerment" brand that Nike attaches to its products in particular. Citing research on the 3000 marketing images most people consume every day, as well as studies linking advertising to an increase in mood disorders, Lasn said rage against the toxic cultural clutter epitomized by Nike ads is going to launch a new kind of revolution.

> **Lasn admits the "ethical sneaker" may not succeed.**

"Twenty-five years ago we woke up to the fact that the chemicals in our food, water and air, even a few parts of a billion, actually will give you cancer," he said. "That was when the modern environmental movement was born. Once people make that connection between advertising and their own mental health, that could be the birth of the modern mental health environmental movement."

When that moment happens, said Lasn, "we will suddenly see the $400 billion worldwide industry collapse to half its size." But for some, Lasn's railing against the Orwellian force of advertising is exactly what makes his decision to market a Black Spot sneaker a bit curious. After all, we live in a world where AIDS, crime and all sorts of global unrest have been turned into fodder for Benetton ads. The medium, as they say, is the message.

This is why people like Naomi Klein, Canadian author of the landmark text "No Logo," aren't quite so enthusiastic about the revolutionary potential of the Unswoosher. "Publications that analyze the commercialization of our lives have a responsibility to work to protect spaces where we aren't constantly being pitched to," she told the *Toronto Globe & Mail*. "This can be undermined if they are seen as simply shilling for a different 'anti-corporate' brand." Lasn disagrees.

"Nike's empowerment is pseudo-empowerment," he says. "But if we are actually able to launch an anti-brand, then the empowerment around the black spot is actually a real kind of empowerment: the power of us the people to have a business climate that is to our liking. It's the most beautiful kind of empowerment I can think of."

> **'Nike's empowerment is pseudo-empowerment,' he says.**

Adbusters launched Buy Nothing Day, says Lasn. "But we never said it's bad to buy something, just bad to buy too much." What's more, promoting the Black Spot sneaker will not be Adbusters' first foray into "real" advertising. The magazine has been raising money to get a Black Spot ad, a series of anti-corporate, anti-U.S. phrases set to Jimi Hendrix's rendition of "The Star Spangled Banner," on television. Although all the major networks have rejected the ad, CNN has aired the Black Spot promo—during the *Crossfire* political debate program.

At Adbusters' offices, located in a Vancouver residential district, the Unswoosher enterprise has something of a Mouse That Roared quality to it. A newly hired business manager is working on locating investors and distributors for the Black Spot. The magazine has already taken preorders for 1,000 pairs, and will use its nest egg of $250,000 to bankroll the initial 10,000 sneakers. According to Lasn, people are "coming out of the woodwork" to offer advice about where the Black Spot should be manufactured—and what kind of labor to use.

Industry watchers are skeptical. "[Adbusters] has absolutely no idea how complicated global production and marketing is," says John Horan, publisher of *Sporting Goods Intelligence*. The magazine could save time and money, he suggested, by selling T-shirts emblazoned with "We want to kick Phil Knight's butt" for $10 each.

Ignoring the naysayers, Adbusters has generated a final list of three possible factories: a factory in Missouri, referred by a former Nike employee who has inspected more than 70 factories worldwide, and two union factories in Asia: one in South Korea, and another in Indonesia. The latter were recommended by Ballinger, whom Lasn has retained to help Adbusters source a union factory for the Unswoosher.

Lasn obviously relishes the idea of manufacturing the sneaker in Missouri. But just as he rejects the argument that there is something problematic about Adbusters advertising shoes, so he has contrarian things to say about some of the anti-sweatshop rhetoric governing the international workers' rights debate. In particular, he says, the "go local" movement is overrated, propelled more by trade unions than activists.

"I have a huge amount of disdain for all those people who are trying to keep all the jobs in North America," he said. "Here we are, the richest part of the world, we're only 5 percent of people in the world, and all of a sudden we're losing a few doldrums in our economy. Let's give the jobs to the Koreans and Indonesians. They need it more, and if we can find a good factory and if we could promote workers' rights worldwide, all the better."

The Estonian-born Lasn recalled a seminal trip he took around the Third World when he was in his 20s. "I know from personal experience that many of those factories that campus people dismiss as sweatshop labor are actually very good factories," he says, "and that the people who live near those factories are just yearning to work in those factories. A good part of those sweatshop people are seriously misguided."

If Lasn's idea of pulling Third World workers up by their bootstraps mimics the language of liberal capitalism—not to mention Phil Knight—it's also an idea that reverberates across segments of the no-sweatshop apparel movement.

> **The magazine could save time and money, he suggested, by selling T-shirts emblazoned with "We want to kick Phil Knight's butt" for $10 each.**

"Globalization is an opportunity to globalize the labor movement," says Ballinger. "Today, the only way to protect a worker's job anywhere is to defend worker's rights everywhere." The Black Spot sneaker represents a clear step forward in the anti-sweatshop movement, says Ballinger. "If the union-made Black Spot sneaker can kick Phil Knight where he feels it—in the pocketbook, we won't get more window dressing from Nike and Reebok; we'll get a real change in policy."

But Marsha Dickson, director of Educators for Socially Responsible Apparel Business, says the Black Spot campaign is naïve in light of efforts that have been made by Nike and other members of the Fair Labor Association, a coalition of industry, university and nongovernmental organizations that issued its first public report in June.

"While the tracking charts clearly show that much work remains to be done," said Dickson via e-mail, "the bottom line is that Nike, Reebok and Adidas are really acting as leaders. If a campaign such as [the Black Spot sneaker] is needed, it should focus attention to the thousands of clothing manufacturers and retailers that are not participating in the FLA. We know nothing or very little about how these companies treat the workers that make their products." The FLA was the recipient of the $1.5 mil-lion Kasky vs. Nike settlement in June. In 1998, Marc Kasky, a California anti-globalization activist, sued Nike for allegedly stretching the truth in its statements regarding contract factory labor practices in Asia. The Cali-fornia Supreme Court agreed with Kasky in a 4-3 ruling. Nike then appealed to the U.S. Supreme Court. Corporate interests had paid close attention to the case, in which Nike claimed that what it said—whether or not it was true—was noncommercial speech protected under the First Amendment.

At its Sept. 22 shareholders' meeting in Portland, Ore., Nike stockholders celebrated their first protester-free gathering in several years. The footwear company registered a record $10.7 billion in revenue in its 2003 fiscal year, and its stock price increased 40 percent, to a high of $62.50 in late September.

Lasn, about to fly off to Indonesia in his newly minted role as factory inspector, is undeterred. The Black Spot sneaker, he says, is part of a larger goal to "tweak the genetic code of corporations": an anti-corporate-globalization process that ranges from rewriting the rules under which corporate charters are reviewed and revoked, to a general "crusade against bigness."

"I grew up in a time when cynicism didn't exist," says Lasn, "that hidden assumption that nothing can change, that you better get used to capitalism, and that cultural revolution is not even possible."

"I don't quite see it that way. I am old enough to have seen a number of cultural revolutions. I believe another one is coming up."

CONSIDER

1. In your opinion, would buying a pair of Blackspot Sneakers be a politically meaningful act? Why or why not? How would you define such an activity?

2. How would you characterize the tone and word choices Kalle Lasn, author of *Culture Jamming*, uses when speaking of Nike and its CEO Phil Knight in quotes attributed to him by Linda Baker? How do Lasn's choices influence your opinion of Lasn? Do you find his comments persuasive? Credible?

3. Visit and study the Blackspot Sneaker Web site. How would you characterize this site's design language? Does the style of the site reinforce or work against the magazine's goal of creating an "anti-brand" product?

COMPOSE

4. Choose a consumer product or organization and study its brand logo or current advertising campaign. Then create a parody ad for that product or organization, using the company's own design language to subvert or criticize the product. Use an image editor to dummy up an actual ad. If you lack the technical expertise to do this, you might sketch the parody you would create and briefly annotate it.

ITEM 7.19 ■ **Torin Boyd for the *New York Times*, Japanese Vending Machine Dress Used as Urban Camouflage, 2007**

This photograph accompanied the *New York Times* story "Fearing Crime, Japanese Wear the Hiding Place" (see page 453). Look closely at the vending machine on the far right and you'll see shoes.

CONSIDER

1. What is your initial reaction to the idea of avoiding crime by using disguises? How would you react to the photograph above if you saw it in *The Onion*?

2. Do you think a person disguised by the vending machine costume might fool potential thieves? Under what circumstances?

7.3 | THE CULTURE AND POLITICS OF DESIGN

Fearing Crime, Japanese Wear the Hiding Place

Martin Fackler
(2007)

> **FYI** Americans reading Martin Fackler's account of the way Japanese inventors have been reacting to a minor crime wave might simply shake their heads. But the story suggests how profound cultural differences—expressed through designs—can be. Fackler reports on Asian issues for the *New York Times*. His story appeared on October 20 (*not* April 1), 2007.

Tokyo, Oct. 19—On a narrow Tokyo street, near a beef bowl restaurant and a pachinko parlor, Aya Tsukioka demonstrated new clothing designs that she hopes will ease Japan's growing fears of crime.

Deftly, Ms. Tsukioka, a 29-year-old experimental fashion designer, lifted a flap on her skirt to reveal a large sheet of cloth printed in bright red with a soft drink logo partly visible. By holding the sheet open and stepping to the side of the road, she showed how a woman walking alone could elude pursuers—by disguising herself as a vending machine.

The wearer hides behind the sheet, printed with an actual-size photo of a vending machine. Ms. Tsukioka's clothing is still in development, but she already has several versions, including one that unfolds from a kimono and a deluxe model with four sides for more complete camouflaging.

These elaborate defenses are coming at a time when crime rates are actually declining in Japan. But the Japanese, sensitive to the slightest signs of social fraying, say they feel growing anxiety about safety, fanned by sensationalist news media. Instead of pepper spray, though, they are devising a variety of novel solutions, some high-tech, others quirky, but all reflecting a peculiarly Japanese sensibility.

Take the "manhole bag," a purse that can hide valuables by unfolding to look like a sewer cover. Lay it on the street with your wallet inside, and unwitting thieves are supposed to walk right by. There is also a line of knife-proof high school uniforms made with the same material as Kevlar, and a book with tips on how to dress even the nerdiest children like "pseudo-hoodlums" to fend off schoolyard bullies.

There are pastel-colored cellphones for children that parents can track, and a chip for backpacks that signals when children enter and leave school.

The devices' creators admit that some of their ideas may seem far-fetched, especially to crime-hardened Americans. And even some Japanese find some of them a tad naïve, possibly reflecting the nation's relative lack of experience with actual street crime. Despite media attention on a few sensational cases, the rate of violent crime remains just one-seventh of America's.

But the devices' creators also argue that Japan's ideas about crime prevention are a product of deeper cultural differences. While Americans want to protect themselves from criminals, or even strike back, the creators say many Japanese favor camouflage and deception, reflecting a culture that abhors self-assertion, even in self-defense.

"It is just easier for Japanese to hide," Ms. Tsukioka said. "Making a scene would be too embarrassing." She said her vending machine disguise was inspired by a trick used by the ancient ninja, who cloaked themselves in black blankets at night.

To be sure, some of these ideas have yet to become commercially viable. However, the fact that they were

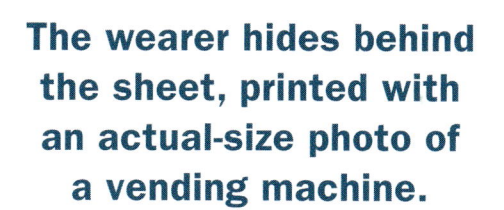

> "The wearer hides behind the sheet, printed with an actual-size photo of a vending machine."

greeted here with straight faces, or even appeared at all, underscores another, less appreciated facet of Japanese society: its fondness for oddball ideas and inventions.

Japan's corporate labs have showered the world with technology, from transistor radios to hybrid cars. But the nation is also home to a prolific subculture of individual inventors, whose ideas range from practical to bizarre. Inventors say a tradition of tinkering and building has made Japan welcoming to experimental ideas, no matter how eccentric.

"Japanese society won't just laugh, so inventors are not afraid to try new things," said Takumi Hirai, chairman of Japan's largest association of individual inventors, the 10,000-member Hatsumeigakkai.

> **In fact, Japan produces so many unusual inventions that it even has a word for them: chindogu, or "queer tools."**

In fact, Japan produces so many unusual inventions that it even has a word for them: chindogu, or "queer tools." The term was popularized by Kenji Kawakami, whose hundreds of intentionally impractical and humorous inventions have won him international attention as Japan's answer to Rube Goldberg. His creations, which he calls "unuseless," include a roll of toilet paper attached to the head for easy reach in hay fever season, and tiny mops for a cat's feet that polish the floor as the cat prowls.

Mr. Kawakami said that while some of Japan's anticrime devices might not seem practical, they were valuable because they might lead to even better ideas.

"Even useless things can be useful," he said. "The weird logic of these inventions helps us see the world in fresh ways."

Even some of the less unusual anticrime devices here reflect a singular logic. A pair of women's sunglasses has wraparound lenses so dark no one can see where the wearer is looking. These are intended to scare off sexual harassers on Tokyo's crowded trains, where the groping of women is a constant problem.

The same is true of some of the solutions for schoolyard bullying, a big problem in Japan. Kaori Nakano, a fashion historian, wrote a book with a chapter on how to ward off bullies with the "pseudohoodlum" attire. Her advice includes substituting a white belt for the standard black one in Japanese school uniforms, preferably with metallic studs or tiny mirrors, and buying short socks with flashy patterns.

"Japan is so fashion conscious that just changing the way you dress can make you safer," Ms. Nakano said. "Culture plays a big role in risk prevention."

Ms. Tsukioka said she chose the vending-machine motif because the machines are so common on Japan's streets. For children, she has a backpack that transforms into a Japanese-style fire hydrant, hiding the child. The "manhole bag" was also her idea.

Ms. Tsukioka said her disguises could be a bit impractical, "especially when your hands are shaking." Still, she said she hoped the designs or some variation of them could be marketed widely. So far, she said, she has sold about 20 vending-machine skirts for about $800 each, printing and sewing each by hand.

She said she had never heard of a skirt's actually preventing a crime. But on a recent afternoon in Tokyo, bystanders stared as she unfolded the sheet. But once she stood behind it next to a row of actual vending machines, the image proved persuasive enough camouflage that passers-by did not seem to notice her.

She said that while her ideas might be fanciful, Japan's willingness to indulge the imagination was one of its cultural strengths.

"These ideas might strike foreigners as far-fetched," she added, "but in Japan, they can become reality."

CONSIDER

1. While designer Aya Tsukioka's experimental fashions may strike you as peculiar, how do fashions in general reflect differences between cultures? Are there reasons a Briton might dress differently from a Parisian, Mexican, or North Korean? Can you identify particular national cultural traits in fashion (or other) products? Provide examples.

2. Fackler explores what the Japanese inventors' anti-crime devices may reveal about their culture—what Fackler describes as "a peculiarly Japanese sensibility." Which of his interpretations of Japanese attitudes toward both crime and "queer tools" do you find most alien or distinctive? Why?

3. Do any of the Japanese strategies for outwitting crime actually make sense to you? Which might you adopt if you lived in a high-crime area?

COMPOSE

4. Have you ever encountered an item or feature that initially struck you as pointless or "over the top," but then found you couldn't live without it? Consider, for example, heated seats in cars or image stabilizers in video cameras. Write a paper exploring the concept of invention and design innovation—its motivations and consequences. What values within a society might encourage creative or even oddball designs? What might stifle innovation?

Writing About Style, Design, and Culture

When you write about or respond to matters of style and culture, your ticket to ride will be meticulous observation backed up by a willingness to learn all you can about a subject. Begin with a **subject** that genuinely intrigues you—a design issue from the past or present that has already piqued your interest. You might find computer interfaces frustrating, video games (or game systems) amazing, fashions for young girls mortifying, political ads degrading. It's fine to start with a topic you already know something about: take advantage of expertise you may have gained through a job, hobby, internship, or coursework. Do a keyword search on the Web to explore potential subjects, too. You'll usually find lots of discussion and plenty of information online—generally enough to decide whether a topic is worth developing.

Look for subjects to which you can bring a fresh perspective or alternative point of view. Maybe you're one of the few people who believe that an obnoxious TV ad campaign works surprisingly well (see "Head Case" on page 421). Or perhaps your forte is history and culture: you could explore how a design evolved and place it within its social and political contexts. Keep a subject and your ambitions under control by considering just how much you can accomplish in the time available for the project.

Explore and develop your topic idea until, by trial and error (and feedback from colleagues), you're confident you can offer a stimulating **claim** or **thesis** statement—that is, a complete sentence that defines what you hope to demonstrate or prove in your project, whether you'll be working in words alone or drawing on the resources of other media. Start with a plan.

Chances are you won't have difficulty finding an **audience** for most papers about contemporary design: everyone's a critic with an opinion about the way the objects they buy, use, and wear should look and function. Your challenge will be to tailor the information you discover to your intended audience. Be careful though: design issues can quickly become quite technical.

In responding to (or even creating) designs, you may have any of a number of **purposes** in mind. You can, in fact, do something as bold as Merlin Mann when he imagined the Hipster PDA (see Item 7.2 on page 401), creating the device as an alternative to designs that solve little problems with big technology. Or you can describe just such an item, listing its features and components. If you need to go into more detail and draw upon research, you might prepare a formal report, looking at the history, contexts, and elements of a design or style—as Linda Baker does with Blackspot sneakers in "Are you ready for some 'unswooshing'?" and Sean Nixon does in Project 7.2 on American architecture. Reports may also follow a problem/solution pattern, chronicling the ingenious way designers face and overcome specific challenges. If the occasion arises, your report might even take the form of an interview with a designer or people who use specific products, recording their ideas and opinions (see "Questions for Niels Diffrient" on page 415).

But you may also find yourself eager to offer arguments about style and culture because that's what most of us like to do: make disputable claims about the quality, effectiveness, beauty, or practicality of designs or design movements. We find Mustangs coolly retro; can't stand Crocs; wish someone would pass a law against marketing sexy clothes to preteen girls. But to persuade audiences, such arguments always need evidence and proof (see Daniel Akst, "Looks *Do* Matter" on page 433). Sometimes, you may want to qualify your initial claims too, limiting them to what you can reasonably defend with the information and data you have.

Be sure always to provide the **context** for understanding a design or style: don't assume that readers will recognize design terminology or movements you pick up as you learn about a subject. Give them simple facts about time, place, people, and—when appropriate—supply helpful images. Even very contemporary subjects need to be surrounded by background information so that your analysis still makes sense when fads and fashions become dated. Seth Stevenson's evaluation of the infamous HeadOn ad campaign, familiar to everyone in 2006-07, might still make sense a decade later simply because he takes the time to describe the ad as if a reader hasn't seen it. Show the same care.

Figuring out how to present your subject in context may also help you decide upon the **genre** and **medium** of your project. Of course, an analysis or argument about design can be presented conventionally through a thesis followed by evidence; through a narrative structure that shows how a fashion developed or evolved; through a classification of types of designs to show similarities, or through comparisons and contrasts to highlight differences (see the way Dylan Ellis compares movie posters in Project 7.1). Almost inevitably, you will need to include images in a project—through a Web site, online videos, or other medium. But stay within your abilities: a few good pictures with informative captions may be all you need to make a point in your project (see Sean Nixon's use of photographs in Project 7.2).

As you develop a draft of your composition, recall a design cliché that applies to any project you might prepare on the subject: *the devil is in the details.* Readers will genuinely want to understand how a design works or why exactly it succeeds or fails. If you're doing your job, you'll take them below the surface, providing the kind of evidence for your claims they will find fascinating or convincing.

Finally, be certain that any information you provide is factually accurate. Furnish the documentation, formal and informal, that will help readers find the sources upon which your projects are based because they *will* check—everyone's work gets Googled these days. And think in terms of multiple *sources*, especially when dealing with popular culture. Use the library too: books and articles are essential to any research project.

Project 7.1

Analyzing the Design of an Everyday Text

This assignment asks you to look closely at an object and to write an analysis or argument about it. Your subject might be a text or an object that you use in your everyday life—a box of cereal, your favorite movie poster, or a pair of $300 jeans, for example. Or it might be a design you are familiar with in your community: a notably successful building, a playground that is both safe and fun, a bridge that couldn't be uglier. Then write a three- to five-page analysis that carefully describes the design and speculates about what messages it sends about identity, values, or culture.

Your purpose in analyzing the text or object you have chosen is to explore the design choices that went into its creation. Don't feel obligated, however, to stop here. Take the next step and offer some claims about how the design elements work together to affect behavior or to suggest particular values or meanings.

If you write about an everyday item, your audience will likely be familiar with what you're discussing: everyone has owned a pair of jeans or read the back of a cereal box. But you will still need to provide detailed descriptions of the particular subject of your analysis: the Calvin Klein low-rise jeans or the box of Honey-Nut Cheerios—or, as shown in the sample paper, an iconic movie poster. Incorporate images into the paper, if possible, to help readers see what you're talking about.

Begin with a close examination of the text or object you are studying: take notes on how it is put together and keep your eyes open for interesting or unexpected patterns. Although most of your material for the project will come from direct observation, you should do background research in the library or online, if needed, to find out basic facts about the text or object you're studying and its creator—as Dylan Ellis does in the sample project.

You already possess many of the analytical skills required for this assignment—you've developed and practiced them throughout this chapter. After studying the text or object carefully and taking notes, identify key design features and come to some conclusions about the messages these features suggest. Then consider the best structure for this project. Typical analysis essays begin with a careful description of the text or object at hand, move on to identify patterns of meaning, and then end with conclusions about the larger implications of those patterns. You may find headings helpful to keep readers on track.

STUDENT PROJECT

Dylan Ellis, "June 29, 1989"

Ellis 1

Dylan Ellis
Professor Ruszkiewicz
RHE 315: Visual Rhetoric
28 March 2007

June 23, 1989

    I remember walking down the corridor of the theatre with dad. I was only three years old and very excited. Finally, I was going to see Batman in a movie! And I loved it. I made my parents buy me every toy and my poor grandparents even had to drive two hours to the closest town with a Wal-Mart to find me the Holy Grail of Christmas toys--the Batmobile. I have many different memories tied to director Tim Burton's Batman (1989)--from seeing it the first time, to ordering it on Pay-per-view, acting it out in my living room, filling in the coloring book, and quoting the lines. The movie became iconic to me. Perhaps no piece of advertising or marketing captures the entire experience and allure of Batman better than its original one-sheet teaser poster. The image speaks volumes by giving away very little, but behind its initial message are layers of meaning tied to both the film and the character of Batman himself.

    Of course the first thing a viewer of the poster notices is the emblem (see fig. 1). It is a completely new interpretation of the Bat-logo, a far cry

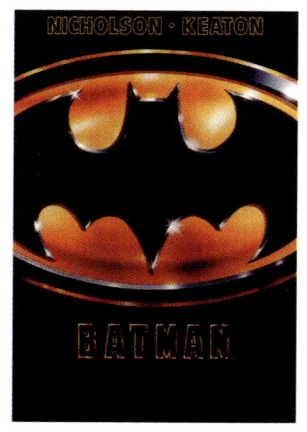

Fig. 1. The original teaser poster carried only the emblem and opening date—not the cast or film title.

Marginal notes:
- The title chosen is intriguing, but would not be immediately clear to most readers.
- The opening ¶ provides a personal context for the forthcoming analysis of a movie poster.
- The final sentence of the opening ¶ provides a thesis for the paper.
- Though the author describes the *Batman* poster meticulously in the paper, readers still need this image.

459

Ellis 2

from the cartoonish item seen in the 1960s television show. Intriguingly, the logo is cut off at the ends, but this slight omission is not a mistake. If the entire logo were displayed on the poster, the image could not be nearly as large and striking. Indeed, the fact that the creator of the poster chose size and boldness over presenting a whole image is significant. In essence, a mere poster cannot contain the Bat-logo: it is too powerful. Eliminating the tips of the emblem even gives it a sense of motion, as if it were bursting out of the poster. To an extent, the creator used the limitations placed on him by the standard dimensions and alignment of a typical movie poster to an advantage.

> **In this ¶ and elsewhere, the author describes an element of the poster and then interprets it.**

A viewer notices, too, that the Batman logo is not placed vertically in the dead center of the frame, but raised slightly above the middle of the poster. Certainly the image could have been centered, and there would have still been room for what little text is at the bottom. Instead, the emblem looms at the top of the poster, much like Batman as he surveys Gotham City perched on building-tops in the darkness. Thus the poster takes on specific attributes of Batman. It is mysterious just as he is, shrouded in secrecy, finding solace in anonymity.

> **Note that every aspect of the simple poster is examined carefully and seriously.**

Of course the emblem also screams ferocity in the way it is made to resemble a bat with its wings open; however, this interpretation is far more stylized than an actual picture of a bat would be. The bottom of the logo looks like the teeth of some monster just before it devours its prey. The top resembles Batman's mask and headpiece with its sharply pointed ears. The sides obviously evoke the image of a bat's wings as it soars. Furthermore, the insignia is razor-sharp. Each point--and there are nine of them--looks as if it would prick you if you could reach your hand into the poster and touch the tip. These serrations convey a feeling of boldness and contrast starkly with the gold behind them.

> **The comparison with Spider-Man here helps to illuminate both the poster and the character of Batman.**

The logo also sparkles in the light. It seems pristine and untouched, perhaps brand new, hinting that this will be an origin story. To me, the gold and the flares of light signify Batman's wealth and his access to so many resources. (Poor college student Peter Parker, also known as

Ellis 3

Spider-Man, surely could not afford a logo this nice.) Moreover, gold is the only color in the entire poster. Much like the film, the image is dark, amplifying what little color there is.

Looking at the original poster as a whole, a viewer sees only the logo and the text, "June 23." The line tells us that the film opens on June 23 while the logo says everything else. Nowhere on the poster does the word "Batman" appear, yet we still know. And though this poster might have been a new design for the Bat-logo, it holds true to key traits so that the viewers would know exactly what it advertises. The creator uses knowledge viewers already have of the character to redefine their ideas about Batman. Advertising firms only dream of this level of brand recognition.

Just as important as establishing trademark identification, the whole poster aligns with the tone of the film. It may have been the first piece of marketing anyone saw for the film, so it had to tell viewers what to expect by igniting their excitement and debunking the previous incarnation of the Caped Crusader-- namely the campy 60s television show with its manufactured sound effects and hokey plot lines. The movie certainly boasted star-power with Jack Nicholson receiving top billing in the film as well as then-young maverick director Tim Burton helming the project fresh off his success with the movie Beetlejuice; yet their names are nowhere on this initial poster though they appear in later versions. Yet this absence of details arouses curiosity and exudes confidence.

In 1989, movies based upon comic books were not nearly as commonplace as they are today. Batman had to have enough gravitas to sustain itself. For audiences to take the film seriously, it had to take itself seriously. The movie went on to be far-and-away the most successful film of 1989 grossing over $250 million at the box office as well as $150 million in video rentals, spawning three sequels, a Saturday morning cartoon show and countless toys. Batman's contributions to the status of comic-book and super hero movies are immeasurable. But everything began with this image. The Batman poster introduced the film to the public. And its influence on poster art can still be seen today: where would Superman (see fig. 2) and Spider-Man (see fig. 3) be without it?

> **The author uses cultural contexts to explain how the poster works.**

> **The concluding ¶ explains the enduring cultural influence of the *Batman* poster. The author supports his claim by comparing it to two more recent film posters.**

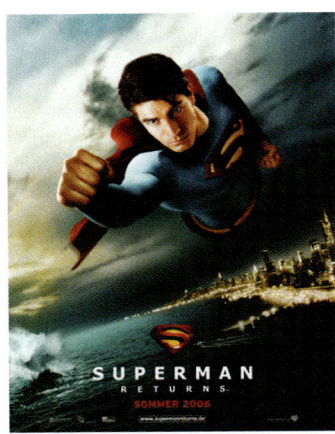

Fig. 2. Superman Returns poster (2006).

Fig. 3. Spider-Man 3 poster (2007).

Project 7.2

Studying Design and Its Contexts

For this assignment, you will conduct research to place a particular design or style into its historical and cultural contexts and explore the relationships and influences you discover. Report your findings in a paper of four to six pages or, alternatively, in a well-developed oral presentation or fully captioned photo essay. The more specific and focused your topic of analysis, the better—though some big questions might intrigue you: for example, how did the great pyramids of ancient Egypt reflect the political power of the Pharaohs who created them? How did murals produced during the Great Depression depict the realities of class conflict? How have political commercials on TV changed in the past thirty years? You can conduct some of your research on the Internet, but you should also use library databases to find scholarly books and articles.

Don't hesitate to choose a topic that speaks to your interests. Style and design intersect with just about every human concern—gender, athletics, economics, politics, social movements. You may be able to make a point about a design simply by placing it in a context: big fins on cars during the booming 1950s, or long hair on men in the 1960s. Or you may want to study a subject that requires you to connect the dots because the relationship between the product and its context may not be obvious.

But be careful about how you explain any connections you discover between design and culture. Different readers will bring their own perspectives and biases to bear on what you have written, so you may have to provide plenty of background information to explain social and political contexts. For example, political murals painted in public buildings in the 1930s inspired some people with their pro-labor themes, but others regarded them as propaganda. That tension is part of the design story that makes these objects interesting and you'd probably need to explore it.

Research, of course, is the key: it will allow you to create a project that ties together design with culture. Some of this research may involve learning more about the evolution of designs—for instance, you might track down information on the development of manmade fabrics (nylon, rayon, polyester) to understand the evolution of some fashions. Or you may need to look deeper into issues of culture—for instance, examining family or racial structures from the 1950s to analyze particular advertising campaigns. Spell out in detail the connections you find.

Use the Internet and some library databases to collect information about your topic. Also locate images that you can analyze. Consider how your readers will react to any positions inherent in your discussion of culture and design. Make sure that a process of analysis shows up in your composition, not just a series of descriptions. Discuss and critique the characteristics of whatever you have found to analyze, make comparisons, explain patterns, and emphasize details that matter. Solicit feedback, and revise your work to make it stronger.

Before beginning, look at Sean Nixon's paper for an example of how one student writer responded to this assignment.

STUDENT PROJECT

Sean Nixon, "The Transformation of American Architecture during the 1920s and 1930s"

Nixon 1

Sean Nixon
Professor Nardgne
English 201
November 22, 2004

The Transformation of American Architecture
during the 1920s and 1930s

    A combination of structure, function, and aesthetics, architecture tangibly illustrates the society of which it is a part. Society dictates which qualities of architecture it most values, and in this way society molds the look, feel, and mood of its buildings. Not only does society affect architecture, but architecture also influences society in a symbiotic relationship. Society "defines the uses of its buildings" and "sets the price it is willing to pay for architecture in competition with other things." In return architecture "acts as a catalyst" in that it "provides symbols, reinforces conservatism or encourages a people to be adventurous" (Burchard and Bush-Brown 4). Architecture can provide a historical snapshot, for often designs can "divulge what the men in power were like who built them, when they were built, and why" (4). An investigation of American architecture during the 1920s and 1930s reveals how architecture relates to the culture that creates it. From the big business internalization of Coolidge to the New Deal progressivism of Roosevelt, this period was marked by severe jolts in the history of America, and architecture responded to changes accordingly.

    By the end of World War I in 1918, the world had witnessed a terrible and violent spectacle the likes of which it had never seen. In America, citizens were disillusioned and their fundamental beliefs disrupted. Despite the irreversible changes the Great War inflicted on American principles, American citizens "tried desperately to pretend that nothing had changed at all, that there had been no entanglement, that the world was just as wide and Europe was just as far away as ever" (Gowans 421). The war gave Americans a vision of a "sick" and "corrupt" Europe, and in the early 1920s a move toward pure Americanism ensued. However, this push was superficial and short-lived. Socially, President Coolidge unsuccessfully attempted Prohibition to purify the soul. In dealing

464   WRITING ABOUT STYLE, DESIGN, AND CULTURE

with foreign affairs the government tried isolation through high tariffs and anti-immigration laws. Politically the idea of "normalcy" prevailed (Gowans 422).

Architecture followed suit in an attempt to revert to a Victorian style of design. The result borrowed an eclectic mix of historical styles that falsely boasted of "modernism" and "Americanism." This form of design was no more than a simplified "colonial" style. The clearest example of this superficial attempt at a unique cultural design is exemplified in the "period house" (see fig. 1). This type of house, resembling a colonial cottage, borrows obvious details from historic styles and presents them in a simplified manner. For many people, these forms portrayed "the concept of American life as somehow distinctly plainer and purer than that of degenerate Europeans" (Gowans 424). Such provincial and insular ideas "made the [early] 1920s a dark [period] of modern architecture in America" (424). Even the "wholly American bred" concept of the skyscraper suffered from this narrowmindedness (Koeper and Whiffen 320). Despite the technologically advanced principles behind these massive new structures, they still derived their design "not from present or future, but from the past" (Gowans 424).

When the time came to take nominations for a skyscraper design for the Chicago Tribune Building (1922), the majority of entries came from European architects. One of the most acclaimed designs was submitted by the Finnish architect Eliel Saarinen, whose plan came in second in the contest. Interestingly, though, Saarinen did not introduce any radical ideas or philosophies, which is the

Fig. 1. Period house, 1926 (Gowans 423).

Fig. 2 Chicago Tribune Building, 1922 (Koeper and Whiffen 322).

key reason his design was so widely accepted (see fig. 2). Only because his "modern architecture" was "so far from radical . . . and so close in spirit to the period house" (Gowans 428) were plans for his buildings approved. The "radical character found in other foreign architects' submissions" would not have an impact on skyscraper design until decades later (Koeper and Whiffen 329).

    The Chicago Tribune skyscraper provides a clear example of architecture clinging to the past. The idea of a skyscraper, a monumental and technologically advanced structure, is contradicted here by the eclectic Victorian columns and ornamental decoration employed in the design. Thus, even in the face of new innovations such as the skyscraper, American architecture in the early 1920s was stagnant and unimaginative. The mood of the Coolidge era seemed as if it would be prolonged indefinitely until the economic crash in 1929. Americans were shaken by the "realization that their society . . . had failed to solve its own internal problems" (Burchard and Bush-Brown 390). They were forced to accept that their ideas were not perfect and that in every society, no matter how strong, there are flaws. In architecture, the year 1929 served as a hinge to close the door on the old eclectic Victorian style and open the door to an age of modernism and imagination.

    Architecture was not totally revolutionized during the 1930s, for a revolution of that scale takes time, but the decade does mark the initial stages of change toward a truly "American" stylistic form. Architecture in the 1930s diverged in two directions. Roosevelt's New Deal administration, which focused on rebuilding the economy and restoring faith in government, served a very functional purpose; architecture of the New Deal perfectly reflected this theme. From the "alphabet soup" of Roosevelt's public programs emerged housing and building projects such as the Federal Housing Administration (FHA), the Public Works Administration (PWA), and the United States Housing Association (USHA). Each of these organizations established by Roosevelt's Works Progress Administration did its best to benefit the general public but did little to further the progress of architecture in the United States. The architecture of the New Deal was aesthetically uninspired and focused mainly on the function of the buildings being built.

During the 1930s Roosevelt and the New Dealers had no incentive to concentrate their efforts on new forms of design, and architecture's "aesthetic aspirations were muffled in the social ideals" of the time (Burchard and Bush-Brown 402).

New Deal architecture served a purely functional purpose on a large scale and contributed little to new styles. However, another simultaneous movement made great progress in terms of public acceptance of radical ideas during the 1930s. During that decade, "European ideas flooded into the United States as they never had since the 1860s" (Gowans 421). Ironically, "it was Europe that supplied answers to the aesthetic problem of American" design (Koeper and Whiffen 320). Streamline Moderne was a major stylistic development with European origins. Streamline Moderne differed greatly from the eclectic style of the 1920s in that "it was stripped of ornament" and was "symbolic of the dynamic twentieth century" (331). The sleek, smooth look of this futuristic style celebrated the use of metal and glass and implied that the age of the machine was here to stay. Frank Lloyd Wright, the most famous of American architects, gave Streamline Moderne an American identity during the 1930s. In his design for the Johnson Wax Company's administration building (see fig. 3), Wright created a harmony between technology and humanism. In an age when many people feared rapid technological development and the use of machines, Wright managed to bring people and machines together in a cohesive unit, thus setting the tone for architecture in the coming decades.

Fig. 3 Johnson Wax Administration Building, exterior, 1936–1939 (Koeper and Whiffen 333).

     Although the two paths of architecture during the 1930s seem drastically different, by the end of the decade it was clear that they shared a common goal: to eliminate the enclaves of eclecticism and create an architectural style unique to American ideals and principles. The New Deal architecture overcame eclecticism through mass production, and many observers believe that modern architecture was "born in the study of structure" and functional necessity (Burchard and Bush-Brown 393). From another perspective, styles such as Streamline Moderne defeated eclecticism by introducing radical new designs manufactured with new technology. The combination of these two approaches eventually phased out eclectic Victorianism altogether by the end of the 1930s.

     Americans realized that buildings were a direct representation of themselves, and they chose to have their structures reflect their power and advancement. Just as Roosevelt's progressive administration saved America from Coolidge's big business conservatism, the progressive designs of the 1930s saved architecture from the stagnant, uninspired styles of the 1920s.

Works Cited

Burchard, John E., and Albert Bush-Brown. The Architecture of America: A Social and Cultural History. Boston: Little, 1961.

Gowans, Alan. Images of American Living. Philadelphia: Lippincott, 1964.

Koeper, Frederick, and Marcus Whiffen. American Architecture 1607–1976. Cambridge: MIT, 1981.

Project 7.3

Using Seth Stevenson's essay "Head Case" as a model (pages 421–422), write a three- to four-page analysis of an advertisement or ad campaign. You can find more about handling such an assignment by reviewing "Writing An Ad Analysis" on pages 72–73. Similar "Ad Report Card" items can be found archived at the Slate.com site. Or try googling "Seth Stevenson."

Project 7.4

Do as much library research as necessary to write a paper in which you examine the context for the style of a written text or musical composition. The text could be anything from a poem to an advertisement. A particular piece of music—from "The Star-Spangled Banner" to "Cry Me a River" (the Justin Timberlake version)—might take a great deal of cultural explanation.

Or, select a video clip of an ad on YouTube or analyze an ad currently running on TV. Write a short paper that places the ad in its cultural context, explaining what knowledge a viewer might need to appreciate it fully. Consider using screen captures to reproduce (with appropriate documentation and credit) any frames that illustrate points you wish to make. Some old political ads worth searching for on YouTube include "Daisy" (for Lyndon Johnson in 1964) and "Bear" (for Ronald Reagan in 1984).

Project 7.5

Explain the design details of some object or item you know well enough to consider yourself an expert—a tennis racquet, a pair of dress shoes, a hunting rifle. In a few pages, share some of your expertise with readers likely to be less knowledgeable by introducing them to design subtleties they probably missed. For instance, you might explain the differences between a fine Swiss mechanical watch and a more inexpensive (and accurate) electronic timepiece.

CHAPTER 8
POLITICS AND ADVOCACY

ITEM 8.1 ■ National Guard Recruitment Ad, *Hooah Magazine,* January 19, 2008

When you hear the words *politics* and *advocacy,* what images come to mind? If you're like many people, the words suggest activities far removed from your daily life: senators plodding through legislation on C-SPAN, angry protesters on a picket line, or pundits shouting at each other on cable news shows. But in fact, most of us regularly find ourselves in situations that call on us to act informally as politicians or as advocates—to make judgments about the policies that shape our country or local communities, or to voice support for a cause that we care about.

The two texts that open this chapter are examples of a kind of political rhetoric that most of us have encountered: the military recruitment appeal. Designed to encourage young people to enlist—an especially complex decision during times of war—these texts embody some common features of political arguments and appeals.

Consider the National Guard advertisement (Item 8.1), which appeared in the January 19, 2008, issue of *Hooah*, a promotional magazine mailed to high school students. Printed advertisements such as this one are a familiar form of political argument. (Most of us can readily conjure up a mental image of classic posters of Rosie the Riveter or Uncle Sam saying "I Want You for the U.S. Army".) With their striking images and hard-hitting slogans, their claims are hard to miss.

But political texts don't always work in such explicit ways. Consider *America's Army* (Item 8.2), an online video game developed by the U.S. Army as an indirect recruitment tool. This popular game—which boasts more than 9 million players to date—immerses players in realistic combat simulations, allowing them to "experience" the rewards and challenges of soldiering. There are no slogans, no directives—the idea is that the vicarious experience of military life will lead players to seek out enlistment more or less on their own.

As these two very different examples illustrate, texts about politics and advocacy take different forms and can carry high stakes. Because these texts are able to inspire us to actions that can quite literally change our lives, they can spark polarized debate and emotional exchanges. Of course, that's also what makes participating in conversations on these issues so exciting.

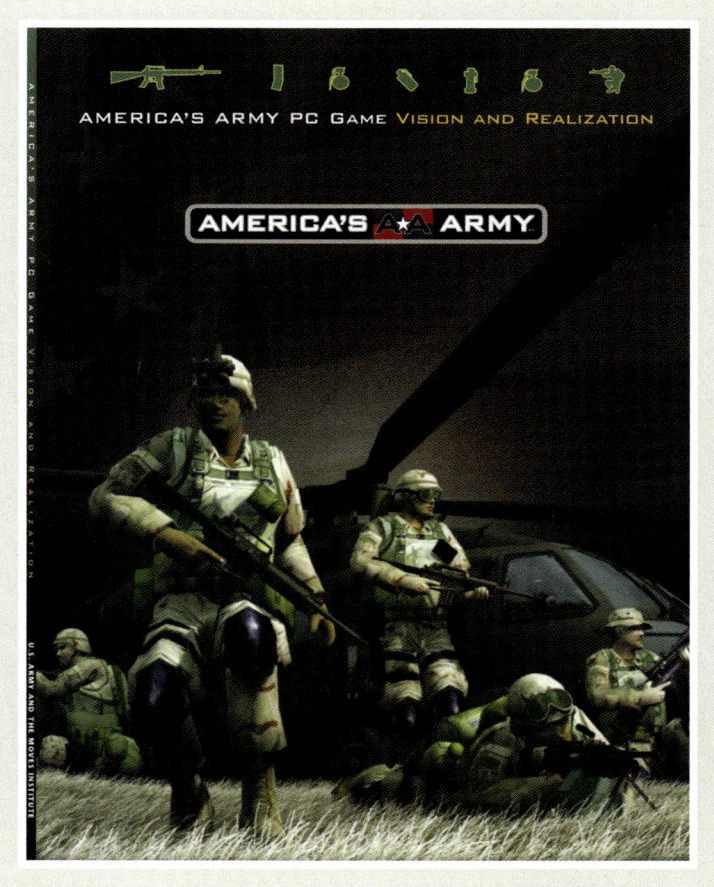

ITEM 8.2 ■ *America's Army: The Official U.S. Army Game,* **Screenshot, 2006**

471

Reading Texts About Politics and Advocacy

There's an important difference between simply reacting to the political texts you encounter and understanding how they work—or ought to work. Understanding such texts means paying close attention to how their different elements work together in addition to the responses they evoke: Why exactly *did* you react in a certain way to an editorial cartoon or a *Daily Show* skit? Was it because a viewpoint was defended powerfully—or just cleverly? Or maybe you rejected a worthy argument because you didn't like its style. Too whiny. Too heavy-handed. Not cool. How might you explain those reactions? That's the point of studying political texts.

When we think about political **subjects,** issues of national policy such as abortion, capital punishment, war, immigration, and global warming naturally come to mind. These important topics inspire passionate claims and opinions. Yet even everyday decisions can affect others, and in this sense even choices about what to buy or eat are also political. The car covered with bumper stickers shown in Item 8.3 suggests the range of political topics you might encounter in a single day's commute: from "Unite for Peace" to "I Recycle," all of the items challenge you to consider how your beliefs and actions affect the larger community.

When writers or artists address political topics, they do so for a **purpose**—typically to move an audience to specific viewpoints or actions. In written texts, this purpose is often expressed in a claim or thesis statement. You probably have plenty of experience with thesis statements. In academic and journalistic writing, thesis statements often combine a claim with a supporting reason or reasons, accompanied by evidence, testimony, or examples.

But visual or multimedia arguments usually work differently: they make claims, of course, but they often do so in ways that are less direct and more visceral. Sometimes an image suggests a claim entirely by its sheer power. That may be the case with Andrew Parsons's photo of a triumphant Iraqi woman displaying her inked finger after voting for the first time (Item 8.4). The contrast between the subject's black veil, her fiercely proud expression, and her outstretched purple-stained finger speak volumes about the promise of democratic reforms in the region. Other times, words and images work together to suggest a text's purpose. For instance, Todd Heisler's photo of soldiers removing a flag-covered coffin from a plane in Reno, Nevada (Item 8.5) is visually compelling; however, the accompanying caption provides context and makes a direct appeal: remember.

Of course, no political conversation exists in a vacuum. Rather, exchanges about public issues unfold among particular **audiences** and within complex personal, historical, and cultural **contexts.** Two millennia ago, Aristotle argued that persuasive texts work by responding to audience and context in three basic ways: by appeals to *pathos* (appeals to the emotions and values of the audience); to *ethos* (appeals to the character, authority, and honesty of the person making the claim); and to *logos* (appeals involving subject matter, including evidence and logic). Ask yourself how a text uses each of these appeals, alone or in combination. (See pages 25–26 for more information about *pathos, ethos,* and *logos.*)

There's no denying that political claims are made more memorable and people are moved to act by appeals to their emotions. Ask yourself: how does a text elicit values and feelings—does it make readers feel happy, fearful, patriotic, generous, amused or angry? To what end? For example, why might the designers of the People for the Ethical Treatment of Animals (PETA) anti-fur poster (Item 8.6) have asked model Kate Ford to hold a rabbit while wearing red gloves? How do you respond to the stern expression on Ford's face? Each of these elements contributes to the poster's appeal to *pathos*.

Still another way to persuade an audience is through *ethos*. In a written argument, the author may cite reliable sources and use unbiased language to elicit your trust—an important first step in getting you to listen to his or her view. *Ethos* is also at work, however, when a celebrity or expert endorses a cause or expresses a viewpoint. PETA, for example, has long used the *ethos* of celebrities who support its opinions to counteract the widespread impression that the group is made up primarily of out-of-the-mainstream radicals. Of course, *ethos* can also be manipulated in dishonest ways, to make an idea or cause seem more reputable than it is. (Consider all the unlucky people fooled into donating money to bogus charities or telemarketing scams.) But the very same kind of manipulation of *ethos* is what makes some parodies and ironic texts work, and they can be compelling and legitimate forms of advocacy. In Margaret Bourke-White's *At the Time of the Louisville Flood* (Item 8.7), for example, we see the irony when the myth of universal American prosperity is stripped bare, displayed as false against the Depression-era hardships documented in the photograph.

Appeals to facts and logic are easy to spot in most media. Does the writer draw on facts reported from reliable sources or gleaned from direct observation and experience? Does the presentation use charts, tables, graphs, or other visual representations of data, as the "pro" editorial in Item 8.8 does to bolster its case?

Political texts take a variety of shapes, so considerations involving **medium** are also important. Words—written or spoken—offer a powerful means for presenting claims and issues. Even in the age of the Internet, politicians still deliver public speeches, serious journals print lengthy articles, and newspaper editorials retain considerable clout. Yet let's be frank—images can deliver an emotional punch more quickly than words alone. They can be shaped, arranged, or combined with words to create persuasive effects. For example, in Dick Locher's Thanksgiving spoof (Item 8.9), words and image work together to cleverly suggest a point about illegal immigration. Though the cartoon's claim is implied, its sentiments come through clearly—leavened by humor and irony.

Whatever their purpose or medium, the majority of texts that address political topics share some basic elements of **structure.** As we've already mentioned, most discussions of such issues stake out one or more claims and present reasons, evidence, or other appeals to support them. Sometimes political texts include rebuttals that acknowledge and respond to opposing viewpoints. In a written text these structures may be easy to see, marked by titles or headings or helpful transitional phrases.

But when a text is mainly visual or aural or some combination of these, structure becomes more complicated. Sometimes the relationship among parts of a visual or multimedia argument is fairly obvious. In other cases, you may need to assemble the pieces yourself, making choices about how to access and absorb the information and its implications. Consider the PotterCast featured in Item 8.10, for example. A reader interested in the Darfur initiative described on the Web page would need to navigate links to several informational sources within and outside the PotterCast site, as well as listen to the accompanying podcast. Noticing where information is located and how easy it is to access on the site will tell you something about the site designers' agenda.

Finally, when you read about politics and advocacy, remember that every **detail** in a text may be important. Design elements representing choices in arrangement, framing, color, image choices, and so on can be just as important as the major claims. Each detail merits scrutiny.

Gallery: Politics and Advocacy

ITEM 8.3 ■ Car with Political Bumper Stickers

A bumper sticker is just a small piece of polyester backed by acrylic glue, yet it's one of the most widespread forms of political expression in our culture. Bumper stickers can address any of a wide variety of causes and present concise arguments, as the collection on the back panel of this 1970s-era Ford Pinto illustrates.

1. What are your thoughts on the medium and genre of the bumper sticker? What kinds of messages can bumper stickers convey? What audiences can they reach? What are some limitations of this medium and genre?

2. In what ways might the message on a bumper sticker be influenced by its context? What do the stickers in Item 8.3 tell us about the owner of the Ford Pinto? What other contextual factors might make a difference?

3. How would you design a bumper sticker for a group or cause you support? How would you respond to the challenges of composing an argument in this medium?

475

ITEM 8.4 ■ **Andrew Parsons, *An Iraqi Woman Shows Her Inked Finger after Casting Her Ballot in a Polling Station in Baghdad*, 2005**

On January 30, 2005, Iraqi voters chose representatives for the newly formed 275-member Iraqi National Assembly. This general election was the country's first since the United States-led 2003 invasion of Iraq and subsequent removal of Saddam Hussein from power, and it marked an important step in the transition of turning control of the country over from United States occupation forces to the Iraqis themselves.

[1] This photo documents a news event—the historic 2005 elections in Iraq. Would it be fair to say that it also makes a political argument(s)? Explain your answer, pointing to specific elements of the image to support your view.

[2] What details in the photo strike you as important? What is the significance of the woman's hand gesture ("V" for victory, or is it a peace sign?), her black veil, her facial expression? Discuss how these details contribute to the overall effect of the image.

[3] Why do you think the photographer chose to focus on this particular voter? Discuss how this choice of subject contributes to appeals based on *ethos, pathos,* and *logos* (see pages 25–26 for more on *ethos, pathos,* and *logos*).

476   GALLERY | POLITICS AND ADVOCACY

ITEM 8.5 ■ Todd Heisler, *Reno, Nevada,* 2005

Todd Heisler won a 2006 Pulitzer Prize for his photographs documenting the return of fallen U.S. soldiers from Iraq. This photograph originally appeared in *The Rocky Mountain News* with the following explanation by Heisler: "When 2nd Lt. James Cathey's body arrived at the Reno Airport, Marines climbed into the cargo hold of the plane and draped the flag over his casket as passengers watched the family gather on the tarmac. During the arrival of another Marine's casket last year at Denver International Airport, Major Steve Beck described the scene as one of the most powerful in the process [of returning the bodies of soldiers]: 'See the people in the windows? They'll sit right there in the plane, watching those Marines. You gotta wonder what's going through their minds, knowing that they're on the plane that brought him home,' he said. 'They're going to remember being on that plane for the rest of their lives. They're going to remember bringing that Marine home. And they should.'"

1. What does Todd Heisler's explanatory caption contribute to your understanding of the image? Point to specific ways in which the text and image work together to tell the story. Would the photo be as powerful without the accompanying text? Why or why not?

2. Consider the composition of the photo. Why do you think Heisler chose to show the row of passengers above the coffin being removed from the baggage compartment? Why might he have chosen not to show the family gathered on the tarmac? What other observations can you make about the composition of the image?

3. Do you think that a viewer who supports U.S. military involvement in Iraq would respond to this image differently than one who opposes the war? In what ways might their responses be similar?

Try telling him it's just a bit of fur trim.

Rabbits and other animals are often beaten and skinned alive for their fur. **Boycott all fur.**

Kate Ford for PETA
FurIsDead.com

ITEM 8.6 ■ **People for the Ethical Treatment of Animals (PETA),** *Fur is Dead* **Poster, 2007**

Animal-rights advocacy group People for the Ethical Treatment of Animals (PETA) often enlists celebrity activists—including musicians, models, and artists—to help promote its cause. This striking poster features well-known British model and actress Kate Ford.

---

1 What are your thoughts on using celebrities as spokespeople for social and political causes? Do you think such appeals are effective? Do they sway you? Why or why not?

2 Consider the use of color in the ad. How does the designer's use of red and white contribute to the message? What else can you say about the use of color in the poster?

3 Examine the text. How do tone and word choices contribute to—or work against—the poster's purpose? How do the words reinforce (or work against) other visual elements in the image?

GALLERY | POLITICS AND ADVOCACY

ITEM 8.7 ■ Margaret Bourke-White, *At the Time of the Louisville Flood*, 1937

Photojournalist Margaret Bourke-White (1904–1971) is best-known for her influential photographs depicting social and political conditions of the 1930s and 1940s. This photo depicting African American residents displaced by the Louisville Flood of 1937 originally appeared in *Life* magazine and is now regarded as an iconic image of the Great Depression.

1. What do you notice first about this photo? What elements of framing or composition does Bourke-White use to draw attention to these focal points? Do you think the people in the photo or passersby on that day would have viewed the scene in the same way?

2. What contrasts do you see between the billboard and the street scene below? What larger point(s) do you think Bourke-White is suggesting? Would it be fair to call this an ironic image?

3. In what ways is the photo valuable as an historical document? In what ways, if any, do you think it might also speak to current issues? Explain.

College Affordability: Boola-boola for Yale
But Ivy tuition cuts don't address broader access to higher education.
By Robert W. Ahrens, *USA Today*

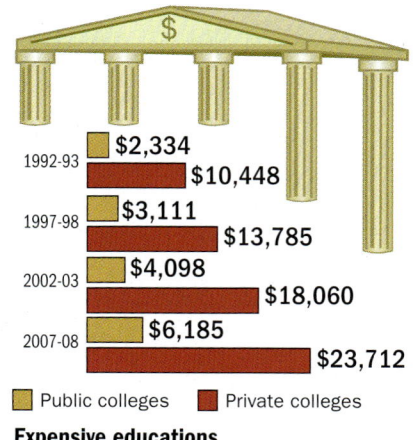

Expensive educations
Average tuition and fees at four-year colleges have more than doubled in the past 15 years.
Source: The College Board
(amounts not adjusted for inflation)

Year	Public colleges	Private colleges
1992-93	$2,334	$10,448
1997-98	$3,111	$13,785
2002-03	$4,098	$18,060
2007-08	$6,185	$23,712

Not all the news on inflation was bad this week. Yale University announced that it is slashing tuition costs for students from families with financial need, matching a similar move by Harvard a month earlier.

Yale deserves a cheer for addressing the sticker stock that discourages applications from brilliant students who lack trust funds. But it's easy to increase aid when your endowment is $35 billion (Harvard) or $22.5 billion (Yale).

The tougher question is what to do about college affordability for the 99.92% of four-year students in the USA who attend institutions other than Harvard and Yale. College costs have been outstripping inflation for years. Average tuition and fees in this school year are $6,185 at public schools (up from $3,111 just a decade ago), and $23,712 at private colleges (up from $13,785), according to the College Board.

When those sorts of numbers scare young people away from higher education, it's a major problem for both them and the nation. An educated workforce is necessary to compete in the global economy, and even many of today's blue-collar jobs require post-high school training.

The affordability issues are difficult, and they vary between public and private institutions:

If big state schools can deliver top educations at affordable prices, the USA can retain its status as the land of opportunity. But public universities are threatened by the recent state announcements of revenue shortfalls. Most worrisome are states, such as New Hampshire, that already charge relatively high tuition but offer modest aid.

Among private schools, Otterbein College in Ohio is more typical than Harvard or Yale. With its modest $100 million endowment, the liberal arts college depends heavily on its $25,000-a-year tuition. Although that price gets discounted for many students, Otterbein President Brent DeVore lacks the option of a dramatic tuition cut. Otterbein and other private colleges depend on the personal touch. The school could raise its 13-to-1 student-faculty ratio, but at what cost to the learning environment?

While affordability questions like these defy easy answers, some steps can be taken.

The federal government can play a role by increasing tuition tax credits and boosting the value of grants that send poor students to college, assuming that offsetting cuts or revenue can be found elsewhere.

Colleges themselves can move faster to cut costs. Collaborating with nearby schools on course offerings, and refusing to join bidding wars for star professors, would help. So would cutting back on professors' esoteric research and raising their classroom hours.

Perhaps the best weapon for controlling college costs is turning students and parents into more informed consumers. Armed with more data about student satisfaction, dropout rates, postgraduate employment and gains in skills, families would be better able to determine whether a selective private college is any better than a nearby, more affordable state school.

There's nothing like a little competition to hold down costs. Just ask Harvard and Yale.

Opposing view: Elite schools drive costs
When Harvard, Yale cut tuition, students elsewhere pay the price.
William G. Durden and Robert J. Massa

Harvard and Yale recently have made pronouncements regarding increased middle-class affordability and access. It is well within their rights to do as they wish, but their decisions could increase costs for the thousands of universities without huge endowments, drive up the tuition price, and reduce access for low- and middle-income students.

Exchanging student loans for grants inflates cost. The "free" grant money must come from somewhere. If one has a large endowment, it comes from taking a greater percentage as payout, leaving the tuition price unchanged. If one has a smaller endowment, or is state- and taxpayer-supported, it is likely to come from tuition increases.

Targeting more grants to upper-income students without a change in how financial aid is determined will also inflate costs. Many colleges, which cannot afford to ignore tuition revenue, will be forced to increase discounts to compete for students. These schools will either have to cut program quality to reduce costs or increase tuition price to fund additional grants. These inflated tuition prices also could force more students into public colleges at a higher cost to taxpayers.

The negative effects of these policies will further be felt as students who cannot get into super-selective universities have their expectations raised regarding a loan-free aid package. When the college to which they apply cannot offer such a package, low-income students might opt out of higher education altogether rather than take out a loan, which they have now been told is "bad."

The elimination of loans by wealthy schools will increase the tuition price students pay "systemwide," not decrease it. Current financial aid formulas are imperfect and expect far more from upper-middle income families than they can afford. Harvard, Yale and other megarich universities should not, however, act unilaterally to "fix" this problem. They are acting because they can afford to do so — not because it is right.

They should be leading a national discussion on reforming the way parent contributions are determined. Flawed policy disguised as affordability and access will do more harm than good, and when Harvard and Yale do it, it has credibility beyond what it deserves.

William G. Durden is president of Dickinson College; Robert J. Massa is Dickinson's vice president for enrollment and college relations.

---

1. In a sentence or two, summarize the main argument in each editorial. Which do you find more compelling? Why?

2. Examine the supporting evidence used in each editorial. What examples or information do you find especially persuasive (or unpersuasive)? How does the bar graph in the first editorial contribute to its overall argument? Does the graph make the first editorial seem more persuasive?

3. What are some reasons that *USA Today* and other newspapers might print opposing editorials alongside each other? Why might the pro-con format appeal to readers? How do you approach texts that offer opposing interpretations of an issue?

ITEM 8.9 ■ Dick Locher, Cartoon, *Chicago Tribune*, November 25, 2003

This cartoon appeared on the editorial page of the *Chicago Tribune* on Thanksgiving Day.

1. This cartoon uses very few words to make its point. Write a paragraph that explicitly spells out the story told in the cartoon and the political argument it implies. Does your paragraph adequately capture all that's going on in the cartoon? Why or why not?

2. How do the words and picture work together to make the cartoon funny? Point to as many specific details as you can.

3. Why do you think Locher might have created this particular cartoon for the Thanksgiving Day edition of the *Chicago Tribune*? Would the cartoon be just as funny on any other day? Explain your response.

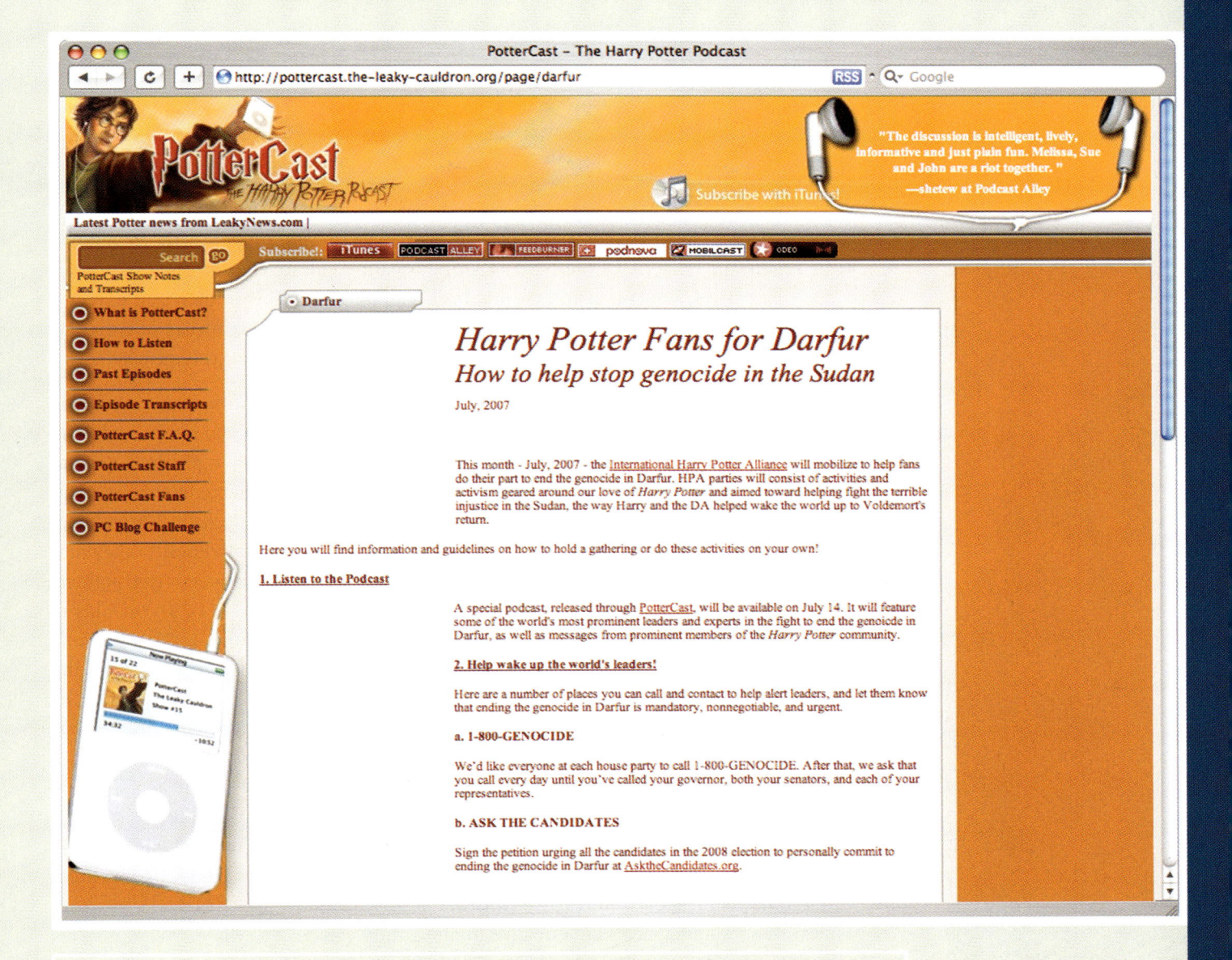

ITEM 8.10 ■ *PotterCast: The Harry Potter Podcast,* Screenshot, 2007

This screenshot captures a 2007 initiative in which the Harry Potter Alliance, an online community for fans of J. K. Rowling's novels, encouraged members to raise donations and pressure politicians to aid genocide victims in Darfur. This project is just one of several activist efforts organized by fans of J. K. Rowling's *Harry Potter* series. Other projects inspired by the novels and developed primarily via online media include voter registration initiatives, petitions protesting international human rights abuses, and advocacy against media-consolidation legislation.

1. Harry Potter Fans for Darfur is just one of many grass-roots political activism efforts that use the Internet to recruit and communicate with supporters. What are your thoughts on this kind of political advocacy? What drawbacks and advantages do you see?

2. How does the Web page use images and references to the Harry Potter novels as part of its political appeal? Why might the designers of this page have chosen to make the informative material about Darfur available as a podcast rather than putting it directly onto the page? What can you say about the appeal in terms of medium and genre?

3. Do you believe that one-time activities such as donation-raising parties are an effective way to make a difference in large-scale political or social problems? Why or why not?

Cluster 8.1
Getting Out the Vote

Demographers have branded people born after 1980 as Generation Y, the first generation of Americans immersed from birth in an information culture characterized by round-the-clock news, infotainment, and multimedia of all kinds. This information overload has made Generation Y the most media savvy in history, with a healthy skepticism of corporate media and politicians. Research suggests that people in this group can't be easily persuaded.

Compared to their Generation X and Baby Boom predecessors, young adults from Generation Y are more likely to do volunteer work, more concerned about environmental issues, and more tolerant of diverse viewpoints. Yet, as a group, they are also less likely than previous generations to vote or be involved in political campaigns. In fact, young people vote in smaller numbers than just about any demographic group except convicted felons. In practical terms, that means that politicians in Washington or City Hall often don't pay much attention to the complaints or needs of young voters. For the past several election cycles, student activists, political parties, and MTV veejays have done what they can to persuade more 18- to 25-year-olds to cast their ballots on election day. Yet despite moderate increases during the last two national elections—an increase sparked especially by enthusiasm for Barack Obama's candidacy during the 2008 presidential campaign—turnout rates among young voters remain relatively low. The texts and images in this cluster explore key issues related to college students' orientations toward voting and political involvement. First, you'll examine an Urban Outfitters T-shirt and a parody piece from the *Onion* that poke fun at media portrayals of young people as politically apathetic or superficial. Next, in Thomas L. Friedman's "Generation Q" and Courtney Martin's "Generation Overwhelmed," you'll encounter two very different explanations for why so many young people don't actively participate in the political process. The cluster ends with examples of outreach initiatives designed to reach young voters. As you assess these texts, ask yourself: What kinds of issues and appeals are effective in motivating college-age voters? What inspires you to get out and vote?

CONSIDER

1. T-shirt designer Foster-Keddie seems to blame everyone for the political environment that makes "Voting is for Old People" possible. Is that sweeping indictment fair? Explain your response.

2. What claim do you think this T-shirt is trying to make? Explain your response, drawing on specific elements from the shirt.

3. How powerful a medium is a T-shirt for making claims and advancing arguments? Within what groups, if any, do you think T-shirt messages would have special appeal?

COMPOSE

4. Describe or design a get-out-the-vote poster that might appeal to a young person inclined to buy the "Voting is for Old People" T-shirt.

ITEM 8.11 ■ **Urban Outfitters, Voting is for Old People T-Shirt, 2004**

When Urban Outfitters produced this $28 T-shirt a few years ago, appalled critics took the franchise to task, accusing them of irresponsibly discouraging young adults from voting. The T-shirt's designer, John Foster-Keddie, countered that the critics just didn't get the joke. He said, "The shirt's real intention is to sum up the current state of political affairs, point a finger at all of us." Urban Outfitters took the shirt off the market nonetheless—so if you own one, hang onto it. It could become a collector's item.

8 POLITICS AND ADVOCACY

Huge Democracy Geek Even Votes in Primaries

The Onion
(October 2, 2002)

FYI This piece parodying young adults' attitudes toward voting was published in *The Onion*, a satirical online news magazine.

NASHUA, NH—Politically engaged citizen David Haas, 25, described by friends and acquaintances as a "big democracy geek," even votes in primaries.

"I can understand voting in the big elections, like for president or governor, or maybe even senator," longtime friend Gregg Becher said Monday. "But David votes in, like, mayoral and county-supervisor elections. How dorky is that?"

The right to vote, as guaranteed in the Constitution, is among the hallmarks of the American democratic system. But Haas has exercised his franchise rights to an embarrassing extreme, voting in every federal, state, and local election since turning 18.

"Normally, David's a reliable, punctual employee," said Dorothy Raubel, owner of Raubel Garden Center, where Haas has worked for the past seven years. "But then there's that occasional Tuesday morning in April or November when he calls in saying he'll be late to work. It's a strange habit, but we've all grown accustomed to it by now."

Haas prides himself on being an informed voter, making sure to familiarize himself with candidates' positions before casting a vote. A self-described "independent" who tends to favor Democratic candidates, he can summarize the basic position of both major parties on most issues. As a result, Haas has endured the mockery and derision of those around him.

"On Sept. 10, he showed up late to work, and you could just tell he'd been voting," coworker Mike Summers said. "He was holding something in his hand, and we were like, 'Hey, Haasenpfeffer, whatcha got there?' He said it was the League of Women Voters candidate guide. So Rob [Mularkey] says, 'League of Women Voters? Now I know why you vote so much—you want to horn in on that hot women-voter action!' David didn't even smile; he just got all huffy and said the guide was from the morning paper and that copies were available to the public."

Richard Prohaska, Haas' next-door neighbor, can attest to Haas' strange dedication to the American political process. Over the years, Prohaska said he has seen him get into numerous doorstep discussions with campaign workers and canvassing local politicians.

"About two months ago, some alderwoman who was up for reelection was going door-to-door passing out leaflets," Prohaska said. "I took one, thanked her, and closed the door as fast as I could. About 30 minutes later, I'm backing the car out of the garage to wash it, and there's David talking to her on his porch. I go to get the hose, and when I come back, he's actually inviting her into his home. I was half-done waxing when she finally came out. Either they had one hell of a quickie, or David cares deeply about local politics. Knowing him, it was definitely the latter."

Though it's not clear why Haas insists on voting in every election, there is no shortage of speculation.

"My guess is, it's his way of hiding from the real world," said Jennifer Thorsten, Haas' sister. "He's always been interested in politics. He was on the debate team in high school and got a B.A. in poli sci in college. I've tried to get him to skip an election, but he never does. *He says that only by exercising our democratic freedoms do we keep our democracy healthy and vital.* Whatever, David."

Source: "Huge Democracy Geek Even Votes in Primaries," *The Onion*, October 2, 2002, Issue 38.36. Reprinted with permission of THE ONION. Copyright © 2008 by ONION, INC. www.theonion.com.

CONSIDER

1. Summarize the argument implicit in *The Onion*'s parody. What reasons does it suggest to explain why many young people don't vote?

2. Does the implied characterization of young people in this piece ring true? Why or why not? Does the accuracy of the portrayal affect whether or not the parody is funny? Explain.

3. This piece was published in 2002. Do you think its points are relevant today? If so, why? If not, what has changed? Point to specific passages to illustrate your claims.

Generation Q

Thomas L. Friedman
(October 10, 2007)

FYI Pulitzer Prize–winning writer Thomas L. Friedman has been writing about foreign affairs for the *New York Times* since 1981. He is also the author of several books, the most recent of which is *Hot, Flat, and Crowded: Why We Need a Green Revolution* (2008).

I just spent the past week visiting several colleges—Auburn, the University of Mississippi, Lake Forest and Williams—and I can report that the more I am around this generation of college students, the more I am both baffled and impressed.

I am impressed because they are so much more optimistic and idealistic than they should be. I am baffled because they are so much less radical and politically engaged than they need to be.

One of the things I feared most after 9/11—that my daughters would not be able to travel the world with the same carefree attitude my wife and I did at their age—has not come to pass.

Whether it was at Ole Miss or Williams or my alma mater, Brandeis, college students today are not only going abroad to study in record numbers, but they are also going abroad to build homes for the poor in El Salvador in record numbers or volunteering at AIDS clinics in record numbers. Not only has terrorism not deterred them from traveling, they are rolling up their sleeves and diving in deeper than ever.

The Iraq war may be a mess, but I noticed at Auburn and Old Miss more than a few young men and women proudly wearing their R.O.T.C. uniforms. Many of those not going abroad have channeled their national service impulses into increasingly popular programs at home like "Teach for America," which has become to this generation what the Peace Corps was to mine.

It's for all these reasons that I've been calling them "Generation Q"—the Quiet Americans, in the best sense of that term, quietly pursuing their idealism, at home and abroad.

But Generation Q may be too quiet, too online, for its own good, and for the country's own good. When I think of the huge budget deficit, Social Security deficit and ecological deficit that our generation is leaving this generation, if they are not spitting mad, well, then they're just not paying attention. And we'll just keep piling it on them.

> **But Generation Q may be too quiet, too online, for its own good, and for the country's own good.**

There is a good chance that members of Generation Q will spend their entire adult lives digging out from the deficits that we—the "Greediest Generation," epitomized by George W. Bush—are leaving them.

When I was visiting my daughter at her college, she asked me about a terrifying story that ran in this newspaper on Oct. 2, reporting that the Arctic ice cap was melting "to an extent unparalleled in a century or more"—and that the entire Arctic system appears to be "heading toward a new, more watery state" likely triggered by "human-caused global warming."

"What happened to that Arctic story, Dad?" my daughter asked me. How could the news media just report one day that the Arctic ice was melting far faster than any models predicted "and then the story just disappeared"? Why weren't any of the candidates talking about it? Didn't they understand: this has become the big issue on campuses?

No, they don't seem to understand. They seem to be too busy raising money or buying votes with subsidies for ethanol farmers in Iowa. The candidates could actually use a good kick in the pants on this point. But where is it going to come from?

Source: Thomas L. Friedman, "Generation Q," *The New York Times* OP-ED, October 10, 2007. © 2007 The New York Times. All rights reserved. Used by permission and protected by the Copyright Laws of the United States. The printing, copying, redistribution, or retransmission of the material without express written permission is prohibited.

> **Martin Luther King and Bobby Kennedy didn't change the world by asking people to join their Facebook crusades or to download their platforms.**

Generation Q would be doing itself a favor, and America a favor, if it demanded from every candidate who comes on campus answers to three questions: What is your plan for mitigating climate change? What is your plan for reforming Social Security? What is your plan for dealing with the deficit—so we all won't be working for China in 20 years?

America needs a jolt of the idealism, activism and outrage (it must be in there) of Generation Q. That's what twentysomethings are for—to light a fire under the country. But they can't e-mail it in, and an online petition or a mouse click for carbon neutrality won't cut it. They have to get organized in a way that will force politicians to pay attention rather than just patronize them.

Martin Luther King and Bobby Kennedy didn't change the world by asking people to join their Facebook crusades or to download their platforms. Activism can only be uploaded, the old-fashioned way—by young voters speaking truth to power, face to face, in big numbers, on campuses or the Washington Mall. Virtual politics is just that—virtual.

Maybe that's why what impressed me most on my brief college swing was actually a statue—the life-size statue of James Meredith at the University of Mississippi. Meredith was the first African-American to be admitted to Ole Miss in 1962. The Meredith bronze is posed as if he is striding toward a tall limestone archway, re-enacting his fateful step onto the then-segregated campus—defying a violent, angry mob and protected by the National Guard.

Above the archway, carved into the stone, is the word "Courage." That is what real activism looks like. There is no substitute.

CONSIDER

1. How does Friedman define Generation Q? What characteristics of the "Quiet Americans" does he find admirable? Problematic? Do you find his description of the group persuasive? Why or why not?

2. Why, according to Friedman, are idealism and community service "no substitute" for political activism? What examples or evidence does he use to support this argument?

3. Do Friedman's references to 1960s activism and icons such as Martin Luther King, Jr. and Robert Kennedy inspire you to act? Who are your generation's icons? Explain the reasons behind your choices.

Generation Overwhelmed

Courtney Martin
(October 22, 2007)

> **FYI** Courtney Martin's writings on gender and political issues have appeared in a variety of news outlets and magazines. Her book *Perfect Girls, Starving Daughters: The Frightening New Normalcy of Hating Your Body* was published in 2007.

At my housewarming party last weekend there was vodka and tonic and indie rock, there were a few, inexpensive cheeses, and there were some 20-somethings with loose tongues and misunderstood hearts.

My friend Molly, an assistant in a big New York publishing house and a fascinating world-wanderer, had sent me the link to Thomas Friedman's *New York Times* op-ed, "Generation Q," earlier in the day. "So what did you think?" she asked. Molly and I met while studying abroad in South Africa together.

"About what?" asked my friend Daniel, a labor organizer destined for Harvard Divinity School next fall. A native of Paul Wellstone's Minnesota, he's spent the years since college on the Hill in Washington, in Harlem sky rises, and Los Angeles barrios and synagogues alike, trying to figure out how to bring people together.

"That Friedman piece where he alleges that our generation is idealistic and 'too quiet, too online, for [our] own good,'" I summarized, I admit, rolling my eyes.

"What's that?" asked Ben, a new friend of mine who works for the Clinton Foundation and who was a speech writer and a campaign organizer before that.

A lengthy, raucous conversation about outrage, its sources and manifestations, ensued. Until of course, we got distracted by a really good dance song . . .

And this, it turns out, is what I'd like to talk to Mr. Friedman about. Not outrage. Not online activism. Not statues of long dead emancipators (which he invokes at the end of his piece as the symbol of what has been lost on us, the young and passive). But distraction. I think that he has mistaken my generation's sense of being overwhelmed, our absolute paralysis in the face of so many choices, so many causes, and so much awareness, for a mere quiet.

We are not quiet. Molly, the passionate environmentalist, Daniel, the bourgeoning theologian, Ben, the political communicator—all of these kids have big mouths and lots of ideas. We don't hesitate to assert opinions. We are often outraged—outraged, in fact, to the point of tears about the war in Iraq. I have lived this outrage since March 20, 2003. And I have had countless conversations with my friends, my mentors, my family, and my own pained conscience about what can possibly be done.

We are not apathetic. What we are, and perhaps this is what Friedman was picking up on, is totally and completely overwhelmed. One of the most critical questions of our time is one of attention. In a 24–7 news climate, it is all but impossible to emotionally engage all of the stories and issues you are taking in, and then act on them in some pragmatic way. So instead, young people become paralyzed. (It seems that all of us are a bit paralyzed. After all, what are Friedman's peers really doing? And aren't his peers the ones with the most straightforward kind of power?)

My generation tries to create lives that seem to match our values, but beyond that it's hard to locate a place to put our outrage. We aren't satisfied with point-and-click activism, as Friedman suggests, but we don't see other options. Many of us have protested, but we—by and large—felt like we were imitating an earlier generation, playing dress-up in our parents' old hippie clothes. I marched against the war and my president called it a focus group. The worst part was that I *did* feel inert while doing it. In the 21st century, a bunch of people marching down the street, complimenting one another on their original slogans and pretty protest signs, feels like self-flagellation, not real and true social change.

When Friedman was young and people were taking to the streets, there were a handful of issues to focus on and a few solid sources of news to pay attention to. Now there is a staggering amount of both. If I read the news today with my heart wide open and my mind engaged, I will be crushed. Do I address the injustices in Sudan, Iraq, Burma, Pakistan, the Bronx? Do I call an official, write a letter, respond to a MoveOn.org request? None of it promises to be effective, and it certainly won't pacify my outrage.

In Friedman's op-ed, he actually hints toward this insight, but falls short of recognizing it. At one point he gives an anecdote of his daughter, who reads about the disappearing ice caps and expresses dismay: "What happened to that Arctic story, Dad?"

What happened is that it was buried in a mountain of other stories about the torture, murder, and blatant disregard for our civil liberties and environmental health. What happened is that none of us can psychologically survive if we pay too much attention or commit ourselves too passionately to affecting change in all of these areas. What happened is that the world became too big and brutal, and we haven't figured out a way to process it all.

We do our best. We pursue careers and seek answers to questions that we believe are important. So many of the young New Yorkers standing around my living room that night were professional activists—social workers and teachers and nonprofit workers. We discuss the latest current events, send one another links to our favorite blogs or videos on the subjects, grab drinks after work and hash it all out. We study like hell. My generation knows so much about so much. We read everything and anything that we think might point us in the direction of some kind of political enlightenment and psychic relief.

But it's not enough. I know that. We know that. Friedman has, in his own patronizing way, pointed that out once again. He's right that our outrage is "in there somewhere." I just wish he and his intellectual literati were suggesting methods for unearthing it and channeling it into effective projects and processes, instead of shaking their heads at us like a bunch of disappointed schoolmarms for not imitating his heyday.

We can't be you, because we don't live in your time.

> **We can't be you, because we don't live in your time. We don't have the benefit of focus, the cushion of cheap rent, the luxury of not knowing just how complicated the world really is.**

We don't have the benefit of focus, the cushion of cheap rent, the luxury of not knowing just how complicated the world really is. Instead we have corporate conglomerates, private military contracts, the WTO and the IMF, school debt, and no health insurance. We are savvy and we are saturated and we are scared.

We are painstakingly composing our Facebook profiles because we did our daily round of news sites, and it left us feeling powerless and unsafe, like the only place to put our energies was inward. We are studying abroad because it feels like the only obvious way to interact with the world we care so deeply about. We are dancing at house parties on Friday nights because we talked about your op-ed, the war in Iraq, rape in Congo, but in the end, we just felt overeducated and underutilized.

You call that quiet. I call that coping.

CONSIDER

1. Martin proposes an alternative to Friedman's explanation for why young adults are politically inactive. Summarize her argument in a few sentences. Do you find her rebuttal of Friedman's argument persuasive? Why or why not?

2. Assess the effectiveness of Martin's essay in terms of *ethos, pathos,* and *logos* (see pages 25-26 for definitions of these terms). What kinds of readers do you think might find the piece most persuasive? Who might find it less persuasive, and why?

3. Martin suggests that Friedman answered his own question with the anecdote about his daughter's reaction to global warming in the news. What is Martin's criticism of mainstream media? Do you agree?

CHALLENGE

4. While Martin disagrees with Friedman on many points, she seems to accept his claim that online engagement with politics—"virtual politics"—is inferior to "real activism." Browse the Web and find a site devoted to a political or social cause that interests you. Track how much traffic it generates over a period of one week, and read any comments made by people who visit the site. Write a few paragraphs summarizing your findings. Would you characterize the activities you observed as "activism"? Why or why not?

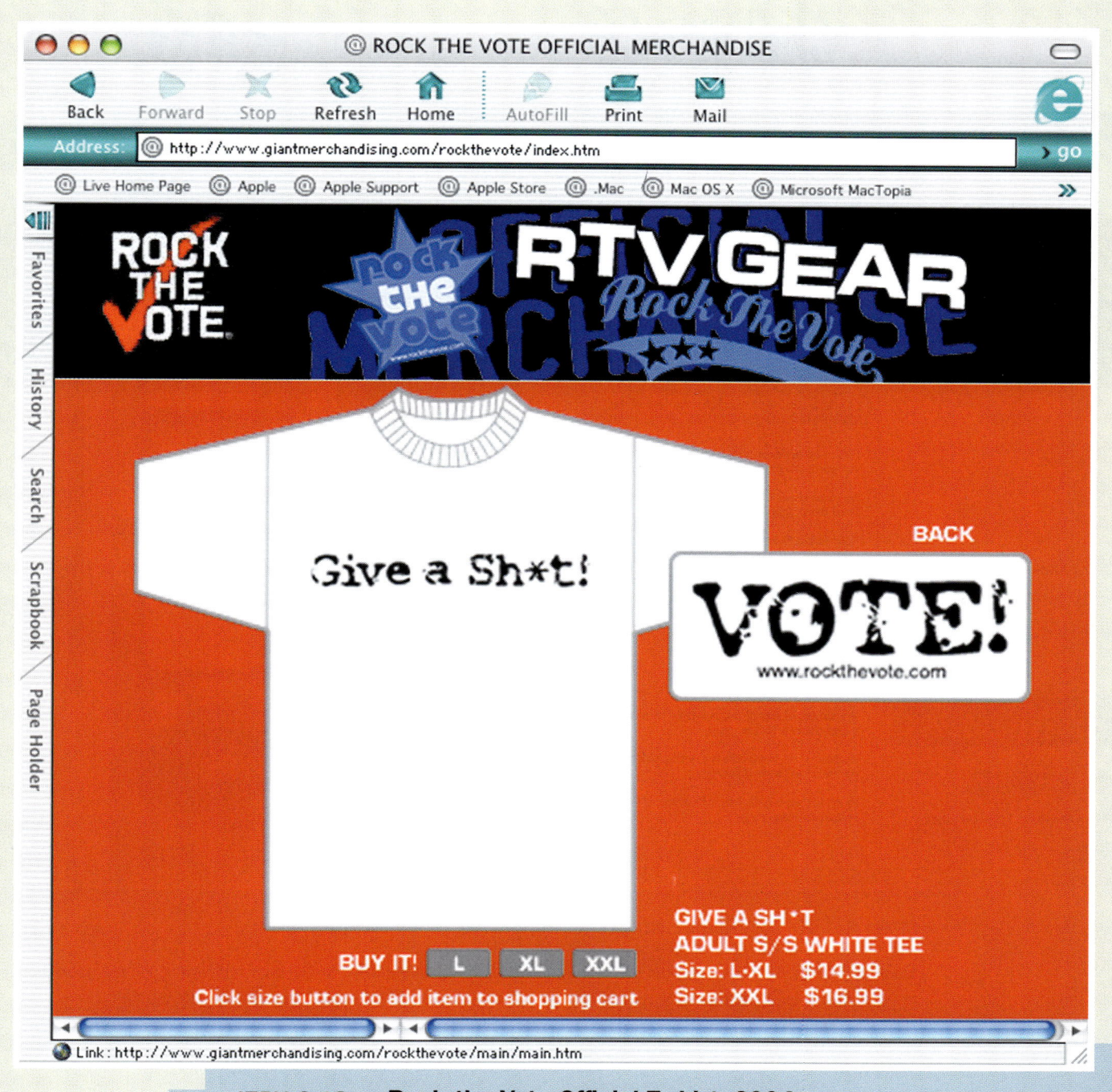

ITEM 8.12 ■ Rock the Vote Official T-shirt, 2004

Founded in 1990 with support from MTV, Rock the Vote is a nonpartisan nonprofit organization that seeks to inspire young people to vote via celebrity-driven voter education initiatives, T-shirts, and other youth-oriented campaigns. The "Give a Sh*t" T-shirt was one of several designs the organization developed and sold during the 2004 Presidential election campaign. To see more T-shirt designs and information about current Rock the Vote initiatives, visit *www.rockthevote.com*.

ITEM 8.13 ■ Redeem the Vote Web Site

According to its Web site, Redeem the Vote is the largest online initiative focused on motivating "young people of faith" to vote. This screenshot comes from its coverage of the 2008 presidential election campaign.

CONSIDER

1. Examine Items 8.13–8.15. How does each of these get-out-the-vote organizations appeal to its target audience? Point to specific aspects of the Web site's text, composition, content, and design elements to support your analysis.

2. Visit each of these organizations' Web sites and peruse the materials and links it offers. Which one do you find most appealing? Why? Did any of the sites persuade you to take action—to read additional material suggested on the site, register to vote, sign a petition, or order merchandise, for example?

3. In general, do you think online sites such as these are more, equally, or less effective than traditional media such as posters and TV ads at motivating people to become politically involved? Explain your response.

8.1 | GETTING OUT THE VOTE

FYI

ITEM 8.14 ■ Voto Latino Web Site

Aimed at young Latino/a voters, Voto Latino "works to promote an enfranchised America by leveraging celebrity voices, the latest technology and youth themselves to promote positive change," according to the group's Web site.

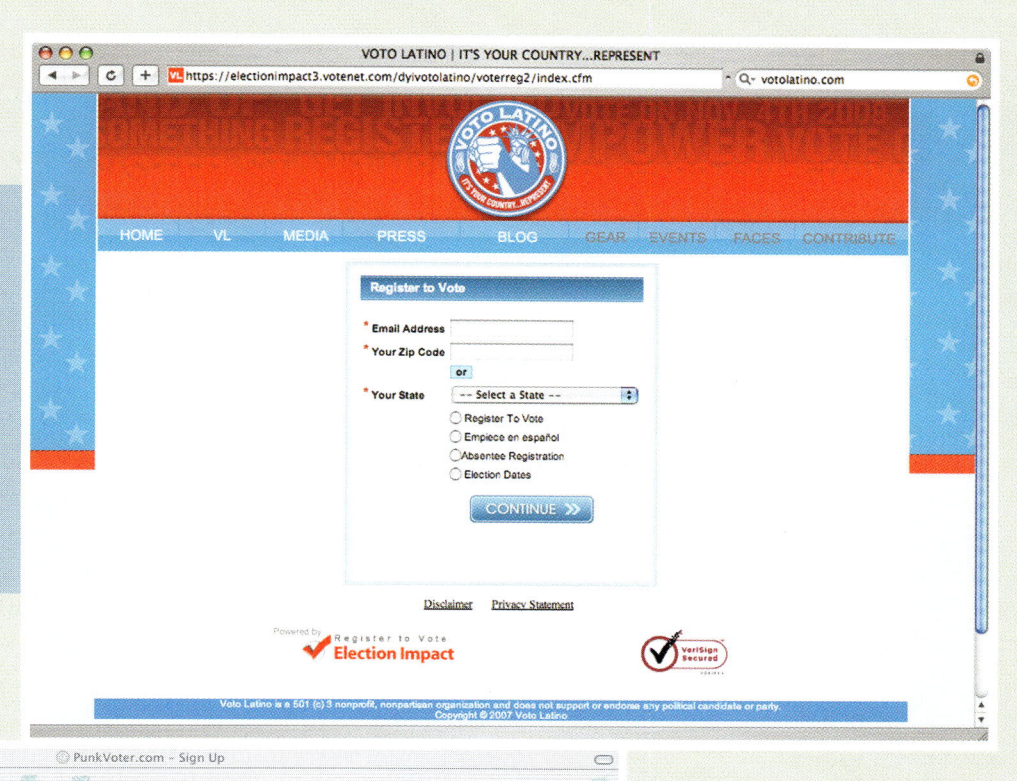

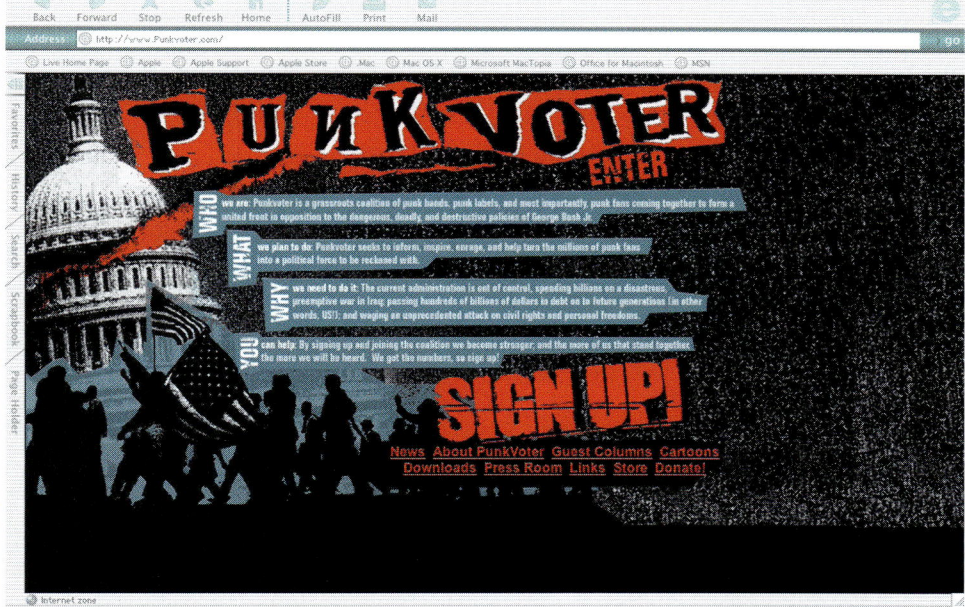

FYI

ITEM 8.15 ■ PunkVoter Web Site

PunkVoter is a political activist organization founded by Fat Mike, frontman of the punk rock band NOFX. Founded during the 2004 Presidential election campaign, the group seeks to bring the "spirit of punk rock rebellion" to contemporary politics. PunkVoter initiatives have included voter registration drives, concerts, T-shirts, and a compilation CD. The group's Web site, which functioned primarily as a news site during the 2008 Presidential election, has gotten up to 15 million hits in a single month.

8 | POLITICS AND ADVOCACY

COMPOSE

4 Efforts like Rock the Vote and Punkvoter are grounded in the assumption that the best way to encourage political participation and voting is to make it seem "cool," by associating these activities with celebrities and youth culture. Is this a valid assumption? Or are there other reasons and appeals that could more effectively motivate voters? If so, what are they? Write two or three paragraphs that explore your views on this question.

CHALLENGE

5 How would you design a Web site to encourage political participation among members of a group that you belong to? Sketch or describe your Web site, then write a few paragraphs explaining and justifying your design and content choices.

493

Journalist Cheat Sheet: Eleven Tips For Reporting the Youth Vote.

Mike Connery
(Blog Post November 18, 2007)

FYI Mike Connery is a writer and activist who is completing a book entitled *Youth to Power* on the role of Generation Y in politics. The following piece appeared on *Future Majority*, a blog focused on progressive youth activism.

It's getting rather tiring, correcting one shoddy media report on the youth vote after another. This really came to a head this weekend when, less than 24 hours after forcing a young UNLV student to ask Hillary Clinton whether she preferred Diamonds or Pearls, CNN un-ironically aired a piece during The Situation Room that made a mockery of young voters and their participation in our electoral process.

So I created this "cheat sheet" for journalists. Basically it's a listing of all the most common mistakes that the media makes when reporting on young voters. Enjoy. Spread widely.

Tip #1: The youth vote is not synonymous with students. In fact, students make up only a small part of the eligible youth vote. Only 21% of all 18–29 year olds are currently attending a college or university. That means that when you report on "students," you are leaving out the other 79% of all the individuals that make up the "youth vote." These people serve in our military, are struggling to raise families—and yes, have very different concerns from college students. I understand that makes it difficult for you to cram them into a cookie-cutter story about student aid activism and tuition costs, but you do them and your readers and our democracy a disservice when you limit your coverage to students.

Source: Current Population Survey[1]

Tip #2: Stop saying that "Howard Dean[2] courted young voters and the youth failed to show up." Fact of the matter is, youth participation quadrupled at the 2004 Iowa Caucus, they just didn't vote for Dean. In case you missed it, young people voted in higher than usual numbers and were 17% of all participants.

Source: Pew Trusts

Tip #3: This tip is directly related to Tip #2. Your cognitive dissonance w/r/t the 2004 Iowa caucus springs from the fact that young people did not vote in a monolithic block like you expected. That's called reality, and it is your job to report it accurately. Young voters chose John Kerry over Howard Dean by almost 2–1. If any candidate in Iowa was the "youth candidate" in the 2004 primary, it was John Kerry, and he won the nomination.

Source: CNN Exit Polling

Tip #4: The idea that "young people don't vote" is patently ridiculous. In 2004, 49% of all voters 18–29 went to the polls. That's millions of voters. In fact, a report by the Harvard Institute of Politics stated that more voters 18–29 went to the polls (20.7 million) than did voters over 65, the so-called reliable seniors (19.4 million).

To spell this out, we may still vote at lower rates than the rest of the electorate, but there are more of us. Millennials are the largest living American generation. In 2004, we were 17% of the electorate. It's estimated that we may well be 25% in 2008, and by 2015, we will be over 30% of all voters. That makes our support valuable, and that's why the Obama, Clinton and Edwards campaigns all have full-time youth outreach staff.

Sources: Harvard Institute of Politics (pdf), CIRCLE (pdf), Young Voter Strategies (pdf)

Tip #5: If you insist on reporting the same old story that young people vote at a lower rate than the rest of the electorate, then you have an obligation to also inform your readers/viewers/listeners that youth turnout has increased for 3 years straight, and is at its highest level in over a decade. You also have an obligation to note that in 2006 the youth vote swung a number of important federal races, including pushing Democratic candidates Jon Tester, Jim Webb, and Joe Courtney[3] over the top.

---

[1]The sources referred to and underscored throughout this piece can be found by following the links incorporated into Connery's original blog post, at *http://www.futuremajority.com/node/794*.

[2]Dean was a candidate for the 2004 Democratic U.S. Presidential nomination, a position eventually won by Massachusetts Senator John Kerry.

[3]Tester (U.S. Senator [D], Montana), Webb (U.S. Senator [D], Virginia), and Courtney (U.S. Representative [D], Connecticut) each won his seat by a close margin during the 2006 legislative elections.

Source: Historical voting patterns (pdf), Impact on Races (pdf), Midterm Turnout (pdf).

Tip #6: If you are going to report on low-turnout among young voters, you also have an obligation to note that young people face more barriers to voting than do older voters. We move more frequently, requiring us to re-register sometimes on a yearly basis, on campus we face a lack of voting machines and long lines, and many university towns actively discourage and try to prevent students from voting.

Source: League of Conservation Voters Education Fund

Tip #7: There are simple fixes to the problems outlined in #6—election day and same-day registration and mail-in voting are two such fixes that can be applied at the state level. These have been proven to bump youth turnout by as much as 14%!!!!! It would be nice if you reported on them occasionally.

Source: CIRCLE

Tip #8: Young voters will participate if they are asked to, particularly by a peer. This is proven. But the system stopped asking long ago by removing resources and manpower away from young voter outreach. Only in recent years have organizations—and a few campaigns—begin to reengage young voters in any serious way. The result is three straight years in which youth turnout increased. In plain terms: young voters are not apathetic. Rather, the system fails to engage them in any meaningful way.

Source: Young Voter Strategies, Voter Mobilization Tactics

Tip #9: Stop reporting on "celebrity activism" as the Rosetta Stone for understanding the youth vote. This is a Boomer and Gen-X construction created for a broadcast TV culture of the 80s and 90s. Today's young voters are interested in peer-to-peer communication and networked action. From Facebook to on the ground, peer to peer organizing at club, bars, barbershops and apartment canvassing, the most effective, and sustainable developments in youth organizing in the past five years have come from new, grassroots organizations doing peer to peer organizing on the ground or online. Stop reporting on celebrities and start doing the work of talking to and reporting on the activities of these organizations. Good places to start include: Forward Montana, The Oregon Bus Project, New Era Colorado, Young Democrats of America, and The League of Young Voters.

There are many more, but let's do this in baby steps. Start with these and we'll work our way deeper into youth organizing together.

Tip #10: Related to #9, "talking to young voters" is not code for "dumbing down." We understand issues. We have thoughts on those issues. We're yelling loudly for the "adults" to take action on those issues. See: Iraq, Global Warming, Global Poverty, Darfur, and college aid. Stop stereotyping us in your reporting by spotlighting frivolous questions.

Moreover, and this is very important, you REALLY need to stop force-feeding us these fluff questions in national forums (see: Mac vs. PC and Diamonds vs. Pearls). If you are going to say that we are frivolous, you shouldn't be enabling—or worse, instigating—that behavior. This habit is doing nothing to build your credibility with a younger audience that is already abandoning you for the internet. So following this rule is not only good for Democracy, it is good for your bottom line.

Source: For more on issues, visit the Harvard Institute of Politics for their annual surveys.

Tip #11: Related to #10, we do not live in a Newtonian Universe. We live in an Einsteinian Universe. Just as the act of observing something changes it, your reporting on the youth vote has an effect on the youth vote. It effects how campaigns, staffers and consultants perceive young voters. When you fail to accurately report on increasing turnout or the impact of youth on an election, these individuals continue to believe that the youth vote is a waste of time. This feeds a vicious cycle in which campaigns put less money into youth outreach, meaning young voters are less likely to turnout because they are not being asked/engaged.

You are not neutral observers. There are no neutral observers. We all exist in a self-referential ecosystem. You are culpable here. With great power comes great responsibility. We rely on you to use it wisely. Please start living up to those not unreasonable expectations.

CONSIDER

1. Do you agree with the criticisms Connery makes of journalists in this piece? Which points do you find most and least persuasive? Why?

2. How would you characterize Connery's tone and style? Point to specific word choices and phrases to support your response. What audiences might find his voice most and least appealing?

Cluster 8.2
The Politics of Food

We're accustomed to approaching the choices we make in our daily lives—what we wear, how we spend our spare time, whom we date, how we interact with friends—as individual matters, guided by our personal tastes and preferences. But in fact, many of our everyday choices are simultaneously personal *and* political. When we decide to walk rather than drive to class, shop at a store that advertises merchandise "made in the USA," or wear a T-shirt bearing a favorite slogan, chances are that we've been influenced as much by wider public issues as by simple comfort or convenience. And that's not surprising, since, as Aristotle once noted, humans are fundamentally political and social beings.

The texts and images in this cluster explore an area of everyday life in which personal and political concerns intersect: food. A few years ago, an advertisement for Subway in Europe caused a stir with its depiction of a bloated Statue of Liberty holding, instead of a torch, a large order of fries. The ad features the caption, "Why are Americans so fat?" The resulting controversy even reached the level of political debate, with one Congressman calling the ad un-American. Associating fast food with America clearly touched a nerve, and it called attention to debates over food, health, and American culture that have been developing for years.

In this section, you'll find texts and images that explore some of the social, political, and cultural issues surrounding Americans' eating practices: Why are Americans more likely to be overweight than their counterparts in other industrialized nations? Michael Rosenwald's "Why America Has to Be Fat" and Lauren Greenfield's photographs from *Thin* and *Camp Shane* suggest some cultural causes. Next, Gary Shteyngart's "Sixty-Nine Cents" and Kim Severenson's "Be It Ever So Homespun, There's Nothing Like Spin" explore the complex ways in which particular kinds of foods and eating practices come to be associated with political and social values. The remaining pieces in this cluster examine ways in which our everyday choices about food affect the public and the global environment. In "Why Bother?" Michael Pollan argues that responsible citizenship lies in rejecting mass-produced foods and living close to the land—a viewpoint that Jonathan Rauch's "Will Frankenfood Save the Planet?" calls strongly into question. The cluster closes with a series of powerful images from Peter Menzel's and Faith D'Alusio's *Hungry Planet: What the World Eats*, which highlight both some vast differences and some surprising similarities in families' eating patterns across the world.

Why America Has to Be Fat

A Side Effect of Economic Expansion Shows Up in Front

Michael S. Rosenwald
(January 22, 2006)

> **FYI** More than 60 percent of Americans are overweight or obese. Is this problem simply a result of individual greed or lack of willpower? In this opinion piece, Michael S. Rosenwald, a staff writer for the *Washington Post*, suggests some broader causes.

I am fat. Sixty pounds too hefty, in my doctor's opinion. Probably 80 pounds, in my fiancee's view.

Being fat makes me a lot of things—a top contender for type II diabetes, for instance, or a heart attack, or stroke, maybe even a replacement knee or hip. My girth also puts me in familiar company, with about two-thirds of the U.S. population now considered overweight.

But in many ways, my being fat also makes me pretty good for the economy.

You've read the headlines: America's problem with bulging waistlines has reached pandemic proportions, according to federal health officials, who warn that obesity is becoming society's No. 1 killer. But as doctors wrestle with the problem, economists have been pondering which corporations and industries benefit, and the role that changes in the overall economy have played in making us fat to begin with.

It turns out, economists say, that changes in food technology (producing tasty, easy-to-cook food, such as french fries) and changes in labor (we used to be paid to exercise at work, now we pay to exercise after work) combined with women's importance in the workforce, not the kitchen, have combined to produce industries able to cheaply and efficiently meet the demands of our busy lives. The cookie industry. The fast-food industry. Potato chips. Soda. The chain-restaurant industry, with its heaping portions of low-priced, high-calorie foods.

In some ways, we are better off in this Fat Economy. Many people work in easier, better-paying jobs, which help pay for their big homes in the suburbs. Women don't have to spend two hours preparing dinner every night; many have risen to unprecedented levels of corporate and political power. Flat-panel plasma TVs hang over fireplaces, which can be lit using the same remote control for flipping channels. But the unintended consequence of these economic changes is that many of us have become fat. An efficient economy produces sluggish, inefficient bodies.

"The obesity problem is really a side effect of things that are good for the economy," said Tomas J. Philipson, an economics professor who studies obesity at the University of Chicago, a city recently named the fattest in America. "But we would rather take improvements in technology and agriculture than go back to the way we lived in the 1950s when everyone was thin. Nobody wants to sweat at work for 10 hours a day and be poor. Yes, you're obese, but you have a life that is much more comfortable."

For many corporations, and even for physicians, Americans' obesity has also fattened the bottom line. William L. Weis, a management professor at Seattle University, says revenue from the "obesity industries" will likely top $315 billion this year, and perhaps far more. That includes $133.7 billion for fast-food restaurants, $124.7 billion for medical treatments related to obesity, and $1.8 billion just for diet books—all told, nearly 3 percent of the overall U.S. economy.

Did you know, according to consumer-research firm Mintel Group, that we guzzled $37 billion in carbonated beverages in 2004? The same year, we spent $3.9 billion on cookies—$244 million of which were Oreo cookies sold by Kraft Foods for about $3.69 a package. In 2003, we splurged $57.2 billion on meals at restaurants such as Denny's, Chili's and Outback Steakhouse (a personal favorite). Potato chip sales hit $6.2 billion in 2004.

"Put simply, there is a lot of money being made, and to be made, in feeding both oversized stomachs and feeding those enterprises selling fixes for oversized stomachs," Weis wrote in 2005 in the *Academy of Health Care Management Journal*. "And both industries—those selling junk food and those selling fat cures—depend for their future on a prevalence of obesity."

> **Put simply, there is a lot of money being made, and to be made, in feeding both oversized stomachs and feeding those enterprises selling fixes for oversized stomachs.**

And the prevalence of obesity won't fade anytime soon. According to David M. Cutler, an economist at Harvard University, Americans' waistlines are caught in a simple accounting quagmire. In a 2003 paper titled "Why Have Americans Become More Obese?" Cutler wrote: "As an accounting statement, people gain weight if there is an increase in calories taken in or a decrease in calories expended."

On the calories-expended side of the Fat Economy, economists have noted that changes in the workplace have caused us to burn fewer calories. Prior to the 1950s, jobs often meant hard labor. We lifted heavy things. We worked outside. Our desks—if we had them—did not come equipped with computers. We lived in urban environments, walking most places.

Now many Americans work in offices in buildings with elevators. If we walk anywhere, it's to lunch—to TGI Friday's or the corner burrito shop. We live in the suburbs, we drive to and from work and—in my case—to and from the mailbox. We pay $60 a month for the privilege of lifting something heavy in a gym we have to drive to. (I belong to two gyms, in the hope that guilt will cause me to visit at least one.) And we also must pay to exercise by giving up our free time. Do we work out, or do we drive the kids to their soccer game, where we can sit and watch? Do we work out, or do we download new songs from iTunes?

"People are just not willing to give up their leisure time," Philipson said. "People don't want to pay to exercise with their leisure time."

Which brings us to the calories-consumed side of the ledger. If we don't expend calories, they add up and turn into pounds. Thirty-five hundred calories generally equals one pound. So behold, for argument's sake, the french fry. An order of large fries at McDonald's puts 520 calories into one's body. It is well known, at least by this consumer, that an order of large fries can generally be placed, filled and consumed in a matter of minutes.

But this was not always so, Cutler said.

Before World War II, if you wanted a french fry, you went to the store, bought potatoes, took them home, washed them, peeled them, sliced them and fried them. "Without expensive machinery, these activities take a lot of time," Cutler said. "In the postwar period, a number of innovations allowed the centralization of french fry production." Now fries are prepped in factories using sophisticated technologies, then frozen at sub-40-degree temperatures and shipped to a restaurant, where they are deep-fried, or to someone's home, where they are microwaved. Either way, they are served up in a matter of minutes.

French fries helped drive up U.S. potato consumption by 30 percent between 1977 and 1995, but they mean more than that—they symbolize the convergence of the economic and technological changes that have made us fat. Cutler and Philipson have noted that when women joined the workplace, they left behind some of the labor that traditionally went into cooking meals. This happened as technology increasingly allowed for mass production and preparation of food. Much of this type of food—be it french fries, potato chips, frozen dinners or quick meals at restaurants—contains more calories.

We expend fewer calories and take more in. The pounds add up. Hence, the Fat Economy.

"The structure of the economy has made us more obese," Cutler said. "That is clearly true. What businesses do is they cater to what we want, whether what we want is really in our long-term interests or not. So people are obese and they want to diet, but they also want things to be immediately there. Manufacturers and store owners make that possible. The upside is nobody spends two hours a day cooking anymore."

So do Americans have to be fat for the economy to thrive? The economy would not exactly crash if people stopped spending money on french fries and meals at TGI Friday's. Economists think the money would just be spent differently or in different places. Specific industries would adapt—as many have already, offering more healthful choices—to meet changing demands. No business can survive by selling things people don't want.

In fact the overall long-term economic costs of obesity are many. The $10,000 of extra medical care that the overweight require over their lifetimes certainly makes a doctor's wallet fatter, but it could bankrupt the health insurance industry. Also, research shows that while more women have entered the workforce, their wages, particularly for white women, sink if they are overweight.

Much of the long-term financial burden for obesity will fall on the shoulders of U.S. corporations, which already fork out billions of dollars a year in sick time and insurance costs related to obesity illnesses, and on American taxpayers, through their contributions for programs such as Medicare and Medicaid. What's more, shorter lifespans will more quickly take millions of educated people out of the workforce.

For that last problem, the Fat Economy has already found ways to innovate and profit. In Lynn, Ind., there is a company called Goliath Casket that makes caskets up to 52 inches wide. The company's Web site, which can be found at http://www.oversizecasket.com/, notes that Goliath's founder quit his job as a welder in 1985, saying: "Boys, I'm gonna go home and build oversize caskets that you would be proud to put your mother in."

CONSIDER

1. Summarize the cause-effect argument Rosenwald makes in this piece. What factors does he believe contribute to Americans' high rates of obesity? What role do media outlets and corporations play? Are you convinced by this argument? Why or why not?

2. How does Rosenwald's admission that he is obese affect his *ethos*? How do you think he might respond to a skeptic who accused him of blaming societal factors in order to avoid taking individual responsibility for his weight problem?

COMPOSE

3. What are your thoughts about lawsuits against fast-food chains or other businesses that promote and sell unhealthy products? In light of Rosenwald's arguments, would you support such lawsuits? Write a short essay or create an issue poster that expresses your opinion on this question.

ITEM 8.16 ■ **Lauren Greenfield, Images From *Thin* and *Camp Shane***

Lauren Greenfield is widely recognized for her photographs and films bringing together interviews and images that document teen life in America. Her collection *Girl Culture* (2002) focuses on teen girls, looking especially at the ways that culture affects attitudes toward popularity and self-worth. Her award-winning documentary *Thin* (2005) follows the struggles of young women battling eating disorders; and her most recent film *Kids and Money* (2007) explores teenagers' spending habits and attitudes toward money. The image below is a still from *Thin*. It depicts a "Mindful Eating" therapy session, in which residents at an eating disorder clinic in Florida must eat a "fear food" such as Pop Tarts, doughnuts, or candy bars and then discuss their feelings. The image at right comes from a photo essay on Camp Shane, a weight-loss camp for young people located in the Catskill Mountains in New York. The photo features Erika, a 14-year-old camper who has decorated the wall behind her bunk with wrappers from her snack foods.

CONSIDER

1. Food packages are prominently featured in both these images. Why do you think Greenfield chose to include these packages in the photos? What can you infer from the packages about the subjects' relationship to food—and to food advertising and packaging?

2. The settings of the two photographs are markedly different—an eating disorder clinic versus a summer camp for overweight teenagers. However, could you argue that these images share common themes or observations about youth culture in America? Point to specific elements in the images to support your answer.

CHALLENGE

3. Would you say that the concerns related to food captured in these images are relevant primarily to young women? Has the media focus on body-image issues for girls and young women caused young men to disappear? By many measures, boys and young men share the same risk for obesity, diabetes, and other eating-related health concerns as girls and women. Do you believe that issues involving the condition of boys and young men should get more attention? Do some research on the subject and then write an argument exploring your views on this question.

4. Explore the resources related to either *Thin* or *Camp Shane* available on Lauren Greenfield's Web site www.laurengreenfield.com. Select two of the photographs and captions, and discuss them in terms of one of the readings in this chapter. Develop an argument that explores how the images add to, complicate, or contradict the ideas in the article.

Sixty-nine Cents

Gary Shteyngart
(September 3, 2007)

> **FYI** Is there something uniquely American about fast-food franchises such as McDonald's? What particular foods have become associated with American lifestyles and identity? Humorist and novelist Gary Shteyngart explores these questions in the following autobiographical essay, which appeared as part of a special issue of *The New Yorker* devoted to food and culture. Shteyngart was born in St. Petersburg, Russia, and has lived in the United States since age seven. He is the author of several books, including his most recent *Absurdistan* (2006).

When I was fourteen years old, I lost my Russian accent. I could, in theory, walk up to a girl and the words "Oh, hi there" would not sound like Okht Hyzer, possibly the name of a Turkish politician. There were three things I wanted to do in my new incarnation: go to Florida, where I understood that our nation's best and brightest had built themselves a sandy, vice-filled paradise; have a girl, preferably native-born, tell me that she liked me in some way; and eat all my meals at McDonald's. I did not have the pleasure of eating at McDonald's often. My parents believed that going to restaurants and buying clothes not sold by weight on Orchard Street were things done only by the very wealthy or the very profligate, maybe those extravagant "welfare queens" we kept hearing about on television. Even my parents, however, as uncritically in love with America as only immigrants can be, could not resist the iconic pull of Florida, the call of the beach and the Mouse.

And so, in the midst of my Hebrew-school winter vacation, two Russian families crammed into a large used sedan and took I-95 down to the Sunshine State. The other family—three members in all—mirrored our own, except that their single offspring was a girl and they were, on the whole, more ample; by contrast, my entire family weighed three hundred pounds. There's a picture of us beneath the monorail at EPCOT Center, each of us trying out a different smile to express the déjà-vu feeling of standing squarely in our new country's greatest attraction, my own megawatt grin that of a turn-of-the-century Jewish peddler scampering after a potential sidewalk sale. The Disney tickets were a freebie, for which we had had to sit through a sales pitch for an Orlando timeshare. "You're from Moscow?" the time-share salesman asked, appraising the polyester cut of my father's jib.

"Leningrad."

"Let me guess: mechanical engineer?"

"Yes, mechanical engineer. . . . Eh, please Disney tickets now."

The ride over the MacArthur Causeway to Miami Beach was my real naturalization ceremony. I wanted all of it—the palm trees, the yachts bobbing beside the hard-currency mansions, the concrete-and-glass condominiums preening at their own reflections in the azure pool water below, the implicit availability of relations with amoral women. I could see myself on a balcony eating a Big Mac, casually throwing fries over my shoulder into the sea-salted air. But I would have to wait. The hotel reserved by my parents' friends featured army cots instead of beds and a half-foot-long cockroach evolved enough to wave what looked like a fist at us. Scared out of Miami Beach, we decamped for Fort Lauderdale, where a Yugoslav woman sheltered us in a faded motel, beach-adjacent and featuring free UHF reception. We always seemed to be at the margins of places: the driveway of the Fontainebleau Hilton, or the glassed-in elevator leading to a rooftop restaurant where we could momentarily peek over the "Please Wait to Be Seated" sign at the endless ocean below, the Old World we had left behind so far and yet deceptively near.

To my parents and their friends, the Yugoslav motel was an unquestioned paradise, a lucky coda to a set of difficult lives. My father lay magnificently beneath the sun in his red-and-black striped imitation Speedo while I stalked down the beach, past baking Midwestern girls. "Oh, hi there." The words, perfectly American, not a birthright but an acquisition, perched between my lips, but to walk up to one of those girls and say something so casual required a deep rootedness to the hot sand beneath me, a historical presence thicker than the green card embossed with my thumbprint and freckled face. Back at the motel, the "Star Trek" reruns looped endlessly on Channel 73 or 31 or some other prime number, the washed-out Technicolor planets more familiar to me than our own.

On the drive back to New York, I plugged myself firmly into my Walkman, hoping to forget our vacation. Sometime after the palm trees ran out, somewhere in southern Georgia, we stopped at a McDonald's. I could already taste it: The sixty-nine-cent hamburger. The ketchup, red and decadent, embedded with little flecks of grated onion. The uplift of the pickle slices; the obliterating rush of fresh Coca-Cola; the soda tingle at the back of the throat signifying that the act was complete. I ran into the meat-fumigated coldness of the magical place, the larger Russians following behind me, lugging something big and red. It was a cooler, packed, before we left the motel, by the other mother, the kindly, round-faced equivalent of my own mother. She had prepared a full Russian lunch for us. Soft-boiled eggs wrapped in tinfoil; *vinigret*, the Russian beet salad, overflowing a reused container of sour cream; cold chicken served between crisp white furrows of a *bulka*. "But it's not allowed," I pleaded. "We have to buy the food here."

I felt coldness, not the air-conditioned chill of southern Georgia but the coldness of a body understanding the ramifications of its own demise, the pointlessness of it all. I sat down at a table as far away from my parents and their friends as possible. I watched the spectacle of the newly tanned resident aliens eating their ethnic meal—jowls working, jowls working—the soft-boiled eggs that quivered lightly as they were brought to the mouth; the girl, my coeval, sullen like me but with a hint of pliant equanimity; her parents, dishing out the chunks of beet with plastic spoons; my parents, getting up to use free McDonald's napkins and straws while American motorists with their noisy towheaded children bought themselves the happiest of meals.

My parents laughed at my haughtiness. Sitting there hungry and all alone—what a strange man I was becoming! So unlike them. My pockets were filled with several quarters and dimes, enough for a hamburger and a small Coke. I considered the possibility of redeeming my own dignity, of leaving behind our beet-salad heritage. My parents didn't spend money, because they lived with the idea that disaster was close at hand, that a liver-function test would come back marked with a doctor's urgent scrawl, that they would be fired from their jobs because their English did not suffice. We were all representatives of a shadow society, cowering under a cloud of bad tidings that would never come. The silver coins stayed in my pocket, the anger burrowed and expanded into some future ulcer. I was my parents' son.

CONSIDER

1. At one level, Shteyngart's piece tells a humorous narrative about a teenage boy struggling to fit into a new environment. Would you say that the essay also makes an argument about the relationship between McDonald's (or fast food in general) and American identity? Where do you think the teenage Shteyngart got his ideas about how "regular" Americans behave and eat?

2. What details does Shteyngart include in the narrative to illustrate contrasts between the cultural and social values of his parents versus the "American" values he wanted to embrace? How do the descriptions of food and eating contribute to this contrast?

3. Do you think Shteyngart still has the same feelings about McDonald's and about what it means to fit into American culture? Explain your answer, drawing on specific words or phrases from the essay.

COMPOSE

4. Write a short essay expressing how food and eating connect to your own cultural, social, or political values.

Be It Ever So Homespun, There's Nothing Like Spin

Kim Severson
(January 3, 2007)

> **FYI** Many Americans who buy products advertised as organic or "healthy" do so not only to improve their own diets, but also to express their social and political views: to undercut the profits of businesses that use pesticides and chemical additives, to support organic and humane farming methods, to safeguard the health of farm laborers, and so on. In the following piece, Kim Severson explores the ways in which companies use marketing and package design to play to these desires. Severson is an award-winning food and culture writer for the *New York Times*, as well as the author of two cookbooks.

Something made me uneasy when I dropped a box of gluten-free EnviroKidz organic Koala Crisp cereal in my shopping cart. But it's hard to suspect a cartoon koala, so I moved on.

The unsettling sensation came back when I bought a bag of my favorite organic frozen French fries. Why did the verdant fields in the Cascadian Farm logo make me feel so smug?

Then I got really suspicious. A bag of natural Cheetos seemed so much more appealing than the classic cheese puff. Why? Was it the image of a subdued Chester Cheetah rising gently from a farm field bathed in golden sunlight?

Like clues to a murder that suddenly point to a single culprit, the mystery in my shopping cart revealed itself. Wheat sheaf by wheat sheaf, sunrise by sunrise, the grocery store shelves had been greenwashed.

And I was falling for it.

The kind of greenwashing I'm talking about is not just a fake environmental ethos. Greenwashing, it seems to me, can also describe a pervasive genre of food packaging designed to make sure that manufacturers grab their slice of the $25 billion that American shoppers spend each year on natural or organic food.

As a design shorthand, it makes subtle use of specific colors, images, typefaces and the promise of what marketers call "an authentic narrative" to sell food. Especially in recent years, greenwashing has spilled out well past the organic section of the grocery store. Even the snack aisle at the gas station isn't immune.

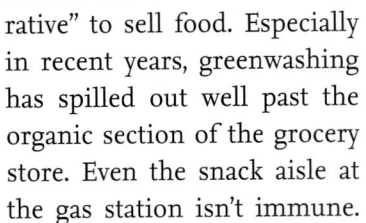

"Somebody becomes successful with a specific point of view, and the consumer begins to identify with it and it spreads like a virus," said Paula Scher, a partner in Pentagram, an international design firm. From there it's only a matter of time before Cap'n Crunch shows up in a hemp jacket, raising money to save the manatees.

Buy a greenwashed product and you're buying a specific set of healthy environmental and socially correct values.

If the package does its work, then the food inside doesn't actually have to be organic, only organic-ish. The right cues on a package free mass-market consumers from doing any homework, said Elizabeth Talerman, a branding analyst. They can assume that a group she calls the green elite—those early adopters who pushed for organic food laws and who helped make Whole Foods markets a success—have done the work for them.

"The mass market wants an instant identifier," said Ms. Talerman, a longtime New York advertising consultant.

So what are the identifiers? After shopping for dozens of products in places as varied as food co-ops and convenience stores, I've uncovered the essential elements of a greenwashed product. Start with a gentle image of a field or a farm to suggest an ample harvest gathered by an honest, hard-working family. To that end, strangely oversize vegetables or fruits are good. If they are dew-kissed and nestled in a basket, all the better.

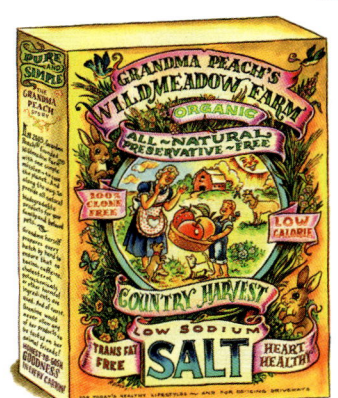

Ross MacDonald

A little red tractor is O.K. Pesticide tanks and rows of immigrant farm laborers bent over in the hot sun are not.

Earth's Best, a baby and toddler food company, offers a delicious example. Its whole grain rice cereal features two babies working the rice fields. One is white and one is black. (A greenwashed package would never show the black child working in the fields alone.) A sign that looks hand-hewn declares "No GMO's." There is a barn, a butterfly and a typeface that could have come from the back room of a general store.

A good greenwashed product should show an animal displaying special skills or great emotional range. Some Organic Valley packages feature a sax-playing, environmentally friendly earthworm. Jaunty cows on Stonyfield Farm yogurt wear sunglasses and headbands. The cows on Horizon's milk cartons dance a bovine jig, despite challenges by organic purists that some Horizon cows see precious little pasture.

A little family history helps, too. My Family Farm of Fort Thomas, Ky., sells packaged cookies and crackers and promises to give some of the money to charity. On the back of the box is a story that begins, "With careers as licensed social workers, my sister and I are committed to improving the lives of children." A carton of Country Hen omega-3 eggs, which cost $3.69 for six, had a fuzzy black-and-white photograph inside showing the company's owner, George Bass, and the entire Country Hen family, along with their favorite eggnog recipe.

A cause is important. Nature's Path, the maker of Koala Crisp, promises that 1 percent of sales will be spent saving endangered species. Barbara's Bakery, maker of Puffins cereal, pays for the National Audubon Society's live "puffin cams" in the Gulf of Maine. Buy a box of Peace Cereal's raspberry ginger crisp, and a percentage of the profit helps pay for International Peace Prayer Day in New Mexico.

The actual health benefits of a product don't always matter. A package of organic Naturepops from College Farm shows a field of lollipops and a barn, suggesting a well-educated farmer tending her candy. The sugar might come from cane juice and tapioca syrup, but it's sugar just the same.

And although "organic" is losing its power as a code word for certain cultural values, it doesn't hurt to flaunt it if you've got it. The word appears 21 times on a box of Cascadian Farm Vanilla Almond Crunch.

Having established a design paradigm that succeeds in selling food that is often more expensive than conventional groceries, the design world should perhaps rejoice. This is not the case. Some top brand and package designers find the cartoonish animals and bad hippie typefaces as grating as a self-righteous vegan at a barbecue.

But then, they didn't like American food package design that much to begin with.

"It's the bottom of the barrel," said Ms. Scher, who works in the New York office of Pentagram design.

Riskier designs, like the clean lettering and curvy bottle of Pom Wonderful pomegranate juice, are rare. Food manufacturers usually agonize over changing the size of a box or shifting the background color from teal to aquamarine.

But when a trend starts to show success, it's a design pileup. That's what happened with the natural and organic category, which makes up about 10 percent of the food at the grocery store and has been growing by more than 20 percent a year since 2000. In the grocery business, a 4 percent jump is considered a victory.

"It's aisle after aisle of design desperation," said Brian Collins, chairman and chief creative officer of the design group at Ogilvy, the international advertising and public relations company. He called the look "phony naïveté" and predicted that its demise was close because consumers are wising up. There is value in telling a story, but it must be true, he said.

Merely dressing up the package is not enough, he

To appeal to consumers' new sensibilities, packaging for pastas and snack foods prominently uses words like "healthy" and "natural."
Tony Cenicola/The *New York Times*

said. Nonetheless, manufacturers are eager to project a wholesome image.

"It's the halo effect," said Caren Wilcox, executive director of the Organic Trade Association. "That's why we encourage consumers to look for the U.S.D.A. organic seal."

But even the organic seal doesn't necessarily offer assurances that the item is produced in a way that jibes with consumer expectations for something that comes in a greenwashed package.

"All the ingredients being used in items with the organic seal are produced using the organic system," Ms. Wilcox said. "It doesn't mean they don't sometimes end up in products some people think other people shouldn't eat."

Design and packaging experts fix the start of sincerity and authenticity in food package design in the 1970s. Mo Siegel began selling Celestial Seasonings tea in boxes with sleepy bears. Tom and Kate Chappell gave up the corporate life to create Tom's of Maine toothpaste. Ben Cohen and Jerry Greenfield sold ice cream in Vermont, using goofy hand-rendered graphics to tell their story.

The trend grew in the 1980s, when corporate America entered a noncorporate phase. "Companies began to try to not look like big companies," Ms. Scher said.

By the late 1990s, anything with a hint of natural organic goodness sold in big numbers. Today, many companies that started with a humble story line have been purchased by larger interests. Unilever owns Ben and Jerry's, the Hain Celestial Group is traded on Nasdaq and Tom's of Maine is controlled by Colgate-Palmolive.

The kind of imagery that once marked a brand as an alternative to corporate food conglomerates has now been incorporated into Lay's potato chips. Consumers can buy classic Lay's in the shiny yellow bag, or Natural Lay's, with a thicker cut, expeller-pressed oil and sea salt. The package has a brown harvest graphic design, old-timey typefaces and a matte bag. The natural chips cost about 10 cents an ounce more than the classics. A handful of either still offers 150 calories and 10 grams of fat.

"When it gets to Lay's," Ms. Scher said, "its time to change."

Ms. Talerman, the New York advertising consultant, predicted that the fascination with what she called the green identifiers will last about five years longer. Then, she said, green-elite food consumers will push companies for even more information about environmental impact, labor practices and community involvement, and mass market consumers will start reading labels instead of just searching out easy identifiers.

Food manufacturers might begin to copy the new nutrition-style labels that Timberland is putting on its shoe boxes. Each one lists the amount of energy it took to make the shoes, how much of that was renewable, whether child labor was used and how many hours per pair Timberland dedicated to community service.

"As soon as the mass market starts to understand these issues more," Ms. Talerman predicted, "we'll get away from the fields and the giant vegetables and get back to better design."

Images of barns, rolling fields, sunshine and happy animals are popular, too.
Tony Cenicola/The *New York Times*

CONSIDER

1. How does Severson define *greenwashing*? What are some of the problems she attributes to this marketing practice?

2. Examine the packages in the photos and the examples of products and packages discussed in the essay. Have you ever bought any of these products, or any products advertised in similar ways? How accurate, in your opinion, is Severson's analysis of the marketers' design strategies?

3. Do you believe that shoppers' choices reflect their desire to purchase a certain set of "social and environmental values," as Severson suggests? Why or why not? If you agree, is there anything wrong with this practice?

CHALLENGE

4. Design a food package that you think would appeal to consumers who hold a particular political orientation. For example, can you envision a breakfast cereal box that would appeal to someone concerned about eradicating global poverty? A milk carton that would appeal to a conservative voter?

Why Bother?

Michael Pollan
(April 20, 2008)

> **FYI** Michael Pollan is a contributing editor to *The New York Times Magazine* and a professor of journalism at the University of California, Berkeley. Penguin Press published his most recent book, *In Defense of Food: An Eater's Manifesto,* in 2008.

Why bother? That really is the big question facing us as individuals hoping to do something about climate change, and it's not an easy one to answer. I don't know about you, but for me the most upsetting moment in "An Inconvenient Truth" came long after Al Gore scared the hell out of me, constructing an utterly convincing case that the very survival of life on earth as we know it is threatened by climate change. No, the really dark moment came during the closing credits, when we are asked to . . . change our light bulbs. That's when it got really depressing. The immense disproportion between the magnitude of the problem Gore had described and the puniness of what he was asking us to do about it was enough to sink your heart.

But the drop-in-the-bucket issue is not the only problem lurking behind the "why bother" question. Let's say I do bother, big time. I turn my life upside-down, start biking to work, plant a big garden, turn down the thermostat so low I need the Jimmy Carter signature cardigan, forsake the clothes dryer for a laundry line across the yard, trade in the station wagon for a hybrid, get off the beef, go completely local. I could theoretically do all that, but what would be the point when I know full well that halfway around the world there lives my evil twin, some carbon-footprint doppelgänger in Shanghai or Chongqing who has just bought his first car (Chinese car ownership is where ours was back in 1918), is eager to swallow every bite of meat I forswear and who's positively itching to replace every last pound of CO_2 I'm struggling no longer to emit. So what exactly would I have to show for all my trouble?

A sense of personal virtue, you might suggest, somewhat sheepishly. But what good is that when virtue itself is quickly becoming a term of derision? And not just on the editorial pages of *The Wall Street Journal* or on the lips of the vice president, who famously dismissed energy conservation as a "sign of personal virtue." No, even in the pages of *The New York Times* and *The New Yorker,* it seems the epithet "virtuous," when applied to an act of personal environmental responsibility, may be used only ironically. Tell me: How did it come to pass that virtue—a quality that for most of history has generally been deemed, well, a virtue—became a mark of liberal softheadedness? How peculiar, that doing the right thing by the environment—buying the hybrid, eating like a locavore—should now set you up for the Ed Begley Jr. treatment.

And even if in the face of this derision I decide I am going to bother, there arises the whole vexed question of getting it right. Is eating local or walking to work really going to reduce my carbon footprint? According to one analysis, if walking to work increases your appetite and you consume more meat or milk as a result, walking might actually emit more carbon than driving. A handful of studies have recently suggested that in certain cases under certain conditions, produce from places as far away as New Zealand might account for less carbon than comparable domestic products. True, at least one of these studies was co-written by a representative of agribusiness interests in (surprise!) New Zealand, but even so, they make you wonder. If determining the carbon footprint of food is really this complicated, and I've got to consider not only "food miles" but also whether the food came by ship or truck and how lushly the grass grows in New Zealand, then maybe on second thought I'll just buy the imported chops at Costco, at least until the experts get their footprints sorted out.

There are so many stories we can tell ourselves to justify doing nothing, but perhaps the most insidious is that, whatever we do manage to do, it will be too little too late. Climate change is upon us, and it has arrived well ahead of schedule. Scientists' projections that seemed dire a decade ago turn out to have been unduly optimistic: the warming and the melting is occurring much faster than the models predicted. Now truly terrifying feedback loops threaten to boost the rate of change exponentially, as the shift from white ice to blue water in the Arctic absorbs more sunlight and warming soils everywhere become more biologically active, causing them to release their vast stores of carbon into the air. Have you looked into the eyes of a climate scientist recently? They look really scared.

So do you still want to talk about planting gardens? I do.

Whatever we can do as individuals to change the way we live at this suddenly very late date does seem utterly inadequate to the challenge. It's hard to argue with Michael Specter, in a recent *New Yorker* piece on carbon footprints, when he says: "Personal choices, no matter how virtuous [N.B.I], cannot do enough. It will also take laws and money." So it will. Yet it is no less accurate or hardheaded to say that laws and money cannot do enough, either; that it will also take profound changes in the way we live. Why? Because the climate-change crisis is at its very bottom a crisis of lifestyle—of character, even. The Big Problem is nothing more or less than the sum total of countless little everyday choices, most of them made by us (consumer spending represents 70 percent of our economy), and most of the rest of them made in the name of our needs and desires and preferences.

> **The Big Problem is nothing more or less than the sum total of countless little everyday choices, most of them made by us (consumer spending represents 70 percent of our economy), and most of the rest of them made in the name of our needs and desires and preferences.**

For us to wait for legislation or technology to solve the problem of how we're living our lives suggests we're not really serious about changing—something our politicians cannot fail to notice. They will not move until we do. Indeed, to look to leaders and experts, to laws and money and grand schemes, to save us from our predicament represents precisely the sort of thinking—passive, delegated, dependent for solutions on specialists—that helped get us into this mess in the first place. It's hard to believe that the same sort of thinking could now get us out of it.

Thirty years ago, Wendell Berry, the Kentucky farmer and writer, put forward a blunt analysis of precisely this mentality. He argued that the environmental crisis of the 1970s—an era innocent of climate change; what we would give to have back that environmental crisis!—was at its heart a crisis of character and would have to be addressed first at that level: at home, as it were. He was impatient with people who wrote checks to environmental organizations while thoughtlessly squandering fossil fuel in their everyday lives—the 1970s equivalent of people buying carbon offsets to atone for their Tahoes and Durangos. Nothing was likely to change until we healed the "split between what we think and what we do." For Berry, the "why bother" question came down to a moral imperative: "Once our personal connection to what is wrong becomes clear, then we have to choose: we can go on as before, recognizing our dishonesty and living with it the best we can, or we can begin the effort to change the way we think and live."

For Berry, the deep problem standing behind all the other problems of industrial civilization is "specialization," which he regards as the "disease of the modern character." Our society assigns us a tiny number of roles: we're producers (of one thing) at work, consumers of a great many other things the rest of the time, and then once a year or so we vote as citizens. Virtually all of our needs and desires we delegate to specialists of one kind or another—our meals to agribusiness, health to the doctor, education to the teacher, entertainment to the media, care for the environment to the environmentalist, political action to the politician.

As Adam Smith and many others have pointed out, this division of labor has given us many of the blessings of civilization. Specialization is what allows me to sit at a computer thinking about climate change. Yet this same division of labor obscures the lines of connection—and responsibility—linking our everyday acts to their real-world consequences, making it easy for me to overlook the coal-fired power plant that is lighting my screen, or the mountaintop in Kentucky that had to be destroyed to provide the coal to that plant, or the streams running crimson with heavy metals as a result.

Of course, what made this sort of specialization possible in the first place was cheap energy. Cheap fossil fuel allows us to pay distant others to process our food for us, to entertain us and to (try to) solve our problems, with the result that there is very little we know how to accomplish for ourselves. Think for a moment of all the things you suddenly need to do for yourself when the power goes out—up to and including entertaining yourself. Think, too, about how a power failure causes your neighbors—your community—to suddenly loom so much larger in your life. Cheap energy allowed us to leapfrog community by making it possible to sell our specialty over great distances as well as summon into our lives the specialties of countless distant others.

Here's the point: Cheap energy, which gives us climate change, fosters precisely the mentality that makes dealing with climate change in our own lives seem impossibly difficult. Specialists ourselves, we can no longer imagine anyone but an expert, or anything but a new technology or law, solving our problems. Al Gore asks us to change the light bulbs because he probably can't imagine us doing anything much more challenging, like, say, growing some portion of our own food. We can't imagine it, either, which is probably why we prefer to cross our fingers and talk about the promise of ethanol and nuclear power—new liquids and electrons to power the same old cars and houses and lives.

The "cheap-energy mind," as Wendell Berry called it, is the mind that asks, "Why bother?" because it is helpless to imagine—much less attempt—a different sort of life, one less divided, less reliant. Since the cheap-energy mind translates everything into money, its proxy, it prefers to put its faith in market-based solutions—carbon taxes and pollution-trading schemes. If we could just get the incentives right, it believes, the economy will properly value everything that matters and nudge our self-interest down the proper channels. The best we can hope for is a greener version of the old invisible hand. Visible hands it has no use for.

But while some such grand scheme may well be necessary, it's doubtful that it will be sufficient or that it will be politically sustainable before we've demonstrated to ourselves that change is possible. Merely to give, to spend, even to vote, is not to do, and there is so much that needs to be done—without further delay. In the judgment of James Hansen, the NASA climate scientist who began sounding the alarm on global warming 20 years ago, we have only 10 years left to start cutting—not just slowing—the amount of carbon we're emitting or face a "different planet." Hansen said this more than two years ago, however; two years have gone by, and nothing of consequence has been done. So: eight years left to go and a great deal left to do.

Which brings us back to the "why bother" question and how we might better answer it. The reasons not to bother are many and compelling, at least to the cheap-energy mind. But let me offer a few admittedly tentative reasons that we might put on the other side of the scale:

If you do bother, you will set an example for other people. If enough other people bother, each one influencing yet another in a chain reaction of behavioral change, markets for all manner of green products and alternative technologies will prosper and expand. (Just look at the market for hybrid cars.) Consciousness will be raised, perhaps even changed: new moral imperatives and new taboos might take root in the culture. Driving an S.U.V. or eating a 24-ounce steak or illuminating your McMansion like an airport runway at night might come to be regarded as outrages to human conscience. Not having things might become cooler than having them. And those who did change the way they live would acquire the moral standing to demand changes in behavior from others—from other people, other corporations, even other countries.

All of this could, theoretically, happen. What I'm describing (imagining would probably be more accurate) is a process of viral social change, and change of this kind, which is nonlinear, is never something anyone can plan or predict or count on. Who knows, maybe the virus will reach all the way to Chongqing and infect my Chinese evil twin. Or not. Maybe going green will prove a passing fad and will lose steam after a few years, just as it did in the 1980s, when Ronald Reagan took down Jimmy Carter's solar panels from the roof of the White House.

Going personally green is a bet, nothing more or less, though it's one we probably all should make, even if the odds of it paying off aren't great. Sometimes you have to act as if acting will make a difference, even when you can't prove that it will. That, after all, was precisely what happened in Communist Czechoslovakia and Poland, when a handful of individuals like Vaclav Havel and Adam Michnik resolved that they would simply conduct their lives "as if" they lived in a free society. That improbable bet created a tiny space of liberty that, in time, expanded to take in, and then help take down, the whole of the Eastern bloc.

> **Going personally green is a bet, nothing more or less, though it's one we probably all should make, even if the odds of it paying off aren't great. Sometimes you have to act as if acting will make a difference, even when you can't prove that it will.**

So what would be a comparable bet that the individual might make in the case of the environmental crisis? Havel himself has suggested that people begin to "conduct themselves as if they were to live on this earth forever and be answerable for its condition one day." Fair enough, but let me propose a slightly less abstract and daunting wager. The idea is to find one thing to do in your life that doesn't involve spending or voting, that may or may not virally rock the world but is real and particular (as well as symbolic) and that, come what may, will offer its own rewards. Maybe you decide to give up meat, an act that would reduce your carbon footprint by as much as a quarter. Or you could try this: determine to observe the Sabbath. For one day a week, abstain completely from economic activity: no shopping, no driving, no electronics.

But the act I want to talk about is growing some—even just a little—of your own food. Rip out your lawn, if you have one, and if you don't—if you live in a high-rise, or have a yard shrouded in shade—look into getting a plot in a community garden. Measured against the Problem We Face, planting a garden sounds pretty benign, I know, but in fact it's one of the most powerful things an individual can do—to reduce your carbon footprint, sure, but more important, to reduce your sense of dependence and dividedness: to change the cheap-energy mind.

A great many things happen when you plant a vegetable garden, some of them directly related to climate change, others indirect but related nevertheless. Growing food, we forget, comprises the original solar technology: calories produced by means of photosynthesis. Years ago the cheap-energy mind discovered that more food could be produced with less effort by replacing sunlight with fossil-fuel fertilizers and pesticides, with a result that the typical calorie of food energy in your diet now requires about 10 calories of fossil-fuel energy to produce. It's estimated that the way we feed ourselves (or rather, allow ourselves to be fed) accounts for about a fifth of the greenhouse gas for which each of us is responsible.

Yet the sun still shines down on your yard, and photosynthesis still works so abundantly that in a thoughtfully organized vegetable garden (one planted from seed, nourished by compost from the kitchen and involving not too many drives to the garden center), you can grow the proverbial free lunch—CO2-free and dollar-free. This is the most-local food you can possibly eat (not to mention the freshest, tastiest and most nutritious), with a carbon footprint so faint that even the New Zealand lamb council dares not challenge it. And while we're counting carbon, consider too your compost pile, which shrinks the heap of garbage your household needs trucked away even as it feeds your vegetables and sequesters carbon in your soil. What else? Well, you will probably notice that you're getting a pretty good workout there in your garden, burning calories without having to get into the car to drive to the gym. (It is one of the absurdities of the modern division of labor that, having replaced physical labor with fossil fuel, we now have to burn even more fossil fuel to keep our unemployed bodies in shape.) Also, by engaging both body and mind, time spent in the garden is time (and energy) subtracted from electronic forms of entertainment.

You begin to see that growing even a little of your own food is, as Wendell Berry pointed out 30 years ago, one of those solutions that, instead of begetting a new set of problems—the way "solutions" like ethanol or nuclear power inevitably do—actually beget other solutions, and not only of the kind that save carbon. Still more valuable are the habits of mind that growing a little of your own food can yield. You quickly learn that you need not be dependent on specialists to provide for yourself—that your body is still good for something and may actually be enlisted in its own support. If the experts are right, if both oil and time are running out, these are skills and habits of mind we're all very soon going to need. We may also need the food. Could gardens provide it? Well, during World War II, victory gardens supplied as much as 40 percent of the produce Americans ate.

But there are sweeter reasons to plant that garden, to bother. At least in this one corner of your yard and life, you will have begun to heal the split between what you think and what you do, to commingle your identities as consumer and producer and citizen. Chances are, your garden will re-engage you with your neighbors, for you will have produce to give away and the need to borrow their tools. You will have reduced the power of the cheap-energy mind by personally overcoming its most debilitating weakness: its helplessness and the fact that it can't do much of anything that doesn't involve division or subtraction. The garden's season-long transit from seed to ripe fruit—will you get a load of that zucchini?!—suggests that the operations of addition and multiplication still obtain, that the abundance of nature is not exhausted. The single greatest lesson the garden teaches is that our relationship to the planet need not be zero-sum, and that as long as the sun still shines and people still can plan and plant, think and do, we can, if we bother to try, find ways to provide for ourselves without diminishing the world.

CONSIDER

1. After reading Pollan's essay, what do you think his major argument is? What passages in the essay make the best case for this argument? What section(s) of this essay would you quote to a friend if you were trying to convince him that it is worthwhile to make small behavioral changes (to "bother")? Which parts of his argument are least convincing? Why?

2. Pollan uses humor to disarm the reader and poke fun at the politics of the issue. What do you think of his tactic? Is it effective? Is it more or less likely to make you open to his arguments? Why?

CHALLENGE

3. Pollan discusses the environmental movement of the 1970s to illustrate his points about what we should do now to respond to global climate and food issues. Research the environmental changes that took place in the 1970s. Be sure to look at public policy events like the creation of fuel economy standards and passage of the Clean Water Act, as well as "personal virtue" choices like recycling and celebrating Earth Day. Now write a short editorial arguing whether and how we can use the lessons of the 1970s to address climate change in this decade.

Will Frankenfood Save the Planet?

Jonathan Rauch
(2003)

> **FYI** Jonathan Rauch is a correspondent for *The Atlantic Monthly* and a senior writer for *National Journal*. He is also a writer in residence at the Brookings Institution and the author of several books, including *Government's End: Why Washington Stopped Working* (1999). The following piece appeared in *The Atlantic Monthly* in 2003 and is still widely cited in debates over the benefits and risks of genetically engineered foods.

That genetic engineering may be the most environmentally beneficial technology to have emerged in decades, or possibly centuries, is not immediately obvious. Certainly, at least, it is not obvious to the many U.S. and foreign environmental groups that regard biotechnology as a bête noire. Nor is it necessarily obvious to people who grew up in cities, and who have only an inkling of what happens on a modern farm. Being agriculturally illiterate myself, I set out to look at what may be, if the planet is fortunate, the farming of the future.

It was baking hot that April day. I traveled with two Virginia state soil-and-water-conservation officers and an agricultural-extension agent to an area not far from Richmond. The farmers there are national (and therefore world) leaders in the application of what is known as continuous no-till farming. In plain English, they don't plough. For thousands of years, since the dawn of the agricultural revolution, farmers have ploughed, often several times a year; and with ploughing has come runoff that pollutes rivers and blights aquatic habitat, erosion that wears away the land, and the release into the atmosphere of greenhouse gases stored in the soil. Today, at last, farmers are working out methods that have begun to make ploughing obsolete.

At about one-thirty we arrived at a 200-acre patch of farmland known as the Good Luck Tract. No one seemed to know the provenance of the name, but the best guess was that somebody had said something like "You intend to farm this? Good luck!" The land was rolling, rather than flat, and its slopes came together to form natural troughs for rainwater. Ordinarily this highly erodible land would be suitable for cows, not crops. Yet it was dense with wheat—wheat yielding almost twice what could normally be expected, and in soil that had grown richer in organic matter, and thus more nourishing to crops, even as the land was farmed. Perhaps most striking was the almost complete absence of any chemical or soil runoff. Even the beating administered in 1999 by Hurricane Floyd, which lashed the ground with nineteen inches of rain in less than twenty-four hours, produced no significant runoff or erosion. The land simply absorbed the sheets of water before they could course downhill.

At another site, a few miles away, I saw why. On land planted in corn whose shoots had only just broken the surface, Paul Davis, the extension agent, wedged a shovel into the ground and dislodged about eight inches of topsoil. Then he reached down and picked up a clump. Ploughed soil, having been stirred up and turned over again and again, becomes lifeless and homogeneous, but the clump that Davis held out was alive. I immediately noticed three squirming earthworms, one grub, and quantities of tiny white insects that looked very busy. As if in greeting, a worm defecated. "Plant-available food!" a delighted Davis exclaimed.

This soil, like that of the Good Luck Tract, had not been ploughed for years, allowing the underground ecosystem to return. Insects and roots and microorganisms had given the soil an elaborate architecture, which held the earth in place and made it a sponge for water. That was why erosion and runoff had been reduced to practically nil. Crops thrived because worms were doing the ploughing. Crop residue that was left on the ground, rather than ploughed under as usual, provided nourishment for the soil's biota and, as it decayed, enriched the soil. The farmer saved the fuel he would have used driving back and forth with a heavy plough. That saved money, and of course it also saved energy and reduced pollution. On top of all that, crop yields were better than with conventional methods.

The conservation people in Virginia were full of excitement over no-till farming. Their job was to clean up the James and York Rivers and the rest of the Chesapeake Bay watershed. Most of the sediment that clogs and clouds the rivers, and most of the fertilizer runoff that causes the algae blooms that kill fish, comes from farmland. By all but eliminating agricultural erosion and runoff—so Brian Noyes, the local conservation-district manager, told me—continuous no-till could "revolutionize" the area's water quality.

Even granting that Noyes is an enthusiast, from an environmental point of view no-till farming looks like a dramatic advance. The rub—if it is a rub—is that the widespread elimination of the plough depends on genetically modified crops.

It is only a modest exaggeration to say that as goes agriculture, so goes the planet. Of all the human activities that shape the environment, agriculture is the single most important, and it is well ahead of whatever comes second. Today about 38 percent of the earth's land area is cropland or pasture—a total that has crept upward over the past few decades as global population has grown. The increase has been gradual, only about 0.3 percent a year; but that still translates into an additional Greece or Nicaragua cultivated or grazed every year.

> **Farming does not go easy on the earth, and never has. To farm is to make war upon millions of plants (weeds, so-called) and animals (pests, so-called) that in the ordinary course of things would crowd out or eat or infest whatever it is a farmer is growing.**

Farming does not go easy on the earth, and never has. To farm is to make war upon millions of plants (weeds, so-called) and animals (pests, so-called) that in the ordinary course of things would crowd out or eat or infest whatever it is a farmer is growing. Crop monocultures, as whole fields of only wheat or corn or any other single plant are called, make poor habitat and are vulnerable to disease and disaster. Although fertilizer runs off and pollutes water, farming without fertilizer will deplete and eventually exhaust the soil. Pesticides can harm the health of human beings and kill desirable or harmless bugs along with pests. Irrigation leaves behind trace elements that can accumulate and poison the soil. And on and on.

The trade-offs are fundamental. Organic farming, for example, uses no artificial fertilizer, but it does use a lot of manure, which can pollute water and contaminate food. Traditional farmers may use less herbicide, but they also do more ploughing, with all the ensuing environmental complications. Low-input agriculture uses fewer chemicals but more land. The point is not that farming is an environmental crime—it is not—but that there is no escaping the pressure it puts on the planet.

In the next half century the pressure will intensify. The United Nations, in its midrange projections, estimates that the earth's human population will grow by more than 40 percent, from 6.3 billion people today to 8.9 billion in 2050. Feeding all those people, and feeding their billion or so hungry pets (a dog or a cat is one of the first things people want once they move beyond a subsistence lifestyle), and providing the increasingly protein-rich diets that an increasingly wealthy world will expect—doing all of that will require food output to at least double, and possibly triple.

But then the story will change. According to the UN's midrange projections (which may, if anything, err somewhat on the high side), around 2050 the world's population will more or less level off. Even if the growth does not stop, it will slow. The crunch will be over. In fact, if in 2050 crop yields are still increasing, if most of the world is economically developed, and if population pressures are declining or even reversing—all of which seems reasonably likely—then the human species may at long last be able to feed itself, year in and year out, without putting any additional net stress on the environment. We might even be able to grow everything we need while *reducing* our agricultural footprint: returning cropland to wilderness, repairing damaged soils, restoring ecosystems, and so on. In other words, human agriculture might be placed on a sustainable footing forever: a breathtaking prospect.

The great problem, then, is to get through the next four or five decades with as little environmental damage as possible. That is where biotechnology comes in.

One day recently I drove down to southern Virginia to visit Dennis Avery and his son, Alex. The older Avery, a man in late middle age with a chinstrap beard, droopy eyes, and an intent, scholarly manner, lives on ninety-seven acres that he shares with horses, chickens, fish, cats, dogs, bluebirds, ducks, transient geese, and assorted other creatures. He is the director of global food issues at the Hudson Institute, a conservative think tank; Alex works with him, and is trained as a plant physiologist. We sat in a sunroom at the back of the house, our afternoon conversation punctuated every so often by dog snores and rooster crows. We talked for a little while about the Green Revolution, a dramatic advance in farm productivity that fed the world's burgeoning population over the past four decades, and then I asked if the challenge of the next four decades could be met.

"Well," Dennis replied, "we have tripled the world's farm output since 1960. And we're feeding twice as many people from the same land. That was a heroic achievement. But we have to do what some think is an even more difficult thing in this next forty years, because the Green Revolution had more land per person and more water per person—"

"—and more potential for increases," Alex added, "because the base that we were starting from was so much lower."

"By and large," Dennis went on, "the world's civilizations have been built around its best farmland. And we have used most of the world's good farmland. Most of the good land is already heavily fertilized. Most of the good land is already being planted with high-yield seeds. (Africa is the important exception.) Most of the good irrigation sites are used. We can't triple yields again with the technologies we're already using. And we might be lucky to get a fifty percent yield increase if we froze our technology short of biotech."

"Biotech" can refer to a number of things, but the relevant application here is genetic modification: the selective transfer of genes from one organism to another. Ordinary breeding can cross related varieties, but it cannot take a gene from a bacterium, for instance, and transfer it to a wheat plant. The organisms resulting from gene transfers are called "transgenic" by scientists—and "Frankenfood" by many greens.

Gene transfer poses risks, unquestionably. So, for that matter, does traditional crossbreeding. But many people worry that transgenic organisms might prove more unpredictable. One possibility is that transgenic crops would spread from fields into forests or other wild lands and there become environmental nuisances, or worse. A further risk is that transgenic plants might cross-pollinate with neighboring wild plants, producing "super-weeds" or other invasive or destructive varieties in the wild. Those risks are real enough that even most biotech enthusiasts—including Dennis Avery, for example—favor some government regulation of transgenic crops.

What is much less widely appreciated is biotech's potential to do the environment good. Take as an example continuous no-till farming, which really works best with the help of transgenic crops. Human beings have been ploughing for so long that we tend to forget why we started doing it in the first place. The short answer: weed control. Turning over the soil between plantings smothers weeds and their seeds. If you don't plough, your land becomes a weed garden—unless you use herbicides to kill the weeds. Herbicides, however, are expensive, and can be complicated to apply. And they tend to kill the good with the bad.

In the mid-1990s the agricultural-products company Monsanto introduced a transgenic soybean variety called Roundup Ready. As the name implies, these soybeans tolerate Roundup, an herbicide (also made by Monsanto) that kills many kinds of weeds and then quickly breaks down into harmless ingredients. Equipped with Round-up Ready crops, farmers found that they could retire their ploughs and control weeds with just a few applications of a single, relatively benign herbicide—instead of many applications of a complex and expensive menu of chemicals. More than a third of all U.S. soybeans are now grown without ploughing, mostly owing to the introduction of Roundup Ready varieties. Ploughless cotton farming has likewise received a big boost from the advent of bioengineered varieties. No-till farming without biotech is possible, but it's more difficult and expensive, which is why no-till and biotech are advancing in tandem.

In 2001 a group of scientists announced that they had engineered a transgenic tomato plant able to thrive on salty water—water, in fact, almost half as salty as seawater, and fifty times as salty as tomatoes can ordinarily abide. One of the researchers was quoted as saying, "I've already transformed tomato, tobacco, and canola. I believe I can transform any crop with this gene"—just the sort of Frankenstein hubris that makes environmentalists shudder. But consider the environmental implications. Irrigation has for millennia been a cornerstone of agriculture, but it comes at a price. As irrigation water evaporates, it leaves behind traces of salt, which accumulate in the soil and gradually render it infertile. (As any Roman legion knows, to destroy a nation's agricultural base you salt the soil.) Every year the world loses about 25 million acres—an area equivalent to a fifth of California—to salinity; 40 percent of the world's irrigated land, and 25 percent of America's, has been hurt to some degree. For decades traditional plant breeders tried to create salt-tolerant crop plants, and for decades they failed.

Salt-tolerant crops might bring millions of acres of wounded or crippled land back into production. "And it gets better," Alex Avery told me. The transgenic tomato plants take up and sequester in their leaves as much as six or seven percent of their weight in sodium. "Theoretically," Alex said, "you could reclaim a salt-contaminated field by growing enough of these crops to remove the salts from the soil."

His father chimed in: "We've worried about being able to keep these salt-contaminated fields going even for decades. We can now think about *centuries*."

One of the first biotech crops to reach the market, in the mid-1990s, was a cotton plant that makes its own pesticide. Scientists incorporated into the plant a toxin-producing gene from a soil bacterium known as *Bacillus thuringiensis*. With Bt cotton, as it is called, farmers can spray much less, and the poison contained in the plant is delivered only to bugs that actually eat the crop. As any environmentalist can tell you, insecticide is not very nice stuff—especially if you breathe it, which many Third World farmers do as they walk through their fields with backpack sprayers.

Transgenic cotton reduced pesticide use by more than two million pounds in the United States from 1996 to 2000, and it has reduced pesticide sprayings in parts of China by more than half. Earlier this year the Environmental Protection Agency approved a genetically modified corn that resists a beetle larva known as rootworm. Because rootworm is American corn's most voracious enemy, this new variety has the potential to reduce annual pesticide use in America by more than 14 million pounds. It could reduce or eliminate the spraying of pesticide on 23 million acres of U.S. land.

All of that is the beginning, not the end. Bioengineers are also working, for instance, on crops that tolerate aluminum, another major contaminant of soil, especially in the tropics. Return an acre of farmland to productivity, or double yields on an already productive acre, and, other things being equal, you reduce by an acre the amount of virgin forest or savannah that will be stripped and cultivated. That may be the most important benefit of all.

Of the many people I have interviewed in my twenty years as a journalist, Norman Borlaug must be the one who has saved the most lives. Today he is an unprepossessing eighty-nine-year-old man of middling height, with crystal-bright blue eyes and thinning white hair. He still loves to talk about plant breeding, the discipline that won him the 1970 Nobel Peace Prize: Borlaug led efforts to breed the staples of the Green Revolution. (See "Forgotten Benefactor of Humanity," by Gregg Easterbrook, an article on Borlaug in the January 1997 *Atlantic*.) Yet the renowned plant breeder is quick to mention that he began his career, in the 1930s, in forestry, and that forest conservation has never been far from his thoughts. In the 1960s, while he was working to improve crop yields in India and Pakistan, he made a mental connection. He would create tables detailing acres under cultivation and average yields—and then, in another column, he would estimate how much land had been saved by higher farm productivity. Later, in the 1980s and 1990s, he and others began paying increased attention to what some agricultural economists now call the Borlaug hypothesis: that the Green Revolution has saved not only many human lives but, by improving the productivity of existing farmland, also millions of acres of tropical forest and other habitat—and so has saved countless animal lives.

From the 1960s through the 1980s, for example, Green Revolution advances saved more than 100 million acres of wild lands in India. More recently, higher

> **If properly developed, disseminated, and used, genetically modified crops might well be the best hope the planet has got.**

yields in rice, coffee, vegetables, and other crops have reduced or in some cases stopped forest-clearing in Honduras, the Philippines, and elsewhere. Dennis Avery estimates that if farming techniques and yields had not improved since 1950, the world would have lost an additional 20 million or so square miles of wildlife habitat, most of it forest. About 16 million square miles of forest exists today. "What I'm saying," Avery said, in response to my puzzled expression, "is that we have saved every square mile of forest on the planet."

Habitat destruction remains a serious environmental problem; in some respects it is the most serious. The savannahs and tropical forests of Central and South America, Asia, and Africa by and large make poor farmland, but they are the earth's storehouses of biodiversity, and the forests are the earth's lungs. Since 1972 about 200,000 square miles of Amazon rain forest have been cleared for crops and pasture; from 1966 to 1994 all but three of the Central American countries cleared more forest than they left standing. Mexico is losing more than 4,000 square miles of forest a year to peasant farms; sub-Saharan Africa is losing more than 19,000.

That is why the great challenge of the next four or five decades is not to feed an additional three billion people (and their pets) but to do so without converting much of the world's prime habitat into second- or third-rate farmland. Now, most agronomists agree that some substantial yield improvements are still to be had from advances in conventional breeding, fertilizers, herbicides, and other Green Revolution standbys. But it seems pretty clear that biotechnology holds more promise—probably much more. Recall that world food output will need to at least double and possibly triple over the next several decades. Even if production could be increased that much using conventional technology, which is doubtful, the required amounts of pesticide and fertilizer and other polluting chemicals would be immense. If properly developed, disseminated, and used, genetically modified crops might well be the best hope the planet has got.

If properly developed, disseminated, and used. That tripartite qualification turns out to be important, and it brings the environmental community squarely, and at the moment rather jarringly, into the picture.

Not long ago I went to see David Sandalow in his office at the World Wildlife Fund, in Washington, D.C. Sandalow, the organization's executive vice-president in charge of conservation programs, is a tall, affable, polished, and slightly reticent man in his forties who holds degrees from Yale and the University of Michigan Law School.

Some weeks earlier, over lunch, I had mentioned Dennis Avery's claim that genetic modification had great environmental potential. I was surprised when Sandalow told me he agreed. Later, in our interview in his office, I asked him to elaborate. "With biotechnology," he said, "there are no simple answers. Biotechnology has huge potential benefits and huge risks, and we need to address both as we move forward. The huge potential benefits include increased productivity of arable land, which could relieve pressure on forests. They include decreased pesticide usage. But the huge risks include severe ecological disruptions—from gene flow and from enhanced invasiveness, which is a very antiseptic word for some very scary stuff."

> **Biotechnology could be part of our arsenal if we can overcome some of the barriers. It will never be a panacea or a magic bullet. But nor should we remove it from our tool kit.**

I asked if he thought that, absent biotechnology, the world could feed everybody over the next forty or fifty years without ploughing down the rain forests. Instead of answering directly he said, "Biotechnology could be part of our arsenal if we can overcome some of the barriers. It will never be a panacea or a magic bullet. But nor should we remove it from our tool kit."

Sandalow is unusual. Very few credentialed greens talk the way he does about biotechnology, at least publicly. They would readily agree with him about the huge risks, but they wouldn't be caught dead speaking of huge potential benefits—a point I will come back to. From an ecological point of view, a very great deal depends on other environmentalists' coming to think more the way Sandalow does.

Biotech companies are in business to make money. That is fitting and proper. But developing and testing new transgenic crops is expensive and commercially risky, to say nothing of politically controversial. When they decide how to invest their research-and-development money, biotech companies will naturally seek products for which farmers and consumers will pay top dollar. Roundup Ready products, for instance, are well suited to U.S. farming, with its high levels of capital spending on such things as herbicides and automated sprayers. Poor farmers in the developing world, of course, have much less buying power. Creating, say, salt-tolerant cassava suitable for growing on hardscrabble African farms might save habitat as well as lives—but commercial enterprises are not likely to fall over one another in a rush to do it.

If earth-friendly transgenics are developed, the next problem is disseminating them. As a number of the farmers and experts I talked to were quick to mention, switching to an unfamiliar new technology—something like no-till—is not easy. It requires capital investment in new seed and equipment, mastery of new skills and methods, a fragile transition period as farmer and ecology readjust, and an often considerable amount of trial and error to find out what works best on any given field. Such problems are only magnified in the Third World, where the learning curve is steeper and capital cushions are thin to nonexistent. Just handing a peasant farmer a bag of newfangled seed is not enough. In many cases peasant farmers will need one-on-one attention. Many will need help to pay for the seed, too.

Finally there is the matter of using biotech in a way that actually benefits the environment. Often the technological blade can cut either way, especially in the short run. A salt-tolerant or drought-resistant rice that allowed farmers to keep land in production might also induce them to plough up virgin land that previously was too salty or too dry to farm. If the effect of improved seed is to make farming more profitable, farmers may respond, at least temporarily, by bringing more land into production. If a farm becomes more productive, it may require fewer workers; and if local labor markets cannot provide jobs for them, displaced workers may move to a nearby patch of rain forest and burn it down to make way for subsistence farming. Such transition problems are solvable, but they need money and attention.

In short, realizing the great—probably unique—environmental potential of biotech will require stewardship. "It's a tool," Sara Scherr, an agricultural economist with the conservation group Forest Trends, told me, "but it's absolutely not going to happen automatically."

So now ask a question: Who is the natural constituency for earth-friendly biotechnology? Who cares enough to lobby governments to underwrite research—frequently unprofitable research—on transgenic crops that might restore soils or cut down on pesticides in poor countries? Who cares enough to teach Asian or African farmers, one by one, how to farm without ploughing? Who cares enough to help poor farmers afford high-tech, earth-friendly seed? Who cares enough to agitate for programs and reforms that might steer displaced peasants and profit-seeking farmers away from sensitive lands? Not politicians, for the most part. Not farmers. Not corporations. Not consumers.

At the World Resources Institute, an environmental think tank in Washington, the molecular biologist Don Doering envisions transgenic crops designed specifically to solve environmental problems: crops that might fertilize the soil, crops that could clean water, crops tailored to remedy the ecological problems of specific places. "Suddenly you might find yourself with a virtually chemical-free agriculture, where your cropland itself is filtering the water, it's protecting the watershed, it's providing habitat," Doering told me. "There is still so little investment in what I call design-for-environment." The natural constituency for such investment is, of course, environmentalists.

But environmentalists are not acting as such a constituency today. They are doing the opposite. For example, Greenpeace declares on its Web site: "The introduction of genetically engineered (GE) organisms into the complex ecosystems of our environment is a dangerous global experiment with nature and evolution . . . GE organisms must not be released into the environment. They pose unacceptable risks to ecosystems, and have the potential to threaten biodiversity, wildlife and sustainable forms of agriculture."

Other groups argue for what they call the Precautionary Principle, under which no transgenic crop could be used until proven benign in virtually all respects. The Sierra Club says on its Web site,

> In accordance with this Precautionary Principle, we call for a moratorium on the planting of all genetically engineered crops and the release of all GEOs [genetically engineered organisms] into the environment, *including those now approved*. Releases should be delayed until extensive, rigorous research is done which determines the long-term environmental and health impacts of each GEO and there is public debate to ascertain the need for the use of each GEO intended for release into the environment. [italics added]

Under this policy the cleaner water and healthier soil that continuous no-till farming has already brought to the Chesapeake Bay watershed would be undone, and countless tons of polluted runoff and eroded topsoil would accumulate in Virginia rivers and streams while debaters debated and researchers researched. Recall David Sandalow: "Biotechnology has huge potential benefits and huge risks, and we need to address both as we move forward." A lot of environmentalists would say instead, "*before* we move forward." That is an important difference, particularly because the big population squeeze will happen not in the distant future but over the next several decades.

For reasons having more to do with politics than with logic, the modern environmental movement was to a large extent founded on suspicion of markets and artificial substances. Markets exploit the earth; chemicals poison it. Biotech touches both hot buttons. It is being pushed forward by greedy corporations, and it seems to be the very epitome of the unnatural.

Still, I hereby hazard a prediction. In ten years or less, most American environmentalists (European ones are more dogmatic) will regard genetic modification as one of their most powerful tools. In only the past ten years or so, after all, environmentalists have reversed field and embraced market mechanisms—tradable emissions permits and the like—as useful in the fight against pollution. The environmental logic of biotechnology is, if anything, even more compelling. The potential upside of genetic modification is simply too large to ignore—and therefore environmentalists will not ignore it. Biotechnology will transform agriculture, and in doing so will transform American environmentalism.

CONSIDER

1. Summarize the argument Rauch makes in favor of biotechnologically modified crops. Do you think he adequately supports his claim that this kind of farming will "save the planet"? Why or why not?

2. On what grounds does Rauch criticize mainstream environmentalists, who advocate conservation and "living close to the land"? To what audiences do you think his comments would be most appealing?

COMPOSE

3. How do you think Rauch might respond to Pollan's criticisms of large-scale corporate farming? Write a few paragraphs exploring this question. Ultimately, which author's views seem more persuasive to you? Why?

CHALLENGE

4. Do some research to find out the "story" of a food product or restaurant meal you regularly purchase: Where is it made? Where do the ingredients come from? Under what circumstances are the ingredients produced? Then write a report on what you learned, focusing especially on any findings that surprised you.

ITEM 8.17 ■ Peter Menzel and Faith D'Aluisio, Images From *Hungry Planet: What the World Eats*, 2005

The following photographs come from the 2005 book by Peter Menzel and Faith D'Aluisio, *Hungry Planet: What the World Eats*, which documents the eating habits of 30 families from 24 nations. Menzel, a photojournalist, and D'Aluisio, a writer and former television producer, told NPR news that they got the idea for the book after noticing that Americans were "expanding" while people in the rest of the world (including wealthy industrialized nations of Western Europe) were not. The photos illustrate some obvious differences in foods and eating practices around the world, but Menzel also notes that food choices are generally becoming less diverse, with families around the world increasingly eating some of the same types of food.

The Revis family in the kitchen of their home in suburban Raleigh, North Carolina, with a week's worth of food. Ronald Revis, 39, and Rosemary Revis, 40, stand behind Rosemary's sons from her first marriage, Brandon Demery, 16 (left), and Tyrone Demery, 14. Cooking methods: electric stove, toaster oven, microwave, outdoor BBQ. Food preservation: refrigerator-freezer. Favorite foods—Ronald and Brandon: spaghetti. Rosemary: "potatoes of any kind." Tyrone: sesame chicken. Food expenditure for one week: $341.98 USD.

The Al Haggan family and their two Nepali servants in the kitchen of their home in Kuwait City, Kuwait, with one week's worth of food. Standing between Wafaa Abdul Aziz Al Qadini, 37 (beige scarf), and Saleh Hamad Al Haggan, 42, are their children, Rayyan, 2, Hamad, 10, Fatema, 13, and Dana, 4. In the corner are the servants, Andera Bhattrai, 23 (left), and Daki Serba, 27. Cooking methods: gas stoves (2), microwave. Food preservation: refrigerator-freezer. Food expenditure for one week: $221.45 USD.

8.2 | THE POLITICS OF FOOD

The Natomo family on the roof of their mud-brick home in Kouakourou, Mali, with a week's worth of food. Cooking method: wood fire. Food preservation: natural drying. Favorite foods—the Natomo family doesn't think in terms of "favorites." Family members: Soumana Natomo, 46 (in blue), sits flanked by his two wives, Fatoumata Toure, 33 (on right) and Pama Kondo, 35. Soumana and Fatoumata's children are daughter Tena, 4 months (in Fatoumata's lap), daughter Fourou, 12 (in front of her mother), son Kansy, 4 (in Soumana's lap), and son and daughter Mama, 8, and Fatoumata, 10 (both at their father's feet). Soumana and Pama's children are son Mamadou, 10 (in front of his mother), son Mama, 13 (far left), and son and daughter Kantie, 16, and Pai, 18 (far right). To Pama's left is Kadia Foune, 33, Soumana's sister-in-law, with her children Kantie, 1 (in her lap), and Mariyam, 8 (squatting). They are living with the Natomos while Kadia's husband works in Ivory Coast. Food expenditure for one week: $26.39 USD.

COMPOSE

1. What details in the three photos and accompanying captions strike you as particularly interesting or compelling? Do you see anything unexpected? Share your impressions with a group of classmates, noting similarities and differences in your responses.

2. Examine the photo of the Revis family. Do their food choices strike you as typical ones for an American family? How do your food choices in a typical week compare and contrast with what you see in the image?

3. What broader social, cultural, political, or economic issues do these photographs raise?

Cluster 8.3
Taking Action

When you're passionate about a cause, it's only natural to want others to share your views—and to act on them. This desire no doubt accounts for why so much writing about political issues takes the form of public advocacy or activism. In this section, we'll introduce you to the work of several writers, speakers, artists—and even a rock star—who use words and images to promote causes they believe in. Their approaches vary widely, from traditional political speechmaking to the guerrilla tactics of street artists. What they all share is their desire to persuade others to join them in solving community problems and creating a better future.

We begin by exploring the phenomenon of celebrity activism, focusing on U2 frontman Bono, whose efforts to fight global poverty have won international acclaim. Mark Yaconelli's "Christian Megastar: Bono on Record" and David Heim's "Breakfast with Bono" examine some ethical and rhetorical dimensions of Bono's activism and assess how successful he's been in persuading political leaders to support his projects. Paul Theroux's "The Rock Star's Burden," in contrast, warns that high-profile initiatives led by entertainment stars may draw attention away from more sustainable, locally organized programs.

The final section of the cluster focuses on grass-roots political activism, looking at the Ghost Bikes Project, an informal effort to create street memorials for bicyclists killed in bike-car accidents. The concluding article, Alex Williams's "Realistic Idealists," documents the growing commitment to community action among high-school and college students, predicting that Generation Y may well become the next "Great Generation."

> **ITEM 8.18 ■ Bono Speaking on Third-World Debt Relief at the U.S. Capitol, 2005**
>
> Paul David Hewson, better known by his childhood nickname Bono, is the lead singer and principal songwriter of the Irish rock band U2. U2 has won more than twenty Grammy awards, including five awards for the 2006 album, *How to Dismantle an Atomic Bomb*. One of the most prominent celebrity activists, Bono is a vocal advocate of several global causes including AIDS prevention and third-world debt relief. Among other projects, he is a co-founder of the ONE Campaign, which aims to eradicate poverty around the globe. He has met with many national and world leaders, including U.S. presidents, the Secretary General of the United Nations, and the U.S. Secretary of Defense.

CONSIDER

1. What are your thoughts on celebrity activism? Do you think that entertainment celebrities are more or less compelling as advocates for humanitarian causes than individuals with a more direct connection to a cause? Discuss several specific examples with a group of classmates—for example, former President Jimmy Carter, Martin Luther King, Jr., and celebrities Angelina Jolie and Brad Pitt immediately come to mind—before deciding on your answer.

2. How important do you think Bono's status as a celebrity is to the success of his political and social activism?

Christian Megastar: Bono on Record

Mark Yaconelli
(March 21, 2006)

When it emerged in the 1980s, the Irish rock group U2, with its lead singer Bono, displayed a spiritual passion that countered the big-haired, "Girls Just Wanna Have Fun" synthesizer pop of that era. The band was sincere and idealistic, and its lyrics sidestepped the standard topics of sex, parties and relationships. The band consciously rejected the detached "cool" that most rock stars sought to embody, exploring instead what Bono refers to as "the nature of awe, of worship, the wonderment at the world around you."

Over the next two decades, U2 became one of the biggest rock acts in the world and Bono a recognizable name not only in music but in international politics. For the past ten years Bono has served as a mouthpiece for such projects as the Drop the Debt campaign, which erased over $100 billion in Third World debt. In 2000 he cofounded, with Bobby Shriver, the organization DATA (Debt, AIDS, Trade, Africa), and he has sought to raise money to fight Africa's AIDS epidemic. His political activism has generated continual press attention, culminating last December in his being named *Time* magazine's "Person of the Year," along with Bill and Melinda Gates.

This book of conversations with Michka Assayas may be as close as we'll get to a Bono autobiography. Bono admits at the front of the book that he isn't prone to introspection. The death of his father and the prodding of his wife led him to enter into a series of discussions with Assayas, a French journalist and longtime friend. Although the book's subtitle uses the word conversation, the exchange is mostly one-way, with the skeptical, introspective, agnostic Assayas throwing out questions and observations for Bono to field.

Assayas wants Bono to analyze his violent working-class childhood, to question his motives behind his political involvement, and to explain how his Christian commitment squares with a life of wealth and fame. Bono half-jokingly refers to Assayas as his therapist.

What emerges is a man aware of his weaknesses, a man with a keen religious instinct, a man of bottomless energy and passion, a man grounded in long-term relationships, and a man for whom prayer and scripture are critical to his understanding of the world.

Bono's early Christian faith was often in tension with his musical aspirations. He and fellow musicians Larry Mullen and "the Edge" lived in Christian community during the early years of the group. Band members shared their resources, attended prayer meetings and engaged in regular Bible studies. "We didn't want the world to change us.... We were kind of zealots." It took years and the near-breakup of the band before they learned that "self-righteousness, self-flagellation" could be as dangerous as sex and drugs.

The subject of Africa evokes Bono's most powerful language. He refers to the AIDS crisis in Africa as "the biggest pandemic in the history of civilization.... And it is not a priority for the West. Why? Because we don't put the same value on African life as we put on a European or an American life. God will not let us get away with this, history certainly won't let us get away with our excuses."

Bono refers to his celebrity status as "silly" and "ridiculous," yet he's learned that "it is a kind of currency" that has given him access to the world's power brokers. He claims to feel few butterflies when meeting with world leaders like Tony Blair, Jacques Chirac,

---

FYI — Mark Yaconelli has written articles on contemporary religion for *The Christian Century*, *Presbyterian Record*, and other publications. He is the author of several books on youth ministry, including *Downtime: Helping Teenagers Pray* (2008) and *Growing Souls: Experiments in Contemplative Youth Ministry* (2007). The following piece is a book review of *Bono: In Conversation with Michka Assayas* (2005), a biographical collection of interviews French writer Assayas conducted with Bono. It appeared as the cover story of the March 21, 2006, issue of *The Christian Century*.

Vladimir Putin and George Bush: "I'm never nervous when I meet politicians. I think they should be nervous because I'm representing the poor and wretched in this world. And whatever thoughts you have about God, who He is or if He exists, most will agree that if there is a God, God has a special place for the poor. The poor are where God lives. So these politicians should be nervous, not me."

His success in winning over political opponents like Jesse Helms is inspired by the work of Martin Luther King. Bono's strategy when dealing with skeptics is to try to make "the light brighter." Like King, he seeks to avoid responding to caricature and instead looks to connect with even his severest political detractors through humor, conversation and an appreciation of the good in each person. "Find the light in them, because that will further your cause." Bono can speak with genuine affection about George Bush and even refers to Helms (whose social agenda is pretty much the opposite of Bono's) as "a beautiful person" while at the same time speaking forcefully against their neglect of the poor.

Bono's struggle with pride, his political activism, his artistic life are all rooted and informed by his Christian faith. Bono claims it's his experience of faith that gives him peace beneath the noise and activity of his life—a sense of God that draws him to try and catch each sunrise and retrieve a sense of being reborn each day. Assayas is sometimes bewildered, sometimes annoyed by this aspect of Bono, yet toward the end of the book appears envious of it.

Bono's genius is in what he refers to as a "religious instinct" that he trusts will lead him toward a greater experience of truth, love and artistic expression. For Bono, this instinct is "more important than intellect." It's an instinct that drives him to pursue art with an almost physical vulnerability ("You put your hands under your skin, you break your breastbone, you rip open your rib cage"), an instinct that drives him to hit high notes that he claims he can reach only in the presence of an audience, an instinct that compels him to construct a life filled with tension and paradox—a life in which he finds himself a friend of both the poor and the rich.

It's this instinct for life that compels Bono to serve in African orphanages, to learn liberation theology from the poor of Central America and to spend New Year's Eve in Serbian refugee camps. His egotistic and self-described "messianic tendencies" seem to be tempered by lifelong friendships and a 25-year marriage to a woman he's known since he was 15. He is drawn to "Sabbath-moments . . . moments when I can be incredibly still and incredibly myself" before God.

The first rock show I ever attended was a U2 concert held in a small theater in Toronto in 1983. When the band was introduced, mayhem broke out. People began climbing over seats, pressing toward the stage. By the second number people were jumping up on the stage, sneaking around the stacks of speakers, grabbing and hugging members of the band. Husky men in yellow jackets appeared from the sides of the auditorium and started dragging people off the stage. Then they leaped into the crowd and began strong-arming people back toward their seats.

Seeing what was happening, Bono stopped the music and asked the bouncers to go back to the stage wings. He then expressed his gratitude for the effort people had made to attend the concert and asked that we all try to stay calm so that no one would be injured or forced to leave.

The security men receded, but it took only a song or two before the stoned and star-struck began scampering back onto the stage. Often Bono didn't see them, and they were caught by the concert security guards and hauled outside. When Bono did notice, he ran to them, pulled them from the guards, hugged them or danced with them, then gently returned the wayward fans to the audience. Soon Bono was alternating between singing to the audience and rescuing people from the bouncers. The concert became so electric and out of control that at one point Bono stopped playing and whispered something to the other band members, who left the stage. Then the lights were cut except for a spotlight on Bono, who brought the crowd to its senses by quietly singing "Amazing Grace."

It was a pleasure to recognize in this book the same Bono I had watched on stage—a man singing full-heartedly while simultaneously seeking to rescue those in trouble. Bono is, in his way, a "community artist." He feels a responsibility to the larger struggles and issues that burden humankind. The tension between artist and public servant keeps Bono open and alive. He may be one of the most important Christian activists of our time.

Breakfast with Bono

David Helm
(March 21, 2006)

> **FYI** David Helm, a graduate of Yale Divinity School, has been executive editor of *The Christian Century* since 1998. In addition to writing articles and editorials for the print publication, he is a frequent contributor to *Theolog,* the magazine's blog. The following piece reports on Bono's keynote address to the National Prayer Breakfast, an annual religious event hosted by the U.S. Congress on the first Thursday in February each year. For the full text of Bono's speech, visit *americanrhetoric.com* and search "Bono."

The National Prayer Breakfast is usually a somewhat self-congratulatory celebration of generic faith, an exercise in civil religion. But when Bono stepped to the podium and objected to the way "self-righteousness rolls down like a mighty stream from certain corners of the religious establishment," one had the sense that this was a prophetic moment, or as close to one as official Washington allows.

Rock star as moral conscience of the world? Bono has an appealing sense of the absurdity of the idea. "There's something unseemly about rock stars mounting the pulpit and preaching to presidents and then disappearing to their villas in the south of France," he admitted to the audience of over 3,000, which included President Bush and many congressional leaders.

Bono's oratorical performance at the February 2 event revealed how he manages to pull off this unlikely role. He was self-deprecating about his fame and earnest about his cause— ending poverty and the ravages of AIDS in Africa. He deftly alternated between praising his listeners and challenging them. And he cited passages from the Old and New Testaments and the Qur'an.

Bono praised the Bush administration for doubling aid to Africa, tripling funding for global health, and saving 700,000 lives with anti-AIDS drugs. Then he outlined how much more there is to do. "There's a gigantic chasm between the scale of the emergency and the scale of the response," he said. "Sixty-five hundred Africans are dying every day of preventable, treatable disease for lack of drugs we can buy at any drug store.

"This is not about charity, this is about justice and equality. Because there's no way we can look at what's happening in Africa and, if we're honest, conclude that deep down we really accept that Africans are equal to us." If the death toll in Africa were occurring anywhere else in the world, Bono suggested, the world wouldn't allow it.

Bono's main interest—and the focus of the One Campaign, for which he is the chief spokesperson—is to persuade the U.S. to give an additional 1 percent of its federal budget to the world's poor, which would more than double the current expenditure. But he also hinted at a more controversial political agenda addressing trade policy, debt relief and pharmaceutical regulations: "Preventing the poorest of the poor from selling their products while we sing the virtues of a free market—that's a justice issue. Holding children to ransom for the debts of their grandparents—that's a justice issue. Withholding life-saving medicine out of deference to the Office of Patents—that's a justice issue."

The prophets of the Old Testament came in an unexpected form and sometimes wore unusual clothes. As for his own attire, Bono had this comment: "I am not here as a man of the cloth—unless that cloth is leather."

ITEM 8.19 ■ Bono greets President George W. Bush after speaking at the National Prayer Breakfast, 2006

CONSIDER

1. Mark Yaconelli suggests that Bono's band U2 inspires fans in part because they convey an *ethos* of "sincerity" rather than the "detached 'cool'" that many celebrities project. Do you agree with this claim? Is Yaconelli's assessment of most celebrities fair? Do you think that people respond more strongly to sincerity than coolness? Cite examples to support your opinion.

2. What does Yaconelli say about how artistic, religious, and political motives connect in Bono's approach to activism? Which of the three, if any, does he imply is most important? Would you agree? Why or why not?

COMPOSE

3. Visit the online speech bank at *www.americanrhetoric.com* and read one or more of Bono's speeches. Then write a few paragraphs analyzing the rhetorical strategies he uses to inspire his audience: In what ways is each speech tailored to the particular audience and occasion? How does Bono—a politically liberal rock star—build common ground with his listeners, whose backgrounds and interests may not match his? Point to specific passages in the speech to develop your analysis.

4. Visit the One Campaign Website at *www.one.org* and examine the various avenues it offers for getting involved. Write a few paragraphs evaluating how successful you think the organization is at inspiring people to take action on global poverty.

The Rock Star's Burden

Paul Theroux
(December 15, 2005)

> **FYI** Paul Theroux is the author of dozens of novels and nonfiction books. He is a Fellow in the Royal Society of Literature and has won numerous literary and editorial awards. He has taught literature at several universities in Asia, Europe, and Africa. As a young Peace Corps volunteer, Theroux participated in the 1964 attempt to overthrow Malawian dictator Hastings Banda. His most recent novel is *The Elephanta Suite* (2007). The following editorial appeared in the *New York Times*.

There are probably more annoying things than being hectored about African development by a wealthy Irish rock star in a cowboy hat, but I can't think of one at the moment. If Christmas, season of sob stories, has turned me into Scrooge, I recognize the Dickensian counterpart of Paul Hewson—who calls himself "Bono"—as Mrs. Jellyby in "Bleak House." Harping incessantly on her adopted village of Borrioboola-Gha "on the left bank of the River Niger," Mrs. Jellyby tries to save the Africans by financing them in coffee growing and encouraging schemes "to turn pianoforte legs and establish an export trade," all the while badgering people for money.

It seems to have been Africa's fate to become a theater of empty talk and public gestures. But the impression that Africa is fatally troubled and can be saved only by outside help—not to mention celebrities and charity concerts—is a destructive and misleading conceit. Those of us who committed ourselves to being Peace Corps teachers in rural Malawi more than 40 years ago are dismayed by what we see on our return visits and by all the news that has been reported recently from that unlucky, drought-stricken country. But we are more appalled by most of the proposed solutions.

I am not speaking of humanitarian aid, disaster relief, AIDS education or affordable drugs. Nor am I speaking of small-scale, closely watched efforts like the Malawi Children's Village. I am speaking of the "more money" platform: the notion that what Africa needs is more prestige projects, volunteer labor and debt relief. We should know better by now. I would not send private money to a charity, or foreign aid to a government, unless every dollar was accounted for—and this never happens. Dumping more money in the same old way is not only wasteful, but stupid and harmful; it is also ignoring some obvious points.

If Malawi is worse educated, more plagued by illness and bad services, poorer than it was when I lived and worked there in the early 60's, it is not for lack of outside help or donor money. Malawi has been the beneficiary of many thousands of foreign teachers, doctors and nurses, and large amounts of financial aid, and yet it has declined from a country with promise to a failed state.

In the early and mid-1960's, we believed that Malawi would soon be self-sufficient in schoolteachers. And it would have been, except that rather than sending a limited wave of volunteers to train local instructors, for decades we kept on sending Peace Corps teachers. Malawians, who avoided teaching because the pay and status were low, came to depend on the American volunteers to teach in bush schools, while educated Malawians emigrated. When Malawi's university was established, more foreign teachers were welcomed, few of them replaced by Malawians, for political reasons. Medical educators also arrived from elsewhere. Malawi began graduating nurses, but the nurses were lured away to Britain and Australia and the United States, which meant more foreign nurses were needed in Malawi.

When Malawi's minister of education was accused of stealing millions of dollars from the education budget in 2000, and the Zambian president was charged with stealing from the treasury, and Nigeria squandered its oil wealth, what happened? The simplifiers of Africa's problems kept calling for debt relief and more aid. I got a dusty reception lecturing at the Bill and Melinda Gates Foundation when I pointed out the successes of responsible policies in Botswana, compared with the kleptomania of its neighbors. Donors enable embezzlement by turning a blind eye to bad governance, rigged elections and the deeper reasons these countries are failing.

Mr. Gates has said candidly that he wants to rid himself of his burden of billions. Bono is one of his trusted advisers. Mr. Gates wants to send computers to Africa - an unproductive not to say insane idea. I would offer pencils and paper, mops and brooms: the schools I have seen in Malawi need them badly. I would not send more teachers. I would expect Malawians themselves to stay and teach. There ought to be an insistence in the form of a bond, or a solemn promise, for Africans trained in medicine and education at the state's expense to work in their own countries.

Malawi was in my time a lush wooded country of three million people. It is now an eroded and deforested land of 12 million; its rivers are clogged with sediment and every year it is subjected to destructive floods. The trees that had kept it whole were cut for fuel and to clear land for subsistence crops. Malawi had two presidents in its first 40 years, the first a megalomaniac who called himself the messiah, the second a swindler whose first official act was to put his face on the money. Last year the new man, Bingu wa Mutharika, inaugurated his regime by announcing that he was going to buy a fleet of Maybachs, one of the most expensive cars in the world.

Many of the schools where we taught 40 years ago are now in ruins—covered with graffiti, with broken windows, standing in tall grass. Money will not fix this. A highly placed Malawian friend of mine once jovially demanded that my children come and teach there. "It would be good for them," he said.

> **There are plenty of educated and capable young adults in Africa who would make a much greater difference than Peace Corps workers.**

Of course it would be good for them. Teaching in Africa was one of the best things I ever did. But our example seems to have counted for very little. My Malawian friend's children are of course working in the United States and Britain. It does not occur to anyone to encourage Africans themselves to volunteer in the same way that foreigners have done for decades. There are plenty of educated and capable young adults in Africa who would make a much greater difference than Peace Corps workers.

Africa is a lovely place—much lovelier, more peaceful and more resilient and, if not prosperous, innately more self-sufficient than it is usually portrayed. But because Africa seems unfinished and so different from the rest of the world, a landscape on which a person can sketch a new personality, it attracts mythomaniacs, people who wish to convince the world of their worth. Such people come in all forms and they loom large. White celebrities busy-bodying in Africa loom especially large. Watching Brad Pitt and Angelina Jolie recently in Ethiopia, cuddling African children and lecturing the world on charity, the image that immediately sprang to my mind was Tarzan and Jane.

Bono, in his role as Mrs. Jellyby in a 10-gallon hat, not only believes that he has the solution to Africa's ills, he is also shouting so loud that other people seem to trust his answers. He traveled in 2002 to Africa with former Treasury Secretary Paul O'Neill, urging debt forgiveness. He recently had lunch at the White House, where he expounded upon the "more money" platform and how African countries are uniquely futile.

But are they? Had Bono looked closely at Malawi he would have seen an earlier incarnation of his own Ireland. Both countries were characterized for centuries by famine, religious strife, infighting, unruly families, hubristic clan chiefs, malnutrition, failed crops, ancient orthodoxies, dental problems and fickle weather. Malawi had a similar sense of grievance, was also colonized by absentee British landlords and was priest-ridden, too.

Just a few years ago you couldn't buy condoms legally in Ireland, nor could you get a divorce, though (just like in Malawi) buckets of beer were easily available and unruly crapulosities a national curse. Ireland, that island of inaction, in Joyce's words, "the old sow that eats her farrow," was the

Malawi of Europe, and for many identical reasons, its main export being immigrants.

It is a melancholy thought that it is easier for many Africans to travel to New York or London than to their own hinterlands. Much of northern Kenya is a no-go area; there is hardly a road to the town of Moyale, on the Ethiopian border, where I found only skinny camels and roving bandits. Western Zambia is off the map, southern Malawi is terra incognita, northern Mozambique is still a sea of land mines. But it is pretty easy to leave Africa. A recent World Bank study has confirmed that the emigration to the West of skilled people from small to medium-sized countries in Africa has been disastrous.

Africa has no real shortage of capable people—or even of money. The patronizing attention of donors has done violence to Africa's belief in itself, but even in the absence of responsible leadership, Africans themselves have proven how resilient they can be—something they never get credit for. Again, Ireland may be the model for an answer. After centuries of wishing themselves onto other countries, the Irish found that education, rational government, people staying put, and simple diligence could turn Ireland from an economic basket case into a prosperous nation. In a word—are you listening, Mr. Hewson?—the Irish have proved that there is something to be said for staying home.

CONSIDER

1. Summarize the criticisms Theroux makes of Bono's activism. What evidence does he use to support his arguments? Do you find his criticisms fair?

2. How would you characterize Theroux's tone in this piece? Does his tone enhance or detract from his argument, in your opinion?

3. Why do you think Theroux chooses to refer to Bono as "Mr. Hewson"? What can you infer about Theroux's general attitude toward entertainment celebrities?

COMPOSE

4. Compare and contrast Bono's and Theroux's views on how people in wealthy industrialized nations can best help to solve problems in developing nations. Which argument do you find the most compelling? Why? Write a few paragraphs explaining your thoughts.

ITEM 8.20 ■ Press Kit Items, The New York City Street Memorial Project/Ghost Bike Project

While activists like Bono work through traditional political channels and media to promote their causes, political street artists have a different style of activism. Such artists use public spaces (usually unofficially or even illegally) as their canvas, creating images that confront passersby with political and social messages. The materials on pages 531–533 come from a press kit created by the New York City Street Memorial Project and the Ghost Bike Project, two loosely organized street art initiatives that advocate traffic safety by creating roadside memorials for pedestrians and bicyclists killed by automobiles. The final photograph comes from the Portland, Oregon, Ghost Bike Project.

8 | POLITICS AND ADVOCACY

The New York City Street Memorial Project

www.ghostbikes.org
www.streetmemorials.org

The Street Memorial Project honors cyclists and pedestrians that have been killed on New York City's streets. We seek to cultivate a compassionate and supportive community for survivors and friends of those lost and to initiate a change in culture that fosters mutual respect among all people who share the streets.

The Street Memorial Project was developed in 2007 to incorporate all the people involved in creating ghost bikes and to include pedestrian memorials. Through the project, volunteers work together to construct the memorials and organize memorial rides and walks to highlight the prevalent safety issues on our streets and remember those killed. As of May 2008, 44 ghost bikes have been placed in New York City.

WHAT IS THE GHOST BIKE PROJECT?

Ghost Bikes are dignified and somber memorials for bicyclists killed on the streets of New York City. A bicycle painted all white is locked near the crash site accompanied by a small plaque remembering the fallen cyclist. We endeavor to recognize every cycling fatality, but limited news coverage, changing statistical counts, and the lack of publicly available information make it difficult to learn about every death. As part of our annual Memorial Ride, we install a ghost bike in remembrance of all the individuals whose names never made the news.

Each installation is meant to be a reminder of a tragedy that occurred on an otherwise anonymous street corner and a quiet statement in support of cyclists' right to safe travel. The first bike memorials were created in St. Louis, Missouri in 2003, and the idea has since spread to at least 40 cities throughout the world. The first New York City ghost bikes appeared in June 2005.

Creating and installing a ghost bike is a sad and moving process. The death of a fellow bicyclist hits home, since we travel the same unsafe streets and face the same risks; it could just as easily have been one of us. Each time we say we hope to never have to do it again—but we remain committed to making these memorials as long as they are needed.

...

WHAT DO WE WANT?

We want a change in culture.
- To encourage mutual respect among all street users.
- To instill the responsibility we share to look out for each other.

We want to incite more humanity in this city.
- To assure that every person is remembered.
- To build solidarity among non-drivers and create a space for mourning and support.
- To acknowledge each death as a tragic, but not isolated, event.
- To recognize the ripple effect that one person's death has on their family, neighborhood, and community and to acknowledge that the loss of one life affects us all.

We want improvements in policy.
- To make the City follow through on necessary improvements in engineering, enforcement, and public education.
- To compel the City to conduct full investigations of crashes and their causes and to take action to improve safety.

We want outrage that makes a lasting difference.
- To encourage the media to report on all deaths in a sensitive, educated manner.
- To hold the City accountable for street safety issues and to force each agency to respond to these tragedies.
- To inspire all New Yorkers to be grieved and angered when someone is killed.

We want to stop having to do this.

ITEM 8.21 ■ **Ghost Bike Memorial, Portland, Oregon, 2005**

CONSIDER

1. The press kit for the Ghost Bike Project explicitly lists the ways in which the artists hope to "change the culture" of urban roads. Do you think these goals are obvious to people who encounter the ghost bikes without having read the document? How effective are the bikes themselves in making the political argument?

2. How do you think the ghost bikes might affect people differently than more traditional public safety campaigns? What audiences might be most and least powerfully affected by the bikes? Why?

3. What design elements can you identify in the ghost bike items? How do these elements (such as color, details, placement, and so on) contribute to their message?

COMPOSE

4. Do some research on political street art, then write a short essay discussing what you see as the strengths and limitations of this kind of activism.

CHALLENGE

5. How do you feel about political activities that involve civil disobedience? For example, ghost bikes and other street art are illegal unless the artist secures a permit to use the public space where the work appears. Write an essay exploring your views on when—if ever—it may be appropriate to bend or break rules in advocating for a cause.

Realistic Idealists

Alex Williams
(September 11, 2005)

> **FYI** What sorts of advocacy and activism are ordinary young people engaging in today? In this article, Alex Williams, style writer for the *New York Times*, suggests that they may be doing more important work than many people would expect.

Lynn Grossman, a writer in Manhattan who is married to the actor Bob Balaban, comes from a long line of social activists. Her mother joined the civil rights movement, and she herself marched in protest of the Vietnam War. But she said that things had changed by the time her eldest daughter, Mariah, now 27, came of age.

For many in Mariah's generation, community service was little more than a requirement that private schools imposed for graduation. Some took brief working vacations in places like Costa Rica, or the Caribbean island of Dominica, where they helped build roads and houses. "These kids had never seen a hammer before," Ms. Grossman said with a laugh. "I don't know what they did aside from get suntans."

Now, she said, "things are completely different."

As an eighth grader, her youngest daughter, Hazel, transformed a basement storage room in a Brooklyn homeless shelter into a library stocked with 5,000 volumes. At 13, she mobilized her fellow students to paint walls, hire librarians and design a functioning library-card system linked to a computer database. "We were floored," Ms. Grossman said. "And it's not just Hazel. A lot of kids out there are like this. They are like C.E.O.'s of community service."

Hazel Balaban, now a freshman at Connecticut College in New London, spent her first days on campus last week trying to organize a bake sale for victims of Hurricane Katrina. "It's almost expected," she said. "With the Internet and 24-hour TV, you just see all these problems. They're everywhere."

Hazel is at the leading edge of a generation whose sense of community involvement was born four years ago on Sept. 11, 2001. The attacks spurred an unprecedented outpouring of donations and volunteerism from Americans. Since then teenagers have witnessed the deadly Florida hurricane season of 2004, the more than 150,000 killed by the tsunami in Asia last December, and now Katrina. Encouraged by an increasing number of high schools with community service requirements and further motivated by college admissions offices looking for reasons to choose one honor student over another, teenagers are embracing social activism with the zeal of missionaries and the executive skills of seasoned philanthropists. Not only are more students participating, educators say, but the scale of ambition seems to be continually increasing.

"We've seen a shift in the zeitgeist away from what you would call 'community service' and more into social action," said Tom Krattenmaker, a spokesman for Swarthmore College near Philadelphia. "It's not just about working in a soup kitchen," he said, but about "creating new programs, shooting higher."

Gregory Pyke, the senior associate dean of admission at Wesleyan University in Middletown, Conn., said that one recent applicant had started a Web-based initiative to collect eyeglasses—thousands of pairs—to be passed along to the needy in underprivileged countries. Another created a large-scale program to collect and refurbish discarded computers before passing them along to the poor. "The number of discussions where a dean is pulling us aside and saying, 'You have to hear about what this kid has done' has also gone up," he said.

While cynics—and not a few colleges—may question whether the young people initiating such grand projects are looking to impress admissions officers, Mr. Pyke said he thought that most of the motivation was altruistic. "These are kids who are aware of many ways in which the world is a pretty lousy place," he said. "They want to exercise more authority in the world than adults give them credit for."

Educators, sociologists and parents explain the outpouring of youthful philanthropy by noting that this generation has been bombarded not only by bad news, all of which seems to demand an immediate response, but by calls to action from political leaders and celebrities. Disaster relief, unlike opposition to the Vietnam War, which stirred many in their parents' generation, is uncontroversial and encourages wide-scale participation. And once roused, young people have greater tools at their disposal, particularly the Internet, to expand projects.

More than 82 percent of high school seniors performed volunteer work, according to the 2004 American Freshman survey, a nationwide poll conducted by a graduate division of the University of California, Los Angeles, compared with just over 74 percent a decade earlier, and 66 percent in 1989.

The Collegiate Challenge program run by Habitat for Humanity in which students spend a week of their summer building housing for the poor in cities throughout the nation, has grown twelve-fold since it started in 1989, said Alynn Woodson, the manager. It has seen a 30 percent growth in participation by high school students in the last two years. "In some ways service has gotten to be kind of a trendy thing to do," Ms. Woodson said.

Katrina is the cause of the moment, and students across the country have responded like seasoned aid workers. By Sept. 2, four days after the storm came ashore in Alabama, Louisiana and Mississippi, students at Westside High School in Houston had raised more than $16,000 for the American Red Cross.

"We have 2,870 students," said Noralea Jordan, the senior class president, who helped organize the drive. "If we made $16,000 in a day, I'm sure in another week we could triple that."

That same day, students at Boiling Springs High School in South Carolina collected 6,000 gallons of bottled water. "We're not very good at our football, but it's been said by rival football teams, 'Whenever it comes to things that matter, Boiling Springs always gets the job done,'" said Jessica Gregg, 17, the student body president.

At many schools students were ready to mobilize because they have had so much practice. Cloydia Garrette, 17, the student council president at Jack Yates High School in Houston and a veteran of drives to raise money for tsunami victims, leukemia research and Ronald McDonald House, collected clothes and other essentials when evacuees from New Orleans began to reach the Astrodome. Charity is infectious, she said, "A lot of kids see us doing it, and they're following along."

> 'These are kids who are aware of many ways in which the world is a pretty lousy place,' he said. 'They want to exercise more authority in the world than adults give them credit for.'

Once rare, community service is now mandatory for an increasing number of schools in all 50 states, said Jennifer Piscatelli, a policy analyst at the Education Commission of the States. Maryland requires every high school student to perform 75 hours of public service to graduate, and similar requirements exist at school districts in Chicago, Los Angeles and Philadelphia. College officials have taken such activity into account when making admission decisions. Bruce Walker, the vice provost and director of admissions for the University of Texas in Austin, said the university, which is faced with an increasing number of qualified candidates, is paying more attention to applicants' public service, or as he said, "what kind of citizen they were, and are."

But even increased basic requirements do not seem to account for the grandiosity of initiatives on the part of many teenagers, educators say. "It's kind of intimidating to see what some kids have done," Mr. Walker said. In Owings Mills, Md., two high school freshmen, Greg Becker and Michael Swirnow, exceeded the McDonogh School's 40-hour community service requirement by doing 500 hours. Starting when they were 14, the boys set out to raise money to build a house for a struggling family in Baltimore through Habitat for Humanity.

"Sometimes, doing everything you can isn't enough," said Greg, who initiated the effort. Through meetings with executives at various foundations and a raffle that raised $42,000 (a Mini Cooper was the top prize), the students collected $88,000.

"At first, I never really thought about it as something for college," said Michael, now 15. "As it went on, though, it suddenly hit me: this is going to be huge on my college application."

Such examples of over-the-top public service can put a competitive pressure on other families who believe colleges are watching. For those who have yet to fall into line with the trend, the anxieties can be great. "I've had three families come in today saying, 'What is this community service thing?'" said Howard Greene, a private college admissions consultant in Manhattan.

But some college admissions counselors have already grown skeptical about what's known in the trade as the "How I Saved the World" essay, as well as about projects that just happen to commence early in a student's junior year. "There are two sides to me," said Jim Bock, dean of admissions and financial aid at Swarthmore, which this past year received 300 more freshman applications than the previous year. "One is the jaded side—is it a strategy? The other side is, is it part of a new generation of students who really are committed to making a better world?"

Mr. Bock noted that his college put a high premium on public service: it highlights Swarthmore students' antigenocide initiatives in Sudan alongside its main features on its Web home page. Two weeks ago Mr. Bock watched a colleague ask nearly 400 freshmen at an orientation seminar how many had done community service projects in high school.

"I'll have to admit I was moved," Mr. Bock said. "Ninety-five percent of the freshmen stood up."

Katherine Cohen, a college admissions consultant who has discussed community service with many high school students in Manhattan, noted that admitting such candidates was in the colleges' self-interest. "Colleges love to see fund-raisers, of course," Ms. Cohen said. "Ding-ding-ding, the bell goes off, because they want to see money raised in the future" for their own endowments.

Teenagers who pull off outsize projects shrug off suspicions that their aims were other than altruistic. Michael Swirnow, the Maryland youth who helped raise $88,000 for Habitat for Humanity, said the motivating factor was to "give back" to the less fortunate. "I think the most important thing is I learned I'm capable of doing something this big," he said. "It's about confidence."

Several educators said that it didn't really matter in the end whether teenagers were expending effort out of self-interest or altruism so long as good deeds were done. Some level of self-interest, after all, is why kids read books and do homework.

"This is a generation that was born after the consciousness revolution" of the 1960's and 70's, said William Strauss, the co-author with Neil Howe of "Millennials Rising: The Next Great Generation," a portrait of Americans born after 1982. "A lot of them are now children of baby boomers, and they look at them as a generation that looked at the self instead of the community. Now they've turned that around. Generations set themselves apart by correcting the mistakes they perceive their parents to have made."

ITEM 8.22 ■ **Students at Westside High School in Houston, Texas, collect money to aid Hurricane Katrina victims, 2005**

CONSIDER

1. In this article, Williams identifies a shift in young people's civic engagement from "community service" to "social action." What's the difference, according to Williams? Do you see a difference?

2. Do you think that social activism that is done partly out of self-interest—because it's required for graduation, or because it will look good on a college application, for instance—is as valuable as social action done for its own sake? Why or why not?

COMPOSE

3. Compare Williams's portrait of the Millennial Generation (Generation Y) with the accounts offered by Thomas Friedman and Courtney Martin on pages 487–490. What similarities and differences do you see in these portrayals? Which do you find most persuasive? Write a few paragraphs exploring your thoughts on this question.

CHALLENGE

4. Consider the various approaches to social action you've read about in this cluster. Which style of advocacy appeals to you the most—the high-profile political activism of Bono, the illicit grassroots art of the Ghost Bike Project, the charitable projects described in "Realistic Idealists," or another approach? Choose the approach that suits you best, then design a campaign for inspiring others to take action on a cause you care about.

Writing About Politics and Advocacy

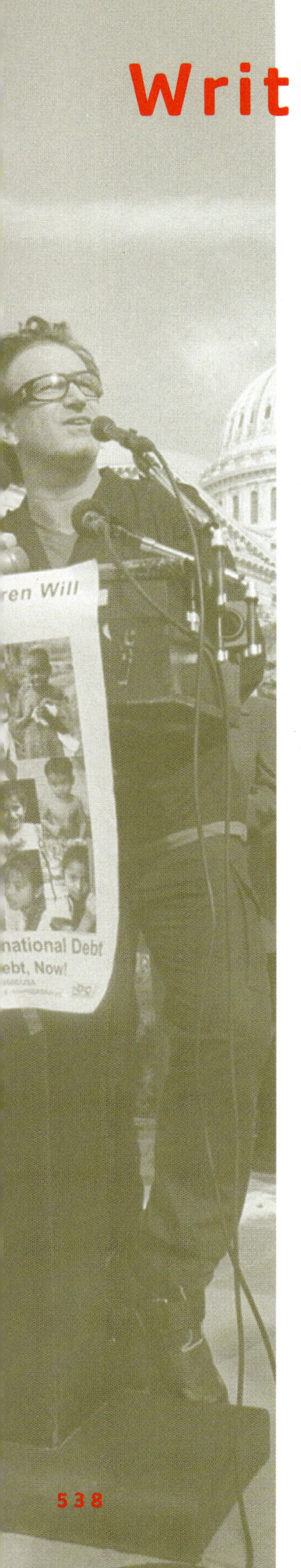

Writing about political or social issues can be challenging. Because such topics affect people's lives, they spark strong opinions, high emotions, and complicated debates. Yet this kind of writing can also be invigorating and rewarding: it gives you the opportunity to raise awareness, shape others' beliefs, even inspire action—and perhaps, in the process, to learn something new about a topic you care about.

When you have the opportunity to write about politics or advocacy, choose a **subject** that you feel passionate about. Perhaps you're a lifelong hunter who feels strongly about protecting gun ownership laws. Or maybe you've been following a debate at your school over whether to use student fees to build a campus child-care center. If you care about a topic and know it well, you'll already have a sense of what arguments are being made about it, and you'll be eager to undertake research to learn more. Having a personal connection to a topic can also help you articulate a unique perspective—a contribution that adds to what others have already said about the issue. In a paper, you might signal this perspective with an introductory personal anecdote, as Courtney Martin does in "Generation Overwhelmed" (see pages 489–490).

Once you've staked out a topic, figure out what **audience** you hope to reach; then plan your project with their needs and responses in mind: What will they already know about your issue? What kinds of background information will they require? What opinions are they likely to have, and what sorts of appeals, examples, and language are most likely to persuade them? Keep in mind that implicit, indirect arguments often work best with resistant audiences, whereas readers who are already receptive to your view will respond well to direct claims. A campus fraternity, for instance, may be far less receptive to a poster that preaches "Keep alcohol off campus!" than to a photo essay that shows a student being treated in an emergency room for the effects of alcohol poisoning after a night of binge drinking. (When you make implicit arguments, though, be sure that they are absolutely clear—you don't want your audience to miss your point.)

The point—or **purpose**—of your project is another key consideration. What do you want readers to think or do as a result of your appeal? Much of the writing people do about political and social issues provides either arguments or analysis. In composing an argument, you express and defend a particular claim about an issue, hoping to alert readers to a problem or persuade them to share your views—as Michael Pollan does in "Why Bother?" (pages 507–511). In an analysis, you invite readers to share your judgment of an argument that someone else has made about an issue—you make an "argument about an argument," as Jonathan Butler does in his analysis of World War I posters in Project 8.1. In either case, you'll need to develop a specific *thesis* or *claim* that reflects your purpose and serves as the focus of your project. (See pages 73–74 for more on writing an argument and pages 71–72 for more on composing a rhetorical analysis.)

Closely related to purpose are your choices about **genre** and **medium**. (If you're writing a paper for a college course, your instructor will likely make some choices for you—be sure to check the assignment and consult with him or her if you have questions.) Will you create a Web site promoting an issue? A flyer that can be photocopied and distributed around campus? A brief video to be posted on YouTube? An academic research report? Your choice will, to a large degree, determine what materials, technology, and rhetorical conventions you'll draw on as you produce your project. Be realistic, however: choose a genre that fits the rhetorical situation, or **context**, your argument will enter.

Whatever shape your project takes, conduct some **research** (see pages 84–87). You'll need to be well informed to understand the complexities of your topic and to come across as credible to readers. Begin with the resources in your campus library, but remember that the Internet and organizations and experts in your community can also provide valuable resources—especially if you're writing about a controversy related to your campus or city. For example, Jonathan Butler's visit to a local museum exhibit yielded many of the examples he cites in his "Visual Images of National Identity."

The information you gather through research will not only shape the major claims you make, it will also help you build a storehouse of **details** and **evidence** that you can draw on. Even if many of the facts, figures, and testimonials you encounter in your research don't appear in the final project, such material will help you make informed choices about how to present your argument. For example, Meixia Huang reviewed a number of articles on the status of boys in our culture before she created her slideshow (see Project 8.2); of these, she quotes only one in the final text. However, this information shaped her opinion that many are unaware of the problems boys face and helped her decide on a call to action: "Pay attention to them."

But don't assume that once you've gathered sufficient information, the pieces of your project will simply fall into place. Although nearly all writing about politics and advocacy will revolve around a central claim, supported with evidence and details, in fact, the **organization** of a particular project can vary greatly, depending on its genre, medium, and the kind of claim it makes:

- A project that develops a *factual claim*—for instance, calling attention to a problem that others have overlooked—must present information in a logical sequence.

- An argument over the *definition* of a term—for example, *Is euthanasia murder?*—might require a totally different structure, one that begins by listing the properties or qualities that make something what it is. Those properties themselves might be debatable, but then controversy is the lifeblood of arguments.

- Or an argument might make a claim about *causes and effects.* (Think about all you've read in recent years about global warming or unemployment.) Such an argument will have to explore the connections between particular phenomena and their origins—sometimes quite complex and multifaceted relationships.

- Or maybe the argument is an *evaluation*, let's say a rebuttal of a published editorial. Somewhere in the argument you'd expect a presentation of criteria or standards, either implied or spelled out.

- Or perhaps the argument makes a *proposal*. Somebody wants to fix a problem. Such an argument, you would expect, should define a problem (*students on your campus can't find convenient parking*), look at alternative solutions (*build a monorail to parking lots on the campus periphery*), come up with a better one (*build parking garages*), and explain why it works (*parking fees can finance the garages*). All these parts would have to follow in logical sequence before readers pay attention to the solution offered.

The point is that different kinds of arguments have different functions and so they will have different structures. When those arguments are mainly written, the structures may be easy to see, marked by titles or headings or helpful transitional phrases. Sometimes a project may be mainly visual or aural or a combination of the two; then, some parts of the argument may be implicit, or they may be suggested by images alone or by images and words working in combination. (See Chapter 2 for more detailed advice on organizing different kinds of projects and papers.)

Once you've generated a draft of your text, assess its effectiveness and identify areas that need **revision** and **editing**. If possible, show the draft to several members of your target audience and ask them to comment on its clarity and effectiveness. Don't forget to cite appropriately any outside sources—including images. Edit the text and fine-tune the design and format before submitting the final version. (For advice on revision and editing, consult Chapter 2.)

Project 8.1

Analyzing a Political Argument

This project asks you to select two or more political texts that address the same issue but are designed to appeal to different audiences. Write a three- to five-page rhetorical analysis comparing and contrasting the persuasive strategies these texts use (for example, how does a political candidate's speech to a college rally compare to her remarks to a gathering of retired military personnel? How do posters produced by an organization such as UNICEF in 1990 differ from those produced in 2009). Your analysis should draw readers' attention to the patterns of similarity and difference you find most interesting: their use of rhetorical appeals to *ethos, pathos,* and *logos*; the ways in which the arguments are structured; the kinds of claims made; the use of evidence or design elements; or any combination of these factors.

When you write your rhetorical analysis, it will obviously be important to study your chosen texts carefully to identify key patterns. It's also essential to lay out for each text the basic facts of the rhetorical situation: *who* is making the argument about *what* issue for which *audience* (or audiences). Do research in the library or on the Internet so that you can accurately identify the texts you've chosen, where and when they appear, in what medium, and so on. You may need to provide a paragraph or more of background information early in your paper to set the context for your analysis.

Before you begin this project, take a look at Jonathan Butler's "Visual Images of National Identity: Propaganda Posters of the Great War." You also may find helpful the material in Chapter 2 on writing a comparison and contrast essay (pages 68–69) and composing a rhetorical analysis (pages 71–72).

STUDENT PROJECT

Jonathan Butler, "Visual Images of National Identity: Propaganda Posters of the Great War"

Butler 1

Jonathan Butler
Professor Friend
English 387
Dec. 8, 2008

Visual Images of National Identity:
Propaganda Posters of the Great War

Although rhetoric has traditionally been thought of as being confined to the realm of language, the art takes other forms as well. As the exhibit of World War I propaganda posters currently on display at the University of South Carolina's McKissick Museum demonstrates, rhetoric happens not just through speech and the written word, but may also work through visuals, or through a combination of words and images that persuade. The dramatic propaganda posters of the Great War seek to evoke emotional and financial civilian support for the war through a variety of persuasive strategies. The posters created in each of the Allied nations were all crafted with the same basic goals; however, each nation employs a distinct style in appealing to its citizens. These different styles in large part reflect the ethos, or preexisting identity, that each nation brought to the table. As the following examples from British and French posters show, each nation's histories and values played a large role in shaping its propaganda.

British posters usually rely on traditional British concepts of honor and the empire to instill nationalism and promote military enlistment. One poster, for instance, shows a male lion, an image traditionally associated with patriarchal royalty, standing on a rock above his pride, his mane flowing, his chest swollen with pride (see fig. 1). The poster associates Britain with the Old Lion who defies his foes with the help of the young lions, presumably the United States and France. Drawing on the sentiments raised by words and images of the empire, United Kingdom posters often also rely on a feeling of honor-bound obligation--one might even say feelings of guilt--for their rhetorical power. Another typical poster features a portrait of field marshal Lord Kitchener, and the

The opening ¶ outlines the general claim and tells readers that an analysis of the posters' visual rhetoric will follow.

Fig. 1. Arthur Wardle, The Empire Needs Men, 1919 ("Posters").

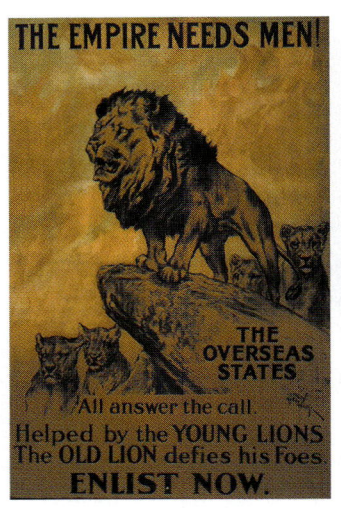

Fig. 2. Lord Kitchener Says: Enlist To-Day, 1915 ("Posters").

following quote, which scolds young men who do not volunteer for military service: "Does the call of duty find no response in you until reinforced--let us rather say superseded--by the call of compulsion?" (see fig. 2). While it's never explicitly stated, one gets the feeling looking at British posters that civilians are being asked to support the war for the Crown, to preserve the history and values of their empire.

The French posters in this exhibit, on the other hand, rely instead on their traditional values expressed in France's motto: "Liberty, Equality, Fraternity." More dramatically symbolic than British posters, French posters create a sense of camaraderie between the Allies, often depicting soldiers representing France, Britain, and the United States collectively defeating a symbolic representation of German forces, usually the black eagle. In one poster, Allied troops in the uniforms of their nations scale a mountain, on top of which the black eagle is perched, its claws red with blood. The inscription reads, "One final effort and we'll have it" (see fig. 3). Even the few French posters that deviate from this "Allies triumphing together" theme still maintain the romanticized style of the

> **Body ¶s draw attention to specific features in each poster and explain how these illustrate cultural differences.**

Butler 3

others, usually depicting images symbolic of French victory over German forces. Not only are the traditional French values of equality and fraternity represented on the posters, but liberty plays a large role as well. Since Liberty has been personified in French culture since the Revolution, it is not surprising that her image was frequently used on French posters. Images of Liberty, resembling a Greek goddess, complete with laurels, abound on posters with and without representations of the other Allied nations. Liberty is often shown posing, huge and specterlike, above a group of soldiers, as in this exhortation to buy liberty bonds (see fig. 4).

While the styles of each nation's posters differ as a result of each country's individual ethos and the stylistic choices of the nation's artists, the posters all have the rhetorical use of imagery and text in common. While French poster illustrators use very dramatic imagery to catch the eyes and stir the emotions of their audiences, for example, British

British and French posters are treated in separate ¶s, to emphasize similarities among each nation's propaganda.

Fig. 3. Un Dernier effort et on l'aura, 1917 ("Posters").

Fig. 4. Lucien Jonas, Emprunt de la Celebration, 1918 ("Posters").

Butler 4

posters tend towards a more realistic, reserved style that reflects their traditional notions of duty and honor. By examining these posters and the various rhetorical strategies their creators employed to reach their audience, we can gain a better understanding of the ways in which both image and text can be manipulated for persuasion--as well as some notion of how a society's cultural features shape the development of its texts.

The conclusion sums up key differences discussed in the body of the paper before wrapping up the central argument.

Butler 5

Work Cited

"Posters of the Great War." Exhibit of posters from the Joseph Bruccoli Collection. McKissick Museum, University of South Carolina, Columbia. Fall 2003. 2 December 2008 <http://www.sc.edu/library/spcoll/hist/gwposters/posterintro.html>.

Project 8.2

Creating a Public Service Announcement

As a college student, you've probably had plenty of opportunities to write persuasive essays and to present argumentative speeches or debates in your academic courses. But you may have had fewer chances to express your views through visual or multimedia compositions. As we've emphasized throughout this book, visual texts are the products of sophisticated rhetorical and design choices—choices at least as complex as those involved in producing a traditional paper or speech. This project invites you to grapple with these choices as you produce a public service announcement (PSA) that makes an argument on behalf of a cause or issue of your choice. PSAs typically make arguments that draw heavily on visual and multimedia elements, because they must quickly capture readers' attention and motivate them to take action.

You may choose the form your PSA will take (check with your instructor for any additional guidelines or limitations). Possibilities include a poster, a flyer, a short video advertisement or documentary film, a Web page, or a brochure.

Before you begin to compose, research your issue thoroughly so that you have comprehensive, current information at hand, and identify the target audience you want to reach. Look for examples of PSAs, such as the PETA anti-fur advertisement on page 478, noting rhetorical and design elements that seem effective. And play to your strengths in choosing a medium and genre: if you have a good eye for visual design, try creating a poster that features dramatic images. On the other hand, if you've never used a video camera and don't know where to procure one, best put aside your documentary film idea in favor of something more manageable, such as a photo essay or brochure.

STUDENT PROJECT

Meixia Huang, "Pay Attention to Them"

Mexia Huang developed this PSA in response to research she had read indicating that growing numbers of boys in the United States now suffer from behavioral difficulties or have problems in school. To raise awareness of this problem, she composed a short video that included a simple but compelling soundtrack and posted it on YouTube. The following stills include the full text and selected images from the video.

Psychologists say that boys' growing dissatisfaction, previously ignored, has been steadily building: Rising numbers of boys are prescribed the drug Ritalin for ADHD. Boys' academic performance has declined, while girls' achievement has risen.

A lopsided gender revolution.
-APA

our boys are being left behind in our schools

8 | POLITICS AND ADVOCACY

Help them become

great men

547

548 WRITING ABOUT POLITICS AND ADVOCACY

Project 8.3

Research the key viewpoints surrounding a current political issue that interests you, and then write a "pro" and "con" pair of editorials that argue on opposing sides of the issue (see the editorials on college costs, pages 480–481, for an example). You may choose a national or global issue such as gun control legislation or health care reform; or you may investigate a controversy in your campus or local community, such as neighborhood crime or arts funding. The challenge in this assignment will be to present the best possible case on both sides of the question so that readers can make an informed decision.

Project 8.4

Do research to learn about a political or social activist whose work interests you, then write a profile that creates a portrait of your subject's life and work. You may focus on someone of historical or national prominence (for example, Bono or Ralph Nader), or you may write about someone known primarily on your campus or in your local community—for instance, the leader of a homeless advocacy group or of a tax watchdog group. (See pages 175–180 for an example of a profile essay.)

Project 8.5

Follow a national or local political campaign to learn about the candidates and issues. Then, choose a text promoting one of the candidates—for example, a speech delivered by the candidate, a television or online commercial, or a brochure or poster—and write an essay evaluating it: How well does it appeal to its target audience? How effectively does it employ appeals to *logos*, *ethos*, and *pathos*? How accurate is the text? Are its arguments fair and ethical? Why or why not?

IMAGE CREDITS

p. v, Chris Jordan; p. vi, Property of Holechek Pictures 2008; p. vii, Cover by Matthew Rolston From *Rolling Stone*, July 13-27. © Rolling Stone LLC 2006. All Rights Reserved. Reprinted by Permission.; p. viii, © Terry Falke; p. ix, (c)Comedy Central/Courtesy Everett Collection; p. x, ODT, Inc.; p. xi Jay B. Sauceda Industries; p. xii, Army National Guard Recruiting-1800GoGuard.com; p. 2, weather.com®. Courtesy of The Weather Channel; p. 4, Scala/Art Resource, NY; p. 5, top, Bildarchiv Steffens/Bridgeman Art Library; bottom, HIP/Art Resource, NY; p. 6, left, Muzammil Pasha/Reuters; right, Sayed Salahuddin/Reuters; p. 8, Chris Jordan; p. 9, left, Chris Jordan; p. 9 right, Chris Jordan; p. 13, Pere Borrell del Caso/Banco de Espanã Biblioteca; p. 14, James H. Evans; p. 15, Donald Judd, 15 untitled works in concrete, 1980-1984, detail. Permanent collection, the Chinati Foundation, Marfa, Texas, photograph by Florian Holzherr, 2002.; p. 19, Courtesy Markos Moulitsas/Daily Kos; p. 20, Image courtesy of The Advertising Archives; p. 21, Courtesy Chrysler LLC. Used with permission.; p. 22, Contemporary Films Ltd./Photofest; pp. 28, 44, Rick Friedman/Corbis; p. 34, Barack Obama Campaign Headquarters; p. 35, BRIAN SNYDER/Reuters /Landov; p. 37, Corbis; p. 42 top, Mark Ulriksen for *The New Yorker*; right, Mark Ulriksen; p. 54, Property of Holechek Pictures 2008; p. 57, Courtesy of Oreck Corporation in its affiliation with Susan G. Komen Foundation for breast cancer awareness.; p. 58, Collection Int. Inst. of Social History, Amsterdam, The Netherlands.; p. 59, Collection Int. Inst. of Social History, Amsterdam, The Netherlands.; p. 62, Cover by Robert Trachtenberg. From *Rolling Stone*, November 16, 2006. © Rolling Stone LLC 2006. All Rights Reserved. Reprinted by Permission.; p. 66, Reproduced from the Collections of the Library of Congress; p. 76, Tony Cenicola/The New York Times/Redux; p. 81, Excerpt from THE 9/11 REPORT: A GRAPHIC ADAPTATION by Sid Jacobson and Ernie Colon. Copyright © 2006 by Castlebridge Enterprises, Inc. Reprinted by permission of Hill and Wang, a division of Farrar, Straus and Giroux, LLC.; p. 91, The Advertising Archive; p. 94, Cover by Matthew Rolston From *Rolling Stone*, July 13-27. © Rolling Stone LLC 2006. All Rights Reserved. Reprinted by Permission.; p. 97, Dorothea Lange, Library of Congress; p. 98, The Advertising Archive; p. 99, Jim Borgman © 1998 Cincinnati Enquirer. Reprinted with permission of UNIVERSAL PRESS SYNDICATE. All rights reserved. p. 100, The Advertising Archive; p. 103, AP/Wide World Photos; p. 104, Edward Hopper, "Nighthawks," 1942. Photograph (c) 2004, The Art Institute of Chicago. All Rights Reserved.; p. 105, Gordon Parks/Getty Images; p. 117, left, Erich Lessing/Art Resource, NY; center, Scala/Art Resource, NY, right, Giraudon/Art Resource, NY; p. 122, Jim Goldberg/Magnum Photos; p. 123, Jim Goldberg/Magnum Photos; pp. 96, 106, 124, 128, 150, 166, Harry Benson/Express/Getty Images; p. 136, Cover by Matthew Rolston From *Rolling Stone*, February 9, 2006 © Rolling Stone LLC 2006. All Rights Reserved. Reprinted by Permission.; p. 136, Cover by Brigitte Lacombe. From *Rolling Stone*, February 23, 2006 © Rolling Stone LLC 2006. All Rights Reserved. Reprinted by Permission.; p.136, Cover by Platon. From *Rolling Stone*, March 9, 2006. © Rolling Stone LLC 2006. All Rights Reserved. Reprinted by Permission.; p. 136, Cover by Sam Jones. From *Rolling Stone*, March 23, 2006 . © Rolling Stone LLC 2006. All Rights Reserved. Reprinted by Permission.; p. 136, Cover by Michael Elins. From *Rolling Stone*, April 6, 2006. © Rolling Stone LLC 2006. All Rights Reserved. Reprinted by Permission.; p. 136, Cover by Sam Jones. From *Rolling Stone*, April 20, 2006. © Rolling Stone LLC 2006. All Rights Reserved. Reprinted by Permission.; p. 136, Cover by Robert Grossman. From *Rolling Stone*, May 4, 2006. © Rolling Stone LLC 2006. All Rights Reserved. Reprinted by Permission.; p. 136, Cover by Matthew Rolston From *Rolling Stone*, June 15, 2006. © Rolling Stone LLC 2006. All Rights Reserved. Reprinted by Permission.; p. 136, Cover by Nick Stevens/Retna. From *Rolling Stone*, June 29, 2006. © Rolling Stone LLC 2006. All Rights Reserved. Reprinted by Permission.; p.136, Cover by Adrian Boot/UrbanImages.tv/Photo illustration by Michael Elins. From *Rolling Stone*, August 10, 2006. © Rolling Stone LLC 2006. All Rights Reserved. Reprinted by Permission.; p. 136, Cover by Matthew Rolston From *Rolling Stone*, October 5, 2006. © Rolling Stone LLC 2006. All Rights Reserved. Reprinted by Permission.; p. 136, Cover by Max Vadukul. From *Rolling Stone*, October 19, 2006. © Rolling Stone LLC 2006. All Rights Reserved. Reprinted by Permission.; p. 136, Cover by Robert Trachtenberg. From *Rolling Stone*, November 16, 2006. © Rolling Stone LLC 2006. All Rights Reserved. Reprinted by Permission.; p. 136, Cover Photo by Max Vadukul From *Rolling Stone*, November 30, 2006 © Rolling Stone LLC 2006 All Rights Reserved. Reprinted by Permission.; p. 137, Cover by Matthew Rolston From *Rolling Stone*, August 24, 2006. © Rolling Stone LLC 2006. All Rights Reserved. Reprinted by Permission.; p. 137, Cover by Matthew Rolston From *Rolling Stone*, September 7, 2006. © Rolling Stone LLC 2006. All Rights Reserved. Reprinted by Permission.; p. 137, Cover by Matthew Rolston From *Rolling Stone*, September 21, 2006. © Rolling Stone LLC 2006. All Rights Reserved. Reprinted by Permission.; p. 137, Cover by Matthew Rolston From *Rolling Stone*, December 14, 2006. © Rolling Stone LLC 2006. All Rights Reserved. Reprinted by Permission.; p. 137, Cover Photo From *Rolling Stone*, January 25,2007 © Rolling Stone LLC 2007 All Rights Reserved. Reprinted by Permission.; p. 137, Cover by Matthew Rolston From *Rolling Stone*, February 8, 2007. © Rolling Stone LLC 2007. All Rights Reserved. Reprinted by Permission.; p. 142, A. Ramey/PhotoEdit, Inc.; p. 143, Uwe Krejci/Getty Images; p. 148, Hulton Archive/Getty Images; p. 149, Metronome/Getty Images; p. 155, Matthias Clamer/Getty Images; p. 161, Impact Visuals/Phototake NYC; p. 162, right, Northwestern University Library, Edward S. Curtis's "The North American Indian": the Photographic Images, 2001. http://memory.loc.gov/ammem/award98/ienhtml/curthome.html; center, Gertrude Käsebier/The National Museum of American History, Smithsonian Institution; left, Northwestern University Library, Edward S. Curtis's "The North American Indian": the Photographic Images, 2001 http://memory.loc.gov/ammem/award98/ienhtml/curthome.html; p. 165, Hulleah J. Tsinhnahjinnie; p. 174, Reproduced from the Collections of the Library of Congress; p. 175, Gordon Parks/Getty Images; p. 176. Reproduced from the Collections of the Library of Congress; p. 180, © Terry Falke, 181, 182, 192, 214, 230, 248; p. 183, Tim Gartside/Alamy; p. 184, Smiley N. Pool/*The Dallas Morning News*; p. 185, David Muench Photography; p. 186, Melissa Ann Pinney/Catherine Edelman Gallery; p. 187, Jon Arnold Images Ltd./Alamy; p. 189, Richard Harrod, http://www.flickr.com/photos/richardharrod/269263130/in/datetaken/; pp. 190–191, Alice Attie; p. 192, Tim Gartside/Alamy; p. 200, left, San Francisco Museum of Modern Art, Accessions Committee Fund: gift of Barbara and Gerson Bakar. ©William Eggleston; right, Hulton|Archive Photos/Getty Images; bottom, New Line/The Kobal Collection/Ralph Nelson Jr.; p. 201, Bill Owens/www.billowens.com; p. 204, Todd Sundsted; p. 213, Ryan Bretag; p. 214, Tim Gartside/Alamy; p. 215, top, Kevin Tuma; middle, Rex Babin/*The Sacramento Bee*; bottom, Signe Wilkinson Editorial Cartoon @ 2006 Signe Wilkinson. All rights reserved. Used with the permission of Signe Wilkinson and the Washington Post in conjunction with the Cartoonist Group.; p. 221, Diane Cook and Len Jenshel; p. 224, Joe Grossinger; p. 225, Joe Grossinger; p. 227, Chad Chase/The New York Times/Redux; p. 230, Tim Gartside/Alamy; p. 231, © Dreamworks/Courtesy the Everett Collection; p. 235, Richard Cummins/Corbis; p. 241, John Cohen/Getty Images; p. 246, Reproduced from the Collections of the Library of Congress; p. 247, Bettmann/Corbis; p. 248, Tim Gartside/Alamy; p. 257, Rudi Von Briel/PhotoEdit, Inc.; p. 262, AP/Wide World Photos; pp. 263, 264, 274, 292, 306, 318, (c)Comedy Central/Courtesy Everett Collection; p. 265, Dave Mirra © 2004 America's Dairy Farmers and Milk Processors; p. 266, Raghu Rai/Magnum Photos; p. 267, Stand Honda/Getty Images; p. 268, DK/Judith Miller Archive; p. 269, Lewis H. Hine/George Eastman House/Getty Images; p. 270, Philip Greenberg; p. 271, Reuters/Nikola Solic/Landov; p. 272, Dentsu/Nippon TV/The Kobal Collection; p. 273, CBS/Landov; p. 278, FDR Library; p. 283, Jim Young/Reuters/Landov; p. 290, AP/Wide World Photos; p. 291, AP/Wide World Photos; p. 293, top, Warner Bros./The Kobal Collection; bottom, Warner Bros./The Kobal Collection; p. 294, MGM/TKC/The Kobal Collection; p. 295, MGM/TKC/The Kobal Collection; p. 300, Universal/The Kobal Collection; p. 301, Universal/The Kobal Collection; p. 304, top, Lions Gate/The Kobal Collection; bottom, Lions Gate/The Kobal Collection; p. 305, top, Focus Features/The Kobal Collection; bottom, Focus Features/The Kobal Collection; p. 313, AP/Wide World Photos; p. 317, DILBERT: © Scott Adams/Dist. by United Feature Syndicate, Inc.; p. 321, Selznick/United Artists/The Kobal Collection; p. 323, Selznick/United Artists/The Kobal Collection; p. 332, ODT, Inc.; p. 333, ODT, Inc.; pp. 334, 341, 344, 360, 374, 386, Frank Lukasseck/ Corbis; p. 335, PocketX Software Inc.; p. 336, David G. Dwhurst Photography; p. 338, Printed with permission from the American Medical Association; p. 339, Image courtesy of Dr. Stephen Smith, Oxford University Centre for Functional MRI of the Brain; p. 340, Mark Scheuern /Alamy; p. 352, Kim Karpeles /Alamy; p. 361, left, Courtesy Everett Collection; right, Comumbia/The Kobal Collection; p. 361, CLADD Company/Warner Bros./The Kobal Collection; p. 364, top, AP/Wide World Photos; bottom, Simon Kwong/Reuters/Landov; p. 365, top, Eduardo Kac, *GFP Bunny, 2000. Alba, the fluorescent rabbit*. Courtesy the artist and Julia Friedman Gallery; bottom left, Bill Scanga; bottom right, Courtesy Daniel Lee and OK Harris Works of Art; p. 369, Philippe Plailly/Photo Researchers, Inc.; p. 373, © CBS / Courtesy the Everett Collection; p. 400, Jay B. Sauceda Industries; p. 401, Jay B. Sauceda Industries; pp. 402, 410, 417, 424, 442, 456, Anthony Scibilia /Art Resource, NY; p. 403, TM & ©20th Century Fox/Courtesy the Everett Collection; p. 404, Courtesy Giro; p. 405, Jay B. Sauceda Industries; p. 406, The Advertising Archives; p. 407, left, RKO/The Kobal Collection; right, Courtesy the Everett Collection; p. 408, left, Jay B Sauceda Industries; right, Jay B Sauceda Industries; p. 409, Jay B. Sauceda Industries; p. 411, Corbis;

p. 414, Courtesy of Humanscale Corporation; p. 420, Jay B Sauceda Industries; p. 425, Courtesy of Unilever; p. 428, Andrea Agelescu/Corbis; p. 432, © Copyright 2005 Christo Komarnitski. All Rights Reserved.; p. 443, © GM Corp.; p. 452, Torin Boyd; p. 459, Courtesy the Everett Collection; p. 462, left, Warner Bros./Photofest; right, Columbia Pictures/Photofest; p. 466, Robert Harding World Imagery/Getty Images; p. 468, Library of Congress; p. 470, Army National Guard Recruiting-1800GoGuard.com; pp. 472, 484, 496, 522, 523, 538, Newscom; p. 475, Mark Gibson/Index Stock Imagery; p. 476, AP/Wide World Photos; p. 477, Todd Heisler/Polaris; p. 478, PETA; p. 479, Margaret Bourke-White/Time-Life Pictures/Getty Images; p. 482, Copyright, Tribune Media Services, Inc. All Rights Reserved. Reprinted with Permission.; p. 485, Courtesy Vintage Vantage; p. 500, AP/Wide World Photos; p. 501, Lauren Greenfield/VII; p. 504, Ross MacDonald; p. 505, Tony Cenicola/The New York Times/Redux; p. 506, Tony Cenicola/The New York Times/Redux; p. 519, Peter Menzel Photography; p. 520, Peter Menzel Photography; p. 521, Peter Menzel Photography; p. 527, AP/Wide World Photos; p. 531, Jonathan Maus/BikePortland.org; p. 533, Fred Conrad/The New York Times/Redux; p. 537, Josh Merwin/The New York Times/Redux; p. 542, left and right Library of Congress; p. 543, left and right, Library of Congress; p. 546, Bettina Salomon/Photo Researchers, Inc.; p. 547, bottom, Laurence Monneret/Stone Allstock/Getty Images; top, Kevin Horan/Mira.com; p. 548, top, Gratton/Photo Researchers, Inc.; middle, Jim Varney /Photo Researchers, Inc.; bottom, David Young-Wolff/PhotoEdit, Inc.

TEXT CREDITS

Chapter 1

p. 19, Screen Shot "Daily Kos" with excerpt from "FISA Fight: Get Ready for Round 3" by mcjoan, January 25, 2008. http://www.dailykos.com © Kos Media, LLC. Reprinted by permission. **p. 27,** Screen shot "Michael Jordan's The Steak House NYC," www.theglaziergroup.com. Used by permission of The Glazier Group. **p. 31,** Seamus Heaney, from "Clearances 3." From *Opened Ground: Selected Poems 1966-1998* by Seamus Heaney. Copyright © 1998 by Seamus Heaney. Reprinted by permission of Farrar, Straus and Giroux, LLC. From *The Haw Lantern*, published by Faber and Faber Ltd. © 1987 by Seamus Heaney. Reprinted by permission of Faber and Faber Ltd. **p. 33,** Screen shot "Lara Croft Tomb Raider Online Game," http://www.tombraider.com. Used by permission of Eidos Interactive, Ltd. **p. 45,** Thomas Washington, "A Librarian's Lament: Books Are a Hard Sell," *Washington Post.com*, January 21, 2007. Reprinted by permission of the author. **p. 50,** From Steven Johnson, "Watching TV Makes You Smarter," *The New York Times Magazine*, April 24, 2005, adapted from *Everything Bad Is Good for You* by Steven Johnson. Copyright © 2005 by Steven Johnson. Used by permission of Riverhead Books, an imprint of Penguin Group (USA) Inc.

Chapter 2

p. 55, Screen Shot from "Cole and Bobby...At the Movies," www.coleandbobby.com. Reprinted with permission. **p. 80,** From *The 9/11 Commission Report*, 2004. **p. 83,** NASA Screen shot, www.NASA.Gov/multimedia/index.html June 13, 2008.

Chapter 3

p. 95, Wikipedia screen shot, Johnny Depp, http://en.wikipedia.org/wiki/Johnny.Depp. **p. 101,** Judy Brady, "Why I Want a Wife," *Ms.* 1971. © 1970 by Judy Brady. Reprinted by permission of the author. **p. 107,** From *I Could Tell You Stories: Sojourns in the Land of Memory* by Patricia Hampl. Copyright © 1999 by Patricia Hampl. Used by permission of W.W. Norton & Company, Inc. **p. 110,** "The Veil" from *Persepolis: The Story of a Childhood* by Marjane Satrapi, translated by Mattias Ripa and Blake Ferris, translation copyright © 2003 by L'Association, Paris, France. Used by permission of Pantheon Books, a division of Random House, Inc. **p. 118,** Alison Stateman, "Postcards from the Edge," *The New York Times*, June 15, 2003. From The New York Times on the Web, © 2003, The New York Times Company. Reprinted with permission. **p. 125,** Annie Dillard, pp. 45-9 from *An American Childhood* by Annie Dillard. Copyright © 1987 by Annie Dillard. Reprinted by permission of HarperCollins Publishers. **p. 129,** Susan Bordo, "The Empire of Images in Our World of Bodies" from *Unbearable Weight: Feminism, Western Culture, and the Body*, Tenth Anniversary Edition. Copyright © 2004, The Regents of the University of California. Reprinted by permission of the University of California Press. **p. 138,** Josie Appleton, "The Body Piercing Project," *spiked-online*, July 2003. Copyright © 2003 spiked Ltd. Used by permission. **p. 144,** Henry Louis Gates, Jr., "In the Kitchen" from *Colored People: A Memoir*. Copyright © 1994 by Henry Louis Gates, Jr. Used by permission of Alfred A. Knopf, a division of Random House, Inc. **p. 151,** Lan Tran, "Lone Stars" as appeared in *Waking Up American: Coming of Age Biculturally* ed. by Angela Jane Fountas. Reprinted by permission of Lan Tran. **p. 156,** Alice Walker, "Everyday Use," from *In Love & Trouble: Stories of Black Women*. Copyright © 1973 by Alice Walker. Reprinted by permission of Houghton Mifflin Harcourt Publishing Company. **p. 163,** Sherman Alexie, "I Hated Tonto (Still Do)", *Los Angeles Times*, June 28, 1998, p. 9. Reprinted by permission of Nancy Stauffer Associates on behalf of the author.

Chapter 4

p. 181, Microsoft Live Labs ™, "Photosynth Technology Preview." © Microsoft Corporation. Used by permission of Alex Daley, Group Product Manager, Microsoft Live Labs. **p. 194,** "Our Sprawling, Supersize Utopia." Adapted with the permission of Simon & Schuster Adult Publishing Group from *On Paradise Drive* by David Brooks. Copyright © 2004 by David Brooks. Originally appeared in *The New York Times Magazine*, April 4, 2004. **p. 202,** Jenny Attiyeh, "My Ghost Town: A Vanishing Personal History," *High Country News*, November 5, 2001. Copyright © 2001 Jenny Attiyeh. Reprinted by permission of the author. **p. 205,** Glenn Reynolds, "The Comfy Chair Revolution" from *An Army of Davids*. First appeared in *TCS Daily*, January 16, 2002. Reprinted by permission of the author. **p. 216,** Charles Bowden, "Our Wall," *National Geographic*, May 2007. © Charles Bowden/National Geographic Image Collection. Reprinted by permission of the National Geographic Society. **p. 222,** Benjamin Alire Sáenz, "The Ninth Dream: War (in the City in Which I Live) from *Dreaming the End of War*. Copyright © 2006 by Benjamin Alire Sáenz. Reprinted with the permission of Copper Canyon Press, www.coppercanyonpress.org. **p. 226,** Randal C. Archibold, "Far From Home, Mexicans Sing Age-Old Ballads of a New Life," *The New York Times*, July 6, 2007. From The New York Times on the Web, © 2007 The New York Times Company. Reprinted with permission. **p. 232,** "Chapter 12" from *The Grapes of Wrath* by John Steinbeck. Copyright 1939, renewed © 1967 by John Steinbeck. Used by permission of Viking Penguin, a division of Penguin Group (USA) Inc. **p. 236,** "Part Three – 9" from *On the Road* by Jack Kerouac. Copyright © 1955, 1957 by Jack Kerouac; renewed © 1983 by Stella Kerouac, renewed © 1985 by Stella Kerouac and Jan Kerouac. Used by permission of Viking Penguin, a division of Penguin Group (USA) Inc. **p. 242,** Holland Cotter, "On My Own Road," *The New York Times*, September 2, 2007. From The New York Times on the Web, © 2007 The New York Times Company. Reprinted with permission.

Chapter 5

p. 271, Screen shot from Human Rights Watch, http://hrw.org. Copyright © 2007 Human Rights Watch. **p. 275,** Gene Santoro, "When No Life Was Touched By War," *World War II*, September 2007. Reprinted with permission of *World War II Magazine*, Copyright © 2008, Weider History Group. **p. 284,** Susan Sontag, excerpt from *Regarding the Pain of Others*. Copyright © 2003 by Susan Sontag. Reprinted by permission of Farrar, Straus and Giroux, LLC. **p. 296,** Amy Taubin, "Fear of Black Cinema" from *Sight & Sound*, August 2002. Copyright © 2002 British Film Institute. Used by permission. **p. 302,** Brian D. Johnson, "The Collateral Damage of *Crash*," *Maclean's*, April 3, 2006. Reprinted by permission of *Maclean's Magazine*. **p. 307,** Henry Jenkins, "From YouTube to YouNiversity," *The Chronicle of Higher Education*, February 2007. Reprinted by permission of the author. **p. 314,** Brad Stone, "MySpace to Discuss Effort to Customize Ads," *The New York Times*, September 18, 2007. From The New York Times on the Web, © 2007 The New York Times Company. Reprinted with permission. **p. 316,** Scott Adams, "Giving Stuff Away on the Internet," *The Wall Street Journal* (Opinion), November 1, 2007. By permission of the author.

Chapter 6

p. 337, Felix Oberholzer-Gee and Koleman Strumpf, from "The Effect of File Sharing on Record Sales: An Empirical Analysis," *Journal of Political Economy*, 115:1 (February 2007). Published by The University of Chicago Press, Copyright © 2007, The University of Chicago Press. Reprinted by permission. **p. 342,** Images from Ready.gov, http://www.ready.gov. **p. 343,** Screenshot from National Geographic website reprinted by permission of National Geographic Maps and

551

Digital. Satellite imagery "Murray-Darling Basin" used courtesy of GeoEye. **pp. 345–347,** Screenshot from National Geographic website reprinted by permission of National Geographic Maps and Digital. Satellite imagery "Murray-Darling Basin" used courtesy of GeoEye. **p. 348,** Evan Ratliff, "Google Maps Is Changing the Way We See the World," *Wired* Magazine, Issue 15.07, June 26, 2007. Reprinted by permission of the author. **p. 353,** "Now on Google Maps: You" by the Denver Post Editorial Board, *The Denver Post*, June 10, 2007. Reprinted by permission of The Denver Post. **p. 354,** Elizabeth Bishop, "The Map" from *The Complete Poems: 1927-1979* by Elizabeth Bishop. Copyright © 1979, 1983 by Alice Helen Methfessel. Reprinted by permission of Farrar, Straus and Giroux, LLC. **p. 355,** Susan Neville, "On Maps and Globes" from *Fabrications: Essays on Making Things and Making Meaning*. © 2001 by Susan Neville. Reprinted by permission of MacAdam/Cage Publishing. **p. 362,** Nicholas Wade, "Genetic Engineers Who Don't Just Tinker," *The New York Times*, July 8, 2007. From The New York Times on the Web, © 2007 The New York Times Company. Reprinted with permission. **p. 366,** Natalie Angier, "Pursuing Synthetic Life, Dazzled by Reality," *The New York Times*, February 5, 2008. From The New York Times on the Web, © 2008 The New York Times Company. Reprinted with permission. **p. 368,** Max Houck, "CSI Reality," *Scientific American*, July 2006, Vol. 295, No. 1, pp. 84-89. Reprinted with permission. Copyright © 2006 by Scientific American, Inc. All rights reserved. **p. 375,** Andrea Foster, "The Avatars of Research," *The Chronicle of Higher Education*, September 30, 2005. Reprinted by permission. **p. 378 left,** Image from website of Idaho State University, Idaho Bioterrorism Awareness and Preparedness Program: Fig. 4 "Potential for Creating Realistic Engaging Scenarios" found at http://www.isu.edu/irh/IBAPP/simulations.shtml Reprinted by permission. **p. 378 right,** Image from website of The Ohio State University Department of Women's Studies: "A Nineteenth Century Woman in a Conservatory in Second Life" found at http://people.cohums.ohio-state.edu/collingwood7/minerva/contest.html. Reprinted by permission of Dr. Sharon Collingwood. **p. 379,** Alan Sipress, "Does Virtual Reality Really Need a Sheriff?" From *The Washington Post*, June 2, 2007. © 2007 The Washington Post. All rights reserved. Used by permission and protected by the Copyright Laws of the United States. The printing, copying, redistribution, or retransmission of the material without express written permission is prohibited. **p. 381,** Steven Johnson, "This Is Your Brain on Video Games" from *Discover Magazine*, July 9, 2007. Reprinted by permission of the author. **p. 392,** Screenshot from "Iamtryingtobelieve.com" website, http://iamtryingtobelieve.com/whatis Reprinted by permission of 42 Entertainment.

Chapter 7

p. 412, Michael Bierut, "To Hell With the Simple Paper Clip," *DesignObserver.com*, July 14, 2004. Reprinted by permission of the author. **p. 415,** "A Machine for Sitting," interview by Pilar Viladas, *The New York Times Magazine*, November 30, 2003. © 2003 The New York Times Company. Reprinted by permission. **p. 421,** Seth Stevenson, "Head Case: The Mesmerizing Ad for Headache Gel," *Slate*, July 24, 2006. Reprinted by permission of the author. **p. 426,** From DOVE® "Campaign for Real Beauty." http://www.campaignforrealbeauty.com. Photo, text, and DOVE® trademark used courtesy of Unilever. **p. 429,** Virginia Postrel, "The Truth About Beauty," *The Atlantic Monthly*, March 2007. Copyright 2007 by The Atlantic Monthly. Reproduced with permission of The Atlantic Monthly in the format Textbook via Copyright Clearance Center. **p. 433,** Daniel Akst, "Looks *Do* Matter," *The Wilson Quarterly*, Summer 2005. Reprinted by permission of the author. **p. 444,** "First Things First Manifesto 2000" from *Émigré Magazine*, No. 51, 1999. Copyright © 1999. Reprinted with permission. **p. 446,** Screen shot from Adbusters website. Courtesy www.adbusters.org. **p. 447,** Linda Baker, "Are You Ready for Some Unswooshing." This article first appeared in *Salon.com*, October 8, 2003, at http://www.salon.com. An online version remains in the Salon archives. Reprinted with permission. **p. 453,** Martin Fackler, "Fearing Crime, Japanese Wear the Hiding Place," *The New York Times*, October 20, 2007. From The New York Times on the Web, © 2007 The New York Times Company. Reprinted with permission.

Chapter 8

p. 471, From *America's Army PC Game Vision and Realization: A Look at the Artistry, Technique, and Impact of the United States Army's Groundbreaking Tool for Strategic Communication* (2004), produced by The United States Army and the MOVES Institute. **p. 480,** "Our View on College Affordability: Boola-boola for Yale" and graph "Expensive Educations" by Robert W. Ahrens, Copyright *USA Today*, January 18, 2008. Reprinted with permission; **p. 481,** "Opposing View: Elite Schools Drive Costs" by William G. Durden and Robert J. Massa. From *USA Today*, January 18, 2008. Reprinted with permission from USA Today and William Durden. **p. 483,** Screen shot from PotterCast website "Harry Potter Fans for Darfur," July 2007, http://pottercast.the-leaky-cauldron.org/page/darfur. Reprinted by permission of PotterCast. **p. 489,** Reprinted with permission from Courtney Martin, "Generation Overwhelmed," *The American Prospect Online*, October 22, 2007. www.prospect.org. The American Prospect, 2000 L Street NW, Suite 717, Washington, DC 20036. All rights reserved. **p. 491,** From Rockthevote, January 2005. Copyright © 2005 Rockthevote. Reprinted by permission. **p. 492,** Redeem the Vote, homepage from www.redeemthevote.com. Reprinted by permission. **p. 493 top,** Screen shot from the homepage of Voto Latino, www.votolatino.org. Reprinted by permission. **p. 493 bottom,** PunkVoter, Homepage, September 2004. www.punkvoter.com. Copyright © 2004 PunkVoter. Reprinted by permission. **p. 494,** Mike Connery, "Journalist Cheat Sheet: Eleven Tips for Reporting the Youth Vote" from blog post November 18, 2007, http://futuremajority.com/node/794. Reprinted by permission of the author. **p. 497,** Michael S. Rosenwald, "Why America Has to Be Fat," *The Washington Post*, January 22, 2006, F01. © 2006 The Washington Post. All rights reserved. Used by permission and protected by the Copyright Laws of the United States. The printing, copying, redistribution, or retransmission of the material without express written permission is prohibited. **p. 502,** "Sixty-Nine Cents" by Gary Shteyngart. Copyright © 2007. First appeared in *The New Yorker*, September 3, 2007. Reprinted with permission of the Denise Shannon Literary Agency, Inc. All rights reserved. **p. 504,** Kim Severson, "Be It Ever So Homespun, There's Nothing Like Spin," *The New York Times*, January 3, 2007. From The New York Times on the Web, © 2007 The New York Times Company. Reprinted with permission. **p. 507,** Michael Pollan, "Why Bother?" from *The New York Times Magazine*, April 20, 2008. Copyright © 2008 by Michael Pollan. Reprinted by permission of International Creative Management, Inc. **p. 512,** Jonathan Rauch, "Will Frankenfood Save the Planet?" from *The Atlantic Monthly*, October 2003. Copyright 2003 by The Atlantic Monthly. Reproduced with permission of The Atlantic Monthly in the format Textbook via Copyright Clearance Center. **p. 524,** Mark Yaconelli, "Christian Megastar: Bono on Record," *The Christian Century*, March 21, 2006, V. 123, I. 6. Copyright © 2006 by the *Christian Century*. Reprinted by permission from the March 21, 2006 issue of the *Christian Century*. Subscriptions $49/yr from PO Box 700, Mt. Morris, IL 61054. (800) 208-4097. **p. 526,** David Heim, "Breakfast with Bono." Copyright © 2006 by *Christian Century*. Reprinted by permission from the March 21, 2006 issue of the *Christian Century*. Subscriptions $49/yr from PO Box 700, Mt. Morris, IL 61054. (800) 208-4097. **p. 528,** Paul Theroux, "The Rock Star's Burden," *The New York Times* OP-ED, December 15, 2005. Reprinted by permission. **p. 532,** From The New York City Street Memorial Project Press Kit. www.ghostbikes.org/new-york-city. Reprinted by permission. **p. 534,** Alex Williams, "Realistic Idealists," *The New York Times*, September 11, 2005. From The New York Times on the Web, © 2005 The New York Times Company. Reprinted with permission.

INDEX

A

Abu Ghraib mural, in Sadr City, Iraq, 262, 263
"A Conversation with Ken Burns" (Santoro), 275–277
Adams, Scott
   Dilbert cartoon, 317
   "Giving Stuff Away on the Internet," 316
Adbuster Web site, 446
advertisements
   branding and, 264, 270
   Dove's "Campaign for Real Beauty," 424–427
   Got Milk? campaign, 264, 265
   "HeadOn: apply directly to the forehead" campaign, 420, 421–423
   Mary J. Blige GAP Red Collection, 406
   military, 470–471
   of Pepsi, David Beckham in, 98
   viral marketing and, 61, 76
   writing an analysis of, 72–73
advocacy, politics and, 472–549
affordability of college education, debate on, 480–481
AIDS Quilt, Washington DC (photo), 161
Akst, Daniel, "Looks *Do* Matter," 433–441
Alexie, Sherman, "I Hated Tonto (Still Do)", 163–164
Al Haggan family (Kuwait), weekly food consumption by (photo), 520
"A Librarian's Lament: Books Are a Hard Sell" (Washington), 45–46
American Gothic (Parks), 105
American Medical Association poster, 338
The American River Ganges (Nast), 37
America's Army: The Official U.S. Army Game (advertisement), 471
analytical texts, 24–25
   "She's very Charlie" (Cruz), 90–93
An American Childhood (Dillard), 125–127
Angier, Natalie, "Pursuing Synthetic Life, Dazzled by Reality," 366–367
animals
   animal rights poster, 478
   genetically engineered, images of, 364
anime, 272
Appleton, Josie, "The Body Piercing Project," 138–141
Archibold, Randal C., "Far From Home, Mexicans Sing Age-Old Ballads of a New Life," 226–229
architecture, 26, 28–29, 416–417
arguments, political. *see* political arguments
arrangement, in text, 39, 40–41
Attie, Alice, Harlem photographs, 190–191
Attiyeh, Jenny, "My Ghost Town: A Vanishing Personal History," 202–203
audience, for texts, 16–23
   reaching, 60–63
   when reading
      about identity, 96
      about places and environments, 182
      about politics and advocacy, 538
      about style, design, and culture, 402
      about technology and science, 334
      media texts, 264
   when writing
      about identity, 166
      about media, 318
      about places and environments, 248
      about politics and advocacy, 538
      about style, design, and culture, 456
      about technology and science, 386
auteur, filmmakers and, 319
"The Avatars of Research" (Foster), 375–378

B

Babin, Rex, immigration cartoon, 215
"Baby, You Mean the World of Warcraft to Me" (Spivey), 385
Bailey, Hannah, "Fitting and Preparing Pointe Shoes," 395–398
Baker, Linda, "Salon.com asks, 'Are you ready for some 'unswooshing' '?", 447–451
balance, in text, 39, 40
ballet slippers, instructions for tying, 394–398
bar graphs, 337
Beckham, David, in Pepsi advertisement, 98
"Be It Ever So Homespun, There's Nothing Like Spin" (Severson), 504–506
Benson, Harry, *Jubilant Clay*, 124
bicycles
   bike helmet design, 404
   Ghost Bike Project, New York City, 530–533
Bierut, Michael, "To Hell With the Simple Paper Clip," 412–413
Bishop, Elizabeth, "The Map" (poem), 354
Blackspot Sneaker, Web page for, 446
Blade Runner (movie), 360–361
Blige, Mary J., in GAP Red Collection advertisement, 406
blogs/blogging, 18–19
   Adams on, 316
Blonsky, Nikki (photo), 428
Blue Marble (photo), 344–345
Blue Marble project, images from, 346–347
body image
   design language and, 424–441
   sample readings, 128–149
"The Body Piercing Project" (Appleton), 138–141
Bono
   Theroux on, 528–530
   on third-world debt relief, 522–523
   Yaconelli on, 524–527
Book of the Dead, 4
borderlands, 214–230
Bordo, Susan, "The Empire of Images in Our World of Bodies," 129–135
Borgman, Jim, *I Want to Be. . . .*, 99
Borrell del Caso, Pierre, *Escaping Criticism*, 12–13
Bourke-White, Margaret, *Breadline During Louisville, Kentucky Flood* (photo), 479
Bowden, Charles, "Our Wall," 216–220
Boyd, Torin, *Japanese Vending Machine Dress Used as Urban Camouflage* (photo), 452
brain maps, 339
branding, 264, 270
Breadline During Louisville, Kentucky Flood (Bourke-White), 479
Bretag, Ryan, "Welcome to the Texas State University Second Life Campus," 213
Brokeback Mountain (movie), 305
Brooks, David, "Our Sprawling Supersize Utopia," 194–199
Buddha statue, Afghanistan, 6
bumper stickers, political (photo), 475
burned soldier, George W. Bush and, 282–283
Bush, George W., and burned soldier, 282–283
Butler, Jonathan, "Visual Images of National Identity: Propaganda Posters of the Great War," 541–544

C

Cadillac Ranch (sculpture), 235
Café Montmartre (Harrod), 189
Campaign for Real Beauty (Dove advertisement), 25
"The Campaign for Real Beauty Background," 426–427
Cans Seurat (Jordan), 8–9
car, with political bumper stickers (photo), 475
Caravaggio, Michelangelo da, *David and Goliath*, 43
car design
   GMC Yukon Hybrid, 442–443
   jeep.com and, 408
   Lexus LCD control display, 336
Carr, David, "Telling War's Deadly Story at Just Enough Distance," 280–282
cartoons
   on immigration, 215, 482
   I Want to Be. . . . (Borgman), 99
   Obesity Planet (Komarnitski), 432
Casablanca (movie), 292–293
cell phone, photo contact displays, 335
child labor, media presentation of, 264, 269, 271
choice, factors influencing, 496–521
"Christian Megastar: Bono on Record" (Yaconelli), 524–527
citing sources, in politics and advocacy writing, 540
Clamer, Matthias, *Young Men Entering Cowboy Saloon* (photo), 155
"Clearances" (Heany), 31
CNN, and YouTube Presidential debates, 267
Cole, Nat King (photo), 149
Cole and Bobby . . . at the Movies!!! (Web site), 55
collage, expressing ideas in, 165
"The Collateral Damage of *Crash*" (Johnson), 302–303
college affordability, debate on, 480–481
Colón, Ernie, and Sid Jacobson, *The 9/11 Report: A Graphic Adaptation*, 80, 81
"The Comfy Chair Revolution" (Reynolds), 205–211
communication
   changing nature of, 2–3
   framework of, 7
   media used for, 3–7
community service, 534–537
comparison and/or contrast project, writing, 68–69
composing texts, 54–93
   audience and, 60–63
   in digital environments, 3
   medium for, 77–83
   purpose and. *see* purpose
   reading and, 2–3
   research for, 84–87
   structure and. *See* structure and composition, of texts
Connery, Mike, "Journalist Cheat Sheet: Eleven Tips for Reporting the Youth Vote," 494–495
context, 36–37
   deciding on, 64–66
   explaining, 65
   when reading
      about identity, 96
      about places and environments, 182

about politics and advocacy, 472–473, 539
about science and technology, 334
about style, design, and culture, 402
media texts, 264
when writing
about places and environments, 248
about politics and advocacy, 539
about style, design, and culture, 457
contrast and/or compare project, writing, 68–69
contrasts, in text, 39, 43
conventions, genres expressed through, 30–31
Cook, Diane, and Len Jenshal, *Tijuana, Mexico* (photo), 220–221
Corner, Donald, and Jenny Young, *Villa Savoye by Le Corbusier* (photo), 416–417
corrido (Mexican folk ballad), 226–229
Cotter, Holland, "On My Road," 242–245
Crash (movie), 304
Johnson on, 302–303
critical reading. *see* reading texts
Cruz, Jacqueline, "She's very Charlie," 90–93
CSI (TV show), still from, 372–373
"*CSI*: Reality" (Houck), 368–372
Cuban poster art, 58
culture
of design, 442–455
everyday choices and, 496–521
writing about, 456–469
Curtis, Edward, Native Americans photos by, 162

D

Daily Kos (blog), 18–19
D'Aluisio, Faith, and Peter Menzel, *Hungry Planet* (photos), 519–521
Damn! (Tsinhnahjinnie), 165
Dargis, Manohla, "Defending Goliath: Hollywood and the Art of the Blockbuster," 47–49
data, visual representation on, 337
David and Goliath (Caravaggio), 43
debate, on college affordability, 480–481
"Defending Goliath: Hollywood and the Art of the Blockbuster" (Dargis), 47–49
delight, texts that, 26
demographics, audience and, 17, 20, 21, 63
The Denver Post, "Now on Google Maps," 353
Depp, Johnny
cover photo of, 94
Wikipedia entry for, 95
descriptions
reading, 182
writing, 67–68
descriptive writing, 67–68
design
analyzing an everyday text, 458–462
context for, 402, 463–468
culture of, 442–455
of everyday things, 410–423
language of, 402, 408
politics and advocacy texts, 474
politics of, 442–455
technology and science texts, 334, 387
writing about, 456–469
design language, 402
and body image, 424–441
from jeep.com, 408
details
examining and interpreting, 11–12
missing, reading for, 12, 15
in text composition, 89
about identity, 167
about places and environments, 249
for politics and advocacy, 474, 539
The Devil Wears Prada (movie), 403
Diffrient, Niels
chair design by, 414
on F-16 fighter jet design, 411
interview with (Viladas), 415–416

digital environments
composing in, 3
reading in, 4
Dilbert cartoon (Adams), 317
Dillard, Annie, excerpt from *An American Childhood,* 125–127
Disney World, Orlando, Florida (Pinney), 186
documenting sources, 87
citing correctly, 540
Dodge, *La Femme* advertisement, 17, 21
"Does Virtual Reality Need a Sheriff?" (Sipress), 379–380
doll, Muslim girl with, 103
Do the Right Thing (movie), 300–301
"The Dover" (floor plan), 193
Dove's "Campaign for Real Beauty"
advertisement, 424–425
background to, 426–427
Postrel on, 429–431
Drought refugees from Oklahoma camping by the roadside, Blythe, California (Lange), 97
Dürer, Albrecht, self-portraits, 117

E

EarthPulse Web site (National Geographic), 343
editing texts, 88–89
in politics and advocacy, 540
in technology and science, 387
editorial cartoons, on immigration, 215
educational texts, 25–26
Eggleston, William, *Memphis* (photo), 200
Eighteen Frogs with Pants Categorized by Color (Scanga), 365
Ellis, Dylan, "June 29, 1989," 459–462
"El Paso Street Art" (Grossinger), 224–225
e-mail, 30
emo fashion, 409
"The Empire of Images in Our World of Bodies" (Bordo), 129–135
environment. *see* places and environments
Escaping Criticism (Borrell del Caso), 12–13
ethnic identity, sample readings, 150–165
ethos, 25, 27, 473, 540
Evans, James, *Hallie's Hands,* 14
"Everyday Use" (Walker), 156–160
evidence. *see* details
experts, learning from, 86

F

Facebook, 306
Falke, Terry, *Trail to Balanced Rock* (photo), 180, 181
family life, images representing, 200–201
fan films, 54, 55
"Far From Home, Mexicans Sing Age-Old Ballads of a New Life" (Archibold), 226–229
Faulkner, Beau, "Year Zero: A Viral Marketing Promotion," 389–394
"Fear of a Black Cinema" (Taubin), 296–299
Feckler, Martin, "Japanese Wear the Hiding Place," 453–455
photo for, 452
F-16 Fighting Falcon (photo), 411
"Fidel" (Martínez), 59
field observation, 86–87, 255–256
Fifteen Untitled Works in Concrete (Judd), 15
figures of speech, 33
film, 72. *see also individual film titles; movie* entries
exploring director's influence upon, 319–326
fan-made, 54, 55
stories told by, 292–305
fine arts, 77–78
"First Things First Manifesto 2000" (Thirty-Three Designers), 444–445
"Fitting and Preparing Pointe Shoes" (Bailey), 395–398

flyers, displaying information, 340
focus/focal point
choosing, 56–59
identifying, 10, 11
when writing about places and environments, 248
food consumption, cultural aspects of, 496–521
Ford, Kate, on animal rights poster, 478
forensic science, 368–373
formality, in writing, 33
Foster, Andrea L., "The Avatars of Research," 375–378
Foster-Keddie, John, T-shirt design by, 484–485
Found Magazine, 36
Frankenstein (movie), 360–361
Freedom Chair design, by Niels Diffrient, 414
Friedman, Thomas L., "Generation Q," 487–488

G

Gable, Scott, on GMC Yukon Hybrid SUV, 442–443
"Gainesville: Selling Small-Town America" (Williamson), 251–254
Garcia, Jose F. and Benjamin, photo of, 227
Gates, Henry Louis, Jr., "In the Kitchen," 144–148
Gattaca (movie), 360–361
Gehry, Frank, architecture of, 28–29
"Generation Q" (Friedman), 487–488
genetic engineering, images of, 364
"Genetic Engineers Who Don't Just Tinker" (Wade), 362–363
genre
choosing, 67–76
identifying, 30–31
for media texts, 264
poems as examples of, 31
for reading
about identity, 96
about style, design, and culture, 402
about technology and science, 387
for writing
about identity, 166
about places and environments, 249
about politics and advocacy, 538–539
about style, design, and culture, 387
about technology and science, 387
Gerson, Michael, "Where the Avatars Roam," 212–213
GFP Bunny (Kac), 365
Ghost Bike Project, New York City, 530–533
Girl Culture (Greenfield), 500–501
Girl Worker in Cotton Mill (Hine), 264, 269
Giro Atmos bicycle helmet, 404
"Giving Stuff Away on the Internet" (Adams), 316
GMC Yukon Hybrid SUV, 442–443
Goldberg, Jim, images from *Raised by Wolves,* 122–123
"Google Maps Is Changing the Way We See the World" (Ratliff), 348–352
"Gordon Parks: Using Photographs to Spark Social Change" (Smith), 173–178
Got Milk? ad campaign, 264, 265
Grand Prismatic Spring, Yellowstone National Park (Muensch), 185
The Grapes of Wrath (Steinbeck), 232–234
graphic arts/novels, 72, 272
The 9/11 Report: A Graphic Adaptation (Jacobson and Colón), 80, 81
graphs, 337
Greenfield, Lauren, *Girl Culture* (photos), 500–501
Grossinger, Joe, "El Paso Street Art" (photos), 224–225
group identity, sample readings, 150–165
Guild Wars (online game), 374

H

Hallie's Hands (Evans), 14
Hampl, Patricia, "I Could Tell You Stories," 107–109
Harlem, New York, photographs of, 190–191
Harrod, Richard, *Café Montmartre* (photo), 189
Harry Potter podcast, political activism and, 483
"Head Case: The Mesmerizing Ad for a headache Gel" (Stevenson), 421–423
"HeadOn: apply directly to the forehead" advertising campaign, 420
  Stevenson on, 421–423
Heany, Seamus, "Clearances" (poem), 31
Heisler, Todd, photo by, 477
Help Build the Gigantic Factories (Mirzoyan and Ivanov), 58
Henry V (Shakespeare production photographs), 40–41
hierarchy, in text, 39
Hine, Lewis, *Girl Worker in Cotton Mill* (photo), 264, 269
Hobo-Dyer Equal Area Map Projections of the World, 332–333
Holding Cell, Maricopa County Jail (Ramey), 142
Holechek Bros., *The 305* (fan film), 54
home life, images representing, 193, 200–201
Hopper, Edward, *Nighthawks*, 104
Houck, Max M., "*CSI*: Reality," 368–372
Huang, Meixia, "Pay Attention to Them," 545–549
"Huge Democracy Geek Even Votes in Primaries" (The Onion), 486
Hungry Planet (Menzel and D'Aluisio), 519–521
Hurricane Katrina, image from, 184–185

I

"I Could Tell You Stories" (Hampl), 107–109
ideas, mapping of. *see* mapping knowledge
identity
  body image expressing, sample readings, 128–149
  of celebrities, 94–95
  group and ethnic, sample readings, 150–165
  memoirs expressing, sample readings, 106–127
  reading texts about, 96–165
  representations of, 97–105
  writing about, 166–179
"I Hated Tonto (Still Do)" (Alexie), 163–164
imagery, in sonnets, 31
images, 4–7. *see also* advertisements; maps; photography
  of brain, 339
  magnetic resonance, 339
  stories in. *see* narratives
  that explain. *see* mapping knowledge
"Images of History: The Hmong" (Lee), 327–329
immigration, cartoons on, 215, 482
immigration issues, reading about, 214–230
"India: A Culinary Experience" (Parekh), 257–260
information
  displaying on kiosk, 340
  gathering through field observation, 86–87, 255–256
  gathering through research, 84–87
  texts providing, 24–25
instructions
  composing set of, 394–398
  visual, 342
Internet, using for research, 85–86
"In the Kitchen" (Gates), 144–148
"Introducing the Hipster PDA" (Mann), 401
iPhone, 400–401
Iraq
  Abu Ghraib mural in Sadr City (photo), 262, 263
  "Most Wanted" playing cards, 264, 268
  prisoners of war (photo), 291
  woman voting in (photo), 476
Ivanov, A. and S. Mirzoyan, "Help Build the Gigantic Factories," 58
I Want to Be. . . . (Borgman), 99

J

Jacobson, Sid, and Ernie Colón, *The 9/11 Report: A Graphic Adaptation*, 80, 81
Japanese Vending Machine Dress Used as Urban Camouflage (Boyd), 452
"Japanese Wear the Hiding Place" (Martin), 453–455
  photo for, 452
jeep.com, design language from, 408
Jelly! Austin (Levine), 204
Jenkins, Henry, "YouTube to YouNiversity," 307–311
Jenshal, Len, and Diane Cook, *Tijuana, Mexico* (photo), 220–221
Johnson, Brian D. "The Collateral Damage of *Crash*" (Johnson), 302–303
Johnson, Steven
  "This Is Your Brain on Video Games," 381–384
  "Watching TV Makes You Smarter," 50–53
Jordan, Chris, *Cans Seurat*, 8–9
"Journalist Cheat Sheet: Eleven Tips for Reporting the Youth Vote" (Connery), 494–495
Jubilant Clay (Benson), 124
Judd, Donald, *Fifteen Untitled Works in Concrete*, 15
"June 29, 1989" (Ellis), 459–462
Juror No. 6 (Lee), 365

K

Kac, Edourdo, *GFP Bunny*, 365
Käsebier, Gertrude, *Zitkala-Sa* (photo), 162
Kerouac, Jack, 241 (photo)
  excerpt from "On the Road," 236–240
Kim Phuc, Pan Thi, photo of, 290
King Kong (movie), 407
kiosk, displaying printed flyers on, 340
knowledge, mapping of. *see* mapping knowledge
Komarnitski, Christo, *Obesity Planet* (political cartoon), 432
Krejci, Uwe, *Teenagers with Facial Piercings* (photo), 143

L

La Femme (automobile advertisement), 17, 21
Lange, Dorothea
  Drought refugees from Oklahoma camping by the roadside, Blythe, California (photo), 97
  Migrant Mother (photo), 65, 66
language
  of design. *see* design language
  as medium, 32
Lara Croft Tomb Raider online game, 33
Lee, Daniel, *Juror No. 6*, 365
Lee, Michael, "Images of History: The Hmong" (photo essay), 327–329
Levine, Jonathan M., *Jelly! Austin* (photo), 204
Lexus LCD screen, 336
library, using for research, 85
life sciences, texts and images in, 360–373
Lindisfarne Gospels, 5
Little Dog (Ulriksen), 42
Locher, Dick, cartoon on immigration, 482
logos, 25, 473, 540
"Lone Stars" (Tran), 151–154
"Looks *Do* Matter" (Akst), 433–441
Love Me Tender (movie poster), 100

M

magnetic resonance imaging, 339
"Make Love Not Warcraft" (*South Park* episode), 263
Mann, Merlin, "Introducing the Hipster PDA," 401
"The Map" (Bishop), 354
mapping knowledge, 344–359
  in life sciences, 360–373
  virtual worlds, 374–385
maps, 344–359
  projections, 332–333
Marley, Bob (photo), 148
Marsh, Stanley, *Cadillac Ranch* sculpture, 235
Martin, Courtney, "Generation Overwhelmed," 489–490
Martínez, Raul, *Fidel*, 59
Marting, Greg, bike helmet design by, 404
McCain, John, 2007 Presidential announcement, 35
McGuigan, Cathleen, "The McMansion Next Door: Why the American House Needs a Makeover," 418–419
McLuhan, Marshall, 7
"The McMansion Next Door: Why the American House Needs a Makeover" (McGuigan), 418–419
media clutter, 9
media/medium
  for communication, 3–7
  for reading
    about identity, 96
    about places and environments, 182
    about politics and advocacy, 472–473
    about style, design, and culture, 402
    about technology and science, 334
  media texts, 264
  for writing
    about identity, 166
    about media, 318–319
    about places and environments, 249
    about politics and advocacy, 473
    about style, design, and culture, 387
    about technology and science, 387
media texts
  citizens making, 306–317
  composing, 77–83, 318–319, 334
  examining, 32–35
  film stories, 292–305
  reading, 264–273
  technology and science, 387
  war coverage, 274–291
  writing about, 318–329
medical research, artwork inspired by, 365
memoirs
  composing, examples of, 167–178
  sample readings, 106–127
Memphis (Eggleston), 200
Menzel, Peter, and Faith D'Aluisio, *Hungry Planet* (photos), 519–521
message(s)
  assessing level of, 17
  media delivery of, 32, 318
  on T-shirts. *See* T-shirt messages
Michael Jordan's The Steak House, N.Y.C. (Web site), 27
Microsoft, Photosynth technology, 181
Migrant Mother (Lange), 65, 66
military recruitment, advertisements for, 470–471
"mindful eating" therapy session (photo), 500
minimalism, 12, 15
Mirra, Dave, in *Got Milk?* ad campaign, 264, 265
Mirzoyan, S. and A. Ivanov, *Help Build the Gigantic Factories*, 58
"Most Wanted" playing cards (Iraq war), 264, 268
movie posters, 100, 231, 361, 407
movies, launch media for, 3
Muensch, David, *Grand Prismatic Spring, Yellowstone National Park* (photo), 185
multimedia, 79

multimedia events, Web pages as, 3
NASA, 82-83
multiple audiences, 60
murals
   of Abu Ghraib, in Sadr City, Iraq, 262, 263
   El Paso Street Art (Grossinger), 224-225
Muslim girl, with doll, 103
My Butt Is Big (Nike), 20, 25
"My Ghost Town: A Vanishing Personal History" (Attiyeh), 202-203
MySpace, 306
   Stone on, 314-315
"MySpace Data Mining" (Stone), 314-315

N

napalm attack, Vietnamese villagers fleeing (photo), 290
narratives, writing, 67-68
NASA
   earth images from space, 344-347
   multimedia page, 82-83
Nast, Thomas, *The American River Ganges*, 37
National Geographic *EarthPulse* Web site, 343
National Guard recruitment (advertisement), 470-471
Native Americans
   images of, 162
   in political cartoon, 482
Natomo family (Mali), weekly food consumption by (photo), 521
A Navaho (Curtis), 162
needs, of audiences, 61
Neville, Susan, "On Maps and Globes," 355-359
Newspaper Rock, 341
news stories, 334
New York City Street Memorial Project, 530-533
Nighthawks (Hopper), 104
Nike, *My Butt Is Big*, 20, 25
The 9/11 Commission Report, 80
The 9/11 Report: A Graphic Adaptation (Jacobson and Colón), 80, 81
Nintendo Wii controller, 405
Nissan Motors advertising campaign, 76
Nixon, Sean, "The Transformation of American Architecture during the 1920s and 1930s," 464-468
"*North by Northwest* and *Spellbound*: Identifibly Hitchcock" (Wooten), 320-326
North by Northwest (movie), 294-295
   exploring director's influence upon, 319-326
"Now on Google Maps" *(The Denver Post)*, 353

O

Obama, Barack, 2007 Presidential announcement, 34
Obesity Planet (Komarnitski), 432
online games, 374
   Lara Croft Tomb Raider, 33
"On Maps and Globes" (Neville), 355-359
"On My Road" (Cotter), 242-245
"On the Road" (Kerouac), 236-240
oral presentations, preparing, 74-75
Oreck Special Edition XL Ultra Vacuum Cleaner, writing about, 56, 57
organization, of material. *see* structure and composition, of texts
"Our Sprawling Supersize Utopia" (Brooks), 194-199
"Our Wall" (Bowden), 216

P

Parekh, Kruti, "India: A Culinary Experience," 257-260
Paris Casino, The Strip Las Vegas (photo), 183
Parks, Gordon
   American Gothic, 105
   "Gordon Parks: Using Photographs to Spark Social Change" (Smith), 173-178

pathos, 25-26, 473, 540
patterns, in text, 38
"Pay Attention to Them" (Huang), 545-549
People for the Ethical Treatment of Animals (PETA), 478
Pepsi advertisement, David Beckham in, 98
Persepolis (Satrapi), 110-116
personal associations, context and, 36
personal memoirs, composing, examples of, 167-178
persuasive texts, 25-26
PETA (People for the Ethical Treatment of Animals), 478
petroglyphs, 341
photo essay, composing, 327-329
photographs, as texts, 8-9, 14. *see also individual photograph titles*
   changing audience and, 18, 22-23
   places and environments, 183-187, 189-191
photography, 78
   "rule of thirds" in, 39, 41
   war. *see* war photography
Photosynth (Microsoft), 181
Pinney, Melissa Ann, *Disney World, Orlando, Florida*, 186
places and environments
   analyzing representation of, 250-254
   borderlands, 214-230
   home and work, 192-213
   observing and analyzing public space, 255-260
   photo images of, 183-187, 189-191
   poetry about, 188
   reading about, 182-191
   road travel and, 230-247
   writing about, 248-261
Pleasantville (movie), 200
PocketX Software, photo contact displays, 335
poetry
   "Clearances" (Heany), 31
   as genre example, 31
   "Route 66" (Troup), 188
   "Sonnet 130" (Shakespeare), 31
   "The Map" (Bishop), 354
   "War (in the City in Which I Live)" (Sáenz), 222-223
point of view, in text, 39, 42
political argument, analyzing, 540-544
political bumper stickers, car with (photo), 475
political activism, 483, 522-537
political announcements, 34-35
political arguments
   analyzing, 540-544
   writing, 73-74
   types of, 539-540
political cartoons, 432
   on immigration, 482
political posters, 57, 58-59
political street artists, 530-531
political texts, 471
   reading, 472-537
   writing, 538-549
politics
   and advocacy, 472-549
   of design, 442-455
Pollan, Michael, "Why Bother?", 507-511
Pool, Smiley N., Hurricane Katrina photo, 184-185
position paper, writing, 70
"Postcards from the Edge" (Stateman), 118-121
posters
   animal rights, 478
   informational, printed flyers as, 340
   movies, 100, 231, 361, 407
   political, 57, 58-59
   public health, 338
Postrel, Virginia, "The Truth About Beauty," 429-431

Pottercast Web page, 483
Presidential announcements, 34-35
Presidential debates, on YouTube, 267
Princess Mononoke (animated film), 264, 272
printed flyers, displaying information, 340
prisoners of war (photo), 291
problem/solution project, preparing, 71
proofreading, technology and science texts, 387
public health poster, 338
public service announcement, creating, 545-549
public space, observing and analyzing, 255-260
Punkvoter Web site, 493
Puppy Love (Ulriksen), 42
purpose, 24-29
   deciding on, 64-66
   when reading
      about identity, 96
      about places and environments, 182
      about politics and advocacy, 472
      about style, design, and culture, 402
      media texts, 264
   when writing
      about media, 318
      about places and environments, 248
      about politics and advocacy, 538
      about style, design, and culture, 456
      about technology and science, 386
"Pursuing Synthetic Life, Dazzled by Reality" (Angier), 366-367

R

racial discrimination, images portraying, 246-247
Raised by Wolves (Goldberg), 122-123
Ramey, A., *Holding Cell, Maricopa County Jail* (photo), 142
Ratliff, Evan, "Google Maps Is Changing the Way We See the World," 348-352
Rauch, Jonathan, "Will Frankenfood Save the Planet?", 512-518
Razanne (doll), 103
reading
   and composing, 2-3
   in digital environments, 4
reading texts, 8-53
   about politics and advocacy, 472-549
   about technology and science, 334-399
   for context and relationship, 36-37
   for missing detail, 12, 15
   rhetorically, 10
   structure and composition in, 38-43
   for subject or focus, 10-15
ready.gov safety images, 342
"Realistic idealists" (Williams), 534-537
"Redeem the Vote" Web site, 492
Regarding the Pain of Others (Sontag), 284-289
reports, writing, 69-70
research
   field observation, tips on, 86-87
   human genome, artwork inspired by, 365
   for text composition, 84-87
      in politics and advocacy, 539
      in technology and science, 386
responses, writing, 70
Revis family (United States), weekly food consumption by (photo), 519
revising texts, 88-89, 319, 387
   media texts, 319
   in politics and advocacy, 540
   in technology and science, 387
Reynolds, Glenn, "The Comfy Chair Revolution," 205-211
rhetorical analysis
   media elements and, 264
   when reading texts, 10
   writing, 71-73
rhetorical situations, in media texts, 264
Riefenstahl, Leni, *Triumph of the Will*, 18, 22-23

556   INDEX

road travel, reading about, 230–247
Road Trip (movie poster), 231
"The Rock Star's Burden" (Theroux), 528–530
"Rock the Vote" T-shirt, 491
role-playing games, online, 374
Rolling Stone cover photos
   audience and, 60, 62–63
   identity and, 94–95, 136–137
Rolston, Matthew, Johnny Depp cover photo, 94
Rosenwald, Michael S., "Why America Has to Be Fat," 497–499
"Route 66" (Troup), 188
rule of thirds, 39, 41

S

Sáenz, Benjamin Alire, "War (in the City in Which I Live)" (poem), 222–223
safety guidelines, 342
"Salon.com asks, 'Are you ready for some 'unswooshing' '?" (Baker), 447–451
Santoro, Gene, "A Conversation with Ken Burns," 275–277
Satrapi, Marjane, *Persepolis,* 110–116
Scanga, Bill, *Eighteen Frogs with Pants Categorized by Color,* 365
science
   new development in, explaining, 388–394
   reading texts about, 334–399
   writing about, 386–399
Sears Catalog, "The Dover" (floor plan), 193
Self-portraits (Dürer), 117
sequences, in text, 38
Severson, Kim, "Be It Ever So Homespun, There's Nothing Like Spin," 504–506
Shakespeare, William
   Henry V (Shakespeare production photographs), 40–41
   "Sonnet 130," 31
Shannon, Alice, "Uncle Duane," 168–171
"She's very Charlie" (Cruz), 90–93
Shteyngart, Gary, "Sixty-nine Cents," 502–503
signals, text audience and, 16–17
Sipress, Alan, "Does Virtual Reality Need a Sheriff?," 379–380
"Sixty-nine Cents" (Shteyngart), 502–503
slogans, 473
Smith, Billy, "Gordon Parks: Using Photographs to Spark Social Change," 173–178
sonnets, 31
Sontag, Susan, *Regarding the Pain of Others,* 284–289
sources, documenting, 87
   citing correctly, 549
South Park (TV cartoon), 263
Soviet poster art, 58
speakers, media texts and, 264
Spellbound (movie), exploring director's influence upon, 319–326
Spivey, Kevin, "Baby, You Mean the World of Warcraft to Me," 385
spoken word, 77
Stata Center, MIT, 26
Stateman, Alison, "Postcards from the Edge," 118–121
Steinbeck, John, *The Grapes of Wrath,* 232–234
Stevenson, Seth, "Head Case: The Mesmerizing Ad for a headache Gel," 421–423
Stone, Brad, "MySpace Data Mining," 314–315
street art, in El Paso (photos), 224–225
street artists, political activism of, 530–533
structure and composition, of texts, 38–43
   choosing, 67–76
   when reading
      about places and environments, 182
      about politics and advocacy, 473–474
   when writing
      about places and environments, 249
      about politics and advocacy, 539
      about technology and science, 387
style, writing about, 456–469
subject
   choosing, 56–59
   defining, 56–57
   identifying, 10–11
   when reading
      about identity, 96
      about places and environments, 182
      about politics and advocacy, 472
      about style, design, and culture, 402
      about technology and science, 334
      in media texts, 264
   when writing
      about media, 318
      about places and environment, 248
      about politics and advocacy, 538
      about style, design, and culture, 456
      about technology and science, 386
surprise, informative texts and, 24
Survivor (TV reality show), 273
Syfers-Brady, Judy, "Why I Want a Wife," 101–102

T

tables, 337
Taipei 101 (photo), 187
tattoos, 424
Taubin, Amy, "Fear of a Black Cinema," 296–299
teach, texts that, 26
technicality, in writing, 33
technology
   new development in, explaining, 388–394
   reading texts about, 334–399
   writing about, 386–399
Teenagers with Facial Piercings (Krejci), 143
television, lure of (photo), 264, 266
"Telling War's Deadly Story at Just Enough Distance" (Carr), 280–282
texts. *see also* images; words
   analysis and effectiveness of, 38–43
   audience for, 16–23
   composing. *see* composing texts
   context in. *see* context
   conventions in, 30–31
   defined, 10
   in everyday environment, 9–10
   poems as, 31
   purpose of, 24–29
   reading. *see* reading texts
   structure and composition of, 38–43, 67–76
   types of, 7
The Onion, "Huge Democracy Geek Even Votes in Primaries," 486
Theroux, Paul, "The Rock Star's Burden," 528–530
"The Truth About Beauty" (Postrel), 429–431
third-world debt relief, Bono on, 522–523
Thirty-Three Designers, "First Things First Manifesto 2000," 444–445
"This Is Your Brain on Video Games" (Johnson), 381–384
The 305 (fan film), 54, 55
Tijuana, Mexico (Cook and Jenshal), 220–221
"To Hell With the Simple Paper Clip" (Bierut), 412–413
tone, 33
topic, of research, 84
   style, design, and culture as, 402
toy cars, branding on, 264, 270
Trail to Balanced Rock (Falke), 180, 181
Trajan's column, 5
Tran, Lan, "Lone Stars," 151–154
"The Transformation of American Architecture during the 1920s and 1930s" (Nixon), 464–468
Triumph of the Will (Riefenstahl), 18, 22–23
trompe d'oeil (fool the eye), 12–13
Troup, Bobby, "Route 66" (song lyric), 188
T-shirt messages
   "Rock the Vote," 491
   "Voting is for Old People," 484–485
Tsinhnahjinnie, Hulleah J., *Damn!* (photo collage), 165
Tuma, Kevin, immigration cartoon, 215

U

Ulriksen, Mark, works by, 42
"Uncle Duane" (Shannon), 168–171
unity, in text, 38
Urban Outfitters T-shirt, 484–485
Ut, Nick, *Vietnam Napalm,* 290

V

Viagra model car, 270
video, 78–79
Vilada, Pilar, interviewing Niels Diffrient, 415–416
Villa Savoye By Le Corbusier (Corner and Young), 416–417
viral marketing, 61, 76
   Dove's "Campaign for Real Beauty" and, 426–427
   sample writing about, 389–394
virtual worlds, 212–213
   living in, 374–385
"Visual Images of National Identity: Propaganda Posters of the Great War" (Butler), 541–544
visual text, analysis of, 90–93
voice, 32–33
voting, 484–495
   arguments and
      in Iraq (photo), 476
"Voting is for Old People" T-shirt, 484–485
"Voto Latino" Web site, 493

W

Wade, Nicholas, "Genetic Engineers Who Don't Just Tinker," 362–363
Walker, Alice, "Everyday Use," 156–160
"War (in the City in Which I Live)" (Sáenz), 222–223
The War (film)
   images from, 278–279
   Ken Burns on, 275–277
war photography
   Carr on, 280–282
   casket of Marine, photo by Todd Heisler, 477
   Sontag on, 284–289
Washington, Thomas, "A Librarian's Lament: Books Are a Hard Sell," 45–46
"Watching TV Makes You Smarter" (Johnson), 50–53
Web pages, 79
   from Microsoft's Photosynth technology preview, 181
   as multimedia events, 3
   NASA multimedia page, 82–83
   Pottercast, 483
   for *The War,* 279
Web sites, 79. *see also individual sites by name*
   Cole and Bobby . . . at the Movies!!! (Web site), 55
   Human Rights Watch, 271
   Michael Jordan's The Steak House, N.Y.C., 27
   National Geographic *EarthPulse,* 343
   Punkvoter, 493
   "Redeem the Vote," 492
   user content on, 306
   "Voto Latino," 493
"Welcome to the Texas State University Second Life Campus" (Bretag), 213
"Where the Avatars Roam" (Gerson), 212–213
White Duck (Curtis), 162

"Why America Has to Be Fat" (Rosenwald), 497–499
"Why Bother?" (Pollan), 507–511
"Why I Want a Wife" (Syfers-Brady), 101–102
Wii controller, 405
Wikipedia entry, for Johnny Depp, 95
Wilkinson, Signe, immigration cartoon, 215
"Will Frankenfood Save the Planet?" (Rauch), 512–518
Williams, Alex, "Realistic idealists," 534–537
Williamson, Jenna, "Gainesville: Selling Small-Town America," 251–254
Wooten, Virginia, "*North by Northwest* and *Spellbound:* Identifibly Hitchcock," 320–326
word choice, 33
words
   history of, 4–7
   as slogans, 473
   spoken and written, 77
working life, images representing, 204
world maps, 332–333
wounded soldiers, images of, 278, 283
writing
   about identity, 166–179
   about media, 318–329
   about Oreck Special Edition XL Ultra Vacuum Cleaner, 56, 57
   about places and environments, 248–261
   about politics and advocacy, 538–539
   about style, design, and culture, 456–469
   about technology and science, 386–387
   descriptive. *see* descriptive writing
   to inform and explain, 334–399. *see also* mapping knowledge
written word, 77

Y

Yaconelli, Mark, "Christian Megastar: Bono on Record," 524–527
"Year Zero: A Viral Marketing Promotion" (Faulkner), 389–394
Young, Jenny, and Donald Corner, and Jenny Young, *Villa Savoye By Le Corbusier* (photo), 416–417
Young Men Entering Cowboy Saloon (Clamer), 155
YouTube, 306
   Jenkins on, 307–311
   Presidential debates on, 267
   videos, 24, 54, 55
"YouTube to YouNiversity" (Jenkins), 307–311
Yukon Hybrid SUV, 442–443

Z

Zitkala-Sa (Käsebier), 162